AID AND POWER
VOLUME 2 CASE STUDIES

The international recession of the early 1980s left many less developed countries in a precarious position as their exports collapsed, private capital flows were sharply reduced and interest rates rose. Major aid donors, in particular the World Bank, responded with fundamental changes in aid policy – the introduction of 'structural adjustment lending'. Under this new policy, financial flows to developing countries were made conditional on changes in policy, generally of a type that reduced the level of government intervention in the economy.

This book examines the implications of this change for both the World Bank and the recipients of aid. For the World Bank, there has been a serious conflict between the objectives of quick disbursement and enforcement of conditions. For developing countries, the Bank's conditions have often posed a political threat; but as the book shows, their governments have worked out ingenious strategies for countering this threat, even in countries where the economic predicament is desperate. As a consequence, the so-called 'counter-revolution' in development policy has found, in spite of the Bank's wishes, limited application in developing countries. The results of some economic reforms have been positive, particularly on external account, but their impact on economic grants and foreign resource inflows has been insignificant and on productive investment negative. Both donors and recipients have learned valuable lessons from the policy-based lending experience, and we move into the 1990s with a more modest and long-term view of what policy reform, and economic policy generally, can achieve in developing countries.

Volume 1 carries the analysis and policy recommendations. It examines the origins of policy-based lending and analyses the essential features of the bargaining process which is at its heart. Criteria for the assessment of the success and failure of programmes are developed, and the results of such programmes across a wide range of countries are examined. Proposals for reform of the system are made in the concluding chapter.

Volume 2 contains the results of nine case studies, involving countries in Asia, Africa, Latin America and the Caribbean. From this volume it becomes clear that each country's experience of structural adjustment is unique and that the relationship between the stimulus of a development loan and the recipient economy's response is conditioned by both donor and recipient bargaining strategies and the political and economic structure of the recipient country.

Paul Mosley is Professor of Development Economics and Policy, and also Director, Institute for Development Policy and Management, at the University of Manchester. **John Toye** is Director, Institute of Development Studies, University of Sussex. **Jane Harrigan**, formerly Pricing Economist, Government of Malawi, is now an independent consultant and Visiting Research Associate, Institute for Development Policy and Management, University of Manchester.

AID AND POWER

The World Bank and Policy-based Lending

Volume 2   Case Studies

Paul Mosley, Jane Harrigan and John Toye

London and New York

First published 1991
by Routledge
11 New Fetter Lane, London EC4P 4EE

Simultaneously published in the USA and Canada
by Routledge
a division of Routledge, Chapman and Hall, Inc.
29 West 35th Street, New York, NY 10001

Printed and bound in Great Britain by Mackays of Chatham PLC, Kent

British Library Cataloguing in Publication Data
Mosley, Paul
Aid and power : the World Bank and policy-based lending.
Vol. 2, Case studies
1. Developing countries. Financial assistance. Loans from
World Bank
I. Title   II. Harrigan, Jane   III. Toye, John *1942–*
332.1532091724
ISBN 0–415–06077–X
ISBN 0–415–06246–2 pbk

Library of Congress Cataloging-in-Publication Data
Mosley, Paul.
Aid and power : the World Bank and policy-based lending
/ Paul Mosley, Jane Harrigan, and John Toye.
p.   cm.
Includes bibliographical references and index.
Contents: – v. 2. Case studies.
ISBN 0–415–06077–X (v. 2). – ISBN 0–415–06246–2 (pbk. : v. 2)
1. World Bank.   2. Loans, Foreign – Developing countries – Case
studies.   3. Developing countries – Economic policy – Case studies.
I. Harrigan, Jane.   II. Toye, J. F. J.   III. Title.
HG3881.5.W57M68   1991
332.1'532 – dc20
90–9153
CIP

CONTENTS

Volume 2   Case studies

CONTENTS

Volume 2   Figures

Volume 2 Tables

APPENDIX TABLES

10

INTRODUCTION AND SYNTHESIS

Paul Mosley

This volume presents the findings of nine case studies of countries which have received conditional programme loans from the World Bank. The selection is intended to provide a balance between different modes of programme lending, between happy and less happy experiences of policy dialogue, and between regions of the world: three of the case studies are from Asia, three from Africa, and three from the Caribbean and Latin America. But the programme of studies was conceived in 1985–6 and so the large Latin American sector loans of the late 1980s are not represented here. Most of the essays are by the principal authors of the study, but two – those for Thailand and Turkey – take advantage of the distinctive insight and local knowledge of nationals of those countries. As a consequence it has been possible to give additional weight to the viewpoint of the recipient in conditionality negotiations – a viewpoint which, in our opinion, has still not been sufficiently articulated or publicised.

The major questions which this study tries to answer are two: the broad question of under what circumstances 'aid' confers 'power' in the sense of enabling a donor to influence a recipient's choice of economic policies, and the narrower question of whether the specific set of liberalising policies which the World Bank has tried to induce developing countries to adopt in the 1980s has done them any good. A number of answers have been offered to these questions in Volume 1, and it is not the purpose of this chapter to recapitulate the analysis of that volume, nor yet to summarise the individual case studies, which speak for themselves. Rather, since a major building-block in our argument is to emphasise that the relationship between the stimulus of a development loan and the recipient economy's response is conditioned by the political and economic structure of the recipient country, we would like to draw attention here to some of those distinctive insights from the country case studies which take us beyond the analysis of Volume 1, and to draw them into relationship with one another. The chapter is short, and no attempt at comprehensiveness is made.

1

A major premiss underlying the approach of Volume 1 is that policy-based lending is in essence a game played out between a 'donor' who provides money and a 'recipient' who is expected, in return, to implement policy conditions. Following through the logic of this metaphor, we duly found that recipients who are in a relatively weak bargaining position, whether because of the gravity of their economic position, their high financial dependence on the Bank or their inability to exert economic or geopolitical reverse leverage, tended to have relatively tight conditionality packages imposed on them and to be treated relatively leniently if they deviated from that conditionality. In general such countries tended also to be more compliant with such conditionality, but we encountered a number of cases where weak recipients gambled, sometimes correctly and sometimes not, that they could none the less get away with high levels of slippage. Where recipients did go through with reform programmes, the regression and modelling exercises of Chapters 7 and 8 suggested that they did in some cases eventually yield a pay-off in terms of weak growth of income and exports, although the independent influence of the *finance* provided by the Bank's programme loans (as distinct from the policy conditions) was at best negligible. There were other disturbing long-term effects to be observed as well, in particular on investment and on income distribution.

What this aggregative, two-person-game approach obscures is that conflicts *within* donor and recipient, and the manner in which they are resolved, may be as significant for the success of policy-based lending operations as the nature of the bargaining relationship between donor organisation and recipient government. This volume provides a rich quarry of material for the study of such conflicts. On the donor side, a tension often appears between the Bank's new structural adjustment-related activities and its old-established project-related activities, as in Malawi (Chapter 15: p. 228) where the Bank personnel responsible for negotiating the Structural Adjustment Loans (SAL) were attempting to secure the removal of a fertiliser subsidy which underpinned the efforts being made by the Bank's project staff to boost the output of maize under the National Rural Development Programme. Sometimes conflict also appeared within the conditionality of a policy-based lending agreement, as in Thailand (Chapter 13: p. 120) where the conditionality for SAL II simultaneously asked for a cut in the average level of import duty and for an increase in the ratio of tax revenue to GDP. It is clear that where such conflicts can be recognised and resolved *ex ante*, the effectiveness of policy-based lending operations will increase.

Still more important for the ultimate impact of such operations is the outcome of the political struggle, documented in all the case studies of this volume, between those who negotiated policy-based lending agreements on behalf of the recipient government and those who expected to lose from the implementation of such agreements. It is common to describe the former group, whose inner core usually lay within the finance ministry and central bank, as a 'technocracy', but any such group, assuming that it did not have the ability to impose its will by brute force as in Chile, needed to broaden its base of support by making appropriate alliances if it had any hope of carrying its policies through. The urban working class, under the stress of devaluation, cuts in subsidies and erosion of social services, has little reason to support such policies; the key interest groups whose support is there to be won or lost are farmers, industrialists and, perhaps most critical, the line agencies of government which have major responsibility for implementation. What governed the ability of the technocracy to build a coalition of support for Bank reforms from within these intermediate groups?

It is worth drawing attention to two elements of the answer which emerge from the following pages. One is that in some of the countries where reforms went furthest, conscious attempts were made by the technocracy to compensate losers within these marginal groups in order to buy their support. This can be done explicitly, as when in the Philippines industrialists were compensated for the removal of import quota restrictions in 1986 by increases in the customs duty exemption which they were able to claim on exports (Chapter 12: p. 70) or implicitly, as in Turkey where 'an increase in the pace of economic growth, with the expansion of the public sector used as the mechanism for distributing the gains, was the primary means by which the government sought to elicit broad support from various strata of the population' (Chapter 11: p. 29). Where the losers are also poor, such measures can also be used to mitigate the social costs of adjustment, as has been attempted for example by PAMSCAD (Programme to Mitigate the Social Costs of Adjustment) in Ghana (Chapter 14: p. 195). The compensation principle may also need to be applied between government ministries, since the line agencies of government – agriculture, commerce, industry, statutory boards, development banks – notoriously have less initial commitment to structural adjustment programmes than the finance ministry – they suffer all the hassle associated with implementation, whereas the finance ministry receives the money and decides on its allocation. This volume is replete with cases (rationalisation of import controls in Kenya, pp. 290–1; privatisation of food marketing in Ecuador, p. 418; elimination of fertiliser subsidies in Malawi, p. 226) where the Bank did a deal with the finance ministry to remove the intervention in question, only to discover that the implementing ministry had scarcely been consulted, much less intellectually persuaded of the need for the change. In such cases line ministries, instead of serving as agencies by which support for reform is 'internalised' within the political economy, find themselves espousing the cause of anti-reform pressure groups in opposition to the technocracy, as in the case of the Philippines Ministry for Industry

3

under Aquino (Chapter 11: p. 62). On the evidence of these case studies, the task of building up an interdepartmental consensus within government in advance of the disbursement of a sectoral adjustment loan is now taken more seriously than it was ten years ago, even at the cost of holding up disbursement. But such a consensus can easily fall apart once the money has been handed over, and there is a case for providing some sectoral loans in kind (e.g. agricultural sector loans in the form of fertiliser or seed) so that the implementing ministry perceives itself as deriving benefit from the transaction.

The degree of momentum behind the Bank's reforms is also obviously influenced by the relations between the Bank negotiating team and the local technocracy. This volume relates cases where the Bank negotiating team put their trust and their money behind a reform programme which had already been designed by the local technocracy (Turkey, Aquino's Philippines), cases where the Bank tried to lay down some priorities which the local technocracy clearly did not share (Kenya, Ecuador, Malawi) and cases where the Bank politely added a number of optional extras to a programme substantially designed in-house, some of which were, politely and without punishment, subsequently ignored (Thailand, Ghana). The key issues are diagnosis and timing. Structural Adjustment Lending was intended to remove critical bottle-necks to an economy's supply-side, but without agreement between Bank and government on where the critical constraint is, little can be done. The institutional arrangements for food-crop marketing, for example, arguably had little to do with accelerating the economic development of either Kenya or Ecuador during the 1980s, and the Bank's preoccupation with that subject tended to erode mutual trust and the possibility for collaborative action in more urgent, export-related areas. Similarly, friction between Bank and the technocracy on the timing of reform emerges in Kenya, Jamaica and Thailand: both parties were united on the need for liberalisation and on tightening of financial discipline, but the central bank and finance ministry wished to be able to choose the opportune moment to obtain the support of the head of state and the operating ministries, rather than be bound by the terms of an agreement with the Bank to (say) remove 229 quantitative import controls by 31 December 1987. On both diagnosis and timing, agreement was made the more difficult by the fact that Bank efforts at structural adjustment were, and remain, improvisations. IMF recommendations to developing countries may have the analytical support of the absorption approach to the balance of payments, but the Bank's structural adjustment recommendations remain based on nothing more precise and scientific than a preference for free markets and an instinct for the way the local economy works – an instinct which may very reasonably be questioned by those who actually live in it and run it.

The effectiveness of policy-based lending in particular countries, then,

4

was significantly influenced by the local technocracy's relations with the Bank and by its ability to build, in Joan Nelson's phrase, a 'fragile coalition' in support of reform amongst interest groups whose allegiance, if given, would necessarily be based on material interest rather than principle. These factors, although exhaustively treated in the following papers, defy quantification of the type that has been attempted in Chapters 6 to 8. However, the case studies reveal other elements of the working of the economy which also varied between countries and which may also help to explain the variation in inter-country response to treatment. These are:

- the existence, and if it exists the internal cohesion, of a 'manufacturing exporters' lobby';
- the response of domestic and overseas investment to the structural adjustment programme (noticeably disappointing, for example, in Kenya, Jamaica, Ghana and Guyana);
- the behaviour of real wages and as a consequence the size of the competitive advantage conferred by devaluation;
- whether or not the structural adjustment exercise was interrupted mid-term by a stabilisation episode (an obvious constraint in Jamaica, Philippines and Kenya).

The first of these was clearly an important contribution to the success of structural adjustment in Turkey, but that it is by no means a necessary condition of dynamism on the export side is demonstrated by the case of Thailand, where a number of Bank-inspired attempts to rationalise the structure of protection ran into the sand between 1983 and 1985 (Chapter 13: pp. 107–9), where tariff levels still remain strewn over a range of zero to 200 per cent, and which nevertheless in recent years (1987–9) has been the most successful manufacturing exporter in the world, with double-figure growth rates of GNP and manufacturing growth. Let us therefore leave this variable on one side, and concentrate on the other three. Figure 10.1 represents these data graphically in relation to the statistical relationship between growth rate and fulfilment of conditionality, which in the multiple regression analysis of Volume 1, Chapter 7 was measured as:

$$\text{GDP growth} = -24.6 + 0.29 \text{ (compliance index unlagged)} +$$
$$1.35^* \text{ (compliance index lagged one period)} +$$
$$0.23 \text{ (compliance index lagged two periods)} +$$
$$\text{terms on other independent variables,}$$
$$r^2 = 0.40 \qquad \text{(Table 7.1)}$$

Reduced to simple two-variable, unlagged terms with all the other independent variables of Chapter 7 removed from the analysis this becomes:

$$\text{GDP growth} = -0.8 + 0.071^* \text{ (compliance index)}, \ r^2 = 0.41$$
$$(2.19)$$

Figure 10.1 Relation between slippage and growth of GDP, with possible explanation of 'outliers'

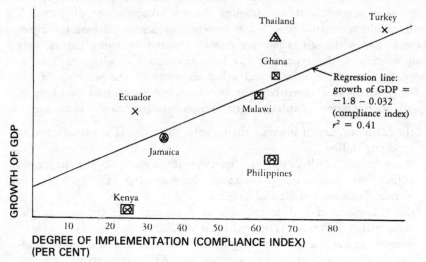

KEY:
Variables in regression:
Level of implementation of World Bank SAL/SECAL measures, from case studies, in this volume, as summarised in Table 5 above. (N.B. 'Slippage' is 100 per cent less 'level of implementation' as measured here).
Growth rate of GDP: annual rate of growth of real GDP between first year of World Bank adjustment lending (three-year moving average) and fifth year after that date (three-year moving average), data from World Bank, *World Development Reports* as summarised in Harrigan and Mosley 1989, annex I, pp 89–96.
Possible explanations of 'outliers':
☐ : negative real growth in private foreign investment during five years after first World Bank adjustment loan: data from World Bank *World Development Reports* as summarised in Harrigan and Mosley 1989, annex I, pp 89–96.
△ : *positive* growth in real manufacturing wages during five-year period after first World Bank adjustment loan as measured in World Bank, *World Development Reports 1989*, appendix table 7.
○ : stabilisation episode involving IMF during five years after first World Bank adjustment loan.

Let us now see whether the variables mentioned above explain any tendency for countries to perform better or worse than this regression line might predict. Malawi, Ghana and Jamaica, of our case-study countries, lie very close to the regression line and so can be disregarded for this purpose. The status of the others in relation to our chosen indicators is as set out in Table 10.1. We must begin by stressing that we are looking at only nine countries, and hence it is not possible to use econometrics as, for example, we did in Chapters 7 and 8. None the less, it does appear as though the less-than-expected performance of foreign investment inflows and the unexpected stabilisation episodes may have something to do with the lower-than-predicted growth rates observed in Guyana and the Philippines; but Kenya, as related in Chapter 16, also experienced a stabilisation episode which it managed to survive without adverse impact on growth. Real wages fell in most LDCs during the 1980s, as related in many of our case studies and Volume 1, Chapter 5; but one of the few in which they rose was Thailand, whose success has already been discussed. At the very least, therefore, it can be said that a fall in real wages did not always constitute a necessary condition for the success of a structural adjustment programme.

Table 10.1 Countries performing much better and much worse than predicted by regression line

	Unfavourable indication in relation to:		
	private foreign investment	real wages	stabilisation during structural adjustment period
Countries performing 'better than predicted'			
Turkey			
Thailand		Yes	
Kenya			Yes
Countries performing 'worse than predicted'			
Guyana	Yes		Yes
Philippines	Yes		Yes

Source: As Figure 10.1.
Note: A *rise* in real wages is treated as an 'unfavourable indication'.

We may conclude by drawing attention to the case of Guyana, by some measure the poorest performer within our sample. Jane Harrigan's case study of this country in Chapter 18 makes it clear that this fiasco is by no means solely due to its failure to implement the policy advice of the World Bank, nor even to the collapse of public expenditure and foreign investment which occurred during the stabilisation episode. Rather, in a country where infrastructure and the export sectors' capital stock had decayed, 'structural adjustment' should have taken the form of rehabilitation of the productive structure, rather than privatisation and liberalisation. As one of the leading actors involved in the process has acknowledged,

Conventional text-book economics is not written for economies in decline, but for static or growing economies. One can structurally adjust an economy which is growing but growing inefficiently, or one that is static. But an economy in cumulative decline forces one to confront a systemic problem. Such an economy requires transformation of a Keynesian type, in which the emphasis is on the quality and quantity of investment, particularly the stimulative role of public

7

sector investment. The Bank's structural adjustment programmes however are rooted in the marginality theories of neo-classical text-book economics with their emphasis placed on price incentives, exchange rate adjustments and trade liberalisation.

(quoted in Chapter 18: p. 391).

The importance of this observation is that it is not, of course, the economy of Guyana alone which is in 'cumulative decline', but of many of the world's poorest countries, including much of sub-Saharan Africa. Mozambique, Sudan, Ethiopia, Somalia, Sierra Leone, Guinea, Zaïre, even Nigeria: all of these, as much as Guyana, require 'transformation of a Keynesian type', plus state intervention to make land and small-holder credit available to those who need them, rather than stimuli for a private capitalist sector which in many of the poorest countries scarcely exists. Our reading of the case studies, then, leads us, in these countries at least, to take inspiration from the Latin American structuralists of the 1950s, who advocated that the state should promote development by itself removing bottle-necks in the economy, rather than from the 'new structuralist' experiments of the 1980s.

It is finally necessary to stress that the World Bank is not a static institution, but one which endeavours to learn from experience, and all of the case studies which follow can be read as studies in institutional learning. In particular, in the country which most closely approximates the condition of Guyana – namely Ghana in 1983–4 – the Bank began not only with an attempted *blitzkrieg* on the apparatus of state intervention but also, and sensibly, with sectoral loans for the rehabilitation of export sectors and their associated infrastructure. For reasons discussed in the early chapters of Volume 1, Bank sector lending has in the 1980s had a bias towards the more progressive, and on the whole the more prosperous, developing countries. It is to be hoped that as this bias is rectified in the 1990s the Bank will build on its insight that poor and declining economies cannot be treated with the same set of remedies as those which are appropriate for countries no longer underdeveloped.

11

TURKEY

Colin Kirkpatrick and *Ziya Onis*

11.1 INTRODUCTION

The relationship between the World Bank and Turkey in the 1980s is characterised by several distinctive features. Turkey and Kenya were the first recipients of the Bank's Structural Adjustment Loans (SAL), both countries signing agreements in March 1980. Second, Turkey emerged as the only country which completed five successive SALs during the 1980–4 period. Third, the scale of the Bank adjustment lending to Turkey during this period was unmatched by any other recipient country.[1] Finally, Turkey is one of the few countries which the World Bank has identified as an example of a successful structural adjustment programme.[2]

These features of the Turkish experience raise a number of substantive issues for investigation. What were the factors which rendered the implementation of five successive SALs feasible? To what extent can the Turkish SAL programme be judged a success? Is it possible to derive certain general lessons from the Turkish experience that are transferable to the World Bank's process of policy dialogue with other developing countries? It will be the objective of this study to shed light on these issues. The starting point is a discussion of the forces that led to the economic and political crisis of the 1977–9 period, which provides the background to the Government's adjustment programme of January 1980 and the subsequent World Bank SALs, beginning with SAL I in March 1980.

11.2 THE CRISIS OF THE LATE 1970s

During the two decades preceding the adjustment programme, Turkey had pursued an inward-oriented development strategy, combined with an extensive involvement by the public sector. Macro planning and import substitution became synonymous, as the import-substituting industrialisation strategy was institutionalised under the First Five Year Development

9

Plan introduced in 1983.[3] In fact, the origins of the inward-oriented industrialisation strategy can be traced back to the étatist period of the late 1930s, corresponding to the first major industrialisation drive in Republican Turkey. The State Economic Enterprises (SEEs) were founded during the 1930s and provided the institutional framework for the major industrialisation spurt under Ataturk.

Judged on the basis of the growth rate of industrial production and overall output, the performance of the 1963–77 period was impressive. The average growth rate of GNP was recorded as 7.0 per cent, while the average growth rate of industrial production was 9.0 per cent. Several exogenous factors exercised a favourable influence during the 1970s and helped to sustain the momentum of rapid growth established during the preceding decade. Three such forces deserve special emphasis. The primary commodity boom was instrumental in the rapid increase of Turkish exports during the early 1970s. Significant inflows of workers' remittances and short-term capital inflows from the Euro-currency market also performed a key role in resolving the foreign exchange problem and maintaining high rates of economic growth.

These forces, however, helped to disguise the principal weakness of the Turkish economy, namely an excessive dependence on imports of intermediate and capital goods, with no corresponding ability to increase export earnings to finance the necessary import bill. A pattern observed in many developing countries was repeated in the Turkish context. The ISI strategy had rendered the economy more vulnerable to external shocks as a result of increased dependence on imported inputs. In contrast, the share of exports in GDP remained constant at around 4–5 per cent throughout the decade.

The crisis of the late 1970s was precipitated by Turkey's inability to meet her external commitments in 1977; which in turn was the combined outcome of domestic and external forces. The reaction of the policy-makers to the oil shock of 1973–4 had been to press ahead with the import-substituting strategy. Public investment was conceived of as the principal mechanism for this purpose. Public sector deficits, which were magnified by the operating losses of the SEEs, were financed by recourse to foreign borrowing. Consequently Turkey's external debts increased from $3 billion in 1973 to $15 billion in 1980.[4]

The economic crisis which manifested itself in 1977 was accompanied by a political crisis.[5] The Republican People's Party (RPP) under the leadership of Ecevit was elected with a majority in 1973 and remained in office until it resigned following a vote of no confidence in 1975.

From 1975 to 1977 the country was ruled by a coalition under Demirel. The elections of 1977 produced a stalemate, with no major party being in a position to secure a majority in the Parliament, in the absence of a coalition. The RPP obtained the largest number of votes in the 1977 elections and formed a coalition with the unlikely partner of the National Salvation Party (NSP). The coalition between the social democratic RPP and the NSP, with an Islamic fundamentalist philosophy, proved to be highly unstable and was unable to deal effectively with the deteriorating economic situation.

A possible solution to the dilemma involved a grand coalition between Ecevit's RPP and Demirel's pro-business Justice Party. The Grand Coalition did not materialise and the period between July 1977 and September 1980 was one of growing political instability, accompanied by mounting levels of terrorism and violence. There were five coalition governments, led alternately by Ecevit and Demirel, between March 1975 and September 1980.

The IMF was involved in negotiations with Turkey throughout the crisis period of the late 1970s.[6] The fifth Demirel administration (July–December 1977) had initiated discussions with the Fund and in the autumn of 1977 negotiated a two-to-three-year stand-by agreement. But the cabinet failed to agree on the pre-conditions of an 18 per cent devaluation and reduction in Government spending, and the administration collapsed in December 1977. The new Ecevit administration reached agreement with the Fund in April 1978, on a two-year stand-by credit of SDR 300 million, with restrictive monetary and fiscal policy, devaluation and better debt management. The performance criteria were relaxed subsequently but negotiations on the release of the third tranche of the stand-by in late 1978 failed to produce an agreement. Negotiations with the Fund were resumed in April 1979, with discussion focusing on devaluation and restrictions on government expenditure. Agreement was reached in July on a new one-year stand-by credit of SDR 250 million, preceded by a 44 per cent devaluation of the lira. In its Letter of Intent, the government committed itself to further stabilisation measures, focusing particularly on the reform of the tax structure. However, the economy's performance continued to worsen in the second half of 1979, while the internal political situation deteriorated with growing civil disorder. The Ecevit administration was replaced by the sixth Demirel administration in November 1979.

The failure of the IMF agreements to halt the deterioration in the economy can be attributed to several interrelated factors. The agreements with the Fund were seen by the Ecevit government as a short-run expediency to deal with the immediate balance-of-payments crisis. Yet, the governments' underlying philosophy of development, as practised during the 1973–7 period, remained unchanged, the objective being to sustain the ISI strategy on the basis of public investment and foreign borrowing. The validity of this observation is supported by the fact that the Fourth Five Year Development Plan, prepared in 1978 for implementation during the 1979–83 period, envisaged a further round of import substitution in capital goods industries, proving to be a linear progression from the Third

Five Year Development Plan.

The government showed no inclination to alter its long-term development strategy. Nor was there any attempt to 'internalise' the stabilisation programme. Rather, the Government presented the programmes as being imposed by external donors against its own will.[7] The external donors had little confidence in the Ecevit Government's ability or commitment to implement what they considered to be the necessary adjustment measures. Consequently the external resources promised by the IMF and bilateral donors were of negligible magnitude as compared with the scale of adjustment assistance made available during the post–1980 period.

11.3 THE POST-1980 STRUCTURAL ADJUSTMENT LENDING PERIOD

The IMF stand-by agreement, 1980

The newly-elected Justice Party under Demirel took up office in November 1979 with Turgut Ozal as the person responsible for economic affairs. The new Government quickly abandoned an early announcement to seek modification of the stabilisation programme, and instead set out to conclude a new medium-term agreement which would represent a fundamental reorientation of economic policy.

The new Economic Stabilisation Programme was announced in January 1980. The main objectives of the programme were a reduction in government involvement in productive activities and an increased emphasis on market forces; the replacement of an inward-looking strategy with an 'export oriented strategy of import substitution' (the Government's own words); and the attraction of foreign investment. A series of measures were introduced. The key decision was a devaluation of almost 50 per cent, which applied to all foreign exchange transactions except for imports of fertiliser and agricultural chemicals where a rate mid-way between the old and new levels was used. A second set of measures concerned internal prices, with reductions in the subsidies on fertilisers and petroleum products. Price controls on most SEE products were removed. The regulation of the prices of private sector manufactured goods was abolished. A third set of measures involved institutional changes. These included the creation of a Money and Credit Committee, chaired by Ozal as Under Secretary of the Prime Ministry, which was given responsibility for decisions on economic policy, previously the prerogative of the Council of Ministers.[8]

By the end of 1979, the inward-looking, étatist approach had been discredited as a viable option and the Demirel administration was converted to the view that a major shift in policy was necessary. The authorities were also fully aware of the willingness of the OECD Consortium to offer substantial external funding to Turkey.[9] This commitment by the OECD countries to a rescue operation in Turkey was motivated to a significant degree by geopolitical considerations. Turkey was seen as a key element in the NATO Alliance and her economic and political weakness would render the NATO southern flank vulnerable to Soviet influence. The Iranian Revolution in February 1979 increased the pressure for a resolution of Turkey's difficulties. The OECD Consortium agreed that external finance was the key to recovery, provided that the appropriate set of policy reforms were implemented, but were unwilling to make major bilateral commitments in advance of Turkey reaching agreement with the Fund on a stabilisation programme. Hence the Fund was under pressure to reach agreement with Turkey, which would act as a catalyst for the release of additional external funding.[10]

At the same time, Demirel recognised that relations with the IMF continued to be a politically sensitive issue, and that it would be to the Government's advantage if the stabilisation programme was seen as having been decided upon independently by the Turkish Government. The Turkish authorities did not enter into formal negotiations with the IMF until March 1980, and were successful in presenting the January policy reforms as an internally formulated programme, decided upon independently of external pressure from the IMF.

However, Demirel had established contact with the IMF shortly after resuming office in November 1979. His officials met with an IMF team during a routine visit to Turkey in early December, and subsequently Ozal was sent to Washington to discuss with the Fund the outline of the proposed stabilisation measures.[11] Thereafter, Ozal and a team of high level technocrats responsible for preparing the new measures maintained informal contact with Fund officials. The key figure in this process of policy reformulation was Turgut Ozal. A former head of the State Planning Organisation during 1965–71, Ozal spent a formative period at the World Bank in the mid-1970s. He subsequently emerged as the main negotiator with the donor organisations during the late 1970s, and became the chief architect of the January 1980 programme.[12] Ozal was supported by a group of technocrats who, through the Money and Credit Committee, were able to change the direction of Turkey's economic strategy and subsequently to retain control over the adjustment process.[13]

In the first six months of 1980 the authorities introduced a series of policy measures aimed at achieving the objectives of the January Programme. These included a restrictive monetary and fiscal policy, restrictions on Central Bank funding of the public enterprise sector; new tax measures; increases in interest rates; and continuous exchange rate adjustments. Throughout this period Ozal was in contact with the IMF resident office officials, and in June 1980 a three-year stand-by agreement for SDR 1.25 billion was signed. This was the first three-year stand-by in the Fund's history. It constituted the highest credit ever extended by the IMF, and it represented 6.5 times Turkey's quota.

The arrangement with the IMF corresponded closely to the January Programme measures, and only two elements were added, relating to interest rate policy and incomes policy (Wolff, 1987: 103).[14] On interest rates, the Government agreed to introduce a significant rise in nominal rates, and on incomes policy, the Government agreed to establish a Labour Contracts Co-ordinating Committee which was intended to encourage employer–employee dialogue. On 1 July the Government removed all controls on commercial bank interest rates and allowed them to be determined by market forces.

The economic situation continued to deteriorate during 1980. Real GDP declined by 0.7 per cent, and consumer prices rose by 110 per cent. Labour unrest and violence continued, and on 12 September 1980 the military dissolved parliament and suspended all civilian political institutions. Significantly, within forty-eight hours of seizing power, the military officially informed the IMF and the World Bank of their intention to continue with the policies of structural adjustment, with Ozal appointed deputy prime minister in charge of economic policy.

In June 1983, an additional one-year follow-on stand-by arrangement was approved for SDR 225 million (75 per cent of quota). This was seen as a continuation of the earlier arrangement, and the conditionality was similar to the 1980 performance criteria. At the end of 1983, the newly-elected civilian government requested cancellation of the existing arrangements. In April 1984, a final one-year arrangement was approved for SDR 225 million (52 per cent of quota) to replace the cancelled arrangement.

The World Bank's structural adjustment lending programme, 1980–4

Between 1980 and 1984, the World Bank extended – in addition to its project lending – five consecutive one-year SALs to Turkey, totalling US $1.6 billion. These five structural adjustment loans were made in support of policy reforms intended to shift the economy from an inward-looking ISI orientation, to an outward-looking strategy emphasising export-led growth.

The Bank's support to the structural adjustment programme in Turkey involved a working relationship with the IMF. There was general agreement between the Fund and the Bank that the adjustment process in Turkey would involve a medium-term period of adaptation, and that stabilisation of the economy was a prerequisite for a return to a sustainable growth path. Both institutions were committed therefore to a medium-term period of financial support to Turkey. Thus, as noted earlier, the

Fund's Stand-by arrangement was for an unprecedented three years, and was extended for a further one year in 1983.[15] Similarly, the Bank provided an uninterrupted succession of SALs, which were seen as 'an incremental set of conditionalities towards achieving the goals of the medium term reform programme' (World Bank, 1983: 15). There was thus an understanding between the two institutions on a division of areas of responsibility, with the Fund's conditionality and responsibilities focusing on monetary and fiscal policy, the exchange rate, and public sector financial management, and the Bank being concerned with SEE reform, trade liberalisation, export promotion, and rationalisation of public investment.

Agreement between the institutions on areas of responsibility does not appear to have extended, however, to a co-ordinated approach to policy implementation. The failure to develop an analytical macro framework which would have enabled the Bank and the Fund to assess the economy-level repercussions of specific policy reforms subsequently contributed to the emergence of unfavourable economic trends which threatened the sustainability of the structural adjustment programme.

From 1980, the World Bank became the dominant partner, with the IMF relegated to a secondary role, in relations with the Turkish authorities. This was due, in part, to the legacy of the 1978–9 period when the Fund had been exclusively involved in negotiations and which was associated with acute economic crisis and disorder. While the World Bank assumed the role of dominant partner in dealings between the Turkish authorities and the international organisations, it also succeeded in maintaining a low public profile. This was a major tactical victory in the sense that the policies adopted were associated in the public mind with the Government itself, rather than with the explicit preferences of external parties.

The Turkish authorities, for their part, were aware of the political damage that would result from a close association with the IMF.[16] Ozal and his advisers also recognised that the qualitative and judgmental nature of much of the Bank's conditionality offered greater latitude in appraising performance than was possible with the Fund's quantitative performance measures, and this further increased the attractiveness of dealing with the Bank. As we shall see, Ozal skilfully used this element of flexibility in the reform process.

The methodological problems involved in attempting to link economic performance to policy reforms were fully discussed in Volume 1. It is theoretically unsound to argue that a particular policy change has a causal and quantifiable effect in a particular area independently of other policy changes undertaken at the same time. Similarly, performance attributable to policy changes is difficult to isolate from exogenous influences (see Volume 1, Chapters 6–8). Here, we restrict the discussion to a summary of the main economic developments during the adjustment period, indicating the major areas in which policy changes can be expected to have influenced performance.

The structural adjustment programme period in Turkey was marked by significant improvements in performance in several major spheres of economic activity. Table 11.1 contains the main macro indicators for this period. Following the marked decline in the growth rate during the late 1970s, culminating in an absolute decline in GDP in 1980, the growth rate of GDP averaged 5.3 per cent over the 1981–6 period. Parallel to the recovery in economic growth, exports also recorded a significant increase. From a mere 4.0 per cent of GDP in the late 1970s, the share of exports in GDP rose to 20 per cent by 1985. Moreover, a major shift occurred in the composition of exports, with the share of manufactures in total exports increasing from 36 per cent in 1980 to 75 per cent in 1985.

The potential contribution of the growth in exports to a reduction in the trade balance was offset by an expansion in imports, and the trade balance remained in deficit. The openness of the economy increased, as shown in the rise in the share of foreign trade in GDP, from 19 per cent in 1980 to 32 per cent in 1986.

The financing of the trade balance involved further accumulation of external debt, and the total external debt to GDP ratio rose from 33 per cent in 1980 to 56 per cent in 1986. A growing share of debt accumulation during the SAL period was in the form of short-term liabilities, which reached 29 per cent by 1986.

During the first two years of the adjustment period a tight monetary policy was followed, which contributed to a fall in the inflation rate, from 110 per cent in 1980 to 45 per cent in 1985. However, the Government failed to meet the SAL objective of reducing the fiscal deficit by increasing tax revenue and reducing public sector investment. In the absence of an adequate tax base, and with restrictions on central bank borrowing, the Government relied increasingly on short-term domestic and external borrowing. The interest rate attached to this borrowing rose in line with the dramatic rise in the general level of interest rates that followed interest rate liberalisation in 1980. As a result, interest payments rose from 1.5 to 4.0 per cent of GDP from 1980 to 1985.

In conformity with the SAL conditions, public sector investment was diverted away from manufacturing into areas regarded as complementary to private investment, namely transport, communications and energy. Aggregate investment increased from 21.9 per cent of GDP in 1980 to 24.8 per cent in 1986. Private sector investment, however, did not increase, but became more concentrated in housing rather than in manufacturing. Public investment continued therefore to be the dominant form of capital formation.

In spite of the substantial progress identified in the context of the SAL programmes, a number of major macro problems emerged during the adjustment period. Several of these macro issues had their origins in the

Table 11.1   Turkey: macroeconomic indicators, 1978–87

	1978	1979	1980	1981	1982	1983	1984	1985	1986	1987
Growth in GDP, at constant prices, %	3.3	-0.9	-0.7	4.2	4.9	3.8	5.9	4.9	8.0	7.4
Growth of exports, at constant prices, %	13.8	-9.3	4.1	85.1	40.1	13.7	19.8	12.3	-1.5	29.1
Exports as share of GDP, in current prices, %	5.2	4.2	6.4	10.3	14.7	15.3	19.2	20.6	17.7	20.1
Growth of imports, at constant prices, %	-33.5	-6.8	2.4	15.0	7.5	17.2	27.7	8.1	11.4	20.1
Imports as share of GDP, at current prices, %	8.9	7.5	14.2	15.7	18.0	19.7	23.4	23.8	20.7	22.7
Current account balance as share of GDP, at current prices, %	-2.4	-2.1	-6.0	-3.4	-2.0	-4.2	-3.3	-2.4	-3.1	-1.9
Total external debt/GDP, %	28.2	22.9	33.4	33.2	37.1	39.6	43.4	49.2	56.4	60.0
Inflation (consumer prices) %	45.3	58.7	110.2	36.6	30.8	32.9	48.4	45.0	34.6	–
Fiscal deficit as share of GDP, at current prices, %	-4.3	-6.3	-3.8	-1.8	-1.8	-2.6	-5.4	-2.9	-3.6	-4.3
Gross domestic investment as share of GDP, at current prices, %	18.7	18.6	21.9	22.0	20.6	19.6	19.9	21.1	24.8	24.1
Real wages (US $ equivalent)	8.23	8.41	5.62	5.08	4.37	4.35	3.63	3.26	3.28	

Source: World Bank (1988).

high interest rate policy. Liberalisation of financial markets and the establishment of positive real rates of interest were core objectives of the structural adjustment programme, and ceilings on deposit rates were lifted in July 1980. Nominal rates rose dramatically to levels in excess of 50 per cent, which conspired with falling inflation to give positive real rates around 20 per cent by mid-1981. The policy of gradual depreciation of the Turkish lira and the financing of the fiscal deficit by external and domestic borrowing kept interest rates high. High real rates increased the servicing cost of the domestic debt, thus widening the fiscal deficit and destabilising the fiscal position. High interest rates contributed to the continued low level of private investment, which in turn limited the expansion of export capacity. With the current account deficit being financed by foreign borrowing, any slow down in export growth was bound to result in a rising debt service ratio. High interest rates also contributed to the fragility of the financial system, and the accumulation of non-performing loans led to the banking sector crisis of mid-1982.[17] The connected problem of macro instability persisted throughout the period and threatened the sustainability of the SAL programme.[18]

These macro problems could have been recognised early in the SAL process, and appropriate corrective measures initiated, if the SAL programmes had been formulated in the context of a medium term macro analytical framework. This did not happen. During SAL II and III the Bank relied on the Fund's analysis of the macro situation, which reported favourably on performance.[19] The Bank's internal audit report concluded:

> One weakness in SAL II and III, however, was the absence of a medium-term strategy document that systematically linked the short-run stabilisation programme to a longer-run development plan. Such a strategy document would have integrated the public investment program and the structural reforms in at least an indicative framework showing a feasible transition to sustainable growth. The strategy document could then have facilitated private sector investment planning, and mobilized aid for private investment.
>
> (World Bank, 1983: 5)

The need for a medium-term planning framework was recognised in SAL IV, which included the completion of the Fifth Five Year Plan as a condition for tranche release. This condition was not met, however, and the Plan did not appear until the last year of the adjustment programme.

The SAL programmes: conditions and implementation

The five SALs to Turkey were designed to bring about a shift from an inward-looking to an outward-oriented development strategy, and the disbursement of loans was conditional on meeting specific policy changes.

There was a continuity in the content of the programmes with four key areas singled out for particular attention – trade policy, involving measures to promote exports and liberalise imports; reform of the state economic enterprise sector; reform of the capital market and financial sector; sectoral measures directed towards energy in particular. At the same time, the relative weight attached to these key policy areas altered, with the design of the programmes evolving from a focus on stabilisation and macroeconomic policies in SAL I, to a focus on sectoral policies under the later SALs.

While each of the SALs contained a comprehensive statement of proposed reform measures, the conditions imposed for tranche releases in most cases were limited in number and highly specific. The formal tranche conditions are set out in Table 11.2.

SAL I was signed in March 1980 and made $250 million available as quick-disbursing funds in support of the reforms announced in January. The main objectives of the programme were to reduce inflation, increase foreign exchange earnings and improve domestic resource mobilisation. A supplement of $75 million was approved in November 1980. SAL I and its Supplement were made in response to Turkey's immediate stabilisation problems. Significantly the agreement was made three months before the IMF stand-by arrangement was concluded. The January 1980 measures conformed closely to the kind of programme that the Bank wished to see introduced under its new structural adjustment lending programme. At the same time, the Bank was under pressure from the Turkey Consortium members to contribute to a rescue operation. Comparison of the January 1980 policy package with the SAL I programme shows that the Bank's programme conformed closely with that of the Government, with the addition of minor conditions relating to various studies that were to be undertaken in co-operation with Bank Staff.[20] The Bank's subsequent comment on the SAL I is illuminating: In contrast to the situation which existed at the time of the first SAL, the Bank was better prepared for the subsequent SALs (World Bank, 1983: v).

SAL II marked the transition to a more comprehensive process of structural adjustment, to be followed by other SALs over a number of years. In addition to new reforms, SAL II continued to support policy reforms initiated under SAL I. Specific conditions for tranche release were set with respect to export promotion, import liberalisation, tax reform, public investment reform, state economic enterprise reform, and energy reform.

SAL III ($304.5 million) was approved in May 1982, before the completion of SAL II in November of that year. The SAL III programme continued the implementation of the reforms set out in SAL II. The programme's tranche conditions were related to progress being made in the areas of SEE reform, public investment, project selection and evaluation, and import liberalisation.

The SAL IV and V programmes continued the agenda set in SAL II. The areas emphasised were: a flexible exchange rate, incentives to encourage producers to export; monetary restraint to control inflation; deregulation of interest rates to encourage private saving; institutional reforms in key sectors (agriculture, energy and finance); rationalisation of the public investment programme; reform of the SEE sector; liberalisation of imports. Tranche conditionalities in SAL IV were: satisfactory progress in development of an annual programme; rationalisation of public investment and concentration on high priority projects; import liberalisation and a reduction in the level of the financial transactions tax. Under SAL V tranche release was conditional upon implementation of the results of the review of the public investment programme; elimination of quantitative restrictions on imports; installation of a computerised debt management system; financial sector reforms; and preparation of an energy sector programme.

Table 11.2 Tranche conditionality and implementation

Conditions	*Implementation*
SAL I (US $250 million: approved 25.3.80)	
1 *Export promotion*	
Export credit insurance scheme and system of export credits to be introduced.	
Reduction in administrative procedures for exports to be implemented.	Export promotion measures introduced in April 1980 included credits from Export Promotion Fund, priorities in foreign exchange allocation and
Comprehensive study on protection to be undertaken.	transfer and customs duty exemption.
2 *Public investment*	
Criteria to be established for selection of priority projects.	Portfolio of public investment projects was revised.
3 *Mobilisation of domestic resources*	
Budget deficit to be reduced.	Fiscal reform begun, designed to revise existing taxes, introduce new taxes
Bank deposit rates to be raised.	and improve tax administration.
Study on reform of capital market to be undertaken.	
4 *Debt management*	
World Bank technical assistance to be provided for computerisation of external debt data.	

Conditions	Implementation

SAL II (US $300 million: approved 15.5.81)

1 *Export promotion*
Adjustment of exchange rate; incentives (credit) for exporters; improvement in administrative structure for exports.

During SAL II the following measures were adopted: exchange rate adjustment, preferential credits at subsidised rates for exports, export tax rebates, duty free importation of goods used in export production. 'Instruments were applied consistently during the SAL II loan period' (Project Completion Report: 107).

2 *Import liberalisation*
Quota list to be abolished and items moved to import licensing system consisting of non-competing and competing commodities.

Quota items transferred to licence lists; commitment to speed up approval of more restricted (List II) items; agreement to undertake study of protection and incentive system, for completion end-1982.
However:
'degree of quota elimination under SAL II–III is ambiguous and requires clarification' (Project Performance Audit Report: 13).

'After the shifts in 1981, there was little movement on import liberalisation until early 1984' (PPAR: 13).

Report on protection and incentive scheme was not completed until February 1984.

3 *Financial policies*
Tax system to be restructured, with introduction of VAT during FY 82, and strengthening of tax administration.

Financial transaction tax reduced from 25 to 15 per cent.
Increase in number of tax offices and officers.

Savings to be encouraged by positive real rates of interest.

Real interest rates on deposits maintained and interest rates on loans deregulated.

Capital market to be developed by establishment of Capital Market Commission.

Increase in budget allocation for tax administration.

Capital Market Board established February 1982.

Table 11.2 continued

Conditions	Implementation
	However:
	Tranche condition on introduction of VAT waived. (VAT was enacted in January 1985).
	Share of tax revenue in GNP remained unchanged.
	Indexing of tax brackets, scheduled for December 1981, was not achieved.
4 *Rationalisation of public investment* Public investment to be reorientated to infrastructure.	Increased share of government investment to infrastructure and lower growth rate in public investment achieved in 1982.
Investment to be concentrated on high priority projects (24 months completion).	'the Government made good progress on this front' (PPAR: 17).
Government to consult with World Bank on preparation of 1982 public investment programme.	However: Delay in preparation of 1982 investment programme.
5 *SEE reform* Government reform package agreed in February 1981 to be implemented.	Quarterly performance reports introduced and considered at prime ministerial level.
Access of SEEs to central bank funding to be restricted.	Limits put on budgetary transfers to SEEs in 1982.
Autonomy in pricing policy for SEEs.	SEE prices raised frequently.
Staffing levels to be reduced and management upgraded.	Vacant posts cancelled. However: Many SEEs engaged in monopoly pricing.
	Internal reforms to improve productivity were not implemented.
	Delay in passing SEE legislation led to delay in release of second tranche of SAL II.
6 *Energy pricing* Investment in development of domestic energy sources.	Frequent adjustments in energy prices.

Conditions	Implementation
Adjustment of energy prices to international levels.	Studies initiated on organisational restructuring of petroleum and coal SEEs.

SAL III (US $304.5 million: approved 16.7.82)

1 SEE reform

Level of budgetary transfers to manufacturing SEEs to be held below 1982 level.	Budget transfers to SEEs in 1982 held to agreed level.
Progress required on SEE legal reforms.	Government approved SEE reform decree in May 1983.

2 Public investment

The rationalisation of the public investment programme was to continue.	Reduction in share of public investment to manufacturing SEEs.
Constraint on level of public investment to be maintained.	Number of ongoing projects reduced.
Private investment to be encouraged.	Limited growth in public fixed investment (0.8% in 1982; 5% in 1983).
Project evaluation capability to be developed.	

3 Import liberalisation

Further progress to be made.	Items shifted from List II to List I 'Levy list' of 25 items introduced, which allowed free importation subject to flexible levy.
	Some simplification of licence procedures for imports.
	Government expressed its commitment to shifting from quota lists to tariffs. Action to follow completion of protection system started under SAL I and scheduled for completion in late 1983.
	However:
	Review mission felt that 'while progress in this area was satisfactory', a 'more systematic approach would be preferable'.

SAL IV (US $300.8 million: approved 23.5.83)

1 Development of 1984 annual programme

To ensure that targets were compatible with medium-term objectives of the Fifth Year Plan, due for publication in autumn 1983.	Not carried out until SAL V period due to delay in completing Fifth Five Year Plan.

Table 11.2 continued

Conditions	Implementation
2 *Further rationalisation of public investment and high priority projects* Mid-year investment review to confirm that at least 85% of funds were programmed to high priority projects.	
3 *Further progress in import liberalisation* Government to set out timetable for shifting from quotas to tariffs, and to begin process in 1984.	Government restated its commitment to import liberalisation over the medium term in its 'Statement of Development Policies' submitted to Bank in support of SAL V application.
4 *Reduction in level of financial transactions tax* To be reduced in steps, between January 1983 and June 1984. Alternative sources of government revenue to be identified to compensate for shortfall.	Financial transactions tax reduced from 15% in 1983 to 3% in 1984 and to 1% in 1986.

SAL V (US $376.0 million: approved 14.6.84)

Conditions	Implementation
1 *Completion of Fifth Five Year Plan*	
2 *Implementation of public investment programme* Government to undertake detailed review of investment programme, with aim of accelerating implementation of high priority projects and improving planning capacity and institutional performance.	Government continued to emphasise priority areas in public investment during SAL V.
3 *Progress in eliminating quantitative control on imports and rationalising the tariff structure*	The number of items on List II was reduced from 821 in 1983 to 523 in 1985. The overall average tariff rate declined to 13.4% by end of SAL V. However: From 1984, increasing use was made of the import levy scheme by the Extra-Budgetary Funds.
4 *Preparation of energy programme* Energy sector plan to be prepared with Bank assistance, by end 1984.	Energy plan completed, September 1984. To support implementation, the Bank extended an Energy Sector Loan ($375m) in 1987.

Conditions	Implementation
5 *Installation of computerised debt management system* Work on designing the system began under SAL I, but progress was slow.	
6 *Financial sector reforms* Progress to be made in the following areas: (i) elimination of tax on inter-bank transactions, (ii) preparation of a review of a standardised accounting system for banks, (iii) issue and diversification of the means of marketing treasury bonds, (iv) preparation of programme for introducing standard system for companies making public issues of stock or bonds, (v) enactment of law on external auditors, (vi) opening of stock exchange, (vii) study of fiscal incentives to induce banks to reduce operating costs.	Most of these measures were already under way at the start of SAL V. The Istanbul Stock Exchange started operations at beginning of 1986.

Table 11.2 also summarises the extent to which programme conditions were met. In spite of the substantial progress in various areas, it is possible to identify a number of spheres where compliance was less than complete. There was a failure to develop a medium-term framework and to build a viable debt management system early in the life of the programme. Import liberalisation proceeded slowly, and the right of the extra-budgetary funds to impose independent import levies acted to counteract the process of import liberalisation. There was no attempt to reduce the level of export subsidies and rebates which rose to excessive levels and encouraged over-invoicing and the associated problem of 'fictitious exports'. Public investment was accelerated in the post-1983 period. There was little effort to implement internal organisational reforms in the SEEs that would have encouraged an improvement in productivity performance.

This 'slippage' in meeting the conditions of the SAL programme was tolerated by the Bank. The release of the second tranches under SAL II was held up because of delays in introducing legislation relating to SEE reform, but otherwise the SALs were agreed to and disbursed without Bank intervention. In a number of instances, conditions were waived, as for example the provision for the introduction of VAT under SAL II. The Bank's tolerance of slippage on conditionality can be explained by considering the unusual nature of the Bank's SAL programme in Turkey. The five SALs were intended to provide a continuous period of financing during which the reorientation of economic policy would occur. The Bank's completion report on SAL II and III, undertaken halfway through the programme, observed that:

25

At the macro-economic level, the program intends to support the necessary structural adjustment measures to be undertaken by the Government as it strives to alter its development strategy; the SAL loans are meant to provide quick disbursing balance of payments support to offset part of the external financial burden created by the implementation of the adjustment program . . . While the SALs successfully supported the structural adjustment process to date, this is not to say that the process is by any means complete. On the contrary, much remains to be done and the current SAL (SAL IV) should be looked upon as another incremental set of conditionalities towards achieving the goals of the medium-term reform program.

(World Bank, 1983).

At the same time it was recognised that many of the structural changes which the programmes were intended to bring about could only be realised over a longer time horizon than the programme's normal life cycle. Conditionality was predominantly qualitative in character, with 'satisfactory progress' in implementing reform measures in designated areas being used to justify a further extension of lending.

However, a willingness of the Bank to tolerate slippage on agreed conditionality embodies its own drawbacks in the sense that it produces moral hazard problems and perverse incentives for the Government implementing the programme. The realisation that Turkey was a test case and that the World Bank had a major commitment to the success of the programme, obviously influenced the Government's perception of the strategic options available. The ways in which this perception influenced the Turkish authorities' response to the SAL conditions on policy reform is examined in the next section.

11.4 COALITION BUILDING, STRUCTURAL ADJUSTMENT AND 'SLIPPAGE'

Policy-making remained highly concentrated and centralised throughout the post-1980 period. The degree of continuity and the centralised nature of the policy-making process is epitomised by the fact that except for a period in 1982 when he resigned following the financial crisis,[21] Ozal remained in charge of the economy during three remarkably distinct phases: the Demirel Government, January to October 1980; the Military Interlude, October 1980 to November 1983; and the Motherland Party Government, November 1983 to the present.

The military intervention in October 1980 clearly facilitated the adjustment effort, by guaranteeing political stability and the exclusion of democratic processes. The presence of the military government resolved the distributional stalemate of the late 1970s, by eliminating the right to

26

strike and subsequently restricting the scope for trade union activity. Consequently, labour was directly excluded from the decision-making process. One of the distinguishing characteristics of the early 1980s concerned the imposition of a compulsory incomes policy which resulted in a decisive shift in income distribution away from wage-earners. The flexibility of real wages, combined with the large inflows of foreign capital, performed a key instrumental role in the recovery process (Onis and Ozmucur, 1988a, 1988b).

The pressure for a return to parliamentary democracy culminated in the General Election of November 1983, which brought Ozal's Motherland Party to power with a decisive majority. The return to a multi-party system by late 1983 confronted the Ozal Government with the task of retaining and consolidating its power base by satisfying the aspirations of the main socio-economic coalition groups. The Motherland party projected an image of a national party, working for a common interest, and tried to dissociate itself from close affinity within any particular socio-economic group. At the same time it had to balance the potentially conflicting demands of these different groups. Growth was seen as the means of walking this tightrope. Rapid economic growth, based initially on export expansion and subsequently on public investment, generated the benefits available for distribution. However, to ensure that these benefits were distributed in a way which preserved the Motherland party coalition base, it was necessary for the authorities to retain control over them. Thus, the policy of structural adjustment was pursued in ways which did not diminish the role of the public sector, but rather increased the state's discretionary power and control over the distribution of economic resources.[22]

This perspective provides an insight into the Ozal administration's approach to implementing World Bank recommended policy reform in the major areas of trade liberalisation, public sector investment and state economic enterprises. Trade liberalisation, as we have seen, was a central component of the structural adjustment programme. Yet, import liberalisation in terms of a substantial reduction of tariff protection occurred at a relatively advanced stage of the programme, after December 1983. In retrospect, the delay in the liberalisation of imports appears to have been motivated by the desire to protect domestic interests from the effects of sudden exposure to foreign competition. The manufacturing sector, which had developed under heavy import protection during the previous two decades, was given time to adjust to the new outward-looking environment by the step-by-step relaxation of the 'List' import restrictions.[23] Simultaneously, the manufacturing enterprises were given major export incentives and subsidies which amounted to 20 per cent of total manufactured export value in the 1980–5 period (Baysan and Blitzer, 1988; Milanovic, 1986).[24] The potential damage of trade liberalisation to domestic manufacturing enterprises was further offset by the Government's policy of encouraging a high degree of concentration in the export-producing sector via the institutional innovation of creating foreign trade companies. Foreign trade companies, which were intended to improve the international competitiveness of the Turkish export sector, increasingly dominated export trade, and in 1986 twenty-four companies accounted for 45 per cent of total exports. Large-scale enterprises, producing for both the internal and external markets, benefited disproportionately from export incentives, and the system of differential tax rebates accelerated the process of concentration in the Turkish export sector. Small businesses, on the other hand, benefited from export incentives only to a limited extent, and furthermore were negatively affected by the high loan rates of interest which emerged with financial sector reform.

World Bank concern with the pace and selective nature of import liberalisation was expressed in the SAL II and III programme reviews, and with the announcement of the 1984 Import Programme in December 1983, the Government introduced major policy changes, the most important being the move to a negative import list system, whereby any import not listed could be freely imported. In addition, licensing procedures were eased. Concurrently, significant reductions in the tariff structure were announced. While the liberalisation of the quota system and the tariff reductions were seen as significant moves in the direction desired by the Bank, several offsetting policy measures were introduced which undermined the credibility of the import liberalisation programme. In particular, the increasing use of the special levy (Fund List) on imports gave protection to an ever increasing number of domestically produced manufactured goods. Second, the Government made increasing use of various import surcharges and deposit requirements for imports to redress its growing budget deficit problem.

A similar reluctance to adopt the World Bank's recommendations is evident with respect to the removal of export promotion measures. In late 1983 the Government announced its intention to stimulate exports through a neutral trade regime of an active exchange rate policy and import liberalisation. The rebate rates were lowered in 1984, but the overall level of export subsidisation fell only marginally, due to the shift in manufactured exports toward high rebate categories, and the introduction of VAT rebates in 1985. Export credits were abolished in January 1985, but reintroduced in November 1986.

A second broad constituency whose support the Government elicited is the state bureaucracy. By the end of the 1970s the SEEs' aggregate losses amounted to 4 per cent of GNP and financing these losses was a major source of the budget deficit. There was agreement between the Government and the Bank from the beginning of SAL I that the SEEs should be reoriented towards improved economic and financial performance. Between 1980 and 1982, the Government implemented a number of measures to improve the short-term financial structure of the SEEs, to redirect their investment programmes and to finance them increasingly from non-budget sources. Legal reforms were undertaken to institutionalise various internal reform actions to increase managerial efficiency and productivity.

The reform of the SEEs came about in three related ways: authorisation of continuous price increases for SEE products and services, the movement off-budget of the SEEs as they reduced their deficits and were allowed to borrow directly from the foreign and domestic banking system, and the redirection of public investment away from manufacturing towards infrastructure. What did not take place was internal restructuring of the SEEs. Despite the conditionality in SAL II requiring its early introduction, the major SEE reform decree was delayed until May 1983. While the deregulation of SEE prices enabled the sector to show positive operating profits after 1980, it is doubtful whether their economic performance improved.[25] Many of the enterprises were operating in monopolistic markets; furthermore, the delayed liberalisation of imports and the subsequent emergence of the extra-budgetary funds in the post-1983 phase helped protect these enterprises from competition and from pressure to improve efficiency. World Bank concern with the failure of the reform measures to improve SEE productivity was expressed in the SAL IV President's Report. A technical assistance loan designed to improve operational efficiency began in March 1984, but was later abandoned when the plans for possible privatisation introduced uncertainty as to the future structure of the SEEs.

The share of the SEE sector in GNP rose during the structural adjustment period, from 15 per cent in 1980 to 20 per cent in 1986, and the SEE share of total investment increased from 33 per cent in 1981 to 40 per cent in 1985. The SEEs contributed significantly to the public investment boom in 1985 and 1986 by raising their fixed investments by almost 10 per cent in each year. Financing of this investment from external and internal borrowing added to the growth of public sector debt.

The paradoxical situation whereby the public enterprise sector increased in relative importance during a time of structural adjustment when the Government had publicly committed itself to reducing the role of the public sector, can be resolved by relating it to the political realities of the post-1983 period. In the absence of electoral constraints imposed by parliamentary democracy, political rationality required the formation and consolidation of a coalition among groups with potentially conflicting interests. Increasing the pace of economic growth, with the expansion of the public sector being used as the mechanism for distributing the gains, was the primary means by which the Government sought to elicit broad support from various strata of the population.

The growth of GDP accelerated during the post 1983 period and reached a peak of 8 per cent in 1986, with public investment increasing as a share of total fixed investment from 56 per cent in 1983 to 58 per cent in 1986.[26]

The constraints on the Government's ability to pursue a high growth strategy were significantly lessened by 1984, due to a combination of two factors. First, from 1983 onwards, the Government's creditworthiness had been re-established, and Turkey could borrow freely from the international financial markets, with the principal component of medium- and long-term borrowing directed to the public sector.[27] Second, the international lending agencies did not impose sanctions on Turkey when the conditionality requirements on macroeconomic aggregates were broken. The SALs did not include explicit conditionality in the areas of fiscal deficits,[28] and the absence of a rigorous macroeconomic analytical framework handicapped the Bank in providing corrections to the macro direction of the adjustment programme. During the early period of the programme monetary targets set by the IMF were adhered to, but in the later stages monetary control was relaxed:

> The structural measures (discussed above) were underpinned by a marked tightening of demand management policies at the outset of the program. Beyond the initial years of the adjustment, however, it proved increasingly difficult to maintain the desired financial policy restraint.
>
> (Kopits, 1987: 17)

The growth of the Extra-Budgetary Funds (EBFs) was an institutional development of the post-1983 period which provided the Government with an important instrument for resolving potential distributional conflicts. The EBFs are off-budget Funds with assigned revenue sources such as levies on particular imports, and a mandate to make expenditures in specific areas, generally of a social nature. The EBFs possessed the following advantages from the Government's point of view. First they enabled the Government to direct expenditure to areas that it considered desirable, in rapid fashion, without prior parliamentary approval. The Mass Housing Fund, which provides credits for construction of small housing units and supports land acquisition, is one of the largest funds and clearly conforms with the Government's objective of legitimising its position among the electorate. Second, the EBFs counteracted the process of trade liberalisation and in that sense can be seen as a response to the demands of inward-looking business and SEEs for maintaining protection from external competition. Finally, the emergence of the EBFs was clearly consistent with the Government's growth objectives with the EBFs' dedicated revenues, as well as their domestic and foreign borrowing, being used to finance the Government's ambitious public investment programme.

11.5 CONCLUDING OBSERVATIONS

The Turkish experience with structural adjustment was unique in at least one respect, namely the willingness of the international donors to assist Turkey in 1980. By late 1979 the major OECD countries were committed to a rescue operation, primarily for geopolitical reasons, to help Turkey out of its acute foreign exchange crisis, with the IMF and World Bank emerging as the intermediate link between the Consortium and Turkey for imposing conditions and monitoring performance. In addition, by the end of the 1970s the World Bank had been converted to adjustment measures oriented towards structural change and the supply-side of the economy and was anxious to introduce its new form of policy-based lending in collaboration with the standard short-run IMF stabilisation programme, by 1980. A test case was needed of a middle income country of a certain standing with a significant likelihood of success. Turkey offered a suitable testing ground for the implementation of the new form of World Bank–IMF cross-conditionality. Considering that Turkey provided the first major test of SAL programmes, the World Bank was clearly committed to the success of the programme.

The scale of extended assistance made available to Turkey was a critical factor in Turkey's recovery from an acute foreign exchange crisis. Between 1980 and 1984 Turkey was in receipt of five successive SAL programmes and three IMF stand-by arrangements. In addition, Turkey received sizeable official assistance from the OECD member countries, Saudi Arabia and the European Resettlement Fund. Additional indirect financing was provided through a number of debt restructuring agreements.[29]

The magnitude of the capital flows generated meant that Turkey did not experience any problems of import compression during the critical adjustment phase.[30] Imports as a share of GDP increased from 14.2 per cent in 1980 to 23.8 per cent in 1985, and Turkey could continue to grow rapidly during the first half of the 1980s without needing to curb her trade deficit.

While the scale of external assistance provided to Turkey undoubtedly facilitated a relatively smooth adjustment process, it is also the case that the success achieved by the programme would not have materialised in the absence of a supporting domestic environment.

Most observers, including those who actively participated in SAL negotiations, agree that a key factor which explains the ability of the Ozal Government to implement the adjustment programmes was the widely-held belief that every other alternative had been tried and discredited.[31] The Demirel Government elected in November 1979 was prepared to abandon long-held views on economic policy, and to adopt an outward-looking, market-oriented strategy. Thus, in marked contrast to the 1972–9 experience, there was a close correspondence between the views of the

31

Turkish Government and its economic policy-makers under the leadership of Ozal, and the type of programme advocated by the World Bank and the IMF. It was no longer a question of a programme being imposed by external donors against the will of the Government,[32] and the Turkish authorities were highly successful in presenting the programme as having been formulated by themselves, assisted by the Bank.

Recent research on the politics of stabilisation programmes suggests that the cohesion and ideological orientation of the bureaucratic elite is an important variable in explaining the fortunes of such programmes.[33] The Turkish case with the example of Ozal is clearly in conformity with this argument. Except for a brief period in 1982, Ozal has been in control of the economy since the inception of the adjustment programme, and policy-making remained highly concentrated and centralised throughout the 1980s.[34]

The Bank's commitment to a programme success story in Turkey, coupled with the Turkish authorities' independent determination to bring about a fundamental shift in development strategy meant that the Ozal administration was able to exercise considerable influence over both the content of the SAL programmes and the speed with which the reform measures were implemented. This autonomy of the Turkish policy-makers was used, especially after 1983, to maximise the discretionary nature of the distribution of resources, and as a means of maintaining a 'broad coalition' of political support among potentially conflicting interest groups.

An interesting feature of the Turkish experiment is the way in which the World Bank assumed the role of the leading external actor, with the IMF operating in the background. The Turkish authorities were aware of the political damage that would be caused by being associated too closely in the public mind with the IMF. The qualitative nature of the World Bank's conditionality, with the emphasis on the direction of policy changes rather than precise quantitative targets, introduced an element of flexibility in programme implementation and was instrumental in eliciting a greater co-operation and commitment on the part of the Government. For their part, the Bank and the Fund were willing to co-operate in this public presentation of their respective roles, while maintaining close institutional contact through regular consultations and joint membership of missions.[35] There was agreement that the Fund's attention would be directed to the country's monetary and fiscal balance and the maintenance of external competitiveness, while the Bank's efforts would concentrate on SEE reform, import liberalisation, export promotion and the rationalisation of public investment. There was little attempt, however, to integrate these two broad areas of responsibility in the form of an overall macro planning framework. The emerging macro difficulties, relating particularly to the relationship between exchange rate policy and interest rate liberalisation, were not recognised. Management, as distinct from mere measurement, of the external debt was not tackled until SAL V. Monetary and fiscal discipline was relaxed after 1983. The Bank tended to rely on the Fund's analysis at the macro level, which became of increasingly limited value. In this sense, the Bank was let down by the quality of the macro advice emanating from the Fund.[36]

The conditionality contained in the SAL programmes was in most instances expressed, as earlier noted, in qualitative and sometimes ambiguous terms, leaving scope for different interpretations by the Bank and the borrower. In the Bank's case, the various President's Reports prepared in support of further SALs merely approved of past performance as showing 'satisfactory progress', or omitted to refer to slippage in meeting targets for the period under review.[37]

It is clear that in spite of important economic achievements, the Turkish experience with structural adjustment was not an unqualified success. Important problem areas persisted, notably in relation to the SEEs, the financial sector, as well as the extra-budgetary funds which counteracted the process of trade liberalisation.

Soft conditionality and tolerance of certain deviations from programme targets might be justified by the Bank on several grounds. First, structural adjustment is by definition a long-term process and the time-horizon for achieving adjustment is likely to be considerably longer than the length of a programme. It is difficult to reconcile this argument, however, with the evident haste with which the Bank moved to disburse the five SALs. By the end of SAL III there was evidence that the reform process was proceeding less rapidly and more unevenly than had been anticipated: the Programme Completion Report on SAL II and III, for example, noted that 'after three years of the structural adjustment process, it is possible to take a broad look at the achievements of the 1980–82 period, which suggest striking success in some areas, less so in others, and some unresolved problems'. The SAL IV programme drew attention to the need for a medium-term macro framework to be established and the lack of progress on stabilisation policy, yet there was no delay in the disbursing of SAL V, in spite of the failure to prepare such a framework. Second, it could be argued that 'qualitative' conditionality and tolerance of slippage were necessary concessions to secure the political environment needed for the structural adjustment process to proceed under Ozal.[38] However, it embodied its own drawbacks, namely that Turkey's awareness of the World Bank's commitment to the success of the programme influenced the Government's perceptions of the room for manoeuvre available to it. In the post-1983 period, with the addition of electoral constraints, Turkish policy-makers were increasingly converted to the view that they could push for rapid growth on the expectation that any budgetary overruns would not be punished by the Bank.

Two general lessons might be drawn from this line of reasoning. First, while a flexible approach to conditionality is desirable to win support for the programme, an excessive relaxation of conditionality may generate perverse incentives for Government policy-making, which in turn may undermine the whole programme and produce serious disequilibrium. Second, a medium-term financial strategy is needed for maintaining fiscal discipline and stability. The persistence of macroeconomic instability can undermine the success of the structural adjustment programme.

A final observation relates to the social and distributional impact of the SAL programme. The implementation of the structural adjustment programme in Turkey was accompanied by a significant increase in income inequality and by a marked decline in the share of wages and other fixed income groups.[39] Real wages fell dramatically. The transfer was achieved by legal and constitutional restrictions on union activity in the 1980–3 period. The process of redistribution assumed a more subtle form in the post-1983 phase, with a rising rate of inflation acting as a forced saving mechanism, thereby transferring income to both the Government and business sectors from fixed income groups. The incorporation of components of those strata that had emerged as significant losers during the reforms of the early 1980s – labour, agricultural work-force, lower state bureaucracy, elements of small business – was a key objective of the rapid growth strategy adopted in the later stages of the programme period. There is no evidence, however, to show that the Government's policy of rapid growth combined with the targeting of public investment expenditure to selected groups brought about a significant improvement in income distribution. What the process of rapid growth did achieve, however, was an acceleration of inflation, a worsening fiscal disequilibrium and a rapid build-up of domestic and external debt. With hindsight, the failure of the SAL programmes to monitor the distributional impact of adjustment and to design countervailing measures to minimise adverse social effects can be seen to present the greatest challenge to the substance and sustainability of the structural adjustment process in Turkey.

Acknowledgements

We are grateful to Jane Harrigan and Paul Mosley for detailed comments on an earlier version of this contribution.

NOTES

1 Between 1980 and 1984, Turkey received US $1556.3 million in SALs. This amounted to over one-third of all Bank policy-based lending in the early 1980s (see Volume 1, Table 2.2) and far exceeded the value of any other Bank adjustment programme of the time. (The next largest, in the Philippines, was worth just over US $500 million between 1980 and 1984). After 1985 the large sector loans granted to Brazil, Argentina and Indonesia began to rival the Turkish programme in size.

2 'Turkey's adjustment program was undoubtedly successful and a major break from past

policies that relied on import substitution, market intervention and reliance on state enterprises' (World Bank, 1988: 84).

3 For a detailed investigation of Turkey's import substituting industrialisation (ISI) experience and the contribution of the ISI strategy to the crisis of the late 1970s, see Onis (1987, 1988). For a broad overview of Turkey's economic and political development since the 1980s, see Hale (1981). A valuable discussion of the link between macro planning and the ISI strategy in Turkey is provided by Yagci (1981).

4 See Rodrik (1986) and Onis and Ozmucur (1988b) for a detailed analysis of the growing fiscal disequilibrium and the debt crisis of the late 1970s.

5 An excellent analysis of the political dimension of the 1977–9 crisis is provided by Sunar and Sayar (1986). For a useful factual study involving the political developments of the late 1970s, see Pevsner (1986).

6 The basic reference on Turkey's relations with the IMF during the 1978–82 period is Okyar (1983). Wolff (1987) is also informative in this respect.

7 Turkey's relations with the IMF during the late 1970s were paralleled in other developing countries where there was a similar absence of domestic commitment to adjusting to internal or external disequilibria (see Haggard, 1985).

8 For details of the January 1980 programme, see OECD (1980), also Okyar (1983).

9 As a Turkish official involved in policy formulation at this time put it to us, 'the international community needed Turkey as much as Turkey needed it'.

10 Chancellor Schmidt of West Germany played a key role in restoring the lines of communication between the IMF and Turkey (see Wolff, 1987: 72).

11 Details in this paragraph are taken from Okyar (1983: 542–3).

12 Many of the measures included in the January 1980 programme had been proposed by Ozal in the Spring 1979 negotiations with the Fund, but were rejected by Ecevit. Much of the 1980 programme, therefore, had already been 'cleared' with the Fund. It is significant that following the January 1980 announcement, the IMF released the remaining tranches of the July 1979 stand-by agreement.

13 This aspect of the Turkish experience is in accordance with the argument of Haggard (1985) and Nelson (1984) that the character and unity of the bureaucratic elite is a critical factor in determining the success of an adjustment programme.

14 Details of the content of the IMF programme are given in Kopits (1987).

15 'The main significance of the January 1980 policy initiatives lies in the recognition that a fresh approach toward economic problems must depend on altering fundamentally previous economic policies and attitudes. If sufficient time can be secured to enable these essential changes to be carried through with determination, the substantial resources which Turkey can potentially mobilise to strengthen its balance of payments should enable it gradually to open up the economy to the full benefits of international trade'.

(IMF (1980), *Turkey – Request for Stand-by Arrangement*, Washington DC, p. 23, quoted in Wolff, 1987).

16 It is interesting to note that in 1987 and 1988 the authorities declined to sign a stand-by arrangement with the IMF on the grounds that this would be associated in the public's mind with the failure of the economic policies which they had attempted to implement almost a decade earlier.

17 Following the financial crash of 1982 deposit ceilings were reintroduced, but the Government aimed at maintaining the rates on time deposits at positive levels in real terms.

18 For detailed discussion of the macro policy dilemmas in Turkey's adjustment programme, see Rodrik (1988) and Celasun (1988).

19 A review by the IMF in March 1982 showed that performance in implementing the stand-by arrangement was satisfactory, and in April 1989 the IMF review concluded

that all performance criteria had been met. These views of the Fund were cited by the Bank in the SAL IV proposal document as supporting evidence.

20 Details of the January 1980 measures are given in OECD (1980).

21 Following the banking crisis of 1982, Ozal resigned and was replaced by the Ulusu administration.

22 For further development of this argument, see Onis (1988) and Waterbury (1988).

23 The timing and sequencing of trade liberalisation was subsequently identified by the Bank as a major issue in programme design (see Edwards, 1984).

24 Export incentives included tax rebates, interest rate subsidies on export credit, and foreign exchange allocations that allowed for the duty-free import of intermediates and raw materials.

25 Ozmucur and Esmer (1988) demonstrate, on the basis of total factor productivity growth estimates, that the overall productivity performance of the public manufacturing sector did not exhibit any improvement during the 1980s.

26 For evidence of the increasing importance of the public sector in the 1983–7 growth period, see Onis and Ozmucur (1988b).

27 See Stallings (1985) for a discussion of how external capital inflows may enhance the autonomy of the state.

28 Details of the fiscal conditionality in Turkey's SALs are contained in World Bank, 1988, Table 3.4.

29 IMF–World Bank programme did not elicit, however, a significant response from the commercial banks and the external funding was provided almost entirely from official sources. For details on the external resources provided to Turkey during the period, see Wolff (1987) and Onis and Ozmucur (1988b).

30 This contrasts sharply with the Latin American experience in the aftermath of the 1982 debt crisis, when in the absence of external sources of finance the major debtor countries were forced to adjust primarily via a compression of imports which exercised a negative influence over their growth performance (see Sachs, 1986).

31 The Ozal administration used the argument repeatedly to consolidate its political support, with Ozal being successfully projected as the only leader capable of managing the economy successfully.

32 As noted earlier, the March 1980 SAL I endorsed the Government's programme of January 1980, and the June 1980 IMF arrangement added only two elements, relating to interest rate policy and incomes policy.

33 See Haggard and Kaufman (1989), Callaghy (1989), and Kahler (1989).

34 The strong state tradition in Turkey and the weakening of internal group organisations, particularly labour, facilitated a high degree of centralisation in policy formulation and implementation (see Heper, 1985).

35 During the SAL I–III period, Bank missions to Turkey averaged about 100 per year.

36 This point was put succinctly in a recent (1987) internal Bank Performance Review: 'In SALs II and III the Bank tended to accept the Fund's analysis at the macro level. Perhaps it should consider developing its own capacity'.

37 For example, SAL IV called for quantitative restrictions on SEE investment and operating profits in 1983. These targets were not met. The quantitative shortfalls were not mentioned in the SAL V documentation which merely cited the need for further improvement in managerial expertise.

38 Ozal resigned following the bankers' crisis of 1982 and was out of office between 1982 and 1983. This was a period of uncertainty for the Bank who wanted continuity in the structural adjustment process. One Turkish official involved in negotiations in this period suggested to us that the Bank used the SALs as a bargaining device by making it known that further SAL loans would be conditional on the holding of multi-party elections and the election of Ozal as Prime Minister.

39 See Celasun (1986).

BIBILIOGRAPHY

Baysan, T. and Blitzer C. (1988) 'Turkey's trade liberalization in the 1980s and prospects for its sustainability', Paper prepared for Conference on 'Turkey's Economic Development in the 1980s: Changing Strategies and Prospects for the Next Decade', Harvard University.

Callaghy, T. M. (1989) 'Toward State capability and embedded liberalism in the Third World: lessons for economic adjustment', Paper prepared for Conference on 'The Politics of Structural Adjustment', Institute of Development Studies, University of Brighton (now published in Nelson, 1989).

Celasun, M. (1986) 'Income distribution and domestic terms of trade in Turkey, 1978–83', *METU Studies in Development* 13(1–2).

Celasun, M. (1988) 'Turkey: fiscal aspects of adjustment in the 1980s', Paper prepared for Conference on 'Turkey's Economic Development in the 1980s: Changing Strategies and Prospects for the Next Decade', Harvard University.

Edwards, S. (1984) *The Order of Liberalisation of the External Sector in Developing Countries*, Princeton, NJ, Princeton Papers in International Finance, no. 156.

Haggard, S. (1985) 'The politics of adjustment: lessons from the IMF's Extended Fund Facility', *International Organisation* 39(3).

Haggard, S. and Kaufman, R. (1989) 'Economic adjustment in new democracies' in Nelson, J. (ed.) *Fragile Coalitions: The Politics of Economic Adjustment in Developing Countries*, Policy Perspectives Series, Washington DC, Overseas Development Council.

Hale, W. (1981) *The Political and Economic Development of Modern Turkey*, Croom Helm, London.

Heper, M. (1985) *The State Tradition in Turkey*, London, Methuen.

Kahler, M. (1989) 'International actors and the politics of adjustment', Paper prepared for Conference on 'The Politics of Structural Adjustment', Institute of Development Studies, University of Sussex. Now published by Nelson (1989).

Kopits, G. (1987) *Structural Reform, Stabilization and Growth in Turkey*, IMF Occasional Paper no. 52, Washington DC, IMF.

Milanovic, B. (1986) 'Export incentives and Turkish manufacturing exports, 1980–87', World Bank Staff Papers, no. 768, Washington DC, World Bank.

Nelson, J. (1984) 'The political economy of stabilisation: commitment, capacity and public response', *World Development* 12(12).

Nelson, J. (ed.) (1989) *Fragile Coalitions: The Politics of Economic Adjustment in Developing Countries*, Princeton NJ, Princeton University Press.

Okyar, O. (1983) 'Turkey and the IMF: a review of relations 1978–82' in J. Williamson (ed.) *IMF Conditionality*, Washington DC, Institute for International Economics.

Onis, Z. (1987) 'Inflation and import-substituting industrialisation: an interpretation of the Turkish case', *Journal of Economics and Administrative Studies* 1(1).

Onis, Z. (1988) 'The dynamics of coalition building, macro-economic instability and growth in Turkey', mimeo, Department of Economics, Bogazici University.

Onis, Z. and Ozmucur, S. (1988a) 'Supply-side origins of macro-economic crisis in Turkey', Paper presented to the World Bank Conference on 'Macro-economic Policies, Crisis and Growth in the Long-run', Madrid.

Onis, Z. and Ozmucur, S. (1988b) 'The role of the financial system in the creation and resolution of macro-economic crisis in Turkey', Paper presented to the World Bank Conference on 'Macro-economic Policies, Crisis and Growth in the Long-run', Madrid.

Organisation for Economic Co-operation and Development (OECD) (1980) *Turkey: Economic Survey*, Paris, OECD.

Ozmucur, S. and Esmer, Y. (1988) 'Total factor productivity in Turkey: a longitudinal and comparative analysis of total factor productivity growth in Turkish manufacturing industries, 1970–1985', mimeo, Department of Economics, Bogazici University.

Pevsner, L. W. (1986) *Turkey's Political Crisis: Background, Perspectives and Prospects*, The Washington Papers, no. 110, Praeger Special Studies, Washington DC.

Rodrik, D. (1986) 'Macro-economic policy and debt in Turkey. A tale of two policy phases', mimeo, Harvard University.

Rodrik, D. (1988) 'Some policy dilemmas in Turkish macro-economic management', Paper prepared for Conference on 'Turkey's Economic Development in the 1980s: Changing Strategies and Prospects for the Next Decade', Harvard University.

Sachs, J. D. (1986) 'Managing the LDC debt crisis', *Brookings Papers on Economic Activity* 2.

Stallings, B. (1985) 'International lending and relative autonomy of the state: a case study of twentieth century Peru', *Politics and Society* 14(2).

Sunar, I. and Sayar, R. (1986) 'Democracy in Turkey: problems and prospects', in G. O'Donnell, P. C. Schmitter and L. Whitehead (eds) *Transitions from Authoritarian Rule – Southern Europe*, Baltimore and London, John Hopkins University Press.

Waterbury, J. (1988) 'Coalition-building, export-led growth and the public sector in Turkey', Paper prepared for Conference on 'Dynamics of a Mixed Economy: Turkey', Middle East Studies Association Annual Meeting, Los Angeles.

Wolff, P. (1987) *Stabilisation Policy and Structural Adjustment in Turkey, 1980–1985. The role of the IMF and the World Bank in an Externally Supported Adjustment Process*, Berlin, The German Development Institute.

World Bank (1983) *Turkey: Structural Adjustment Loan II and III*, Project Completion Report, Washington DC, World Bank.

World Bank (1988) *Adjustment Lending: An Evaluation of Ten Years of Experience*, Policy and Research Series no. 1, Country Economics Department, Washington DC, World Bank.

Yagci, F. (1981) 'Macro planning in Turkey: A critical evaluation', *METU Studies in Development*, Special Issue, 'Two Decades of Planned Development in Turkey'.

12

THE PHILIPPINES

Paul Mosley

12.1 INTRODUCTION

During the 1980s, the principal focus of this essay, the Philippine economy diverged dramatically from the scenario originally visualised by the international agencies. Instead of emerging from a phase of macroeconomic crisis and stabilisation at the beginning of the decade into a period of microeconomic structural adjustment, it remained in a state of virtually continuous macroeconomic crisis until the middle of the decade, which eventually culminated in the replacement of the Marcos by the Aquino regime; it therefore found itself having to undertake structural adjustment in the midst of stabilisation. This, we shall argue, is one of the distinctive factors which shaped the pattern of the government's and the economy's response to the World Bank's intervention. But there are others lying much further back in time, which form the main subject matter of this introductory section. These are: the relative failure of the development strategy followed during the 1960s and 1970s; the political economy of the Marcos regime; the previous history of relations with the IMF and World Bank during this same period; and the special relationship with the United States. All of these, we shall argue, exhibit characteristics so distinctive as to make the Philippines case, fascinating though it is in its own right, a particularly risky one from which to generalise.

Our point of departure is that the Philippine economy, one of the most dynamic in the Third World in the 1950s when its manufacturing output rose by 12 per cent per annum in real terms, gradually lost this dynamism in the 1960s and 70s, and became the sick man of Asia. As illustrated by Table 12.1, the Philippines growth rate gradually fell below that achieved, not only in the 'Four Little Tigers' of the Far East, but also other neighbouring South-East Asian countries.

Table 12.1 Growth rates of GDP per capita in East and South-East Asian LDCs, 1950–80

	1950–60	1960–70	1970–80	1950–80
East Asian NICs				
Taiwan	4.0	6.3	6.7	5.7
South Korea	3.1	6.0	8.0	5.7
Singapore	n.a.	6.7	7.7	6.2
Hong Kong	4.5	7.2	6.4	6.0
ASEAN countries				
Malaysia	1.0	3.3	5.3	3.2
Thailand	2.8	4.7	5.1	4.2
Indonesia	1.9	2.3	5.7	3.3
Philippines	3.6	2.2	3.4	3.1

Source: H. Oshima (1983) 'Sector sources of Philippines post-war growth', *Journal of Philippine Development*, 1st semester.

The roots of this relative decline are both internal and external, since the Philippines correspond neither to the standard 'import-substituting industrialisation' nor the 'export-oriented industrialisation' models. Domestically the growth of demand was constrained by a relatively backward agriculture – which achieved self-sufficiency only briefly in the late 1970s – and by notoriously low wage levels which were the direct consequence of the low living standards of the rural mass. In 1986 it was estimated that three-fifths of the 56 million Filipinos lived beneath a poverty line that was officially set at \$120 a month for a family of six; this proportion has not changed substantially since the 1960s, and is well below that achieved in the other East and South-East Asian countries of Table 12.1.[1] And if the home market was limited by deficiency of domestic purchasing power, the external market was restricted by the narrow front on which export penetration was achieved. Aside from the staples of plantation agriculture – sugar, coconut, pineapple, and bananas – the only significant Philippine exports are in the areas of garments and electronics. These non-traditional exports have made rapid progress, as recorded in Table 12.2; however, just like traditional import-substituting industrialisation they are import-intensive, as they consist of small labour-intensive strata within a complex multinational manufacturing process.[2]

As a consequence, the stimulus they have been able to impart to domestic development has been limited. Of the value of garment exports in 1979 it is estimated that 56 per cent was imported and 44 per cent was domestic value added, whereas in the electronics industry only 13 per cent consisted of domestic value added.[3] As the appraisal document for the Bank's First Structural Adjustment Loan conceded,

Table 12.2 'Non-traditional' exports as proportion of total ($ millions at current prices)

	1970	1976	1981	1983	1986
'Non-traditional exports' of which:	205	546	2374	2537	2685
Electrical equipment and components	30	85	838	1054	903
Garments	106	185	618	542	750
Total exports	2157	2600	5790	4974	4881
'Non-traditional' as % of total exports	9.5	21.1	41.2	50.7	55.5

Source: *Philippine Statistical Yearbook*, various issues.

'due to the high cost and low quality of domestic inputs, non-traditional exports are largely dependent on imports and, as a result, have remained enclaves with only few backward linkages to the domestic manufacturing sector. Consequently value added is only 25 per cent of output.'[4]

If domestic inputs were of 'high cost and low quality' some of the blame certainly lay with the climate of oligarchy fostered by Ferdinand Marcos as President during the twenty years to 1986. Democratically elected in 1966, he imposed martial law in 1972 and thereafter sought to retain the necessary power base through two strategies: the first a broad-based populist appeal mediated through programmes of land reform and community development, and the second a network of relationships with clients who, on the classic feudal model, delivered political support in return for selective economic benefits. Some of these clients were relatives of the Marcos family, such as Benjamin and Alfredo Romualdez, both brothers of the First Lady, mostly involved in retail trade and consumer goods manufacture. Edwardo Cojuangco, the estranged cousin of Mrs Aquino, took charge of Unicom, a monopoly established to administer coconut exports. Hermino Disini received a 500,000 acre logging concession from the President, and was able to take over other distributorships and manufacturing enterprises through 'behest loans' made at Marcos's personal request from the two state-owned banks, the Philippines National Bank and the Development Bank of the Philippines. Roberto Benedicto controlled the National Sugar Trading Corporation and so determined the price and quality of the country's sugar exports. As this list implies, 'the dominant political coalition' – to quote Haggard – 'was not built around export-promoting industry as it was in [South Korea]'.[5] Nor yet was it built around the rural estate-owning aristocracy. It was built, rather, around the conferment of rents to selected barons in the agribusiness, trade and consumer goods sectors, whom Marcos hoped to build up in due course into the leaders of industrial conglomerates on the

East Asian model. These rents were created not only through the classical instruments of protection – tariffs, quotas and subsidised credit – but also through *selective exemption* from these instruments, as when Herminio Disini was authorised, in 1975, to import cigarette filters with an import duty of only 10 per cent in face of a prevailing tariff of 100 per cent.[6] An important additional vehicle of patronage was the fostering of state-owned enterprises, which grew in number from 70 to 245 between 1972 and 1984; such enterprises were exempt from the personnel rules and pay scales governing the regular civil service and could in consequence be used to provide rewards of flexible size to government clients.

To the extent that the inefficiencies described above surfaced as balance-of-payments deficits, which occurred with increasing frequency after the mid-1970s, the role of the IMF and, later, the World Bank, became crucial. From 1970 to 1985 a condition of chronic balance-of-payments deficit was treated by chronic recourse to Fund stand-bys, 1982 being the only year when no such operation was recorded. But as Table 12.3 records, there is very little evidence that the appropriate medicine for such an affliction, namely a real devaluation of the exchange rate, was actually swallowed in spite of the Fund's constant supervision. Rather, it appears, the Fund allowed its conditionality on the exchange rate, which appreciated in real terms by 18 per cent between 1970 and 1983, to be evaded by recourse to high-cost foreign borrowing,[7] which it may have done the more readily through unawareness of the extent to which the foreign exchange reserves were being window-dressed by means of short-term overseas borrowing.[8] This overvaluation imposed on Philippine exporters an additional competitive burden which the Bank, when it came to involve itself in macroeconomic issues at the beginning of the 1980s, was to find less than welcome.

For its part, the Bank had expanded its project-lending enormously in the 1970s, from $39 million in 1972 to $561 million in 1979 or about sixfold in real terms, most of it in the agricultural and infrastructure sectors, as illustrated by Table 12.4. In terms of long-term objectives, this aid was highly successful: productivity in rice was increased enormously, to the extent that the country was a net exporter by the end of the decade, and these were also the years of the shift to non-traditional exports, as indicated in Table 12.2. But at project level, worrying signs soon began to appear, in the shape of a decline in project rates of return.[9] Such a decline, of course, was beginning to worry the Bank world-wide, and to be ascribed to policy deficiencies within central government.[10] At the same time, disbursement rates on projects within the Philippines had fallen to a disturbingly low level. The obvious solution to both problems was programme assistance in support of the project portfolio, with policy conditions attached: in other words, Structural Adjustment Lending.

Table 12.3 Balance of payments, IMF stand-bys and exchange rates, 1970–85

Year	Balance of payments on current account (% of GNP)	Exchange rate against US dollar (1980 = 100)		IMF operations
		Nominal (pesos/ US dollar)	Real effective* (index 1980 = 100)	
1970	−0.4		95	Stand-by
1971	−0.6		90	Stand-by
1972	−1.3		86	Stand-by
1973	−5.1	6.7	93	Stand-by
1974	−1.2	6.8	111	
1975	−5.2	7.2	102	Stand-by
1976	−5.9	7.4	100	Stand-by
1977	−3.6	7.4	97 ⎤	Extended Fund
1978	−5.0	7.4	88 ⎬	Facility
1979	−5.6	7.4	96 ⎦	SDR 217m
1980	−5.2	7.5	100	Stand-by
1981	−5.4	7.9	103	Stand-by SDR410m
1982	−8.5	8.5	107	
1983	−6.8	11.1	90	Stand-by SDR315m CFF SDR183m
1984	−0.1	16.7	89	Stand-by SDR615m
1985	2.9	18.6	98	

Source: Nuqui *et al*. (1987).
Note * An increase implies *appreciation* of the real effective exchange rate.

Table 12.4 The World Bank project-lending portfolio, 1971–82

Sector	Value in $ millions	Percentage of portfolio
Agriculture and rural development	889	31.9
Industry	325	11.7
Transport	446	16.0
Power and electrification	217	7.8
Water supply	149	5.3
Education	164	5.9
Health and population	65	2.3
Development finance companies	402	14.4
Urban multipurpose	122	4.3
Total	2779	100.0

Source: World Bank (1983).

The final theme of the overture, inevitably, is the Philippines' special relationship with the United States. From 1898 to 1946 the colonial power, the United States retains a relationship with the Philippines that is not only developmental but also military, in the shape of Clark Air Force Base and Subic Bay Naval Base, both north-west of Manila. Since its withdrawal from Vietnam these bases represent America's only outpost in the Pacific; in particular they protect the Indonesian Straits of Malacca and Sunda, through which almost 90 per cent of Japan's oil is shipped from the Gulf. Directly and indirectly, they employ almost 69,000 Filipinos on a payroll second only to that of the Philippines Government. In addition, the USA is still the leading market for Philippines goods, the chief supplier of Philippine imports, the foreign investor with the largest stock of accumulated assets and home for about one million Filipino emigrants. The situation creates considerable bilateral leverage in both directions. On the one hand, after the declaration of martial law by President Marcos the United States progressively cut its bilateral development aid (though not its 'security assistance') from $125 million in 1973 to $72 million in 1979 (a financing gap which was filled, as we saw, by the World Bank) in the hope of exercising some influence over human rights in the Philippines. It was the American Government which finally advised Marcos to resign and flew him and his entourage out to Hawaii, and the US Air Force which in the week this final draft was written (December 1989) intervened to prevent rebel aircraft from taking off and thus to frustrate the sixth and most serious attempted coup against Corazon Aquino's Government. For its part the Philippine Government has been able to raise the 'rental' (or security assistance payment as the Americans see it) for the bases from $500 m for the period 1979–84 to $1.14 billion already committed for the period 1984–9, with one year of the agreement still to go. The possibility of terminating the agreement in 1991 is a powerful bargaining card in the Philippine Government's hand.

Whereas it will be made clear in what follows that the interests and policy preferences of the World Bank and US Government can by no means be treated as identical, it remains the case that in the Philippines the possibility of independent leverage by one bilateral donor is far greater than in most of the other countries which supply case studies for this volume. The implications of this fact are picked up in the concluding section 12.5.

12.2 THE SAL PHASE 1980–5: DEFINITION OF CONDITIONS

The World Bank in 1980, then, found itself dealing with an economy in which the balance-of-payments deficit was already over 5 per cent of GNP; the IMF, on the Bank's own diagnosis, was not dealing effectively with the problem of exchange rate overvaluation,[11] a very high ratio of investment to national income was, as a consequence of astronomical capital-output ratios,[12] leading to rather modest growth rates of national income, and even the Bank's own investment portfolio was being affected by the general malaise.[13] To make matters worse, foreign capital, which had been happy to make short-term bank loans from recycled petro-dollars in the late 1970s to cover the Philippine balance-of-payments deficits, was reluctant to enter the country in the form of direct foreign investment.[14]

Of this complex of problems the Bank's First Structural Adjustment Loan, (SAL) finally approved in September 1980, set out, as illustrated in Table 12.5, to tackle just two: the uneven and personalised structure of protection and the low return on public investment. Broadly speaking, the initiative in the first area came from the Philippines Government and in the second area from the Bank. The Government spontaneously undertook, in a letter of intent from the Finance Minister of August 1980, to lower the average level of tariff protection and to confine rates within a band of 10 to 50 per cent; to remove over 1,000 items from the list of products subject to import control over the coming three years; and to institute various measures for export promotion. For its part, the Bank expressed anxiety over, in particular, that part of the public investment programme known as the 'eleven major industrial projects'. Announced just after the oil crisis broke, in late 1979, they consisted of a serious attempt to switch the basis of the economy from light (export-oriented) to heavy (import-substituting) industry.[15] The Finance Minister, Roberto Ongpin, attempted to disarm inevitable criticism from the Bank by claiming that projects such as the fertiliser factory and aluminium smelter were export-oriented, and that they were intended to attract inward investment from overseas; however, he was forced to promise the Bank as a part of its conditionality for SAL I that the projects would go ahead 'only if found viable by rigorous economic analysis'. It seems clear from the testimony of Bank staff that they regarded the economic philosophy of the entire package as misconceived and wished to have it thrown out, but this feeling concerning the 'spirit of the condition' nowhere emerges from the courteous prose of the loan document.

The first tranche of $100 million was released at once. The supervision mission for the second tranche arrived surprisingly soon, in January 1981, waited for four months only to see that the first batch of 590 items were liberalised on schedule, and then released the second tranche also. Following two years in which the macroeconomy (with the exception of inflation) did not improve[16] but implementation, at least on the trade side, appeared to Bank staff to be reasonable, SAL II, for $300 millions, was approved in April 1983. As Table 12.5 shows, it picked up unfinished business from SAL I in the area of trade liberalisation; in addition it asked for the system of industrial incentives to be simplified and stripped of its capital-cheapening bias, and for energy policy to be reformed with a view to eliminating, in particular, the various subsidies on power tariffs. There

Table 12.5 Philippines: World Bank policy-based lending: implementation of conditions, 1980–9

Original condition	Beneficiaries (+) or losers (−) from application of condition	Level of implementation as assessed by World Bank (mark on scale 1 to 5 in brackets*)	Remarks
First Structural Adjustment Loan (Sept. 1980) $200 m			
Lower overall level of protection and even out the spread in tariff rates within and between sectors	Importers protected by high tariff rates (−) Consumers of protected goods (+)	Average tariff rate reduced from 43% to 29%, 1980–3, but some 33 tariff rates remained below 10% in 1984 (4)	Temporary 3% revenue surcharge imposed on all imports December 1982, increased to 5% in 1983. Currency appreciating in real terms (see Table 12.3)
Liberalisation of import licensing	Importers protected by quota (−) Non-crony business sector (+)	870 items liberalised in 1981–2; but scheduled liberalisation of 87 items in 1983 scaled back to 48. Little liberalisation on investment goods (3)	
Implementation of various export promotion measures	Exporters (+)	Some improvements, but Export Credit Corporation and standardisation of import duty drawbacks for exporters not yet implemented (4)	
Eleven major industrial projects to be subjected to economic appraisal and implemented only if review satisfactory	Selected industrialists, mostly Marco's cronies (−, if projects found to be unviable)	Six projects under construction (in 1984), remainder postponed (no mark awarded)	
Reorganisation of Ministry of Trade and Industry		Substantially implemented (4)	
Second Structural Adjustment Loan (April 1983) $200 m			
Legislation to eliminate protective effect of indirect tax system		Implemented (4)	

Reform of industrial incentive system		9 out of 15 incentives, including those with major capital-cheapening bias, discontinued (4) Numerous exemptions on advertised rates
Upward adjustment of low tariff rates and further elimination of import restrictions	Importers protected by quota (−)	Temporary 10% import surcharge imposed following balance-of-payments crisis, 1983 (1)
Continued liberalisation of import licensing		No implementation of 1984 programme (1)
Energy policy reform programme	Urban consumers (−)	Upward adjustment in electricity prices (4). But no progress on promised study of country-wide prices tariff structure (1)
Economic Recovery Loan (Feb. 1987) $315 m		
Internal reorganisation of Development Bank of the Philippines and Philippines National Bank	Institutions and their new customers (+) Dismissed employees of banks; beneficiaries of bad loans (−)	Complete**
Tax reform, including completion of studies for value added tax. Raise tax/GNP level to 11% in 1987 and 12% in 1988	Holders of tax exemptions (−)	Tax reform complete; but tax yields have not risen as hoped.** Value added tax introduced ahead of schedule
Complete ongoing trade liberalisation programme	Importers protected by quota or prohibition (−) Consumers of protected goods (+) (incl. many exporters)	Initial programme of liberalisation complete; 94 further items liberalised since beginning of 1988
Agree public investment programme for 1987–8 with Bank and establish monitoring system for public investment; aim at a target level for public investment in 1987–8 and 1988–9 of 5–6 per cent of GNP		Public investment well below budget

Source: For SALs I and II: World Bank, Structural Adjustment Loans I and II: Project Completion Report
For ERL: interviews in Washington and Manila.

Notes: * Mark on scale from 1 (poor) to 5 (excellent). Source is Project Completion Report mentioned under 'sources' above, Annexe 1.
** Author's assessment, nor World Bank's.

was no further mention of the Eleven Major Industrial Projects. The SAL was assembled as part of a financial package which contained a contribution from major New York banks for a further $300 million and an IMF Compensatory Finance Facility (CFF) of 188 million SRD's; Haggard argues that this was put together in a way which 'suggests co-ordinated backing from the United States'.[17] The second tranche was released, without delays, in December 1983.

In assessing all this from the Bank's point of view it is first of all necessary to stress that to get the Marcos Government to consider liberalisation of any sort was a notable achievement. The Government's previous responses to balance-of-payments crises, in 1962 and 1970, had been essentially deflationary rather than liberalising in spirit,[18] and Marcos's instincts were all towards intervention in the market either directly or through clients rather than towards *laissez-faire*. Also germane is the fact that SAL I represents a package originally conceived as a sector loan and then given a new suit of clothes as a SAL when the new form of lending was announced with a flourish of trumpets in 1980.[19] Having said this, the two initial SALs do appear with hindsight, on the Bank's own admission, as 'somewhat narrowly based'.[20] They ignored not only the agricultural sector with its lagging performance and its export taxes and monopolies,[21] but also the inefficiency of a state financial sector based on special relationships, a nettle which the Bank was to grasp with notable success, for example, in Malawi.[22] They were unspecific in their guidance as to which imports should be liberalised. Perhaps most seriously, they failed to make any provisions regarding the macroeconomic framework, assuming this to have been dealt with by the current IMF Stand-by. As a consequence, the real exchange rate of the peso continued to appreciate, by 7 per cent between 1980 and 1982;[23] in this sense, the Fund let the Bank down. However, it is questionable whether tariff reductions on the scale which the Philippine Government was proposing in 1980 should have been encouraged at that time of severe fiscal deficit; for, as subsequent theoretical writing within the Bank has subsequently elucidated,[24] such reductions may deplete the revenue side of the public accounts to such an extent that the public sector deficit, the level of inflation and of interest rates remain locked at levels which preclude other policy-induced changes in relative prices from having their proper effect. The consequences of letting the macroeconomy ride will be discussed in the following section.

From the point of view of the Philippine Government between 1981–3, the conditions set out in Table 12.5 cannot have appeared burdensome. First of all, the sheer number of the conditions it was asked to satisfy was not large: only six for each of the two SALs, by comparison with fourteen or fifteen for a number of developing countries. Second, in respect of the conditions related to liberalisation there was a powerful group of gainers, namely those businessmen who were not Marcos's clients and whose access

Table 12.6 Basic economic indicators, 1980–8

	1980	1981	1982	1983	1984	1985	1986	1987	1988*
Real growth in GNP %	5.0	3.5	1.9	1.3	−7.1	−4.2	1.5	5.0	5.9
Growth in dollar value of exports %	25.8	−1.2	−12.2	−0.3	7.7	−14.1	4.6	5.4	7.6
Growth in dollar value imports %	25.8	2.8	−3.5	−2.4	−18.9	−15.1	−1.3	35.4	8.7
Current account balance (% of GDP)	−5.4	−5.4	−8.5	−8.1	−4.0	—	+0.9	+1.5	+1.2
Public expenditure (% of GDP)	10.0	—	—	12.4	11.4	12.2	16.1	17.3	—
Public revenue (% of GDP)	13.6	—	—	10.4	9.5	10.3	11.7	—	10.9
Public sector deficit (−), or surplus (+) (% of GDP)	−3.1	−6.2	−6.5	−4.7	−3.0	−2.6	−4.4	−2.8	—
Inflation %	18.2	13.1	10.2	10.0	50.3	23.1	5.0	3.7	9.9
Investment (% of GDP)	30.7	30.7	28.8	27.1	19.2	16.2	16.9	12.7	14.8
Debt (current $ billions)	8.4	10.1	17.0	19.1	19.9	19.8	—	—	28.0
Debt service ratio (% of GDP)	12.9	18.1	33.9	32.9	33.6	38.0	44.0	—	51.0

Source: Philippines Economic Yearbook, various issues.
Note: * = provisional.

to foreign exchange became easier once imports were decontrolled. So long as the loyalty of the clients was assured, it made excellent political sense for Marcos to court this uncaptured group of businessmen, much as in an orthodox two-party political system it makes sense for governments of whichever ideological stripe to court the floating voters in the centre rather than their own committed supporters.[25] Third, a number of the conditions, as we shall see in the next section, could be easily dodged or subverted.

In terms of the tightness of the conditionality imposed on it,[26] then, the Philippines Government between 1981 and 1983 got an easy ride. This almost certainly reflects the strength of its bargaining position in relation to the Bank at that time: its balance of payments and debt position were not yet desperate; it could foresee positive advantages in complying with some of the conditions, and the possibility of dodging others; the United States was still providing strong material and moral support[27] to the regime, and had not yet switched horses. But combined with the IMF's and its own failure to anticipate the consequences of ever-expanding fiscal and overseas deficits, it paved the way for one of the most painful deflationary episodes to have been observed in a developing country during the 1980s.

12.3   THE SAL PHASE 1980–5:   IMPLEMENTATION

A summary picture of the level of implementation of the Bank's conditions to 1984 is set out in the upper part of Table 12.5, with the mark awarded by the Bank's internal evaluator attached. Not all the performance criteria set out in the original loan documents were assessed in quantitative terms, but on those which were the compliance rate works out at 25/40, or 62 per cent (38 per cent slippage), a figure remarkably close to the Bank's more recent conclusion based on world-wide data that 'about 60 per cent of the conditions in SALs and Sectoral Adjustment Loans (SECALs) are implemented fully or more than fully'.[28] Overall, the programme represented by SALs I and II was described as 'largely well-designed and successful'.[29]

In analysing compliance by category, it is appropriate to make a distinction, recently stressed by the report just quoted, between 'key conditions' and others.[30] In the case of the Philippines it is clear that both donor and recipient saw the key conditions as being those attaching to trade policy and to the public investment programme.

Broadly speaking, compliance was much higher on the non-key conditions. Under SAL I, the reorganisation of the Ministry of Trade and Industry was carried through and a system of import duty refunds for exporters instituted; under SAL II, the indirect tax system was modified to remove the differential tax treatment of imported and domestically produced goods, the system of industrial incentives was revised so as to reduce the total number of incentives from 15 to 6 and remove the bias towards capital intensity in the existing system,[31] and power tariffs were raised by 40 per cent in real terms between 1982 and 1984. In all of this, the only major sufferers, but an influential pressure group, were electricity consumers, most of them in the cities; the businessmen who lost money through the termination of investment subsidies were in most cases able to recoup their losses through the new tax credits on net value earned and on net local content of export products instituted under the SAL agreement.[32]

On the 'key conditions' the progress made by the Bank, though substantial in each case, was clouded both by overt slippages and by actions which cancelled out a part of such policy changes as were made. Of the 'eleven major industrial projects' the Philippine Government was persuaded to cancel four – the steel mill, the aluminium smelter, the paper mill and the petrochemical complex – leaving the others to go ahead, albeit on a reduced scale.[33] Since the Bank had given its blessing for these projects to go ahead 'if justified by rigorous economic appraisal'[34] this decision did not necessarily constitute breach of the letter of the Bank's conditions; it certainly represented a breach of their spirit, since the Bank had made clear to the Philippine Government verbally and informally that the switch to heavy industry implied by the Eleven Major Projects was questionable, the more so at a time of serious macroeconomic disequilibrium. The Bank was additionally irritated not to be involved in such 'rigorous economic appraisal' as was done, except in the case of the steel mill.[35] But having shown its pique it decided, when SAL II was negotiated, not to make an issue of the public investment programme. The Major Industrial Projects did not figure at all in the conditionality for the Second Structural Adjustment Loan, and the Government's rather dubious compliance with what had originally been a key condition was neither mentioned nor quantitatively assessed in the Bank's summary of performance issued at the end of the SAL II period.[36]

All the signs point, indeed, to a decision by Bank staff to focus increasingly on the issue of tariff reduction and trade liberalisation as the loan period wore on. At first, progress in both areas was rapid. The maximum tariff rate was reduced to 50 per cent by August 1981, bringing down the average nominal tariff rate from 43 per cent in 1980 to 29 per cent in 1983, and the average effective protection rate from 52 per cent to 28 per cent. However, it remained possible for industrialists who had a personal connection with the President or his family to petition him for exemption from a particular tariff in order to have access to cheap imports.[37] Of 960 quantitative restrictions on imports scheduled to be removed under a Monetary Board resolution of 15 August 1980 (i.e. *before* the final award of SAL I) 263 were liberalised in 1981 and 610 in 1982, leaving only 87 outstanding. Most of these were items of final consumer demand. At this point macroeconomic crises conspired with growing opposition among domestic industrialists to thwart further progress. Opposition to the weakening of the protective shield had always been there, both in the form of voice (in the shape of counter-pressures from the Philippine Chamber of Industry, with the backing of the Ministry of Industry) and exit (most notoriously Dewey Dee, the textile manufacturer who in early 1981 slipped out of the country, leaving about $100 million of bad debts and several ailing garment and textile firms). These pressures Marcos had felt well able to resist, as previously explained, as coming in large part from a protected industrial sector which continued to be beholden to him for favours; and resisted they were through 1981 and 1982. This stance was altered by two key events. The first was the assassination of Benigno Aquino, the banned opposition leader, on his return from exile on 21 August 1983, which caused a large number of overseas commercial banks to terminate their short-term lending to the Philippines on fears for its political stability. International reserves fell by over $1 bn between July and October 1983. In the second place the IMF, which for a dozen years had been condoning overvaluation of the peso, increases in the budget deficit and cosmetic improvements to the reserves achieved through short-term borrowing,[38] suddenly turned hawkish and imposed upon the Government in 1984 a deflationary package featuring a float of the peso, rigid controls on monetary growth, a 10 per cent import surcharge and the issue of central bank bills carrying maturities of 30 to 270 days (known as 'Jobo Bills' after the new governor of the central bank, Jose Fernandez) carrying 40 per cent interest.

In terms of the standard objectives of stabilisation policy, this cold turkey treatment was successful – inflation was brought down from 50 per cent to 5 per cent within two years, and the balance of payments, in deficit for over fifteen years, went into surplus within twelve months.[39] But it very nearly killed the patient. The issue of 'Jobo bills' in particular, as may be expected in an underdeveloped financial system, provoked a stampede of savings deposits out of what were often already distressed financial institutions, and the closure of a number of banks, including the largest savings bank in the country;[40] in the real economy, GDP fell by over 10 per cent between 1983 and 1985, investment fell from 27 to 16 per cent of GDP, and measured unemployment rose from 7.9 to 11.1 per cent.[41] In the process the moves towards tariff reduction which the Bank had been supporting under SALs I and II were thrown into reverse, as the Government, to raise revenue, imposed a 10 per cent emergency surcharge on all imports. At the same time the programme of import liberalisation was halted at the end of 1983; indeed, some controls were reimposed during the two subsequent years. The Bank, which for years had been trying to urge the Fund to insist on a competitive exchange rate and budgetary restraint, suddenly saw its programme of microeconomic reform swept aside by the Fund's macroeconomic overkill. In the circumstances the observation of the Bank Project Completion Report that 'both SAL I and SAL II were carefully co-ordinated with the IMF, particularly in the areas of fiscal . . . and exchange rate policy'[42] defies adequate commentary.

It was not only the Fund with whom the Bank found itself at odds after 1984. The United States Government, which had openly played a role in assembling the financial package which accompanied SAL II and may have played a part in the strange decision to release the second tranche of that loan on the nod in December 1983[43] when the Philippines Government's performance was clearly going off track, began to qualify its support for the Marcos regime after Benigno Aquino was assassinated, and by 1985, aware of the strength of armed resistance to Marcos within the Philippines, it was acting as a powerful braking force on the international agencies. It held up $19 million of its own bilateral assistance following attempts by Marcos to obstruct reform in the distribution of wheat and flour, backed the temporary suspension of IMF drawings in 1985 over failure to implement reform of the sugar and coconut monopolies, and openly expressed its opposition, in the Executive Board of the World Bank, to a $150 million Agricultural Inputs Loan from the Bank. Although, under Congressional pressure, it in addition shifted the composition of Economic Support Fund assistance from military to economic, it resisted all appeals to cut off its own aid altogether.

The Marcos regime, then, was receiving in 1985 a conflicting variety of signals from the international agencies; encouragement in its deflationary efforts from the IMF, a more muted encouragement from the Bank tempered by awareness that many of its microeconomic slippages were the result of belated efforts to please the Fund,[44] and from the United States a still more muted support bordering on unsteadiness. It is interesting that in face of this disunity and a decline in the flow of policy-conditioned foreign money, it none the less persisted in many important areas with its programme of microeconomic reform. The spontaneous removal of price controls on food and the removal of a number of export taxes in 1984 owe nothing to *direct* financial pressure from the Bank (although, of course, a policy dialogue was continuing at the time, in the absence of structural adjustment finance) and more to the continuing reformist pressure of technocrats within the Marcos Government. Although the President himself almost certainly adopted the language of liberalisation purely as a flag of convenience, there were many within his Government – particularly the Ministry of Finance and central bank – whose commitment to the cause was more genuine, and whose support he continued to need.

Not all of the enthusiasm which the Marcos Government showed for the Bank's structural adjustment programmes, then, consisted of a reflex conditioned by the stimulus of money to come, as some interpreters of the experience would have it. That slippage on the agreed programme was substantial owed something, to be sure, to the forces emphasised in the previous volume – the relative failure of previous liberalisation efforts,[45] the Government's expectation that liberalisation would be a temporary phase, the Government's ability – until late 1983 – to obtain concessional finance from a number of sources and to conduct arbitrage between them. But much of the slippage was enforced rather than willed – enforced by the macroeconomic crisis of 1983–5, which interrupted and pre-empted above all the tariff reduction and import liberalisation components of the Bank's planned structural adjustment sequence. As we have seen the Bank had long been aware of the dangers of trying to act on aggregate supply whilst aggregate demand remained out of balance; their failure to translate that awareness into adequate pressure on the Fund between 1980 and 1985 robbed their own programme of much of the effectiveness which it otherwise might have had. On a harsh interpretation, the beginnings of true structural adjustment – described in the next section – came after the end of the period of formal Structural Adjustment Lending.

12.4 THE POST-SAL (ECONOMIC RECOVERY) PHASE, 1985–8

(a) Design of conditions

The events by which Ferdinand Marcos was ousted from power in February 1986, following a disputed election and a mass desertion by his armed forces, and replaced as President by Corazon Aquino have been well described by a number of commentators, outstandingly so by Hodgkinson (1988). This so-called 'peaceful revolution'[46] was, in many spheres, incremental and even reactionary. Not only were a number of decision-makers, including the Minister of Defence and the Governor of the Central Bank, taken over from the old regime to the new, but the change of government brought back to positions of power many representatives of the old estate-owning aristocracy (including the President herself)[47] who under the previous dispensation had been pushed aside by the entrepreneurial group whom Marcos had raised up. In addition, however, it contained a number of human rights lawyers; industrialists both of the free-enterprise, anti-special privileges variety (such as the Finance Minister, Jaime Ongpin) and of the nationalist, protectionist school (such as the Trade and Industry Minister, José Concepcion). All in all, the make-up of this new Aquino cabinet owed more to a desire to reward the loyalty of people who had helped her in opposition than to a desire to advance any particular class, interest group or economic philosophy.

None the less, a distinctive economic policy manifesto quickly emerged. By early May, less than three months after the change of government, an agenda for reform entitled *Economic Recovery and Long-term Growth* (Philippines Institute for Development Studies, 1986) had been produced on the instructions of the Planning Minister, Solita Monsod. The document, known as the 'Yellow Book' was jointly produced by staff of the planning ministry (NEDA), the Philippines Institute for Development Studies which is attached to NEDA, and the University of the Philippines. Its theme could be summed up as: liberalise, decentralise, and redistribute from the resulting growth. Many of its ideas had been common currency in opposition circles long before the fall of Marcos and hence needed little working-up to be incorporated in the new manifesto. Specifically, it requested:

- a more open trade regime, with an exchange rate determined on the free market;
- reform of government financial institutions, and a limitation of the involvement of the central bank in development finance;
- elimination of government intervention in the labour market (including minimum wages) and a movement to local-level wage bargaining;
- a substantial extension of land reform;
- and a limitation of debt service payments to what the Government could afford to pay.[48]

With the exception of the last provision (which has not yet become formal government policy, and to which the central bank for example is firmly opposed) all of the above represented a voluntary espousal of policies which the World Bank had been advocating for years. The first three provisions were to find their way, as we shall see, into the conditionality for the 1987 Economic Recovery Loan. The 'Yellow Book', much of it written by individuals who were semi-detached from the formal policy-making process, always retained the status of a discussion document, rather than a formal government manifesto. But it was on several occasions publicly praised by the President, and formed the basis for the subsequent *1987–92 Development Plan*. Naturally the unpicking of a number of the special economic privileges created by the Marcos Government, in particular the abolition of the sugar and coconut monopolies, represented for the new government a particularly attractive way of carrying out the philosophy of the Yellow Book. But by no means all of its economic actions during its first Hundred Days consisted of the extinction of rents to particular Marcos cronies. During the course of 1986, before negotiations with the Bank on new money had reached an advanced stage, they had in addition abolished the remaining export taxes, carried out a major tax reform, liberalised over 800 restrictions on imports, and published a new investment code designed to attract foreign companies.

In such an environment, the World Bank could see that it was pushing at an open door.[49] It took a golden opportunity to implement three lessons from its experience of the previous ten years. It handed over to the Philippine Government the policy initiative in determining the next steps to be taken within the reform programme. It co-ordinated its recovery package and attached conditionality very closely with the IMF and with other donors, in particular the Japanese. And it confined its conditionality to a few key policy issues, which noticeably related to the allocative rather than the redistributive part of the Yellow Book.[50] Three of them represented issues which had formed part of the agenda of the first two Structural Adjustment Loans: trade liberalisation, tax reform and the public investment programme. The fourth, which although not labelled as such[51] was the linch-pin of the entire Bank reform package, was new: this was the reform of the Government financial institutions. The details of the conditionality eventually attached to the Bank's so-called Economic Recovery Loan[52] of March 1987 are set out in the bottom part of Table 12.5. The loan was of $300 million, to be disbursed in three equal tranches in 1987, 1988 and 1989.

The simplest of the reforms requested by the Bank was the amendment of tax structures. Leadership in designing the reforms lay with the Fund, and there was cross-conditionality on this issue between the two institutions. The essential problem lay at the macro level, namely the fall in tax ratios between 1980 and 1985 from 14 to 10 per cent, which had become a major cause of the persisting public sector deficit.[53] As identified by the Bank, the principal cause of the problem lay not so much with low rates of tax as with the enforcement of those taxes that were due and with the failure to tap particular tax bases, in particular rural property.[54] The Philippine Government, as noted above, had already carried out a number of reforms in July 1986 to simplify and increase the revenue elasticity of the tax structure, including abolition of most exemptions from income tax and a shift to an *ad valorem* basis for all indirect taxes. Under the terms of the Economic Recovery Loan the Philippine Government was asked to initiate studies in the area of capital gains tax and property tax, and (following up a theme from SAL II) the further rationalisation of tax incentives. In addition, it was asked, by April 1988, to introduce a value-added tax.

In the area of public investment, also, the problem lay at the macroeconomic level, in the shape of a catastrophic decline during the years preceding the change in government. Between 1983 and 1985, following a common pattern in developing countries,[55] the Government development budget had taken almost the entire weight of the fiscal adjustment to the economic crises of that time, so that public investment fell from 7.7 per cent to 3.6 per cent of national income, or about 50 per cent in real terms,[56] with particularly heavy cuts in the industry, transport and energy sectors. Overall investment had fallen from the high (if unproductive) level of around 30 per cent at the beginning of the decade to 16 per cent in 1986, and the Bank saw an urgent need for pump-priming activity by the public sector. It asked the Government to maintain a public sector investment rate at the 5–6 per cent level over the years 1987–90 and to maintain operation and maintenance expenditures in the economic and social sectors at least at their 1982 real levels.[57]

In the trade area, the essential business was to undo the damage done to the reform programme during the 1983–5 crisis, during which a 10 per cent import surcharge had been imposed and the planned programme of liberalisation interrupted and indeed reversed. Of the 25 per cent of total imports covered by prohibition or by a requirement for 'prior approval' from government agencies, about half, or 936 items, had already been scheduled for liberalisation by the Aquino government when negotiations with the Bank began. These were mainly consumer goods and raw materials; the Bank focused its attack on intermediate products, and asked for a further 292 restrictions to be removed by April 1988.[58] In addition it asked for a new programme of liberalisation and a review of the tariff structure to be presented before release of the second tranche.[59]

It remains to consider the real innovation in the conditionality attached to the Economic Recovery Loan, which was the proposed reform of the Government financial institutions, many of which, it will be recalled, had been damaged by being used as instruments of political patronage and generalised scattering of rural favours during the Marcos period. The severest problems lay with the Philippine National Bank (PNB) and the Development Bank of the Philippines (DBP) which between them accounted for nearly half of the country's total banking assets, but had become technically bankrupt, with some 80 per cent of their combined portfolios being treated as non-performing.[60] Ten others were in some kind of financial difficulty, including six which had been taken over from the private sector because of liquidity deficiencies but not yet fully rehabilitated. The problems had been perceived and discussed with the Bank as early as 1985, as part of a projected financial sector loan which ended by being absorbed into the ERL package. There was agreement even at this stage between Bank and Philippine Government negotiators (mostly within the central bank and the Ministry of Finance) as to the principle which should guide the reform of the financial institutions, namely that they should be allowed to operate on strictly commercial lines rather than as instruments of political patronage. However, there were differences of opinion concerning how this common end should be approached, which may be summarised by Table 12.7. As the table indicates, in those cases where there was disagreement on strategy, the Philippines Government view prevailed on all major issues save in the matter of the DBP's capital:asset ratio, which in the final outcome was targeted more conservatively than government negotiators had wished. Amicable agreement between both parties had, however, been negotiated on all but minor details by early 1986, so that there was an institutional reform package ready to take off the shelf by the time that the Bank felt ready to initiate

Table 12.7 Alternative approaches to financial sector reform, 1985–6

Reform category	Initial Bank position	Initial Philippine Government position	Policy eventually adopted
1 Allocation of assets of DBP and PNB	Privatise completely	Merge institutions and dispose of non-performing assets	Rationalise institutions separately and dispose of non-performing assets
Once (1) agreed:			
2 Portfolio restrictions on DBP	Confine to agriculture and small industry*	None (i.e. retain existing business in large industry and real estate)	None
3 Private equity in DBP and PNB	Yes	No	No
4 Capital:asset ratio for DBP	1:3	1:5	1:3
5 DBP Board of directors to be reappointed:	Annually	Every 3 years	Annually

Source: Interviews, January 1989.
* View held by visiting mission only.

negotiations on a large programme loan in support of the new regime's reform efforts.

(b) Implementation

A subjective interim assessment of implementation may have some value in identifying the extent to which the blockages to policy reform identified under the Marcos regime persist under the present one.[61] This is as follows: the reforms to the tax structure and government financial institutions have been carried through ahead of time, although the tax reforms have not yielded the hoped-for increase in tax effort; meeting the public investment target is currently causing serious difficulties but may become easier; trade liberalisation, after the initial burst, is becoming more difficult all the time. What is interesting about this is that whereas in normal Bank experience 'push-button' reforms – i.e. those which involve changing a price or removing a control – are easier to implement than institutional changes,[62] recent Filipino experience has been the opposite. It is instructive to try and understand why.

The key to the success of the Government financial institution (GFIs) and tax reforms was twofold. At the administrative level, most of the hard work of designing the blueprint for reform, and indeed much of the hard work of implementation, had been done before the loan agreement was signed; at the political level, the special interests whom the reforms deprived of protection (i.e. holders of large non-performing loans from the GFIs, and holders of tax exemptions) were precisely the interests whom the incoming regime was most anxious to deprive of such protection. In the case of the GFIs, indeed, the reform operation consisted of little else, and has achieved a remarkable transformation. The DBP, for example, has halved its work-force, sold off its non-performing assets through an Asset Privatisation Trust at discounts varying from zero to 50 per cent, and reduced its number of branches from sixty-nine to fourteen; nor, under the new regime, has it yet come under any pressure to give (or forgive) loans on any but the strictest commercial criteria. The tax reforms – involving a shift towards a direct tax base – have, at the level of monitorable policy actions, been fully accomplished, and in the case of the introduction of VAT accomplished ahead of time. They have not delivered the expected increase in tax effort,[63] but since this may derive as much from a faster than expected growth of GNP as from a slower than expected growth of tax revenue, this may simply illustrate the inadvisability of setting performance criteria for policy-based loans in terms of variables which are not fully under the Government's control.[64]

Somewhat similar observations apply to the Bank's conditionality on public investment, which was partly procedural (e.g. 'establish a monitoring system for public investment')[65] but which also asked the Government to achieve at least the 5–6 per cent ratio of investment to national income mentioned in the Letter of Development Policy[66] 'over the next three years', i.e. 1987–90. The level actually achieved in 1988 was 3.3 per cent. This is alleged to be 'one of the major issues the World Bank will raise before it releases the third tranche of the ERL'.[67] There is, however, an irony here. For whereas the thrust of the World Bank's policy advice on public investment has generally been to get rid of wasteful projects – implying a *downward* pressure on the total[68] – here the advice is to scale it *upward*. And whereas the tools for the first job lie ready at hand – namely more intensive cost-benefit analysis – it is precisely the enthusiastic application of these methods, *on Bank advice*, which is currently making the second objective difficult of achievement. At the present time, with the economy growing fast, it is very common to read accusations in the Philippine press that this runway extension, or that power station, is being held up by the requirements of project appraisal or by NEDA's intricate committee structure; but these requirements have been imposed by technocrats to maximise the return on public investment, and lie at the heart of the micro-reforms the Bank has tried to introduce to move the aggregate supply curve of developing countries. In the short term, it seems, attempts to 'mimic the market' within the public sector may jeopardise the achievement of the Bank's macro targets – and may also, incidentally, cause overshoots on the Fund's targets for public sector deficit and inflation.[69]

In trade liberalisation, also, the pace of reform has been slackening fast, and falls somewhat short of the Bank's hopes. The summary picture is given in Table 12.8. Of the 1,306 items on which import restrictions had been removed by early 1989, 936 had been liberalised as part of the 'down payment' in mid-1986 and a further 292 were decontrolled in 1987 as a condition of second tranche release. Of the 673 items which remained controlled at the beginning of 1988, NEDA has announced that 114 are non-negotiable for reasons of national security, and 104 more will certainly be liberalised; 94 of these controls had in fact been removed by January 1989, including a number relating to artificial fibres within the intermediate goods sector which has always been the hardest to crack.[70] This leaves 455 on which, it is expected, public hearings are to be held. These contain a number of the key intermediate goods which enter into the entire cost structure, including that of exporters: steel, cement, coal, cotton fabrics.

And whereas in principle the traditional outcry of the home market-based part of the manufacturing sector against 'foreign dumping' ought to be counterbalanced by a contrary outcry from exporters – for example, garment manufacturers who cannot compete against Hong Kong without a cheaper supply of imported cotton cloth – no such counter-pressure exists. The Philippines Exporters' Association is politically almost silent,[71] and no match for those elements in the manufacturers' lobby – Philippines

Table 12.8 Progress on trade liberalisation

	1980	1981	1982	1983	1984	1985	1986	1987	1988
Liberalisation of import controls:									
Number of controls:									
removed		263	610	48	—	—	936	292	94
reimposed		—	—	20	210	50	—	—	—
Changes in tariff structure:									
Average tariff rate	43	34	30	29	28	31	30	32	33
+ surcharge			3	5	10	10			
Total average import tax	43	34	33	34	38	41	30	32	33

Source: World Bank (1984, 1987), NEDA.

Chamber of Commerce, American Chamber of Commerce – who retain an interest in control. The latter have the support of the trade unions, and also a representative in the cabinet – the Industry Minister, Jose Concepcion, a flour miller and food manufacturer, who is also pressing for the minimum rate of tariff, currently 50 per cent, to be raised to 75 per cent.[72] Changes in tariff rates and import controls now, contrary to the Marcos years and the first year of the Aquino regime, have to pass through an increasingly reluctant legislature. Defenders of liberalisation within the Government now speak increasingly in terms of euphemisms such as 'removal of administrative discretion over imports'. In short, there are few votes in further liberalisation, and not very much money either, since the Government has made so large a 'down payment' in this policy area that the World Bank seems ill-disposed to make the issue a sticking-point. The key point is that whereas in the case of reforms which were implemented easily – above all, the GFIs – almost everyone who lost from the reform was associated with the Marcos regime and hence could be snubbed at small political cost by its successor, this is by no means true of trade liberalisation. The 'old money' which the Aquino regime re-established in power brought back with it a strong dose of old-fashioned protectionism, which is now well-entrenched.

Many of the characteristics of economic policy in the Aquino period are easily explainable in terms of the approach of Volume 1. The small number of conditions attached to the ERL is indicative of the donors' strong need of the Aquino Government in 1986. The relatively high overall compliance rate reflects the continued dependence of the Philippine Government in 1987–8 on official sources of finance whilst foreign investors were still unwilling to lend, and also the willingness of a new government to dissolve rents deriving from special privileges granted by a disliked predecessor. For the latter reason, the early Aquino Government provides an exception to Ranis and Fei's generalisation that

> a growth activist LDC Government is typically anti-liberalisation in its reactions since, in an evolutionary perspective, 'liberalisation' essentially means moving in the direction of the advanced countries' organisational choice, i.e. featuring an increasing role for markets.[73]

However, as we have seen, its more recent actions suggest a shift of the pendulum in the opposite direction.

12.5 EFFECTIVENESS: INITIAL ASSESSMENT

It is facile to state that the Philippine economy, during the period of Structural Adjustment Lending delivered less than the Bank hoped, and less than what had been achieved in the previous period. As Table 12.9 indicates, levels of GNP growth, balance of payments, export growth, domestic and overseas investment were all lower during the SAL period (1980–5) than had been planned by the architects of the SAL, or previously achieved, and export growth was actually negative by 4 per cent per annum in dollar terms. Both comparisons, as noted in Volume 1, are arbitrary,[74] and in particular the economy could be expected to do worse during the international slump of the early 1980s than during the boom of the late 1970s. But if the Philippine performance during the slump is compared with the performance during that period of three potential control groups – middle-income countries, highly-indebted countries and Thailand, as a country similar in level of income and industrialisation to the Philippines – the comparison is in all cases save investment levels to the disadvantage of the Philippines. The external factor which most often blew structural adjustment programmes off course, from the analysis of Volume 1, was an unfavourable trend in terms of trade, and this did indeed affect the Philippines worse than developing countries as a whole.[75] But in the Philippines the clinching factor appears to have been the macroeconomic crisis of 1983–5, which played havoc with the growth rates of GDP and exports, the level of investment and ultimately the liberalisation programme itself. For these reasons it is difficult to identify quantifiable benefits to the Philippine economy from the SAL programme proper, although it must be emphasised that we have made no attempt to simulate what would have happened to the Philippine economy in the absence of the money which the World Bank lent or the policy changes which it caused to be implemented. In the absence of such simulation, any judgement must remain guarded.[76]

The Aquino (or post-stabilisation) period, 1986–9, presents a brighter picture, with a disappearance of the balance-of-payments deficit and growth rates of exports and GDP which are now respectable by the standards of highly-indebted countries, if still short of those achieved elsewhere in the Far East. However, investment remains depressed – both public investment, to the World Bank's chagrin,[77] and the inward investment by foreign companies and banks that it was hoped the adjustment lending exercise would pull in.[78] It seems clear that the return on adjustment lending in the post 1986 period has been positive, although we may note from Table 12.9 that it has so far fallen short of what the Bank's Philippine staff of 1983 hoped to achieve even *without* a structural adjustment process.

It would be tempting to conclude from the above account that structural adjustment (and lending for such adjustment) only has a chance of working when the macroeconomic environment is right; and then to leave it at that. But this would be to understate both the Bank's achievement and the constraints to its operations which persist within the microeconomic sphere. In many ways the Bank's Philippine policy agenda is a somewhat untypical one, since whereas much of its effort elsewhere (and the job which it seems to have done most successfully) consists of 'getting the

Table 12.9 Philippines: comparisons of economic performance during SAL period with previous performance, plan projections and 'control groups'

Performance indicators: (annual averages)	Philippines						International comparisons (1982–6)		
	1976–80		1981–5		1986–90		Thailand	All Middle income	All highly-indebted
	actual	planned	actual	planned	planned 'With structural adjustment'	planned 'Without structural adjustment'	actual 1986–8		
Annual GDP growth (%)	5.9	3.4	−0.9	6.5	4.0	4.1	4.5	2.2	1.9
Annual export growth (%)	10.0	5.2	−4.0	8.5	6.5	5.9	9.4	6.6*	2.9*
Current account/GDP (%)	−6.8	−4.0	−5.2	−2.9	−7.5	+3.6	−0.9	−4.5	−3.7
Investment/GDP (%)	25.6	27.7	24.4	28.0	27.0	14.8	22.5	19.2	17.9
Foreign private capital inflow/GDP (%)	0.3**		0.15**				0.4**		

Sources: All Philippine actual figures from Philippines Statistical Yearbook; Philippines planned figures from World Bank (1983) Table 2: 38; Thailand comparisons from Fei and Ranis (1988); other comparisons from World Bank (1988) Table 2.6: 45.

Notes:
* 1982–7.
** Net foreign private investment only.

prices right',[79] very little of the Philippine programme consisted of push-button adjustments to government-determined prices. Most of it consisted of institutional change, which it has historically found more difficult to achieve; and also of its own attempts at macroeconomic intervention, first to restrict and then to stimulate the level of public investment. And a great deal of the institutional transformation which has taken place since 1986 has been highly successful, in particular because blueprints for change in financial and tax systems had already been worked out before that date and because it was very much to the political advantage of a new regime to publicly eliminate the rents and special privileges which had enriched its predecessors. In these areas the Bank acted, substantially, as a policy adviser rather than a wielder of leverage or initiator of reform. In trade policy, also, progress has been substantial, in terms of the sheer volume of controls removed (see Table 12.8); however, quantity has been at the expense of quality, or to put the same point another way, the politically expedient sequence of liberalisation has been adopted in preference to the economically optimal one. The lists of items to be liberalised both in 1981 and 1986, as set out in Table 12.8, were prepared by the Philippine Government; but the consequence of letting the Government take the lead has been that the controls which have been liberalised first consist mainly of final consumer goods which by definition have no effect on the rest of the industrial sector, whereas the controls which represent a real obstacle to export competitiveness (for example those on cotton fabrics, cement and steel), being politically sensitive, remain in force. Similarly, it might have been economically desirable for the Bank's advice on tariff policy to concentrate less on the *absolute* level of tariffs, and more on the relative discrimination within the tariff structure against the agricultural, and in particular the agro-exporting, sector. This again would have raised its political profile. The principle of compensating the losers, already involved on an *ad hoc* basis to facilitate liberalisation in artificial fibres, would appear to hold the key to further progress in this area.

Opinion is divided both inside and outside the Philippines about whether the economy, as the result of its efforts in recent years, has now 'crossed the hump' separating it from the more dynamic economies of South-East Asia, or whether it is now destined to slip back again as the result of adjustment fatigue and a resurgence of mercantilist pressures. Opinion is also divided on whether the key to crossing the hump rests on further liberalisation (as argued within the Philippines for example by USAID, and at an academic level by Fei and Ranis, 1988) or on the implementation of the structuralist solution of state-backed export promotion backed by a competitive exchange rate (as argued for example by Helleiner, 1987). The World Bank has of course backed both horses in the Philippines, pushing for trade liberalisation with one hand and for investment expansion with the other. Having had the good luck to catch a reformist tide at the flood in 1986, it now finds that the 'easy phase' of liberalisation is over, and that the current is beginning to turn against it within the legislature and business community. The key to its continued influence may be its willingness to continue to 'walk on both legs' and to back those policy initiatives in the Yellow Book which deal with redistribution and decentralisation, as well as those which simply involve the removal of state controls.

Acknowledgements

The author acknowledges with warmest thanks the help of the following people: in Washington, Norman Hicks, Isabel Guerrero, Israel German; in Manila, Rolando Arrivillaga, Paul Deuster, Jesus Estanislao, Armando Fabella, Mario Lamberte, Wilfredo Nuqui.

GLOSSARY

CFF   (IMF) Compensatory Financing Facility
DBP   Development Bank of the Philippines
ERL   Economic Recovery Loan
GFI   Government Financial Institution
IMF   International Monetary Fund
NEDA National Economic and Development Authority
PNB   Philippines National Bank
QR   Quantitive restriction
SAL   Structural Adjustment Loan

NOTES

1 The percentage of families living below the poverty line is estimated at:
   1961   57.9
   1971   44.9
   1975   53.2

   Source: World Bank, *Poverty, Basic Needs and Employment*, Washington DC, 1980: 36.
2 For example, in the case of semiconductor manufacturing Filipino workers only perform one of the operations involved in the production process – the assembly stage, involving a combination microscope and soldering iron. Similarly in the garment industry fabrics are woven on machine looms in Japan and the US, then sent to the Philippines for making-up and embroidery on Singer sewing machines.
3 World Bank (1979: I: 32).
4 World Bank (1980: 15).
5 Haggard (1988: 25). The combination, in the Philippines under Marcos, of rural-based oligarchy, import-substituting industrialisation, military involvement in government and spiralling debt – and a love-hate relationship with the United States to boot – is distinctively Latin-American rather than Asian, as befits the country's ancestry as a Spanish colony prior to 1898.
6 Haggard (1988: 39).

7 This augmented the Philippine debt problems substantially in the medium term (see Pante, 1983, and Mosley, 1987).
8 The most notorious example of this was in 1982 when the reserves were exaggerated by the central bank to the extent of some $600 m (see section 12.3 below).
9 Whereas the Bank regarded 30 per cent of all projects as 'problem projects' in 1977, the proportion had risen to 63 per cent in 1979, or well above average for the East Asian and Pacific region.
10 See, for example, World Bank, *Rural Development Projects: A Retrospective View of Bank Experience in Sub-Saharan Africa*, Report No. 2242, Washington DC, 1978.
11 Nor was the IMF dealing effectively with the other problems it had set itself in the late 1970s. Of the three other objectives which the Fund set for the Philippines Government under the Extended Fund Facility of 1976–9 – an increase in tax effort, removal of import controls and a removal of controls on internal prices, including interest rates – none was carried out (see Montes, 1988: 8).
12 The Philippines incremental capital-output ratio for 1974–80 was 17 per cent higher than that in South Korea, 29 per cent higher than that in Malaysia, 31 per cent higher than Thailand's and 69 per cent higher than Indonesia's, according to UNCTAD data cited by Haggard (1988: 36).
13 See passage keyed by note 9.
14 The average net annual inflow of direct foreign investment into the Philippines between 1972–81 was $184 million, or about half of one per cent of GNP, by comparison with 2–3 per cent of GNP for the Philippines' East Asian neighbours.
15 The projects were: a copper smelter, an aluminium smelter, a phosphate fertiliser plant, diesel-engine manufacturing, cement industry expansion, coconut industry rationalisation, an integrated pulp and paper mill, a petrochemical complex, a heavy engineering industry, an integrated steel project, and alcogas (fuel made from sugar cane) production.
16 The balance of payments deficit, public sector deficit and GDP growth rates all deteriorated during this period; see Table 12.6.
17 Haggard (1988: 43).
18 The previous measures and their impact on the balance of payments may be thus summarised:

Measure	Growth of exports in subsequent 3 years (%)
1962 Removal of exchange controls	18.5
1970 Devaluation, removal of some import controls	11.8
Average annual rate of growth of exports, post-liberalisation periods (1962–4 and 1970–2)	15.1
Average annual rate of growth of exports, other periods (i.e. 1965–70 and 1973–9)	−2.2

19 The Philippines SAL I was the second Structural Adjustment Loan which the Bank approved world-wide (the first, for Kenya, is discussed in Chapter 16).
20 World Bank (1984: 36).
21 In the loan appraisal report the performance of the agricultural sector was described as 'satisfactory relative to the other sectors of the economy, and the need for structural reform is not as critical' (World Bank, 1983: 34).

22 See Jane Harrigan's chapter in this volume (Chapter 15). Note also that the nettle was eventually grasped in the Philippines as part of the Economic Recovery Loan package (see section 4 below).

23 See Table 12.2.

24 For example, Edwards (1984).

25 On this see for example Downs (1957).

26 For alternative definitions of 'tightness' and for the pitfalls underlying each of them see Volume 1, Chapter 4.

27 An interesting example of the latter was the eulogy, by Vice-President George Bush in September 1982, of Marcos's 'adherence to democratic principle and the democratic process'.

28 World Bank (1988: 89).

29 World Bank (1984: 36).

30 See, for example, World Bank (1988: 103, para. 5.15).

31 For example, the existing arrangements for accelerated depreciation of capital equipment and for tax deduction on reinvestment were deleted under the SAL II agreement, thereby removing a couple of subsidies to the use of capital equipment.

32 Oral information, Department of Trade and Industry.

33 For the full list, see note 15.

34 See Table 12.5.

35 World Bank (1984: 27).

36 In the table at the end of the evaluation document (World Bank, 1984: Annexe I) there is no mention of the Major Industrial Projects.

37 Cf. the case of Herminio Disini (passage keyed by note 6).

38 'Much of this debt was going into continued investment by state-owned enterprises, including particularly the nuclear power project', Haggard, 1988: 44. It remains a matter of contention how sudden the IMF's discovery of 1983 was.

39 See Tables 12.3 and 12.6.

40 On the macroeconomics of the Philippine experience between 1983 and 1985, see Montes (1987) and Taylor (1988: 104–7). Taylor comments:

> According to simulations carried out on a rather monetarist econometric model, gradualism (i.e. a slower reduction of aggregate demand and money supply) could have offset the major GDP losses which occurred with $1 billion or so of higher payments deficits.
>
> (Taylor, 1988: 107)

41 Data on GDP and investment from Table 12.6; on unemployment from Nuqui et al. (1987: Table 6).

42 World Bank (1984: 34).

43 Ibid.

44 None the less, the collapse of the macroeconomy after 1984 caused an indefinite postponement of plans for a proposed Third Structural Adjustment Operation. On this cancelled operation planned for Fiscal Year 1986 see World Bank (1984: Annexe III).

45 See analysis of note 18.

46 A phrase used for example by USAID (1987).

47 The President's family own a large sugar estate at Tarlac, north of the capital.

48 See executive summary at Philippines Institute for Development Studies (1986: i, ii).

49 For similar cases where the World Bank found itself financing a reform programme which had already been published as the manifesto of a new government, see the cases of Jamaica and Turkey, both described by essays in this volume.

50 In particular the Bank's conditionality did not involve itself in any way with the Yellow Book's proposals for land reform – which has become the major issue in Philippine politics during the Aquino years.

51 Recall the recommendations of the Bank's internal review that the 'key conditions' attached to a programme should in future be identified explicitly (World Bank, 1988: 103).

52 In spite of its changed name, it was identical in function to the previous Structural Adjustment Loans, and as argued in the text took up unfinished business from the loans. Co-financing of a further $300 millions from the Overseas Economic Co-operation Fund and Export-Import Bank of Japan was attached.

53 See Table 12.3.

54 World Bank (1987: 14).

55 See for example Hicks and Kubisch (1984).

56 World Bank (1987: 18).

57 World Bank (1987: 19).

58 The position as at March 1987 was as follows:

	Already liberalised	Scheduled for liberalisation by April 1988
Raw materials (iron and steel, basic chemicals, fish and fish products)	189	29
Intermediate goods (fibres and yarn, fabrics and textiles, paper, glass)	51	217
Consumer goods	696	46
Total	936	292

59 World Bank (1987: 18).

60 World Bank (1987: 22). The Bank had invested some of its own money in the DBP in the 1970s but had cut off lending to it in 1983; none the less, it had more than the usual amount of self-interest in wishing to see the institution restored to a sound financial footing.

61 At the time of writing (December 1989) the Economic Recovery Loan has only just been fully disbursed.

62 See for example World Bank (1988: Chapter 4).

63 Taxes as a proportion of GNP in 1988 are estimated at 10.9 per cent against a targeted 12 per cent (see Table 12.3).

64 See Mosley (1987: 34).

65 World Bank (1987: 48).

66 World Bank (1987: 21, 56).

67 Oscar Quiambao, *Philippine Daily Inquirer*, 26 January 1989, p. 13. The issue was indeed 'raised' but the Bank was forced to accept that changes in the aggregate public investment level could only be achieved over the long term, and could not be produced by magic to satisfy a tranche release condition.

68 This was of course precisely the advice given by the Bank to the Marcos Government under SAL I (see page 45).

69 At the time of writing (end of 1989) inflation is just crossing over into double figures and the balance-of-payments surplus is just disappearing. Agreement on an IMF Extended Facility is held up pending agreement on forecasts for the growth rate and the budget deficit for the next couple of years.

70 These concessions were facilitated by offering to users of imported artificial fibres an increase in the drawback which they were able to claim on customs duties attached to their exports: in other words by compensating them against the loss of the QR. This

principle is further discussed in the conclusion to volume 1 (Chapter 9).

71 Interview, World Bank (Manila), 23 January 1989.

72 His brother is a manufacturer of refrigerators and air conditioners. Imports of both products are still subject to control.

73 Fei and Ranis (1988: 55).

74 See Volume 1, Chapter 6.

75 The annual change in terms of trade during the 1980s was as follows:

	1981	1982	1983	1984	1985	1981–5
Philippines	−12.0	−2.9	4.4	−2.5	−6.6	−3.7
All developing countries	3.6	−0.8	−3.5	1.8	−2.4	−0.3

Source: World Bank (1988: Table 2.1: 34).

76 A simulation model of the Philippines does exist within the World Bank (Hwa, 1986) but it has so far only been used for *ex ante* forecasting, and has not yielded reliable results. Another model at the University of the Philippines has been used to simulate the effects of the 1983–5 policy package; this is described in Montes (1987).

77 See pp. 59–60 above.

78 Rodrik (1988) argues, with reference to the Philippines and other countries, that private investment expenditures may have been depressed in the wake of World Bank-inspired structural reforms *because* the reforms were seen by the business community as 'unsustainable', i.e. likely to be reversed, the moment the World Bank's financial leverage was removed.

79 World Bank (1988: Chapter 4).

BIBLIOGRAPHY

Bello, W., Kinley, D. and Elinson, E. (1982) *Development Debacle: the World Bank in the Philippines*, San Francisco, Institute for Food and Development Policy.

Downs, A. (1957) *An Economic Theory of Democracy*, New York, Harper & Row.

Edwards, S. (1984) *The Order of Liberalisation of the External Sector in Developing Countries*, Princeton, NJ, Princeton Papers in International Finance, no. 156.

Fei, J. C. H. and Ranis, G. (1988) *The Political Economy of Development Policy Change: A Comparative Study of Thailand and the Philippines*, unpublished paper, Economic Growth Centre, Yale University.

Haggard, S. (1988) *The Political Economy of the Philippine Debt Crisis*, unpublished paper.

Helleiner, G. (1987) 'Comment on Chapter 2', in V. Corbo, M. Goldstein and M. Khan (eds) *Growth-oriented Adjustment Programs*, Washington DC, IMF/World Bank.

Hicks, N. and Kubisch, A. (1984) *Finance and Development* 21, 35–42.

Hodgkinson, E. (1988) *The Philippines to 1993: Making up Lost Ground*, Economist Intelligence Unit Special Report no. 1145, London, Economist Intelligence Unit.

Hwa, E.-C. (1986) *Simulating Economic Recovery Strategies of the Philippines*, unpublished paper, World Bank Economic Analysis and Projections Department.

Lamberte, M. (1984) *The Development Bank of the Philippines and the Financial Crisis: A Descriptive Analysis*, Philippines Institute for Development Studies Staff Paper 84–07.

Medalla, E. M. (1985) *The Protection Structure, Resource Flows and the Capital-Labour Ratio in Philippine Manufacturing: A Short Empirical Note*, Philippines Institute for Development Studies Staff Paper 85–01.

BIBLIOGRAPHY

Montes, M. F. (1987) *Macro-Economic Adjustment in the Philippines 1983–5*, Philippines Institute for Development Studies Working Paper 8701.

Montes, M. F. (1988) 'A review of structural adjustment in the Philippines', unpublished paper, November, forthcoming in *Philippine Development Review*.

Mosley, P. (1987) *Conditionality as Bargaining Process: Structural Adjustment Lending, 1980–6*, Princeton, NJ, Princeton Essays in International Finance, 168.

Nuqui, W., Bermal, N. B., Quiarbo, V. V. and Tayson, F. M. (1987) 'The Philippines: external shocks, adjustment policies and impact on selected development concerns 1973–85', *Journal of Philippine Development* 14(1), 173–217.

Pante, F. (1983) *Exchange Rate Flexibility and Intervention Policy in the Philippines 1973–81*, Philippines Institute for Development Studies Staff Paper 83–01.

Philippines Institute for Development Studies (1986) *Economic Recovery and Long-Run Growth: Agenda for Reforms* (the 'Yellow Book'), Manila, PIDS.

Power, J. H. (1989) *Investment Incentives in a Protectionist Regime: The Philippines*, unpublished paper, University of the Philippines.

Rodrik, D. (1988) *Liberalisation, Sustainability and the Design of Structural Adjustment Program*, unpublished paper, Harvard University.

USAID (1987) *Philippine Structural Adjustment and Selected Policy Reforms*, Manila, November.

World Bank (1979) *Industrial Development Strategy and Policies in the Philippines*, 2 vols (Report no. 2513-PH), Washington DC, 29 October.

World Bank (1980) *Report and Recommendation on a Proposed Structural Adjustment Loan* (Report no. P-2872-PH), Washington DC, 21 August.

World Bank (1983) *Report and Recommendation on a Proposed Second Structural Adjustment Loan* (Report no. P-3389-PH), Washington DC, 1 April.

World Bank (1984) *Structural Adjustment Loans I and II: Project Completion Report*, 30 July.

World Bank (1987) *Report and Recommendation on Two Loans for an Economic Recovery Program* (Report no. 4466-PH), Washington DC, 23 February.

World Bank (1988) *Report on Adjustment Lending*, Country Economics Department (Report no. R88–199), Washington DC, World Bank.

13

THAILAND

Chaipat Sahasakul, Nattapong Thongpakde
and Keokam Kraisoraphong

13.1 INTRODUCTION

(a) Objective of the project

The main objective of this chapter is to evaluate the World Bank's first and second Structural Adjustment Loans (SALs) made to Thailand in 1982 and 1983 respectively. To meet this objective, at least two key questions have to be answered. First, why were some measures attached to SALs to Thailand implemented? Why were some not? Second, what was the impact on the Thai economy of those measures that were implemented?

To answer the first question, we hypothesise that the likelihood of implementing the measures depends on (1) whether the measures or their elements were new or had been tried in previous years, (2) whether those measures would have been implemented in the absence of conditionality, (3) the World Bank's specific role in Thailand, and (4) other political and economic factors.

The second question focuses on the impact of quantifiable SAL measures on aggregate economic variables such as real gross domestic product, export and import values, current account deficits, and Government deficits.

(b) Organisation of the chapter

This chapter is divided into five sections. Section 1 gives an introduction and an overview of macroeconomic performance. Section 2 presents a historical summary of structural adjustment loans in Thailand starting from policy recommendations made by the World Bank in 1980 to selected SAL issues. Section 3 is devoted to presenting details of findings from the interview method. Section 4 details the modelling method and its empirical results with some simulations. The paper ends with a summary and gives lessons from the SAL experience in section 5. Appendix A supplements section 2 by giving a summary review of recommendations, measures and implementation related to structural adjustment loans. Appendices B and C supplement section 3 by describing in detail the interview methodology, summarising interviewees' responses.

(c)   An overview of macroeconomic performance

Table 13.1 reports selected macroeconomic variables from 1970 to 1987. Table 13.2 presents growth rates and shares of exports classified by selected sector for 1979 to 1987 and Table 13.3 gives growth rates of selected items of principal exports for 1970 to 1987.

1970–8: A period of strong economy

The Thai economy was relatively strong between 1970 and 1978 despite experiencing adverse effects resulting from the first oil shock in 1973 and 1974. Its current account deficit, international reserves, external debt and central government budget deficit remained throughout the decade in the manageable and acceptable range.

The growth rate of real gross national products (GNP) for 1970–8 averaged 7.1 per cent per year, well above the level achieved in most developing countries. The first oil shock in 1973–4 had some adverse effects on the economy as it directly raised the energy costs facing the industrial sector and the country's import bill. The inflation rate measured by the GNP deflator rose from an average of 2.9 per cent per year for 1970–2 to an average of 14.3 per cent for 1973–5 and the growth rate of imports of goods and services for 1973–5 averaged 30.3 per cent per year, a substantial jump from an average of 7.0 per cent per year for 1970–2 (see Table 13.1).

Fortunately, the prices of farm products which constituted Thailand's major exports also rose sharply in 1973 and 1974. As shown in Table 13.3, the growth rate of export values of farm products – rice, rubber, maize, tapioca products and sugar – during this period ranged from 38 per cent to 89 per cent per year. The Thai economy was thus blessed with (1) a relatively high growth rate of 23.9 per cent per year of exports of goods and services for 1973–5, (2) a low (1.7 per cent) current account deficit to GNP ratio, and (3) comfortable international reserves covering at least half a year's imports during 1973–5. Partly as a consequence, Thailand never experienced a 'debt problem': the debt service ratio was only 11.2 per cent between 1973 and 1975.

1979–81: a period of economic weakness

Unlike the first oil shock, the world farm prices during the second oil shock in 1979–80 were unfavourable, and the average GNP growth rate for

73

Table 13.1 Thailand: selected macroeconomic variables, 1970–87

	1970–87 average	1970–2 average	1973–5 average (1st oil shock)	1976–8 average	1979–81 average (2nd oil shock)	1982–4 average (SAL I SAL II)	1985–7 average	1987
Gross National Product (GNP)								
1 Growth Rate of Real GNP (in %)	6.2	4.2	6.5	9.6	5.3	6.3	4.8	7.0
GDP share at current factor cost (in %)								
2 Agriculture	25.4	27.9	30.4	28.2	25.7	21.5	18.6	18.1
3 Manufacturing	18.2	14.9	16.8	17.8	19.3	19.6	20.8	21.3
4 Services	13.2	12.6	11.6	11.9	13.1	14.4	15.3	15.3
Inflation and interest rate (%)								
5 Inflation rate (GNP deflator)	6.6	2.9	14.3	6.7	9.7	2.4	3.5	6.5
6 Inter-Bank lending rate	11.0	8.8	10.4	9.7	15.2	12.6	9.3	6.5
7 Real interest rate (= line 6 − line 5)	4.4	5.9	−3.9	3.0	5.5	10.2	5.8	0.0
International transactions								
8 Current account/GNP (in %)	−3.6	−2.1	−1.7	−4.2	−7.1	−5.0	−1.6	−1.4
9 Growth rate of exports of goods and services (in %)	18.4	18.5	23.9	20.4	23.4	6.4	18.0	22.4
10 Growth rate of imports of goods and service (in %)	17.0	7.0	30.3	19.3	25.3	4.9	12.0	32.5
11 Ratio of international reserves to imports of goods and services (in number of months)	5.2	7.9	6.7	5.3	3.8	3.1	4.2	4.6

Exchange rates								
12 Baht/US $	22.02	20.91	20.45	20.38	20.86	23.14	26.36	25.74
13 Baht/100 yen	9.22	6.24	7.20	8.00	9.32	9.69	14.88	17.71
External debt								
14 Public external debt/GNP (in %)	12.0	4.5	3.9	6.0	12.5	18.6	26.6	27.0
15 Debt service ratio (in %)	15.2	14.4	11.2	12.7	14.7	18.6	19.7	16.0
Central Government (in %)								
16 Budget deficit GNP	3.5	4.3	3.8	3.5	3.1	3.7	2.6	0.0
17 Debt/GNP	24.0	21.7	17.9	18.2	21.5	27.8	37.1	37.0
18 Growth rate of revenue	15.5	7.0	23.1	18.7	19.8	10.2	11.1	19.0
19 Growth rate of expenditure	13.9	9.0	16.9	19.6	20.0	10.9	5.3	3.0

Notes: Data on inter-bank lending rate (line 6), international reserves (line 11), exchange rates (lines 12 and 13); public external debt that includes government obligations (line 14), and central government variables (lines 16–19) are from Bank of Thailand, *Monthly Bulletin*, various issues. Data on debt service ratio were directly obtained from Bank of Thailand. Data on (ex-post) real interest rate are from inter-bank lending rate (line 6) minus inflation rate (line 5). The rest of the data were constructed from data in National Economic and Social Development Board, *National Income of Thailand*, New Series 1970–1987.

1979–81 dropped to 5.3 per cent per year. The major adverse effect of the second oil shock was a high current account deficit and low international reserves. The ratio of current account deficit to GNP rose from an average of 4.2 per cent for 1976–8 to an average of 7.1 per cent for 1979–81. As the current account deficit rose, international reserves dropped from an average of 5.3 months' import coverage to 3.8 months between 1979 and 1981. The second oil shock also raised the inflation rate from an average of 6.7 per cent per year for 1976–8 to an average of 9.7 per cent per year for 1979–81 and raised the inter-bank lending rate from an average of 9.7 per cent per year to 15.2 per cent per year for the same period. The debt service ratio rose from 12.7 per cent to 14.7 per cent during the same period.

The deterioration in these indicators provoked an increasing pressure on the Thai Government to restructure the economy. Consequently, the Government formulated a structural adjustment programme and initiated negotiations with the World Bank for a Structural Adjustment Loan.

1982–84: a period of world-wide recession and structural adjustment

Since the world economy was relatively weak, the average growth rate of exports was low at 6.4 per cent per year for 1982–4, and by comparison 18.4 per cent per year for 1970–87 as a whole. Similarly, the growth rate of imports averaged 4.9 per cent per year for 1982–4, in relation to an average growth rate of 17.0 per cent per year for 1970–87 as a whole.

The Bank of Thailand, faced with increasing levels of balance-of-payments deficits, initially chose to deal with this problem by restriction of domestic credit rather than devaluation, but in November 1984, it eventually devalued the baht by 14.8 per cent against the US dollar and then pegged it to a basket of major trading partners' currencies instead of the US dollar. These adjustments restored Thailand's competitiveness in the world market. It should be noted that the baht devaluation measure was not part of the conditionality attached to the Bank's Structural Adjustment Loans, but the IMF played an important role in encouraging the Bank of Thailand to devalue its currency against the US dollar. The 1982–4 period was also a period of high real interest rates.

Given the low growth rate of exports and imports, the average ratio of current account deficit to GNP was still high at 5.0 per cent for 1982–4, with an alarming fall in international reserves to three months' imports. The Bank's SALs, totalling US $325.5 million (approximately 12.4 per cent of the average annual international reserves for 1982–4), played a crucial part in preserving Thailand's rating on the international credit market.

INTRODUCTION

1985–7: a period of slow recovery

Helped by the 1984 devaluation, the growth in export values rose to 18.0 per cent per year between 1985 and 1987, whilst import growth was restricted to 12.1 per cent. These growth rates substantially improved the current account situation, and the balance-of-payments deficit dropped to 1.6 per cent of GNP between 1985 and 1987. The period was one of exceptional growth in manufacturing exports at an average rate of 35.5 per cent per year between 1985 and 1987, by comparison with an average rate of 12.2 per cent per year for the SAL period of 1982–4 (see Table 13.2). During this period Thailand evolved from a primary product exporting economy into a newly-industrialising country (NIC). The leading export items of manufacturing products were textiles, integrated circuits and precious stones with their corresponding growth rates of 37.0 per cent, 28.7 per cent and 24.6 per cent per year for 1985–7 (see Table 13.3).

Table 13.2   Exports classified by selected sector, 1979–87 (in per cent)

	1979–87	1979–81 Average	1982–4 Average	1985–7 Average	1987 Average
Growth rate					
All exports of goods and services	15.9	23.4	6.4	18.0	22.4
Agriculture	8.9	21.4	3.0	2.3	4.9
Manufacturing	26.0	30.4	12.2	35.5	48.0
Tourism	22.0	35.1	8.4	22.6	34.0
Share					
Agriculture	34.6	40.2	36.7	26.9	23.5
Manufacturing	35.6	28.0	33.7	45.2	53.0
Tourism	12.2	10.6	12.8	13.3	14.1

Notes: Data on all exports of goods and services are from Table 13.1. Data on other variables were calculated from data in Bank of Thailand, *Monthly Bulletin*, various issues.

Finally, tourism has become a leading foreign exchange earner for Thailand since 1982 (see Table 13.2). The world-wide recovery and the 1984 baht devaluation helped raise the growth rate of tourism export from an average of 8.4 per cent per year for 1982–4 to an average of 22.6 per cent per year for 1985–7, rising to 34 per cent in 1987, which was designated as Visit Thailand Year.

The turnaround of the external balance and government budget situation for 1985–7 was the result of world-wide recovery, the SAL measures (see Section 2 for details) and other government policies (such as the baht devaluation and IMF Stand-by agreement). It is, as a consequence, relatively difficult to evaluate the success or failure of the SAL measures. First, attempts have been made in this study using the interview and econometric approaches whose findings are presented respectively in sections 3 and 4.

77

Table 13.3 Growth rates of selected items of principal exports, 1970–87 (in per cent)

	1970–87 Average	1970–2 Average	1973–5 Average (1st oil shock)	1976–8 Average	1979–81 Average (2nd oil shock)	1982–4 Average (SAL I, SAL II)	1985–7 Average	1987
Rice	21.4	34.1	37.6	26.8	36.6	1.2	-3.7	11.8
Rubber	19	-8.5	41.6	33.0	13.9	7.4	17.2	35.9
Maize	10	3.7	47.0	-4.6	25.2	7.1	-20.5	-57.6
Tapioca products	20.7	13.1	45.0	35.8	17.3	2.0	8.6	8.3
Prawns	25.7	24	53.1	22.1	16.6	10.8	27.2	30.9
Tin	9.5	1.5	15.7	48.1	10.2	-15.5	-5.9	-24.3
Sugar	59.5	268.6	89.0	-5.9	68.2	-11.2	18.0	17.9
Precious stones	32.3	70.8	30.1	31.3	38.1	11.9	24.6	41.7
*Integrated circuits	**28.2				49.1	6.7	28.7	18.4
*Textile products	**25.2				22.7	15.8	37.0	55.3

Notes:
*   Nor classified by Bank of Thailand as one of principal exports until 1977.
**   Average of 1979–87.
     Data were computed from data in Bank of Thailand, *Monthly Bulletin*, various issues. Items that were classified by Bank of Thailand as principal exports before 1977 but excluded afterwards are jute and kenaf, tobacco leaves, mung beans, fluorite, sorghum, cement and teak.

13.2   THE BACKGROUND TO STRUCTURAL ADJUSTMENT LENDING IN THAILAND

(a)   Objectives

This chapter is written for the reader who is not familiar with the historical dimension of structural adjustment in Thailand. The players in the structural adjustment episode, besides the Thai Government, were the International Monetary Fund (IMF) and the World Bank. We begin with a discussion on the roles of the IMF in Thailand in the early 1980s in sub-section (b) and discuss the role of the World Bank in sub-sections (c) to (h).

(b)   The role of the International Monetary Fund in Thailand in the early 1980s

After being affected by adverse external shocks in 1979–80, Thailand experienced rapidly increasing current account deficits as discussed in section 13.1(c). Besides the Structural Adjustment Loans from the World Bank, Thailand also initiated discussions with the IMF on an appropriate policy response.

The IMF's involvement during 1981–3 included (1) purchases under the Compensatory Financing Facility of SDR186 million, (2) a buffer stock financing facility of Special Drawing Right (SDR) 58 million and, most importantly, (3) a two-year Stand-by arrangement of SDR814.5 million. The two-year Stand-by arrangement was approved in June 1981 with the general objectives of restructuring demand, reducing the public savings-investment gap, and limiting the growth of foreign indebtedness. The arrangement included undertakings on monetary and credit policy, fiscal policy, and external debt. However, as discussed in the World Bank (1983: 31), the central government revenue shortfall in Financial Year 1982 led to an increase in the budgetary deficit, which, in turn, caused a non-observance of the subceiling on net credit to the Government of Thailand. In the circumstances, the initial two-year Stand-by arrangement was replaced in November 1982 by a new fourteen-month Stand-by in an amount of SDR272 million (at that point 100 per cent of quota) which was subsequently increased to SDR386.6 million under the 1983 general review. Under this new agreement, particular attention was paid to interest and exchange rate policies.

(c)   The World Bank's policy recommendations in 1980

Following the conclusion of the agreement with the IMF, a mission from the World Bank visited Thailand in February/March 1980 to discuss policies and programmes to alleviate emerging economic problems and to improve Thailand's longer term prospects for sustaining high rates of growth and reducing poverty. The mission resulted in a report, International Bank for Reconstruction and Development (1980a). This report's analysis of the emerging economic imbalances in Thailand also incorporated the results of the International Bank for Reconstruction and Development (1978, 1980b, 1980c, 1980d).

On the Bank's analysis, the accelerating inflation, growing dependence on foreign borrowing, and large budgetary deficits of the late 1970s were due not only to adverse external factors, but also to internal problems within the economy, including failure to fully adjust energy prices, price distortions, and excessive liquidity creation. The Thai Government had initiated some corrective measures, but the deficits seemed likely to continue growing into the 1980s on unchanged policies.

Major reforms, in fact, were necessary in the areas of:

1   Resource mobilisation, particularly in the public sectors.
2   Monetary policy, including measures to maintain high rates of private saving and to manage external debt and the capital account.
3   Energy policy and conservation, with particular attention to pricing.
4   Industrial policy and measures to promote industrial exports.
5   Agricultural policy and measures to maintain high rates of growth of agricultural production and exports.

(d)   The down payment or actions taken

The Thai Government decided in the autumn of 1980 to opt for a course of action to improve Thailand's external balance (which had deteriorated from 1.7 per cent of GDP in 1973–5 to 7.1 per cent in 1979–81) (see Table 13.1), largely through medium-term structural adjustments to the economy (see Letter of Development Policy (LDP), dated 4 February 1982 and Wibulswasdi, 1987).

It should be clear that the Thai Government in 1980 had a strong intention to restructure its economy even before submitting its first LDP for the first Structural Adjustment Loan. Two obvious evidences are (1) the policy framework of structural adjustments outlined in the Fifth Plan and (2) actions already taken in the direction of structural adjustments.

Substantial progress had been made in the agricultural sector as the Government lowered or eliminated export taxes or restrictions on Thailand's major agricultural exports (rice, rubber, maize, cassava and sugar) and started the land certification and reclassification programmes. In the industrial sector, most of the actions were committee establishment and study initiation. However, an important measure to promote Thai exports was a devaluation of the baht (within the context of the ongoing IMF Stand-by) by approximately 10 per cent against the US dollar in 1981, given the large appreciation of the US dollar against other major currencies. Substantial progress was also made in the energy sector when the Government substantially raised power tariffs and petroleum prices by April 1981 to remove all subsidies.

The above actions taken before the Thai Government's submission of its first LDP were considered by the World Bank as a down payment for applying for the first structural adjustment loan and were seen by it (International Bank for Reconstruction and Development, 1986), as one of the key factors making Thailand a success story in structural adjustment. The discussions in section 13.3 also confirm this point.

(e) Proposed measures in SAL I

The major concern of the Thai Government when requesting the World Bank to extend the first Structural Adjustment Loan (SAL I), as revealed in the first LDP of 4 February 1982 was rising current account deficits. The measures or actions planned for SAL I were discussed in the first LDP and also tabulated in Table A.3 of Appendix A of this paper. The planned actions for SAL I should be seen as a continuation of the above measures or actions taken in the sectors of agriculture, industry and energy and the policy areas of fiscal policy and institutional development.

Two more measures in the agricultural sector were added to the actions already taken, i.e., the deregulation of livestock marketing and the fertiliser marketing study. Many measures in the industrial sector were new since most measures in this area that had already been taken were committee establishment and study initiation. These new measures were broad-based improvements in the organisation and operation of the Customs Department, establishment of export processing zones and more bonded warehouses, general tariff reform, *ad hoc* arrangements for large-scale project evaluation, and new studies.

Although many measures in the area of institutional development and development of a medium-term fiscal strategy as proposed in the first LDP were not specific, those in tax policy were specific, for example, measures of restructuring of personal and corporate income taxes.

It is interesting to see that, as structural adjustment in Thailand developed over time, the detailed measures shifted from the sectors of agriculture and energy into the sector of industry and the area of tax policy between 1981 and 1982. As will be seen in section 13.2(f), the focus finally moved to public sector management when submitting the second Letter of Development Policy in 1983.

One final remark regarding the first LDP is that, since the proposed measures in SAL I involved many governmental departments, good co-ordination among them was extremely crucial. Therefore, the Thai Government, ensuring systematic implementation of the proposed measures, instituted a high-level Economic Structural Adjustment Committee, one of whose functions was to undertake regular reviews of progress achieved in co-operation with the World Bank.

(f) Proposed measures in SAL II

Originally, the Thai Government had hoped to rely on exports to alleviate external deficits and to provide the main driving force in the manufacturing and agricultural sectors, but as prospects for the world economy worsened, it changed its reforms towards restrictive medium-term institutional measures aimed at the containment and regulation of the public finances. Measures introduced at this time (tabulated in Table A.3 of Appendix A) ranged from fiscal strategy, medium-term fiscal reform, tax administration, state enterprises and foreign debt. The most striking and, probably, most effective measure in bringing down budget and current account deficits was the reduction in the ceiling of annual public borrowing from abroad by approximately 14 per cent – from US $2,400 million to US $2,060 million. This 'public' borrowing included borrowing by not only the central government, and local governments, but also state enterprises.

Other new SAL II measures worth mentioning were a measure to explore the feasibility of export credit and guarantee schemes in the industrial sector; a reduction in fuel price differential, energy conservation measures and the establishment of an Energy Conservation Centre of Thailand (ECCT) in the energy sector; and studies of a land bank and water resource development and management in the agricultural sector.

The deterioration in the world economy not only shifted the focus of the Thai Government's structural adjustment effort towards public sector management but also caused two targets proposed in SAL I to be amended. First, the target for FY 1986 of central government revenue/GDP ratio was dropped from 18 per cent to 16 per cent and, second, for FY 1983, the Thai Government imposed a one-year temporary import duty surcharge of 10 per cent of existing duties and the Ministry of Finance was authorised to temporarily increase export duties.

(g) The World Bank/IMF co-operation in SALs

The World Bank and the IMF staff have generally co-ordinated their activities closely through frequent consultations on matters of joint interest. In the context of SALs, as discussed in International Bank for Reconstruction and Development (1983: 31), the World Bank did not cover any of the areas in which the IMF was active, except for fiscal strategy and policy.

The division of work in the fiscal policy area followed the comparative advantage of the two institutions: the IMF handled short-term macro management and budgetary issues and strengthened the administrative arrangements for resource mobilisation and the World Bank concentrated on medium-term and structural issues, including efficient utilisation of public revenues and incorporation of an appropriate fiscal strategy in the planning framework of the country.

This close collaboration helped achieve complementarity between SALs and Stand-by programmes, even on specific targets. For instance, as discussed in International Bank for Reconstruction and Development (1986: 31), the November 1984 devaluation of the baht against the US dollar, in which the IMF was instrumental, has turned out to be an important helping hand to SAL measures in promoting exports.

(h) World Bank's assessment and current status of implementation of SAL measures

This section gives an overall picture of the proposed measures, the World Bank's assessment of their implementation as of July 1984 and their current status (as of February 1989). Table 13.4 contains a summary of the above overall picture where the first column lists the originally proposed SAL conditions in the first LDP of 4 February 1982 and the second LDP of 7 March 1983 (their detailed conditions are also reproduced in Tables A.2 and A.3 of Appendix A). The second column presents a brief summary of the World Bank's assessment as of July 1984. The third column provides our additional comments based on information in the interviews (see section 13.3) and documents, and the last column presents new developments of the implementation of SAL measures up to February 1989. New developments are from the interviews and Sahasakul (1987). Below are the highlights of Table 13.4.

A land-use policy and a reduction and/or an elimination of export restrictions on major farm products are two key measures achieved in the agricultural sector. The World Bank's assessment as of July 1984 was that substantial progress had been made in land certification and classification, export duties for rice and rubber had been lowered and other restrictions on the export of maize, rice, and partly, sugar, had been lifted. However, we may comment that the progress on land certification and reclassification have been slow when SAL counterpart funds used for these purposes ran out. The new development in this area is that the land bank study was completed and the Government has been considering an establishment of a land bank in the Bank for Agriculture and Agricultural Co-operatives (which is a state enterprise). The progress on the reduction/elimination of

83

Table 13.4 A summary of implementation of SAL conditions

Original SAL conditions	Level of implementation as assessed by World Bank as of July 1984	Comments	New developments up to February 1989
AGRICULTURE			
Land use policy: land certification and reclassification in forest reserve areas; land bank study.	Land certificates had already been issued to one-third of a million farm families; surveys for the purpose of land reclassification had been completed or were under way in almost two million ha of pre-reserved forest but procedures for approval of classification recommendations were proving too cumbersome; the feasibility study of a land bank was due for completion in November 1984.	Land certification and reclassification have been slow once the SAL counterpart funds used for those purposes ran out.	From 1933–5, land certificates were issued to 378900 farm families; the government has been considering an establishment of a land bank in the Bank for Agriculture and Agricultural Co-operatives.
Marketing and pricing policy: reduction and/or elimination of export restrictions on major farm products; improvement in the rice price support programme; deregulation of livestock marketing; fertiliser marketing study.	Export duties for rice and rubber had been lowered and other restrictions on the export of maize, rice and, partly, sugar had been lifted: the costly and ineffective rice price support programme was substantially eliminated: authorisation of private slaughterhouses for beef and hogs, primarily for export purposes, fertiliser marketing study nearing completion.	Total export duties dropped from 2619 million baht in 1983 to 806 million baht in 1986: or from 22% of total taxes of central government in 1963 to 6.6% in 1986.	Duties and premiums on rice exports have dropped to zero per cent since 25 September 1985 and 31 January 1986 respectively: a reserve requirement for rice exports was abolished on 12 May, 1982; there was consideration of establishing the National Fertiliser Corporation.

Water resource development and management: studies, staff and institutional support

Cabinet established the National Water Resource Board to oversee the management and development of water resources.

INDUSTRY

Export promotion: broad-based improvements in organisation of the Customs Department and in procedures for implementing the import tax drawback Act: establishment of export processing zones and adding five bonded warehouses: decision on the financing and operations of the Export Development Fund: a feasibility study to set up the export credit and guarantee schemes.

The export rebate and duty drawback systems were overhauled; an attempt was made to move towards duty-free status for export production in a few selected areas; an Export Development Fund was established in 1982, followed in 1983 by the creation of an Export Development Committee: number of bonded warehouses was expanded and the Export Service Centres were upgraded: a feasibility study of an export credit guarantee was completed in 1984.

Average growth rate of manufacturing exports was 12.2% per year for 1982–4 but rose to 35.5% per year for 1985–7 partly because of the export promotion policy but partly because of the baht devaluation and recovery of the world economy.

Reform of the Protective Structure: tariff rates would be modified so that all rates would lie between 5% and 60%.

The general tariff reform undertaken in the SAL context was successful; a somewhat scaled-down programme of subsector studies has been under way since 1982 (electrical goods study finalised in 1982, automotive industry study completed and reviewed in 1983, chemicals and plastics study was nearing completion):

The 1988 import tariff rates ranged from zero % to 300%; recommendation of reducing import tariff rates on electrical goods was implemented but recommendation of reducing local content and protection on automotive industry was not; recommendations in other studies were not considered.

Subsector studies on electrical goods, automotive industry, chemicals, plastic products, machinery and other equipment and textiles have been completed.

Table 13.4 continued

Original SAL conditions	Level of implementation as assessed by World Bank as of July 1984	Comments	New developments up to February 1989
Investment incentives: plan for the reform of the Board of Investment's activities: a study of the economic and fiscal consequences of the present and proposed incentives.	In early 1983 the Government issued policy guidelines for investment promotion and for tax privileges as an explicit framework for Board of Investment's activities: a study of the fiscal implication of investment incentives was scheduled for completion within 1984.		There has been an attempt to revise various investment incentives as part of a tax reform package: the study on the fiscal implication of investment incentives and promotion efficiency was completed in 1984.
Large-scale projects: *ad hoc* arrangements would be made for reviewing whether large scale projects met the criterion of economic viability.	A study on the evaluation of large-scale projects was completed in mid-1984 and a series of seminars have been held to review it.		A committee has been set up to evaluate large-scale projects. However, there has been only one meeting since then.
ENERGY Pricing: a study of the relative price structure of petroleum products; appropriate steps to gradually moderate the large price differential between gasoline and diesel fuel.	The range of retail prices for the various petroleum fuels has been narrowed and the Oil Fund has had a surplus since late 1983; a comprehensive energy pricing study was completed in late 1983.	Since late 1983, petroleum product prices were hardly changed until 21 February 1986 when the range of retail prices for gasoline and diesel was narrowed. Also note that there has been a substantial decline in world crude oil prices since 1983.	The range of retail prices for gasoline and diesel has been subsequently narrowed. For example, the price ratio of premium gasoline to high-speed diesel dropped from 1.82 on 2 December 1981 to 1.39 on 25 November 1988 with several downward adjustments in price differential in between.

Conservation: a study on energy conservation: formulation of policies and implementing measures on reduction in energy consumption; establishment of the Energy Conservation Center of Thailand (ECCT); transport energy conservation studies.

Strategy formulation: studies on the energy master plan, gas utilisation, domestic nonconventional energy, and energy conservation; formulation and implementation of the energy strategy based on findings in the studies; strengthening of the National Energy Authority (NEA)'s ability in medium-term energy strategy.

A study of incentives for energy conservation in industry was getting under way; the ECCT was formally established by Cabinet in mid-1984; an action plan for energy conservation in the transport sector was approved in principle by Cabinet in 1983.

Two separate studies have been completed.

A substantial decline in world crude oil prices since 1983 has relieved the pressure on energy conservation. As a consequence, the ECCT has not been as active as originally planned.

PUBLIC SECTOR MANAGEMENT

Consolidated public sector finances: medium-term projection for the financial operations of public enterprises, extra-budgetary funds and local government would be integrated into an overall financial strategy for the entire public sector; broadening and intensifying the role of the Fiscal Policy Office (FPO) of the Ministry of Finance as a central fiscal planning unit.

An integrated fiscal plan was first prepared in 1982/83 and the National Economic and Social Development Board (NESDB) has updated development expenditure programme and financing plan since then on a routine basis; proposal incorporated all major elements of fiscal planning for the entire public sector with FPO as a central role in leading co-ordination effort.

Establishment of the National Energy policy Office, responsible for energy policy planning, in the Office of the Prime Minister.

Table 13.4 continued

Original SAL conditions	Level of implementation as assessed by World Bank as of July 1984	Comments	New developments up to February 1989
Tax/revenue policy: the target of FY1986 central government revenue/GDP ratio was 18% in SAL I but dropped to 16% in SAL II: restructuring of personnel and corporate income taxes; simplification of business taxes and excise duties; enactment of selected revisions of the revenue code, customs laws and the new consolidated excise tax law; a feasibility study of introducing value-added tax; development of an action programme to strengthen local finances.	Robust revenue projection model developed for multi-year revenue planning and annual budgeting purposes: annual tax packages introduced in 1981, 1982 and 1983 increased the central government revenue/GDP ratio from 13% in FY81 to 15% in FY84; a change to *ad valorem* rates for various excise taxes; an adjustment in tax rates on business tax to reduce cascading effects; extensive adjustments in export and import duties; numerous studies and measures carried out to strengthen local government revenue.	The target ratio of central government revenue to GDP of 16% was not reached in FY1986.	The target ratio of the central government revenue to GDP of 16% has been reached since 1987. There has been a plan to implement a value-added tax in 1988 which will replace most of the existing business tax; local property tax has been implemented, i.e. a land transfer through inheritance is exempted from being taxed but the transfer is taxed once the land is sold.

Tax administration: setting up of area tax offices in Bangkok; decentralisation of operational functions of the Revenue Department's headquarters to the area tax office; reorganisation of the Revenue, Customs and Excise Departments; rationalisation of import/export forms and documents; erection of a tax training Institute; establishment of a tax rulings committee.

Expenditure policy: improvement of methods to project central government outlays.

Establishment of district tax offices in Bangkok and reorganisation of the Revenue Department headquarters' functions; various operational reform of Revenue, Customs and Excise Departments including effective separation of Customs Department headquarters' functions from customs administration at port of Bangkok; study to assess need for centralised tax training with a conclusion that decentralised training functions developed by the three Ministry of Finance (MOF) departments provided an adequate initial response to training needs of MOF staff.

Central government expenditure growth for items other than debt service was significantly reduced: two studies were carried out to provide guidance for further improvements of comprehensive public expenditure programming.

There has been no separation of the function of the Chief Customs Office at the port of Bangkok from the function of the Director General of the Customs Department. However, this separation will soon be possible when more new ports outside Bangkok are commercially used; establishment of the tax training institute is still far from a reality.

Table 13.4 continued

Original SAL conditions	Level of implementation as assessed by World Bank as of July 1984	Comments	New developments up to February 1989
State enterprises (SEs) financing and management: a classification of the SEs into commercially-oriented, public utilities, loss incurring and other SEs with appropriate policies attached to each classification (the policies aimed at reducing subsidy from the central government).	A programme of tariff increases for most SEs was not implemented for 1981–August 1984 because of political obstacles: some small manufacturing SEs were liquidated or put up for sale to the private sector; private bus operators were licensed to compete with loss-making public bus company; corporate planning was introduced for all SEs; financial revitalization programmes for major loss-making SEs were being prepared; Bangkok oil refinery reorganisation planned.	The SAL counterpart funds were partly used to finance SE deficits, which might have partly relieved pressure to raise tariffs.	Tariffs on water supply and bus fare were substantially raised in 1985; tariff on electricity was substantially reduced in 1987 after the world oil price has substantially declined since late 1983.
Extra-budgetary funds: a study reviewing the operations and effectiveness of the extra-budgetary funds.	Study concluded that no major importance needs were attributed to reform of extra-budgetary funds at this point.	The study was not completed yet by the time of the World Bank assessment in July 1984. See Thanaporapun (1988: 64).	The study was completed and the on-going funds that were no longer necessary have been abolished.
External debt management: formulation of a three-year rolling plan for planning, evaluation and monitoring of the government's external borrowing programme; improvement of data base and analysis; improvement of co-ordinating mechanism for external resources mobilization; reduction of the ceiling on public	Comprehensive three-year rolling programme for public foreign borrowing was introduced; FPO acquired computer facility for improved public debt analysis and monitoring but lacked analytical capability to utilise them effectively; the original annual public borrowing ceiling was reduced in 1983 from US $2.6		The annual borrowing ceiling was then reduced to US $1 billion and recently in 1989 was raised to US $1.2 billion.

external borrowing from US $2.4 billion to US $2.06 billion per year.

INSTITUTIONAL DEVELOPMENT
Policy analysis and co-ordination: strengthening the in-house capabilities of the core agencies (primarily NESDB, MOF and Budget Bureau) responsible for economic and fiscal policy analysis and advice; creation of an autonomous economic and social policy research institute to provide research support and consulting service to NESDB and other government agencies.

Programme formulation, evaluation and implementation: consultants would assist the NESDB to design, test and introduce new planning and programming systems (investment programming system, project preparation and investment appraisal system, programme monitoring and evaluation system).

billion to US $2.04 billion.

The mechanisms for policy supervision and implementation of the SAL programme were significantly improved with a committee structure and a joint NESDB-MOF secretariat, which became effective in September 1983; Thailand Development Research Institute (TDRI) was set up in early 1984 as a private foundation.

A project appraisal/investment planning system has been developed in NESDB; consultants failed to produce an appropriate blueprint for the development of a monitoring and evaluation system; FY1984 was the first year of implementation of government-wide programme budgeting; consultants' recommendations on provincial accounting system of the government were largely found to be unimplementable at this point; establishment of new performance

Co-ordination among key planning agencies in terms of management information system has now improved substantially.

Table 13.4 continued

Original SAL conditions	Level of implementation as assessed by World Bank as of July 1984	Comments	New developments up to February 1989
	auditing division in the Office of the Auditor-General.		
Personnel management: studies of the organisation, management and compensation of the civil service; a formulation of staff training programmes in all of the central management functions in 1983.	Two studies of the organisation/management and compensation of the civil service were scheduled for completion in February 1985; a planned study of the staffing needs for planning agencies besides NESDB was not undertaken; a staff development/ training programme was under way.		

Note: Information in the first column is extracted from the Letters of Development Policy of 4 February 1982 and 7 March 1983 whose proposed measures are also reproduced in Tables A.3 and A.4 of Appendix A of this paper. Information in the second column is extracted from International Bank for Reconstruction and Development (1988: 97–103) which is reproduced in Table A.5 of Appendix A of this paper. Comments in the third column and new developments in the last column are from interviews, Sahasakul (1987) and other documents as cited in the table and text.

export restrictions on farm products has continued after SAL II as duties and premiums on rice exports have dropped to zero per cent and a reserve requirement for rice exports has been abolished. Consequently, total export duties dropped from 2.619 million baht in 1983 to 806 million baht in 1986.

In the industrial sector, two key policies were export promotion and a reform of the protective structure on which the World Bank's assessment as of July 1984 was favourable. We agree with the World Bank that the export promotion policy has been successful, indeed the average growth rate of manufacturing exports soared to 35.5 per cent per year between 1985 and 1987 from 12.2 per cent per year for 1982–4 (Table 13.2), although part of this impressive result comes from the baht devaluation in November 1984 and a recovery of the world economy. Unlike the export promotion policy, we judge that the planned reform of the protective structure is far from being a success. The SAL condition on this reform is to modify the import tariff rates so that the rates ranged from 5 to 60 per cent with few exceptions but, in practice, few modifications have been made to import tariff rates, and few recommendations, from subsector studies, on selected industries have been implemented with the exception of electrical goods.

A reduction of the large price differential between gasoline and diesel fuel, and energy conservation, were the main proposed measures in the energy sector. The World Bank's judgement, as of July 1984, was that they had made progress. In fact, the retail prices on gasoline and diesel fuel, so far from being revised to reflect changes in import cost, remained unaltered from 1 December 1983 to 21 February 1986, during which period the world price of crude oil dropped substantially. The prices of gasoline and diesel fuel have been adjusted downward a couple of times since February 1986, and the price differential between gasoline and diesel fuel was progressively narrowed from 1.82 in 1981 to 1.75 in 1983 to 1.52 in 1986 and finally to 1.39 on 25 November 1988. This represented the gradual but not total unwinding of a concession to commercial vehicle operators entirely unmotivated by economic efficiency, and in general, the progress of energy conservation measures since the World Bank's assessment in 1984 has been negligible.

Public sector management, as earlier noted, became the major policy area in SAL II. It involved many measures in the subareas of consolidated public sector finances, tax/revenue policy, tax administration, expenditure policy, state enterprise (SE) financing and management, extra-budgetary funds, and external debt management. All these measures were aimed at reducing government expenditure, raising government revenue and reducing government budget deficits and external borrowing. The World Bank's judgement on the progress of these measures was generally favourable except for the measures on SE financing and management in which the Government had failed to raise tariffs for most SEs during the SAL period of 1982–4. We generally agree with the above judgement although we would like to add that (1) the tariff increases for many SEs were eventually implemented after the time of the World Bank assessment in 1984 when the political obstacles subsided and the Thai economy improved; for example, tariffs on water supply and bus fares were substantially raised in 1985 (see more details in section 13.2) and (2) the measure of setting the target of the 1986 central government revenue/GDP ratio at 18 per cent in SAL I and then dropped to 16 per cent in SAL II was not reached in 1986 but has eventually been reached since 1987 (see Table 13.5 and section 13.2(i)). In our view, the most successful measure in keeping government finance in control was the ceiling on public external borrowing, discussed in some detail in section 13.2(f) above.

Table 13.5   Ratio of central government revenue to GDP, 1981–8

Date	Ratio of central government revenue to GDP (in %)	Annual growth rate of central government revenue	Annual growth rate of nominal GDP
1981	14.7	—	—
1982	14.1	3.7	7.9
1983	15.8	23.7	11.0
1984	15.2	3.4	7.0
1985	15.8	8.4	4.2
1986	15.5	5.8	7.9
1987	16.6	18.9	11.5
1988	18.4	27.8	14.7

Notes: Data on central government revenues are from Bank of Thailand, *Monthly Bulletin*, various issues. Those on nominal GDP are from National Economic and Social Development Board, *National Income of Thailand*, new series, 1970–87. Data on nominal GDP in 1988 was calculated by assuming that the annual growth rate of nominal GDP in 1988 was 15 per cent.

Finally, the measures in the policy area of institutional development aimed at co-ordination among core government units and an establishment of an independent research institute, but greater emphasis was placed on various studies concerning programme formulation, evaluation, implementation, and personnel management. The World Bank's assessment in this policy area as of July 1984 was that, with respect to studies, the consultants either failed to produce an appropriate system or recommended impractical solutions. We believe that institutional development is in fact a difficult, if not an inappropriate, task for quick-disbursing policy-based lending.

(i) Selected SAL issues

There remain many issues concerning SALs in Thailand but we would like to consider three important ones here, i.e. (1) the tranching issue, (2) the consistency issue between various tax measures at the micro level and the target of the central government revenue/GDP ratio at the macro level, and (3) the bargaining relationship in SAL negotiation between the World Bank and the Thai Government.

Tranching

It is interesting to note that there was no tranching of both SAL I and SAL II; this is a special feature of the SAL approach in Thailand, very seldom adopted by the Bank in other countries. As discussed in International Bank for Reconstruction and Development (1986: 83), the reasons for the absence of tranching were, on one hand, the Government's reluctance to accept a tranched SAL, in the belief that tranching would be seen in Thailand as an unacceptable degree of external intervention and would thus endanger the entire process of SAL operations by undermining the political consensus surrounding the SAL dialogue. On the other hand, the absence of a tranching provision was acceptable to the Bank in this case since the Thai Government had in the past been willing and able to honour commitments of the kind that would be embodied in the SAL and, especially, since it was thought that leverage in support of the structural adjustment programme would be more effectively applied through a series of relatively small and frequent SALs than through larger and tranched ones. In addition, with a significant 'down payment' element implicit in a succession of SALs, tranching was in any case an almost redundant mechanism.

Consistency issue of various tax measures

One of the SAL measures in the policy area of public sector management was to set the target of a central government revenue/GDP ratio at 16 per cent in FY 1986 in SAL II, a reduction from a target of 18 per cent in SAL I. Besides this target at the macro level, SAL conditions also imposed other tax measures at the micro level. It is interesting to see how far these tax measures contributed to the macro objective of raising the revenue yield to 16 per cent of GDP. However, before we investigate the contribution of these tax measures, a close look at the time series of the actual ratio of central government revenue to GDP may give some clues to what these measures did contribute.

Table 13.5 presents time series ratios of central government revenue to GDP for 1981–8. As shown in the table, the Government revenue/GDP ratio for 1981–6 was below 16 per cent, the target in SAL II. The ratio in 1987 was above 16 per cent but still below 18 per cent which is the target

95

in SAL I. However, in 1988, the ratio rose, for the first time, to 18.4 per cent.

To see how the ratio changed over time, let us consider the ratio (R) whose numerator is the central government revenue (REV) and whose denominator is the gross domestic product (GDP),

$$R = \frac{REV}{GDP} \tag{1}$$

Now, let us take a logarithm of equation (1) and then take total derivatives, we obtain

$$\frac{dR}{R} = \frac{d(REV)}{REV} - \frac{d(GDP)}{GDP} \tag{2}$$

According to eq.(2), if the revenue changes in the same proportion as the change of GDP, then the revenue yield to GDP will not change, To raise the revenue yield to GDP to 16 per cent from 14.7 per cent in 1981 (see Table 13.5), the percentage increase in the revenue must be greater than the percentage increase in the GDP. Therefore, in the case of SALs, we wonder whether the tax measures at the micro level helped raise the growth of government revenue at a rate which is faster than that of GDP. To answer this question, an in-depth analysis of tax revenue is necessary.

Theoretically, tax revenue (T) can be simplified as the product of a proportional tax rate (p) and a tax base (y) or

$$T = py \tag{3}$$

Once again, taking a logarithm of eq. (3) and then differentiating, we obtain

$$\frac{dT}{T} = \frac{dp}{p} + \frac{dy}{y} \tag{4}$$

According to eq. (4), a percentage increase in tax revenue comes from either a percentage increase in tax rate or a percentage increase in tax base.

In the case of Thailand, tax revenue contributed approximately 80–86 per cent of central government revenue for 1981–8. Other categories of government revenue include, for example, sales and charges, contributions from government enterprises, and dividends. Therefore, changes in the tax rate (p) and tax base (y) have a substantial impact (approximately 80 per cent) on government revenue.

Various tax measures in SALs, on theoretical grounds, tend to give an ambiguous combined result on tax revenue. For example, a reduction in export duties for rice and rubber $(dp/p < 0$ in eq. (4)), which was part of the SAL conditionality in the agricultural sector, tended to lower tax revenue[1] and, consequently, government revenue. And the general tariff reform, a part of SAL conditionality for the industrial sector, yielded an ambiguous effect on tax revenue since tariff rates on some imported items were intended to be raised but those on other items were lowered. Other measures, especially changes in tax administration such as an establishment of district tax offices in Bangkok and reorganisation of the Revenue, Customs, and Excise Departments were intended to increase the efficiency of tax collection and, therefore, raise the tax base ($dy/y > 0$ in eq. (4)).

In reality, it is difficult to pin-point the revenue effect of each micro tax measure on the macro target of the central government/GDP ratio. The most difficult measurement exercise, in our opinion, would be the empirical test of the revenue effect of tax administrative changes and this subject can be a separate study of its own. However, it is easier to conjecture the revenue effect of changes in tax rates as discussed below.

A growth rate of central government revenue of 3.7 per cent in 1982 as shown in Table 13.5 was lower than that of nominal GDP of 7.9 per cent which, therefore, lowered the revenue/GDP ratio from 14.7 per cent in 1981 to 14.1 per cent in 1982. The Thai Government for revenue reasons and contrary to the wishes of the World Bank imposed in 1983 a one-year import duty surcharge of 10 per cent of the 1982 duties. This action sharply raised import tax revenue by 38.8 per cent in 1983 and contributed to the 23.7 per cent increase in central government revenue, which resulted in a revenue/GDP ratio of 15.8 per cent in 1983 (see Table 13.5). In other words, the Thai Government was only able to approach fulfilment of the Bank's macro-conditionality by breaching one of its micro-conditions. When the import duty surcharge was removed in 1984, the revenue growth rate dropped to 3.4 per cent and the revenue/GDP ratio declined to 15.2 per cent. In 1985, the growth rate of government revenue was 8.4 per cent which just doubled the growth rate of nominal GDP and brought the revenue/GDP ratio back to 15.8 per cent. However, approximately 60 per cent of the total growth rate of government revenue came from an increase in the contribution of state enterprises and dividends.

The rapid growth of Thai nominal GDP in 1987 and 1988 of 11.5 per cent and 14.7 per cent respectively (see Table 13.5) has substantially raised the size of the tax base ($dy/y > 0$ in eq. (4)) both by raising income and increasing the number of taxpayers. Examples are taxpayers of the corporate income, business, excise and import taxes. Moreover, in case of progressive tax rates like the personal income tax and export duty on rubber, an increase in the tax base will push some taxpayers into a higher tax bracket ($dp/p > 0$ in eq. (4)) and thus bring in more tax revenue as a percentage of the tax base. In 1987, the annual growth rates of corporate income, business, excise and import taxes were 13.3 per cent, 23.4 per cent, 23.4 per cent, 28.6 per cent respectively, and in 1988, 27.6 per cent, 55.5 per cent, 49.2 per cent and 46.7 per cent respectively.

Bargaining relationship in SAL negotiations

The last issue that we would like to address is the bargaining relationship in SAL negotiations between the World Bank and the Thai Government.

Since 1981, the World Bank was in a strong bargaining position in its negotiation in SAL I and SAL II in relation to the Thai Government – because, as discussed in section 13.1(c), the Thai economy had been suffering from the second oil shock in 1979 with the result of current account deficit to GNP ratio soaring sharply, international reserves falling at an alarming rate, and a consequent deterioration in the Government's international credit rating.

By 1985, when the proposed third structural adjustment operation was partially appraised, growth had resumed, and with it the Government's ability to obtain bank credit[2], in particular on the Tokyo market. This strengthened the Thai Government's bargaining position. Since the implementation of SAL II slipped more than that of SAL I, the World Bank, when negotiating an intended SAL III, insisted on the continuation of the conditions that failed in SAL II, such as a restructuring of state enterprise finances. Some of these proposed conditions in SAL III were still politically unpopular and, therefore, rather than conclude an unfavourable agreement, the Government broke off negotiations. Subsequently, the economy has turned favourable as the growth rate of real GNP grew at the annual rate of 4.3 per cent in 1986 and 7.0 per cent in 1987; the current account turned into surplus for the first time since 1970 in 1986, and the international reserves rose to 4.5 months of import value in 1986. From this point on, Bank programme finance, with its associated political costs, was no longer necessary for Thailand, strongly though the Bank tried to persuade the Government to accept it. It may be that the Bank overestimated its bargaining position in 1985, tried to make too much of the relatively small slippage on SAL II, and as a consequence missed an opportunity to make the kind of low-conditionality, front-loaded export development loan which it has subsequently employed in countries such as Indonesia and Mexico.

13.3 FINDINGS FROM INTERVIEWS

(a) Objectives and organisation

The previous section gave a broad factual account of SALs in Thailand since 1980. However, it may leave out some important details and insights which will be revealed once one talks to government officials involved in SAL negotiation and implementation and to key persons in affected private business. Findings from our interviews with the principal actors in the drama are presented in this chapter. The interviews aimed at answering the following four key questions:

1 Were the SAL measures new or had they been tried in previous years?
2 Would the measures have been implemented even in the absence of World Bank finance?
3 What contribution did the World Bank make to structural adjustment in Thailand? and
4 What political and economic factors affected the implementation decision?

The section will start with a brief discussion on the interview methodology in sub-section (b); fuller details are given in Appendix B. Sub-section (c) reports the main findings from interviews by focusing on answering the above four questions. Appendix C gives detailed responses of individual interviewees to each of the above four questions.

(b) Brief discussion on the methodology

We chose twelve organisations to be included in our sample size; nine of them are public organisations and the other three are private organisations. The total number of our interviewees is thirty-seven, many of whom came in a group when we interviewed them. Before any interview, we also informed our interviewee that s/he would not be cited as a source of information.

(c) Findings from interviews

We strongly believe that our policy of keeping interviewees' identities and their views apart, results in a non-distorted opinion. The opinions expressed below are those of policy-makers, technocrats and businessmen. The findings are grouped according to the above four questions as follows:

Whether the SAL measures were new or had been tried in previous years

Thirteen out of fourteen groups or individuals of our interviewees responded that some or most SAL measures were not new. The fourteenth mentioned specific SAL measures that were new but did not say whether other SAL measures were or were not (see Table C.1 of Appendix C for details of responses to this question). The broad consensus among interviewees was as follows:

Many SAL measures were not new. Some were ongoing projects or programmes. Others were part of an implementation plan waiting for government's financial support. However, a few SAL measures were new. The fact that many SAL measures were not new, or perceived as being imposed on the Government, is an important answer to the question of why SALs in Thailand were (generally perceived to be) successful.

From 1979 onwards, Thai policy-makers had been discussing ideas for the restructuring of the economy. Many such ideas (one interviewee suggested 30–40 per cent) were incorporated in the Fifth Economic and Social Development Plan (FY 1982–6). In particular, Thailand's industrial policy was geared towards export promotion and away from import substitution even before SAL implementation. Even in 1981, there were four manufacturing items in the top twenty of Thai export earners i.e. textile products, integrated circuits, canned pineapple, and canned fish. Textile products are an ideal example of a used-to-be import substitution item but now an export item. Other examples of ongoing measures are land certification and reclassification (whose origins can be traced back to 1961), tax privileges promoting export industries (which were initiated in 1977), and changes in excise tax rates (which were moved to an *ad valorem* basis from 1981 onwards). Not all of them could be implemented at that time, since the government budget was suffering a serious budget deficit; the money made available by the SALs allowed these supplementary measures to be carried out.

Some measures, however, did come up as new ideas during the SAL negotiations; these were generally the least successfully implemented. For example, the idea of a restructuring of petroleum product pricing was a new measure with an aim of making their prices consistent with the structure of costs, likewise the ideas of tariff nationalisation and price increases for water and bus services.

Although many SAL measures themselves were not new, some interviewees pointed out some new aspects of the SALs. One said that the new macroeconomic management technique was generated by SALs. This new technique involved a good co-ordination of various government agencies and required a common target, a similar methodology and a check and balance system. In this sense, the Bank acted as an external chairman co-ordinating the different branches of the Thai economic policy-making machinery. Furthermore, it was also the first time in the history of Thailand that academics played an important role in influencing government policies through studies, seminars and conferences.

Whether the SAL measures would have been implemented without SALs, and what was the contribution of the World Bank

Since, as discussed above, many SAL measures were not new, it is natural that a majority of those measures would have been implemented even without SALs. Eight groups or individuals (interviewees) responded to this question and all of them confirmed that, even without SALs, many measures would have been implemented. However, their responses varied somewhat in terms of what would have happened to the measures if without SALs (see Table C.2 of Appendix C for details). Some said that the coverage of measures would have been less (for example, that only 40,000 farm families per annum would have received land certificates by comparison with over 100,000 each year between 1983 and 1985). Others believed that some measures would have been delayed due to lack of international funding, or that SALs had caused government priorities to be reordered (for example, the decentralisation of loan administration became a top priority in the SAL period). One of the respondents said that the implemented measures would have been piecemeal and less co-ordinated without SALs, buttressing the role of the Ministry of Finance and National Economic and Social Development Board in this respect.

Some interviewees argued that Thailand, if revenue shortfall was the problem, could have borrowed more from the international credit market; but at least one of our interviewees argued that the interest rate charged by the international credit market would have been higher than that charged by the World Bank, so that the financial cost advantage had to be balanced against the political disadvantage of accepting the SAL. This argument was true in 1982 if we use the London InterBank Offer Rate (LIBOR) on one-year maturity of US dollar deposit as a guideline for the interest rate charged by the international credit market. The LIBOR averaged 13.69 per cent per year in 1982 which is clearly higher than the interest rate on SAL I of 11.60 per cent per year. In fact, Thailand would probably have had to pay at least 1–1.5 per cent premium per year on LIBOR if borrowing from the international credit market at that time, so that the interest cost advantage of borrowing via the SAL route was at least 3 per cent per annum. The same interviewee argued further that the Bank's SALs had the added advantage of raising Thailand's creditworthiness in the international credit market and enabling it to secure credit more cheaply from other sources.

Nevertheless, some of our interviewees raised an interesting dilemma about SALs. On the one hand, the SALs aimed at restructuring the economy with an emphasis on using market forces. On the other hand, many SAL measures did not use funding from SALs as they were part of the ongoing projects or programmes; a majority of the loans, rather, were used to finance state enterprises, thus relieving them of pressure to raise their service charges. By increasing the Thai Government's room for manoeuvre, in other words, it postponed the need for a financial restructuring of state enterprises.

The political and economic factors affecting the implementation decision

Our interviewees cited various political and economic factors affecting the implementation decision. Table C.4 of Appendix C details their responses. Selected points are discussed below.

Many SAL measures in Thailand, especially those which formed part of the SAL I conditionality, were implemented; others, particularly in the later stages of the relationship, slipped. One of our interviewees estimated that the level of implementation of SAL measures was approximately 60 per cent of the proposed measures, which is precisely the average level reported by the World Bank (1988: Chapter 9). Various reasons explaining the implementation decision include (1) whether the measures would have been implemented without SALs, (2) whether there was a leading organisation on the Thai side, (3) whether there was an 'international commitment', (4) whether the measure was politically popular, (5) whether there was a liquidity constraint in the Government budget, and (6) whether the economic environment changed in a manner unfavourable to the reform in question.

Thailand had launched more than one-half of the measures listed in the SAL conditionality before it signed an agreement with the World Bank; its 'down payment', in other words, was substantial. This action of launching many SAL measures before the agreement was reached increased the trust which the Bank felt in relation to the Thai Government and made the negotiation between Thailand and the World Bank easier (see related discussions on modelling the bargaining process in Mosley, 1986: 12–20). As a consequence, Thailand was the only country in the 1980s where SALs were not tranched. Structural adjustment tasks could be classified into two types: the tasks of which the Thai Government had full knowledge and understanding and those where it was inexperienced. For the first type of tasks, Thailand initiated its own measures without prior consultancy studies. One example was the Ministry of Agriculture and Co-operatives' STK (or right to farm certificates). An important factor contributing to their success in SAL I was that there was a leading organisation taking part in organising, screening, reviewing and monitoring measures scattered over various implementing agencies. In the Thai case, the leading organisation was the Ministry of Finance. Some of our interviewees also counted the National Economic and Social Development Board as a leading organisation in SAL planning. Unlike SAL I, there was no such leading organisation under SAL II, which might explain why SAL II measures slipped more.

For the second type of tasks, Thailand began with a consultant's feasibility study. Unfortunately, those studies were not monitored closely and not synthesised within a single framework. The Ministry of Finance, a leading organisation in the process, did not have time to follow up these studies. Examples of the second type of tasks were energy policy, sectoral studies of industrial protection, and some tax issues. As a consequence, results or findings from the studies under SAL I were either incomplete or inappropriate for the new environment under SAL II. For example, the energy studies were initiated in 1982 when the world oil price was relatively high but, by the time the studies were completed, the world oil price had dropped substantially. Therefore, recommendations in those studies, designed for a period of rising oil prices, had become inappropriate before the implementation phase began.

Some measures, especially those under SAL II, slipped because of their unpopular nature among influential pressure groups and members of the legislature. Examples of these measures were pricing policies on petroleum products (especially diesel), bus fares, and user charges for electricity and water supply. Raising prices of these products and services exposes the Government to militant opposition, magnified by the media, which in many countries has been sufficient to bring about the fall of governments. As a result, prices of these products and services in some periods were kept substantially lower than their actual cost. The World Bank attempted, under SAL II, to change these pricing policies towards efficiency – that is, the principle that prices should reflect real resource costs. We now consider some examples.

Figure 13.1 gives time series of the world price of crude oil in US dollars and domestic retail prices in baht of premium gasoline and high-speed diesel for 1977–87. As the world price of crude oil rose sharply in 1979–80 and peaked in 1981, the Thai Government also raised domestic retail prices of various types of petroleum products. However, the increase in domestic prices was slower than the rise in the world oil price for 1979–81 as shown by, when compared with the slope of the world oil price line, the flatter slope of the broken line representing retail prices of premium gasoline and high-speed diesel in Figure 13.1. During the SAL implementation years of 1982–4, the retail price of premium gasoline was adjusted upward but that of high-speed diesel was kept low while the world oil price dropped. It appears that the Thai Government tended to use premium gasoline to absorb the high cost of energy with the consequence of a big gap between the retail price of premium gasoline and that of high-speed diesel, which was consumed by the influential domestic manufacturers' and transporters' lobby. Interestingly, when the world oil price dropped further in 1985–7, the downward adjustment in the retail price was mostly on premium gasoline, thus closing the gap between the retail prices of premium gasoline and high-speed diesel. One of the SAL recommendations in the energy area pressed hard by the World Bank was to narrow down the range of retail prices for the various petroleum products; in this it was unsuccessful during the SAL period of 1982–4, but had more success after 1986.

Figure 13.2 plots time series of the world price of crude oil in US dollars and domestic user charges of public utility and bus services in Baht for 1977–87. The electricity rates, bus fares, and water supply charges were slowly adjusted upward in 1979–80 when the world oil price rose sharply. However, their rates were raised sharply in 1981 immediately before SAL I agreement. Since then, both bus fares and water supply charges were

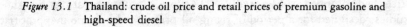

Figure 13.1   Thailand: crude oil price and retail prices of premium gasoline and
high-speed diesel

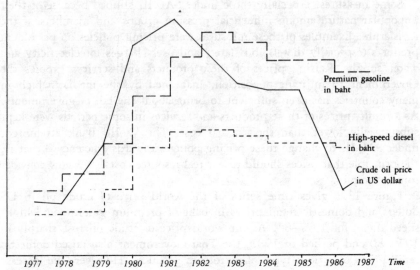

Premium gasoline
in baht

High-speed diesel
in baht

Crude oil price
in US dollar

1977   1978   1979   1980   1981   1982   1983   1984   1985   1986   1987   *Time*

Note: Data on crude oil price are from International Monetary Fund, *International Financial Statistics*,
various issues. Those on premium gasoline and high-speed diesel are from Table D.1 in
Appendix D.

scarcely changed during the SAL period 1982–4 but electricity charges
were raised to an economic level in 1982. The condition imposed by the
World Bank, in relation to public utilities, was that public utility
enterprises were supposed to raise their tariff rates so that the nominal rate
of return on total assets was at least 8 per cent per year. Note that the
World Bank did not specifically set the tariff rates for the Thai
Government; it simply gave a broad guideline on the minimum rate of
return on capital. It appears that bus fares and water supply charges were
still below costs up to 1984, but they were raised to an economic level in
1985 at a time when the World Bank was no longer exerting any leverage.
The fact that compliance was least on the above conditions (reduction in
the fuel price differential and an increase in public utility tariffs) explains
why the World Bank's pressure on these conditions was most strident. But
it yielded little: the conditions which were pressed hardest by the World
Bank were those with the least compliance.

Now, let us go back to the next factor affecting the SAL implementation
decision, i.e. the liquidity in the Government budget. The funding from
SALs created liquidity that was needed when the Government budget was
in severe deficit. This newly-created liquidity facilitated an introduction of
various policies that might be expected to reduce government revenue in
the short run. Examples of those policies were a reduction in export duty

Figure 13.2 Thailand: crude oil price, electricity rate, water supply charge and bus fare
(index 1977 = 100)

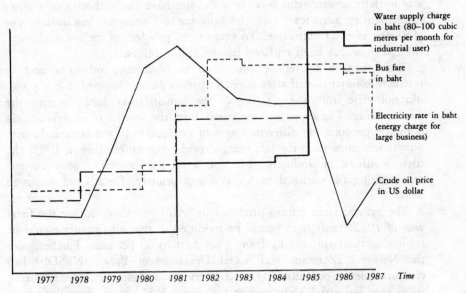

Water supply charge
in baht (80–100 cubic
metres per month for
industrial user)

Bus fare
in baht

Electricity rate in baht
(energy charge for
large business)

Crude oil price
in US dollar

1977   1978   1979   1980   1981   1982   1983   1984   1985   1986   1987   *Time*

Note: Data on crude oil price are from International Monetary Fund, *International Financial Statistics*,
various issues. Those on electricity rate, water supply charge and bus fare are from Table D.2,
D.3 and D.4 in Appendix D.

rates on rice and rubber and an elimination of export duty on maize (for
more discussions on taxes, see Sahasakul, 1987). For the same reason of
liquidity in relation to an expected government revenue shortfall, some
SAL measures were reversed once implemented. In 1982, for example, the
Government reduced import tariff rate differentials across commodities
with an aim to reducing distortion. The result was that an average import
tariff rate and the Government revenue fell in 1982. Some argued that the
revenue shortfall was due to a slow growth period of the Thai economy. In
any case, the Thai Government was alarmed by this revenue shortfall and
reversed the measures by imposing surcharges on imports in 1983.

Finally, changes in the domestic and international economic environment also affected the implementation decision. A slow growth of the Thai
economy in 1982 coupled with the revenue shortfall are two reasons that
changed the Government decision on the target of government revenue to
GDP ratio as it lowered the target from 18 per cent under SAL I to 16 per
cent under SAL II. Another example is the Energy Conservation Centre
that was first established in 1982 for finding alternative technologies for
conserving energy, but lost urgency when world oil prices declined in
1986, so that the Centre is operating on a reduced budget.

The Export Development Fund was not so successful in promoting
exports because the funding provided of 300 million baht, 0.15 per cent of

the average annual export value for 1982–4, was insufficient for any serious export promotion effort. Similarly, the Export Development Committee was initially unsuccessful because it did not have any authority over other implementing agencies – i.e., the Minister of Commerce was initially the chairman of the Committee. To correct the problem of lack of authority, the chairman has been replaced by the Prime Minister.

The measures to reduce protection on domestic industries and to restructure import tariff rates slipped in most cases. However, the slippage did not arise from the pressure of the industrialists' lobby against the restructuring. The slippage came partly from the conflict of interest among domestic producers at different stages of production in the same industries but mostly came from the fact that, after the general election in 1983, the then Minister of Industry did not give the objective of industrial restructuring (as outlined in SALs) a top priority. Details are discussed below.

The general tariff reform proposed in SAL I was that, during the fiscal year of 1982, tariff rates would be modified so that all imports would be subject to the ratio ranging from 5 per cent to 60 per cent. Furthermore, the National Economic and Social Development Board (NESDB) had commissioned a consultant team to carry out an industrial restructuring study (see Industrial Management Co. Ltd., 1985, as an example) whose objective was to provide policy guidelines and recommendations for the NESDB in preparing action plans for the implementation of the industrial restructuring programmes as set out in the Fifth National Economic and Social Development Plan. Part of the study, concerning the distortion created by import tariffs and protection of reforms, was expected to reduce effective protection rates for all sections and also to rationalise rates across sectors. Phase 1 was implemented without difficulty (see Table 13.6) because it involved only small changes from the existing rates. The effects of phase 1 were then ascertained to determine whether phases 2 and 3 were desirable and feasible. It should be noted that moving from phase 1 to phase 3 would have led to a greater uniformity of tariff rates which was part of the SAL II proposal in the industrial area.

Table 13.6   Proposals for general tariff reform

Category of imported item	Phase 1	Phase 2	Phase 3
Final products	50	40	35
Intermediate products	40	30	30
Machinery	20	25	25
Raw materials	10	15	20
		(in per cent)	

Source: Industrial Management Co. Ltd. (1985) 7.

Initially, industrial restructuring got a good start and gained momentum, especially the stage of carrying out the industrial restructuring study (financed by SAL counterpart funds) and other subsector studies (financed by UNIDO/UNDP) because the then Minister of Industry had assigned one of the Deputy Ministers of Industry to oversee the industrial restructuring under SALs. In order to minimise any opposition from domestic producers whose interests might be adversely affected by the restructuring and to compromise any conflict of interest among domestic producers in the same sector or across sectors, the Thai Government always held consultations with the private sector in the Joint Public-Private Consultative Committee on Economic Development Policy. This Committee then submitted the matter for consultation to the vested interest groups. In the case of industrial restructuring, it submitted the matter to the then Thai Industries Association (now the Federation of Thai Industries) which was also a member of the Joint Committee. The Thai Industries Association was composed of various associations of more specific sectors such as textiles, electrical goods and so on. Any general tariff reform, for example, would affect various sectors differently and, even for the same sector, it would have different impacts on various domestic producers at different stages of production (see more details in the discussion on subsectors below). At that point, most industrialists generally agreed with the Government that an industrial reform at the macro level was necessary and that, since personal interests at the micro level had endless power to block reform, this would have to be orchestrated from above.

The most important factor that put the industrial restructuring under SAL proposals on ice was a change in the Minister of Industry after the general election in 1983. The incoming Minister of Industry put aside measures and recommendations under SALs but gave priority to the sugar industry and other agri-processing interests. As a consequence, the mechanism to translate technical work in the studies into actual plans for implementation came to a halt. Since a minor reform in 1984, no changes to the tariff structure have been carried out.

It is also interesting to see the development of trade liberalisation for specific sectors. One of the SAL II conditionalities was to conduct subsector studies whose recommendations would be considered by the Government and private sector for implementation. Those subsectors were electrical goods, automotive, chemical and plastic products, ceramics, iron and steel products, machinery and other equipment, and textiles. Details of developments for specific sectors are as follows:

1 *Electrical goods sector*

The intention behind restructuring the electrical goods sector was to reduce distortion created by differential import tariff rates on imported final products and parts and components. A move to a more uniform tariff rate would have had differential effects on different producer groups: for example, a reduction in tariff rates on imported parts and components would benefit those domestic firms which imported parts and components for their assembly lines but would reduce the competitive position of those domestic firms whose production lines were more complete and relied little on imported parts and components. The first group of domestic firms would favour the measure but the second group would oppose it as their competitors' costs were lowered. However, if it was a reduction of tariff rates on imported final products, all domestic firms would oppose. There had been many meetings between the public and private sectors but they finally in 1984 reached a solution of tariff reductions although the reduced rates were not as uniform as initially planned, and favoured intermediate imports to the electrical industry. The reason that domestic producers agreed with these reductions was that these tariff reductions would lower the incentive to smuggle electrical goods from abroad, which then increased the sales of domestic firms.

2 *Automotive industry*

The finding of a consultant team was that Thailand did not have a comparative advantage in producing automobiles. The team recommended that protection should eventually be phased out by, first, freezing the existing tariff rates and required local content in assembled automobiles and, then, slowly lowering the tariff rates and required content over a certain period. Unfortunately, after the general election in 1983, the then Minister of Industry proposed just the opposite – that is, an increase in the required local content up to 100 per cent and an increase in imported tariff rates. These opposing options were discussed many times in meetings of economic ministers (i.e. industry, finance, transport and communications, etc.) resulting in a compromise agreement to restore the status quo, i.e. all existing required local content regulations and tariffs would be unchanged. In this case the local manufacturers' lobby was able to beat off opposition from the representatives of international capital.

3 *Textile industry*

In similar manner to the conflict of interest in the electrical goods sector, domestic producers such as spinners, weavers and garment producers in the textile industry at different stages of the production process were affected differently by the tariff reform; in general, producers of finished clothes lobbied for maximum protection on finished goods and minimum protection on imports and producers of fabrics resisted this. Once the Thai economy started to pick up in 1985, the focus of government shifted from the protection issue to the issue of investment for exports; at the same time, many former import-substitution industries have become export industries since 1986, including cotton fabrics and carpets. From this moment on all government activity towards rationalisation of the protective structure was suspended.

13.4 QUANTITATIVE COMPARISONS

(a) Objective and organisation

This chapter presents the methodology and findings of the modelling approach whose objective is to investigate the impact of broadly defined SAL measures on Thailand's aggregate economic variables. In particular, it makes use of findings in Thongpakde (1989).

(b) World Bank's projection results and international comparison

The World Bank (1984) has projected Thailand's macroeconomic performance under alternative circumstances – that is, with and without structural adjustment – using the World Bank's SIAM I model. Its selected results are presented in Table 13.7, items (b), (c), (g) and (h).

Table 13.7   World Bank's (1984) projection results and international comparisons

| | Average of annual real growth rate (%) | | | |
	GDP	Export	Import	Investment
Thailand				
(a) 1976–81: actual[1]	7.1	11.0	9.1	10.0
(b) 1982–6 (SAL I in 1982 and SAL II in 1983)				
– Projection with structural adjustment[2]	5.2	6.9	6.2	6.4
– Projection without structural adjustment[2]	5.0	4.8	5.6	6.9
– Actual[3]	5.7	9.1	7.7	3.3
(c) 1986–90				
– Projection with structural adjustment[2]	5.5	6.8	5.7	6.0
– Projection without structural adjustment[2]	4.5	4.9	4.9	6.0
– Actual (1986–87)[3]	7.1	14.5	24.4	9.3
International comparison				
1982–6				
(d) All middle-income developing countries	2.2[4]	6.6[4]	−2.4[5]	−2.3[6]
(e) All highly indebted developing countries	1.9[4]	2.9[4]	−7.2[5]	−6.3[6]

Table 13.7 continued

| | *Ratio to GDP (%)* | | |
	Investment	*Current account deficit*	*Foreign capital inflow*
Thailand			
(f) 1981: actual	24.7[1]	7.0 [1]	6.2[3]
(g) 1986			
– Projection with structural adjustment[2]	26.2	2.5	—
– Projection without structural adjustment[2]	26.8	4.7	—
– Actual[3]	19.7	(2.1)[7]	1.6
(h) 1990			
– Projection with structural adjustment[2]	26.9	1.8	—
– Projection without structural adjustment[2]	28.6	6.0	—
International comparisons			
(i) All middle-income developing countries[6]			
1980	26.8	4.6	—
1986	21.3	0.3	—
(j) All highly indebted developing countries[6]			
1980	25.2	4.8	—
1986	19.0	1.4	—

Notes: 1 From International Bank for Reconstruction and Development (1984) 47, Table 3.1.
     2 From International Bank for Reconstruction and Development (1984) 53, Table 3.3.
     3 Data on GDP, investment, import and export of goods and services are from *National Income of Thailand*, new series, 1970–1987, Account 6, Tables 7 and 9. Data on foreign capital inflow and import and export unit values are from Bank of Thailand, *Monthly Bulletin*. Current account deficit was computed as the difference between exports and imports of goods and services. Data on real export and import growth were constructed by deflating import and export values by their corresponding unit values.
     4 From Fei and Ranis (1988).
     5 From International Bank for Reconstruction and Development (1988a) Table 1. Imports include only those of merchandise trade and the average growth was for 1980–6.
     6 From International Bank for Reconstruction and Development (1988a). Data on investment are from Tables 4 and A.7. Those on current account deficit are from Table 1.5 and on GDP are from Table A.3.
     7 Thailand experienced a current account surplus in 1986.

The World Bank's simulation forecast that average annual growth rates of real GDP, exports and imports with structural adjustment would grow faster than the case without adjustment. However, the growth of investment without structural adjustment for 1982–6 was projected to be higher than that with adjustment measures. When comparing actual figures with the projected ones for 1982–6, one finds that actual growth rates of GDP, exports and imports were higher than the with-adjustment projections, but the actual growth of investment was lower than that projected in either the with-adjustment or the without-adjustment scenario.

The World Bank also projected that structural adjustment would improve the current account deficit in 1986 and 1990, i.e. the ratio of current account deficit to GDP would decline. In the event, the current account in 1986 turned from deficit into surplus.

Table 13.7 also provides international data for comparison (see items (d), (e), (i) and (j)). It will be seen that for the first half of the 1980s, during which the economy was exposed to SALs, the Thai economy outperformed those of middle-income and highly indebted developing countries as a group in terms of the indicators listed. The data we have precludes us from being able to infer how much of this is due to SAL finance, and how much to the fulfilment of policy conditions, but it seems clear from the analysis of the text that the SAL finance relieved the Government of having to plunge the economy into recession at a time of serious external payments crisis.

13.5 SUMMARY AND LESSONS

This project has aimed to answer two key questions regarding the World Bank's first and second Structural Adjustment Loans: (1) why were some measures attached to SALs to Thailand implemented, and some not? and (2) what was the impact on the Thai economy of those measures that were implemented?

The project utilised three approaches to answer the above two key questions. First, it utilised information and data from various documents published in Thailand and by the World Bank. Second, it utilised information from interviewing government officials (involved in SAL negotiation, design, and implementation) and affected businessmen. Finally, it made statistical comparisons between the economic outcome and that which materialised in comparable countries. The interview approach is the core of this project to answer the first key question of why some SAL measures were implemented. However, data and information from various documents substantially help form a background to interviewees' arguments and the overall picture of the structural adjustment process in Thailand.

The logic of structural adjustment in Thailand came from the fact that Thailand, after being adversely affected by the second oil shock in 1979–80, experienced rapidly rising current account and government budget deficits in the early 1980s. The world economy at that time was also in a bad shape dominated by world-wide recession, high real interest rates and high inflation. Therefore, the solution of reviving the Thai economy from the above twin deficits by depending on a recovery of the world economy, at that time, seemed hopeless. Structural adjustment of the Thai economy appeared as the only available option.

The SAL measures agreed between Thailand and the World Bank were only part of an overall programme for structural adjustment in Thailand. The Thai Government itself had formulated broad policies in various areas into the Fifth National Economic and Social Development Plan for Fiscal

111

Year 1982–6. In addition, the Thai Government also took other measures which were not included in the SAL agreement. An important one was a devaluation of the baht against the US dollar in 1981 and again in 1984. The Thai Government was not alone in launching these structural adjustment measures. Various international institutions had lent Thailand a hand. Two of them playing a very important role are the IMF with Stand-by arrangements and, of course, the World Bank with its Structural Adjustment Loans. Although the amount of both SAL I and SAL II combined was not substantial, slightly above US $325 million, the proposed measures covered a wide range of areas and policies namely, agriculture, industry, energy, fiscal policy and institutional development.

To answer the question of why some SAL measures were implemented and why some were not, we hypothesise that the likelihood of implementing the measures depends on (1) whether the measures or their elements were new or had been tried in previous years, (2) whether those measures would have been implemented with or without SALs, (3) the World Bank's distinctive role in Thailand, and (4) political and economic factors. We tested our hypotheses by interviewing more than thirty-five people in eleven organisations. The findings are quite encouraging since the responses from our interviewees were generally in the same direction. The main findings are as follows. First, many SAL measures were not new. Some were ongoing programmes or projects. Some were implemented before Thailand signed the SAL agreement and were considered by the World Bank as the down payment. Finally, some were part of the Fifth National Economic and Social Development Plan.

Second, the SAL measures would have been implemented without SALs. However, the coverage and the speed would have been less and slower, respectively. Third, the World Bank made substantial contributions ranging from the finance itself, through indirect influence on the Thai policy-makers, to technical assistance. Finally, the changing economic environment is an important factor affecting the degree of success or failure of the implementation of SAL measures. As important are the views of the general public and the press towards measures.

To answer the second key question of what was the impact on the Thai economy of the SAL measures that were implemented, we have set up a simple statistical comparison between plan and outcome in Thailand, and between the outcome in Thailand and what was achieved in other countries. The results are generally such as to suggest that the combination of money and policy change implemented under the SAL had a positive effect, although it is difficult to separate the one from the other.

The main lesson regarding the generally perceived success of the SALs in Thailand, in our view, is that success came mainly from a true commitment of the Thai Government to restructure the economy as evidenced from (1) the down payment of various actions taken before signing the SAL agreement, (2) a vigorous implementation of SAL measures during the SAL period of 1982–4, and (3) a continuation of the implementation of the measures even after the SAL period. However, the Thai authorities retained throughout a clear conception of what measures were politically compatible with their restructuring items, and politely but firmly resisted any external advice – including from the Bank – which did not fit in with that conception. The resulting policy slippage did not prevent Thailand from emerging from the 1980s as the most dynamic of all developing countries, a 'new newly-industrialising country' which through its newly acquired status had by the end of the decade largely outgrown the need for the type of financial transfer which this book analyses.

Acknowledgements

Part of the research involved obtaining data from and interviewing many government officials and businessmen. We gratefully appreciate their time and views. Their names in alphabetical order of their last names are as follows: Dr Narongchai Akrasanee, Prachaya Arreeraksa, Nibhat Bhukkanasut, Krishna Brikshavana, Thapana Bunnag, Prangtip Busayasiri, Pisit Chatvachirawong, Jiraporn Chewaprecha, Prachitt Kambhu, Premsri Katewongse, Machima Kunjara-Na-Ayudhya, Wichan Kwanchadr, Somthep Lacharroj, Vanee Lertdumrikarn, Nalinee Luerngthada, Thongchai Lumdubwong, Thamrong Mahajchariyawong, Vanchai Mahatanangkoon, Saijin Mayakarn, Vichai Mittongtare, Dr Charnchai Musignisarkorn, Yukta Na Thalang, Viroj Nelayothin, Dr Bunyaraks Ninsananda, Dr Direk Patmasiriwat, Sommai Phasee, Satri Pradipasen, Vittaya Praisuwan, Nongluk Rangnoi, Dr Phadej Rojanasakul, Pisit Samahito, Yoottaphol Singhaumpai, M. R. Chatumongkol Sonakul, Hansa Sri-ityawit, Tayaporn Srisung, Amnuay Sujarittham, Dr Suchart Thada-Thamrongvech, Dr Phaichitr Uathavikul, Suvit Wanglee, and Prani Yasasindhu.

Comments of participants in a workshop on this project at the Thailand Development Research Institute on 19 May 1988 were helpful. Paul Mosley and John Toye kindly provided invaluable comments on various drafts of this paper. Dr Vuthiphong Priebjrivat helped interview at the beginning of the project, Suvadee Kovatana and Darunee Suwatanakriengkrai enthusiastically prepared the manuscript.

Finally, we would like to thank Dr Virabongsa Ramangkura not only for his substantial contribution to this project but also for his consistent encouragement. Without his encouragement, we think this project could not have been completed.

NOTES

1 This result generally holds for a low tax rate which, in our judgement, is the general case of Thailand. However, for a high tax rate, a reduction in the tax rate may result in an increase in tax revenue. This relationship between tax revenue and a tax rate is often called a Laffer curve. See details in, for example, Barro (1987: 366–9).

2 The country risk score for Thailand quoted by *Euromoney* rose from 16.0 in 1982 to 70.6 in 1985 and 77.0 in 1988.

APPENDIX A

Table 13A.1 Actions taken for structural adjustment before submitting the Letter of Development Policy for the first World Bank Structural Adjustment Loan (SAL I)

Sector or policy area	Actions taken
Agriculture	
1 *Land-use policy*	
(a) Land-use study	The government had prepared, for the Fifth National Economic and Social Development Plan, a study on land-use and development policy and the magnitude and regional distribution of the problem had been identified.
(b) Land certification	The decision was made to issue 'right to farm' certificates (or 'STK') to farmers who were cultivating soils suitable for agriculture.
(c) Land reclassification	The government had begun the process of land reclassification with the 1982 fiscal year budget of baht 73 million and had prepared a broad programme for land reclassification aimed at covering the majority of the problem area during the Fifth Plan period.
2 *Marketing and pricing policy*	
(a) Export restriction on cassava, maize, and sugar	Export quota system for cassava had been eliminated and that for maize had been made more flexible. Ban on sugar exports had been lifted.
(b) Export tax for rubber	Reduced from 25% to 11%.
(c) Rice programmes on price, distribution, and reserve requirement	The efficiency and effectiveness of the rice price support programme had been improved; paddy prices to the farmers increased by about 20–25% over 1981.
	The effectiveness of the cheap rice distribution programme meeting the needs of poverty groups had been improved by limiting quality and eligibility for purchases and by increasing the proportion of cheap rice marketed outside Bangkok from 40% in 1980 to 65% in the first half of 1981.

Sector or policy area	Actions taken
	In December 1981, rice reserve requirement was halved, resulting in a reduction of its effective burden on rice exports from an estimated 20% down to 10%.

INDUSTRY

1 Discussions and seminars

Broad-ranging discussions on industrial development policies had begun between officials of the agencies concerned, industrialists, private bankers and manufacturers.

Public seminars were held on
(1) rationalisation of industrial protection policies,
(2) productivity improvement,
(3) export promotion, and
(4) energy conservation.

2 Committee establishment

Setting up a permanent high level interdepartmental committee to co-ordinate, implement and monitor industrial development.

3 Export promotion

The dollar value of the baht was reduced in 1981 by about 10%.

A new export tax drawback Act was approved by Parliament.

Legislation had been passed to establish an Export Development Fund to provide technical and promotional support for exports.

4 Reform of the protective structure
(a) Subsector study

Arrangements had been made for the World Bank to assist with the study on the electrical goods sector.

5 Investment incentives
(a) A study

Under the UNDP/IBRD technical assistance arrangement to the Board of Investment (BOI), a comprehensive study had been completed on the system of investment incentives and on the functions and procedures of BOI.

(b) Committee establishment

A high level committee had been set up to review the existing system of investment incentives, based on the policy recommendations of the above study.

Table 13A.1   continued

Sector or policy area	Actions taken

ENERGY

1 *Pricing and tariffs*

By April 1981, average power tariffs and petroleum prices had been raised by about 120% over the average level in March 1979 to reduce underpricing of energy.

2 *Supply-side*

Availability of natural gas in the Gulf of Thailand since September 1981 had reduced the dependence on imported oil.

FISCAL POLICY

1 *Measures to reduce budget deficits*

In fiscal year 1981 and in the budget for fiscal year 1982, the government had started (1) to increase discipline over public spending and (2) to impose selected tax measures and substantially increase public enterprise tariffs.

2 *Short-term fiscal stabilisation measures*

The government had the Stand-by Agreement with the International Monetary Fund (IMF). Its amount was SDR814.5 million over a two-year period which started in May 1981.

3 *Tax policy*
  (a) Tax administration

As of January 1982, the Revenue Department had set up five Area Tax Offices in Bangkok.

The IMF had provided extensive technical support in the area of tax administration.

  (b) Tax Policy Board

The Board had recently been set up. Its functions were to identify an appropriate long-term tax structure and develop a programme of phased-movement towards it.

INSTITUTIONAL DEVELOPMENT

1 *Policy analysis and co-ordination*

A permanent high-level National Economic Policy Steering Committee was formed in November 1980 under the chairmanship of the Prime Minister and with the NESDB functioning as its secretariat.

2 *Programme formulation, evaluation and implementation*

Since March 1980 a consultant firm had been working with the Budget Bureau to improve the national budget system. The first phase of this undertaking was completed in September 1981. The second phase of this project was initiated at the end of 1981 for the conversion of the entire government to full programme budgeting.

Note: Extracted from the Letter of Development Policy no. MF.0304/4460, dated 4 February 1982, from Mr Sommai Hoontrakul, Minister of Finance, to Mr Clausen, President of the World Bank; Re: Thailand Structural Adjustment Loan.

Table 13A.2 Specific actions planned for SAL I

Sector or policy area	Planned actions
AGRICULTURE	Actions aimed at increasing productivity through the improvement of incentives to farmers.
1 Land-use policy	Work on land certification and reclassification was continued. By March 1982, the Ministry of Finance would prepare a more detailed work programme for land reclassification.
2 Marketing and pricing policy	
(a) Rice programmes	Further improvements in the procurement and distribution.
	Further reductions in the overall burden of rice taxation.
(b) Deregulation of livestock marketing	Permitting the establishment of private slaughterhouse facilities for export by April 1982.
(c) Fertiliser marketing study	Reviewing the public sector programme for supplying fertiliser to farmers, paying particular attention to pricing issues and distribution mechanisms and objectives.
INDUSTRY	Action aimed at inducing efficient growth.
1 Export promotion	
(a) Customs department	Broad-based improvements, implemented in 1982, in organisation of the Customs Department and in procedures for implementing the import tax refund scheme and the new export tax drawback Act.
	Customs stations would be created at industrial estate locations and in major regional cities.
(b) Bonded warehouses and export processing zones	Five additional bonded warehouses would be created in 1982.
	Export processing zones would be set up in Bangkok and Sattahip early in the Fifth Plan period (1982–6).
(c) Export Development Fund	Details concerning the financing and operations of the Fund would be decided by June 1982.
2 Reform of the protective structure	
(a) General tariff reform	During the fiscal year of 1982, tariff rates would be modified so that all imports would be subject to the ratio ranging from 5% to 60%. Exceptions would only be granted in special cases.

Table 13A.2 continued

Sector or policy area	Planned actions
	By mid-1982, further appropriate changes in both tariff and non-tariff restrictions.
(b) Subsector studies	Plan for automotive industry in 1982; chemical, plastic products, and ceramics in 1983; iron and steel products, machinery and other equipment in 1984.
3 *Investment incentives* (a) Board of Investment	By March 1982, the government would formulate a more detailed programme and phasing for the reform of the investment incentives.
(b) A study	By mid-1982, the Ministry of Finance, in co-operation with the BOI, would initiate a study of the economic and fiscal consequences of the present and proposed incentives.
4 *Large-scale projects*	*Ad hoc* arrangements would be made for reviewing whether large-scale projects met the criterion of economic viability as long as the National Economic and Social Development Board (NESDB) and BOI were not yet in a position to fulfil their functions for all large projects.
ENERGY	Actions aimed at reducing the demand for largely imported energy and eliminating underpricing of energy.
1 *Pricing* (a) A study	A study of the relative price structure of petroleum products.
(b) Pricing changes	Plan to initiate appropriate changes in the price structure in 1982.
2 *Energy strategy formulation* (a) Energy studies	Studies on the energy master plan, gas utilisation, domestic non-conventional energy, and energy conservation.
(b) Strategy formulation	Based on the findings in the above studies, the National Energy Authority (NEA) in consultation with other concerned agencies would formulate and implement the energy strategy.

Table 13A.2 continued

Sector or policy area	Planned actions

FISCAL POLICY

1 *Tax policy*

   (a) Tax measures

Restructuring of personal and corporate income taxes, and a progressive income tax on sales of property.

Selective increases in import duties on goods now exempted or taxed at low rates.

Increases in excise taxes on certain sumptuary items and the change in the excise tax on cement from a specific to an *ad valorem* base.

   (b) Tax administration

By March 1983, the Revenue Department would have set up the total of eight Area Tax offices in Bangkok.

By mid-1982, regulatory action required for the Revenue Department to implement a separation of headquarters from operational functions and to organise its headquarters along functional lines would be completed.

2 *Development of a medium-term fiscal strategy*

   (a) Integrated fiscal planning

Preparing phased implementation programme for attainment of the expenditure and revenue targets and of the broad fiscal policies identified in the Fifth Five-Year Plan for the entire public sector. Specifically, central government revenues would be raised from 14% to 18% of GDP over the Plan period.

   (b) Public enterprises

Establishing realistic financial targets for all major public enterprises and a phased programme for the achievement of these targets. Operational losses in these major public enterprises would be eliminated.

   (c) A study

Reviewing the operations and effectiveness of the extra-budgetary funds with the objective of establishing clear performance criteria and a central monitoring system and considering whether they should continue to operate as separate entities.

INSTITUTIONAL DEVELOPMENT

1 *Policy analysis and co-ordination*

   (a) In-house capabilities

Strengthening the in-house capabilities of the core agencies (primarily NESDB, Ministry of Finance and Budget Bureau) responsible for economic and fiscal policy analysis and advice.

Table 13A.2   continued

Sector or policy area	Planned actions
(b) Outside capabilities	With effect from fiscal year 1983, provision of regular budget resources to permit the greater utilisation of analytical capabilities outside the core agencies in the conduct of key policy studies.
	The creation of an autonomous economic and social policy research institute early in 1982 to provide research support and consulting services to NESDB and other government agencies.
2 *Programme formulation, evaluation and implementation*	Consultants would assist the NESDB to design, test and introduce new planning and programming systems which comprised a three-year rolling investment programming system, a uniform project preparation and investment appraisal system, and a comprehensive programme monitoring and evaluation system.
3 *Personnel management* (a) Studies	The Prime Minister's office would initiate studies of the organisation, management and compensation of the civil service during 1982.

Note: Extracted from the Letter of Development Policy no. MF.0304/4460, dated 4 February 1982, from Mr Sommai Hoontrakul, Minister of Finance, to Mr Clausen, President of the World Bank; Re: Thailand–Structural Adjustment Loan.

Table 13A.3   Specific actions planned for SAL II

Sector or policy area	Planned actions

PUBLIC SECTOR MANAGEMENT

1 *Fiscal strategy*

(a) The revenue side	Strengthening of the link between the new revenue targets and the tax policy and tax administration changes. The target of central government revenue/GDP ratio was dropped from 18% as stated in SAL I to 16% in FY 1986.
(b) The expenditure side	Improvement of the methods to project central government outlays.
(c) Public enterprises, extra-budgetary funds, and local government	Medium-term projections would be made for the financial operations of public enterprises. These projections and those for extra-budgetary funds and for local government would then be integrated into an overall financial strategy for the entire public sector.

Table 13A.3 continued

Sector or policy area	Planned actions
(d) Role of the Fiscal Policy Office (FPO)	With IMF assistance, a programme for broadening and intensifying the role of the FPO of the Ministry of Finance as a central fiscal planning unit.
2 *Medium-term fiscal reform*	
(a) Tax measures	The implementation of a phased programme for simplification of business taxes and excise duties.
	The enactment of selected revisions of the revenue code and customs laws to enhance their scope and impact.
	The enactment of the new consolidated excise tax law.
(b) A study	The initiation of a study on the feasibility of introducing value-added taxation on selected items.
(c) Local finances	The development of an action programme to strengthen local finances by bringing up to date land housing assessment values, local fines and fee structures.
3 *Tax administration*	
(a) The Revenue Department	Computerising its operations and further decentralisation on the basis of evaluation of experience gained from area offices already established.
(b) The Customs Department	Rationalising import/export forms and documents to eliminate unnecessary papers.
	Decentralising and reorganising this Department to facilitate trade flows.
(c) The Excise Department	To be reorganised during 1983, based on IMF proposals and following the enactment of the new excise laws, to eliminate overlaps in several departments and enhance efficiency.
(d) Tax Training Institute	Its creation for tax, excise and customs specialists.
(e) Tax Rulings Committee	In October 1982, a high level Committee for Tax Rulings was established to help solve assessment and tax liability problems and to formulate a tax arrears policy. Its establishment aimed towards a fairer tax system.
4 *State enterprises* (SEs)	
(a) Commercially-oriented SEs	No new SEs competing with the private sector would be set up in the future.

Table 13A.3 continued

Sector or policy area	Planned actions
	Existing SEs would have to stand on their own feet or be liquidated. In 1983, the government would formulate an action programme to implement this policy.
(b) Public utilities SEs	In 1983, the government would determine which SEs it would be willing to assist financially, and to what extent.
(c) Other SEs	Would have to earn appropriate returns on assets by the end of the Fifth Plan.
(d) SEs incurring considerable losses	The government would assess and project forward the overall magnitude of the losses.
	The government would develop, with World Bank assistance, a firm medium-term plan to reduce these losses gradually over 1983–6 through rate increases and efficiency improvements. With respect to the latter, the new policy directions were (i) each major SE would be subjected to a comprehensive programme of efficiency-enhancing measures, (ii) salary structures would be reviewed to attract capable managers, (iii) technical efficiency would be improved by better maintenance, modernisation of accounting and billing systems, and (iv) operations would be decentralised and management by objectives (including programme budgeting) would be introduced.
(e) A study	To introduce the new policy directions, regarding the efficiency improvements, on a more systematic and permanent basis, particularly in the major enterprises.
5 *Foreign debt*	
(a) Three-year rolling plan	The formulation of a three-year rolling plan for planning, evaluation and monitoring of the government's external borrowing programme, in conjunction with the formulation of the three-year (1984–6) fiscal strategy discussed under (1) above.
(b) Data base and analysis	An improvement in the external debt data base and analysis.
(c) Co-ordination	Improvement in the co-ordinating mechanism for external resources mobilisation which had been put into operation by the Committee on External Debt Policy in June 1982.
(d) Reduction in the ceiling on public external borrowing	From US $2,400 million to US $2,060 million per year, a reduction of approximately 14%.

Table 13A.3 continued

Sector or policy area	Planned actions

INSTITUTIONAL DEVELOPMENT

1 *Continuation of SAL I*

   (a) Assistance of a consultant team — The design and implementation of new project proposal and rolling investment systems.

Monitoring and evaluation systems to meet the needs of central core and line agencies.

   (b) A programme budget system — Had been designed and would be implemented in FY1984. This system would be linked with the planning systems.

   (c) A report on accounting system — A comprehensive report on necessary changes in the governmental accounting system would be completed in 1983.

   (d) Improvement in systems for provincial financial reporting — Based on recommendations, it was implemented.

   (e) Auditing — New procedures and standards for performance auditing had been designed by the office of the Auditor General.

A study on the introduction of comprehensive auditing would be undertaken.

   (f) Staff training programmes — Would be formulated during 1983 in all of the central management functions.

2 *New actions*

   (a) Studies — A broad study on the organisation, compensation and personnel administration of the civil service. The study would also identify weaknesses of the governmental machinery in departmental reorganisation procedures and processes.

A reorganisation study for a realignment of several of the NESDB functions.

A study of the staffing needs and arrangements for NESDB and of selected ministerial planning units.

   (b) Policy analysis and formulation — Encountering difficulties in establishing an independent research/development institute, the government enhanced the NESDB's capacity to co-ordinate and manage the conduct of policy research.

INDUSTRY

1 *Continuation of SAL I*

   (a) Export promotion — Reduction of the bias against exporting *vis-à-vis* import substitution.

Table 13A.3 continued

Sector or policy area	Planned actions
	Establishment of export processing zones in industrial estates.
(b) Reform of the protective structure	Overall reduction and greater uniformity of effective protection through general and/or subsectoral actions.
	Arrangements with UNIDO to implement a programme of restructuring feasibility studies, per subsector.
	A study on the textile industry was added.
	Expanding the scope of subsector studies to include the nature and extent of incentives to be granted by the BOI.
	Implementation of appropriate non-tariff reform policies in the subsectors under review.
(c) Investment incentives	Plan for the reform of BOI activities started to be implemented.
	A study on the fiscal and investment consequences of the revised investment promotion structure was initiated.
(d) Large-scale projects	*Ad hoc* arrangements had been put in place to undertake comprehensive economic and technical evaluations.
	The NESDB short-listed a number of consulting firms and invited proposals for in-depth technical and economic reviews of the remaining large industrial projects.
2 *New actions*	
(a) Export credit and guarantee schemes	Exploring its feasibility in order to provide the financial needs of new exporters especially of non-traditional manufactured items.
(b) A study	Recommendations on the ways in which NESDB's capacity to undertake preliminary evaluations of proposed major investments could be strengthened.
ENERGY	
1 *Continuation of SAL I*	
(a) Studies	On energy pricing, conservation and strategy formulation became available around September 1983.
(b) Implementation	Based on findings in the above studies.

124

Table 13A.3 continued

Sector or policy area	Planned actions
2 *New actions*	
(a) Reduction in fuel price differential	Appropriate steps to gradually moderate the large price differential between gasoline and diesel fuel prices.
(b) Reduction in energy consumption	Formulating policies and implementing measures.
(c) Strengthening NEA's ability	To prepare, maintain and update the medium-term energy strategy.
(d) Establishment of the Energy Conservation Centre of Thailand (ECCT)	Providing limited technical and technology assistance to industries for energy conservation.
(e) Transport energy conservation studies	Two studies on energy policies and on road-user taxation had been completed. An action programme would then be prepared to implement appropriate recommendations on transport energy conservation.

AGRICULTURE

1 *Continuation of SAL 1*

(a) Land-use policy	Issuance of 'right-to-farm' (STK) certificates in forest reserve areas. The certificates were legally limited to 15 rai per family but landholdings of up to 50 rai would be recognised. However, land rights for areas in excess of 50 rai per family occupying forest reserves would not be recognised.
	During implementation of the land reclassification programme in each forest reserve area, the government would ascertain (1) the extent and location of excess land in holdings over 50 rai and (2) encroachment in areas determined to be unsuitable for sustained-yield agriculture.
(b) Marketing and pricing policy	No increase in the taxation of agricultural exports beyond the levels in March 1983.
	The Rice Policy Committee would conduct an evaluation of the 1982–3 rice price support programme and propose measures to improve it.
	A new committee had been established to review the whole marketing infrastructure and to develop an agricultural trade information system.

Table 13A.3 continued

Sector or policy area	Planned actions
2 New actions	
(a) Land Bank study	Aimed at the feasibility and desirability of establishing a Land Bank. The study would be carried out under the supervision of the National Rural Development Committee's Land Policy Subcommittee. The Land Bank would enable transfer of land covered by STKs and leases and thereby improve access to credit by STK certificate holders. It would also function as the financial arm of the government's land tenure and land reform policies.
(b) Water resource development and management	
(i) Studies	On organisational, legal, development potential and information needs would be initiated.
(ii) Staff and institutional support	Would be strengthened.

Note: Extracted from the Letter of Development Policy, dated 7 March 1983, from Mr Sommai Hoontrakul, Minister of Finance, to Mr Clausen, President of the World Bank; Re: Second Structural Adjustment Loan.

Table 13A.4 Summary review of SAL I and II programme components as assessed by World Bank in 1984

Sector/policy area	Status of implementation
I. AGRICULTURE	
1 Land-use policy	In 1982 the Cabinet issued a comprehensive set of guidelines on land use and land rights policy aimed at bringing land use and classification better in line with land suitability.
(a) Land certification	STK ('right to farm') certificates have already been issued to one-third of a million farm families who previously had no rights over their land. Forestry Department continues with the certification programme which is expected to affect one million families.
(b) Land reclassification	Surveys have been completed or are under way in almost two million ha of pre-reserved forests in order to determine what the more appropriate classification would be, prior to proceeding with land certification/titling. Procedures for approval of classification recommendations are proving too cumbersome and the Land Reclassification Committee, as a result, has become a bottle-neck.

Table 13A.4   continued

Sector/policy area	Status of implementation
(c) Socio-economic survey	Two rounds of surveys have been carried out and their results are shedding new light on the socio-economic characteristics of the farmers in the forest.
(d) Land Bank study	This study of the feasibility of a land bank is due for completion in November 1984.
2 *Marketing and pricing policy*	The Government's commitment to deregulation of agricultural exports has manifested itself in liberalisation measures across the board.
(a) Export duties	Step-by-step reductions in export duties for rice have lowered the burden on rice exports from over 30% (in early 1981) to the current 5% of FOB prices, eliminating the burdensome reserve requirement in the process. The tax on rubber exports was also reduced from 25% to 11% (of September 1981 FOB prices), and further reduced in 1984.
(b) Export quotas and licensing	Restrictions on the export of maize, rice, and (partly) sugar have been lifted since 1982.
(c) Domestic intervention	After several modifications, the costly and ineffective rice price support programme was substantially eliminated with effect in the 1983–4 season.
	A start towards deregulation of livestock and meat marketing was made in 1982 with the authorisation of private slaughterhouses for beef and hogs, primarily for export purposes.
(d) Marketing study	A major study to identify improvements in agricultural marketing information and infrastructure was completed in mid-1984 and an action plan is now being prepared on the basis of its findings.
(e) Fertiliser study	A study of the fertiliser marketing system (involving a large-scale survey of distributors) is nearing completion. Due to delays in its initiation its findings may turn out to have been overtaken by development of the National Fertiliser Corp.
3 *Water resources*	Cabinet established, in 1983, the National Water Resources Board (chaired by a Deputy Prime Minister) to oversee the management and development of water resources. Problems in setting up a permanently staffed secretariat have delayed initiation of the related programme of studies.

127

Table 13A.4 continued

Sector/policy area	Status of implementation

II INDUSTRY

1 *Protective structure*

(a) General tariff reform

The general tariff reform undertaken in the SAL context was successful in terms of (i) substantially reducing overall levels of protection; (ii) decreasing the bias of the protective structure against exporting industries; and (iii) narrowing down the range of rates of protection. Most of the progress across the board was made in 1982 with reform continuing more selectively and at a slower pace in 1983 and 1984 and in 1985 was slightly revised for revenue reasons.

(b) Subsector studies

A somewhat scaled-down programme of subsector studies has been under way since 1982. The electrical goods study, finalised in 1982, has already resulted in tariff reforms. The automotive industry study was completed and reviewed in 1983 and some of its recommendations have already been implemented (e.g., a freeze on the domestic content requirements progression). The chemicals and plastics study is nearing completion. And, in the textile subsector, the government is proposing to establish an 'intelligence unit' to prepare a reform programme.

2 *Investment incentives*

(a) Board of Investment

In early 1983 the government issued policy guidelines for investment promotion and for tax privileges as an explicit framework for Board of Investments (BOI) activities. Even though the guidelines were largely restating existing policies, disseminating them served a useful purpose and it was followed by the approval of an action plan for BOI which included an effort to design specific subsectoral and product group promotional packages and which will also involve changes in incentive administration to be reflected in a revision of BOI's Act.

(b) Fiscal impact

A study of the fiscal implications of investment incentives is now under way (and scheduled for completion within 1984), after being repeatedly delayed by disagreements on its scope between BOI and the Ministry of Finance.

128

Table 13A.4 continued

Sector/policy area	Status of implementation
3 *Export promotion*	The export rebate and duty drawback systems were overhauled and procedural changes made so that the schemes are now working well – though their reach needs to be expanded. In addition, through tariff reforms, an attempt was made to move towards duty-free status for export production in a few selected areas (e.g., electronics and footwear). An Export Development Fund was established in 1982, followed in 1983 by the creation of an Export Development Committee. During the same period the number of bonded warehouses was expanded and the Export Service Centres were upgraded as well. Finally, a study of the feasibility of an export credit guarantee was completed in 1984 and the Government is reviewing its recommendations.
4 *Large-scale projects*	A study on the evaluation of large-scale projects was completed in mid-1984 and a series of seminars have been held to review it.
III ENERGY	
1 *Pricing and taxation*	As a result of the introduction of a number of modifications in the petroleum price structure, the range of retail prices for the various petroleum fuels has been narrowed and the Oil Fund has had a surplus since late 1983. A comprehensive energy pricing study was completed in late 1983, as well, and is now under review by the steering committee – which will prepare recommendations for the appropriate policy-making bodies (including the Cabinet) by the end of 1984.
2 *Conservation* (a) In industry	A study of incentives for energy conservation in industry is now getting under way, after having been delayed to ensure co-ordination with ADB-sponsored energy audits which were carried out during 1983.
(b) In transport	An action plan for energy conservation in the transport sector was approved in principle by Cabinet in 1983 and considerable progress was made subsequently in designing programmes for specific policy action, including a new structure of road-user charges.

Table 13A.4   continued

Sector/policy area	Status of implementation
(c) National centre	The National Energy Conservation Centre was formally established by Cabinet in mid-1984, under the auspices of the Association of Thai Industries, with initial supervision from the National Energy Administration (NEA), and with government (SAL) funding.
3 *Strategy formulation*	Two separate studies have been completed. An energy assessment has been completed as a collaborative task supported by UNDP/World Bank/NESDB/CIDA and is expected to be an important input into the Sixth Plan. A strategy formulating study has been completed for the NEA, after substantial delays, and is now being reviewed.

IV   FISCAL POLICY

1 *Consolidated public sector finance*

(a) Integrated fiscal planning	An integrated fiscal plan was first prepared in 1982–3 jointly by the National Economic and Social Development Board (NESDB), the Bureau of the Budget (BOB) and the Ministry of Finance (MOF) in collaboration with World Bank, for the Fifth Plan period. NESDB has updated the development expenditure programme and financing plan since then on a routine basis. New comprehensive expenditure programme being prepared for Sixth Plan. As a result of revenue and expenditure measures undertaken, total public sector deficit as a proportion of GDP fell from 7.9% in FY80 to an estimated 5.9% in FY84.
(b) Role of fiscal policy office	Stronger capacity developed for central government revenue projections. Proposal prepared for fiscal planning committee structure incorporates all major elements of fiscal planning for the entire public sector and all core agencies as committee participants, following recommendations of Bank Report no. 4366-TH. FPO is to have central role in leading co-ordination effort. Implementation of proposal currently under review; may be incorporated in future SAL programme.

2 *Tax policy*

(a) Revenue projections	Robust revenue projection model developed for multi-year revenue planning and annual budgeting purposes, replacing purely *ad hoc*

Table 13A.4 continued

Sector/policy area	Status of implementation
	annual extrapolation previously used. The need for discretionary tax measures can thus now be clearly defined in advance, to ensure gradual acheivement of revenue target.
(b) Tax measures	Annual tax packages introduced in 1981, 1982 and 1983 increased the central government revenue/GDP ratio from 13% in FY81 to 15% in FY84. This is the first significant increase in Thailand's revenue/GDP ratio in 15 years and represents substantial progress towards achieving the government's target of a 16% ratio for 1986. (The revenue target ratio was reduced from 18% originally postulated under SAL I to 16% under SAL II, on the ground that the latter provided a more realistic goal, given a less buoyant outlook for the Thai economy.)
(c) Tax structure improvements	Change to *ad valorem* rates for various excise taxes;
	Adjustment in tax rates on business tax to reduce cascading effects;
	Extensive adjustments in export and import duties (see under agriculture and industry headings);
	Study carried out on indirect tax reform (with IMF assistance); and
	legislation submitted to Parliament for overhauling motor-vehicle taxation.
(d) Local government revenues	Numerous studies and measures carried out to strengthen local government revenue base (including property tax mapping, road-user charges, fees, etc.).
3 *Tax administration*	
(a) Revenue department	Establishment of District tax offices in Bangkok and reorganisation of headquarters functions; introduction of uniform tax identification numbers, computerisation of tax files, automatic mailing of tax notifications, stop filer programme and increase of audit programme. The programme represents a far-reaching reform of Revenue Department operations, following technical assistance provided by IMF.
(b) Customs Department	Various informal changes in operations following advice of IMF experts, including effective separation of headquarters functions from customs administration at port of Bangkok.

Table 13A.4 continued

Sector/policy area	Status of implementation
(c) Excise Department	Enactment of bill reforming operations of Excise Department and transferring selected business taxes to Excise Department for administration. (Latter provision may not serve long-term objective of rationalising tax structure and may lead to fragmentation of business tax domain, thus making it more difficult to transform the business tax into a broad-based sales tax).
(d) Tax training	Study carried out to assess need for centralised tax training concluded that decentralised training functions developed by the three MOF departments provide adequate initial response to training needs of MOF staff, although selective training functions can eventually be taken over by small central MOF training unit.

4 *Expenditure policy*

(a) Public expenditure programme	Comprehensive public expenditure programme review carried out in 1982. As a result, the investment programmes of state enterprises were progressively scaled back in 1982 and 1983. NESDB prepared for the first time a priority projects list for budget preparation, and on this basis engaged in effective discussions with BOB on reflecting Plan priorities in the annual budget. Central government expenditure growth for items other than debt service was significantly reduced compared with the Fourth Plan expansion, in both nominal and real terms.
(b) Expenditure strategy	Comprehensive expenditure programme developed for Fifth plan period, consistent with macroeconomic targets and based on agency-specific expenditure plans. NESDB now periodically prepares development expenditure programmes; BOB prepares multi-year recurrent expenditure forecasts. Two studies were carried out to provide guidance for further improvements of comprehensive public expenditure programming; their findings are currently under review.

5 *State enterprises financing and management*

(a) Programme of tariff increases	Substantial tariff increases were carried out in a number of state enterprises in 1980 and 1981. A programme of further tariff increases was developed, and accepted in principle by the Cabinet in October 1982, with implementation delegated to individual enterprises and their supervising ministries. However, the

Table 13A.4　continued

Sector/policy area	Status of implementation
	programme was not implemented as of August 1984, because of political obstacles. Minor tariff increases have been implemented for the Bangkok water company (MWWA) as part of a programme of small monthly increases initiated in June 1984, and small railway tariff increases were introduced. Further tariff measures in the four major loss-making enterprises are urgently needed still. Electricity tariffs were maintained roughly unchanged despite substantial reductions in costs of imported fuels.
(b) Improvements of SES financial management and operations	NESDB carried out overview study of state enterprise financial management practices and problems, and identified various measures to improve SE management in principle. The recommendations received Cabinet endorsement, and were submitted to the high-level Administrative Reform Committee for review and the preparation of detailed reform proposals. Progress to date has been made in the following areas:

   (i) Some small manufacturing SEs have been liquidated or put up for sale to the private sector; private bus operators are licensed to compete with loss-making public bus company;

  (ii) Corporate planning has been introduced for all SEs, as a means to increase management accountability of state enterprises;

 (iii) Financial revitalisation for major loss-making SEs is being prepared; in some agencies (esp. the Provincial Water Works Authority) substantial operational improvements have been made.

 (iv) Bangchak oil refinery reorganisation planned with Bank assistance, and agreed upon by all parties concerned.

| 6 *Extra-budgetary funds* | Study identifying all extra-budgetary funds, found that only a few are individually of any substantial size, and that all combined do not amount to a significant portion of total financial flows of the public sector. Therefore, it was concluded that no major importance needs to be attributed to reform of extra-budgetary funds at this point. |

Table 13A.4 continued

Sector/policy area	Status of implementation

7 *External debt management*
  (a) Foreign borrowing strategy — Comprehensive three-year rolling programme for public foreign borrowing introduced as a management tool for controlling total public foreign borrowing. A strategy was adopted to limit total public borrowing in line with macroeconomic and balance-of-payments constraints; the original annual public borrowing ceiling for the Fifth Plan period was reduced in 1983 from US $2.6 billion to US $2.04 billion, reflecting more stringent international capital market conditions and revised outlook for Thailand's debt-carrying capacity.

  (b) External debt monitoring — FPO acquired computer facility for improved public debt analysis and monitoring. However, it still lacks analytical capability to utilise these facilities effectively.

V INSTITUTIONAL DEVELOPMENT

1 *Systemic changes* — A series of consultant studies initiated in the context of SAL I led in most cases to action plans to implement the relevant recommendations.

  (a) Planning — A project appraisal/investment planning system has been developed in NESDB, but its full implementation has been awaiting approval of NESDB's reorganisation by the Administrative Reform Committee. Meanwhile a related staff development/training programme is under way. A planned study of the staffing needs of other planning agencies has not been undertaken.

  (b) Monitoring and evaluation — The consultants failed to produce an appropriate blueprint for the development of a monitoring and evaluation system but NESDB has come up with its own system development programme, which will be stretched over four years.

  (c) Budgeting — FY84 was the first year of implementation of government-wide programme budgeting, and refinements/adjustments continue to be introduced. BOB's task for years to come will be to take 'on board' the rest of the financial management system and to deepen the understanding of programme budgeting among budget staff in line agencies. BOB developed accordingly a 3-year training programme with an annual throughput of 120 of its own staff and 200 line agency staff.

Table 13A.4   continued

Sector/policy area	*Status of implementation*
(d) Provincial finances	The consultants' recommendations on provincial accounting are being implemented, albeit at a slower pace than was anticipated. Faster progress appears to have been made in improving financial cash management.
(e) Central government accounting	A set of consultant reports on the accounting system of the central government was reviewed by the Controller-General's Department and its recommendations were largely found to be unimplementable at this point; in a number of cases minor modifications of the accounting procedures will be implemented. The main stumbling block is that computerisation, a keystone of the consultants' proposed reform, does not appear practicable, given existing staff skills and advisory capacity in Thailand.
(f) Performance auditing	The establishment of a new performance auditing division in the Office of the Auditor-General has been finally approved by the Administrative Reform Committee. Meanwhile a performance auditing manual to guide staff is being finalised.
2 *Institutional infrastructure*	
(a) Civil Service	A study of organisation, management and compensation in the civil service was planned for 1982. Opposition by some government agencies to the size of the budget proposed by the consulting groups which bid for the contract led to the study's scope being reduced and to two separate teams being hired for the compensation and organisation/management components. Both studies are now scheduled for completion in February 1985.
(b) TDRI	The Thai Development Research Institute was set up in early 1984, with the legal issues that delayed its inception resolved by its being formed as a private foundation (with bilateral grants providing a trust fund) governed by a board chaired by NESDB's Secretary General.
(c) Structural adjustment process	The mechanisms for policy supervision and implementation of the SAL programme were significantly improved with a committee structure and a joint NESDB-MOF secretariat, which became effective in September 1983.

Source: International Bank for Reconstruction and Development (1986) Annexe 2: 97–103.

APPENDIX B

DESCRIPTION OF THE INTERVIEW METHODOLOGY

B.1 *An introduction*

This appendix describes the methodology of the interview approach. We believe that the methodology such as sample selection and the way we conduct interviews may affect the answers from our interviewees and consequently the results. Therefore, we first present in this appendix details of our methodology so that the reader can judge whether results are biased because of the methodology. Our methodology starts with sample selection, coupled with a list of interviewees, and, then, moves to some ground rules that we followed during the interview.

B.2 *Sample selection and a list of interviewees*

We first chose the public and private organisations that intuitively should be involved in SALs decision and implementation. For example, the fiscal policy area under SAL agreement is obviously the area of the Ministry of Finance. As a result, twelve organisations were chosen to be included in our sample. Nine of them are public organisations and the other three are private organisations. The nine public organisations are (1) the Bank of Thailand, (2) the Board of Investment, (3) the Bureau of Budget, (4) the Royal Forestry Department of the Ministry of Agriculture and Cooperatives, (5) the Fiscal Policy Office, (6) the Revenue Department, (7) the Excise Department, (8) the Customs Department[1] and (9) the National Economic and Social Development Board. Organisations nos 5 to 8 are in the Ministry of Finance.

The other three private organisations are (1) the Board of Trade of Thailand, (2) the Federation of Thai Industries, and (3) the Thailand Development Research Institute (TDRI). We chose these private-sector organisations because many SAL measures affected their economic behaviour and, therefore, their views should be heard. One exception is TDRI. That is, we did not choose TDRI because it has been affected by the SAL measures. We chose it because the interviewees there were key persons when SALs were negotiated and implemented.

Letters requesting an interview with key persons who know about SAL negotiation and/or implementation were, then, delivered. In a few cases, we identified interviewees but, in many cases, we left the matter of selecting interviewees up to the decision of the organisation. Out of the above twelve organisations, the Federation of Thai Industries declined to be interviewed. The others accepted.

A list of our interviewees in alphabetical order of their affiliations is shown below:

Bank of Thailand
Prangtip Busayasiri, Pisit Samahito, Yoottaphol Singhaumpai, and Hansa Sri-ityawit

Board of Investment
Vanee Lertdumrikarn, Premsri Katewongse, Prani Yasasindhu, Thamrong Mahajchariyawong, Jiraporn Chewaprecha, Wichan Kwanchadr, Nongluk Rangnoi, Tayaporn Srisung, Vanchai Mahatanangkoon, and Nalinee Luerngthada

Board of Trade of Thailand
Yukta Na Thalang, Suvit Wanglee, Thapana Bunnag, Amnuay Sujarittham, and Dr Phadej Rojanasakul

Bureau of Budget
Prachitt Kambhu, Thongchai Lumdubwong, Satri Pradipasen, and Vittaya Praisuwan

Ministry of Agriculture and Cooperatives − The Royal Forestry Department
Krishna Brikshavana and Somthep Lacharroj

Ministry of Finance
  − *Fiscal Policy Office*
  Nibhat Bhukkanasut, Sommai Phasee, Machima Kunjara-Na-Ayudhya, Dr Charnchai Musignisarkorn, and Vichai Mittongtare
  − *Revenue Department*
  M. R. Chatumongkol Sonakul
  − *Excise Department*
  Prachaya Arreeraksa
  − *Customs Department*
  Pisit Chatvachirawong

National Economic and Social Development Board
Dr Bunyaraks Ninsananda

Thailand Development Research Institute
Dr Phaichitr Uathavikul, Dr Narongchai Akrasanee, Dr Virabongsa Ramangkura, and Dr Direk Patmasiriwat (Ex-World Bank staff in Thailand)

Though our interviewees are grouped by their affiliations, their views on the World Bank's Structural Adjustment Loans may not necessarily represent the views of their affiliations.

B.3   *Some ground rules during the interviews*
Before conducting the interviews, we briefed our interviewees on the following subjects: (1) How TDRI obtained the research grant to evaluate SALs (see Preface of this paper); (2) TDRI has requested a permission to conduct SAL evaluation in Thailand from the Permanent Secretary of the Ministry of Finance; (3) Objectives of the project (see section 13.1 of this paper); and (4) our strict confidentiality policy of not citing each individual as source of information. We also asked our interviewees' permission to tape the interviews and were willing to stop taping during the course of interview as they wished. Furthermore, we promised to send copies of this paper to them and disseminate findings to the general public.

When asking questions, we focus on our four key questions listed in the section of 'Objectives of the project' in Chapter 1. That is, whether the SALs measures were new or had been tried in previous years, whether those measures would have been implemented with or without SALs, what contribution the World Bank made to the structural adjustment in Thailand, and what political and economic factors affected the implementation decision.

APPENDIX C

INTERVIEWEES' RESPONSES

Table 13C.1   Interviewees' responses to the question, 'Were the SAL measures new or had they been tried in previous years?'

Interviewee	Response
A	Not new. However, packaging and managing SAL measures were new.
B	Many SAL measures were not new as they had been discussed among Thai policy-makers such as an idea to restructure the Thai economy. However, those measures could not have been implemented due to lack of funding. The SAL proceeds helped provide liquidity. However, some measures were new, i.e., a restructuring of petroleum product pricing to reflect their cost structure.
C	Some SAL measures such as export promotion policy were not new as Thailand was pursuing them when negotiating SAL. Other measures were planned to implement, therefore, they were included as part of SAL measures. However, a

Table 13C.1 continued

Interviewee	Response
	measure suggested by the World Bank but not included in the SAL measures was a close co-operation between public and private sectors in managing the economy. This idea, nevertheless, was developed independently by the Thai government to be 'the Joint Public and Private Sector Consultive Committee'. Many people think that this committee has helped resolve many conflicts between public and private sectors.
D	More than one half of SAL measures initiated by the Thai officials were not new. They were ongoing measures used to solve the existing problems in the early 1980s. For example, in the agricultural area, Thailand has diversified its farm products even before it implemented SAL measures. Similarly, in the industrial area, Thailand started to switch from the policy of import substitution to export promotion before implementing SAL measures.
E	Many SAL measures were those of the Fifth Economic and Social Development Plan. They initially could not be implemented because of lack of funding. However, the SALs provided liquidity and, therefore, were used to finance those measures.
F, G	Not all SAL measures were new. However, some new measures were initiated during the negotiation between the World Bank staff and Thai officials.
G	Approximately 30–40% of the SAL measures came from the Fifth National Economic and Social Development Plan.
H	Some SAL measures such as land certification and reclassification were not new. They were ongoing measures. The land certification was initiated by the Cabinet Ruling on 28 August B.E. 2522 (or in 1979). The Ruling gave the 'Right to Farm' certificates to farmers occupying the reserved forest areas. It was estimated that there were approximately one million families occupying the reserved forest areas. The land certification started in 1982 with limited government budget allocation. However, when the SAL agreement was reached, this measure was also included as part of SAL measures and therefore it received a larger budget financing.
	Similarly, the land classification was not new since it was included in the First National Economic and Social Development Plan in 1961.
I	Some SAL measures such as the export promotion policy were not new. Producers in exporting industries could obtain tax privileges from the Board of Investment. This policy was contained in the Investment Promotion Act in 1977.
J	Some SAL measures were not new. For example, in 1981, the Excise Department added *ad valorem* rates to the existing specific tax rate schedule where the applicable rate depends on whichever tax rate generates higher tax revenue. This action took place before the SAL implementation but it was included as part of the SAL measures.
K	Reduction of tariff and premium rate on rice export was new. This measure was sensible as the world price of rice had declined substantially in the early 1980s.
M	Some measures were new, some were not. However, SALs helped broaden the coverage of issues, sharpen the idea and speed up many measures. For example, SALs helped speed up issues of energy pricing, tariff liberalisation

Table 13C.1   continued

Interviewee	Response
	and export-oriented policies. Many studies were completed, using the SAL proceeds.
	In fact, both SAL measures and the Fifth National Economic and Social Development Board shared the same principle of using the market mechanism which was based on the World Bank's studies. However, when the World Bank's staff conducted research in Thailand, they always talked to and consulted their Thai counterparts. Therefore, it was quite difficult to nail down who really originated the idea. Probably, the World Bank and the Thai government contributed evenly.
N	Most of the SAL measures were ongoing programmes. However, the new outcome that was generated from SALs was the macroeconomic management technique of the Thai government which involved a co-ordination of various government agencies. The most important impact was to raise consciousness of economic decision-making among Thai officials. This macroeconomic management technique required, from various government agencies, a similar target, a similar methodology, and a check and balance system. Furthermore, it also opened the working of government policies to academics. Their contributions mainly came from studies and discussions in seminars and conferences.

Table C.2   Interviewees' response to the question, 'Would the SAL measures have been implemented without SAL?'

Interviewees	Response
A	The SAL measures would have been implemented if without SALs. However, the measures would have been piecemeal, not systematic or organised. Furthermore, the coverage of measures would have been less because, if without SALs, Thailand would not have international commitments to introduce sensible but unpopular measures.
B	Some SAL measures would not have been implemented if without SALs because those measures might lower government revenue in the short run and, therefore, worsen the government deficit situation. The SALs removed this constraint as the loans provided liquidity during the revenue shortfall in the short run. However, some may argue that, if Thailand at that time needed liquidity, it could borrow from the international credit market. Two disadvantages of doing so are (1) the interest rate charged by the international credit market was higher than that charged by the World Bank and, (2) more importantly, the international credit market required no conditions or measures that benefited the Thai economy. Moreover, the success in SAL implementation later on became an evidence of prudently responsible government and, therefore, raised Thailand's creditability in the international credit market once additional loans were needed.
C	Even without SALs, Thailand would have implemented similar measures anyway. However SALs helped speed the process of designing programmes and measures, the process of co-ordination and the process of monitoring implementation of measures.

Table C.2 continued

Interviewees	Response
	There is a point regarding the counterpart funds of SALs. As few SAL measures really require additional funding over and above the government budget, a majority of counterpart funds were used to finance state enterprises. Therefore, there was less pressure on those state enterprises to raise their product or service prices.
D	Thailand had set up various projects or measures to cope with internal and external imbalances. However, if without SALs, it might not have sufficient government budget to finance all measures. SALs helped finance many measures and reorder the priority of the measures. For example, the tax policy reform and the establishment of district tax offices in Bangkok became the first priority measure in SALs. Furthermore, SALs helped keep the implementation of measures as planned.
H	Even without SALs, the measures would have been implemented. However, the scale of operations would have been much smaller due to limitations on the government budget.
I	If without SALs, the implementation would have continued. However, the measures were more effective with SALs since SALs provided additional funding and advisory committees.
M	The SAL measures would have been implemented if without SALs. However, the implementation process would have been slower.
N	If there were no SALs, Thailand would still have implemented the measures. However, the coverage would have been more limited and the speed of implementation would have been slower.

Table C.3 Interviewees' response to the question, 'What contribution did the World Bank make to structural adjustment in Thailand?'

Interviewee	Response
A	Many contributions: (1) the loan proceeds; (2) the World Bank team included staff with high calibre and experience, which reduced transaction costs in negotiating the SAL terms; (3) the World Bank involvement was an international commitment among Thai politicians, which helped implement sensible but unpopular measures; (4) the World Bank involvement also helped raise co-operation among Thai government officials; (5) the World Bank helped design approximately one-half of the measures; and (6) the World Bank provided some technical assistances.
B	Two contributions: (1) the loans boosted Thailand's international reserves when the reserves were substantially low; (2) with World Bank involvement, Thai government officials gave more weight to the SAL measures; (3) the World Bank lobbied for and reminded of the measures to implement, which helped speed implementation; and (4) technical assistances provided by the World Bank have long been beneficial to Thailand especially those on

Table C.3 continued

Interviewee	*Response*

macroeconomic analysis and on suggesting various measures since the drafting of the Fourth National Economic and Social Development Plan.

C First, the loans were used to raise international reserves. Second, the Ministry of Finance and the National Economic and Social Development Board whose aim was to co-ordinate structural adjustment used the SALs to commit other governmental agencies to adopt the structural adjustment measures. Third, the World Bank helped design the measures although more than one-half of the measures were designed by the Thai authority. Fourth, the World Bank indirectly helped the Thai government to set the priority of measures. Finally, the World Bank helped point out which government agencies should be responsible for each measure and which structure should be changed. In fact, the Energy Conservation Centre was an original idea of the World Bank.

D The World Bank played many roles. First, the loans were used to raise international reserves. Second, the World Bank helped adjust some measures so that they were more practical. For example, Thailand initially set the target of government revenue to GDP ratio at 18% but, later on, the World Bank helped adjust the target down to 16%. Third, the loan proceeds created a commitment among Thai policy-makers. This commitment helped speed the decision process. Finally, the World Bank and the International Monetary Fund urged the Thai government to adopt a fiscal discipline that focused on a realistic forecast of government revenue, a control on expenditure and a reduction in government deficits.

E The loans were used to supplement both international reserves and the government budget. They also helped finance many projects. Furthermore, the Thai technocrats, especially those in the Ministry of Finance, National Economic and Social Development Board, Bank of Thailand and the Budget Bureau, used SALs to indirectly influence Thai policy-makers. This indirect influence started with the Thai side laying down the groundwork of the measures. Then they worked closely with the World Bank staff to arrive at the consensus. The World Bank staff, then, submitted the case to the World Bank executives who, in return, had influence on policy-makers in Thailand. Without SALs, the Thai technocrats would have found it more difficult to influence Thai policy-makers.

F The loans were used to supplement the government budget. Many projects would not have been implemented if without SALs. Most of the counterpart funds were spent on studies and hiring consultants.

G The loans were used to supplement the government budget and international reserves. The counterpart funds were spent on studies and financing state enterprises.

L The World Bank gave a general guideline but the Thai government worked out details. The loans were used to supplement the government budget and international reserves. Part of the counterpart funds were used to finance state enterprises.

M Many contributions: (1) providing loans, (2) speeding the implementation of the SAL measures, (3) sharpening the SAL measures such as the energy policy and educating the Thai technocrats, (4) directly discussing with Thai

Table C.3 continued

Interviewee	Response
	policy-makers about the structural adjustment and their implementation, and (5) SALs were used to supplement international reserves and the government budget.
N	The loans were used to supplement international reserves. The World Bank's contribution was approximately 50–60% of the inputs, especially studies. Although the Thai officials did not have time to conduct studies, they also helped to formulate measures as the World Bank staff when doing research collated information and then discussed with Thai officials. Therefore, it is not so surprising that many measures were originated by Thai officials. In return, Thai officials used the World Bank's studies to support their arguments when proposing structural adjustment measures to policy-makers.
	The World Bank involvement in Thailand was perceived by some as a surrender of sovereignty of the nation to the World Bank.

Table C.4 Interviewees' response to the question, 'What political and economic factors affected the implementation decision?'

Interviewee	Response
A	All SAL measures were implemented. The main reason is that Thailand really had a strong intention and commitment towards structural adjustment as shown by the fact that Thailand had launched many measures even before signing the first SAL agreement with the World Bank. Those measures launched accounted for more than one-half of the SAL measures mentioned in the first Letter of Development Policy. This action raised the probability that Thailand would comply with the World Bank's conditions and eased the negotiation process. As a result, Thailand was the only country, among those countries receiving SALs, on which tranching of the loans was not imposed.
	Structural adjustment tasks can be classified into two types. First, those that Thailand had sufficient information and understanding about and, second, those that Thailand did not have. Thailand designed its own measures for the first type of tasks and implemented them immediately with success. Examples of these tasks are a restructuring of customs tariff system that narrowed down tariff rates across commodities and the land certification or 'STK'. The Ministry of Finance took a leading role in implementing the first type of tasks. In contrast, Thailand started with research studies for the second type of tasks it had incomplete information and understanding about. Unfortunately, the Ministry of Finance did not have time to follow up/monitor the studies; therefore, results of the studies were either incomplete or unsuited for the new economic environment. Examples of studies are those on energy policy and some tax issues.
	Another factor contributing to the success of SAL implementation is an international commitment made among Thai politicians.
	Although SAL I could be considered a success story, SAL II was less successful. Under SAL I, many studies were conducted but, under SAL II, recommendations in those studies should have been implemented. However,

Table C.4 continued

Interviewee	Response
	they were not because (1) as mentioned above, results or findings from the studies under SAL I were either incomplete due to lack of monitoring on the Thai side or inappropriate as the world and Thai economies had changed and (2), more importantly, there was no leading organisation on the Thai side to take roles in reviewing and monitoring SAL measures under SAL II especially when economic environments had changed.
B	SAL I measures, the majority of which were studies, were implemented. But SAL II measures the majority of which were concrete actions slipped because of political and economic reasons. For example, the measure of raising petroleum product prices, bus fares, electricity rates and water supply user charges to reflect real cost of resources was a good measure. However, it was politically unpopular among political party members as the measure was generally opposed by the public.

Other examples of successful and slipped measures when implemented are

(1) Success story: The Thai government could reduce export duty on rice and rubber and eliminate export duty on maize although the measure created a shortfall in government revenue and although Thailand still experienced a relatively slow growth because the SALs supplemented international reserves and provided liquidity to the government budget.

(2) Slippage story: a measure to narrow down import tariff rates across commodities slipped because of changes in economic environment. In 1982, the Thai economy experienced a relatively slow growth, which created a government revenue shortfall. This shortfall surprised the Thai government which responded by temporarily imposing surcharges on imports. However, this reversal of policy was acceptable to the World Bank.

(3) Slippage story: another slippage story because of changes in economic environment is the SAL measure of setting the target of central government revenue to GDP ratio at 18% under SAL I. The fact that other tax system adjustments tended to reduce government revenue and the Thai economy experienced a relatively slow growth in 1982 had altered the target of revenue to GDP ratio down to 16% under SAL II. Actually, up to 1986, the target was never reached.

(4) Success story: the SAL measure of setting a ceiling of external public borrowing was successful in implementation because the Thai government realistically set the ceiling by taking into consideration the ongoing projects of the government that needed funding. Initially, the ceiling was set above US $1,000 million because there were many ongoing projects. However, when some projects were completed and new projects were not initiated, the ceiling could be lowered to US $1,000 million.

(5) Slippage story: losses in some state enterprises required some forms of financing from the central government, which worsened the budget deficit. The SAL measure of raising service or product charges of those state enterprises was one solution to solve their losses. However, the implementation of this measure slipped because doing so might trigger public unrest and, consequently, destabilise the government. Interestingly, part of SAL money was used to help finance losses of some state enterprises.

Table C.4   continued

Interviewee	Response

C   The fact that SAL measures in Thailand were generally considered as a success story came from two factors: (1) the screening of planning agencies, the Ministry of Finance and the National Economic and Social Development Board and (2) many SAL measures were initiated by the Thai government officials. The former factor, screening of the planning agencies during the negotiation with the World Bank mission, resulted in SAL measures that, from the Thai view, had a high probability of getting cabinet approval. The latter factor, measures initiated by the Thai officials, resulted in flexible measures very few of which had to be changed because of changing political and economic environments.

Details of some SAL measures are as follows:
(1) Up to now, the study on the fertiliser marketing system has not been completed.
(2) New pricing of state enterprises' services (electricity, water supply and bus) was not successful in implementation during 1982–4 but was recently successful because a recovery of the Thai economy in recent years has raised the purchasing power of the public so that they can afford higher prices of utilities.
(3) The establishment of the Energy Conservation Centre, whose purpose is to suggest alternatives to conserving energy and reducing oil import bills, was a successful measure. However, when the world energy situation has changed as the world oil price has declined, the need to conserve energy is less important and, therefore, the Centre was not as fully supported as it used to be.
(4) Thailand had adjusted its pricing on petroleum products but the adjustment was not along the lines of what the World Bank would like to see. The Thai government's policy on the pricing of petroleum products was to subsidise the low income class but the World Bank's view was to move toward commercial pricing. The Thai government agreed with the World Bank in principle that pricing of petroleum products in the long run should not be subsidised. However, in the short run, as the low income people were subsidised in the past, a drastic change in pricing policy might result in an adverse effect on inflation and costs of production which, in turn, might make Thailand less competitive in the world market.
(5) One of the SAL measures was to set up a government organisation overlooking the pricing policy of petroleum products. This measure was fully supported by the Thai government. Eventually, the Thai government set up 'The National Energy Policy Office' in the office of the Prime Minister although the set-up was after the period of SAL II.

D   Details on implementation:
(1) The Export Development Fund was established by imposing 0.5% surcharge on imports. The total amount of the fund turned out to be 300 million baht. This amount was used to promote exports. The Export Development Fund was not so successful in promoting exports because the fund amount was limited.
(2) The Export Development Committee was not successful because it lacked authority over other implementing agencies. Later on, there was a structural adjustment which mainly replaced the Minister of

Table C.4 continued

Interviewee	Response
	Commerce by the Prime Minister as the Chairman of the Committee.
	(3) Bonded warehouse was successful because it resolved the delay of tax rebate to exporters.
	(4) There was a delay in the implementation of the Export Credit Guarantee because initially there were arguments over forms of organisation. Later on, when it was decided to form the Export Credit Guarantee Fund, participants argued over the activities that the Fund should promote.
	(5) External debt management was successful as the Thai government reduced the debt ceiling and government expenditures.
	(6) The protection of domestic producers has been reduced. The rate of protection across industries has been lowered since 1982. Even the protection on products receiving the Board of Investment promotion has also been reduced. For example, the number of imported items on which the Board of Investment imposes surcharges has been reduced from 30–40 items per year to less than 10 items per year. The protection rates for the protected items have been frozen or reduced. For example, the rates on chemical and plastic products have been frozen at 40% in spite of a lobby for a rate of more than 40%. Another example is textiles whose protection rate has been reduced from over 40% to now almost zero per cent.
	(7) Two or three years ago, automobile imports were generally banned but now imports are allowed. However, imported automobiles are taxed. The purpose of taxing imported automobiles is not to protect domestic producers but to keep the trade deficit from worsening.
	(8) Since 1982, there has been an attempt to eliminate the tax burden on exporters by giving tax rebates on raw materials or intermediate products used in the production. In the past, the rebate was based on some fixed formula that did not reflect actual uses but now it is based on the physical coefficient which is more realistic. The industries that use this new rebate method are automobiles and most canned foods.
G	The effectiveness or accomplishment of SAL implementation is approximately 60% of the proposed measures.
I	In the case of reducing protection on import substitution products, it is natural that adversely affected producers have a tendency to put pressure on the government so that the measure can be reversed. However, the SAL measure of reducing protection on import substitution products was eventually implemented. Its success depends on various factors. First, the Thai government always consulted private sector organisations such as the Thai Industries Association (now, the Federation of Thai Industries) before implementing the measure. Second, the domestic producers also benefited from the export promotion policy as they switched from import-substitution products to export products. Finally, many used-to-be import substitution industries now become exporting industries for Thailand, for example, textiles and garments, footwear, furniture, iron structures such as pipes, bicycles, electrical appliances, and carpets.
M	Examples of success and slippage stories:
	(1) The implementation of raising the energy pricing and service charge of

146

Table C.4 continued

Interviewee	Response

state enterprises was slow mainly because doing so was usually objected to by the public.

(2) Reductions of export taxes and other structural adjustments for export promotion were slow in implementation in 1982 since the world economy was in recession which, in turn, reduced government revenue. Reductions of export taxes and other adjustments might worsen the government budget further. Therefore, the government slowed down implementation.

N   Political conflicts are common when there is a structural change. There were a couple of political battles with respect to implementing SAL measures:

(1) The industrial policy that dropped import substitution policy and promoted export industry involved changes in tax policy, subsidy policy, financial assistance, import quotas and the Board of Investment's investment incentives. These changes of course were objected to by import-substituting industrialists. However, the Thai government insisted on export and gave various incentives to export such as reducing export taxes and impediments to exports. Many industries had moved from import substitution industries to exporting industries. However, in some industries such as automobiles, the battle continues.

(2) Agriculture has been a major sector of Thailand. The majority of population depend on agriculture and they are relatively poor, therefore, when one considers the agricultural sector, he/she always takes into consideration the equity or distribution of income and, consequently, supports the policy of farm price supporting programme and ignores the market force or market mechanism. The SAL measures in the agricultural sector aimed to change the traditional farm price support programme. As Thailand has been a country of rice monoculture, the SAL measures tried to change from rice monoculture to cash cropping and tried to diversify the crops from a few major farm products to various fruits and vegetables. The objection to these new SAL measures, of course, came from the farmers. However, the Thai government, like the policy for industry, insisted on export and also reduced export taxes and premiums on those major farm products to promote exports and to allow the market mechanism to change the structure of the agricultural sector. However, this battle is still ongoing.

(3) There has been a perception among politicians and journalists that prices of petroleum products should be kept low and it is the role of the government to subsidise those products. As a result, raising petroleum product prices has been a political issue and, in the past, many Thai governments had to resign from the post after raising petroleum product prices. Even now, this battle has not ended. However, Thai officials have tried to depoliticise the issue by imposing the maximum tax rates on petroleum products and then trying to rationalise the pricing.

(4) It is generally perceived that services of state enterprises are public goods and, therefore, the service price should be kept low. In case of losses, the government should subsidise those state enterprises. The

Table C.4   continued

Interviewee	*Response*
	SAL measures with respect to state enterprises did just the opposite. That is, the measures asked for an increase in the service charge (and an improvement in management) of state enterprises so that the central government could eventually terminate its subsidy. This, of course, reduced government expenditures and deficits. At that time, the state enterprises also agreed on the measures. However, resistance came from the public. As a result, the increase in service charges of many state enterprises has been slow.
(5)	The next battle was to improve the tax system. It has two problems. First, at the policy level, both politicians and businessmen did not favour tax increase. Second, tax collectors resisted changes in their routine work and were reluctant to work under the new system. One solution was to change the philosophy of tax collectors and taxpayers. This battle, however, continues.

It can be seen that many SAL measures affected more or less everyone and the difficult task of Thai officials was to sell their cases to the cabinet. The way they did was to use findings in the studies under SALs to support their cases. Furthermore, the SAL proceeds under the counterpart funds also helped finance various programmes and studies that lacked government budget support, this financing turned out to help get support from various government agencies on the SAL measures. At that time, the Thai government handled the political conflict by taking the line of least resistance.

BIBLIOGRAPHY

Adulyapichet, A., (ed.) (1986) *Official Listings Thailand 1986*, Bangkok, Thailand, Tawanna Holdings Ltd.

Bank of Thailand, various issues, *Monthly Bulletin*, Bangkok, Thailand.

Bank of Thailand (1987) *Important Economic Indicators*, Bangkok, Thailand, December (in Thai).

Bank of Thailand (1988) *Thailand: Economic Conditions in 1987 and Outlook for 1988*, Bangkok, Thailand.

Barro, R. J. (1987) *Macroeconomics*, 2nd edn, New York, John Wiley & Sons.

Board of Investment (n.d.) *Thailand: the Climate and Incentives for Investors*, Bangkok, Thailand.

Economic Report of the President (1986) Washington DC, United States Government Printing Office, February.

Euromoney, various issues, London, Euromoney Publications PLC.

Fei, J. C. H. and Ranis, G. (1988) 'The political economy of development policy change: a comparative study of Thailand and the Philippines', unpublished paper.

Industrial Management Co. Ltd. (1985) *Industrial Restructuring Study: Summary*, Bangkok, Thailand, National Economic and Social Development Board, September.

International Bank for Reconstruction and Development (World Bank) (1978) *Thailand: Toward a Development Strategy of Full Participation* (Report no. 2059–TH), Washington DC, 1 September.

International Bank for Reconstruction and Development (World Bank) (1980d) *Thailand: Energy Issues and Prospects* (Report no. 2813–TH), Washington DC, May.

International Bank for Reconstruction and Development (World Bank) (1980a) *Thailand:*

Coping with Structural Change in a Dynamic Economy (Report no. 3067a–TH), Washington DC, 23 December.

International Bank for Reconstruction and Development (World Bank) (1980b) *Income Growth and Poverty Alleviation* (Report no. 2566–TH), Washington DC, 20 June.

International Bank for Reconstruction and Development (World Bank) (1980c) *An Industrial Development Strategy for Thailand* (Report no. 2804a–TH), Washington DC, 5 June.

International Bank for Reconstruction and Development (World Bank) (1983) *Report and Recommendation of the President of the International Bank for Reconstruction and Development to the Executive Directors on a Second Structural Adjustment Loan in an Amount Equivalent to $175.5 Million to the Kingdom of Thailand* (Report no. P–3481–TH), Washington DC, 10 March.

International Bank for Reconstruction and Development (World Bank) (1984) *Thailand: Managing Public Resources for Structural Adjustment*, A World Bank Country Study, Washington DC, June.

International Bank for Reconstruction and Development (World Bank) (1986) *Program Performance Audit Report Thailand – First and Second Structural Adjustment Loans* (Loans 2097-TH and 2256-TH) (Report no. 6085), Washington DC, 28 February.

International Bank for Reconstruction and Development (World Bank) (1988a) *World Development Report*, New York, Oxford University Press, June.

International Bank for Reconstruction and Development (World Bank) (1988b) *Report on Adjustment Lending* (Report no. R88–199), Country Economic Department.

International Monetary Fund, various issues, *International Financial Statistics*, Washington DC.

Letter of Development Policy (1982) no. MF.0304/4460, Re: Thailand Structural Adjustment Loan, from Mr Sommai Hoontrakool, Minister of Finance, to Mr A. W. Clausen, President of the World Bank, dated 4 February.

Letter of Development Policy (1983) Re: Second Structural Adjustment Loan, from Mr Sommai Hoontrakool, Minister for Finance, to Mr A. W. Clausen, President of the World Bank, dated 7 March.

Loan Agreement (Structural Adjustment Loan) between Kingdom of Thailand and International Bank for Reconstruction and Development, Loan Number 2097 TH, dated 15 March 1982.

Loan Agreement (Second Structural Adjustment Loan) between Kingdom of Thailand and International Bank for Reconstruction and Development, Loan Number 2256 TH, Dated 27 April 1983.

Mosley, P. (1988) 'Conditionality as bargaining process: a study of World Bank Structural Adjustment Lending, 1980–86', unpublished paper, University of Manchester, revised draft, October. Published in the *Princeton Papers in International Finance* (1987).

National Economic and Social Development Board (n.d.) *National Income of Thailand*, new series, 1970–87, preliminary, Bangkok, Thailand.

Sahasakul, C. (1987) *Features of the Tax System in Thailand*, Thailand Development Research Institute, Bangkok, Thailand, December.

Thanapornpun, R. (1988) 'The process of policy formulation', *1988 TDRI Year-end Conference on Income Distribution and Long-term Development*, 17–18 December 1988, The Regent Cha-am Beach Hotel, Thailand Development Research Institute, Thailand, December (in Thai).

Thongpakde, N. (1989) *Economic Effects of Fiscal Policies*, Thailand Development Research Institute, Bangkok, Thailand, forthcoming.

Wibulswasdi, C. (1987) 'Recent Thai experience in economic management', paper presented to Malaysian Economic Association Ninth Convention, 'Strategy for Growth: Towards a More Competitive Economy', Kuala Lumpur, Malaysia, 17–19 November.

14

GHANA

John Toye

14.1 GHANA'S POLITICAL ECONOMY BEFORE 1983

A proper understanding of the way in which Ghana's Economic Recovery Programme has developed in the period since the IMF was called in in April 1983 must be based on a careful examination of the pre-existing political economy. Such an examination will be important to understand two things. First, one must be clear what it was that had to be stabilised and adjusted. Second, one must be clear how the decision to stabilise and adjust was made, and how the Fund and Bank became involved in the ERP. Stabilisation and structural adjustment programmes do not necessarily involve the Fund or Bank; they can also be indigenous in conception and execution. The indigenous programmes of Botswana and Papua New Guinea are discussed by Harvey (1986). When the Fund and Bank are involved, it can occur in very different ways, as a comparison of Ghana's ERP with Nigeria's 1987 Structural Adjustment Programme vividly illustrates (Callaghy, 1987: 47–50)

The questions which lie behind all the country studies in this volume are several. What form have relations between the Bretton Woods institutions and developing country governments taken when programme lending is conditional on policy change? Is it more accurate to describe these relations as policy dialogue, bargaining, coercion or something else again? Where bargaining is involved, what are its dynamics? To answer these questions it must be clear what the Bank and Fund were trying to do (recognising the possibility of occasionally conflicting aims) and how Bank/Fund objectives connect with the political aims of the regime with which they are dealing.

(a) Ghana's trajectory since 1960

Before coming to that, however, a brief look at the historical context is necessary to give perspective to the economic crisis which confronted the

Rawlings government in 1982. Fortunately for the non-specialist in recent Ghanaian history, the main lines of the story emerge clearly from the literature, and are not particularly complex or controversial.

It may seem harsh to say so, but, just as Ghana pioneered political independence from colonial masters in Africa, so also has she pioneered a set of self-destructive economic policies which many more recently decolonised African countries have also followed. After only fifteen years of independence, and before the aggravating factors that led to the economic implosion of the early 1980s, key features of a counter-productive development strategy were visible (Killick, 1978: 185–208). In Ghana they can be seen with a classic starkness, without the complications imposed by copper nationalisation in Zambia or indigenous oil supplies in Nigeria.

Their key feature is the failure to provide adequate incentives for producers in the primary product sector which generates the bulk of the country's foreign exchange via exports. In Ghana's case this sector was, and still is, the cocoa sector. Using administrative machinery developed in the late colonial period ostensibly to stabilise cocoa producers' income from year to year, a permanent and sizeable wedge was driven between the world fob cocoa price and the price paid to the producer. This price wedge was composed of (a) internal marketing charges and (b) internal taxation of cocoa producers. The excessive size of this price wedge, going well beyond necessary minimum marketing costs and rates of taxation applied to other sectors, was the fundamental policy 'error'.

Its consequences for the economy could, however, have been mitigated in time if, when the overtaxation of cocoa producers had produced an investible surplus, that had been used to create profitable non-traditional export industries, or efficient domestic import-substitution industries. Generally speaking such industries were not created. Instead, the new industries could survive only with high and continuing levels of protection. Tolerance of poor financial results became endemic, with annual losses being made up from public expenditure. This placed additional pressure on Ghana's public finances, just when the discouragement of cocoa production began to have its impact on volume and hence on the tax revenue derived from cocoa. Without additional tax revenue from other sources, the budget deficit must increase, or more worthwhile expenditure on infrastructure and social welfare must be cut back.

Acceptance of financial and commercial failure in state enterprises had some additional pernicious effects. It was a standing temptation to corruption and embezzlement. In the name of 'employment-creation' it permitted gross overmanning, eroding both the incentive to work (rather than just 'be employed') and to acquire and exercise genuine skills.

This was approximately how matters stood at the beginning of the 1970s. The economic malaise was evident by the mid-1960s and facilitated the toppling of Nkrumah in 1966. Neither the military National Liberation Council (1966–9) nor the civilian government of Busia succeeded in solving the persistent and underlying economic problems which had emerged. Busia did tinker with them by devaluing the cedi and beginning to privatise some state enterprises. But the fragile economy was vulnerable to the 1971 decline in the cocoa price, and so in 1972 was Busia to another military coup.

That the economic and political turbulence of this early period of independence was not more severe can be explained by several favourable factors. At the start, export prices of cocoa and timber were buoyant, while export volumes were still going up. Apart from the ill-chosen industrial investment, the Nkrumah Government also spent more lavishly than the colonial regime on health and education. So the physical indicators of welfare all showed significant improvement: life expectancy and school enrolment went up and infant mortality came down, while the income generation needs implied by population growth still remained a problem for the future. Internationally, some cushions still remained. Sterling balances accumulated in the late colonial period as a result of war were still there to be drawn down, while various other capital inflows had not yet dried up (Green, 1987: 3).

On the political side, the pattern of income distribution which the chosen economic policies brought about favoured urban organised workers. These were the people who had brought Nkrumah to power and in the early independence period both made and broke Ghanaian governments. The political economy of urban bias had a certain degree of stability until economic malaise degenerated in the 1970s into an economic crisis.

(b) From economic malaise to economic crisis

Before Colonel Acheampong's take-over in 1972, economic policy-making could be criticised as makeshift, slipping all too easily from one expedient to another without tackling essential problems. One is reminded irresistibly of the motorist who said to the garage mechanic: 'My brakes are no longer working, so please repair the horn'. Basic problems of incentive distortions and poor industrial productivity cannot be solved merely by import protection and budgetary deficits. But after Acheampong's arrival, all attempts at economic policy-making suffered paralysis, while the General and his military henchmen proceeded to plunder the economy of the country which they had undertaken to govern. Ghana fell under the rule of a kleptocracy. In such circumstances it is hardly surprising that a new and more damaging series of economic problems superimposed itself on those which already existed. What happened next is the most convincing vindication possible of Myrdal's concept of 'vicious circles of circular and cumulative causation'.

152

Ghana's gathering economic crisis took the following form:

1   Domestic saving and investment fell away increasingly rapidly both in the public and the private sectors. Private investors were frightened off by an increasingly risky environment, while public investment was eroded as corruption bled the budget.
2   As a result of (1), the growth dynamic of the economy all but vanished. Combined with the growing loss of cocoa production (or its illicit smuggling to neighbouring countries), output began a slight but steady decline.
3   Population continued to grow strongly. (Because of inconsistent official statistics and uncertainty about migration numbers, estimates vary from 2.5+ to 3+ per cent a year – see Green, 1987.) This led to a substantial erosion of per capita income and consumption, with reinforcing effects on the decline in domestic saving. It was in the 1970s that Ghana changed from a middle-income into a low-income country – with Nigeria, the only African country known to have made such an unhappy transition (ODI, 1988: 4, Table 2).
4   As the crisis of legal cocoa production intensified and cocoa revenues fell, the government resorted increasingly to budgetary deficits and the printing of money to finance them. Unsurprisingly, inflation began to accelerate, and production problems in the domestic food sector led to food prices inflating much faster than the average. Wholesale prices rose by 37 per cent (1973–7) and 56 per cent (1977–9) during this time, showing strong acceleration.
5   Since Ghana's domestic inflation was dramatically greater than that of her trading partners while nothing (or little) was done to devalue the nominal value of the cedi in terms of foreign currencies (i.e. to depreciate the nominal foreign exchange rate), the cedi became grossly overvalued. From an approximate parity rate of 1.15 cedis to the US dollar in February 1973, the only devaluation was a small one (compared to what was required) to 2.75 cedis on 26 August 1978, shortly after the replacement of Acheampong by Akuffo. The cedi's overvaluation created its own additional disincentive to exporters, both traditional and non-traditional. This would have intensified the withdrawal from cocoa production or its cross-border smuggling.
6   The overvalued cedi created other problems, in the context of the imposition early in the Acheampong period of a system of administrative foreign exchange allocation (in response to recurring balance-of-payments deficits). Imports became progressively cheaper in real terms; but this benefit was confined to those who could secure import licences. Rent-seeking behaviour was encouraged and corruption among the upper echelons of the military, the wealthy traders and importers and civil servants grew further.

7   The various price controls which were instituted in the vain hope of 'controlling' an inflation which the Government itself was fuelling with the printing press had a similar effect of driving goods into parallel markets and creating rents, rent-seeking behaviour and corruption.

8   Policy inaction in the face of inflation was, however, evident with respect to the nominal interest rate. Large negative real rates of interest were allowed to emerge. Windfall gains accrued to those who could secure credit, and the domestic banks inevitably themselves became involved in corruption, the more easily since (excluding foreign banks) their audit procedures were so lax. There was a positive disincentive to saving.

9   Policy inaction during inflation (i.e. disregarding the ineffective price controls) allowed the real level of wages and salaries to fall below the point at which employees could live from them alone. Accordingly public functions, from university teaching to the collection of customs duties, were not performed properly, because the people employed to do so were forced to develop other occupations, including rent-seeking and petty corruption, in order to live.

10 As the economic crisis spread and deepened, not only did money capital dry up, but human capital also exported itself. Those Ghanaians with genuine marketable skills to offer, including doctors, lawyers, engineers, teachers and administrators, voted with their feet. Loyalty went unrewarded, voice was ignored or punished, so only exit remained for many of the best of the professional middle class. Their destinations were the developed countries, the oil-rich states of West Asia and other better-placed African countries.

When the effects of this vicious circle of policy mistakes were manifesting themselves with ever-increasing strength, a further series of external shocks brought the economy near to its nadir.

The production problems in the domestic food sector were compounded by a very serious drought between 1982–4, requiring large additional food purchases on a commercial basis. The drought also affected the production of hydroelectric power, which further reduced capacity utilisation in industry down to 20–25 per cent by late 1983 and provoked fires which reduced both cocoa and timber exports through widespread destruction of trees and bushes. The 1979–80 oil price rise further intensified the ongoing decline in Ghana's terms of trade. Finally in 1983, between one-half and one million expatriate Ghanaians were expelled back into Ghana by Nigeria, and had to be rapidly reabsorbed into the rural areas. Although they provided an extra supply of labour to an agriculture with labour shortages, in the short run they just added to the demand for food and consumption imports.

The devastated and distressed state of the Ghanaian economy in 1983 was, then, the result of three compounding sets of causes:

1 A flawed development strategy since the 1960s;
2 Gross economic mismanagement and corruption in the 1973–81 period;
3 A simultaneous set of severe external shocks in the early 1980s.

(c) The origin of the Rawlings Regime and the ERP

That a self-proclaimed 'revolutionary' government, with strong anti-neocolonialist rhetoric, has accepted help from the Fund and Bank to create Africa's most successful stabilisation and structural adjustment programme has caused much puzzlement. Some resolve this puzzle by describing the regime which J. J. Rawlings leads as 'schizophrenic' – able to pursue two contradictory objectives simultaneously. Others see the Provisional National Defence Council (PNDC) as 'patient revolutionaries', whose journey to a complete transformation of the social order has taken a very necessary detour through internationally-assisted economic reconstruction. Others again see some truth in both these images (Callaghy, 1987: 22).

There is another interpretation – that the regime's objectives have in fact changed over time, in response to the pressures of government. To see the PNDC as a 'Marxist regime' was never very apt. Its early rhetoric was more populist and nationalist than Marxist-Leninist, and it always lacked a Leninist revolutionary party to control the revolution's trajectory. Technically, the PNDC may be 'a Marxist-led revolutionary movement' in that it has some leaders (e.g. Kojo Tsakata) who call themselves 'Marxist' and their political project a 'revolution'. But to take these labels at face value and then to construct a 'Marxist' account of the entire regime, as Ray (1986) uncritically does, gives a misleading overall interpretation which stands at odds with significant transitions of the regime's history, which Ray has so carefully and competently described.

Rawlings burst on the scene as the leader of a failed coup by Air Force lower ranks on 14–15 May 1979. His apparent purpose was to punish corrupt officers and their Syrian and Lebanese trader friends who had voted themselves an indemnity from prosecution, to take effect when they handed back power to a civilian government. That was why Rawlings acted just at the moment when elections for the civilian regime were about to take place. His failed effort did chime with a popular mood, especially in the lower ranks of the Services, and an Army mutiny on 4 June 1979 released him from prison and put him at the head of the short-lived Armed Forces Revolutionary Council. The AFRC carried out eight summary executions, including those of three former heads of State (Acheampong, Akuffo and Affrifa), an action entirely without precedent in Ghana's history and traditions (Yankah, 1986: 29–33). He then handed over power to the little-known diplomat, Dr Hilla Limann, who emerged from the elections as the new civilian President.

As a result of these events, the elected Limann Government was placed in an impossible position, which it could hardly have resolved even if it had been stronger and more experienced than it was. Rawlings remained on the scene, still popular but unwilling to submit to any electoral process and clearly threatening to repeat the AFRC episode of 'clean-up' if Limann 'failed'. Limann opted to try and buy off, then frighten off, Rawlings, while procrastinating over calling in the Fund and the Bank for fear of exciting popular opposition. This was a disaster on both counts. Rawlings did not frighten easily, but the deepening economic crisis gradually discredited civilian politics. After 27 months of this, a second armed forces coup (31 December 1981) installed Rawlings in power as Chairman of the Provisional National Defence Council (PNDC).

Two crucial turning points for the regime occurred in 1982. At least one PNDC member was linked to the brutal murder of three judges and a retired manager of the Ghana Industrial Holdings Corporation. This act recalled the summary executions of the AFRC, and seriously eroded the regime's legitimacy in the eyes of many Ghanaians. The second event was the power struggle within the PNDC over whether or not to call in the Fund and the Bank. The June the Fourth Movement (JFM) members in the PNDC opposed a Fund/Bank deal, using classic dependency arguments, despite the failure of missions seeking financial support for Ghana from the Soviet Union, Eastern Europe and Libya. (The latter was a particular disappointment.) Kwesi Botchwey (notwithstanding his PhD thesis criticising international monopoly capital), P. V. Obeng and the New Democratic Movement were in favour of a deal and were already drafting what became the Economic Recovery Programme and discussing it with the Fund.

These two sources of stress were resolved simultaneously by Rawlings, after a period of considerable political confusion, in late November 1982. JFM members and sympathisers failed in an apparent coup to oust Rawlings and left the PNDC. At the same time, the PNDC member later executed for the three judges' murder confessed to this crime, and another PNDC member resigned in protest against 'indiscipline' (Ray, 1986: 104–8). Originally, the PNDC was a coalition of leaders of the four elements of Rawlings support in the 1979–81 period – the lower ranks of the forces, a variety of left-wing student organisations, some of the unionised workers in Accra and some sections of military intelligence. Before the PNDC had lasted a year, it had lost most of those who had been closely involved in the second coup. The 'radical' (or 'Utopian') students had gone into exile and the leaders of the lower ranks left the PNDC to begin a long series of abortive coups which lasted until 1985. The 'revolution' was now eating its children.

The historical resonance of these events is, however, not really with Marxist revolutions. Rather these events resonate with the Bonapartism which Marx (1973) analyses in *The Eighteenth Brumaire of Louis Bonaparte*. The failed coup; the sudden turn of events which brings mass popularity at a time of disorder; the second, successful coup; the overthrow of the existing constitution and the muzzling of the press; the loss of legitimacy and the search for respectability through a combination of economic development and a grandiose and backward-looking foreign policy – one could make many parallels between the careers of J. J. Rawlings and Louis Napoleon Bonaparte. If the former had more personal charisma and financial integrity, the latter had more camouflage in managed national assemblies and popular plebiscites.

Why did Rawlings and the NDM pragmatists decide in mid-to-late 1982 that an IMF deal should be done? In the first place, the idea of such a deal had been 'on the cards' at least since the previous year when it was extensively contemplated by the Limann government. Even at that time, stabilisation measures were long overdue and could not be effectively implemented without new sources of external finance. In April 1981, the Limann government started discussions with the IMF. The IMF indicated the policy conditions that a deal would entail – devaluation, increased cocoa producer prices, increased interest rates, increased repayment of foreign debt (including by 1982 $580 m of arrears) and reductions in government expenditures and payrolls (Ray, 1986: 123). The Government also approached the World Bank at the same time with a proposal for an Export Rehabilitation Credit, and the Bank indicated that this would hardly happen without a thorough restructuring and reform of the Ghana Cocoa Marketing Board. The Bank also prepared a study in 1981 to outline the kinds of fiscal reforms which would be required in Ghana if it was to raise significantly its level of exposure to the country.

But the shadow of Rawlings the Avenger deterred Limann from bringing these discussions to a positive conclusion. It has therefore been argued that, far from advancing the Fund/Bank deal, the events of Rawlings's first and second comings actually set it back by a year (Boahen, 1988(2): 7). There may be some truth in this. On the other hand, whether the programme would have worked as well if it had been introduced earlier under Limann, must remain a very open question.

The conventional view, that the international financial institutions were finally summoned by Ghana 'because its disaster was complete' (*The Economist*, 1988: 54) turns out not to be a very helpful one. There is always some lower depth to which a country can sink. In Ghana's case, her disaster was more complete in 1983 and 1984 than it was in 1982, when the Fund/Bank decision was made.

By mid-1982 it was crystal clear that stabilisation measures were long overdue, and that these needed large financial inflows to sustain them. The only question was whether these could be obtained except from the Fund and Bank, and it soon became evident that they could not. Rawlings must have judged that, having overthrown elected civilian rule because of its inaction during the economic crisis, his own regime would rapidly be in danger if he did not achieve better economic results soon. Since none of the quick initiatives taken by the PNDC in the first half of 1982 showed any sign of turning the trick, the Fund and Bank were at long last summoned with their money and their conditionalities, all the denunciations of neo-colonialism notwithstanding. But those who still believed in those denunciations had to be out-manoeuvred before the regime could begin to change its face. The timing of the decision was determined by the volatile political situation, given the relentless economic pressures.

When the time came, the path had to be eased. Fund officials and Dr Botchwey both state that the PNDC formulated an economic recovery programme and then sought Fund/Bank support for it (Chand and van Til, 1988: 33; Ray, 1986: 36–7). While this is surely formally correct, one need not doubt that there was a great deal of informal assistance provided by the Fund and Bank. Ghana had very few technocrats capable to do it – perhaps only Dr J. S. Abbey, who had been Commissioner for Finance and Economic Planning (succeeding Robert Gardiner in that role), possessed all the technical expertise that the design of such a programme would have required. In addition, the Fund officials involved have written as follows:

> The basic elements of an adjustment program were clear. It was more difficult, however, to establish the precise policy actions to be adopted and their phasing each year, taking into account political and social constraints in addition to these concerning the availability and efficiency of policy instruments in an economy that was beset by structural deficiencies.
>
> (Chand and van Til, 1988: 33)

It is a fair assumption that the Ghana Government would not have been able to do all of this on its own, and would have been given considerable Fund/Bank technical support on an informal basis.

If the 31 December 1981 revolution was ever 'Marxist' in the sense of intending the overthrow of capitalism and capitalists, it soon embarked on a path which has taken it ever farther away from that aim. Indeed by now the PNDC sees Ghana's problems as arising from the absence of sufficient private saving, private investment, banking services and stock exchanges. The PNDC has turned full circle, without schizophrenia and without secret reservations about a future switch back. But the Bank and the Fund did not initially induce this change; it emerged from internal conflict. Both institutions have, needless to say, very assiduously nourished it and sustained it, once it was made. Ghana's own ability to shape the ERP was, however, almost non-existent, despite some official claims to the contrary. As one veteran and sympathetic observer of Ghana has put it:

> Given the 1966–83 (or, as the external financial sources saw it, 1957–83) record, the Ghana Government had very limited credibility for bargaining on the parameters of the programme, and, given the chaotic and disintegrating state of the economy, it also had very little time to seek to negotiate alterations.
>
> (Green, 1987: 34).

14.2 THE ERP, THE IMF AND THE WORLD BANK 1983-8

Ghana's post–1983 Economic Recovery Programme (ERP) is a large and complex one, as befits the economic problems which it set out to address. From the beginning it was designed with a series of (partially overlapping) phases; stabilisation was to give way to the rehabilitation of the economy and this in turn was to give way to a phase of economic liberalisation (World Bank, 1984a: xvii,73). Support in the form of external finance was intended to come from many sources, the IMF, the World Bank, bilateral aid donors and, eventually, private foreign investors. The economic recovery which Ghana has undoubtedly experienced since the ERP was introduced is also the result of many different influences. These include factors outside government control, inflow of external finance and policy changes made in response both to Fund conditionalities and to Bank conditionalities.

We will proceed to a detailed examination of World Bank conditional lending to Ghana in the next section. But before doing so it is important to place World Bank policy reform loans clearly in the wider perspective of the Economic Recovery Programme and its external financing. It is also important to try and assess how much of Ghana's revival in economic fortunes should be attributed to policy reforms of all kinds. The argument is that World Bank policy reform loans are a smallish part of the whole story, whose results are only just beginning to show.

(a) The roles of the Fund and the Bank

The first ERP ran from 1984 to 1986. Its purpose was to get output rising, and to export a higher percentage of that output; to control inflation and improve international creditworthiness; and to rehabilitate Ghana's infrastructure with the help of increased domestic and foreign finance. The second ERP (1987–9) aims at continuing the emphasis on growth and balance-of-payments soundness, while also raising saving and investment rates and upgrading the quality of management in the public sector.

In the period of ERP I, the main provider of additional foreign financial inflows was the IMF. For the four years 1983–6, an additional US $ one billion was channelled to Ghana, and about 60 per cent of this was provided by the Fund. The World Bank, by contrast, supplied a mere 14 per cent (Loxley, 1988: 24). The bilateral aid donors at this time lagged some way behind the Bank.

This division of financial responsibility was appropriate at this phase of the recovery programme. The first requirement was to make progress on macroeconomic stabilisation, narrowing the gap between the official and the parallel exchange rate, curbing inflation by cutting budget deficits, removing price controls and providing the foreign exchange to ease import strangulation. The Bank's role was very much as a junior partner in support, providing additional foreign exchange for imports to rehabilitate the export sectors and beginning to look at some of the microeconomic problems of the leading export sector – cocoa.

With the shift to ERP II, the respective roles of the Fund and the Bank have begun to change. Initially the Fund supported ERP I through three successive Stand-by arrangements. This created a major debt-servicing problem for Ghana in the years 1987 and 1988: in those years she would have required about one-quarter of her export proceeds just to deal with IMF charges and repurchases (see Table 14.1).

Table 14.1   Ghana's debt-service ratios, actual and estimated, 1984–9

	1984	1985	1986	1987	1988	1989
Excluding IMF	32.1	46.8	37.0	26.3	27.5	25.0
Including IMF	36.3	53.4	46.5	51.9	59.2	46.2
Including IMF and arrears	46.4	61.8	46.9	55.0	67.3	53.6

Source: World Bank (1987) p. 69, Table 16.

The finance role of the Fund for ERP II has thus been to find mechanisms effectively to reschedule Ghana's debts to it. From November 1987 this was done by allowing Ghana access to its Extended Fund Facility and Structural Adjustment Facility (EFF and SAF). In late 1988, these arrangements were in turn replaced by even more favourable ones. Ghana gained access to the Extended Structural Adjustment Facility (ESAF). ESAF's loan term is ten years, not seven, with a 5+ year grace period and a substantially lower interest rate (*West Africa*, 1988a: 1737). Besides Ghana, only Malawi and Senegal in Africa enjoy ESAF loans. The Fund's exposure in Ghana can now be expected to rise until 1991.

Since 1987 the Fund has maintained a watching brief on cocoa producer prices and the foreign exchange rate system. It has remained in the lead on the key macroeconomic parameters – the aggregates of government expenditure and revenue (and hence the budget deficit); the overall ceiling on domestic credit creation (and hence the state of liquidity and the dynamics of inflation); aggregate limits on public sector wages and salaries and the management of Ghana's external debt. All these responsibilities are exercised in close consultation with the Bank. Sometimes differences of policy arise between the Fund and the Bank, arising from their different primary objectives and the trade-offs inherent in conflicting objectives.

The simplest way of contrasting the Bank's role in Ghana with that of the Fund is to say that, while the Fund supervises macroeconomic policy, the Bank handles microeconomic issues of development policy. This is helpful, if not taken too rigidly. The 'meso' area where macro and micro meet leaves plenty of scope for territorial disputes. In Ghana, the early flaws in her development policy (see section 14.2(a)) were in the micro domain – pricing and incentive errors in the cocoa sector, inefficient import substitution in the new industrial sector and the failure to establish sound economic criteria for public investment. These major problems thus fall to the Bank. Other micro problems from the Acheampong period included ineffective price controls, negative real rates of interest, excessively low public utility prices and the erosion of real remuneration in the civil service. They also fell to the Bank (although the Fund also has a strong interest in interest rates and price controls). In its more traditional vein, the Bank focuses on individual development projects; in Ghana's case, this often meant rehabilitating existing decayed pieces of infrastructure.

During ERP I the Bank's lending fell roughly into two categories: programme aid support for the balance of payments and a revival of project lending for rehabilitation (after a lending hiatus in 1981–3). The details of each category of loan are given in Table 14.2(a). After 1986, the two categories become three, when sectoral adjustment loans begin to proliferate alongside the two existing types of loan (Table 14.2(b)).

Table 14.2(a) World Bank loans to Ghana, 1983–6 (US million dollars)

Year	Type and purpose	Amount (less cancellations)	Undisbursed (at 31.3.88)
	Programme Aid		
1983	Reconstruction import (1)	40.00	0.00
1984	Export rehabilitation	35.88	7.73
1984	Export rehabilitation	40.12	1.40
1984	Export rehab: tech. asst.	17.10	2.60
1985	Reconstruction import (2)	60.00	16.00
1986	Health and education rehab.	15.00	11.10
		208.10	38.83

Table 14.2(a)   continued

Year	Type and purpose	Amount (less cancellations)	Undisbursed (at 31.3.88)
	Project Aid		
1983	Water supply rehabilitation	13.00	2.51
1983	Petroleum	11.00	6.16
1984	Oil refinery rehabilitation	6.90	1.40
1984	Oil palm II	25.00	14.06
1985	Urban development	22.00	11.27
1985	Roads maintenance	40.00	21.72
1986	Power system rehabilitation	28.00	11.77
1986	Ports	24.50	16.32
		170.40	85.21

Table 14.2(b)   World Bank loans to Ghana, 1986–8 (US million dollars)

Year	Type and purpose	Amount (less cancellations)	Undisbursed (at 31.3.88)
	Programme Aid: SAL		
1987	Structural adjustment	80.89	35.44
1987	Structural adjustment	14.66	14.66
1987	Structural adjustment	34.00	23.50
1987	Institutional support	10.80	9.09
1988	PAMSCAD priority works	10.60	10.60
		150.95	93.29
	Programme Aid: SECAL		
1986	Industrial sector adjustment	24.95	6.42
1986	Industrial sector adjustment	28.50	8.46
1987	Education sector adjustment	34.50	23.29
1987	Agric. services rehabilitation	17.02	16.03
1988	Financial sector adjustment	100.00	100.00
1988	Public enterprise: tech. asst.	10.50	9.85
1988	Cocoa rehabilitation	40.00	40.00
		254.97	204.05
	Project Aid		
1987	North grid extension	6.30	4.40
1987	Refinery and distrib. rehab.	15.00	15.00
1988	Transport rehabilitation	58.87	58.87
1988	Telecommunications		
		80.17	78.27

As Table 14.2(a) shows, programme aid was somewhat greater than project aid under ERP I, although project aid was by no means insignificant. It also shows that programme aid did disburse much more rapidly than the traditional variety. Only 20 per cent of the 1983–6 programme aid remained unspent in early 1988, as against 50 per cent of project aid of the same period.

It has to be admitted that the grouping of loans into the categories in Tables 14.2 involves an element of arbitrariness. No two loans are exactly alike, and certainly their titles alone ('sector adjustment' or 'rehabilitation') provide no conclusive guide to similarities. Judgements based on a loan's purpose, scope and type of conditionality are unavoidable in creating categories.

The above groupings are however, robust enough to indicate that, from 1986, the Bank's two previous loan modalities – programme and project – both diminished somewhat in quantity while a new modality, the 'sector adjustment loan' made a striking entrance on the Ghanaian economic reform scene. The SECAL is intermediate between policy-conditioned programme aid and project aid, in that it aims at funding policy reforms within a given sector of the economy. The figures in Table 14.2 indicate that it is also intermediate between programme and project aid in terms of its speed of disbursement, although, given such a short time period, this result may not be very reliable. In any case, the SECAL rather than the SAL seems to have been chosen by the Bank as its primary instrument for the liberalisation phase in Ghana.

(b) Problems of Bank–Fund co-operation

The Bank and the Fund both have resident representatives in Accra, and the co-operation of both institutions in support of the PNDC Government and its ERP is broadly speaking very good. An improvement dating from mid-1987 is the joint production by the Fund, the Bank and the Ghana Government of a 'Policy Framework Paper' setting out joint intentions for the future development of the ERP and its financing. This paper formed the basis for the move to EFF and SAF finance late in 1987 and a similar one did the same for the move to ESAF finance at the end of 1988.

Co-operation is most in demand at the point where macro and micro meet. Where problems have arisen between the Fund and the Bank, it has been at sensitive points along this frontier. Not all points are sensitive, however: the Fund passed across to the Bank the leading role on cocoa producer prices quite amicably. The same applies to foreign exchange arrangements, although here the Fund seems to. have been in favour of rather more speedy rate unification.

A more contentious area is the government budget. The Fund has to be satisfied with the size of the budget aggregates, but the Bank takes the lead on the difficult management aspects of the budgetary process. One of the Bank's major tasks has been to get produced a Public Investment Programme with a strong potential to induce economic growth.

The Bank sees the need for a larger PIP than the Fund believes is feasible while preserving macro-balance. The Fund insists that the PIP has the Bank's approval and has no strong views on which projects should have 'core' or 'super-core' status, but is adamant that the Bank's view of how much public investment in total can be afforded is over-optimistic.

Public consumption has given problems, as well as public investment. The Government wage bill has become a disportionately large element of public consumption and the Fund and Bank have had different objectives which impinge on the wage bill. The Bank's concern for improved public sector management leads it to policies which raise real salary levels in the public service and expand differentials, which have become highly compressed. The Fund meanwhile is trying to create budget surpluses as contribution to squeezing more excess liquidity out of the system. The resolution of this conflict has been an agreement on the share of the public sector wage bill in GDP: 5 per cent in 1988, rising to 6 per cent in 1991.

The Fund's squeeze on excess liquidity has brought it into conflict with the Bank on another issue. A recurring feature of IMF stabilisation exercises has been the additional requirement for working capital that is created, especially as a result of devaluation. The Bank detected a number of sound, productive enterprises being unable to secure the extra credit they needed for their new, higher working capital needs. It pressed the Fund, therefore, for a relaxation of the existing ceiling on credit creation. The Fund acknowledged the phenomenon of credit starvation, but suggested a different remedy – one that the Bank should implement and not the Fund. The Fund analysis was that the problem was caused by a failure of the banking system to provide adequate financial intermediation. Banking reform, not looser credit ceilings, was the suggested remedy. It has been taken up by the Bank. A Financial Sector Adjustment Credit was granted to Ghana in mid-1988.

The Fund and the Bank did not have any great difficulty in agreeing their projections for the cocoa price: they both thought that an average price of 1600 SDRs per ton would be right. This is a pity, because the market thought quite differently. By September 1988, the London futures market was only two-thirds of that, at £785 per ton. The prospects of the International Cocoa Organisation defending a higher price successfully did not look bright. This is bad news for Ghana, since revived cocoa exports had been at the centre of its recovery strategy. It also poses a particular conjunctural problem. The Bank has pursued a policy of ensuring that the producer price takes a growing share of the world price: the eventual aim is 55 per cent. The falling cocoa price would put an intolerable squeeze on tax revenue from cocoa if the agreed progress in raising the producers' share of the world price were now to go ahead as planned. Ironically, the Bank could only achieve its price aim if the deterioration in terms of trade were offset by additional devaluation of the cedi. But both Fund and Bank seem to have agreed that this would be too drastic a solution, especially in the light of the accelerating inflation since 1986.

It should be emphasised that none of these opposed objectives and opinions caused lasting division between the Fund and the Bank, or seriously damaged their joint support of the ERP. The point is that there are multiple sources of tension in the relationship, and differences of priority and judgement need to be continuously reconciled. It appears, on balance, as if these reconciliations have tended to favour the Fund's initial positions over the Bank's. This may indicate that the macroeconomic imperatives are still seen as fundamental, and that faster growth simply cannot be bought at the expense of macroeconomic imbalance.

The debates between the Bank and Fund are also interesting because they highlight the more problematic areas of the ERP – rationalising public investment, remotivating the civil service, stimulating private investment and relying very heavily on export proceeds from cocoa. These are looked at more closely in the next subsection.

Finally, these debates throw up an important aspect of the measurement of 'slippage' by the borrower in performance of policy conditions in the loan. Slippage cannot necessarily be measured accurately by comparing the performance required by the condition with the actual state of affairs at the due date. Changes in the economic conjuncture may have occurred in the meanwhile which make it no longer desirable to the Bank that the condition be performed as originally agreed. Total slippage is the sum of 'desired' slippage and 'undesired slippage', although it is usually only the former that is thought of when the term slippage is used. This introduces an important complication in any assessment of the practical working of policy reform loans.

(c) The ERP's successes and failures, 1983-7

A broad measure of agreement unites the independent commentators who have assessed the first phase of the Economic Recovery Programme. Two thorough and perceptive overviews have come from Green (1987) and Loxley (1988). Agricultural aspects are the focuses of Seini, Howell and Commander (1987) and Smith (1987). Social and regional aspects are particularly well covered by Norton (1988).

Ghana has experienced five years of continuous economic growth since 1984, bringing real Gross Domestic Product back to the level of the early 1970s. Because of population increase in the interim, real per capita income, though growing again at about 2 per cent per annum since 1984, remains at about 80 per cent of 1975 levels.

Table 14.3   Ghana's Gross National Product, 1983–7

Year	GNP at 1975 prices		Per capita national Income at 1975 prices	
	C million	Percentage change	Cedis	Percentage change
1983	4,717	−4.4	366	−7.1
1984	5,103	+8.2	394	+7.6
1985	5,345	+4.7	400	+1.5
1986	5,601	+4.8	408	+2.0
1987	5,870	+4.8	412	+1.0

Source: Quarterly Digest of Statistics, March 1988, Table 74, p.82.

The impulse of growth was felt in most of the subsectors of industry and agriculture. In Table 14.4, a breakdown of the main types of economic activity is given, with 1970 values to indicate the extent of recovery.

Table 14.4   GDP by type of activity, 1979 and 1983–6 (constant 1975 million cedis)

	1970	1983	1984	1985	1986
A. *Agriculture*	2713	2534	2780	2802	2952
Agriculture and livestock	1472	1763	2035	2001	2102
Cocoa production marketing	899	370	339	384	427
Forestry and logging	263	309	313	313	316
Fishing	79	92	93	104	107
B. *Industry*	1033	550	600	707	752
Mining and quarrying	130	52	59	66	66
Manufacturing	679	328	370	452	483
Electricity and water	16	41	39	47	51
Construction	208	129	132	142	152
C. *Services*	1466	1798	1917	2064	2152
Transport, storage, communications	156	192	217	238	247
Wholesale, retail trade	629	463	510	557	591
Finance, insurance business	302	415	453	495	514
Government and other	379	728	737	774	800
D. *GDP at market prices* (= A + B + C adjusted for import duties)	5349	4747	5158	5420	5705

Source: World Bank (1987) p. 105, Table 2.03.

The structure of the growing national product was also successfully altered. The share of gross fixed capital formation rose from a mere 4 per cent in 1983 to over 10 per cent in 1987 (Loxley, 1988: 22). The bulk of the new capital formation was transport equipment and other machinery and equipment. The share of exports in GNP also rose from 6 per cent in 1983 to over 10 per cent by 1987. This in turn allowed a *pari passu* growth in imports, relaxing somewhat the previous import strangulation. The continuing deficit on the balance of payments was financed by the inflow of IMF and World Bank assistance.

The central government's finances were put on a much sounder footing. A combination of tax reform and the use of very vigorous methods of tax enforcement produced a remarkable rise in the share of GDP accruing as tax revenue. In 1983, the tax share was only about 5 per cent, but it then rapidly climbed to 15.3 per cent (i.e. net of grants) in 1987. Government expenditure was allowed to grow less rapidly, with the result that by 1986 the budget deficit was eliminated and a small surplus generated (Chand and van Til, 1988: 34). The main public finance aggregates as shares of GDP are set out in Table 14.5. The move to a budget surplus sharply contracted the contribution of the Government to the expansion of the money supply, although the rate of expansion of M2 rose to over 50 per cent in 1985–6.

Table 14.5 Public finance aggregates and money supply indicators, 1983–7

	1983	1984	1985	1986	1987
Tax revenue and grants (% GDP)	5.5	8.3	10.8	14.4	17.4
Expenditure (% GDP)	8.0	9.8	12.2	13.8	16.4
Development expenditure (% total)	8.0	12.3	15.2	13.4	16.7
Real development expenditure (1983=100)	100.0	131.2	182.4	180.0	191.9
Overall deficit (% GDP)	−2.7	−1.8	−2.0	0.1	0.2
% Change in M2	38.1	40.9	59.5	53.7	
% Change in M2 explained by government borrowing	45.4	24.0	14.4	8.2	
M2 (% GDP)	11.1	13.0	15.1	16.9	

Source: Loxley (1988) p. 25, Table 7.

Key prices in the economy (see Table 14.6), which had been allowed to get grossly out of line with scarcity values, were pushed back in the right direction. The devaluation of the cedi against the US dollar from 2.75 to 228 by September 1988 has already been noted. The nominal fall of over 8,000 per cent has to be adjusted for inflation. But the real depreciation to less than one-third of its 1983 value is dramatic enough. At the same time the real producer price for cocoa exports, which had been allowed to fall to one-third of its 1972 level, was restored to that level by 1987. Adjustment of the interest rate was not quite so well managed: after achieving positive real rates in 1985, a small negative rate has re-emerged. The real wages of the civil service rose again from 1985.

Table 14.6   Key prices in the Ghanaian economy (adjusted for inflation), 1983–7

	1983	1984	1985	1986	1987
Real exchange rate (1983=100)	100.0	69.2	57.1	30.2	34*
Real producer price of cocoa exports (1972=100)	34	38	62	80	100*
Real interest rate:					
(a) short-term deposits	−51.1	−20.4	6.0	−6.1	
(b) maximum lending rate	−49.5	−16.8	8.7	−3.3	
Real civil service wages (1977=100):					
(a) Senior management	10	7	13	36	
(b) Accountant	16	12	24	55	
(c) Clerical grade	26	22	43	64	
(d) Unskilled labour	32	27	55	56	

Source: Loxley (1988) pp. 24–5, Table 6 and 7.
* Indicates Loxley's estimate.

It would be a mistake, however, to conclude that because sensible policies were followed on public finance and the setting of key prices, they alone were responsible for the observed economic growth. They certainly played a part, but only a part, in Ghana's recovery. The initial response to the policy changes was disappointing, a phase which lasted well into 1984 (Chand and van Til, 1988: 34). Then a spontaneous recovery occurred in agriculture, as the rains returned after the severe drought. Two other external shocks of 1983 also unwound themselves. Ghana's terms of trade improved by no less than 37 per cent, as cocoa prices rose and the price of imported oil fell. No less than 60 per cent of the increased export proceeds of 1984–6 can be attributed to the terms of trade shift. Finally the returned Ghanaians from Nigeria, who were promptly transported to the rural north were beginning to ease some of the labour shortages in agriculture just when agriculture was bouncing back from the drought.

The disaggregated growth figures in Table 14.4 show that the first phase of growth came in 1984 in non-cocoa agriculture. Industry did not revive significantly until the following year, benefiting from the additional imports made possible by the start of Fund and Bank financial inflows. It was not until 1986 that cocoa showed a marked growth response, and to secure that, the real producer price had to be doubled. What has happened in Ghana, therefore, is that necessary policy reforms have been floated up by a rising tide of non-policy developments. After an unhappy eighteen months when the PNDC Government hung on through continuing economic deterioration, the Government, the Fund and the Bank took the flood tide and were led on to fortune. They were able to expand into change and avoid the serious and prolonged further reductions in living standards which would have left the ERP vulnerable to political turbulence.

The failures of ERP I are as generally agreed as are its remarkable successes. Perhaps the most obvious weakness is non-cocoa agricultural policy, which has been largely neglected. The Fund and the Bank seem to be relying on 'market forces' to reverse the fall in per capita production of food items (Loxley, 1988: 28). But the raising of the real producer price for cocoa has, in the medium term and until the hoped-for market forces materialise, created a relative price disincentive to produce food. The effect of this is not entirely clear, given that agricultural supply response is determined by many other influences besides product price: getting prices wrong is not a cause of immediate disaster any more than getting prices right is a cause of overnight abundance. Nevertheless, if the removal of subsidies on inputs like fertiliser and pesticide is taken into account, the absolute position of food-crop producers appears to have worsened under ERP I (Smith, 1987: 35). The particular groups thus negatively affected are northern farms and southern women (Norton, 1988: 42).

A second widely-perceived failure of ERP I is its approach to the distributional effects of the economic reforms. It is true that no social group has lost out massively in Ghana, but it is equally true that those who have lost, even if not massively, are those with relatively poor ability to withstand such losses. The example of the poor northern farmers and women food farmers in the south has already been mentioned. Another example would be petty retail traders (again often women) whose reduction in margins between 1983 and 1987 is attested by the huge difference between the rise in wholesale and the rise in retail prices. A third example would be the retrenched workers from the civil service and state enterprises who, as usual, largely came from the lowest-paid grades. The Fund and the Bank appear to have made no studies of income distribution, and were quite tardy (waiting until 1986) before trying to tackle the collapsed health and education systems. In 1988, sensing the possible onset of 'adjustment fatigue', the Bank has led the way on funding the PAMSCAD initiative, to mitigate the social costs of adjustment. But it is far from clear that PAMSCAD is properly designed to address those social costs. Food for work programmes are not really appropriate in areas of agricultural labour shortage, for example, whereas improved water supplies and health care would be (Norton, 1988: 41).

The poor suffer worst from inflation. As Paul Streeten (1987: 22) has said: 'the poor have no assets whose value goes up with inflation, and their money incomes tend to lag behind price increases, especially of the goods mainly consumed by them, such as food'. Some of the claims made for control of inflation under ERP I have been exaggerated. Bank officials have claimed that the ERP succeeded in bringing inflation down from 122 to 10 per cent between 1983 and 1985. Such a fall did indeed occur. But both peak and trough are attributable to the drought – the peak to its arrival and the trough to its departure. Since 1985, the rate has climbed back to just under 40 per cent, and the average for the whole period 1982–8 has been just over 40 per cent. This is an improvement on the late 1970s, but slightly worse than the period 1973–7. Thus self-congratulation under this heading needs to be moderated. This is particularly so because Ghana enjoyed two important initial advantages in the battle against inflation. The fiendishly difficult problem of removing food subsidies or food price controls did not have to be faced, as none existed. Also, the prices of many imports (though not oil) reflected already the parallel exchange rate rather than the official rate, so the large depreciations of the cedi did not spark off powerful new inflationary pressure.

Apart from food, income distribution and inflation, a variety of other economic issues remained unaddressed under ERP I. But some at least of these were tackled under ERP II (1987–9), as part of the move to a broader liberalisation of the economy under the explicit banner of 'structural adjustment'. Structural adjustment issues, and the role of Bank conditionality therein, form the subject of the next section.

14.3   THE WORLD BANK'S POLICY-CONDITIONED LOANS

(a)   Introduction: the definition of policy conditions

In two important respects, the World Bank's 1987 Structural Adjustment Credit represented a watershed in the evolution of the Economic Recovery Programme. In the first place, it marked the crossover point in the Fund/Bank relationship with Ghana, at which the Bank moved out of the junior and support role which it had previously played. From 1987, if not in finance, then at least in shaping policy, the Bank began to dominate the presence of the Fund. Second, and as part of this change, the Bank broadened out the range of policy issues with which it concerned itself. The Bank had always lead on the cocoa export sector budget management and the control of public investment. From 1986, it had begun to make the running on foreign exchange management and trade policy. From 1987, major new policy areas were opened up – the reform of state enterprises, public sector management generally, the financial sector, the education sector and the mitigation of the social costs of adjustment.

Nevertheless, the 1987 SAC did not mark the start of World Bank policy reform lending in Ghana. An analysis of policy conditionality in Ghana requires us to look at all types of World Bank loans, and not merely that explicitly labelled 'structural adjustment'. That label is, as noted before, not very informative.

Almost every World Bank loan to Ghana since 1983 contains some 'special conditions'. But not all special conditions are policy conditions. All Bank loans carry standard conditions, covering the detail of Bank requirements of borrowers on matters of report, audit, access, procurement etc. 'Special conditions' may merely make some additional, non-routine stipulation on such matters – an extra report, a fancier form of accounting and so on. Or they may specify some other accompanying agreement on the activation of which the main loan agreement is contingent. The special condition is then an 'effectiveness condition' of the loan.

Policy conditions are a subcategory of special conditions which go beyond this to specify actions which the borrower has agreed to take to alter the policy environment. Since the early days of Bank lending, policy conditions have been attached to project loans, e.g. tariff reforms have been conditions for electricity generation project loans. The facts that since 1983 Ghana has received an increased number of project loans and that 'getting prices right' is one of the Bank's objectives, make it only to be expected that some of the burden of policy conditionality in Ghana has been placed on the project loans. A recent example is the November 1987 Transport Rehabilitation Credit. One of the seven 'actions agreed' in this Credit is the elimination of operating subsidies to the railways by 1991. Looking at the policy conditions of structural adjustment loans (SALs), or even at SALs and sector adjustment loans (SECALs) together, omits the project-linked pressures for economic reform. At the same time, it is not the case that every project credit to Ghana carried a policy condition: the Northern Grid Extension Project of January 1987 limited all its five special conditions to specifying financial procedures for the Volta River Authority.

Policy conditions, as they appear in the SAL and the SECALs, are very heterogeneous. They include the classical 'dated action': the Government to perform action 'X' by a stated date in the future. They include undated actions: the Government must do action 'Y', but the timing of it is left completely open. They include new procedures: 'Z' will be reviewed regularly by both parties, but with the aim in mind left unstated. Sometimes studies of problems are called for; sometimes studies plus the implementation of the recommendations of the studies not as yet undertaken (surely a somewhat rash promise to make!). Sometimes the Government is required to come to an agreement with IDA about some issue (not the sort of condition which it is always easy to fulfil unilaterally). Some conditions are so broadly phrased that it would be quite difficult not to fulfil them: others are so detailed that they relate to the arrival of a particular officer at his desk. Quantifying such disparate things could only mislead. Even deciding whether some have been met or not is a far from easy task.

To complicate matters further, the Bank's practice of policy conditionality has not remained static over the 1983–8 period. The initial conception it relied on was too simple, too rigid and too ambitious, the fundamental idea being that should the Government fail to perform agreed dated actions it would forthwith be financially penalised. Something much more flexible than this soon proved to be necessary. Interestingly, the very term 'condition' falls out of the Bank's vocabulary in dealing with Ghana just after the time when the SAC was negotiated, in March 1987. A new format is adopted in which 'agreed actions' by the Ghana Government are recited, accompanied by an explanation of the thrust of government policy on the issues with which the credit is concerned. This may seem a minor presentational change, but there is a clear difference between being in breach of a condition of a loan and being behind in the execution of agreed actions. The exceptions to this were the SAC I itself and the Financial Sector Adjustment Credit, both of which still included explicit 'conditions'.

Neither the policy conditions nor the list of agreed actions tell the whole story of the Bank's relations with the Ghana Government. The Bank is careful not to announce policy aims of its own if they go beyond what the Ghana Government has already agreed to. It also tends to endorse publicly government policies which it has tried to stop, and failed. The Bank's studied public diplomacy plus the confidentiality of its files means that the arenas of Bank/Government conflict have to be inferred, rather than demonstrated. But they are as much a part of the picture of policy reform conditionality as the conditions and actions that have been agreed.

One further device may be used to hide policy disagreement from prying eyes. This is the device of the annual mission of inspection. A credit may merely stipulate that such a mission must be satisfied with the progress of reforms before the next year's money is released. Here no individual agreed actions are listed at all. The causes of Bank satisfaction and dissatisfaction and the balance between them need be known only to the Bank and its borrower. In Ghana, the 1987 Education SECAL embodied this device.

Thus the loan conditions themselves merely crystallise one point in a continuous process of negotiating economic reform in return for external finance. Just as a succession of still photographs can be used to create the impression of movement, so the knowledge of a succession of loan conditions can be used to create a rough-and-ready reconstruction of this process of negotiation. This is the method employed in the analysis which follows. But it must be recognised that the precise degree of unanimity, the unspoken threats on either side, the nods and the winks cannot be recaptured.

(b) Themes of policy conditionality

In such a complex and changing set of loan conditions, it would a Herculean labour to establish in each and every case whether any slippage occurred in the performance of the condition or agreed action. Apart from anything else, mere non-performance does not, as already noted, necessarily represent culpable slippage. In default of a condition-by-condition accounting, the method here is to identify the major policy issues which recur through the numerous Bank credits to Ghana and to concentrate discussion on them. Evident slippage in the central reforms, where it has happened, can provide an adequate foundation for exploring whether political resistance or administrative incapacity has contributed more to delays in the reform programme.

The major themes of policy conditionality in Ghana between 1983 and 1988 were the following:

1 the producer price of cocoa;
2 the cocoa marketing costs of the Ghana Cocoa Marketing Board;
3 the removal of subsidies and price controls;
4 the trade and foreign exchange regime;
5 cost recovery and removal of subsidies in health and education;
6 public expenditure programming;
7 state enterprise divestiture;
8 public sector management;
9 banking reform.

For each of these nine policy themes, one can trace the forms which loan conditionality took. This sketch then provides the basis (a) for speculating about whether the policy actions would have been taken anyway, even without conditionality and (b) for setting out any evidence of slippage in the performance of conditions or agreed actions.

1   *The producer price of cocoa*

The first Reconstruction Import Credit (RIC 1) of June, 1983 prescribes that cocoa producer prices be reviewed and adjusted annually in consultation with IDA. Given the centrality of low producer prices in the collapse of the pre-1983 development strategy, it is entirely understandable that the Bank would wish to participate in their regular review and ensure their (upward) adjustment. This condition, or a variant on it, is, however, constantly repeated. It reappears in credits for December 1983, March 1985, March 1987 and October 1987. What does this repetition imply?

It certainly does not imply that the Ghana Government was unwilling to review the cocoa producer price, or to see it move significantly upwards. That is one of the few specific reforms of the ERP which the PNDC had indicated that it favoured before the Fund and Bank became involved in Ghana. In his second broadcast as Chairman of the PNDC, Rawlings had condemned the urban exploitation of rural cocoa producers and spotlighted the need for better incentives in agriculture (n.d. (a): 4–5, 7–8). Nor do the repeated conditions imply significant slippage in raising the producer price. As already noted in section 14.2(b), the real producer price of cocoa increased steadily and sizeably throughout the ERP I period, markedly ahead of the rise in the world cocoa price f.o.b. The reason for repetition seems to be that until 1987 no mechanism existed for periodic, automatic review and adjustment. Until then, each change was essentially *ad hoc*, and had to be prompted. The Bank may also have been worried that the Government, although approving the principle of increases, might be deterred by the difficulty of squeezing down the Marketing Board's share to make room for an increased producer share without hurting its own cocoa tax revenue. Some pressure, via conditionality, may have been applied for that reason.

2 The cocoa-marketing costs of the GCMB

At the time of RIC 1 (June 1983), the Ghana Government assured the Bank that it intended to produce comprehensive and far-reaching measures aimed at reducing the current marketing costs of the Ghana Cocoa Marketing Board (GCMB or Cocobod). The Export Rehabilitation Credit (ERC) of December 1983 contained the first conditions on the GCMB, that it should be converted to a commercial body with financial autonomy and a corporate plan, that it should devise a staff retrenchment programme and that it should produce plans to divest itself of its cocoa plantations, cocoa products factories and insecticide formulation plants. It was a condition for release of the second tranche of the ERC that actual staff reductions should have taken place.

The GCMB then reappears in the policy conditions of SAC 1 (March 1987). Release of the second tranche was conditional on the implementation of Cocobod restructuring measures in 1986–7 and agreement on a three-year Corporate Plan. In October 1987, the Cocoa Rehabilitation Project credit was aimed at reorganising the Cocoa Services Division and the Cocoa Research Institute of the Cocobod as well as supporting transport and storage investments. The agreed actions of this credit included actions to privatise farm input distribution and storage as well as restructuring Cocoa Research Institute management, revitalising the extension service and agreement on the staffing of key positions in the Cocobod headquarters.

Before the launch of the ERP, the GCMB had been criticised by the PNDC leadership. But the criticism was moralistic, exposing the methods by which Board employees exploited the cocoa farmers. The PNDC had a general understanding that the Board had got out of control and needed to be cut down to size. But it did not have a programme for doing so, and certainly not the kind of programme that is outlined in the Bank's loan conditionalities.

Some slippage in carrying through this programme is evident. By the end of 1984, a start had been made on studies of retrenchment and privatisation. By the end of 1985 the first phase of retrenchment had been carried out, although the number affected was 16,000 rather than the anticipated 19,000. Some 10,000 'ghost workers' were removed from the payroll in February 1987 and by the end of 1987, a further 14,000 workers were made redundant in a second phase of retrenchment. By late 1988, the Cocobod still had just under 50,000 staff left, but some have argued that this is still far too many (Green, 1987: 32). Almost certainly, the Bank had hoped for faster progress of de-manning than this in the five years since the ERP first placed it on the Government's agenda.

Progress towards privatisation has also been frustratingly slow for the Bank. An early (1983) Bank aim had been to involve more private hauliers in the transport of cocoa: in 1987 it still felt that the participation of private hauliers needed further facilitation. By late 1987, the Bank had achieved its 1983 objective of a financially autonomous Cocoa Board equipped with an initial three-year corporate plan (Ghana Cocoa Board, 1987). But the plan itself went only part of the way towards the kind of privatisation sought by the Bank. The Board would divest itself of fifty-two of its ninety-two plantations: the desirability of divesting the other forty would only be studied. The Board's insecticide plant would not be sold. Instead, it would be converted into a joint venture with Bayer A.G. (the majority shareholder) which guaranteed the Board a fixed percentage of the factory's production. The Board's cocoa processing factories (producing cocoa butter, liquor and cake) would not be privatised outright. Instead, they will be refurbished and subjected to tighter financial discipline while the pros and cons of privatisation are studied. The Board will run down its subsidies on the farm inputs which it supplies but only as and when the farm input supply function is itself privatised.

The 'comprehensive and far-reaching measures' foreshadowed in 1983 had by 1988 been subject to some dilution. In part this was because the Bank had been convinced that the private sector option was not as easy to implement as it had thought. At any rate, the 1983–8 Cocobod changes were replete with compromises.

3 The removal of subsidies and price controls

A programme for the gradual removal of subsidies on fertilisers was the Bank's very first policy condition in RIC 1 (June 1983). 'Gradual' turned out to be the operative word. The Bank claimed a swift success, stating categorically that 'the subsidy on fertiliser was removed in stages resulting in a selling price of c.450 per bag in April, 1984' (World Bank, 1984b: 76). But this seems to have been premature. When fertiliser prices were raised again in June 1986, the Bank noted that 'a subsidy remained to cover distribution and handling costs' (World Bank, 1987: 71). As has already been noted, the removal of subsidies on farm inputs was an important issue in the Cocobod's corporate plan for 1987–8 to 1990–1. It also reappears as one of the key objectives of the Agricultural Services

Rehabilitation Credit of April, 1987. An agreed action contained in the conditionality for this credit was the elimination of the fertiliser subsidy by the end of December 1989.

If indeed the fertiliser subsidy had been fully removed in April 1984, it was quick to reappear and persistent thereafter. Thus although fertiliser price increases were made, and kept the subsidy to less than would otherwise have been the case, one has to conclude that some slippage has occurred here, compared with what the Bank thought that it had agreed in 1983.

RIC 2 (March 1985) had, as a condition of effectiveness, the requirement that the number of items subject to price control be reduced from seventeen to eight. The Government had already started to move in this direction, decontrolling four items in December 1984. The reduction from seventeen to eight happened in July 1985, leaving subject to price control only imported rice, sugar, baby food, cement, textiles, drugs, matches and soap (World Bank, 1985: 99).

Similar prompt compliance occurred with another RIC 2 condition: that prices of petrol products be raised in line with exchange rate depreciation. This was done in April and August 1985. In fact, the effect of devaluation was over-compensated, by between 5 and 25 per cent (World Bank, 1985: 99). Thus there was no slippage on the RIC 2 condition. Further increases (and one small, brief reduction) in petrol prices were made in 1986 and 1987 (World Bank, 1987: 73). These changes more or less reflected the combined effects of changing world oil prices and the devaluation of the cedi. It is, however, in the nature of key parametric prices like that of imported fuel that they must be kept under continuous review and adjusted whenever the need arises. Even apparently easy reforms like 'getting prices right' in fact need institutional underpinning. The Petroleum Refining and Distribution Project Credit (May 1987) reflects this need. One of its agreed actions was the implementation of a pricing system that will permanently maintain petrol prices at or above world levels.

The PNDC's record of compliance on price decontrol is all the more remarkable in the light of its actions and philosophy in its first months of power. This was the Government which ordered the burning down of the Makola No. 1 Market, the chief market-place in central Accra, in order to curb high prices. (This was later explained as an action to prevent market women being murdered by crowds angry at high prices (Rawlings, n.d.(c): 94–5).) Rent control for workers' housing was also instituted, in line with the philosophy of ensuring that 'prices are within manageable limits' set by the purses of the poor (Rawlings, n.d.(a): 7–9). Such a government would never have decontrolled prices without pressure from the Fund and Bank.

4 *The trade and foreign exchange regime*

Reform of the exchange rate began in April 1983 with a system of bonuses and surcharges which produced multiple exchange rates with a weighted average value of US $1 = 25 cedis (compared with an official rate of 2.75 cedis) (Addo, n.d: 25). When negotiating RIC 1, the Ghana Government promised to unify these rates, and did so at a value of 30 cedis in October 1983.

In the period between 1983 and 1986, the question of trade and Forex makes only two brief appearances in the conditions of World Bank credits. Taking the more significant, but later, instance first, the Industrial Sector Adjustment Credit (March 1986) had, as conditions for the release of the second tranche, the approval of a phased programme of import liberalisation acceptable to IDA and the implementation during 1986 of agreed export promotion measures. The ERC of 1985 had stipulated only that the year's foreign exchange budget be submitted for IDA's approval.

Thus during ERP 1, the reform of the foreign exchange rate itself was handled outside the area of formal Bank conditionality. At first this was by regular devaluations. By the end of 1983, the cedi had fallen against the US dollar from 2.75 to 30: seven further devaluations brought it down to 90 cedis to the dollar by early 1986. Then in September 1986 the central bank (Bank of Ghana) set up an auction market for 'second-tier' foreign exchange, while the higher, officially administered rate continued to be used for cocoa sales, petroleum purchases and debt service. In February 1987, this dual exchange rate was unified and the auction market rate was applied to all officially-funded transactions. These changes were very much at the initiative of the Government of Ghana. Green (1987: 52–3) concluded that the Forex auction system was launched 'more to show dramatically that the Treasury was still able to influence events than because . . . of external pressure'. The detailed study of Bank loan conditionality reinforces that conclusion.

Once the new Forex system was in place, however, its further development did become a subject of loan conditions. SAC 1 (March 1987) was conditional, in part, on the announcement of a timetable for phasing consumer goods imports into the Forex auction, and implementing related trade and tax reforms. The latter had already been announced in the February 1987 budget, and their implementation does not seem to have been a problem. The incorporation of consumer goods imports into the auction was accomplished by the 1988 budget (Republic of Ghana, 1988a: 30).

What is of interest in Ghana's reform of its trade and foreign exchange regime is the discontinuity of the process, and the small extent to which Bank loan conditions were employed as an instrument for directing it.

5 *Cost recovery and subsidy removal in health and education*

Loan conditions concerning cost recovery and subsidy removal in the health and education sectors changed suddenly between one credit and the next – from visibility to invisibility. The Health and Education Rehabilitation Project (December 1985) produced a credit which required the Ministry of Health to meet 15 per cent of its total recurrent expenditures from cost recovery in 1986, 1987 and 1988. The underlying idea was that the essential drugs whose import the credit would finance should not be distributed free, but that a system of user charge should form the launching-pad for a permanent system of cost recovery to support the health care budget.

Unfortunately, the health side of this project was little short of a disaster. The existing mechanisms for acquiring and distributing essential drugs were too weak to cope with the project. Much of the Credit remained at March 1988 undisbursed, and has now been partially diverted to an attempt to strengthen management in the health system.

Before this credit was agreed, the Ghana Government had, with effect from 5 July 1985, sharply raised hospital fees. The fee for a hospital bed in an open ward had jumped from 7.5 to 40 cedis (adult) and from 5 to 20 cedis (child), while the charge for general hospital consultation was increased fifteenfold, from 5 to 75 cedis (World Bank, 1985: 99). This suggests that the Government needed no pushing from the Bank to embrace the principle of cost recovery in health care.

Nevertheless, when the Bank *did* insert loan conditions on health cost recovery into its Credit (which incidentally had been requested of the Bank at the highest levels of the PNDC), there was almost total slippage. No further progress was made on health charges, it appears. Nor was there any threat to cut off the credit for this default – it was not disbursing properly anyway. This fiasco had two implications. One was that the Ministry of Health was in a sufficiently sickly state that it could not be entrusted with the administration of further conditional Bank Credits for a while. The other was that a different approach to conditionality was called for in the education sector.

The 1987 Education Sector Adjustment Credit did not have the usual list of conditions or agreed actions. Instead, its single requirement was that an annual inspection mission agreed that the results in the previous year of the education reforms were satisfactory to IDA. The expected results cover a wide range of issues, which are linked in that they are all designed to improve the cost-effectiveness of the school and university system. These issues include the more intensive use of school buildings, curriculum reform and the speeding up of teacher training. Cost recovery and subsidy removal are just two components in a large package. Cost recovery on textbooks is aimed at getting simpler, cheaper textbooks back into the classrooms without the Bank having to be responsible for their recurrent cost. The removal of food and boarding subsidies in stages from schools and universities is designed to get educational expenditure spent on education, and not on social welfare. The results to date are that parents now have to pay a higher charge for the new textbooks, but appropriate textbooks are now available. The food and boarding subsidy has now been withdrawn from 80,000 pupils in secondary schools and halved for students at Ghana's three universities. The Ministry of Education and the Ghana Education Service are evidently better able to design (with much Bank help) and administer a reform programme than the Ministry of Health and the powerful consultants who control the health service.

6 *Public expenditure programming*

The Bank's concern with public expenditure programming first appears in the Export Rehabilitation Credit (December 1983). Its second tranche release was conditional on IDA agreeing that the size and composition of the Development Budget in the 1985 fiscal year was indeed consistent with the medium-term investment programme. The same concern was evident again in SAC 1, of which one condition was agreement with IDA on the 1988–9 public expenditure programme. These concerns are best understood in the light of the virtual collapse of the budgetary process after 1983. The budget itself represented past decisions rather than contemporary priorities, while the link between a budgetary allocation and the release of cash was often tenuous, with cash releases being dictated – essentially on an emergency basis – by the inflow of revenue (World Bank, 1984b: 38–9).

In 1984, the Ghana Government decided to make a three-year rolling medium-term programme, a capital and recurrent development budget. A Bank mission to review public expenditure policy in April-May 1985 recommended the preparation of a more comprehensive Public Investment Programme (PIP) than what had been developed at that time. The PIP for 1986–8 was then drawn up, covering 80 per cent of the development expenditures of the central government, plus investments of the major parastatals – 162 projects in all.

Although the PIP represents a big step in the attempt to develop coherent public investment priorities, many weaknesses remain. Major ones clearly visible are:

(a) the fact that appraisal methods used were inadequate to secure a consistent and optimal ranking of projects (Tribe, 1988: 25);
(b) the PIP was the work of a special Task Force, not integrated with the Ministry of Finance and Economic Planning, and some lack of co-ordination with the regular budgetary process must certainly exist;
(c) the PIP is still not automatically linked to cash release, even when

179

budget allocation has been made; if it were, the Bank's efforts to 'protect' twenty so-called super-core projects in the PIP would not be necessary.

While the Bank's conditions on public expenditure were neither numerous nor apparently difficult to comply with, they were a cause of more upset in Bank-Government relations than others that looked tougher. The cause of the problem was the Government's erratic behaviour in April 1986 in announcing large wage and benefit increases – without seeing their implications for the public investment/GDP ratio, given the strict IMF ceiling on credit creation. This seems to have been the one occasion when both the Fund and Bank resorted to sanctions in the 1983–8 period. The Bank imposed a 90-day warning delay in the release of credit funds, until the Government was able to extract itself partially from the mess it had created.

7   State enterprise divestiture

An early indication of the Bank's attitude to failing Ghanaian state enterprises was provided by a condition in the 1983 Export Rehabilitation Credit. The State Gold Mining Corporation was required to enter into a management contract to manage the SGMC mines with an international mining consortium. It agreed to do so (World Bank, 1984b: 77). The contract was awarded to a Canadian company and became effective in November 1985 (World Bank, 1985: 16).

But a major push on state enterprise (SOE) divestiture did not come until SAC 1 (March 1987) – if the Cocobod divestiture programme is ignored in this context. SAC 1 required five SOEs (including the State Fishing Corporation) to be put up for sale, five inactive SOEs to begin liquidation proceedings and ten SOEs to have corporate plans completed (four of these with draft performance agreements). The release of the second tranche of SAC 1 was conditional on all of this, among other things. In fact, the programme which the Government agreed with IDA covered more than the twenty SOEs listed in the conditions: some thirty SOEs were involved in all.

Before it became clear whether there would be any slippage, SAC 1 was followed up with the Public Enterprise Project Credit (August 1987). The agreed actions for this Credit did not expand the number of SOEs involved in the exercise. But it did expand on the various procedures which the exercise would require – guidelines, progress reports, detailed dossiers, reviews of this and that, and finally, adequate budgetary provisions.

The Ghana Government was quite amenable to all of this: it did not have to be coerced to agree – although whether if left to itself it would have tackled the issue so energetically is doubtful. All the same, less than a year after the launch of the Public Enterprise Project, both the Bank and the Ghana Government were agreeing that much too much had been attempted. The Ghana Government had not done its homework properly, and in this instance the Bank's own homework was no better. One unsuspected problem was that the SOEs have failed to make provision for terminal payments of redundant staff. To try and sell SOEs encumbered with its unfunded liability would not be attractive to the private sector, yet if the Government were itself to find the money, its budgetary projections would be thrown into disarray. Another unsuspected problem was the extent of inter-SOE indebtedness: thus the valuation of a single SOE depends on the value of many others, and cannot be easily established without a large-scale untangling of cross-debts.

The Bank has accepted that these are real problems and not invented excuses for the slippage. It is ready to renegotiate the conditionality to fit a smaller and less ambitious divestiture programme. Ironically, these softer conditions could probably have been obtained in the first place, if the Ghana Government had been in a position to argue its case properly in early 1987.

8 Public sector management

The Bank's concern for improved management in the public sector was the origin of the Technical Assistance Project which accompanied the 1983 Export Rehabilitation Project, and the condition that proper project management units be set up for the 1986 Health and Education Rehabilitation Project. But, as with the SOEs, it was not until SAC 1 of March 1987 that the issue was opened up on a broad front.

The aspect which the Bank included in its conditionalities was the retrenchment of civil servants; 15,000 were to go in 1987 and more in 1988. The background agreement envisaged 15,000 in 1988 and another 15,000 in 1989. The rationale was that overmanning at the lower levels of the service made it impossible to create adequate incentives for work at the higher levels: differentials had become very tightly compressed indeed. For the purpose of counting job losses, the civil service includes the Ghana Education Service.

The PNDC Government, in the days before arrival of the Fund and Bank, had denounced the public service for its corruption, singling out the GES for special mention in the connection. The redeployment criteria adopted show that the Government in part saw retrenchment as an opportunity to be rid of 'officers whose work and conduct have been persistently negative'.

Slippage of about 20 per cent on the 1987 target of 15,000 job losses has occurred. By 7 January 1988, 4,011 civil servants had been retrenched, receiving 480 m. cedis in compensation. Some 4,069 non-teaching staff of the GES and 87 teaching staff had been retrenched, with 450 m. cedis paid in compensation. The remainder of the total of 12,462 was made up of over-aged personnel who were found to be still in the service and who were then pensioned off under normal pension arrangements. Additionally, about 15,000 'ghost workers' were discovered on the civil service payroll when the first serious census of the civil service was conducted in August 1987 (by ODA consultants) and these names have now been struck off (*People's Daily Graphic*, 29 September 1988: 6). For 1988, the announced target has been reduced to 12,000 on account of the discovery of further over-aged personnel; to date (September), some 7,257 had been retrenched. SAC 1 included an Institutional Support Project. Attempting to avoid overreliance on foreign consultants (and raise indirectly civil service rewards), the Bank intends to pay local civil servants as its consultants and to try and attract back to Ghana *émigré* talent.

It was not the Bank, but the UK ODA that was selected to supply the major study on civil service reform, covering grading, pay structure, training, personnel management and management services. These studies were completed by mid-1988, and their implementation started in early 1989.

9   *Banking reform*

Anxieties about the soundness of the Ghanaian banking system have a number of sources. One was the Fund/Bank debate about the tightness of credit ceilings: this was resolved by agreement that the credit shortage for creditworthy borrowers arose because the banks were not performing their financial intermediation role efficiently. They could not do so because of unsound loans made in the past (often corruptly) which had never been properly audited and had never been written down as bad debts. Another confirmation of this came when the SOEs' relations with the banks began to be unravelled. The conditions of the Financial Sector Adjustment Credit of May 1988 revolve around the promulgation of new banking regulations, particularly in respect of accounting and audit, and their enforcement. Later tranches are conditional on progress in the restructuring of the banks' assets and liabilities. A study for a stock exchange is also asked for. It is too early yet to determine whether this Credit's conditions have slipped.

Table 14.7 summarises the extent of slippage in the areas of conditionality discussed above, to the extent that it can be ascertained. If the ambiguous cases (marked with a query) are excluded and partial slippage is awarded half marks, the Ghana Government's performance in relation to Bank conditions comes out at 7/12 (58 per cent) compliance, or 42 per cent slippage – not by any means the miracle of collaboration and implementation that has sometimes been implied.

Table 14.7   Compliance with Bank conditionality, 1983–8

Conditions (in chronological order)		Slippage?
(1983)	Cocoa Producer price increases	No
	GCMB privatisation	Some
	Removal of subsidies and price controls	No (except on fertiliser)
*	Trade and foreign exchange reforms	?
	Health and education cost recovery	Yes
*	Public expenditure programming	?
	(Non-cocoa) state enterprise divestiture	Some
	Civil service reform	Some
*(1988)	Banking reform	?

* Denotes an area of conditionality jointly apportioned between Bank and Fund.

The most obvious explanation of the extent of slippage which emerges from this survey is that compliance is easier when conditions ask for price changes and more difficult when conditions ask for institutional changes (but for a contrary case, see the Philippines, Chapter 12). This is the basis for the frequently-heard observation that economic reform gets harder the further it has already gone. Even this simple generalisation must be qualified, however. Price changes themselves require institutionalisation, if they are not to be forever externally prompted. And other factors are at work, so that some price changes are easier to make than others: it is easier to raise cocoa output prices than to abolish cocoa input subsidies, for example.

One oddity of Ghana's record to date is that new institutional constructions – like the Forex market or the Public Investment Programme – were achieved *without* formal Bank loan conditionality. Leaving aside the education sector, where slippage is hard to detect, Bank requirements for institutional changes have been subject to much slippage. Staff retrenchment is the most successful aspect, and success here was much aided by the discovery of many over-age workers on the public payroll. One hypothesis on the cause of slippage can be rejected. The policy stance of the PNDC before Fund/Bank intervention is not a reliable predictor of compliance. The abolition of price controls is a dramatic example of good compliance with loan conditions which cut right across the grain of previous policy. On some issues the PNDC has genuinely changed its mind.

14.4   THE CAUSES OF SLIPPAGE

A variety of answers exist to the cynic's question why, if reforms are truly advantageous to a developing country, they have to be incorporated as conditions in a World Bank loan before they are adopted. These answers boil down to the following:

1 divergent *information*, about current facts, causal relations or the future (as embodied in forecasts);
2 divergent *objectives*, including the weighting and time-phasing of objectives;
3 divergent *attitudes to risk*, including that which arises from differences of interests;
4 *strategic behaviour*, e.g. for the purpose of shifting the opprobrium for the reforms from the reformers on to the Bank.

All of these explanations have different implications for the occurrence of slippage. From the details of the slippage that has occurred in Ghana, it may be possible to infer which of these explanations is most relevant in the Ghanaian case.

One can start by ruling out the 'scapegoating' form of strategic behaviour, for two reasons. The more obvious is that the Ghana Government has taken full public responsibility for the ERP/SAP, and has not resorted to criticising the Fund or Bank when reforms run into difficulties. The second reason is that scapegoating does not imply slippage, rather the reverse, and some slippage there has been.

Divergent information, by contrast, has not been entirely absent in Ghana. This is evidenced by the frequency with which loan conditions do not prescribe actions or dated actions, but studies and agreement on action plans. Another sign is the emphasis on achieving satisfactory results rather than using particular policy instruments, as for example in the education sector adjustment loan. Divergent information can cause slippage, if inadequate time is scheduled for research, discussion and reaching agreement (the 'policy dialogue').

But that does not seem to have been the serious problem in Ghana. On the contrary, a more powerful cause of slippage might be called 'insufficiently divergent information'. The most obvious example here is the slippage on the SOE divestiture programme. Both the Bank and the Ghana Government believed that the implementation of the agreed actions would be straightforward and rapid. But both sides were misinformed. The Ghana Government tends to be overreliant on the technical expertise of the Bank (Loxley, 1988: 48–9). When the Bank then loses sight of the limitations on its own local knowledge, the problem of insufficiently divergent information comes to the fore. The Ghana Government clearly needs to diversify its sources of advice, while the Bank needs to reflect on the fact that, however great its technical sophistication (and that can be exaggerated), knowledge of the local policy context is often even more vital to success.

Divergent objectives are to some extent noticeable between the Ghana Government and the Bank. The general picture is still governed by the decision of the PNDC, taken in 1982 after considerable infighting, to put economic policy in commission to the Fund and the Bank. But despite all the visible anxiety to comply with the main lines of policy agreed (often on insufficient information) with the Fund and Bank, the Ghana Government has not entirely abandoned the pursuit of independent objectives. Thus signs of some conflicts of objectives can still be detected, and these have caused a certain amount of slippage.

Three examples can illustrate the extent of conflict of objectives. Perhaps the most significant concerns the development planning system itself, which at least for the period since 1985 has been being redesigned to fit in with the forthcoming establishment of 110 district assemblies and associated decentralised functions and resources. The Ghana Government sees the setting up of a new National Development Planning Commission as the fulfilment of a commitment to popular participation in decision-making made in the early days of the regime. The World Bank sees the NDPC as too *dirigiste*; as a premature attempt to move away from crisis management; and as objectionable because it separates the planning function institutionally from finance and budgeting. The Bank has also indicated that, in its view, the task of assigning permanent responsiblity for managing the public investment programme 'has been complicated by the recent decision to put in place a national planning system'. It noted, without further comment, that as of early 1987, 'the modalities to implement this decision have yet to be worked out' (World Bank, 1987: 45). These coded remarks indicate considerable Bank unhappiness with the NDPC concept. Nevertheless, the NDPC is going ahead and, in late 1988, the Bank seems to be taking the line that the change will perhaps not have such a big impact after all, and must be verbally supported for the public record.

The PNDC Government has over the years of the ERP shed the support of the groups on which it originally relied (students, urban workers) without having gathered in the support of originally hostile or indifferent groups – the urban middle class and the farmers in rural areas (Gyimah-Boadi, n.d.: 8). The decentralisation exercise and the forthcoming district assembly elections are a delicate attempt to mobilise rural support without giving too much scope to urban opposition to organise and strengthen itself (cf. Callaghy, 1987: 27). If this very limited move to democratisation and legitimation were to succeed (which does not seem likely) it would strengthen the PNDC's hand in relation to the Bank and Fund as well as entrenching more deeply the ERP.

The Bank, however, is more concerned with the short-term costs of this political manoeuvre. It sees these costs as diversion of effort from the manifold economic policy problems and the weakening of integration between planning and budgeting. Although, as previously noted, the Bank has used its conditionality sparingly in relation to public expenditure management, in a loose sense, the Bank sees 'slippage' occurring in this area because of uncertainty surrounding the birth of the NDPC. All the same, the Bank has at best secured some amendments and guarantees: it has not been able to block the whole development.

The second arena of conflict has been discussed already – the future of the Ghana Cocoa Marketing Board. The Bank wanted cocoa marketing privatised and the Board disbanded. The Ghana Government refused. The Board still exists as a commercial entity, with plans for the privatisation of some of its functions – but not enough to suit the Bank. Although dialogue proceeds on the basis of a shared objective – lower cocoa marketing costs – and differences about means, it seems more reasonable to suppose that the Ghana Government sees the continuation at least of the Board's purchasing monopoly as an objective, while the Bank sees the breaking of that monopoly (and any others held by the Board) as desirable in itself. The Government continues to fight a successful rearguard action on behalf of the Board.

The third example of conflicting objectives is not so clear, and it could be argued with more plausibility than in the last example that the conflict is about means and not ends. The Ghana Government is dismayed at the extent to which World Bank loans involve the use of foreign consultants – to make studies, to design new systems, to lead special task forces and so on. It believes that the use of foreign consultants on the scale required by the Bank is unnecessary, expensive and demoralising for its own civil service. The Bank, *per contra*, believes that it is necessary to strengthen the capacity of the civil service and that the expense is unavoidable. To make its point, the Government has refused to use certain Bank loans to buy foreign consultancy services, and obliged the Bank to find a bilateral donor willing to supply the same service financed by a grant. The ODA study of civil service reform was provided in just this way. The Bank has also been obliged to fund a somewhat optimistic 'skills mobilisation scheme for Ghanaians' to minimise use of expatriate consultants (World Bank, 1987: 66–7).

It is worth noting that in cases where the Government has taken the view that its vital interests are involved – because of the link between planning and attempted democratisation, the link between cocoa marketing and government revenue and the link between consultancy and the reversal of Africanisation – the Bank has given ground.

Strategic behaviour, divergent information, differing objectives and risk preferences are all causes of slippage that are rooted in lender/borrower conflict of one kind or another. But slippage can also be caused by other factors when there is total unanimity between lender and borrower on policy issues. One such factor is cash. Reforms of institutions usually require to be financed, particularly if they have been financially mismanaged or have become grossly overmanned. Availability of finance for reforms in the hands of the Government is determined by the macroeconomic situation and the external events which influence it. The current fall in the world cocoa price, if uncompensated either by more devaluation or additional foreign aid, will squeeze the Government budget (since budget deficits are to be avoided). This will in turn slow down expensive reforms – e.g. de-manning the civil service, privatising SOEs and introducing a more realistic public sector pay structure.

Apart from cash to meet the short-term cost of institutional reform, the biggest cause of slippage is a widespread lack of administrative capacity. Ghana has been fortunate in having a small group of ministers and top civil servants who, as a team, have guided the ERP, since its inception – one thinks particularly of the trinity of P. V. Obeng, Kwesi Botchwey and Joe Abbey. The stability and continuity of the top economic leadership in Ghana has been unusual and very positive. But the middle and lower levels of the civil service provide precious little support for the top team. The Chairman of the PNDC put his finger on the problem when the ERP started, and in the last five years very little has changed. He said: 'too many people (in the bureaucracy) still stand waiting to be told what to do next, waiting for authorisation to do the obvious, afraid to act in case someone higher up disapproves' (Rawlings, n.d. (c): 31). This is not just a result of civil servants needing a second occupation because of the low purchasing power of their salaries. In addition to that, counter-productive behaviour is much in evidence – the withholding of necessary information from colleagues, constant referral upwards of all decisions, even the most trivial and innocuous, and failure to co-ordinate with other units working in a related field. A particular weakness is failure to undertake preparatory policy analysis, setting out and appraising all relevant policy options. The inevitable result is instant, on-the-spot decision-making by the top leadership, which often commits the Government publicly to policies that are well-intentioned but ill-conceived. PAMSCAD was one notable example of this. The plans for decentralisation are another. The lack of public debate on policy options intensifies this weakness (Loxley, 1988: 49–50).

The decade before the ERP began did very serious damage to Ghana's social and political life. Corruption permeated very widely and very deeply. The PNDC leadership is not itself corrupt and it has striven, both by example and by taking punitive action, to roll corruption back. But clearly – just judging by the regular newspaper exposés – the roll-back of corruption still has a long way to go. Meanwhile, the process of reform is retarded every time some new, unexpected aspect of this general corruption emerges as a particular impediment to action. The corruption of the domestic banking system (collusion in the circulation of worthless cheques; loans made to family, or to those who will bribe – without hope of recovery, etc.) provides a good example. Rehabilitation of sound enterprises has been held back because their managers cannot borrow enough domestic currency to be able to bid for Forex for imports in the auction. They cannot borrow because people still are afraid to deposit much money in the bank, and what they do deposit is often dissipated in irrecoverable loans. Again, the interaction of a corrupt banking system with ill-run SOEs has created such a financial tangle that SOE divestiture cannot go swiftly ahead.

Rather like the workman who came to put up new wallpaper, and found that the plaster beneath was crumbling and the brickwork and timber beneath that was rotten, so the World Bank has been drawn into an ever more comprehensive scheme of institutional reforms. Loxley (1988: 36–7) wondered why the Bank 'is pressing so hard for reform in the face of . . . obvious concerns' about the strain on administrative capacity. The answer seems to be twofold. One answer is that it has become clear that some of the initial reforms will fail unless validated by later reforms (e.g. of the financial sector). The new wallpaper cannot go up until the plaster, timber and brickwork are restored. The second answer is that, with the failure of foreign private investment to respond to the reforms to date, the Bank and the Fund will have to continue for longer as Ghana's major international creditors, and these financial inflows need a series of reform 'vehicles' to carry in the foreign exchange. At all events, more and more reform is being attempted with, if anything, less in the way of public support and administrative competence – a process which clearly has limits. The Limann regime bequeathed to Ghana a large number of half-constructed buildings. The Rawlings regime is in some danger of bequeathing a large number of half-finished reforms.

14.5   THE CONSEQUENCES OF CONDITIONALITY

Whether slippage occurred or not in the performance of agreed actions, consequences ensue for the economy. It would be a mistake to assume that only those conditions which were implemented have an impact. Ghana's sad history between 1973 and 1983 shows vividly that doing nothing is an option which can inflict terrible social costs, and slippage is just another word for doing nothing. If we are interested in second-guessing whether the policy agreed with the Bank was the right one, the consequences both of performance and of non-performance help to do this. This question is examined for the first eight policy themes below.

1   *The producer price of cocoa*

Loxley (1988: 30) suggests that, by 1987, the process of raising the producer price of cocoa had become counter-productive. His reasons are twofold. First, he sees a demand-pull effect of higher cocoa producers' incomes fuelling inflation. Second, he notes the substantial deterioration of the price incentive to produce food relative to cocoa and queries whether this has contributed to the decline in per capita food production.

These points are perhaps a little academic. All observers are agreed that the price increases up to 1985–6 were an important cause of the 22 per cent increase in cocoa production between 1982–3 (179,000 tons) and 1985–6 (219,000 tons). It seems also to be the case that the 1986–7 price of 85,000 cedis per ton just crossed the threshold that made new planting of cocoa profitable (Seini, Howell and Commander, 1987: 30–1). Even at this price the rehabilitation of old trees remained unprofitable. The incentive to smuggle cocoa to Côte d'Ivoire also remained (World Bank, 1987: 19). Hence the move to 156,000 cedis per ton.

How much further to raise the cocoa producer price beyond the 1987–8 season level of 156,000 cedis per ton has been made somewhat academic by the precipitate fall of the world cocoa price in late 1988. As the world price falls, the producer's share automatically rises while the purchasing price and the exchange rate remain constant. The target of a rapidly rising producer share thus becomes attainable without nominal price rises. A falling world market price is also likely to lead to a drastic cut in the 1987–8 producer price in the Côte d'Ivoire (*West Africa*, 1988(b): 1830). The need to match an unrealistic price in a country to which smuggling is feasible should disappear.

The 'failure' to allow relative prices to shift back in favour of food crops is not a convincing complaint. By the early 1980s, Ghana's internal cocoa price was suffering extreme distortion and that had to be put right (Lipton, 1987: 199). But it is to other instruments of policy than relative prices – better research, better inputs, better rural welfare – that policy-makers must look in order to achieve significant productivity gains for food crops (Green, 1987: 8–9).

2 *The cocoa marketing costs of the GCMB*

That in aggregate the GCMB was overmanned, probably grossly so, is rarely denied. Even after the labour retrenchment already accomplished, some still complain of overmanning (e.g. Green, 1987: 32). That the Board and the cocoa industry has benefited from the retrenchment and accompanying discovery of massive payroll fraud is undeniable. What is not known is how this loss of employment and loss of fraudulent income has been adjusted to by those concerned, and the impact of that adjustment on the rural economy. Are they a welfare burden that has been shifted to the peasant economy, or have they become a productive resource to be utilised by it? Nobody seems to know, yet this is the true process of structural adjustment.

Doubt about the GCMB reforms has centred not on retrenchment, but on privatisation. Apparently, the World Bank's initial position (though never formalised in any loan condition) was that the Board should be disbanded, and cocoa marketing be entirely privatised (Loxley, 1988: 37). The Ghana Government successfully resisted this solution, which was completely at odds with the functions envisaged for the Board in PNDC law 81 of 1984 (Ghana Cocoa Board, 1987: 5–6). The many compromises embodied in the Board's 1987 Corporate Plan thus reflect the resolution to date of this basic conflict. In the medium term, the agreement is that the Cocobod should do only those things which the private sector cannot do more efficiently. In the longer run, however, the Bank insists that 'it is necessary to assess the effectiveness of the entire operation' (World Bank, 1987: 20–2).

The current doubt is whether the efficient parts of the Board's operation are being unnecessarily privatised. Specifically, the existing *extension* service of the Cocoa Services Division of the Board and the cocoa *purchasing* function of the Produce Marketing Board neither appear to be overmanned, nor seem to be failing the farmer in the discharge of their duties (Seini, Howell and Commander, 1987: 19–22). Yet the input supply function of the extension service has been earmarked for rapid privatisation and the purchasing function for the same at a somewhat later date. If this goes ahead as planned, there may be a negative impact on the quality of the Ghanaian cocoa crop. Private merchant purchasing could increase crop adulteration, as happened recently in Nigeria. Also an extension service confined to technical advice may prove less effective in promoting improved cultivation practices – particularly spraying for capsid and black pod disease.

Although negative consequences from the agreed privatisation plans have not yet materialised, they are seen by the Ghana Government as a serious possibility.

3 *The removal of subsidies and price controls*

The main consequence of the partial removal of the subsidy on fertiliser has been a sharp contraction in farmers' demand for fertiliser (Seini, Howell and Commander, 1987: 16). This is unfortunate for two reasons. One is that fertiliser is very little used on any crop, a mere 5 per cent of the cultivated area having in the recent past been fertilised. The other is that the yields of the traditional varieties of most crops have been shown by agronomic research to respond well simply to fertiliser application. The reason for the low usage is said by the farmers to be inadequate returns to fertiliser at the current input and output prices (Seini *et al.*, 1987: 33). When the subsidy is completely withdrawn, something will have to be done to alter the marginal returns to fertiliser, or the private traders will find that they have little business to do.

Insecticide use is different. It is used by most cocoa farmers, but not by growers of other crops. The withdrawal of subsidy has led to a fourfold price increase to 600 cedis per litre. It is not clear how demand has been cut back. It is clear, however, that the cocoa harvest of 1987–8 has not attained its target of 230,000 tons and that diseases (swollen shoot and black pod) are said to be responsible for this disappointing result.

The changes in the petrol price to keep it in line with international levels have had very little impact on the general rate of inflation. The consumer price index for transport and communications did rise 3.6 times between 1983 and 1987, while the combined index rose only 2.5 times. But the weight of this component in the whole index is very slight, a mere 3.2 per cent. More significant in fuelling inflation was an even larger price rise for clothing and footwear, which accounts for nearly one-quarter of the total index weight (Republic of Ghana, 1988 (b): 50).

In any case, both for petrol and for other products whose prices were completely decontrolled, changes in official price indices overstate the effect of permitted price increases or price decontrol. Ineffective price controls are accompanied by active parallel markets. The effect of increases in official market prices must be measured from a base which is the average of the official price and the (usually much higher) parallel market price. This necessarily reduces the measured impact. The difficulty with actually following this ideal procedure is our ignorance of the volume of transactions in the parallel market, which in the nature of things tends to be concealed. Without knowing this volume, a weighted average of prices cannot be calculated. At the very height of Ghana's crisis in 1983, quite a few products vanished both from official and parallel markets. Prices in both, to that extent, ceased to have economic meaning at all.

4 The trade and foreign exchange regime

Ghana has succeeded in bringing its foreign exchange rate down to a level which is much closer to purchasing power parity than it has been for fifteen years. As a result it has eliminated most of the disincentive to export and most of the massive windfall gains that accrued to those having access to allocations of foreign exchange. Additionally, progress has been made in simplifying and rationalising the tariff structure around a standard tariff of 20–25 per cent (World Bank, 1987: 17).

Without in any way belittling these valuable reforms, it must be noted that Ghana is still some way from a market-determined exchange rate applied to all foreign transactions and from a tax and tariff regime which is non-discriminating between different types and sources of production (except for selective, targeted interventions).

Signs of government management of the weekly Forex auction are not hard to detect. There is a curious regularity in the results of the auction. The established rate varies very little for three or four months at a time and then drops suddenly (see Table 14.8). The result is a series of stepwise devaluations, separated by plateaus of increasing stability. That an auction should produce such a pattern without management is implausible. Discretion presumably enters the process when the 'eligibility' of each bid is determined in advance of the auction. The motivation is presumably the fear that an unbroken descent might accelerate speculatively and undermine public confidence in the auction mechanism. The differential between the auction and the parallel rate actually widened in the first year of operation, but fell again slightly to stand at 1:1.32 at the end of September 1988. The failure to eliminate this differential is not so surprising if the auction is indeed being managed. The licensing of non-auction Forex bureaux which trade at a near-parallel rate as of June 1988 may be seen less as an attempt to finally close the action/parallel rate gap and more as a device to tax a trade which may be around for some while yet.

Table 14.8 Marginal auction rates, 1986–8
(Cedis/US $)

Weekly auction nos.	Lowest rate	Highest rate
3–25	145	152
36–47	161	164
49–65	170	176
70–83	184	186
93–98	226	228

Source: Bank of Ghana.

Exports responded strongly to improved incentives, as well as to the progress of infrastructure rehabilitation, with a quantity increase overall of 42 per cent between 1983 and 1986 (Loxley, 1988: 24). The most spectacular export growth was, however, in timber, where the export volume tripled (World Bank, 1987: 14). Such a rapid increase has some worrying environmental and economic aspects to it. Up to this point, logging has taken place without the Government having a survey of the forest or a plan of exploitation. The locations for felling are randomly chosen. The methods of felling and transport are crude, wasteful and ecologically unsound. The rate of offtake which is sustainable has not been calculated, and the obligation placed on loggers to replant is often simply ignored. Fortunately donors have realised that timber exports are being bought at a heavy price and a forest survey has now been started. The economic concerns are the low value added in exporting logs, and the possible malpractices such as under-invoicing which timber exporters may be responsible for.

The heavy concentration of attention and effort on traditional exports –

cocoa, gold and timber – has led to the relative neglect of the urgent need to diversify Ghana's exports and to produce and market successfully a range of non-traditional exports. The 1988 Budget has now highlighted this need – spurred on by falling cocoa prices – but the measures announced so far to this end do not appear to be sufficiently detailed and concrete.

5 *Cost recovery and subsidy removal in health and education*

Price indices do not show the cost of medical care and health in Ghana rising any more rapidly than the general rate of inflation in the period 1983–7 (Republic of Ghana, 1988b: 50). None the less, the cost recovery measures in health and education have been unpopular. The PNDC, like other governments elsewhere, has found that health and education charges touch an extremely sensitive nerve in the general public's political consciousness. Dr Botchwey, the Finance Minister, felt obliged in his 1987 Budget Speech to mount a spirited defence of 'the much misunderstood emphasis on cost recovery' (n.d.:2).

Because cost recovery has been pursued more vigorously in education than in health, its repercussions have been more noticeable. They have been good and bad. The good has been the reappearance in school classrooms of low-cost textbooks – even if parents have had to pay more than before to get them there. The bad has been the lack of adequate scholarship funds to protect the children of the poorest from educational deprivation. In the tertiary sector, the loss of half of the food and boarding allowance has been strongly resisted by the students. There was trouble in the three universities on this issue in 1987 and again in 1988, which resulted in their being closed by the university authorities. However, university closures are a pretty frequent occurrence in Ghana. This reflects the fact that the students are one of the few organised groups outside the Government who remain politically powerful. It would be difficult to argue that the universities would certainly have remained open, and tertiary education proceeded according to plan *but for* the decision to cut half of the food and boarding subsidy.

6 *Public expenditure programming*

It is hard not to be a little alarmed by the apparent disarray in public expenditure management in Ghana five years into the Economic Recovery Programme. After an extensive Public Expenditure Review shown to the Ghana Government in August 1985, but not otherwise available, it was decided to focus effort on producing a Public Investment Programme for 1986–8 (PIP). So far, so good, but:

1 the PIP is not comprehensive, excluding 20 per cent of the Government's development expenditure (World Bank, 1987: 37);

2 by no means all the PIP projects are yet financed from internal or external resources (World Bank, 1987: 68);
3 despite the 'careful consideration' exercised in choosing them, not all the projects included are worthwhile. This is partly because there is no mechanism for getting bad projects *out* of the PIP if the ministries succeed in smuggling them in, and partly because of already noted weakness in appraisal methods;
4 to the extent that the PIP has any operational significance, it is either (a) achieved by relying on erratic cash releases or (b) the result of the imprest account mechanism devised for the super-core projects.

The Bank is aware of the need to move beyond a primitive revenue in/expenditure out system of expenditure control. A medium-term planning document, which informs the negotiation of budget allocations, and budget allocations which in turn under delegated powers can be turned into cash are what is required. It is not at all clear why the Bank has taken so long to get round to the view that an integrated budgeting system is vital. The cost of delay is continuing incoherence in spending priorities and wasteful resource allocation.

7 State enterprise divestiture

Central Government transfers to public boards, institutions and corporations constituted in 1983 some 16 per cent of its total expenditure. By 1986, the latest date for which a comparable figure is available, the percentage was only half of this. This falling share reflects the rapid increase in capital expenditure as tax revenues sharply recovered. But even at 8 per cent of expenditure, the deficits of public sector institutions add up to a large burden for the central government to bear.

The consequence of delaying the divestiture of state-operated enterprises is twofold. In the short term, divestiture incurs costs – for planning, negotiation, settlement of residual liabilities, sale or demolition. In the long run, the perpetual drain on the budget of loss-making enterprises is ended. Thus the failure to move faster on divestiture of SOEs has postponed some short-run costs, but also the long-run savings which in a few years would have more than compensated for them.

8 Public sector management

The major blemish to the 1987 retrenchment exercise (apart from the slippage itself) was the delay in making the terminal payments to those who had been retrenched. The Accountant-General's office took about six months after termination to make the due payment. In the middle of 1987, considerable resentment built up, especially in those retrenched from the

GES. A makeshift 'alimentary allowance' had to be devised, but the damage had been done. A difficult exercise had been made needlessly more difficult and the purpose of the terminal payments – to soften the immediate distress of redundancy – was lost.

No one is really very sure of the condition of those who have been retrenched. Provision has been made for retraining programmes, and the use of abandoned state lands in the Northern and Eastern regions for resettlement farms. Despite the Government's glowing accounts of redeployed workers 'leading new lives in new spheres of economic activity which they never imagined possible for them', it would be surprising if resource constraints and the lower educational level of those redeployed do not combine to frustrate most of the good intentions.

The Programme of Actions to Mitigate the Social Costs of Adjustment (PAMSCAD), while not intended to compensate directly the losers in the adjustment process, is meant to do so indirectly by creating employment for unskilled labour, particularly in the rural areas. PAMSCAD has excited much international interest as an unusual, but very welcome, effort to give the adjustment process a 'human face'. Unfortunately, despite three years of gestation, the programme (of twenty-four disparate components) has been poorly designed, and details of implementation strategies for most of the components have not been forthcoming. Apart from the Bank's own funding of the Priority Works Project, implementation has not begun and donors were still fighting shy in September 1988.

It is too early to assess the ODA consultants' study on civil service reform, which has still to be acted on, and is anyway outside the framework of Bank conditional lending. But the prospects for the Bank's attempts to secure the return of émigré Ghanaians to work in the civil service seem doomed to certain failure. The current pay differential between a permanent secretary and a driver is, after all the adjustments so far, still only 3:1. Moreover, even if the ODA consultants' suggested pay scales were put in place, a permanent secretary would still earn less than one-sixth of the pay of a locally based UNDP consultant. It is highly implausible that any émigré Ghanaian would be tempted by that to return to the civil service, even if he or she believed that a ready welcome would be waiting for them from Ghanaian colleagues who did not emigrate in the bad times. The prospect is better of dissuading some now in the service who might still be tempted to leave: 'topping-up' consultancies may be helpful here. Obviously, to have a beneficial effect such consultancies would need to be awarded very strictly on merit. Otherwise, given that retrenchment has so far been entirely confined to the lowest grades of worker, the end result could even be counter-productive.

14.6 IMPLICATIONS FOR DONOR POLICIES

Making some suggestions for changes in donor policies is quite consistent with endorsing the general thrust of donor policies in Ghana. The economic reforms which Ghana has undertaken since 1983, using World Bank and Fund advice and finance have been, by and large, purposeful moves in the right direction, aimed at putting right a wide range of policy errors committed in preceding years. It is not necessary to claim, with *The Economist's* leader writer, that the reforms themselves have caused Ghana's 5–6 per cent growth rate or that they are a prophylactic against coups, to agree that reforms of the broad type that have been undertaken are beginning to resolve some of the serious economic muddles in which Ghana had got itself involved.

Further, the conditionality that has been used by the Bank in the reform lending has not been particularly harsh or coercive – at least in relation to the PNDC Government. After a struggle, it decided to go down the road to which the Fund and Bank beckoned. Once it had done so, it did not find the discipline of the Bank's loan conditions unreasonably harsh (although the Fund's conditionality is quantitative and strict). The Bank attempted to establish a genuine policy dialogue in advance of laying down particular loan conditions. The limitations inherent in such a policy dialogue do not come from the Bank's lack of sincerity, but from the Ghanaians' weak ability to make use of it to push their own policy preferences. In most instances of slippage, the Bank's response has been renegotiation rather than financial punishment.

Yet all is not quite serene. It is a structural feature of the Bank-Ghana Government relationship (and not anybody's *fault*) that the Bank dominates by virtue of its superior reservoir of technical skills and its superior ability to organise itself for policy initiatives. This places a heavy burden of responsibility on the Bank to ensure that its technical advice is indeed the best available.

One area where the Bank appears to show some technical weakness is in the task of forecasting commodity prices. This can be a serious drawback in cases, like that of Ghana, where structural adjustment revolves around the rehabilitation of a primary commodity export industry – cocoa. The Bank has clearly overestimated the cocoa price by somewhere between 30 and 50 per cent. This is a little difficult to do, given that cocoa demand is not speculative and cocoa supply not greatly responsive to the vagaries of the weather. Some have claimed that the Bank made the elementary mistake of not taking account of the additional Ghanaian supply its policies were designed to elicit, when making its global price projection (Green, 1987: 53). If this is true, it is quite scandalous.

In case anyone should miss the irony in this, the Bank's relentless pressure to privatise the Ghana Cocoa Board should be recalled to mind. The Bank argued that the Board's functions could be performed better by the private sector. But when it comes to making commodity price forecasts, the Bank forgets the principle of using the private sector if it can do the job better. It maintains an in-house commodity division whose work is clearly inferior to the best private sector forecasters. Apart from this simple efficiency point, the use of in-house Bank forecasts is dangerous because the Bank has a vested interest in commodity price optimism. It appears to validate the export-led growth strategy for primary product exporters, and it minimises initially (but not ultimately) the size of the financial inflow needed to make structural adjustment viable. The Bank should in future use forecasts from sources which are entirely independent, and which have no interest in sustaining either price optimism or price pessimism.

Another area of concern is the Bank's judgement of policy priorities. Not everyone would place the same degree of emphasis as the Bank on the pursuit of privatisation. This is not for ideological reasons, but because of practical doubts about the medium-term potential of the private sector to respond to opportunities that are opened to it. For example, the pressure to involve private hauliers in the Cocoa Board's cocoa transport function ignored the fact that private hauliers are only prepared to operate over good quality roads and many of the feeder roads to cocoa farms are in a very bad condition. The bid to privatise the Board's cocoa processing activities failed because, in the end, it became clear that no private sector operator was likely to be able to do the task more efficiently. The very notion of 'private sector' blurs important ethnic cleavages in Ghana, and in the medium term there are likely to remain serious doubts about the moral standards of private sector operators – doubts which are not allayed by the behaviour of the private logging companies.

Some of the energy spent on the search for privatisation might have been better devoted to a stronger intervention in the reform of public expenditure management. This central function of government remains in considerable disarray, with effective control over the total secured at the expense of much control over the composition of expenditure. When highly selective promotion of public investment is the need of the hour, the present 'system' is hopelessly inadequate. One wonders whether the Bank has pulled its punches with the Ministry of Finance and Economic Planning in its own affairs because it needs to work with MFEP in reforming other departments of government. One also wonders how much *practical* expertise the Bank commands in public expenditure control.

Moving from priorities to process, some comment is called for on the Bank's own internal co-ordination. The Bank's local office in Accra has only a handful of senior staff, who cannot possibly co-ordinate and manage the two or three dozen missions from headquarters which arrive each year. Such co-ordination must be provided, then, from Washington itself. A very active Bank programme, as is Ghana's, runs the risk that this kind of remote control will not work well, and the Bank will appear to have multiple positions on issues – never mind co-ordination between the Bank and the Fund. Some of the advice offered on tax reform and trade policy has suffered from insufficient co-ordination.

The remote control technique is also hampered because mission personnel are often short on local knowledge. They come with neatly analysed technical prescriptions based on other countries' experiences and an in-built unwillingness to be convinced that the scheme will not work to plan in Ghana as well. At the same time, local knowledge which *could* be drawn on is not lacking. But it tends to be in the embassies of the bilateral donors, who sometimes maintain more than just one or two senior aid personnel each: together they constitute a sizeable pool of local knowledge. At present it tends not to be used, because the bilaterals rely on the Bank to negotiate policy reform and set conditions. The bilaterals then endorse these.

Some new way of drawing in the local resources of bilateral agencies needs to be devised by the World Bank as a way of strengthening its policy advice. At present aid co-ordination between donors consists of a Consultative Group which should (but does not always) meet monthly and which exchanges information rather than plans common activities. This may provide a starting point for a more concerted approach to policy advice and the negotiation of more solidly-based policy conditionality.

If this does not prove possible – and to be possible the Bank would really have to want to make it work – the bilaterals can still improve the situation by commissioning assessments of the policy reform process by knowledgeable and independent outsiders, along lines already suggested by Streeten (1987: 39). This idea has already borne fruit in Ghana, thanks to CIDA's willingness to fund the studies of Loxley (1988) and Seini, Howell and Commander (1987). As Ghana hopefully continues to make progress down the long, long road to full recovery and then further development, other bilateral donors may wish to shoulder more of the evaluation burden which, until now, has been carried with distinction by Canada. The main need of the moment is to temper Ghana's heavy reliance on World Bank expertise by diversifying the available sources of advice.

Acknowledgements

Officials of the Government of Ghana, the Bank of Ghana, the Ghana Cocoa Marketing Board and of many donor agencies operating in Ghana responded helpfully to my enquiries. But the responsibility for the facts and interpretations set out in the chapter is solely that of the author. Reg Green willingly made available his encyclopaedic knowledge of Ghana and Paul Mosley assisted in innumerable ways in the completion of this portion of our joint research project. Warm thanks are due to both.

GLOSSARY

AFRC	Armed Forces Revolutionary Council
ASRC	Agricultural Services Rehabilitation Credit
CIDA	Canadian International Development Authority
EFF	Extended Fund Facility
ERC	Export Rehabilitation Credit
ERP	Economic Recovery Programme
ESAC	Education Sector Adjustment Credit
ESAF	Extended Structural Adjustment Facility
Forex	Foreign Exchange
FSAC	Financial Sector Adjustment Credit
GCMB	Ghana Cocoa Marketing Board (Cocobod)
GES	Ghana Education Service
GHIC	Ghana Industrial Holdings Corporation
HERP	Health & Education Rehabilitation Project
IDA	International Development Association (of World Bank)
ISAC	Industrial Sector Adjustment Credit
JFM	June the Fourth Movement
NDM	New Democratic Movement
NDPC	National Development Planning Commission
NGEP	Northern Grid Extension Project
PAMSCAD	Programme of Action to Mitigate the Social Costs of Adjustment
PIP	Public Investment Programme
PNDC	Provisional National Defence Council
PRDPC	Petroleum Refining & Distribution Project Credit
RIC	Reconstruction Import Credit
SAC	Structural Adjustment Credit
SAF	Structural Adjustment Facility
SECAL	Sector Adjustment Loan
SOE	State-owned Enterprise
TRC	Transport Rehabilitation Credit

BIBLIOGRAPHY

Addo, J. S. (n.d.) *The State of the Economy 2: Major Speeches on the Economic Recovery Programme*, by Mr J. S. Addo, Governor of the Information Services Department, Bank of Ghana.

Boahen, A. (1988) 'The Ghanaian sphinx: reflections on the contemporary history of Ghana, 1972–1987', J. B. Danquah Memorial Lectures, three lectures, Ghana Academy of Arts and Sciences.

Botchwey, K. (n.d.) *The State of the Economy 4*, Bank of Ghana, Information Services Department.

Callaghy, T. M. (1987) 'The politics of economic stabilization and structural change in Africa: Ghana, Zambia and Nigeria', mimeo.

Chand, S. K and van Til, R. (1988) 'Ghana: toward successful stabilization and recovery', Finance and Development, March.

Economist, The (1988) 'Africans who can be saved, and those who can't', 20 August 1988.

Ghana Cocoa Board (1987) Corporate Plan (1987/88–1990/91), Accra, September.

Green, R. H. (1987) *Stabilization and Adjustment Policies and Programmes: Country Study 1, Ghana*, Helsinki, World Institute for Development Economics Research.

Gyimah-Boadi, E. (n.d.) 'The political implication of ERP/SAP and towards a programme of action for the mitigation of political costs', mimeo.

Harvey, C. (1986) 'Successful macroeconomic adjustment in three developing countries: Botswana, Malawi and Papua New Guinea', mimeo.

Killick, T. (1978) *Development Economics in Action: A Study of Economic Policies in Ghana*, London, Heincmann.

Lipton, M. (1987) 'Limits of price policy for agriculture: which way for the World Bank?', *Development Policy Review* 5, 197–215.

Loxley, J. (1988) *Ghana: Economic Crisis and the Long Road to Recovery*, Ottawa, The North-South Institute.

Marx, K. (1973) 'The eighteenth Brumaire of Louis Bonaparte', in *Surveys from Ex.6*, London, Allen Lane.

Norton, A. (1988) 'Ghana social profile', mimeo, London, Overseas Development Administration, May.

ODI (Overseas Development Institute) (1988) *The Rich and the Poor: Changes in Incomes of Developing Countries since 1960*, ODI briefing paper, London, June.

Rawlings, J. J. (n.d) (a) *A Revolutionary Journey, Selected Speeches of Flt-Lt. Jerry John Rawlings Chairman of the PNDC, Dec 31st 1981 – Dec 31st 1982*, 1, Tema, Ghana Publishing Corporation.

Rawlings, J. J. (n.d) (b) *Forging Ahead, Selected Speeches of Flt-Lt. J. J. Rawlings Chairman of the PNDC, January 1st 1983 – December 31st 1983*, 2, Tema, Ghana Publishing Corporation.

Rawlings, J. J. (n.d) (c) *The New Direction and Purpose, Selected Speeches of Flt-Lt. Rawlings Chairman of the PNDC, January 1st 1986 – December 31st 1986*, 5, Tema, Ghana Publishing Corporation.

Ray, D. I. (1986) *Ghana: Politics, Economics and Society*, London, Frances Pinter.

Republic of Ghana (1988a) *The PNDC Budget Statement and Economic Policy for 1988*, Accra, Ghana Publishing Corporation, 16 January.

Republic of Ghana (1988b) *Quarterly Digest of Statistics* VI(1), Accra, Statistical Service, March.

Seini, W., Howell, J. and Commander S. (1987) 'Agricultural policy adjustment in Ghana', mimeo, London, Overseas Development Institute.

Smith, S. (1987) 'Structural adjustment in Ghana: its impact on smallholders and the rural poor', mimeo, Rome, IFAD, 31 July.

Streeten, P. (1987) 'Structural adjustment: a survey of the issues and options', mimeo, London, Overseas Development Institute.

Tribe, M. (1988) 'Project rehabilitation in Ghana's economic recovery programme', mimeo, University of Bradford Project Planning Centre, April.

West Africa (1988a) 'Ghana's new deal with the IMF', 19–25 September.

West Africa (1988b) 'Cocoa's double edge', 3–9 October.

World Bank (1984a) *Ghana: Policies and Program for Adjustment*, Washington DC, World Bank.

World Bank (1984b) *Ghana: Managing the Transition*, 2 vols (Report no. 5289-GH), Washington DC, World Bank, 7 November.

World Bank (1985) *Ghana: Towards Structural Adjustment*, 2 vols (Report no. 5854-GH), Washington DC, World Bank, 7 October.

World Bank (1987) *Ghana: Policies and Issues of Structural Adjustment* (Report no. 6635-GH), Washington DC, World Bank, 30 March.

World Health Organization (Division of Strengthening of Health Services) (1988) *Health Economics: A Programme For Action*, Geneva.

Yankah, K. (1986) *The Trial of J. J. Rawlings, Echoes of the 31st December Revolution*, Tema, Ghana Publishing Corporation.

15

MALAWI

Jane Harrigan

15.1 INTRODUCTION

Malawi was one of the earliest recipients of a World Bank Structural Adjustment Loan (SAL) and in the eyes of the Bank provided a favourable testing ground for its new mode of programme lending. The country possessed a strong, highly-centralised political regime and an economic ideology which appeared receptive to the types of structural reforms advocated by the Bank, whilst the macroeconomic disequilibrium experienced by Malawi in the late 1970s and early 1980s, and the structural weakness consequently exposed, appeared to be moderate in comparison with the problems faced by many other sub-Saharan countries. Hence it was expected that Malawi's adjustment experience would illustrate the potential of new adjustment lending instruments in the sub-Saharan region.

By the late 1980s, however, there was an air of disillusion amongst Bank staff and the Malawian authorities regarding the impact of the extensive adjustment reforms undertaken. Malawi is one of only a handful of countries to have received a series of three consecutive SALs, and with the SAL period covering a six year period, 1981–6, this provides an adequate time span to assess the effects of the medium-term supply-side reforms implemented under the SALs. The outcome is far from favourable. The export base remains narrow and the economy is still highly vulnerable to exogenous shocks; the public sector continues to run a large deficit; investment, in both public and private sectors has fallen; and the decline in GDP per capita is still to be arrested. Does this disappointing outcome, in a country which seemed both willing and able to carry out the Bank's policy recommendations (liberalisation of agricultural prices and markets; consumer price decontrol; subsidy removal; parastatal reform; tax reform; public expenditure reductions; and public sector institutional and management reform), imply that such reforms are inappropriate for tackling the structural problems faced by similar sub-Saharan economies? Or was it, as one Bank analyst has implied, simply an unfortunate case of 'promising reforms, bad luck' (Gulhati, 1989)?

This case study attempts to address such questions. The answers are more complex than allowed for by either of the above extremist responses. On the one hand, Malawi did implement a number of promising reforms. The expected positive impact on macro-indicators failed to occur partly due to 'bad luck' in the form of a continued and severe deterioration in the external economic environment. Important lessons emerge from this. Adjustment programmes in low-income, highly vulnerable, aid-dependent economies, such as Malawi, must be sensitive to changes in a potentially hostile external environment such as commodity price shocks, dislocations caused by political events in neighbouring countries, reductions in anticipated aid flows, and drought. This necessitates programme flexibility in terms of reassessing policy recommendations and performance targets. The latter need is particularly pertinent in the case of the rigid performance targets of IMF stabilisation programmes.

Malawi's disappointing economic performance under the three SALs, however, cannot be attributed purely to bad luck. In important reform areas, notably agricultural pricing and marketing and fiscal policy, the Bank's policy prescriptions proved to be inappropriate. In the former case, this led to protracted conflict between the Bank and the Government, and intransigence on the part of the Bank throughout the SAL period. In the latter case, the Bank responded by altering, albeit slowly, their policy recommendations. An analysis of these two areas of policy reform provides important insights into the adjustment requirements of predominantly agriculturally-based African economies struggling with the dual, and often conflicting, objectives of achieving food self-sufficiency and increasing agricultural export revenues, whilst facing tight constraints on the Government expenditures needed to promote these development objectives. The Malawi experience clearly illustrates that in such circumstances the interfacing of policy-based lending with donors' traditional project lending activities is crucial. It will be argued that under Malawi's three SALs this requirement was not adequately fulfilled. Potential conflicts between programme and project lending, which emerged in the areas of agricultural and fiscal policy, were not initially addressed, so lowering the returns to both forms of aid.

The importance of the sequencing of policy reform also emerges strongly from the analysis of Malawi's adjustment attempts. Part of the disappointing outcome in Malawi can be attributed to poor sequencing of the SAL reform process. Sequencing problems occurred in the phasing of the following reforms: consumer price decontrol and trade liberalisation; and agricultural price reform and liberalisation of agricultural marketing.

The sequencing issue highlights a difficulty caused by the interaction of the two components of programme aid, namely, finance and the attached policy reform conditions. A low-income, aid-dependent, vulnerable economy such as Malawi faces large, and occasionally unexpected, balance-of-payments financing gaps creating pressure on donors to provide rapid disbursements of balance-of-payments support in the form of programme aid. Yet this tends to result in conditionality being equally rapidly devised without due regard for the appropriateness and sequencing of reforms.

Finally, it will be argued that SAL reforms in Malawi yielded less than promised because the Bank's characterisation of the Malawian political economy as a free-market, non-interventionist, private-sector dominated regime was misplaced. In certain areas, most notably the reform of the President's massive holding company, Press Holdings Ltd, the Bank showed an acute awareness of political parameters, so enabling one of the most successful reforms of the SAL programme. In other areas, such as smallholder agricultural policy and consumer-price policy, Bank staff did not fully appreciate the political economy context of the reform process. This resulted in misguided bargaining strategies, inappropriate reform prescriptions and sequences, and failure to tackle a fundamental structural reform, namely, adjustment of the relationship between smallholder agriculture and estate agriculture. The analysis of Malawi's adjustment experience shows that even in a country which appears receptive to the types of reform advocated by the Bank, an in-depth understanding of the political economy, and an attempt to internalise the reform process within this context, is essential to success.

The six years of SAL-guided reforms in Malawi provide ample material from which to draw general policy lessons regarding structural adjustment in sub-Saharan economies similar to Malawi. Policy lessons clearly emerge in the following general areas: the role of the external environment; the interaction between programme lending and project lending; the appropriateness and sequencing of reforms; the importance of the political economy; and the need to internalise the reform process.

15.2 ECONOMIC AND POLITICAL DEVELOPMENTS: 1964–81

At independence in 1964 the Malawian economy was characterised by three main sectors: the colonial estate sector which produced 43 per cent of the country's merchandise exports (mainly tea and tobacco); the smallholder sector producing for subsistence, providing a marketed food surplus, and producing export crops amounting to 50 per cent of merchandise exports; and a labour reserve sector which supplied estate labour and migrant labour to neighbouring countries. The economy was predominantly agricultural (agriculture accounting for 55 per cent of GDP and 90 per cent of domestic employment), lacked mineral resources, capital and skilled labour and possessed a limited, small domestic market (McCracken, 1983).

In acknowledgement of the above constraints, the post-independence development strategy focused on export-orientated agro-based expansion, with import-substituting industrialisation (ISI) playing only a secondary role and restricted to a narrow range of consumer goods which were already afforded a high degree of natural protection by the country's land-locked position. The trade regime was determined by the overriding aim of stimulating agricultural exports. Tariffs were generally low and direct restrictions on imports were minimal. Emphasis was placed on maintaining exchange rate competitiveness and the currency overvaluation and appreciation witnessed in most other sub-Saharan countries outside the French franc zone was avoided.

The Government's wages and incomes policy, and public sector expenditure, were also important components of the outward-looking agricultural development strategy. Public sector wage restraint helped suppress wages throughout the economy and avoided both wage-led inflation and high rates of rural-urban migration, so providing the expanding estate sector with cheap supplies of labour. In contrast to many other post-independence African states, the Government's development expenditures were concentrated in the economic sectors, namely agriculture, transport and infrastructure, with the social sectors accorded a low priority. The economic policy environment and the stability of the political regime was conducive to the inflow of both foreign manpower and capital. High levels of foreign capital were attracted in the form of private investment in the estate and the manufacturing sectors and donor grants and loans. This inflow of foreign capital contributed to the Government's ability to pursue conservative fiscal and external payment policies through to the mid-1970s.

It is on the basis of the above type of summary description of the post-independence development strategy that many commentators, including Bank staff, have described Malawi as a free-market, non-interventionist, capitalist economy (Acharya, 1978, 1981a,b; Agarwala, 1983; World Bank, 1983a).[1] It is true that Malawi stands in stark contrast to many other sub-Saharan economies: trade policies, the exchange rate, prices and taxes have not overprotected industry or been biased against agriculture; prior to the late 1970s the public sector did not appear to be overextended; and there was comparatively little in the way of *direct* government intervention in the economy.[2] However, a closer look at the development of Malawi's political economy during the late 1960s and 1970s shows that the 'free market' characterisation is inaccurate.

The Malawian polity is most aptly characterised as a centralised, efficient, personal dictatorship in the form of the Life President, Dr K. H. Banda – President since the formation of the Republic in 1964. In the early years of the regime, coercion and political patronage were extensively used for the establishment of Banda's power. The legislature, Judiciary, and Congress Party (Malawi is a single-party state) were all subverted into subordinate arms of the Executive and a large body of bureaucrats and politicians was created – lacking an independent power base and indebted to the President's political patronage (Williams, 1978). During the 1970s Banda's position was consolidated by a populist, patrimonial appeal to all strata of society, largely based on continued criticism and exposure of the hardships faced by all groups under the colonial regime.

The strength of Banda's personal dictatorship has two important implications for Malawi's political economy. First, the country has avoided the repeated post-independence legitimacy crises faced by many African states (Sandbrook, 1985). This has enabled Banda to pursue his own vision of appropriate programmes of social and economic change. Eschewing political and economic ideology, Banda believed that neither the capitalist nor socialist models were appropriate to Malawi's needs (Short, 1974: 175). Malawi required a unique solution to its development problems and the resulting outcome can best be described as a mixed economy. Second, the strength of Banda's power base was such that extensive recourse to economic patronage was not required to maintain legitimacy and support. Consequently, Malawi cannot be characterised as a 'rent-seeking' political economy, in which vested interest groups compete for rents created by government economic interventions (Krueger, 1974).

Despite the absence of rent-seeking, Banda's mixed-economy approach to development, and his use of parastatals and large holding companies to promote estate agriculture and to support his populist political platform, resulted in a wide range of state economic activity. Although this activity is often indirect and hard to observe it is extensive and pervasive. Intervention has been particularly prevalent within the agricultural sector. Although Malawi avoided an anti-agricultural policy bias, there was a severe bias *within* the agricultural sector, with government policies favouring the estate subsector at the expense of the smallholder subsector. The rapid expansion of estate agriculture, which occurred during the 1970s was assisted by the availability of cheap labour, and land, made possible by the Government's wages and incomes policy and by the ability to annexe smallholder customary land. Finance was provided by heavy implicit taxation of smallholder cash-crop production, implemented by ADMARC, the State Marketing Corporation. Prices paid by ADMARC for smallholder tobacco, cotton and groundnuts were well below export-parity levels throughout the 1970s (Harrigan, 1988: 418). The bulk of the resulting large surpluses made by ADMARC on the crop trading accounts, particularly the tobacco account, was channelled into investment in estates. Between 1971 and 1979 ADMARC extracted MK 181.9 million[3] from the smallholder sector, of which 14 per cent was used to cross-subsidise smallholder food production and consumption, (maize and rice) the remainder being used for investment and loans, only 4.3 per cent of which were related to the development of smallholder agriculture (Kydd and Hewitt, 1982: 368).

Investment in estates also occurred via a more circuitous route established by the complex relationship between the corporate, financial and parastatal sectors of the Malawian economy. At the centre of these interactions lay Press Holdings, a large, private holding company owned by the President with equity interests in virtually every sphere of the Malawian economy, including majority shareholdings in the country's commercial banks. Two important parastatals, ADMARC and the Malawi Development Corporation (MDC) also held shares in the banks. The relationship between Press, the parastatals and the banks was complex, but has been succinctly summarised by Mhone: 'All three organisations were intertwined through interlocking directorates in which final authority and control resided in Dr. Banda through Press Holdings' dominance' (Mhone, 1987: 63). This structure was used to siphon ADMARC's profits into the estate and agro-industry sectors whilst Press, with easy access to financial resources, borrowed heavily domestically and abroad often under government guarantees, in order to finance Banda's control over tobacco estates. Press's influence over the commercial banks was similarly used to encourage politicians and bureaucrats to follow Banda's example and establish themselves as pioneering tobacco farmers assisted by easy access to commercial bank funds. Between 1970 and 1980 commercial bank lending to the agricultural sector increased from MK 2 million to MK 93 million, such that by 1980 agriculture accounted for 54 per cent of domestic bank advances (Kydd and Hewitt, 1982: 368).

Government intervention in the agricultural sector also took the form of a wide range of restrictions on smallholder production. Smallholders were legally barred from growing a number of high-value traditional estate crops such as burley and flue-cured tobacco, certain types of cotton, tea, and sugar. ADMARC's monopsony was used to enforce the restrictions as well as to regulate market outlets for crops in certain geographical areas. Likewise, 'Achikumbe' (progressive farmer) certification, and government provision of inputs, credit, and extension services were used to control and segment the pattern of agricultural production (Mhone, 1987: 67).

In addition to direct and indirect government intervention in agriculture, intervention was prevalent in other areas of the economy. The Government possessed considerable regulatory powers, facilitated by licensing arrangements, which covered all sizes of enterprise and extended to all people who owned or rented land. Extensive use was made of such powers to prevent the local Asian business community from operating in areas outside of the three main urban centres and hence from competing with the rural trading and distribution activities of Banda's Press Holding Company. The non-transparent system of foreign exchange allocation was similarly used in favour of Press and parastatal companies. During the 1970s, parastatals such as ADMARC and the MDC grew to become large holding companies, which, along with Press, acquired extensive shareholdings in Malawi's supposedly private sector, including multilateral and expatriate-owned companies in the textile, brewing, distilling, banking, insurance and fuel retail industries. Finally, as part of the Government's wages and incomes policy, the prices of over sixty consumer goods were controlled by the Government, and Trade Unions were assimilated into the Malawi Congress Party and effectively suppressed.

The parastatals and Press have also played a central role in Banda's cultivation of a unique brand of patrimonial populism. This has resulted in a curious mix of private and public sector activity. Somewhat bogusly, the President, in his capacity as Minister for Agriculture, constantly stressed the broad-based benefits of government provision of agricultural services to the smallholder population and of the attainment of food self-sufficiency in contrast to colonial agricultural policy. Price control, the benefits of which were genuinely widely spread, was likewise contrasted to the monopolistic exploitation by expatriate-owned companies during the colonial era. Parastatals such as ADMARC, the State Trading Corporation, and those providing subsidised utility services, developed into hybrid organisations, partly expected to operate according to commercial criteria, yet simultaneously required to carry out a range of developmental functions in order to bolster Banda's populist appeal. ADMARC, for example, was expected to maintain an extensive network of rural markets providing subsidised inputs and purchasing crops at guaranteed pan-territorial prices.

The Press Holding Company, although a supposedly private company owned by Banda, was also used as an instrument of public policy to promote the populist platform. Profits from Press, and government-guaranteed loans contracted by Press, were used to construct the Kamuzu Academy and to finance the development of the Malawi Women's League, whilst Press's financial involvement with ADMARC and MDC contributed to the developmental activities of these parastatals.

Banda's export-orientated state-led agricultural strategy, combined with his personal brand of patrimonial populism has resulted, not in a paradigm free-market economy, but an economy which is so mixed that it is often difficult to distinguish the public and private sectors. In the words of a USAID mission analysing the private sector: 'Malawi's private sector is alive, doing well, and owned by the Government'. In many ways, this state-led export development strategy, the indirect manner in which state intervention has occurred, and the resulting blurring of the private and public sector, is not dissimilar from the development strategies of the Asian NICs, and like the NICs Malawi's mixed economy approach produced an outstanding growth record.

Between 1967 and 1979 Malawi's real GDP grew at an average rate of

5.5 per cent per annum and real GDP per capita by 2.5 per cent, with growth accelerating in the 1970–9 period to 6.3 per cent and 3.9 per cent respectively (Table 15.1). High growth rates were recorded in all sectors of the economy, with the exception of subsistence agriculture. The rapid expansion of wage employment in all sectors indicated a labour intensive growth pattern. These growth rates compared favourably with the sub-Saharan region (excluding Nigeria) where average real GDP per capita fell by 0.5 per cent during the 1970s (Harvey, 1983). However, Malawi's impressive growth rate was from a low GDP base, such that by the end of the 1970s, GNP per capita stood at only US $200, and the country remained one of the poorest in the world.

The sectoral growth rates, however, disguise an important intrasectoral structural shift which took place within the agricultural sector. The policy bias towards estates was such that whilst estate output grew at an average of over 17 per cent per annum, smallholder output grew at less than 3 per cent per annum, with subsistence production stagnating. Consequently, smallholder contributions to export earnings declined over the period and export revenues became increasingly dependent on estate production of tobacco and tea.

Malawi's achievements relating to capital formation and its financing were also impressive. At independence, investment constituted only 8.6 per cent of GDP, domestic savings stood at 0.3 per cent of GDP and capital formation was predominantly foreign financed. Between 1967 and 1979, gross domestic investment grew at an average rate of 22 per cent per annum, increasing as a share of GDP to 30.7 per cent. Domestic savings rose even faster resulting in an increase in the share of domestic financed investment such that by the end of the 1970s, the Government financed over 25 per cent of its capital expenditures, and the private sector over 90 per cent (Table 15.1). This successful record of internal accumulation is largely attributable to the Government's interventionist policies outlined above: 'The logic of Malawi economic policy lies in the government's ability to manipulate wage policy, labour flows, agricultural price and subsidisation policies, and monetary policies to the maximisation of forced savings which are directed into productive investment' (Mhone, 1987: 80).

Performance in terms of the Government accounts was also satisfactory until the late 1970s with the central government budget deficit remaining below 10 per cent of GDP throughout most of the period (Table 15.1). Despite the lack of a taxable mineral sector and a developed manufacturing sector, government revenue increased at an average rate of 16 per cent per annum between 1967–70. By 1971, government savings on the recurrent account had become positive, eliminating the need for UK grants-in-aid.

Balance-of-payments performance also gave little cause for alarm prior to 1977. Satisfactory export growth and stable terms of trade limited the

Table 15.1 Key macroeconomic indicators: 1970–80

	1970	1971	1972	1973	1974	1975	1976	1977	1978	1979	1980
GDP growth rate	0.47	16.23	6.22	2.29	6.13	4.18	5.83	9.07	6.99	5.11	0.23
Total investment as % of GDP	26.10	19.40	24.70	22.70	24.00	28.40	16.40	21.90	37.30	30.70	21.80
Domestic savings as % of GDP	13.30	9.30	12.20	13.70	13.60	10.10	10.70	17.60	20.90	15.10	10.90
Central government budget deficit as % of GDP	15.46	9.17	9.44	7.97	8.99	12.64	9.88	6.63	8.52	9.89	12.58
Net government borrowing from domestic banks (MK millions)	n.a.	5.50	7.30	−1.00	−3.30	18.00	17.20	−9.30	25.00	27.20	62.60
Balance-of-payments current account deficit as % of GDP	10.22	7.88	10.53	7.84	7.04	12.88	9.82	6.71	16.81	19.61	16.77

Sources: World Bank (1982) statistical appendix, Tables 2.01, 2.02, 2.04, 9.01; IMF, *Government Finance Statistics Yearbook*, various issues.

increase in trade deficits. The expansion of exports was greatly assisted by exchange rate policy and by relatively low rates of domestic inflation, including wage inflation, which maintained the competitiveness of Malawi's exportables. The factor and non-factor service account displayed an increasing deficit, but until 1977 this was limited by substantial remittances from migrant labour working in the mining and commercial agricultural sector of neighbouring countries.[4] Although the current account deficit increased in the early 1970s, it remained at an average of 7–10 per cent of GDP and net capital inflows in the form of foreign grants, loans, and investment more than covered the deficit, so enabling growth of foreign currency reserves (Table 15.1).

In the late 1970s Malawi suffered the impact of a series of exogenous shocks. These shocks exposed several fundamental structural weaknesses in the economy and highlighted the high long-run opportunity costs of what had, until then, appeared to be a successful post-independence development strategy. Exogenous shocks took the form of: a dramatic deterioration in the terms of trade; a sharp rise in international interest rates; drought conditions in 1979–80; and disruption to Malawi's traditional trade route to the sea due to civil war in Mozambique.

The crisis precipitated by the shocks was clearly manifested in terms of a burgeoning of the balance-of-payments current account deficit, which by 1979 had reached 19.6 per cent of GDP. A large trade account deficit was brought about primarily by a 35 per cent decline in the terms of trade between 1977 and 1980. Much of the terms of trade decline was accounted for by a drop in tea and tobacco prices, in particular a 36 per cent fall in the 1979–80 auction price of flue-cured tobacco. This illustrated the economy's increased vulnerability resulting from an estate-led export strategy which had intensified the concentration of the export base – by 1979 tobacco accounted for 54 per cent of Malawi's export earnings. The development strategy had also fostered many estates which made extensive inefficient use of high cost imports – fuel, fertiliser, chemicals, machinery – and the 54 per cent increase in import costs in the late 1970s exposed the low *net* contribution of the estate sector to the balance of payments (Kydd and Hewitt, 1986a: 539). The agricultural policy bias against a smallholder sector which had high domestic value-added also contributed to the deteriorating trade account. Small-holder exports fell, and the country's balance of trade in staple food became negative in 1976. The adverse food situation was highlighted by the need to commercially import large quantities of maize following the drought conditions of 1979–80. The decline in the factor and non-factor services account was even greater than that on the trade account and was caused by a hardening of loan terms, increasing international interest rates, and an escalation in transport costs due to civil disturbances in neighbouring Mozambique and Zimbabwe.

Symptomatic of the emerging crisis of external imbalance was the recourse to undesirable methods of financing the current account deficit. By the end of the 1970s, the Government was increasingly resorting to commercial borrowing and foreign reserve run-down in an attempt to maintain import, production and employment levels. Between 1977 and 1980 net foreign exchange reserves fell from MK37 million to MK33 million, publicly-guaranteed debt more than doubled, and the debt service ratio increased from 7 per cent to 19 per cent.

The external imbalance of the late 1970s coincided with a historic high on the Government's budget deficit, which by 1981 had reached 16.5 per cent of GDP, compared to a steady average of 9 per cent in the early 1970s. This was predominantly due to a rapid rise in Government expenditure which more than doubled between 1978 and 1981. Recurrent expenditure expanded due to a series of large civil service pay awards, the need to import maize and increasing interest rate payments. This pattern of expansion led to underfunding of recurrent expenditures on education, health, transport, and agriculture so lowering the returns to public sector capital (World Bank, 1982: 23). The increase in government development expenditures was largely the result of a series of prestige projects – construction of a new capital city, international airport, presidential palaces, defence installations and an elite academy, resulting in a reduced allocation to the agricultural sector. Although government revenue as a percentage of GDP increased in 1979 and 1980, following a series of *ad hoc* tax increases, revenue failed to keep pace with the growth of expenditures. Hence, the Government resorted to domestic borrowing, which by 1981 financed 57 per cent of the fiscal deficit, whilst extensive international eurocurrency borrowings were used to finance the Government's prestige projects. Due to the short-term nature of these loans and the high import content of the associated government expenditures, the adverse impact on the balance of payments was quickly felt.

The Government's budgetary position was worsened by the financial deterioration experienced by most parastatals from 1977 onwards. By 1980, the ten major parastatals were operating at a loss, having developed unfavourable medium-term debt profiles, and facing managerial problems, falling profits in their subsidiaries, and suffering from the inflexibility of the Government's system of price controls at a time of increasing domestic inflation. ADMARC, in particular, suffered heavily due to the 1979 decline in tobacco auction prices and due to the sharp increase in the producer price of maize, announced by the Government following the 1979–80 harvest failure. Hence, ADMARC's use of tobacco profits to cross-subsidise food production, a central plank of Banda's 1970s development strategy, no longer appeared viable. Despite sharp cut-backs in parastatal investment levels, many were forced to seek relief from the central government in the form of higher subsidies, new loans, deferral of servicing on existing government loans, and calling on government loan guarantees.

Press Holdings was also drawn into the ambit of the Government budget. By the late 1970s, Press had become severely over-extended having borrowed heavily from the domestic banking system as well as contracting large government-guaranteed foreign loans to finance Banda's projects such as the construction of the Kamuzu Academy. With Press undercapitalised and facing large financial losses, its potential insolvency threatened to destroy both the domestic banking system (Press Holdings was the major shareholder in the country's two commercial banks, as well as their largest debtor) and ADMARC who had re-lent large overseas loans to Press Holdings. MDC and ADMARC faced similar problems of a liquidity crisis in the face of undercapitalisation. By 1980, it was obvious that the intricate relationships between Malawi's corporate, parastatal, and banking sectors, used by Banda to foster the estate boom of the 1970s, were no longer sustainable. Structural relationships in the economy were such that, in the words of Gulhati: 'The financial crisis of this triumvirate (Press, MDC, and ADMARC) had a major adverse impact on commercial banks, the government budget and Malawi's external creditworthiness' (Gulhati, 1989: 17). The viability of the domestic banking system was also threatened by bad debts in the private sector, namely in many of the tobacco estates formed during the 1970s. Most of these estates had a highly-geared financial structure, with no equity invested, and were capitalised with what were effectively overdrafts from the commercial banks and loans from ADMARC. With the collapse of tobacco prices in 1979 many of the poorly-managed politicians' tobacco estates faced bankruptcy.

The severe internal and external imbalances afflicting the Malawian economy in the late 1970s rapidly translated into a declining investment level and GDP growth rate. The Government's budgetary policies had led to a crowding-out of the private sector due to a rapid increase in government expenditures (34 per cent of GDP in 1981), in the public sector's share of total fixed capital formation (70 per cent in 1979) and its share in domestic credit (44 per cent in 1980). This crowding-out, combined with high inflation, price controls and a heavy tax burden, gave rise to production disincentives, such that a large part of disabsorption was taken up by declining investment levels. By 1981 private sector fixed investment was lower in real terms than in 1973 and total gross fixed capital formation had fallen to half the 1979 level – substantially below the level needed to maintain the country's capital stock. Domestic savings had also fallen considerably, standing at only 11 per cent of GDP in the early 1980s. The down-turn in investment had a marked impact on GDP growth rates which declined from 5.1 per cent in 1979 to 0.2 per cent in 1980, with the decline spread across all sectors except utilities. Whereas GDP per capita had stood at an historic high in 1979, between 1980–2 it had fallen by a total of 12 per cent.

In early 1979 the Government acknowledged that the balance-of-payments current account deficit could no longer be funded under existing policies and opened negotiations with the IMF. A two-and-a-half-year stand-by providing US $32.9 million was agreed in June 1979, with a further US $23.8 million provided from the IMF's Compensatory Finance Facility and US $7.1 million from the Trust Fund. The Stand-by conditions included a range of short-term demand management measures: government expenditure restraint; measures to increase government revenue (increased excises, import duties and petroleum duties); increased interest rates and ceilings on total domestic credit, government credit, and external borrowing. However, further exogenous shocks in late 1979, namely complete closure of all traditional external transport routes through Mozambique, the need for commercial food imports following drought and a worsening of ADMARC's financial position and credit requirements due to the increase in maize procurement costs following the drought meant that the Government was unable to adhere to the Stand-by conditions and the arrangement broke down in early 1981.

The unsustainability of the Stand-by in the face of further exogenous shocks underscored the need for a programme of structural adjustment covering the whole economy in order to complement the stabilisation efforts, and to avoid the sacrifice of growth under short-run stabilisation policies. Imports were constrained and threatened the operating level of the productive system, pressures were mounting on government development expenditures in order to stabilise internal accounts, the Government's recurrent account was severely underfunded, Press Holdings had become insolvent, the domestic banking system was on the verge of collapse, and investment had fallen to a level which jeopardised the maintenance of the existing capital stock. It was under these circumstances that the Government requested the Bank to consider Malawi for a Structural Adjustment Loan.

15.3 THE BANK'S DIAGNOSIS AND PRESCRIPTIONS

Preparatory work for the first SAL identified six structural weaknesses in the economy: the slow growth of smallholder exports; the narrowness of the export base, in particular the increased reliance on tobacco; dependence on imported fuel and on a declining stock of domestic fuelwood; the rapid deterioration in parastatal finances; the increasing budget deficits of the late 1970s; and the inflexible system of government-administered prices and wages. Although one cannot take issue with this list of structural problems, the Bank's background analysis (World Bank, 1981: 1–10) did not demonstrate a clear understanding of Malawi's post-independence development strategy and the associated political economy or the manner in which many of the structural weaknesses were the by-products of this strategy.

The review of the smallholder sector was focused entirely on export crops and attributed disappointing performance solely to ADMARC's pricing policies. Little mention was made of the role played by more general policies implemented under the Integrated Rural Development Projects (IRDPs) or the more recent National Rural Development Plan (NRDP). Yet these Bank- and donor-funded smallholder development projects supported and complemented Banda's estate expansion strategy at the expense of smallholder export crop production. The projects helped to strengthen infrastructure and smallholder market networks, and to provide credit, extension services, and subsidised inputs to smallholders. The main beneficiaries were a relatively small number of progressive smallholder farmers – the Achikumbe, or kulak peasant class, who possessed enough land to meet their own food requirements and to produce a marketed crop surplus. Pricing policies, the types of inputs and services provided and the perpetuation of a rigid colonial productive pattern, whereby smallholders were prevented from growing high-value exportable crops, ensured that the Achikumbe's marketed surplus increasingly took the form of the major food crop – maize. Such policies facilitated Banda's estate expansion strategy in two ways. First, the majority of smallholder subsistence producers, unable to participate in the cash economy and hence benefiting little from the rural development programmes and facing growing land scarcity, became increasingly impoverished. This forced many to enter estate wage employment despite declining real wages in the estate sector throughout the period.[5] Second, this increase in wage employment at the expense of smallholder subsistence production required a concomitant increase in the marketed surplus of food crops in order to feed the new estate labourers. The Achikumbe were central to providing such a surplus. Hence, by the late 1970s, Malawi's agricultural sector was essentially trimodal (Mhone, 1987; Harrigan, 1988) with the smallholder sector subdivided and relegated to providing the country's food requirements and the estates' labour requirements.

Although SAL policies attempted to redress the policy bias against smallholders, the Bank's failure to appreciate the trimodal nature of Malawian agriculture led to inappropriate policy prescriptions. In particular, the failure to appreciate the centrality of the food self-sufficiency drive to Banda's policy agenda was such that SAL diagnostic work overlooked a trend in smallholder agriculture which was even more alarming than the disappointing export crop production, namely, declining subsistence production in the increasingly impoverished third sector of the trimodal agricultural economy.

An equally glaring omission in the Bank's diagnostic work was the summary treatment of the estate sector. Although narrowness of the export base and the concentration of foreign exchange earnings in estate tobacco and tea was stressed, the nature of the previous estate expansion, and the structural and financial problems it had created, were not appreciated. As late as 1980, in its Malawi Economic Report, the Bank had summarised the performance of estate agriculture as 'very efficient' (World Bank, 1980: Annexe I: 61), despite the fact that a large number of tobacco estates faced bankruptcy to an extent which threatened the survival of the domestic commercial banking system. The Bank's limited knowledge regarding the estate sector was to some extent understandable. Bank project lending during the 1970s had concentrated on smallholders, whilst Banda's estate-led growth strategy had not featured in any of the Government's official development policy statements and had been implemented 'behind donors' backs' via circuitous methods of state intervention (Kydd and Hewitt, 1986b: 536). Government agencies, such as the Ministries of Agriculture and Finance with whom Bank staff were involved, themselves had limited dealings with, and knowledge of, the estates. However, the oversight was to prove costly in the form of inappropriate, simplistic, and peripheral policy prescriptions for the agricultural sector.

Regarding parastatal finances and the system of administered prices and wages, the Bank correctly identified important problems: parastatal finances were deteriorating due to the Government policy of subsidising a range of parastatal goods and services; the inflexible and unpredictable system of administered prices created production disincentive effects; and the *ad hoc* nature of public sector wage adjustments had placed unanticipated strains on the Government's recurrent budget. Again, however, there was a failure to comprehend the underlying economic and political rationale for such policies. Parastatal tariffs and consumer prices had been held down in order to maintain minimal living standards in the face of the Government's low wage policy, and in order to contain inflation. Low wages and inflation rates were both essential to the promotion of estate expansion, since, in conjunction with exchange-rate policy, they preserved the international competitiveness of estate exports. In addition, tariff and price control over a wide range of goods and services consumed by low-income groups conveniently supported Banda's attempts to cultivate a populist appeal

In the areas of energy problems and the growing government budget deficit, the Bank's analysis was, on the whole, sound. The Government's management of the two oil price shocks, in the form of passing costs on to consumers, was appropriately commended, and the rapid depletion of domestic fuelwood, which represented 80 per cent of energy consumption, was highlighted. In terms of budgetary policy, the Government's inability to track the recurrent cost implications of the rapid expansion in donor-assisted development expenditures was identified as a major policy problem, leading to underfunding of recurrent expenditure in agriculture, health and education. Nothing was said, however, regarding the implications of this for the Bank's own past and future activities as a project-donor in Malawi.

The most striking feature which emerges from a general assessment of the Bank's diagnostic work is the fact that the most fundamental and central structural problem was ignored, namely, that the previous estate-led export-orientated development strategy was no longer viable. Lack of continued viability was not just due to the exogenous shock in the form of the collapse in tobacco prices and the resulting exposure of inefficiencies in the sector. The requirements for continued expansion and much needed diversification – finance, land and labour – were no longer available. The weak financial position of most estates meant that few were able to expand using internally generated funds. At the same time, the commercial banks, having seriously over-exposed themselves in the estate sector, had retrenched, and funds were no longer available from Press Holdings or ADMARC. This lack of finance was exacerbated by the credit ceilings required under the IMF Stand-by. By the early 1980s cheap land and labour were also in short supply. Following high rates of population growth throughout the 1970s, productive customary land in most areas was under immense pressure so limiting the ability to annexe smallholder customary land into the estate sector.[6] Finally, given the growing impoverishment of the majority of the population, further suppression of real wage rates in order to compensate for the decline in commodity prices and the inefficiencies of estate management represented a high-risk political strategy.

Related to the limits on further estate expansion was a crisis of viability in the smallholder sector. By the 1980s the central plank of Banda's estate development strategy, namely the exploitation of the smallholder sector to promote estate expansion had run its course. The decline of the smallholder sector was such that ADMARC could no longer extract a surplus, land and cheap labour could not be continually annexed and food self-sufficiency, either nationally (marketed) or individually (subsistence) could no longer be achieved.

True structural adjustment of the Malawian economy hence required a fundamental reassessment of the relationship between smallholder and estate agriculture in the form of land policies, tax policies, price policies, the focus of smallholder rural development projects, and the restrictions on crops grown by smallholders and estates. In short, a readjustment of a trimodal system of colonial production which had been perpetuated by Banda's post-independence development strategy. This had implications, not just for agricultural policy, but in other policy areas. In terms of budgetary policy, the high costs of the attempt to achieve food self-sufficiency needed to be reviewed, the untapped tax revenue potential of the estates needed exploration, the high recurrent costs of largely unsuccessful donor-funded smallholder development projects required questioning, and the costs of consumer subsidies needed to be addressed. Bank reforms implemented under the three SALs failed to address this central adjustment issue. Consequently, policy prescriptions were *ad hoc* and were not integrated into an overall assessment of Malawi's past and future development options.

Following the Bank's diagnostic work during 1980 and early 1981, Malawi's first SAL was approved in June 1981 and provided US $45 million on International Bank for Reconstruction and Development (IBRD) terms. Policy reform conditions were targeted at five general objectives: improving the balance of payments; adjusting price incentives and incomes policy; strengthening resource management; rationalising the Government investment programme; and institutional improvements. SAL I policy reform conditions under each of these headings are summarised in Table 15.2, along with the associated conditions of SALs II and III.

SAL conditionality was characterised by several important general features. Under the balance-of-payments heading most of the emphasis was placed on increasing smallholder export crop production – to be achieved by increasing producer prices towards export parity levels. Conditions relating to the estate, energy and agro-industry sectors' contribution to the balance of payments were less tangible and enforceable. The lack of specificity regarding agro-industrial and estate policies was unfortunate, since it resulted in the considerable balance of payments potential of these sectors being underexploited throughout the SAL period.

One notable feature of the first SAL is the generally weak nature of its conditionality with a large number of conditions related to the conducting of studies, reviews and plans which were to provide inputs to subsequent SAL operations. Most of the remaining conditions consisted of 'quick fix' measures (price, tariff, and tax increases) aimed more at rapid financial stabilisation than at medium-term structural reform (Kydd and Hewitt, 1986b: 354). This approach was understandable, since prior to 1980, Bank lending to Malawi had been entirely project related, and its general macroeconomic work (World Bank, 1973; 1980) contained little in the way of rigorous analysis of the macroeconomic structure. Not only was the Bank's analytic position weak, the few *ad hoc* prescriptions it had previously suggested in areas of project related macro-policy, such as smallholder producer prices, recurrent account underfunding and the budgetary cost of consumer subsidies had been ignored by the Government (World Bank, 1977). Hence the Bank required a learning period on structural and bargaining issues and judiciously avoided an over-rapid pressing of reform.

SAL II was approved in December 1982 and provided US $55 million on International Development Association (IDA) terms. In contrast to SAL I, the conditionality of SAL II was tighter and incorporated the findings of some of the studies conducted under the first SAL. An important new condition was added, namely removal of the subsidy on fertilisers supplied by ADMARC to smallholders. SAL II also contained more specific

Table 15.2 SAL policy matrix

Economic issue	SAL I policy measures	SAL II policy measures	SAL III policy measures
I IMPROVEMENTS IN BALANCE OF PAYMENTS			
A Smallholder production			
Slow output growth and export stagnation	Annual review of smallholder prices using Bank-approved methodology.	Continued use and improvement of the price-setting mechanism.	Continued use of the price-setting mechanism, with Bank approval of 1986–7 prices.
	Increase in 1981–2 cotton producer price.	80% reduction in the 1984–5 fertiliser subsidy with complete removal by 1986–7.	Fertiliser subsidy to be removed by 1989–90, with Bank approval for 1986–7 prices.
	Review of livestock sector prospects and incentives.		Bank monitoring of the Fertiliser Project.
	Review of ADMARC's marketing and storage operations.		Acceleration of ADMARC's rationalisation. Relieve ADMARC of the financial burden of certain developmental activities. Expand the role of private traders in agricultural marketing.
B Estate production			
Excessive reliance on tobacco and tea exports. Rising input costs, shortage of management talent and land.	Study on tobacco market prospects and on tobacco estate diversification.	Revision of the proposed programmes for estate extension, management training and credit provision.	Set up a pilot estate credit scheme. Prepare management training and extension programmes.
C Energy			
Rapid rise in petroleum import bill and depletion of domestic fuelwood supplies.	Energy sector survey on prospects, new investments and price policy. 1982–3 fuelwood price increase.	Preparation of Energy Action programme and medium-term Energy Investment Programme.	No policy actions proposed.

D *Agro-industrial investments* Need to exploit investment opportunities to earn and save foreign exchange.	Reform of Press Holdings and MDC to enable them to undertake new investments. Adoption of appropriate price incentives and wages and incomes policy.	Conditionality the same as under SAL I.	Conditionality the same as under SAL I.

II PRICE AND NON-PRICE INCOME POLICIES:

A *Wages, prices and institutions* Need for more frequent adjustments to maintain incentives and prevent distortions.	Government review of price control system to improve flexibility. More frequent parastatal tariff increases in line with cost evaluation. Increase 1981 Blantyre Board tariffs. Prepare plan for implementing economic housing rentals.	Prepare price liberalisation programme and decontrol substantial number of items. Annual review of parastatal financial accounts and tariff increases where needed. Address issue of housing subsidies.	Complete price liberalisation programme by end of 1985. Review 1964 Industrial Development Act to encourage competition and restrict protectionist use of industrial licensing system. Ensure importance of goods that compete with domestically produced goods. Strengthen Export Promotion Council, prepare an export promotion policy, set up an Export Financing facility.
B *Exchange rate* Need for periodic review.	Period review under IMF Stand-by.	Periodic review under IMF EFF.	Government to continue an active exchange rate policy.

Table 15.2 continued

Economic issue	SAL I policy measures	SAL II policy measures	SAL III policy measures
III RESOURCE MANAGEMENT:			
A *Interest rates*	Periodic review under IMF Standby.	Adjustments to keep real interest rates positive.	No policy actions proposed.
B *Public enterprises* Need to improve profitability and operational efficiency.	Develop investment programme for Air Malawi and Malawi Railways. Review MDC's financial position including debt and equity needs. Review management budgeting of MDC and its subsidiaries and prepare long-term plans.	Implement findings of various studies on operational and financial improvement in individual parastatals. Strengthening and clarify the role of the Dept. of Statutory Bodies. Implement recommendations of the MDC studies.	Improve effectiveness of Dept. of Statutory Bodies in monitoring parastatal operations. Prepare action plan to remove parastatal deficits and improve efficiency. Continued monitoring of MDC investments in agro-industry.
C *Press Holdings Ltd* Need to improve Press Holdings management, budgeting and profitability so that it can undertake new agro-industrial investments.	Complete the review of Press Holdings management performance, finances and corporate structure. Develop a plan for long-term financial restructuring.	Implement Press Holdings restructuring programme, adhere to new corporate guidelines, carry out studies in sale of assets.	Ensure that asset rationalisation proceeds satisfactorily.

D	*Government revenue*			
	Need to improve revenue performance to finance recurrent expenditures and local component of development expenditures, whilst reducing government reliance on domestic borrowing.	15% increase in all specific excise and import duties, 10% hotel and restaurant tax, 3% across-the-board tariff increase to be introduced in 1981–2 budget.	Government revenue to be maintained at current ratio of GDP. License fees and tariffs to be reviewed prior to each budget. Review, and if necessary increase, public sector user charges and improve fees and charges collection systems. Improve buoyancy of tax system under IMF EFF.	Adopt a strategy towards restructuring the tax system. Introduce initial changes in 1986–7 budget.
E	*Government borrowing*			
	Need to limit domestic borrowing to reduce inflation and increase private sector credit. Need to limit foreign commercial borrowing.	Adherence to IMF's domestic and foreign credit ceilings. Strengthen government's ability to monitor and manage public debt. Establish a target debt-service ratio.	Ensure debt monitoring system is operational. Develop borrowing strategy to achieve target 20% debt-service ratio.	Revise the external borrowing plan.

IV GOVERNMENT EXPENDITURE AND INVESTMENT PROGRAMME

A	*Recurrent expenditure*			
	Need to correct under-funding in agriculture and expand expenditure in key economic and social sectors in line with on-going investment programme.	Commit additional MK2.8 million to agriculture in 1981–2 budget. Real growth in recurrent expenditures in key economic and social sectors during 1981–6.	Review recurrent budget allocations with Bank and ensure agricultural requirements are not under-funded.	No policy actions proposed.

Table 15.2 continued

Economic issue	SAL I policy measures	SAL II policy measures	SAL III policy measures
B *Public sector investment programme* Need to increase shares allocated to key economic and social sectors and reduce shares in low priority investments.	1981–6 Public Sector Investment Programme (PSIP) to increase shares to agriculture, water, education, health and housing. Maintain share to government buildings. Provide Bank with 3-year PSIP.	Review PSIP with Bank and make necessary modifications in view of changing circumstances.	Prepare a PSIP for the period 1986–7–1988–9.
C *Budgetary planning*	No policy actions proposed.	Develop a system of forward budgeting with 3-year projections of revenue and expenditure by April 1984. Improve the guidelines for revenue estimates and budgetary allocations.	Update the revenue and expenditure projections to cover 1986–7 to 1988–9. Make changes to give the budget a more programmatic content.
V INSTITUTIONAL IMPROVEMENTS			
A *Economic monitoring* Need to monitor all investments to ensure economic and financial viability.	Preliminary review of all large investment co-ordinating committee and detailed review by independent consultants. Strengthen expertise in Treasury, Economic Planning Division and Ministry of Agriculture under technical assistance programme to assist with public debt, Government finance, macro and agricultural planning and statistical resources.	Strengthening Economic Planning Division to assist medium-term strategy development and project identification, evaluation, monitoring and co-ordination.	Strengthen and reorganise policy-making staff of the Office of President and Cabinet and Ministry of Finance.

conditions on consumer price decontrol, placed greater emphasis on measures to increase government revenues, and included tough conditions in the form of restructuring programmes for Press Holdings and MDC.

SAL III was approved in December 1985, and provided US $70 million, US $30 million from IDA and US $40 million from the Bank's African Facility. In addition, Special Joint Financing of US $22.6 million was provided by Japan and US $6.4 million by Germany, with US $15 million provided by USAID on a bilateral parallel basis. Hence in total, the financing associated with SAL III amounted to US $114 million. Despite the high level of funding, the conditionality of SAL III, as with SAL I, was relatively mild, and in many cases represented a continuation of the policies initiated under the previous SALs. The target date for fertiliser subsidy removal was extended to 1989–90 in view of cost increases caused by new disruptions to external transport routes. In addition to the continuation of previous reform measures, SAL III contained several new policy initiatives: a restructuring of the tax system; measures to stimulate competition and exports within the industrial sector; and redefinition of ADMARC's role along with attempts to stimulate private trading in smallholder agricultural markets. The severity of ADMARC's financial crisis during 1985–6 was such that the Bank granted a US $42 million supplement to SAL III in order to provide financial assistance for the rehabilitation and restructuring of ADMARC.

15.4 AGRICULTURAL REFORMS[7]

In view of the weakness of the Bank's diagnostic work on the agricultural sector, the most important sector of the Malawian economy, it is not surprising that it is in this area that SAL policies deserve the greatest criticism. The Bank's agricultural reforms can be faulted in five respects. First, there was relative neglect of the estate sector and of the relationship between estate and smallholder production patterns. Second, within the smallholder sector, Bank policy focused exclusively on increasing export crop production without appreciating and attempting to reconcile the direct conflict with the Government's food self-sufficiency objective. Third, SAL policy objectives also conflicted with the Bank's own project-lending activities in Malawi, the central focus of which was to promote smallholder uptake of improved, fertiliser-responsive, varieties of maize in order to increase the productivity of food production. Fourth, the Bank's excessive reliance on price policy instruments to increase export crop production, in conjunction with the SAL price policy of input subsidy removal, exacerbated the food crop versus export crop conflict. Finally, policy reforms were inappropriately sequenced – price liberalisation occurred in advance of market liberalisation, so placing a financial strain on ADMARC and contributing to the collapse of the formal marketing system in 1985–6.

The Bank's conditions on agricultural price policy, under which producer prices of smallholder export crops were to be raised towards export parity levels in order to redress the previous incentive bias towards maize production, represented one of the most tangible and enforceable components of SAL conditionality. However, such conditionality was over-optimistic. The 1979–80 maize harvest failure had resulted in economically and politically costly imports of maize for the first time since 1949–50. Under these circumstances, it is difficult to understand how the Bank failed to acknowledge the potential conflict between their price policy conditions and Banda's food self-sufficiency objective. Yet, as Kydd and Hewitt have noted:

> The first SAL report does not suggest that the Bank addressed itself in a rigorous way to balancing the objectives of increased food production and increased exports by peasant producers. The document contains not a single reference, either direct or oblique, to the issue of how to maintain food supplies during the period of the first SAL, even though this was at the time a major preoccupation of Malawi's political leadership, receiving frequent mention in Malawi's national media.
>
> (Kydd and Hewitt, 1986b: 357)

In view of this conflict, which was equally ignored under the second and third SALs, Bank optimism regarding the willingness of the Government to comply with the pricing conditions was misplaced.

The Bank was also over-optimistic in its implicit belief that price policy alone could stimulate an *aggregate* increase in smallholder production. Although Malawi's smallholders were highly price responsive (Brown, 1970; Mills, 1983), prevailing technological, land, and credit constraints were such that price increases alone, in the absence of complimentary non-price policies, were unlikely to elicit an aggregate supply response (Harrigan, 1988; Lipton, 1987; Streeton, 1987). Rather, the change in relative price incentives proposed by the Bank threatened to increase export crop production via the displacement of food crops.

It is hardly surprising, therefore, that under the first SAL, the Government ignored the Bank's agricultural price policy conditions. Prior to the SAL I loan approval, the official producer price of maize had been increased by 32 per cent in order to ensure that ADMARC could compete with private traders following the 1979–80 harvest failure. A decision had also been taken in 1980 to construct an 180,000 metric tonne (MT) strategic grain reserve. This was followed by a direct violation of SAL conditionality, with the 1981–2 maize producer price raised by a further 68 per cent. Hence, the Government's policy of instituting price incentives biased towards maize production at the expense of smallholder export crop production, and the associated use of ADMARC's profits on the export crop trading accounts to cross-subsidise food crops, was intensified. The nature of this policy violation indicated that the dictatorial nature of Malawi's political regime created considerable problems for the Bank in areas of policy conflict. Although civil servant bureaucrats appeared to have reached agreement with Bank staff on the methodology to be used by the Interministerial Producer Price Advisory Committee in setting relative smallholder prices, this agreement at the technical level was overridden by Banda, in his capacity as Minister for Agriculture, without consultation with either civil servants or Bank staff:

> Final decisions . . . were taken by President Banda. . . . the decision to raise maize prices sharply in 1982 had little to do with methodological issues. It reflected the President's preoccupation with food security against the background of drought experiences. Civil servants' recommendations on the basis of the agreed methodology were ignored.
>
> (Gulhati, 1989: 49–50)

Government price policies implemented under SAL I had the desired effect in terms of the Government's policy objectives. Between 1980–1 and 1982–3 maize sales to ADMARC more than doubled so enabling the filling of the strategic grain reserve. This was at the cost of a halving of sales of the main smallholder export crops of tobacco, groundnuts, cotton and rice (Table 15.3).

Table 15.3 ADMARC crop purchases (metric tonnes)

	Maize	Tobacco	Groundnuts	Cotton	Rice	Total (exc. maize)
1978–9	116,025	23,732	11,145	24,219	31,103	90,199
1979–80	82,404	19,516	24,296	22,411	20,634	86,857
1980–1	91,205	11,340	31,484	23,096	16,863	82,783
1981–2	136,591	12,756	19,490	21,740	14,629	68,615
1982–3	246,086	8,708	10,620	14,629	12,623	46,580
1983–4	244,916	9,279	10,218	13,370	8,810	41,677
1984–5	296,443	19,163	9,667	32,122	10,201	71,951
1985–6	272,275	20,815	18,251	32,717	10,799	82,582
1986–7	111,331	17,168	53,050	21,033	12,073	103,294
1987–8	113,409	13,286	49,064	19,454	7,821	89,625

Source: Harrigan (1988) Table 2.

The SAL II loan agreement repeated the conditionality on smallholder crop pricing and added new conditionality in the form of the fertiliser subsidy removal programme. The latter was undoubtedly the most controversial aspect of the entire SAL programme, causing protracted, bitter and unresolved conflict between Bank staff and policy-makers in

Malawi's Ministry of Agriculture. It also caused an intense division within the Malawi Government.

The negotiation process on the fertiliser subsidy issue illustrates a tension, inherent to programme-lending activities, between the need for rapid disbursement of finance and the need to devote time to devising appropriate conditionality and to forging consensus between government agencies with differing mandates and objectives. During the SAL II loan negotiations of late 1983 Malawi's balance of payments and public finance problems had intensified. In addition, tight budgetary conditions had been stipulated as part of the new IMF Extended Fund Facility approved in September 1983. Hence, in urgent need of foreign exchange to support the balance of payments and Government budget and with the fertiliser subsidy constituting 6 per cent of the budget deficit in the form of subventions to ADMARC, the Ministry of Finance, acting as the lead SAL negotiation agency, willingly and hastily agreed to the Bank's fertiliser subsidy removal conditions without consulting the Ministry of Agriculture, despite the fact that the latter was expected to implement the reform. Subsidy removal was presented as a measure designed to reduce the budget deficit and remove the 'allocative inefficiencies' caused by subsidies and price distortions. No attempt was made, however, until 1985–6, to provide a comprehensive analysis of the effects of subsidy removal on fertiliser uptake, on the adoption rates for improved maize varieties (all of which required fertiliser applications), on maize productivity, or on the general levels of food-crop production. In short, there was a complete failure, by both Bank and Ministry of Finance staff, to view the fertiliser subsidy issue in the broader context of the Government's *multiple* policy objectives and to quantify the opportunity costs and trade-offs between these objectives.

Throughout SAL II and during most of SAL III, the Government complied with Bank conditionality in the area of smallholder pricing policy. Several factors explain this newly co-operative stance. The disbursement of the SAL I second tranche had been delayed by six months, partly because of the Government's failure to comply with agricultural price conditions, so providing a clear signal that continued non-compliance would not be tolerated. The deterioration in internal and external accounts and the associated increased dependence on the SAL balance-of-payments support further strengthened the Bank's leverage. In addition, the Government's independent maize price policy implemented under SAL I appeared to have rectified the food-deficit crisis by enabling ADMARC to stock the MT180,000 strategic grain reserve, so reducing the conflict between Government and Bank objectives.

Although a 10 per cent maize producer price increase was announced for the 1983–4 growing season against the advice of the Bank, this was followed by a period of constant nominal maize prices through to 1987, implying a decline in the real price. At the same time, producer prices for smallholder export crops were substantially increased. Between 1983–4 and 1987–8 ADMARC's top grade prices for cotton increased by 55 per cent, rice by 80 per cent, groundnuts by 25 per cent, and tobacco by 43 per cent, in all cases reaching a level close to farmgate export parity. Fertiliser prices also escalated. Between 1983–4 and 1987–8 the weighted average price for the three main types of smallholder fertiliser increased by 87 per cent. Despite the dramatic increase in fertiliser prices, a significant revision was required in the subsidy removal programme. The increase in 1984–5 fertiliser selling prices had effectively eliminated the subsidy based on import costs via the traditional transport routes through Mozambique. However, 1984 witnessed further disruption of these routes necessitating importation via more costly routes through South Africa and Tanzania. As a result, the actual subsidy level remained above 20 per cent. Acknowledging the importance of these exogenous factors, Bank staff adopted a flexible and realistic position and negotiated a new schedule for subsidy removal under which subsidies were to be gradually phased-out by 1989–90.

On the evidence of ADMARC purchase data, the impact of the Bank's policy prescriptions under SALs II and III appeared successful. Between 1983–4 and 1985–6 maize sales to ADMARC increased slightly despite the decline in real producer price (Table 15.3). In addition, in response to the large producer price increases, sales of export crops (tobacco, rice, groundnuts and cotton) to ADMARC more than doubled from MT41,677 to MT103,294 between 1983–4 and 1986–7. The alarming pattern of events which emerged in the 1986–7 marketing year, however, illustrated the fragility of this earlier success and confirmed the Ministry of Agriculture's fears regarding the Bank's price policy package. ADMARC purchases of maize fell by 59 per cent – the lowest level since the late 1970s. At the same time, ADMARC's domestic maize sales were at a record level of MT286,400. The combined result was a run down of the country's maize stocks and the need for maize imports in excess of MT140,000 – the highest import level since the early 1970s. In addition, the following season, 1987–8, witnessed a 13 per cent decline in the sale of smallholder export crops to ADMARC.

Part of the above crisis can be explained by exogenous shocks. An influx of over 700,000 refugees fleeing the civil war in Mozambique increased the demand on ADMARC's maize stocks, whilst drought in the southern half of the country contributed to a regional decline in ADMARC's maize purchases. However, the nation-wide decline in ADMARC's purchases resulted from the effects of inappropriate and poorly-sequenced reforms implemented under the SALs.

The Bank's emphasis on stimulating export crop production overlooked the fact that increased food crop production was a prerequisite for success in terms of a favourable balance-of-payments effect. For a land-locked country such as Malawi, the use of export crop income to purchase bulky maize imports is not an economically viable development strategy. Hence, an increase in export crop production needed to coincide with increased maize production and sales, combined with confidence, on the part of export crop producers, in ADMARC's maize marketing capacity. The events of 1986–7 showed that Bank policies had failed on both counts.

The Bank's insistence that ADMARC's maize purchase price be held constant at a time of rapidly increasing fertiliser prices, necessitated by the subsidy removal programme, resulted in a continued decline in the gross margin on maize production.[8] As the Ministry of Agriculture had constantly argued, the eventual effect was a displacement of maize, previously grown as a cash crop by the Achikumbe, by exportable cash crops, which contributed to the dramatic decline in ADMARC's maize purchases in 1986–7. In addition, the Bank's attempts to monetise and diversify Malawi's smallholder agricultural sector bypassed the large preponderance of farmers who remained subsistence producers. Given the importance of this subsistence subsector and the country's severe land constraint, increased smallholder contribution to the balance of payments first required a substantial increase in the productivity of subsistence food production if land was to be released for other crops without jeopardising individual food security. In this respect, Bank policies perpetuated, albeit in a different form, the Government's own policy mistakes. Both placed an excessive emphasis on the achievement of *marketed surpluses* – of export crops in the case of the Bank and of maize in the case of the Government – whilst ignoring trends in *production*, particularly in the key subsistence subsector. As a result, there was a tendency on the part of the Bank to regard input and output price instruments as symmetrical in impact with the belief that higher producer prices would compensate for higher input prices. Although such symmetry applied to those farmers able to produce for the market, subsistence producers derived no benefit from higher producer prices yet faced increasing input prices.

The effects of asymmetries in input and output pricing contributed to the failure of the focal objective of the Bank-supported National Rural Development Plan, namely, promotion of the uptake of improved fertiliser-responsive maize varieties, particularly amongst subsistence producers. The failure is shown by the fact that the share of such maize varieties in total maize production declined by over 50 per cent between 1984 and 1987 (Harrigan, 1988: Table 4). Clearly, there was a stark lack of co-ordination between the Bank's role as a traditional project donor in Malawi, in which it aligned with the Ministry of Agriculture, and its new role as a programme aid donor in which it aligned with the Ministry of Finance and insisted on such policies as input subsidy removal. In addition, despite the existence of the NRDP, Ministry of Finance budget cut-backs implemented under the SALs meant that insufficient resources were devoted to non-price policies such as provision of credit for low-income and subsistence producers in order to encourage input uptake at a time of rapidly rising input prices.

As a result of the 'pricist'[9] policies adopted during the 1980s a pattern of development came about whereby an increased marketed 'surplus' of both export and food crops was achieved up until 1986–7, without eliciting any substantial increase in total smallholder production. The dramatic expansion of marketed surpluses coincided with a fall in the growth rate of smallholder production to 2.3 per cent per annum. Not surprisingly, disappointing production was particularly marked in the case of maize. Over the decade 1976–7 to 1986–7 maize production displayed a growth rate of −0.8 per cent (Harrigan, 1988: Table 5). Increased sales to ADMARC did not therefore reflect a true marketable surplus. The achievement of food security at the aggregate national level, in the form of the filling of the strategic grain reserve prior to 1986–7, occurred at the expense of worsening food security at the individual level in the form of declining per capita maize availability.

In addition to the general inappropriateness of Bank price policy prescriptions and their conflict with project lending and government policy priorities, SAL policies in the agricultural sector were poorly sequenced, with poor sequencing contributing to the food crisis of 1986–7. Not only did liberalisation of input prices occur in advance of liberalisation of the maize producer price, the moves towards general agricultural price liberalisation occurred in advance of market liberalisation and contributed to the collapse in ADMARC's marketing capacities. During the 1980s ADMARC was faced with the demand that producer prices be substantially increased − first for maize by the Government, then for the major export crops by the Bank. Yet it was not relieved of the burden of its developmental activities which part of the previous implicit taxes on smallholder produce had been used to finance − subsidising an extensive network of markets and employment, defending pan-territorial prices for producer goods and inputs, cross-subsidising maize and rice producer prices, and defending subsidised consumer prices. Indeed, extra developmental burdens were added during the 1980s, namely, maintaining the strategic grain reserve and defending subsidised consumer prices during a time of increasing producer prices. Although Bank staff constantly stressed the adverse effects of higher maize producer prices on ADMARC's financial position as a reason for holding maize prices constant, they failed to acknowledge the similar effects of higher export crop prices. The result was the creation of a hybrid and unsustainable parastatal, which was expected, under Bank and IMF conditionality, to operate as a commercial organisation, in the sense of making a healthy profit on its trading activities whilst paying parity prices for smallholder crops, while at the same time continuing many of its costly developmental activities in an

229

otherwise unliberalised smallholder market. In the absence of widespread private trading, ADMARC continued to be legally charged with purchasing all crops offered for sale at rigid pan-territorial prices fixed in advance for the entire agricultural season regardless of the vagaries of world market prices.

The impact of the poor sequencing of reforms placed financial strain on ADMARC and contributed to the collapse of the formal marketing system in 1985–6, with ADMARC unable to purchase the maize harvest or to guarantee the timely distribution of inputs. The superimposition of a marketing crisis upon the disappointing pattern of smallholder production compounded the country's food deficit problem. Smallholder fertiliser uptake declined in absolute terms in 1985–6 and in the face of market uncertainties many risk-averse farmers shifted their cash cropping pattern out of improved maize and towards groundnuts – a crop not usually fertilised by smallholders, with a more favourable gross margin than improved maize, more easily storable, and enjoying a well-developed informal market. The upshot was the dramatic decline in ADMARC's maize purchases in the 1986–7 marketing year.

In response to the ADMARC crisis, the Bank was forced to hastily devise the SAL III Supplement to ADMARC which provided US $42 million of untranched financial support for ADMARC restructuring. Prior to the Supplement, there was little attempt to comprehensively revise the role of the state marketing board in the light of SAL price reforms within the smallholder sector. The 1983 consultant study on ADMARC, commissioned as a condition of SAL I, had recommended a number of fundamental reforms, only two of which, however, had been implemented prior to 1985. ADMARC's financial management had been strengthened and the Corporation had divested itself of a number of investments not related to agricultural marketing and processing via asset swaps with Press Holdings and MDC. However, by 1985, the most far-reaching recommendations of the study, namely that the Government compensate ADMARC for its non-commercial developmental activities and that smallholder marketing be opened to increased competition from private traders, had not been implemented.

The re-evaluation of ADMARC's functions following the 1985–6 crisis resulted in a number of significant reforms. The cost of fertiliser subsidisation was shifted to the Smallholder Fertiliser Revolving Fund with US $12 million support for the Fund provided by USAID's parallel financing to SAL III. The Government also purchased the strategic grain reserve from ADMARC and took over the financial responsibility of its maintenance. In December 1986 a series of market liberalisation reforms were announced: a public notice was gazetted confirming the legality of private trade in all crops except tobacco and cotton; ADMARC floor purchase prices were differentiated with a wholesale price introduced to encourage private traders to undertake direct purchase and haulage functions; the Government agreed to devise a programme to assist private traders with credit, training and information; 224 out of 1,419 ADMARC markets were to be closed and 148 markets to be operated on a reduced basis; and the Government agreed to increase the maize consumer price to a cost recovery level by April 1987 in order to increase ADMARC's trading margins. In addition, the Government pledged to speed up the USAID-assisted ADMARC divestment programme which by mid-1986 had fallen behind schedule with shares in only two of six agreed companies having been sold.

The reforms announced, at the end of 1986 represented an attempt to redefine ADMARC's role as one of scaled-down buyer and seller of last resort defending a band of producer and consumer prices. However, the timing of the new market liberalisation measures was disastrous. ADMARC's new role was premised on the supposition that ADMARC would possess the necessary maize supplies to defend the ceiling consumer price of maize. Following the marketing crisis and stock run-down of 1986–7 this was patently not the case. Consequently, consumer prices escalated in the following year, resulting in considerable hardship for Malawi's net food purchasers and intensifying political opposition to the reforms on the part of MPs and Ministry of Agriculture staff. As with the price policy reforms of SAL II, the Ministry of Agriculture, an effective and vocal ministry, strongly opposed many aspects of the 1986 reforms to ADMARC. Ministry staff argued that more time was needed to resolve largely unaddressed issues: the effects of ADMARC market closures on the availability of inputs, consumer maize supplies, and producer market access in remote areas unlikely to be served by private traders; the effects on smallholder credit recovery when marketing occurred via private traders – credit previously having been collected at ADMARC markets; the effectiveness of the new marketing system in arbitrating price differences over time and space; the Government's ability to maintain adequate domestic supplies of exportable food crops in the face of relaxed export controls; and the ability of ADMARC to defend floor producer prices and ceiling consumer prices, particularly for maize, and the relationships this would necessitate between ADMARC and the now government-owned strategic grain reserve.

The scale of ADMARC's financial crisis in 1986 and 1987 was such that the Ministry of Agriculture's fears were ignored. In the words of one senior Ministry of Agriculture official:

Market liberalisation was done by trial and error. Despite strong opposition, the Government was forced to agree due to the desperate need for the US$42 million Supplement for ADMARC – the Ministry of Agriculture was told to agree by the Treasury. In retrospect, the

Bank now admits that they made mistakes in trying to dismantle a working system too quickly and without forethought.

(Personal interview, Lilongwe, May 1987)

Not surprisingly, the inappropriately timed *ad hoc* market liberalising reforms were only partially implemented by the Government and were largely unsuccessful. The Government applied highly restrictive criteria in licensing private traders and private grain handling capacity failed to develop with traders facing credit, transport, and information shortages (Lele, 1988). Seventy ADMARC markets scheduled to be closed were kept open, and in those areas where markets were closed private traders, as feared by the Ministry of 'Agriculture, failed to fill the gap. ADMARC, lacking maize supplies, was unable to defend the ceiling consumer maize price, already increased by 25 per cent, such that unofficial prices rose much more sharply. ADMARC divestment proceeded at a slow pace and the Government's continued desire to control consumer prices via ADMARC, understandable in the food-deficit circumstances and in the absence of clearly thought-out alternatives, confounded the objective of making ADMARC a commercial self-sustaining enterprise. ADMARC's financial difficulties remained, therefore, a considerable drag on the Government's fiscal performance.

Government resistance to the 1986–7 ADMARC reforms was facilitated by the fact that the SAL III supplement was untranched, with implementation to be monitored under SAL IV. The proposed SAL IV, however, was abandoned before the loan agreement stage, and was replaced with a series of SECALs. Three years later, the agricultural SECAL is still under negotiation. This hiatus in programme aid policy conditionality in the agricultural sector reduced the Bank's ability to enforce and monitor the ADMARC reforms. This is to be seen as fortunate, since it has provided both the Bank and government with a much needed breathing space in which to reappraise not just ADMARC's new potential role, but also the general policy approach to the entire agricultural sector.

This reappraisal occurred within the context of a complete failure of Bank policies in the smallholder sector in terms of both sustained implementation and impact. By 1987, the Ministry of Agriculture had convinced most government agencies, including the Ministry of Finance, that the arguments it had been forwarding since 1981 against SAL price policy prescriptions were well founded. Maize production and eventually procurements had declined, maize stocks were depleted, ADMARC's cash-flow position had failed to improve, the objectives of the NRDP were unfulfilled, and the net contribution to the balance of payments from the smallholder sector had deteriorated. The latter is perhaps the strongest indictment against Bank policies. The main thrust behind such policies had been to diversify the smallholder sector in order to increase foreign exchange earnings. Not only had such diversification failed to take place, but the neglect of food-crop production had ultimately resulted in costly maize imports which, had they occurred on an entirely commercial basis, would have more than outweighed the earlier foreign exchange earnings derived from the increase in smallholder export crop production. The Bank's failure to anticipate this medium-term adverse balance-of-payments effect is all the more surprising since the Bank itself had, in 1983–4, developed a Multi-Market Agricultural Pricing Model for Malawi's smallholder sector. Simulations carried out on this model by the present author, and reported in Volume 1 of this publication, clearly show that Bank pricing policies, in contrast to the Ministry of Agriculture's own preferred pricing scenarios, had an unfavourable net foreign exchange effect via the creation of a food-deficit situation. Yet Bank staff failed to use this model to provide a similar medium-term projection of the impact of differing price policy scenarios on the multiplicity of government and Bank objectives, including balance-of-payments improvement.

In response to the manifest failure of SAL pricing policies, the Ministry of Agriculture, now backed by the front-line ministries, carried out a complete U-turn on price policy in direct violation of SAL conditionality. In mid-1987 a 36 per cent post-harvest producer price increase for maize was announced. This was followed by the announcement of fertiliser prices for the 1988–9 season which set the weighted average subsidy level at 22 per cent – in excess of the level at the start of the subsidy removal programme. The strength of the Government's convictions on the subsidy issue are indicated by the fact that conditionality was violated despite a high opportunity cost, namely, the withdrawal of USAID's programme aid support to the Smallholder Fertiliser Revolving Fund.

In contrast to the smallholder subsector, reforms to estate agriculture were not vigorously pursued under the three SALs by either Bank or Government staff. Conditionality regarding estates under SAL I consisted of a range of studies on potential diversification. The conclusion was that there was no obvious alternative to continued reliance on tobacco. Although a range of subsidiary crops was identified, caution was recommended in the uptake of such crops in view of potential managerial and technological problems. In addition, the recovery of tobacco prices in the early 1980s, and a movement by estates out of flue-cured tobacco, which placed heavy demands on the country's dwindling fuelwood supply, into air-cured burley, reduced the urgency of estate diversification (Kydd and Hewitt, 1986a: 358).

Under SALs II and III, it was acknowledged that diversification required support in the form of provision of management training and extension services to estates, and increased availability of credit. Under SAL III, an estate management and extension service was set up for tobacco estates. However, the scheme was slow to develop and was not extended to other types of estates. In addition, attempts to establish an Agricultural Development Bank proved unviable, with credit provision left instead to the two commercial banks and the Industrial and Development Bank (INDEBANK). Hence, estate owners were provided with little incentive or support to develop new activities and the disruption to traditional transport routes continued to depress the profitability of new export crops. With the concomitant failure to develop agro-industry, Malawi's export base remained heavily concentrated. In 1987, agricultural commodities provided 90 per cent of exports, 80 per cent of which consisted of tobacco, sugar, and tea, with tobacco alone accounting for 61 per cent of total merchandise exports.

The Bank itself, in an internal evaluation of SALs I and II, had commented on the relative neglect of estate agriculture: '. . . it would appear that these provisions for strengthening estate agriculture should have been included and implemented sooner' (World Bank, 1987: 9). The same report also notes that such provision – management training, extension, and credit services – might better be 'handled through conventional project lending. Even these project-type reforms, however, are unlikely to be capable of solving the severe structural problem of Malawi's narrow export base. An effective solution requires the readjustment of Malawi's colonial pattern of agricultural production entailing a reappraisal of the relationship between smallholder and estate agriculture. Idle land on estates is currently excessive and beyond the requirements of crop rotation and fallow, with only 6–7 per cent of estate land cultivated each year in contrast to 33 per cent within the smallholder subsector (Gulhati, 1989: 24). The encouragement of estate diversification requires forceful policies to increase land use, such as a sharp increase in the currently low estate land taxes and rentals, as well as tax incentives for diversification, and the implementation of crop-by-crop action plans. In addition, the colonial system of preventing smallholder production of high-value export crops, the restrictive nature of share-cropping tenant schemes, and the discouragement of smallholder production activities in certain geographical areas urgently needs dismantling, whilst land as well as crop redistribution demands attention. Such fundamental structural reforms would produce doubly beneficial effects. First, increased smallholder competition with, and pressure on, the estates would stimulate efficiency – including diversification attempts – within the estates. Second, such non-price policies would help promote the much-needed increases in smallholder food-crop productivity and in *aggregate* smallholder production.

That the Bank shied away from such policy issues can be attributed partly to the weakness of the SAL diagnosis of Malawi's structural problems in the agricultural sector. However, in fairness to the Bank, such reforms would undoubtedly have confronted considerable political opposition from Malawi's powerful estate interests – Banda, politicians, civil servants, and military personnel: 'With the regrowth of estates in the 1970s, they were able to exercise an influence on government at least as powerful as that wrought by the European planters at the heyday of their influence on the colonial government' (Kydd, 1988: 73). Unfortunately, however, the issue of political viability of such reforms appears not to have been considered by the Bank despite the fact that under SAL II Bank staff had successfully implemented an equally sensitive and politically challenging series of reforms, namely, the restructuring of Banda's Press Holdings.

15.5   REFORMS IN THE CORPORATE AND PARASTATAL SECTORS

In contrast to agricultural reforms, SAL reforms in the corporate and parastatal sectors (with the exception of those directed towards ADMARC) met with a large measure of success. Most notable was the restructuring of Press Holdings.

Although a private holding company owned solely by the President, Press's pivotal position in the Malawi economy cannot be overemphasised. As the largest corporation in the private sector, Press and its subsidiaries employed 10 per cent of the country's paid labour force and in 1981 had a turnover of MK400 million – equivalent to 36 per cent of the country's GDP. Its portfolio encompassed twenty-two wholly-owned companies, twenty-three subsidiaries in which Press had majority shareholdings and a lead management role, as well as 44 per cent and 40 per cent ownership of the country's two commercial banks. Hence, Press's activities extended to most sectors of the economy, and were virtually monopolistic in certain areas of export trade, wholesale and retail trade, energy and transportation. The central role played by Press in Banda's estate-led development strategy had created close linkages between the Corporation and the Government, parastatals, and commercial banks. Press held joint ownership with ADMARC and MDC in over twenty companies. In addition, it owed MK54 million to ADMARC, over MK80 million to the two commercial banks (making Press their largest debtor) and had borrowed over MK20 million in unsecured and government-guaranteed foreign loans.

By 1980, Press faced a severe financial crisis and was unable to service most of its loans. The crisis was the culminative result of: adverse conditions in the agricultural sector, in particular, the 1979–80 collapse of tobacco prices, Press having invested heavily in tobacco estates; mismanagement; excessive payment of dividends and excessive withdrawal of funds by the President to finance prestige projects such as the construction of Kamuzu Academy; and overrapid and imprudent expansion during the late 1970s. The magnitude of Press Holdings' crisis had implications for the entire economy.

Quite literally, Press's insolvency posed the prospect of bankruptcy of the two commercial banks, as well as threatening the financial viability of ADMARC, and jeopardising the country's international creditworthiness. The Corporation's activities had restricted domestic credit to the remainder of the private sector, and its operational difficulties implied a major adverse impact on the country's output, employment, and exports.

There was an urgent need to avert the financial collapse of Press Holdings and to ensure that potentially profitable assets remained operational. The issue of Press restructuring, however, implied Bank involvement in highly sensitive political areas, since a key implication of restructuring was a reduction in Banda's control over Press's economic and political activities and in his personal monetary gains from the Corporation:

> Thus, in seeking the legal and financial restructuring of Press, the Bank was not engaged in a purely technical exercise. Effectively, the Bank was seeking far-reaching changes in the political economy of the country, and in particular in the operation of mechanisms of resource control and political patronage.
>
> (Kydd and Hewitt, 1986a: 360)

As the Bank itself has retrospectively acknowledged, the reform of Press was: '. . . an area in which IDA dared to tread despite the potential risk this intervention posed to our relationship with Malawi' (World Bank, 1987: 82). Two questions immediately arise. Why was the Bank willing to take this political risk, whilst shying away from other politically sensitive issues such as reform of the colonial pattern of agricultural production? Second, how did the Bank manage to elicit successful and sustained implementation of the Press reforms when other politically controversial reforms, such as agricultural price policy, were marked by lack of sustainability and violations of SAL conditionality?

The Bank's decision to tackle Press arose from the acknowledgement that: '. . . the structural adjustment of Malawi could not be separated from the restructuring of Press Holdings Ltd.' (World Bank, 1987: 16). In addition, the nature of the problem, although inextricably linked with the country's medium-term structural difficulties, took the form of an acute financial crisis. Not only was it impossible to overlook such an immediately pressing crisis, but if political agreement could be secured, the beneficial impact of restructuring would be both extensive and rapidly felt. By contrast, other politically sensitive reforms were not characterised by such crisis management requirements. Hence, in the case of Press, the political stakes were high, but the benefits promised to be tangible, tractable and immediate.

Bank staff skilfully exploited this unique aspect of the Press problem. A series of studies was commissioned by the Bank in order to quantify the implications of allowing Press to become bankrupt. The studies established Press's assets to be worth MK86 million, and its liabilities MK126 million, and represented the first clear quantification of the Corporation's insolvency. The impact of restructuring on the Government budget parastatals and banks was assessed and contrasted to the alternative of allowing the bankruptcy of Press whilst insulating the banks and viable subsidiaries. The latter scenario forecast 'extraordinary damage to the economy' and the credibility of its presentation undoubtedly helped to persuade Malawian policy-makers, particularly the President, of the urgent and inevitable need for a salvage operation.

Although Press held a pivotal position in the Malawian economy and was crucial to the Bank's structural adjustment programme, the fact that it was a single, private, corporate entity, owned by one individual, albeit the country's President, also assisted the Bank's reform efforts. It was principally the President who faced personal loss from the proposed reform of Press, and it was Banda alone, as the sole shareholder, who needed to be convinced of the need for reform. If this could be achieved there was little else, in the form of political stumbling blocks, which stood in the way of restructuring. Again, Bank staff fully exploited the uniqueness of this situation by adopting an equally unique bargaining strategy. Negotiations largely bypassed civil servant bureaucrats, utilising instead Presidential advisers, particularly Banda's personal lawyer who acted as an envoy between Washington and the presidential palace. Furthermore, the Bank displayed a pragmatic willingness to compromise and accept a second-best solution in order to obtain the President's acquiescence. The compromise solution involved the establishment of a Trust to which Banda transferred his shares and of which he became the Senior Trustee. Under the new legal arrangements, the restructured Press was legally bound to pay an annual fee of MK1 million into the Trust, with this fee being the first priority charge on Press's accrued income each year. The Bank has subsequently been criticised for establishing such an arrangement whereby the President continues to derive large personal gains from the operations of Press. However, it is doubtful whether Banda's co-operation, which was essential to the implementation of reform, could have been secured in the absence of such a compromise:

> It was deemed by the Bank to be a necessary cost to obtain the co-operation of the owner, and an enforceable way of controlling future withdrawals and ensuring that they were in no way excessive, as they had been in the past.
>
> (World Bank, 1987: 17)

A further factor, unrelated to the Bank's bargaining strategy, also helps to explain Banda's willingness to accept the reform of Press. Although Press's profits were rapidly eroded in the late 1970s, senior management of the Corporation, unwilling to face the political consequences of being the harbingers of bad news, failed to inform Banda of the magnitude of Press's financial deterioration and the President continued to withdraw large sums despite the Company's poor balance sheet. It was the IMF Stand-by negotiations of 1979 and the SAL I appraisal mission which alerted Banda to Press's insolvency. The magnitude of Banda's shock is evidenced by the subsequent gaoling of Press's general manager. Hence, Banda's hand was forced by this eleventh-hour immersion in a crisis management situation. At such a stage in the crisis, the options facing Banda were limited and stark: allow the bankruptcy of Press with a possible political backlash and scandal; or accept the Bank's offer of tactful and diplomatic negotiations for a restructuring plan.

Prior to the SAL I loan agreement, Press had already suspended dividend payments, closed down the operations of several loss-making subsidiaries, and reduced its work-force by 20 per cent. Conditionality on Press under SAL I consisted of the commissioning of studies and reports, and the resulting restructuring plan formed a central part of the SAL II conditions. The restructuring entailed the formation of a new holding company, Press Group Ltd., and an overhauling of senior management. Shares in a number of agro-industries were sold to ADMARC, and further asset rationalisation occurred through a series of share swaps with ADMARC and MDC. As a result, the number of companies in which Press held shares was reduced from twenty-four to fourteen. New corporate guidelines covering price policy, investment criteria, overdraft arrangements, and rules for inter-company loans were drawn up to ensure that the new PGL operated on a commercial basis. The restructuring involved considerable cost to the Government, with the Government taking over Press's liabilities to the commercial banks through the issue of MK54 million Special Stock. In return the Government received preference shares and income notes from the new PGL. Following the restructuring, PGL owed MK64.5 million to the Government and MK40 million to ADMARC. Although the first claim of future annual income of PGL was the MK1 million annual payment to the Presidential Trust Fund, Press was legally obligated to repay government debts before investing or paying other dividends.

Initially there was some delay in the legal enactment of Press restructuring. This resulted in a five-month delay in the disbursement of the SAL II second tranche. However, by the end of 1984, the restructuring was largely completed, and resulted in a rapid improvement in Press's operational, management and financial position. In 1984, the new PGL made a pre-tax profit of MK4 million, followed by an MK16 million profit in 1985 and in 1985 Press began to repay debts to the Government and ADMARC and to pay taxes.

Although by 1985 Press's financial viability had been restored, certain reservations remain regarding aspects of the restructuring arrangement. The insistence that proceeds of divestment be used to meet liabilities reduced potential profit and the incentive to sell assets. Consequently, from 1985 onwards PGL's progress in selling assets in order to repay the Government was slow. The series of share swaps with ADMARC and MDC also had the effect of passing many of Press's problems, in the form of unprofitable subsidiaries, on to these parastatals. Hence, by 1986 ADMARC, having inherited many of Press's problems, itself stood in urgent need of a large restructuring operation. In a sense, therefore, the Press package avoided a true and fundamental restructuring of Malawi's corporate and parastatal sector. Such a restructuring would have required extensive share purchases by private sector organisations, including medium and small-scale Malawian enterprises, in addition to the share swapping with public enterprises. The failure to divest to the private sector and to involve domestic partners in Press's ventures now threatens to jeopardise the strengthening of Malawi's entrepreneur class. Given PGL's size, its access to resources, its monopolistic position, the smallness of Malawi's domestic market and the large number of parastatals already operating in this market, the scope for the development of an indigenous private sector remains limited. As the Bank itself has asked: 'Has this commercial and industrial giant been perpetuated to the permanent detriment of local private enterprise and Malawian entrepreneurship?' (World Bank, 1987: 25).

The Bank's general neglect of Malawi's emerging indigenous private sector is a marked feature of the SAL programmes and stands in stark contrast to most of the Bank's adjustment operations elsewhere. Despite the smallness of this sector, it held considerable potential in the area of development of small and medium-scale agro-industrial businesses which could have provided a valuable boost to the attempts to diversify Malawi's narrow export base.

Within the parastatal sector an important restructuring of the Malawi Development Corporation (MDC) occurred under the SAL programme. The objective was to return this wholly government-owned holding company to its original role as a development banking parastatal. During the 1970s, MDC had expanded rapidly, retaining share interests in a wide range of ventures whilst developing an unfavourable debt structure. By the late 1970s losses in a large number of subsidiaries, high interest payments, and weak management confronted MDC with severe financial problems. The SAL-guided restructuring involved the conversion of much of MDC's debt into equity, the selling of a number of subsidiaries, and the swapping of shares with Press and ADMARC, which reduced the number of companies in which MDC held interests from thirty-two to eighteen. The management, planning and budgeting functions of MDC and its subsidiaries were also strengthened.

The immediate impact of MDC's reform was favourable. The Corporation made a post-tax profit of MK6 million in 1984 and MK11 million in 1985, in contrast to the losses incurred in the previous six years.

However, much of this profit resulted from the 'once-off' gains derived from the sale of MK4.8 million of assets and the conversion of MK13 million of government debt into equity. Despite the restructuring and rationalisation of MDC's portfolio and debt, its longer-run prospects remained precarious, with real trading profits falling below MK1 million in 1986 and 1987. MDC continued to hold a controlling interest in eight companies, despite the fact that its policy guidelines prohibited majority shareholdings, and many of these companies continued to face financial losses. As with the restructuring of Press, a major problem confronting the Bank in the reform of MDC was the lack of a dynamic private sector which was needed to facilitate both MDC's divestments and to help MDC develop small and medium-sized net foreign-exchange-earning manufacturing projects in association with the private sector. Hence, although SAL reforms successfully restored MDC's financial viability, further policy efforts are required to stimulate Malawi's dormant private sector if MDC is to successfully fulfil its original mandate of becoming a dynamic, profitable, mixed public-private development bank.

In contrast to the major restructuring operations covering MDC and ADMARC, SAL policy reforms directed at other parastatals were less ambitious, focusing on cost-recovery tariff increases, managerial reorganisation, improved financial monitoring and planning, periodic review of parastatal financial accounts by the Department of Statutory Bodies, and improvements in debt/equity structure. This resulted in improvement in the management and finances of several major parastatals. Others, however, continued to face financial difficulties.

Overall, Bank-guided reforms in Malawi's corporate and parastatal sectors, with the exception of the belated attempt to restructure ADMARC, were relatively successful, particularly in the case of Press and MDC, in that their financial burden in the Government budget was reduced. However, reforms largely took the form of *ad hoc* measures aimed at specific enterprises rather than an attempt to improve the effectiveness of the parastatal sector as a whole and to reduce its role in the economy. Fundamental reforms in terms of scaling-down the activities of Press and the parastatals and improving their efficiency via increased competition required a concomitant strengthening of private sector activity in the Malawian economy. Bank-guided attempts, however, to stimulate such competition in manufacturing and industry were largely unsuccessful.

15.6 TRADE AND INDUSTRIAL REFORMS

Policies directed at the trade and industrial sector were accorded a low priority during the SAL programme. Substantive conditionality in this area took the form of a programme of consumer price decontrol, which was a second tranche release condition of all three SALs.

During the 1970s, government control over consumer prices had intensified. Although formal control existed on over sixty commodities, most of which were important components in low-income household expenditures, and a growing number of items were subject to informal control, with the Ministry of Trade, Industry and Tourism requiring firms 'to consult' prior to price increases. By the late 1970s, most manufacturing output fell within the ambit of the Ministry's formal and informal controls. Such price controls were implemented using a cost-plus criterion, often with extensive delays in the processing of applications. In the inflationary environment of the late 1970s and early 1980s the inflexibility of the system created disincentive effects. Firms switched production away from rigorously controlled essential items, cost-plus pricing undermined incentives to reduce costs, delays in approvals created financial hardships for firms in the face of rising costs, and consumer and producer responses to changing demand and supply conditions were reduced.

Although the Government acknowledged the above problems during the SAL negotiations, there was considerable resistance to the dismantling of a system which had played an integral role in the Government's development strategy. Due to the smallness of the domestic market, low domestic purchasing power, and economies of scale in many of the consumer goods industries, the Government's import-substituting industrialisation (ISI) strategy inevitably intensified the oligopolistic industrial structure inherited from the colonial period. By the early 1980s, 86 per cent of firms were oligopolies and accounted for 91 per cent of total sales (World Bank, 1988a: 5). Hence, Government control of consumer prices was used to protect consumers from oligopolistic exploitation and to contain inflation, and as such was an essential component of the ISI strategy. It was equally essential to the Government's wages and incomes policy, with the restraint of real wages, in turn, playing an important role in Banda's estate expansion strategy. With real wages falling rapidly throughout the 1970s and early 1980s, consumer price control on basic commodities was used to soften the impact on vulnerable groups.

The position was clearly articulated by the Malawi Government in a memorandum to Bank staff on the proposed SAL II measures:

As the Bank pointed out in nearly all reports about Malawi, price and wage restraint have played important roles in restraining inflation, maintaining international competitiveness, providing incentives for employment creation, and moderating the rural-urban income gap and hence the rate of internal migration . . . at present our economy is not so strong that we could recommend a total reduction of subsidies, especially as it would be contrary to our incomes policy.

(Government of Malawi, 1983: 3)

As a result of the Bank's failure to fully appreciate the role played by consumer price control in the Government's overall industrial and agricultural development policy, inappropriate bargaining strategies were used. Arguments focused on the distortive effects and allocative inefficiencies created by the system's inflexibility. Although disincentive effects did exist, the dogmatic 'allocative inefficiency' argument was inappropriate to an economy characterised by oligopoly, where, in accordance with the Theory of the Second Best, *ad hoc* distortion removal had no ready justification in terms of allocative efficiency arguments. In addition, the neo-classical 'rent-seeking' political economy paradigm, so often used in support of the Bank's distortion removal arguments, was not applicable to Malawi. The nature of government intervention in Malawi's industrial sector contrasted to that in many other countries where the Bank was involved with SAL operations. The economy possessed little in the way of production of intermediate goods used as industrial inputs. Consequently, the government was not in the position to license the sale of, and control the price of, high value intermediate goods in a manner which creates high rents, pervasive patron-client networks, and the 'purchasing' of political support within the industrial sectors. Hence, in contrast to a country such as Turkey, Malawi cannot be characterised as a rent-creating and rent-seeking political economy (Krueger, 1974). Rather, the benefits of price control over a range of final consumer goods were thinly spread across a large number of consumers. The political motivation behind such controls was the desire to protect consumers from oligopolistic exploitation, and as such formed an important part of Banda's populist political platform. Clearly, a more effective Bank bargaining strategy would have addressed Banda's populist concern for consumer exploitation and stressed the high budgetary costs of using subsidies to control inflation and labour costs as part of what had patently become an unsustainable development strategy.

Despite the populist resistance to consumer price decontrol, and the economic arguments forwarded by the Ministry of Trade, Industry and Tourism, Bank conditionality prevailed, although in response to government concerns regarding domestic inflation, decontrol occurred gradually. During SAL I, the number of items subject to price control was reduced from over eighty to fifty-six. Significant progress was made under SAL II with the Bank using delay in second tranche disbursement as leverage to effect the decontrol of forty-eight goods. A further four items were decontrolled under SAL III, leaving only four goods subject to formal price controls.

Although there was no blatant reversal of formal price decontrol by the government, a large number of items continued to be subjected to effective informal controls. Bank staff were aware of this violation of the spirit of the agreement, but no attempt was made to follow up on the issue or to systematically study the impact of formal decontrol. This lapse is probably explained by the fact that many of the government's fears were shown to be correct. The availability of some goods increased following price decontrol, but at the cost of a significant increase in the price of items prominent in the cost-of-living index, hence bringing latent inflationary pressures into the open. The problem was intensified by a failure to synchronise price decontrol with reforms to the Government's wages and incomes policy. Nominal public sector wages, for example, remained constant between 1982 and 1985, and real wages in both the public and private sector declined rapidly in the face of inflation.[10]

In addition to the failure to integrate consumer price decontrol with an appropriate wages and incomes policy, there was no attempt to sequence price liberalisation with effective trade liberalisation. Given the oligopolistic structure of domestic industry, any attempt to stimulate efficiency in order to avoid consumer exploitation and inflationary pressures required a concomitant effort to increase competition. Yet the SAL programme did little to encourage more local production or to increase the competitive use of imports, the trade liberalisation issue being entirely ignored throughout SALs I and II.

Under SAL III there was a belated realisation that effective structural reform of Malawi's industrial sector required much more than consumer price decontrol and the restructuring of Press Holdings and parastatals. More was needed, not only to reduce the threat of oligopolistic exploitation following consumer price decontrol, but also because, by 1985, it had become obvious that the viability of the government's ISI strategy required reassessment. Although the economy was free of quantitative trade restrictions, and tariff rates were moderate, the protected manufacturing sector was creating a growing strain on the balance of payments, importing two-thirds of its raw material needs and absorbing 40 per cent of Malawi's export earnings whilst exporting only 3 per cent of its total sales. Hence, there was a need to increase competition from imports, to develop and expand the indigenous private sector, and to foster the growth of agro-industrial export activities.

In 1985, the government agreed, as a condition of SAL III, to review industrial licencing policy in order to reduce entry barriers and to ensure that the foreign exchange allocation mechanism was not used to restrict import competition. In addition, there was agreement to strengthen the Export Promotion Council, to devise an export promotion policy, and to establish an export financing facility. However, progress in these areas was slow, resulting in a delay in the release of the SAL III second tranche. Government reluctance to proceed with some of the measures was partly due to potential conflict with IMF conditionality. Within the context of the growing foreign exchange shortages of 1985 and 1986, and with the need to meet IMF external account targets, the industrial licensing of new entrants became even more restrictive. The Government also started to rely heavily on quantitative import restrictions and on discretionary foreign exchange allocations which restricted the entry of competing imports.

The measures introduced under SAL III to broaden the scope of industrial sector policies beyond price liberalisation were largely unsuccessful, with minimal impact in terms of increased competition and output. Many of the previously neglected problems, however, are now being addressed under a Bank Sectoral Adjustment Loan (SECAL) to Malawi's trade and industrial sector, which became operational in 1988. The SECAL represents a much more integrated approach to policies in the sector than its SAL predecessors. The tariff structure has been rationalised and lowered and foreign exchange allocation mechanisms made more transparent in order to increase competition; the Government's wages and incomes policy is being reviewed in the context of the price and trade liberalisation programme; export promotion policies are being pursued more vigorously; and measures are being devised to provide credit and other forms of support for medium- and small-scale private sector producers, particularly in the area of non-traditional exports.

15.7 PUBLIC SECTOR FINANCE REFORMS

Public sector financial reform received high priority throughout the life of the three SALs, with the public sector targeted to bear most of the disabsorption required to reduce external payments pressures. The SAL programme focused on reducing the budget deficit, whilst at the same time improving the selection of public investments and maintaining adequate recurrent outlays.

A key institutional problem, identified by the Bank, was the Government's inability to co-ordinate development and recurrent expenditure decisions. Prior to the SAL activities, the Government possessed no formal Public Sector Investment Programme (PSIP) under which projects were prioritised according to resource availability, developmental objectives, and recurrent cost implications. As a highly-aid-dependent country, most development projects were donor funded, with control over capital outlays determined by sectoral ministries and parastatals, each attempting to obtain as much donor financing as possible. Recurrent expenditures, however, were controlled by the Ministry of Finance, which lacked the ability to estimate the recurrent expenditure requirements of projects. The Ministry's main objective was to minimise outlays in order to achieve a surplus on the recurrent budget. Such a surplus was regarded as a measure of economic viability by the President — largely because it had enabled the elimination of UK grants-in-aid to the current budget during the mid-1970s.

As a result of the above system, capital expenditure growth had outstripped recurrent expenditure growth, in a manner detrimental to the productivity of public sector investments. In response to this problem, SAL conditionality included a stipulation that the Government prepare a three-year rolling PSIP to be reviewed and approved by the Bank. The Government's preparation of the PSIP progressively improved under the SALs, resulting in the use of revenue and expenditure projections, greater selectivity in acceptance of donor finance, and improved allocations of capital expenditures. Shares to agriculture, health and education were maintained, whilst allocations to the programme of building presidential residences, defence installations and government buildings were reduced. Delay in the release in the second tranche of SAL II was effectively used to bring about reduced expenditures on the presidential palaces and to create a separate account to monitor such outlays.

The problem of recurrent expenditure underfunding was addressed under the SALs by government commitment to achieve real growth in recurrent expenditures in key economic and social sectors between 1981 and 1986. Particular emphasis was placed on the agricultural sector, with SAL I containing a specific condition that an extra MK2.8 million be allocated to this sector in the 1981–2 budget. During the SAL period, the overall pattern of government expenditure shifted away from capital expenditure in favour of recurrent expenditure, with recurrent outlays to agriculture doubling between 1979 and 1984–5, and with outlays to transport, education and health increasing. However, much of the increase in recurrent expenditures was due to the growing burden of debt servicing, and despite higher allocations to key sectors, there remained evidence of substantial underfunding (World Bank, 1988b).

SAL measures to reduce the overall budget deficit focused on both reducing expenditures and increasing revenues. Expenditure reduction under SALs I and II was successfully implemented. Between 1980 and 1984 real expenditure net of debt service fell by 27 per cent, and cuts had occurred whilst maintaining expenditure levels in the priority economic and social sectors. Attempts to increase government revenue under the SAL programme occurred through a series of *ad hoc* tax increases combined with measures to improve cost recovery. The result was an increase in central government revenue which, net of grants, increased from MK187 million in 1979–80 to MK465.1 million in 1985–6. Despite this impressive performance, revenue increases failed to keep pace with the sharp rise in government expenditure which occurred under SAL III. Between 1984 and 1986, expenditures increased from MK294 million to MK358 million such that 1986 witnessed a sharp rise in the budget deficit. Much of the deficit increase can be attributed to exogenous factors, namely the impact of the Mozambiquan civil war in the form of a rapid escalation in external transport costs and the influx of over 700,000 refugees, and the impact of debt-servicing obligations. Nevertheless, after three SALs, the central structural problem of a high budget deficit remained unsolved.

The disappointing impact of SAL reforms on the budget deficit cannot be attributed solely to exogenous factors. Part of the problem arose from weaknesses in the Bank's policy prescriptions, particularly under SALs I and II. The Bank's desire to reduce the overall deficit, whilst increasing recurrent expenditures in key sectors implied a cut-back in capital expenditures and/or a sharp increase in revenue. Given the structure of the Malawian economy, neither requirement could be fulfilled to the extent needed to achieve these dual objectives. The SAL programme expected the central government deficit to be sharply reduced. During the same period, however, recurrent expenditures increased by 50.3 per cent as a result of the need to meet Bank conditions on recurrent allocations and as a result of exogenous factors. A sharp compensating cut-back in development expenditure was therefore required, with outlays falling from MK167 million in 1980 to MK86 million in 1983. However, given the importance of public sector investment to the country's capital formation, this level of reduction could not be sustained without severely jeopardising future growth prospects. Consequently, in 1984 and 1985, government capital expenditures were permitted to increase.

Given the limitations on the extent to which capital expenditures could be continuously cut, the SAL programme was forced to place excessive emphasis on revenue-increasing measures. Although *ad hoc* tax increases were successfully implemented under SALs I and II, other cost recovery measures were less successful. There was considerable delay in the implementation of parastatal tariff increases, and the Bank encountered strong and successful resistance to its attempts to greatly increase user charges in housing, health, and education, the latter proposal representing a sudden reversal of the policy stance adopted by Bank staff during the 1970s.

In retrospect, it is clear that Bank expectations regarding government revenue increases were excessively optimistic. The structure of the Malawi economy limited the extent to which the growth rate of public revenue could be continually increased. Given the Government's wages and incomes policy, sharp increases in parastatal tariffs and social sector user charges threatened to restrict access amongst large numbers of the population, and, given the low base levels of many tariffs and charges, had only minimal revenue-raising capacity. Reliance on *ad hoc* tax increases also created problems. The recessionary economic environment of the 1980s led to declining receipts from company taxation and import duties, despite increases in duty rates. Hence, most of the burden of extra taxation fell on consumers and income-earners at a time of high inflation and declining real wages. This undoubtedly created disincentive effects which counteracted the Bank's attempts to provide incentives to stimulate smallholder cash-crop production and lowered savings and investment levels. In addition, the *ad hoc* nature of tax reforms intensified the complex and distortive structure of Malawi's tax system.

In response to problems created by some of the public sector finance reforms undertaken during the first two SALs, SAL III incorporated several new policy thrusts. In March 1985 a Bank-supported tax study was launched. The study recommended: a broadening of the tax base and a reduction of rates in order to increase the buoyancy of the system; shift of taxes from external trade to domestic transactions and from production to consumption; and increased taxes on domestic manufacturers and elimination of taxes on intermediate goods in order to remove protective elements of taxation. The government maintained a co-operative stance on the tax reform issue, and steps to improve the system were initiated in the 1986–7 budget.

SAL III also included more concerted efforts to improve expenditure planning and budgeting, following the Bank's belated realisation that 'quick fix' revenue raising measures and reductions in development expenditures were not viable solutions to the budget deficit problem. The Bank recommended the gradual introduction of a new approach to budgeting, designed to give the budget a more programmatic content and to achieve optimal resource allocation. Expenditures were to be tabulated under designated programme headings, with recurrent cost implications of development expenditures clearly itemised. A new unit was created in the Office of President and Cabinet and was made responsible for public investment screening, investment co-ordination, and intersectoral policy analysis. The Ministry of Finance's external debt monitoring unit was also strengthened in an attempt to improve the capacity to develop an external borrowing strategy and to achieve the targeted 20 per cent debt service ratio. It was hoped that this would enable an eventual reduction in recurrent outlays on debt servicing.

The approach to public sector finances adopted under SAL III and the subsequent tripartite Bank/IMF/Government Policy Framework Paper of 1986 stood in marked contrast to the approach under SALs I and II. The early years of the adjustment programme had emphasised revenue increases and cut-backs in development expenditures in order to reduce the overall deficit whilst permitting increases in recurrent outlays. From SAL III onwards, revenue increases were accorded less priority in acknowledgement of the economy's limited tax base and the problems of sharply increasing parastatal tariffs and social sector user charges. Development expenditures were now targeted for *increase*, reflecting the realisation that further cuts would threaten long-term growth prospects. Hence, it was now recurrent expenditure reductions which were to bear the brunt of bringing about a reduction in the overall deficit.

The new approach represented a much more viable strategy, which attempted to ensure that the need for short-term stabilisation of the government deficit did not conflict with the growth objective through the disincentive effects of high tax and tariff rates and declining public sector investment. Undoubtedly, the use of the tripartite Policy Framework Paper contributed to this improved co-ordination between IMF stabilisation policies and the Bank's adjustment for growth policies. The long delay in the adoption of this improved strategy, however, gave rise to difficulties. From 1986 onwards, recurrent expenditures were under considerable strain due to a number of exogenous factors – an increase in the cost of debt service, transport disruptions, refugee influx, and the need to import maize. As a result, the government was unable to achieve targeted budget deficit reduction through recurrent expenditure cut-backs and the Fund's ESAF and Stand-by facilities proposed for 1986 could not be activated.

Two questions arise from the above analysis. First, why did it take so long for Bank staff to accept that reliance on revenue increases and on development expenditure reduction did not represent a viable strategy for achieving the dual objectives of reducing the budget deficit and stimulating economic growth? Second, what was required in order to bring about the much-needed reduction in recurrent expenditures? The two answers are closely related. Significant cut-backs in the current budget required a highly critical review of recurrent expenditures in order to identify those items which were not providing priority social services and which were failing to effectively support production. The obvious implication was the need to assess recurrent expenditure commitments created by donor-funded investment projects. The bulk of Malawi's development expenditure account consisted of projects which attracted donor funding and the ready availability of donor finance during the 1970s and early 1980s had given rise to high recurrent expenditure commitments in a large number of government agencies and departments. This was particularly so from the mid-1980s onwards, when many projects came to the end of their period of donor-supported development account funding. The Bank's unwillingness to tackle the issue of recurrent expenditure reductions in the early years of the SAL programme resulted from a reluctance to critically appraise its own past project-lending activities in Malawi. The Bank's failure to integrate its roles as a project donor and a programme aid donor in Malawi was a major oversight, and gave rise to a situation whereby: '. . . the Bank's attitude to spending commitments may have been shaped by its past and continuing project lending' (Kydd and Hewitt, 1986b: 362).

Lack of integration between the Bank's two roles was also closely related to the Bank's failure to adopt a fundamental programme of structural reform within Malawi's agricultural sector. A prime candidate for recurrent cost scrutiny was the massive National Rural Development Plan. The Plan, in which the Bank had been the lead donor, absorbed considerable recurrent expenditures. Yet there was growing evidence that, like its Integrated Rural Development Plan predecessors, the high cost NRDP was not resulting in a significant impact on smallholder production (Kydd and Hewitt, 1984: 150–8). A major weakness of the NRDP was the fact

248

that it continued to be implemented within the context of a perpetuation of a colonial pattern of agricultural production biased against smallholders. In addition, the sole SAL policies aimed at redressing the bias, namely export parity pricing for smallholder non-food crops, further jeopardised the NRDP's attempts to achieve the essential increase in maize productivity.

Despite the shortcomings of the NRDP, the Bank refused until 1987 to conduct a comprehensive analysis of the costs and effects of the Plan with a view to scaling-down recurrent expenditures. Indeed, under SALs I and II, the reverse occurred, with the Bank insisting on *increased* recurrent expenditure allocations to the agricultural sector, including the specific condition of an extra MK2.8 million allocation under SAL I.[11] In retrospect, the Bank has acknowledged the inappropriateness of this prescription:

> The Bank seemed to suggest that this be an additional expenditure . . . without identifying equivalent savings, possibly in the form of waste and extravagance which could have been excised. In the eyes of Malawi officials, this condition was no more than a safeguard devised by Bank agricultural projects staff to ensure the full counterpart funding of on-going Bank financed project activity.
>
> (World Bank, 1987: 11)

Fundamental structural adjustment within Malawi's agricultural sector would have assisted in tackling the budget deficit problem not only through a critical review of the NRDP's recurrent costs, but also through a release of the considerable untapped tax potential within the estate sector. Given the lack of a mineral sector and a developed manufacturing sector Malawi's tax base was extremely limited, and by 1980 the modern sector was already heavily taxed. Taxation on estates, by contrast, was negligible. There was no export or land tax imposed on estates, land rentals were charged at a low flat rate of MK1 per acre in 1980, rising to MK3 in 1983, and the government was lax in the collection of corporate taxes from this sector. A SAL effort to increase estate taxation would have produced doubly beneficial results. First, government revenue increases could have been achieved without excessive reliance on distortive and disincentive-producing *ad hoc* increases in import duties, taxes on intermediate inputs and on personal income. Second, estate taxation policies were a potentially important instrument in the bringing about of a much needed change in the pattern of agricultural production – required to tackle the problems of suppressed smallholder production capacity.

Following the disappointing fiscal impact of the three Structural Adjustment Loans, and the problems encountered in implementing the measures contained within the 1986 Policy Framework Paper, the Bank has in recent years taken initial steps to rectify some of the shortcomings of its previous fiscal policy prescriptions. In 1987 a major Bank review of the

NRDP was launched with a view to isolating the reasons for its disappointing results and identifying cost reduction measures. This forms part of a more thorough and critical review of public expenditure priorities by the Bank, Fund and government. Initial moves have also been made to increase the tax burden on the estate sector. The 1985–6 budget included a 10 per cent levy on tea and tobacco exports, a 35 per cent increase in land rent, and an acceleration of the payment of corporate taxes in all sectors including the estates. This estate taxation policy is likely to be intensified under the proposed 1990 agricultural SECAL which will incorporate, for the first time, significant Bank non-price measures to adjust Malawi's structure of agricultural production in favour of smallholders. The Bank is also placing pressure on other donors to increase the flexibility of their project finance systems in order that finance can be made available to cover, not only project investment costs, but also the Government's recurrent expenditure needs, particularly in the social services sector.

As in other areas of policy reform, SAL policies aimed at public sector finances achieved important institutional improvements. Formulation of the PSIP and the system of budget preparation were greatly improved; a system for monitoring public debt was created; monitoring and planning of parastatal finances improved; and reform of the tax system was initiated, albeit belatedly. In addition, the provision of SAL financial resources helped to alleviate pressure on the government's development programme and recurrent spending. The shift away from project lending towards programme lending also enabled donor funds to be used more flexibly to help maintain recurrent outlays rather than to solely finance new investments. However, in the absence of close co-ordination between the Bank's programme and project-lending activities, and an associated fundamental structural reform of Malawi's key agricultural sector, such institutional reforms and the provision of SAL finance were unable to bring about any significant improvement in the public sector budget deficit.

15.8 COMPLIANCE WITH SAL CONDITIONALITY

Compared to many other SAL recipients, Malawi Government compliance with SAL conditionality was generally high in most areas of policy reform. The exception was the direct violation of policy prescriptions for smallholder agricultural pricing under SAL I and in the latter stages of SAL III, although under SAL II the Government did implement the Bank's desired agricultural pricing reforms despite continued opposition from the Ministry of Agriculture.

Satisfactory compliance was facilitated by the highly-centralised nature of the political system and by the structure of the country's political economy. The lack of organised and politically influential interest groups (with the exception of those within the estate sector which was in any case neglected under the SAL programme) and the concentration of power in the President simplified the Bank's policy bargaining task. The main need was to convince Banda and his advisers of the desirability of the proposed reforms. In addition, Banda's power was vested not only in his ultimate decision-making authority, but also in his prominence in terms of ownership of the means of production: 'Malawi does not even have autonomous capitalist interests which can assert themselves independently of Banda. Banda himself is the premier monopoly capitalist' (Mhone, 1987: 79). Hence, there was a sense in which many of the SAL reforms, such as the restructuring of Press, ADMARC and MDC, and price changes, were akin to the reform of a giant corporate enterprise requiring only the approval of the Corporation's chairman. The high level of commitment found in Malawi was, therefore:

> a commitment of an extraordinary kind which did not require consensus building of the nature normally encountered . . . it is sufficient in Malawi if they [reforms] are pragmatic and are presented convincingly enough so as to appeal to and obtain the consent of the Life President. It is almost inconceivable that implementation failure would stem from resistance from affected parties.
>
> (World Bank, 1987: 24)

The Bank rapidly learnt of the essential need to win Banda's support for proposed reforms and of his willingness to contemptuously override agreements reached between civil servants and international agencies. The early days of the first SAL had provided clear evidence in the form of Banda's violation of smallholder price-policy agreements. Following this episode, Bank staff were acutely aware of the need to appease Banda and put this awareness to good use in the bargaining strategies adopted, and the compromises reached, over such delicate issues as the reform of Press Holdings and cut-backs in expenditures on Presidential residences.

The fact that Malawi was not a typical sub-Saharan rent-creating and rent-seeking political economy also assisted the implementation of what, in many other countries, would have been politically controversial and risky reforms. The fact that parastatals, Press Holdings, and government price interventions were not used to create rents and economic patronage helps explain why Banda acquiesced to reforms in these areas without fear of loss of political support from economic rent receivers. The suppression of trade unions and the smallholder population also meant that reforms in the areas of wages and incomes policies and smallholder agriculture primarily required presidential approval rather than consensus building amongst affected parties.

It is ironic, however, that one of the effects of the SAL programme was to slightly modify and improve the parameters of the country's decision-making process in a manner which complicated the Bank's bargaining strategies. Prior to the Bank and IMF's programme aid activities in Malawi, macro-policy decisions were taken by Banda on a largely intuitive basis with neither Banda nor civil servants possessing the analytical capacity to trace the *ex ante* consequences of these decisions (Giles, 1979). In addition, civil servants were reluctant to suggest policies which conflicted with Banda's preconceptions or to convey 'bad news' to the President. This had the effect of delaying and limiting policy responses to emerging problems, the case of Press Holdings and the presentation of fictitious surpluses on the Government's current account in the late 1970s being classic examples (Gulhati, 1989: 35). Hence, the advantages of a centralised decision-making system, in the form of the ability to make quick decisions without the need to compromise with competing power groups, was offset by disadvantages in the form of the failure to report and correct adverse policy consequences and the lack of stimulative competition of ideas.

The Bank's SAL programme and IMF activities played an important part in reducing the above problems. Both agencies played a galvanising role in the evolution of Malawian policy. Many of the institutional and macro-planning reforms implemented under the SAL programme helped civil servants and technocrats to define and analyse alternative policy options and provided them with confidence, along with donor backing, in the presentation of such policies to the President. However, this decentralisation and internalisation of the SAL policy-formulation process strengthened the bargaining position of the civil service not only in relation to the President, but also in relation to the Bank itself, such that the Government's ability to confront the Bank and to shape its own adjustment programme progressively increased. During SAL II, for example, the Government successfully resisted Bank proposals to significantly increase health and education user charges, comprehensively presenting their case in terms of the minimal anticipated economic impact and the adverse social consequences. During the SAL III appraisal, all ministries drafted comprehensive reviews and critiques of the relevant policy proposals which were used by the Ministry of Finance in negotiations with the Bank. The policy internalisation process was particularly effective in the case of the Ministry of Agriculture, which, in contrast to the Ministry of Trade and Industry, was strong and vocal having benefited greatly from manpower strengthening under the SAL programme. As a result, during SAL III this ministry was able to win support from both the front-line ministries and the President for its views against continuation of SAL pricing policies in the smallholder agricultural sector. The upshot was the Government's complete abandonment of such policies in direct violation of SAL conditionality. Increased government confidence and a greater appreciation of the margin within which bargaining could occur was also evidenced by the preparation of a comprehensive Special Studies Document on the proposed fourth SAL which represented the government's equivalent of the Bank's President's Report and which clearly outlined the types of adjustment policies which the government *itself* wished to see implemented (Government of Malawi, 1987a).

Despite the high level of political commitment to most SAL reforms, the Bank nevertheless encountered implementation difficulties. These often arose because implementing ministries did not fully appreciate, and were not fully prepared for, the reform implications of agreements reached with the Bank by front-line ministries. Three factors greatly assisted the Bank in overcoming these implementation difficulties and in overcoming problems caused by political resistance to such reforms as agricultural price changes: the major role played by Bank programme aid finance in the Malawian economy; extensive cross-conditionality between the SAL programme and IMF and bilateral programmes; and the Bank's highly effective use of delays in second tranche disbursement as a leverage mechanism.

During 1981–5, the period of the SAL programme, Overseas Development Assistance (ODA) flows to Malawi declined sharply and non-commercial loans and suppliers' credits dried up completely (Table 15.4). As a result the country became increasingly reliant on a narrow range of donors both to support the balance-of-payments financing gap and to enable debt-servicing obligations to be fulfilled. Most notable amongst these donors were the Bank and IMF (Table 15.4). Consequently, by 1986, 54 per cent of publicly-guaranteed long-term debt outstanding and disbursed was owed to the Bank Group. The position did not substantially change until 1986, when a donor Round Table Group successfully elicited substantial new aid pledges, many of which took the form of support for Malawi's continued adjustment efforts.

Table 15.4 Gross aid commitments and commercial transfers to Malawi, 1981–6 (million US $)

	1980	1981	1982	1983	1984	1985	1986
World Bank Group	14	115	11	55	99	127	25
IMF	36	38	12	36	38	23	0
Bilateral ODA	105	105	96	85	75	78	193
Bilateral other	29	7	n.a.	13	n.a.	8	67
Commercial banks	22	33	9	n.a.	3	3	0
Suppliers' credits	23	2	1	n.a.	3	2	0
Total	229	300	129	189	218	241	285
Bank and IMF as % of Total	21.8	51.0	17.8	48.1	62.8	62.2	8.8

Source: Gulhati (1989) Table 7.

At the same time as Malawi was becoming more dependent on a narrow range of donors (the Bank; IMF; EEC; UK; West Germany; and in the latter years USAID) many of these donors were increasingly shifting their aid priorities in the direction of supporting the Bank's adjustment programme. This occurred through increased bilateral provision of programme aid, such as the US $44 million in bilateral support to SAL III from USAID, Germany, and Japan, and also through the overlapping of SAL conditions with conditions attached to bilateral funded projects. The most important example of the latter was the attaching of fertiliser subsidy removal conditions to the USAID/IFAD Smallholder Fertiliser Project such that this project became an integral part of the Bank's adjustment programme.

Cross-conditionality was intensified by the close co-ordination between the Bank's SALs and the various IMF stabilisation programmes. The Fund's second two-year Stand-by covering 1980–1 to 1981–2 coincided almost exactly with implementation of the first SAL, and the Fund's Extended Fund Facility, which commenced in late 1983, coincided with the implementation of SAL II. During the 1980s, the Fund became increasingly aware that structural issues and reforms were essential to the sustained success of stabilisation in low-income countries, hence giving rise to the greater use of Extended Fund Facilities (EFFs), Structural Adjustment Facilities (SAFs) and the tripartite Policy Framework Paper (PFP) approach. The Fund's more medium-term structural approach to stabilisation was put into practice in Malawi, and this led to close collaboration with the Bank. As a result, many key conditions of the SAL programme, such as smallholder producer pricing, input subsidy removal, the restructuring of Press and ADMARC, and government expenditure allocations were also regarded as essential to the success of the Fund's programmes.

The fact that SAL conditions were also conditions of Fund programmes and of bilateral programme and project aid, greatly assisted the Bank's leverage in Malawi. This was particularly so in the case of agricultural pricing conditions, especially the controversial fertiliser subsidy removal condition. During negotiations with the Government, the Bank consistently pointed out that the Ministry of Agriculture's desire to breach these conditions would violate, not only the SAL agreements, but also the requirements of IMF and USAID programmes. This combined weight of the Bank, IMF, and USAID helps to explain why it took the Ministry of Agriculture over six years to convince front-line ministries, as well as many Bank staff, of the desirability of abandoning agricultural pricing conditions.

The government's high level of dependence on Bank finance and extensive cross-conditionality was supported by the Bank's effective use of appraisal missions and tranche delays in order to enforce compliance. The mid-term appraisal of each SAL was comprehensive and rigorous. The missions identified areas in which the reform programme had fallen behind schedule, and drew up a detailed list of measures which were required before the second tranche could be disbursed, with a strict timetable appended to the list. Under all three SALs, second tranche release was delayed by five to six months to ensure that the Government complied with the missions' stipulations and where necessary, additional technical assistance was provided to assist the Government.

The above general factors influencing compliance, namely, the nature of the political regime; the role played by Bank finance; the use of cross-conditionality; and the use of tranche delay, interacted with changes in the external economic environment to determine the tightness of conditions and the level of compliance under each of the three SALs. Under SAL I, compliance was fairly low, with the authorities and Banda showing little urgency to implement reform. The government, experiencing SAL-type conditionality for the first time, was unable to anticipate the Bank's willingness to take punitive measures in the form of tranche delays having been able to successfully ignore the macro-policy suggestions forwarded by the Bank during the 1970s. In addition, 1981 witnessed a peak in ODA commitments (Table 15.4) such that the Government could not yet anticipate the increased reliance on Bank finance which was to materialise from 1982 onwards. For its part, the Bank was yet to fully appreciate the importance of securing direct Presidential approval for reform proposals.

SAL II was characterised by much higher conditionality and higher compliance: Press was restructured; Bank agricultural price policies were implemented; and consumer price decontrol took place at a rapid pace. By this time, the Government had experienced Bank willingness to delay the disbursement of the SAL I second tranche, as well as the suspension of two IMF Stand-bys. Given the increased reliance on both Bank and Fund finance the Government was anxious not to jeopardise either the SAL II loan agreement or the recently agreed IMF Extended Fund Facility. In addition, a range of external factors facilitated implementation, namely, improvements in the terms of trade and the ability to export maize to neighbouring countries, which greatly improved ADMARC's financial position. These external factors resulted in a significant economic recovery between 1982 and 1984 in terms of both export and GDP growth rates, which undoubtedly improved the Government's willingness and ability to intensify adjustment reform efforts. Implementation was also assisted by the Bank's new realisation of the need to enlist Presidential approval for SAL conditions.

SAL III represented a return to a situation of relatively mild conditionality and less satisfactory government compliance. Informal control of consumer prices intensified, exchange allocations were increasingly used to restrict imports, Press, ADMARC and MDC divestments slowed down, and in 1987 the government completely violated agricultural price conditionality. By this time, the government had become adept at formulating, and tracing the macro-impact, of its own desired policies, particularly in the area of smallholder agriculture. In addition, 1986 witnessed a major increase in bilateral aid pledges, so reducing the government's dependence on Bank and IMF finance. This was important in the case of the fertiliser subsidy issue. By 1986 the Government had secured significant bilateral support for the Smallholder Fertiliser Project in the form of grant-aid fertiliser from the EEC, Canada, West Germany and Japan, and many of these donors were themselves expressing disquiet over the adverse impact of subsidy removal. Hence, the government was able and willing to abandon the programme despite the resulting loss of USAID support to the project which had been provided as a bilateral component of SAL III. A range of adverse exogenous factors also reduced the government's ability and willingness to comply with SAL III conditions: declining terms of trade; drought; external transport disruption; and the influx of refugees. The resulting poor economic performance was compounded by the negative impact of the earlier cut-backs in investment and imports implemented under Bank and IMF programmes.

The role played by exogenous factors throughout the SAL period raises important questions regarding the appropriateness and flexibility of both Bank and IMF programmes in Malawi. Time and again reform objectives were frustrated by unexpected exogenous shocks. Under both SALs I and III rising interest rates and fuel prices, cyclical swings in export prices of tea, tobacco and sugar, poor weather, and transport disruptions, led to a serious deterioration in the government's budgetary position and the balance of payments.

Under such circumstances, one must question the Bank's rigorous use of tranche disbursement delays to enforce pre-existing agreements on conditionality. In certain important policy areas the changing external environment was such that these enforced conditions were no longer appropriate – for example, fertiliser subsidy removal at a time of escalating fertiliser costs caused by intensification of transport disruptions, suppressing the maize price in times of drought, liberalising consumer prices at a time when the government was forced to restrict competing imports due to balance-of-payments pressures, and liberalising agricultural marketing at a time when ADMARC was unable to defend ceiling consumer maize prices due to maize shortages caused by drought and refugees. A similar criticism can be levelled against the Fund's strict use of performance targets in the face of an unpredictable and rapidly changing external environment. The Fund's attempts to achieve stabilisation through cuts in the real volume of government expenditure were consistently frustrated, and government outlays as a proportion of GDP increased. This largely resulted from a tension between macro-fiscal targets and micro- and sector-level expenditure requirements, with the latter continually requiring revision due to unexpected exogenous shocks which necessitated increased outlays on transport, on maize imports, on debt servicing, and on feeding refugees. The problems created by lack of Fund flexibility have been succinctly summarised by Gulhati:

> How useful in this context were the very precise, time-bound targets adopted by the government and the IMF? Given the uncertainties Malawi faced and the lack of sufficient reserves, the need to adhere to these targets imposed an unnecessary rigidity in macro-economic management. Also, these macro-targets likely overestimated the speed with which public outlays could be adjusted.
>
> (Gulhati, 1989: 59–60)

As a result of this rigidity on the part of both the Fund and Bank, several categories of public recurrent expenditure that were essential for efficient use of the existing stock of public capital remained suboptimal, and public investment remained at a low level (7.9 per cent of GDP in 1984–6 compared to 13.1 per cent in 1977–80). The upshot was a sacrifice of long-term development and growth in order to obtain performance targets and conditions.

Several commentators, such as Gulhati, have suggested that, in view of the extremely hostile environment, Malawi's undertaking of SAL reforms represented an 'heroic endeavour' with the inability to perform a 'policy miracle' being regrettable but understandable. Although it is true that the Bank expected a policy miracle, this was not so much because heroic efforts were expected in the face of adverse external circumstances, but rather because the heroic and fundamental structural reforms which the changing external environment of the 1980s demanded were not tackled under the SAL programme. The regret is that neither the Bank nor the Fund fully utilised the breathing space provided by SAL and IMF finance to devise a deep-cutting reform programme. Instead, the colonial agricultural system remained largely unchallenged, as did the ISI strategy and the monopolistic dominance of parastatals and Press Holdings. Most commentators have also stressed the receptive policy environment and the lack of ideological conflict between the Bank and Government (Gulhati, 1989; Harvey, 1983; Kydd, 1987; Kydd and Hewitt, 1984, 1986a, 1986b). They omit, however, the fact that this lack of conflict occurred, not because Malawi epitomised a market-orientated non-distorted economy, but because the Bank's adjustment programme did not understand, address, or challenge in any significant way, the structure of the pre-SAL economy. In the Bank's own words:

> The economic crisis highlighted the need for addressing mainly *institutional* issues relating to economic and parastatal sector

management and the need to *improve incentives* for growth and diversification. No truly serious distortions had been highlighted during sector work or during preparation of the SALs.

(World Bank, 1987: 41)

This then was the source of both the Bank's success and failure in Malawi – success in that Malawi, in comparison to many other SAL countries, was a compliant and co-operative recipient; failure in that the resulting *ad hoc* reform programme produced an insignificant impact on overall economic performance.

15.9 ECONOMIC IMPACT OF THE STRUCTURAL ADJUSTMENT PROGRAMME

The SAL programme in Malawi produced a varied outcome in terms of sustained positive impact on key macroeconomic indicators. A slight improvement in government revenue as a percentage of GDP was sustained throughout the programme, along with a significant improvement in the balance-of-payments current account deficit. This was offset by a failure to permanently reduce the Government budget deficit, by a sharp decline in GDP and export growth rates towards the end of the SAL period and by a chronic deterioration in investment levels and the debt service ratio (Table 15.5). This somewhat disappointing outcome was the combined result of the economy's exposure to exogenous shocks, the programme's failure to address the fundamental structural weaknesses of the economy, and the adverse impact of certain SAL measures such as agricultural pricing-policy reforms.

Following the recessionary years of 1980 and 1981, the period of SAL I and II, 1982–4, produced signs of a mild economic recovery. By 1984, the GDP growth rate had reached 4.4 per cent compared to −5.2 per cent in 1981. This was matched by an impressive increase in exports, the growth rate of which increased from −13.3 per cent in 1982 to 23.2 per cent in 1984, and, in conjunction with declining import levels, this resulted in a reduction in the balance-of-payments current account deficit from −24.3 per cent of GDP in 1980 to −1.4 per cent of GDP in 1984. There was also a moderate improvement in fiscal performance. In terms of GDP percentages, government revenue increased and expenditures fell, resulting in an improvement in the central government deficit from −13.9 per cent of GDP in 1980 to −8.8 per cent of GDP in 1984.

How much of the 1982–4 recovery, however, can be ascribed to the SAL programme? Much of the GDP growth rate recovery resulted from domestic policy initiatives which were independent of the SAL programme. 1981 and 1982 witnessed an upturn in the performance of estate agriculture which made an important contribution to GDP growth rates. This improved estate performance resulted from the Government's own

Table 15.5 Key macroeconomic indicators, 1980–6

	1980	1981	1982	1983	1984	1985	1986
GDP growth rate at 1978 factor cost of which:	−0.4	−5.2	2.7	3.6	4.4	4.3	−0.3
agriculture total	−6.5	−8.1	6.4	4.4	5.4	1.1	0.1
smallholders	−8.5	−8.9	2.5	3.7	7.2	1.2	0.4
estates	3.3	4.9	22.4	7.1	0.8	0.6	−1.1
manufacturing	0.3	3.6	−0.3	7.1	2.4	0.5	5.3
Central government revenue as % of GDP	18.9	20.0	19.6	19.9	20.7	21.9	21.4
Central government expenditure as % of GDP	34.3	35.6	32.2	30.1	29.5	31.8	34.6
Central government deficit as % of GDP	−13.9	−15.6	−12.5	−10.2	−8.8	−10.0	−13.2
Exports	21.6	0.5	−13.3	2.8	23.2	−19.3	−2.6
Imports	9.1	−19.6	−11.8	−0.9	−11.5	1.0	−0.1
Balance-of-payments current account deficit as % of GDP	−24.3	−15.5	−12.6	−11.8	−1.4	−8.2	−6.9
Debt service ratio	21.9	n.a.	23.3	21.5	21.4	29.5	40.1
Gross domestic investment as % of GDP	24.5	17.7	21.5	22.8	13.9	17.9	10.1

Source: Government of Malawi, 'Economic Report, 1987'.

solution to the financial and managerial problems facing a large number of tobacco estates in the late 1970s. Instead of allowing politicians' estates to go into receivership, or writing off their debts to the banks, Agricultural Advisory Units were set up in the two commercial banks. These units took over management of the estates, and although ownership legally remained with Banda's entourage of politicians they were effectively denied any further managerial role and were excluded from financial gains. The adoption of this 'state-led' farming model, along with a recovery in tobacco prices, accounts for improved performance in a sector largely ignored by the SAL policies.

A second essentially *domestic* supply-side initiative was the sharp increase in the 1980 and 1981 maize producer price, implemented by the Government in direct violation of SAL I conditionality. This was a major factor in the recovery of growth rates in the smallholder sector. In addition, the resulting income gains amongst smallholders widened the market for basic consumer goods and led to considerable buoyancy in the import-substituting manufacturing sector. The upshot was marked improvement in the growth rate of both the smallholder and manufacturing sectors (Table 15.5).

The economic recovery of 1982–4 was further assisted by exogenous factors which were unrelated to the SAL programme. The domestic initiatives in the estate sector were facilitated by a recovery in tobacco prices, whilst drought in neighbouring countries enabled much of the build-up in ADMARC's maize stocks, resulting from the producer price increase, to be profitably exported. These exogenous factors were largely responsible for the recovery in export growth rates and the sharp reduction in the balance-of-payments current account deficit.

SAL policies, in conjunction with IMF measures, did however play an important role in the improved fiscal performance of 1982–4. The series of *ad hoc* tax increases, combined with parastatal tariff increases, boosted government revenue, whilst Bank review of the PSIP and SAL-guided improvements in budget preparation reduced government expenditures. Expenditure restraint was further assisted by a series of debt rescheduling agreements made possible by increased creditor confidence in an economy undertaking both Bank and IMF reform programmes. Consequently, by 1984, the central government deficit had reached a satisfactory −8.8 per cent of GDP.

In summary, the economic recovery of 1982–4 was brought about by domestically-initiated supply-side reforms, favourable exogenous factors, and Bank and IMF measures which aimed to rapidly stabilise fiscal performance. Following 1984, however, these circumstances were not sustainable and the recovery stalled. By 1986, the GDP growth rate had fallen to −0.3 per cent and per capita GDP was 11 per cent lower than its historic high point of 1979. The major cause of the GDP growth rate decline was a sharp fall in both smallholder and estate output (Table 15.5). At the same time, the Government budget deficit again increased, and by 1986 stood at almost the same level as it had done in 1980. The balance-of-payments current account deficit also increased, reaching −8.2 per cent of GDP in 1985 and −6.9 per cent in 1986.

Under the tighter conditionality of SAL II, the Government was no longer able to continue with its own smallholder pricing policies. Instead, a sharp increase in the producer price of smallholder export crops was announced. This temporarily maintained the buoyancy of the sector and contributed to export earnings. However, the impact of the simultaneous SAL policies of suppressing the maize producer price and input subsidy removal, along with the failure to synchronise these policies with project aid, gave rise to a rapid deterioration in smallholder performance. By 1986, the growth rate of smallholder output had stagnated at 0.4 per cent. The adverse impact of SAL agricultural pricing policies was felt, not only in terms of the sector's contribution to the decline in the GDP growth rate, but also in terms of the post-1986 adverse impact on the balance of payments in the form of the need for massive levels of maize imports.

By 1985, Bank and Fund measures which had successfully achieved rapid fiscal stabilisation had begun to produce negative effects which rendered the earlier growth rate recovery unsustainable. The 'quick-fix' *ad hoc* tax increase measures were beginning to produce disincentive effects and the reduction in government expenditures had occurred through cut-backs in development expenditures. In conjunction with the IMF's credit ceilings, this had resulted in a dramatic decline in overall investment levels, with investment as a percentage of GDP falling to 10.1 per cent in 1986 compared to 24.5 per cent in 1980. In addition, part of the balance-of-payments improvement had been achieved through forced reductions in imports, with a negative import growth rate registered throughout most of the SAL period (Table 15.5). The impact of tax increases and investment and import reductions was clearly felt through a renewed decline in GDP growth rates, and a reduced capacity to diversify the country's export base. Adverse exogenous factors also contributed to the stalling of recovery after 1984: drought; refugee influx; further disruptions to external transport routes; and the inability to obtain further favourable debt rescheduling arrangements.

Table 15.5 clearly shows that in terms of most macroeconomic indicators, with the exception of the balance-of-payments current account deficit, performance in 1986 was little better than it had been at the commencement of the SAL negotiations in 1980. This is not to deny, however, that the SAL programme produced important economic benefits. In particular, there was significant and sustained improvement in the form of public sector management and policy formulation capacity brought about by SAL institutional reforms. The planning of the PSIP was greatly improved, with sectoral allocations made more compatible with overall development policies and recurrent cost implications detailed. The system of budget preparation was greatly improved upon, as was the Government's external debt-monitoring capacity. The Department of Statutory Bodies was strengthened, enabling the parastatal sector to become increasingly integrated into the central government's financial planning, and MDC and Press were both successfully restructured.

It is also important to note that the most significant and successful reform of the entire SAL programme, namely the restructuring of Press, essentially averted an impending large-scale financial and economic crisis. The fact that this reform took the form of prevention rather than cure means that the favourable impact cannot be seen simply by looking at trends in economic variables. A clear specification of the impact of the counter-factual scenario of allowing Press to collapse is required in order to quantify the benefits of this SAL reform. The Bank's study on Press prior to the salvage operation quantified the counter-factual impact and clearly indicated that the upshot of collapse would be a decline in production and employment, reduced credit availability, bankruptcy of the two commercial banks and possibly ADMARC, and a deterioration in the country's external creditworthiness, all of which would have contributed to a further decline in GDP growth rates. Hence, one must conclude that the restructuring of Press produced significant economic benefits.

Finally, the provision of SAL financial resources produced significant economic benefits, which again cannot be quantified without an analysis of the potential counter-factual scenario. Between 1981 and 1986, disbursements of SAL finance averaged 3.1 per cent of annual GDP. This financial inflow prevented what would otherwise have been an even more dramatic cut-back in import levels and government development expenditures.

Throughout this study it has been pointed out that despite institutional improvements and price-policy measures implemented under the SAL programme a significant sustained macroeconomic improvement failed to materialise because the SAL programme neglected to tackle fundamental structural reform requirements. This, however, raises a second important counter-factual question. What would have happened had the Bank pushed for a more comprehensive and meaningful adjustment programme? Would non-price measures designed to redress the imbalance between estate and smallholder agriculture, and attempts to stimulate private sector activity through a reduction in the economic power of Press and the parastatals have met with political resistance – resulting possibly in complete abandonment of the SAL programme? As yet, it is too early to answer this question. Since 1987, the Bank had adopted a new approach to adjustment lending in Malawi in the form of a series of Sectoral Adjustment Loans. The conditionality attached to these loans contains initial steps to address some of the country's more deep-rooted structural problems. It is encouraging to note that the initiative in this direction came as much from the Malawian authorities (Government of Malawi, 1987a) as from Bank staff, and as such, undoubtedly reflects the gains from improvements in government macro-planning capacity which resulted from the SALs. It remains to be seen, however, whether the politically-controversial reform proposals can be carried out through the SECAL programme.

15.10 CONCLUSION: A NEW APPROACH TO ADJUSTMENT LENDING

The abandonment of the proposed fourth SAL in 1987 was not the result of a Bank desire to take punitive action against a government which had violated important components of conditionality in the latter months of SAL III. It arose, rather, from a Bank realisation that a new approach to adjustment lending was required in Malawi. It is encouraging to note that under the new SECAL approach many of the lessons derived from Malawi's six years of SAL experience are beginning to be put into practice.

Under the new approach there is a stronger realisation of the need to allow for unexpected changes in the external economic environment. There is also a much greater internalisation of the reform process, with many of the new adjustment initiatives coming from the Government itself – supported by, rather than imposed by, the Bank. Most important of all, many of the new reform proposals reflect the realisation that Malawi's past forms of estate-led export expansion and ISI policies no longer offer a viable development strategy. This has necessitated a review, by both the Bank and the Government, of the country's past and future development options. The upshot is a new willingness to begin much-needed and much-delayed fundamental structural reforms, particularly in the key agricultural sector. For its part, the Bank has accepted that this will require an attempt to reconcile the conflicting objectives, found in so many sub-Saharan countries, of food self-sufficiency and increased agricultural export earnings. This has led to Bank willingness to abandon its previous 'pricist' and 'state minimalist' approach to agricultural policy, to an appreciation of the essential need to co-ordinate project- and programme-lending activities, and to a realisation that the estate sector and the smallholder sector cannot be treated in isolation from each other.

Sectoral adjustment lending to Malawi commenced in 1988 with the signing of a Trade and Industry SECAL. This was followed by lengthy negotiations on an Agricultural SECAL during which both the Bank and Government reappraised development options for this sector. The agricultural SECAL is due to be signed by 1990, and there is the possibility of further SECALs in the early 1990s. In all, the finance allocated to Malawi's SECALs exceeds that which was planned for the fourth SAL. This higher financing level, along with the greater flexibility of the SECAL approach, reflects a stronger awareness on the part of the Bank of the difficulties confronting Malawi in the face of an extremely hostile, and rapidly changing, external environment. The higher financing level will provide much needed balance-of-payments support for an economy continually faced with the adverse impact of exogenous shocks. The use of SECALs will also enable a more flexible response when exogenous shocks create unavoidable difficulties in the implementation of loan conditions. Implementation problems within a particular sector can now be tackled through tranche delay for the relevant SECAL, rather than through the more financially disruptive mechanism of suspending disbursements for the entire adjustment lending programme, as occurred under the SALs. This approach has considerable benefits for a highly aid-dependent vulnerable sub-Saharan economy such as Malawi.

The use of SECALs will also enable a much greater internalisation of the policy reform process, and will reduce the potential internal conflicts between the country's negotiating and implementing ministries. Under the SECAL approach the implementing ministries in the relevant sector will be involved in loan negotiations from the outset. Hence, conflicts between ministries with differing mandates, and between the multiplicity of government policy objectives can be addressed at the loan design stage so resulting in loan conditions which are more attuned to the Government's overall development plans. Again, such an approach promises considerable benefits to sub-Saharan economies where government resources are extremely limited and yet development needs and objectives are many-fold. It also provides an improved mechanism through which to address the inherent conflict contained within programme-lending, namely, the pressure on front-line ministries in aid-dependent vulnerable economies to accept rapid disbursements of programme finance regardless of conditions, and the need to devise appropriate and correctly sequenced reform conditions. The increased involvement in implementing ministries at the loan negotiation stage will help to ensure that the latter need is not bypassed in the attempt to secure donor finance.

The first SECAL was granted to the Trade and Industry sector, since, in contrast to the agricultural sector, less was needed in the way of fundamental structural reform of this sector. Nevertheless, the Trade and Industry SECAL embodied the realisation that Malawi's previous consumer-orientated ISI strategy was no longer viable in view of its high balance of payments cost implications. Unlike the SALs, the SECAL acknowledged that price liberalisation needed to be closely sequenced with trade liberalisation, in order to stimulate competition and to increase the private manufacturing sector's contribution to export revenues. Policy measures aimed to put exporters in a free-trade position, to reduce the general tariff level, and to ensure that the tariff structure was not unduly biased against exporters. Similarly, comprehensive reform of the tax structure was undertaken to facilitate the export drive, and export promotion measures were strengthened. Although the economic dominance of Press Holdings and the parastatals was not directly confronted under the SECAL, the measures to strengthen private sector manufacturing and agro-industrial activities have the potential to increase the number of economic agents in the Malawian economy. This is the correct sequence of activities, since direct actions to reduce the role of Press and the parastatals cannot be taken *until* the private sector has been adequately strengthened to a level which will enable it to fill the gap left by a scaling-down of public sector economic activity.

The most radical departure from the SALs, in the form of an attempt to address fundamental structural issues, occurred in the agricultural sector. The proposed agricultural SECAL represents a first attempt to adjust Malawi's colonial pattern of agricultural production. The most significant reform in this area consists of proposals to increase land rents in the estate sector, and to remove the legal restriction against smallholder production of burley tobacco, a high value export crop previously reserved for estate production which represented the most important restriction on the production pattern. In addition, the SECAL abandons the SAL's excessive emphasis on smallholder price policy and addresses the crucial need to increase smallholder food-crop production. The main thrust of the SECAL is to address the non-price constraints which have limited the supply response from the smallholder sector, particularly amongst subsistence maize producers. The new land rental and burley tobacco policies will assist in this respect by removing two important non-price constraints which existed under Banda's previous estate-expansion strategy, namely, reduced smallholder land availability and highly restricted smallholder crop options.

Non-price and non-marketing reforms will take the form of new land, extension and research policies. In particular, the Government will be assisted in the development and introduction of a new high-yielding variety of local maize which will involve a close co-ordination between the Bank's project- and programme-lending activities. There is also an acknowledge-ment that, in view of the need to stimulate increased maize productivity, particularly amongst impoverished subsistence producers, rapid fertiliser subsidy removal is not an appropriate policy. Hence, the Bank has accepted that in 1990–1 the weighted average fertiliser subsidy will remain at 25 per cent. Similarly, the SECAL is devoid of any policy prescriptions relating to suppression of the maize producer price, whilst the only stipulation relating to smallholder export crop pricing consists of a recommendation that smallholders receive no less than 45 per cent of the tobacco auction price.

During the SECAL negotiations the Bank conducted a comprehensive review of the most important component of its project-lending portfolio in the smallholder sector, namely, the National Rural Development Plan. The aim was to isolate the reasons for the NRDP's disappointing impact, and to identify possible cost savings, especially in the recurrent budget. The upshot of this exercise is a much improved co-ordination between the Bank's project-lending and programme-lending activities in Malawi, as reflected in the conditionality attached to the agricultural SECAL. Consequently, the Bank will no longer be a schizophrenic actor in Malawi policy formulation, with its project-lending attempting to increase food-crop production and its programme-lending attempting to increase export-crop production. The two objectives will be pursued, in a more appropriately sequenced manner, under *both* types of Bank lending. Rectification of these previous conflicts will provide greater scope for reduction in government expenditures. The Bank will no longer be in the position of having to direct high levels of government recurrent expenditures to the agricultural sector in an attempt to support a National Rural Development Plan under threat from other conditions in the Bank's own programme-lending policies.

Under the new SECAL lending strategy, the Bank is making a greater effort to improve the flexibility, not only of its own aid to Malawi, but also that of other donors. Throughout the sub-Saharan region, the Bank is attempting to convince donors of the need to provide greater support for government's recurrent expenditure requirements, rather than to simply pump money into the development account in a manner which often produces unsustainably high recurrent commitments for the government.

The new adjustment policies proposed for Malawi are rooted in a much clearer understanding of the country's political economy and of the nature of the development strategy pursued by Banda during the 1970s. The result is a reform package which acknowledges that this past strategy is no longer viable and that true structural reform will require much more than institutional strengthening and adjustment of price incentives. Having confronted the fact that Malawi is not a paradigm free market sub-Saharan economy and that government non-price interventions have created major structural problems within the economy the Bank must now confront the possibility that its new programme of fundamental structural reform will encounter considerable political opposition. Such opposition can be expected from Banda's entourage of politicians, military personnel, and advisers who hold substantial personal interests in the estate sector. The success of the Bank's structural adjustment programme will largely be dependent on a continuation of the strength of Banda's personal power. In view of the life President's age and the growing prospect of the country's first legitimacy crisis since independence, the long delay in a Bank attempt at true adjustment of the Malawi economy may carry a high cost, not only in terms of the adverse impact of the inappropriate policy prescriptions of the past, but also in terms of the country's political ability to implement the much-delayed programme.

NOTES

1   Agarwala (1983) calculated a composite price distortion index for thirty-one developing countries and Malawi was found to have the lowest composite index. Malawi's pricing of products, labour, and foreign exchange had low distortions, whilst the pricing of capital had medium distortions.
2   The World Bank's Accelerated Development Report (1981a) attributes much of the disappointing sub-Saharan growth record during the 1970s to these types of anti-agricultural, interventionist domestic policies.
3   The currency unit in Malawi is the Malawi kwacha (MK). The following represents the annual average exchange rate of MK to £1:

1973	2.00	1981	1.82
1974	1.98	1982	1.85
1975	1.90	1983	1.78
1976	1.62	1984	1.89
1977	1.58	1985	2.21
1978	1.61	1986	2.73
1979	1.74	1987	3.80
1980	1.87	1988	4.76

4 In 1975 migrant remittances amounted to MK30 million, making them the second largest foreign exchange earner after tobacco.
5 Kydd and Hewitt (1982, 1986a, 1986b) and Mhone (1987) provide a large body of evidence regarding the declining returns to smallholder agriculture and the associated increase in estate wage employment.
6 In 1981, under the prevailing technological conditions, only 38 per cent of the land area was suitable for cultivation, of which 95 per cent was already in use (Kydd, 1987).
7 A more detailed critique of the Bank's policy prescriptions for Malawi's smallholder agricultural sector is contained in Harrigan, 1988.
8 In 1986, Malawi's smallholder maize producer price was only 50 per cent of Kenya's and 60 per cent of Tanzania's at purchasing parity exchange rates (Lele, 1988).
9 Lipton (1987) outlines what he refers to as the 'extreme state-minimalist and pricist positions' held within certain quarters of the World Bank, particularly those concerned with Bank programme aid such as SALs. Malawi's experiences during the 1980s provide empirical support for many of the points raised by Lipton in his general critique of the Bank's pricist and non-interventionist school of thought.
10 Although the Bank acknowledged the need for a more flexible wages and incomes policy, the Government had already reached an agreement with the IMF, under the Extended Fund Facility, to restrain wages. In general, Bank/Fund activities in Malawi were marked by a lack of conflict, but in this rare case of conflict on the wages issue the Bank did little to address the anomaly.
11 The sectoral allocation of the Bank's project-lending adversely shaped its view of recurrent cost requirements in the early years of the SAL programme. The Bank asserted that recurrent underfunding was most critical in the agricultural sector (World Bank, 1982: Annexe no. 3). Alternative evidence, however, suggests that the social sectors (health and education) suffered from even greater recurrent underfunding problems (Kydd and Hewitt, 1984: section 2.3). The fact that these social sectors had received less in the way of past Bank project aid compared to the agricultural sector helps explain the relative neglect of their recurrent underfunding problems under the SAL programme.

BIBLIOGRAPHY

Acharya, S. N. (1978) 'Perspectives and problems of development in low income sub-Saharan Africa', *World Bank Staff Working Paper* 300.

Acharya, S. N. (1981a) 'Perspectives and problems of development in sub-Saharan Africa', *World Development* 9(2).

Acharya, S. N. (1981b) 'Development perspective and priorities in sub-Saharan Africa', *Finance and Development* 18(1).

Agarwala, R. (1983) 'Price distortions and growth in developing countries', *World Bank Staff Working Paper* 575.

Brown, C. P. (1970) 'Aspects of smallholder decisions regarding the allocation of farm resources in Malawi', unpublished research paper, University of Malawi.

Fardhi, M. A. (1988) *Malawi: Background Country Paper for Adjustment Lending Policy Paper*, Washington DC, World Bank.

Giles, B. D. (1979) 'Economists in government: the case of Malawi', *Journal of Development Studies* 15(2).

Government of Malawi(1983) 'Malawi government memorandum to the World Bank on government policy measures for the proposed SAL II programme', *Government Memorandum*.

Government of Malawi(1987a) 'Adjustment with growth and development: a proposed fourth structural adjustment programme', *Government of Malawi Special Studies Document* 1986(2).

Government of Malawi (1987b) *Statement of Development Policies 1987–1996*, Zomba, Malawi, Government Press.

Gulhati, R. (1989) *Malawi: Promising Reforms, Bad Luck*, World Bank EDI Development Policy Case Series, no. 3.

Harrigan, J. (1988) 'Malawi: the impact of pricing policy on smallholder agriculture 1971–88', *Development Policy Review* 6, London, Sage.

Harvey, C. (1983) 'The case of Malawi', *IDS Bulletin* 14(1).

Krueger, A. (1974) 'The political economy of the rent-seeking society', *American Economic Review* 64, (June), 291–301.

Kydd, J. and Hewitt, A. (1982) 'Structural change in Malawi since independence: consequences of a development strategy based on large-scale agriculture', *World Development* 10(5).

Kydd, J and Hewitt, A. (1984) 's Study of the effectiveness of aid to Malawi', *Study for the Task Force on Concessional Flows of the World Bank/IMF Development Committee.*

Kydd, J. and Hewitt, A. (1986a) 'Limits to recovery: Malawi after six years of adjustment, 1980 to 1985', *Development and Change* 17.

Kydd, J. and Hewitt, A. (1986b) 'The effectiveness of structural adjustment lending: initial evidence from Malawi', *World Development* 14.

Kydd, J. (1987) 'Policy reform and adjustment in an economy under siege: Malawi, 1980–87', *IDS Bulletin.*

Kydd, J. (1988) 'Malawi's export crop boom: a reappraisal', *IDS Bulletin* 19(2).

Lele, U. (1988) 'Structural adjustment, agricultural development and the poor: some lessons from the Malawian experience', *World Bank*, mimeo.

Lipton, M. (1987) 'Limits of price policy for agriculture: which way for the World Bank?', *Development Policy Review* 5, 197–215.

McCracken, K. (1983) 'Planters, peasants and the colonial state: the impact of the native tobacco board in the central province of Malawi', *Journal of Southern African Studies*, 9.

Mhone, G. (1987) 'Agriculture and food policy in Malawi: a review', in T. Mkandawire (ed.), *The State and Africulture in Africa.*

Mills, J. C. (1983) 'Technology in the subsistence sector of Malawi', Paper presented to the University of Edinburgh Conference on Appropriate Technology.

Sandbrook, R. (1985) *The politics of Africa's economic stagnation*, Cambridge University Press.

Short, P. (1974) *Banda*, London, Routledge and Kegan Paul.

Streeten, P. (1987) *What Price Food?*, London, Macmillan.

Williams, T. D. (1978) *Malawi: The Politics of Despair*, Cornell University Press.

World Bank (1973) *Recent Economic Developments and Prospects of Malawi* (Report no. 67a – MAI).

World Bank (1977) *Memorandum on the Economy of Malawi* (Report no. 1677a – MAI).

World Bank (1980) *Malawi Basic Economic Report*, Washington DC, World Bank.

World Bank (1981a) *Accelerated Development in sub-Saharan Africa: An Agenda for Action*, Washington DC, World Bank.

World Bank (1981b) *Report and Recommendation of the President of the International Bank for Reconstruction and Development to the Executive Directors on a Structural Adjustment Loan to the Republic of Malawi* (Report no. P– 3024a – MAI).

World Bank (1982) *Malawi: Growth and Structural Change, A Basic Economic Report* (Report no. 3082a – MAI).

World Bank (1983a) *World Development Report 1983*, Washington DC, World Bank.

World Bank (1983b) *Report and Recommendation of the President of the International Development Association on a Proposed Credit of SDR 51.9 Million to the Republic of Malawi for a Second Structural Adjustment Project* (Report no. P-3663-MAI).

World Bank (1985) *Report and Recommendation of the President of the International Development*

Association to the Executive Directors on a Proposed Credit of SDR 22.0 Million and a Proposed African Facility Credit of SDR 37.4 Million to the Government of Malawi for a Third Structural Adjustment Operation (Report no. P-4172 – MAI).

World Bank (1986a) *Malawi: Request for Supplemental Financing for the Third Structural Adjustment Operation*, Washington DC, World Bank.

World Bank (1986b) *Malawi: Policy Framework Paper* (Report no. Sec M86–958).

World Bank (1987) *Project Performance Audit Report: Malawi – Structural Adjustment I, Structural Adjustment II and Technical Assistance I* (Report no. Sec M87–699).

World Bank (1988a) *Malawi Industrial Sector Memorandum* (Report no. 7402).

World Bank (1988b) *Malawi Public Expenditure Review*, Washington DC, World Bank.

16

KENYA

Paul Mosley

16.1 BACKGROUND

The relations between Kenya and the World Bank in the 1980s are riven with paradox. At the level of policy statements, the approach of both parties towards the removal of long-term constraints to growth seems identical. Yet few country lending experiences have given the Bank so much cause for frustration. To understand why, it is necessary to go back into the colonial period, long before the Bank was founded, to trace the origins of the policy framework which it found itself obliged to challenge.

Kenya was one of the African 'colonies of European settlement', in which Europeans became involved in landownership and agricultural production as well as administration. From 1931 until 1959, indeed, about half the high-potential land in the country was reserved for exclusive European occupation. However, from the 1920s onward, African exports of cotton, maize, wattle, sugar and livestock products came to assume equal importance with exports from the European plantations as a basis for the colony's economy; and it was also during the inter-war period that one sees the beginnings of import-substituting industrialisation, much of it funded not by the capital of European settlers, but of Asian shopkeepers and traders.[1] Kenya was therefore already, before the Second World War, some distance away from the 'dependency school' stereotype of a foreign capital-dominated economy at the mercy of trends in world commodity prices. After the war its government became involved in economic management in three respects relevant to the theme of this essay. *First*, it erected a structure of protective tariffs that can only be described as personalised, i.e. tailor-made to the needs of the particular transnational which it was trying to attract, so that to this day there is a higher import tariff on tomato paste than on tinned tomatoes, and a higher tariff on corrugated iron sheets than on steel tubes – economically, a mess, but politically, a masterpiece of accurate targeting of favours.[2] Once Kenya became involved in a formal customs union agreement with Uganda and Tanzania in 1963 it became more difficult to confer such favours by means of tariff increases, since these would have had to be agreed with her partners; from this time on, therefore, selective import quotas replaced selective tariffs as the principal instrument of protection. *Second*, the Kenya Government encouraged, especially from the later 1950s onward, the growing of coffee, tea and pyrethrum by African smallholders; these people were to be important, not only as the basis of the country's agricultural development, but also as a market for import-substituting industry. (Under-consumption on the Latin American model has never represented a serious barrier to development in Kenya; the memorable phrase used to describe the country by a former Assistant Minister in 1974, 'a country of ten millionaires and ten million beggars' had in fact ceased to be accurate twenty years previously.)[3] *Third*, initially under pressure from white settler-farmers it established a system of marketing boards which paid at least export realisation for all crops, and often well *above* export realisation for those crops which were grown by the most vulnerable farmers – maize and wheat.[4] Thus Kenya, thanks to the political power in the hands of settler farmers, never suffered seriously from the world-wide problem of 'urban bias' by which a part of the rural surplus was siphoned off to subsidise urban consumption and capital formation;[5] however, the Kenyan marketing boards were to become, as we shall see, a major issue in their own right in the 1980s.

In the 1960s and early 1970s, the decade after independence, the Kenya economy grew at a rate which, as indicated by Table 16.1, stood comparison with any in the developing world. Of its two 'leading sectors' agriculture was boosted by the ability of African farmers to acquire good land at low cost from departing European settlers, and industry was able to make hesitant steps from import-substitution towards export-orientation through its discovery of new markets in neighbouring less developed countries of Africa, particularly Uganda and Tanzania with which it was, effectively, the senior partner in a customs union agreement. As a very open economy, Kenya has always been vulnerable to external shocks, and the first cloud to darken the post-independence horizon was the oil crisis of 1974–5, which put a brake on the growth rate and gave rise to the first inflationary problem in Kenyan history;[6] but this negative shock was quickly followed by the stimulus of the coffee and tea boom of 1976–7, to which the Government responded in a pro-cyclical fashion, allowing the benefits to come through to the private sector.[7] At this time Kenya appeared to be graduating rapidly from low-income to middle-income status, and to celebrate the fact the Government allowed itself to borrow heavily on the international capital markets, partly through 'hard' World Bank loans tied to ambitious civil engineering projects,[8] but also, in common with other middle-income countries, through short-term borrowing of recycled petro-dollars from private banks at what were often punitive interest rates.[9] In addition, it allowed itself expansive gestures on recurrent account, as when President Moi, on 1 May (Labour Day) 1979, decreed that employment in all public sector establishments should be increased by 10 per cent.

Table 16.1   Economic performance: Kenya in relation to other developing countries

A.   Average real GDP growth rates (% per year)

		1950–9	1960–9	1970–5	1975–80	1980–6
1	Taiwan	6.7	7.9	← .... →		5.9
2	South Korea	3.3	6.9	← 9.5 →		5.1
3	Colombia	3.7	3.9	← 5.9 →		2.5
4	Mexico	11.3	6.1	← 5.2 →		2.0
5	Thailand	4.8	7.0	← 7.2 →		6.2
6	Kenya	6.1	5.9	10.0	5.9	3.4
7	Sub-Saharan Africa, total	....	4.9[a]	5.6	3.5	0.0

[a]:   1965–70 only

B.   Investment as a ratio of GDP

1	Taiwan	28.5	34.1	31.2	33.1
2	South Korea	22.2	27.9	30.9	32.5
3	Colombia	15.9	18.7	24.8	18.0
4	Mexico	21.8	17.9	27.6	21.1
5	Thailand	20.1	24.2	26.8	21.3
6	Kenya	20.5	23.2	25.3	24.4
7	Sub-Saharan Africa, total	15.9	20.4	23.6	18.2

Source: For Kenya and sub-Saharan Africa, World Bank (1989b) Table 1.1: 3; for international comparisons, Fei and Ranis (1988) Table 1.

What was less clear at the time, and was concealed by the coffee boom, was that the Kenyan economy was experiencing a gradual decline in its growth potential throughout the later 1970s. As shown by Table 16.2, the decline was most serious in agriculture, in spite of the stimulus of the tea and coffee price boom:

Table 16.2:   Sectoral growth rates 1964–80

	Whole economy	Agriculture	Industry	Services and other
1964–73	6.6	4.0	9.0	6.5
1974–80	4.2	0.3	3.2	5.4

Source: Kenya, Economic Surveys, various.

The cause of this decline was certainly not a shortage of overall investment which, as may be seen from Table 16.1, remained throughout the period at a high level by international standards as well as those of sub-Saharan Africa. Rather, it appears to have been a decline in the productivity of investment. In the industrial sector, the incremental capital-output ratio deteriorated by more than 50 per cent between the early 1970s and early 1980s,[10] and in agriculture the decline was even more severe. One aspect of this which particularly worried the development agencies, pre-eminently the World Bank, was that the rate of return on their own projects was falling as well. Within the Bank's portfolio, the average *ex post* realised rate of return on projects fell from 16.8 per cent between 1976–9 to 11.2 per cent between 1980–3,[11] and by 1982 only one of its twelve projects in the agricultural sector was rated 'relatively free from problems'.[12] In other words, it was becoming increasingly difficult to disburse money effectively for development in Kenya in the late 1970s.[13] Exactly why remains in dispute. The dissolution of the East African Community in 1977 (which deprived manufacturing industry of most of its export market),[14] the disappearance of the margin of high-potential land left behind by the European settlers, the involvement by the Bank in large-scale 'poverty-focused' projects (e.g. Integrated Agricultural Development I and II; Livestock I and II) for which no proper technical and organisational basis existed in the country – all of these played a part in pulling down returns on capital. But the structural change which was to be most heavily blamed for the economy's relative decline was the sudden rapid growth in the public and parastatal sector. In the aggregate, the share of public sector output in GDP rose from 24.7 per cent in financial year 1976–7 to 35.4 per cent in 1980–1,[15] much of this accounted for by the operations of the 147 parastatal organisations. Over and above this, any reader who thinks of Kenya as a model of African capitalism may be surprised to learn that the Government owned shares in a further 176 companies, including textiles, shoes, sugar, tyres, alcohol, pharmaceuticals, canning, mining, salt, drilling, paper, hotels, cement, batteries, vehicles, radios, fishing, engineering, beverages and food processing.[16]

It was not only the World Bank and IMF who were to see this expansion of the public sector as having efficiency costs. A Kenya Government commission on government expenditures reported in 1982 a 'marked decline' over the years in standards of management performance and government control. It proceeded:

The collapse of financial discipline in project implementation has seriously undermined the capacity of the Government to plan and use the scarce resources available in an efficient manner. The result . . . [has been] that Government facilities and structures have been neglected and allowed to fall into disrepair. Government contracts have invariably been more costly than need be and excessive cost escalations in Government programmes have almost been taken for granted. In certain instances cases of gross misuse of Government resources have been noted and often not punished.[17]

It was, of course, precisely this kind of inefficiency at microeconomic level which the conditionality on the Bank's Structural Adjustment Lending was intended, world-wide, to eliminate.

The crisis which was to give the Bank its opportunity was not long in coming. In late 1979 the Kenya economy was hit by a sharp fall in the price of coffee — in effect, the final collapse of the late-1970s primary commodity boom — as well as by a doubling in the price of imported oil.[18] Its first response to the consequent balance-of-payments problem was to go to the IMF, as it had previously done on two occasions since 1975. Terms for a new stand-by agreement (conditional on the observance of ceilings for domestic credit creation, government borrowing and an 'understanding' with the Fund on exchange rate policy) were agreed in August 1979, but disbursements were delayed for a year, requiring the drawing up of a completely fresh agreement, initially because the ceilings on government borrowing from the central bank proved unworkable, and then because of a legal technicality concerning a decision in the 1980 budget to double the rate of export subsidy.[19] The delay left the Kenyan Government in urgent need of quickly available, low-interest programme finance: precisely the function which the World Bank's Structural Adjustment Lending programme was intended to fulfil.

16.2 THE SAL PHASE, 1980–4: DETERMINATION OF CONDITIONS

In early 1980 the World Bank was at the very beginning of its venture into policy-based lending. Although it had been aware for some years that the success of projects was related to central government policy and in consequence had begun to attach policy conditions to a number of project agreements,[20] its staff had severe misgivings, reinforced by the Executive Board, about moving into medium-term balance-of-payments support, which was traditionally the territory of the IMF and in particular its Extended Facility. What made the great leap into Structural Adjustment Lending possible was that when the oil crisis broke, various Bank country desks had sector-based operations more or less ready, which claimed to make a quick contribution to the balance of payments and hence to respond to the new crisis in the world economy. One such was a planned industrial sector operation for Kenya, designed to build on indications by the Kenya Government in the Fourth Development Plan (1979–83) that industrialisation strategy would be moved to a more outward-oriented approach. A programme of suggested policy changes, including the replacement of quantitative restrictions with tariffs, the rationalisation of the tariff structure and the boosting of export incentives, had been agreed by the summer of 1979. Converting it into a SAL involved no more than the addition of a couple of conditions relating to budgetary control and the monitoring of external borrowing.[21] It could well be argued that the sharpening of incentives to the industrial sector, which accounted for less than a quarter of Kenyan GDP in 1979, was not the most urgent priority for dealing with the growth and balance-of-payments problems of an agricultural country; but the preparation of a comprehensive package would have taken another year, and the Kenyan Government, facing a balance-of-payments deficit of 10 per cent and a rapid growth in its debt obligations (see Table 16.3) needed the money right away. The projections attached to the loan document, which show exports increasing and the debt service ratio stabilising almost immediately after loan disbursement, suggest that the Kenyan balance-of-payments problem was seen as being transient,[22] and that 'rationalisation of industrial protection and improvement in export incentives could quickly contribute to better balance of payments performance'.[23] The formal conditions attached to the loan are set out in Table 16.4.

It shortly became apparent that the Kenyan economic crisis was to be more severe and protracted than the Bank had hoped: exports, so far from reviving, declined through both 1981 and 1982, private sector investment began to dwindle and inflation rose to over 20 per cent in 1982. In the circumstances the Government was forced to return to the IMF for a further stand-by at the beginning of 1982, linked like its predecessors to ceilings on government borrowing and domestic credit expansion, but also, in an early example of cross-conditionality, to a 'programme of progressive import liberalisation in the medium term'. During the period of this agreement two policy changes of great macroeconomic importance took place. In the first place the exchange rate, which had been pegged to the SDR throughout the 1970s, was sharply devalued, by 15 per cent in September 1982 and by 14 per cent in December, and thereafter managed on a crawling-peg basis so as to ensure a slight depreciation in the real value of the shilling through the 1980s (see Table 16.5). In the second place, the central bank began for the first time to exert serious control over monetary aggregates, with the result that the central bank discount rate, which had been static through the 1970s, rose sharply and by 1983 had become positive in real terms. In an atmosphere of financial crisis, the central bank governor, Philip Ndegwa, and the permanent secretary to the Treasury, Harris Mule, found their bargaining position in relation to the rest of the Government enormously strengthened; by 1982 their position had been strengthened still further by the promotion of Simeon Nyachae to the position of permanent secretary to the Office of the President and in 1984 head of the Civil Service. From 1982 to 1986 this triumvirate of civil

Table 16.3   Kenya: main macroeconomic indicators, 1978–88

	1978	1979	1980	1981	1982	1983	1984	1985	1986	1987	1988
Real growth in GNP %	6.8	5.2	5.3	4.1	0.9	1.7	2.1	3.8	6.4	5.1	3.5
Growth in dollar value of exports %	1.7	−4.6	5.4	−4.2	−0.4	1.6	1.9	5.9	10.2	−2.7	4.9
Growth in dollar value of imports %	27.5	−19.0	10.0	−21.0	−16.5	−18.1	17.9	−6.2	17.3	5.8	4.4
Current account balance (% of GDP)	−13.9	−9.5	−12.6	−8.4	−4.7	−0.7	−2.0	−3.5	−3.4	−7.7	−8.5
Public expenditure on recurrent account (% of GDP)	23.0	26.4	32.5	33.7	35.2	29.6	28.7	29.1	29.0	32.1	33.0
Public revenue on recurrent account (% of GDP)	25.4	24.8	26.9	29.1	29.7	27.7	26.7	28.0	27.6	28.0	28.5
Public sector deficit (−) or surplus (+) (% of GDP) (includes transactions on capital account)	−8.4	−6.0	−9.5	−11.1	−10.3	−9.1	−6.7	−4.9	−7.2	−7.1	−7.5
Inflation %	16.9	8.0	13.8	11.8	20.4	11.5	10.2	13.0	4.0	5.2	9.5
Investment GDP %	29.8	22.7	30.0	28.4	22.4	21.1	21.0	21.8	25.7	24.7	18.8
Debt (current US $ billions)	0.6	1.2	2.3	3.6	3.8	3.6	3.9	4.2	4.6	5.8	8.9
Debt service ratio (% of exports)	6.4	5.4	12.2	17.9	23.6	24.8	13.9	19.3	23.2	34.1	36.0
Central Bank discount rate %	6.8	4.6	6.0	10.1	13.4	15.1	14.5	14.1	11.1	13.0	15.0

Source: Kenya Government, *Economic Surveys*, various.

Table 16.4 (a) IMF high-conditionality credits and World Bank structural adjustment loans, 1975–82

IMF agreements	World Bank agreements	Conditionality	Implementation of conditionality	Remarks
July 1975: IMF Extended Fund Facility, SDR 67.2 m.		Ceilings on government borrowing and on total domestic credit.	Ceilings exceeded after 3 months.	
November 1978: IMF stand-by, SDR 17.2 m.		Ceilings on government borrowing from the banking system and on total domestic credit; wage restraint.	Observed.	
August 1979: IMF stand-by, SDR 122.5 m.		Ceilings on domestic assets of the central bank and on government borrowing from the banking system; understanding on exchange rate policy and on elimination of the import deposit scheme to be reached by end of 1979.		Credit cancelled before first disbursement.
	March 1980: World Bank First Structural Adjustment Loan, US $55 m.	*Overseas trade*		

Table 16.4 (a) continued

IMF agreements	World Bank agreements	Conditionality	Implementation of conditionality	Remarks
		1 Recommend time schedule for replacing quantitative restrictions with tariffs by April 1980; begin replacing QRs by June 1980; begin reducing tariffs by April 1981; complete rationalisation process by December 1983.	New quota classification introduced 1981; replaced 1982 by system of weekly foreign exchange allocations; replaced 1983 by modified version of original quota classification. Some *increase* in tariff levels 1981.	'The structural adjustment of industrial enterprises under the programme has made little progress' (World Bank, 1984: 7).
		2 Improve existing system of export compensation payment and examine proposal for export insurance scheme.	Level of compensation payments increased from 10% to 20% of value of exported goods. Insurance scheme not introduced.	Coverage of scheme limited (see text p. 287).
		Budget 3 Set up programme for monitoring and controlling external borrowing during 1980–1.	First plan prepared in April 1982.	
		4 Prepare forward budget for years 1980–1 to 1982–3.	Budget prepared for years 1981–2 to 1983–4, not containing parastatal bodies.	'Criteria for evaluating projects were vague and little attention was given to economic analysis' (World Bank, 1984: 9).

IMF agreements	Conditionality	Implementation of conditionality	Remarks
October 1980: IMF stand-by, SDR 241.5 m.	Ceilings on central bank's net domestic assets and net public sector borrowing; undertaking to reach an agreement on exchange rate policy and on import liberalisation.		Only SDR 90 m. drawn.
January 1982: IMF stand-by, SDR 151.1 m.	Ceilings on budget deficit and on net credit to the government; and a commitment to a programme of 'progressive import liberalisation in the medium term'.		Only SDR 90 m. drawn.

(b) IMF high-conditionality credits and World Bank policy-based operations, 1982–8

IMF agreements	World Bank agreements	Conditionality	Implementation of conditionality	Remarks
	June 1982: World Bank Second Structural Adjustment Loan.	Shift 20% of items presently subject to quotas to free import status each year from 1982 to 1986.	About one-third implemented (see Table 16.6).	Some tariffs lowered in 1984 and 1985 budget (see text, Table 16.6).
		Prepare action programme for export promotion by June 1983.	Institutions exist but little has been done to make exporting more attractive (see text p. 287).	
		Undertake review of maize marketing and implement its recommendations.	Review recommended that NCPB should confine itself to 'buyer and seller of last resort'.	

Table 16.4 (b) continued

IMF agreements	World Bank agreements	Conditionality	Implementation of conditionality	Remarks
		functions. Not implemented, but grain buying by one large co-operative allowed.		
		Monitor annual price review to confirm that prices are based on export parities.	Price level satisfactory (see Table 16.5).	
		Prepare programme for subdivision of co-operative and group-owned farms.	Not done.	
		Pass on increases in energy costs to consumer.	Implemented.	
		Establish National Population Council and set up specific targets for family planning, average family size and population growth.	Implemented.	
			Not implemented.	
		Establish positive real interest rates.	Implemented.	Also an IMF condition.
		Improve machinery for recording of external debt.	Partially implemented.	
March 1983: IMF stand-by, SDR 175.9 m.		Devaluation: fiscal adjustment and reduction in government borrowing from banking system.	Condition observed.	

Facility	Conditions	Outcome
February 1985: IMF stand-by, SDR 85 m.	Ceiling on budget deficit and on government borrowing from banking system.	
June 1986: World Bank Agricultural Sector Credit.	Increase fertiliser availability; expand number of distributors; announce fertiliser prices in January each year; adopt a new fertiliser pricing framework based on world prices.	Availability rose 40% in first year but has since flattened out.
	Increase fees for livestock services.	Implemented.
	Restructuring of NCPB, SONY and NIB to make satisfactory progress.	
	Implement budget rationalisation plan in Ministry of Agriculture. Begin implementation of plan to rehabilitate AFC.	Little progress (see text, p. 293).
February 1988: IMF stand-by, US $85 m. plus US $90 m. Structural Adjustment Facility.	Reduce overseas borrowing; reduce budget deficit; maintain positive real interest rates.	Little reduction in budget deficit to February 1989. Positive real interest rates maintained.

Table 16.4 (b) continued

IMF agreements	World Bank agreements	Conditionality	Implementation of conditionality	Remarks
April 1989: IMF Enhanced Structural Adjustment Facility.		Various measures to reduce budget deficit including introduction of user charges; removal of price controls.		School and hospital user changes introduced, autumn 1989. Price controls removed on 15 items, July 1989.
	July 1989: Financial Sector Adjustment Credit.	Positive real interest rates; increase in Central Bank of Kenya's regulatory powers; establishment of a capital markets Development Authority.	Implemented. Implemented. Implemented.	
		Reduction in public sector fiscal deficit to 4 per cent in 1992–3.		No decline to end of fiscal 1990.

servants ran economic policy in Kenya, thus 'making the cabinet redundant' as one high-ranking member of the Government subsequently put it. Nyachae served as the conduit, both recommending to the President policy measures which the other two – both of them economists – wished to promote and also conveying to them the presidential veto on whatever proposal was thought to be politically infeasible. All three were members of the *Working Party on Government Expenditures* (Kenya, 1982), from which we have previously quoted, which drew attention to waste and overspending within the Government sector and made recommendations for stricter budgetary control and selective privatisation.

By early 1982 the World Bank was ready with new proposals for a structural adjustment programme. In spite of evidence that the programme of reforms under SAL I was proceeding slower than planned,[24] the new draft programme was a great deal more comprehensive and administratively demanding than its predecessor. Its conditions reached into virtually every sector of the economy, picking up the unfinished trade-policy business of SAL I, adding an important agricultural component, and additionally requesting actions in the areas of interest rates, energy, the parastatal sector, and family planning. They even asked the Government to consider

Table 16.5 Government macro-policy instruments, 1976–88

	Exchange rate		Interest rate		Maize price		
	Shillings per US $	Real effective (1981=100)	Commercial bank savings deposits (%) Nominal	Real	Nominal per 100 kg	As % of export price	As % of urban wages (1964=100)
1976	8.36	95	5.0	−5.7	65.00	106	86
1977	8.27	103	5.0	−8.6	80.00	86	93
1978	7.72	121	5.0	−10.3	80.00	93	84
1979	7.47	119	5.0	−2.8	65.00	76	67
1980	7.42	120	6.0	−6.9	80.00	110	72
1981	9.04	100	10.0	−1.6	90.90	68	65
1982	10.92	94	12.5	−6.6	125.00	*	79
1983	13.31	83	12.5	+0.9	154.00	78	91
1984	14.41	81	11.0	+0.8	175.00	70	95
1985	16.43	77	11.0	+0.3	187.00	134	93
1986	16.22	80	11.0	+5.3	198.00	154	91
1987	16.45	78	11.0	+3.9	209.00	133	89
1988	17.75	74	12.5	+1.7	222.00	127	87

Source: Kenya Government *Economic Surveys*, various.
Note: * No exports of whole maize in this year.

the issue of land reform, but in such vague language as to make almost any actions, or lack of them, by the Government appear consistent with the recommendation.[25] In general, however, the conditions of SAL II were not only more numerous but more specific than those of SAL I; for example, the request of SAL I that government 'implement its agreed liberalisation programme' was replaced, in SAL II, by a request that 20 per cent of the items then subject to quota be shifted to free import status each year from 1982 to 1986.

The agricultural conditions appear, at least in hindsight, to have been seen by the Bank as the 'key conditions', although it is a matter of dispute how clear this was to the Kenyan negotiators at the time. For some while, as noted earlier, the Bank had been attaching policy conditions to its agricultural projects, as when disbursements for the South Nyanza Sugar Rehabilitation Project in 1977 were linked to an undertaking to raise the price of sugar by a fixed percentage each year for five years, or when the Kenya Meat Commission was required to phase out all price controls in respect of the production and marketing of beef cattle within three years as a condition attached to the Second Livestock Development Project. (Neither condition was met.) The Bank returned to this arena with SAL II, requesting that 'all farm prices should be based on export and import parities and provide adequate incentives to producers'. But they then decided to go further, and asked the Government to consider the privatisation of the marketing of maize. This needs to be seen in historical context. Since the early years of the Second World War Kenya's main food crop has been subjected to a system in which the right to purchase from farmers and sell to millers has been monopolised by a state marketing board which fixes producer and consumer prices, and has the right to veto all private sales of maize in bulk[26] between districts. This system has tended, for nearly half a century, to open up a large gap between producer and consumer prices of maize and, as a consequence, to inhibit regional specialisation in the production of the crop, since consumers have found it cheaper to grow maize themselves, however unsuitable the soil and climate, than to pay a retail price containing an element of monopoly profit. Described as early as 1942 as 'the most barefaced and thorough-going attempt at exploitation the people of Africa have ever known since Joseph cornered all the corn in Egypt',[27] the system of maize marketing has since that date been subjected to commissions of inquiry in 1946, 1952, 1955, 1958, 1963, 1966 and 1972, each of which has recommended some diminution of the scale of state involvement in the interests of lowering the price to the consumer, encouraging specialisation of maize growing in the best areas and making the large black market redundant.[28] Each has been unsuccessful. In the first place large maize farmers, from the President downwards, make profits out of the persistence of controls; for so long as controls exist, it is possible for those who hold permits to move maize from surplus to deficit areas at a higher price than would prevail in a free market, and for those who hold political power to wield patronage by influencing the allocation of permits. Maize control, in other words, confers oligopoly rents; and those who receive the rents have always been able to defend them by arguing that decontrol would reduce food security and augment the economic stake of the Asian population. Both arguments are specious, but command substantial political support. In asking, as a centre-piece of the conditions of the second SAL, that the Kenya Government should 'undertake a review of maize marketing in order to develop recommendations on the appropriate roles of the public and private sector . . . and implement its recommendations', the World Bank was therefore attempting, from outside the country, a feat of political muscle which had defeated all liberalising pressures from inside for over forty years.

In assessing a programme such as this there are three criteria we can use: was it sensible (i.e. were the conditions appropriate and in the right order)? Was it politically feasible? Was it administratively possible? If these criteria 'fit inside' one another, then one approach to sensible design, as we have argued elsewhere,[29] is to begin with an economically rational package (i.e. the entire set of measures that will bring the economy closer to its production frontier, in a sensible order), then narrow this down by applying the tests of political and administrative feasibility in sequence. Beginning at the level of economic appropriateness, therefore, it is doubtful whether the SAL programme needed *both* to aim at world parity prices for farmers *and* to decontrol maize, on the grounds that if the former objective is achieved, the latter becomes unnecessary. And indeed border prices usually have been obtained by Kenyan farmers, contrary to their counterparts in the rest of Africa, simply because they have inherited from their colonial predecessors a system in which they have substantial political leverage and 'urban bias' has never represented a significant source of distortion.[30] In the specific case of maize the consultant's report commissioned by the Kenya Government in fulfilment of the SAL II conditionality duly concluded that the average national producer price under control was virtually the same as the producer price in 'free market equilibrium';[31] in other words, it might have been more sensible for the Bank to concentrate their conditionality on the prices offered to farmers, where they were in any case pushing on an open door, and leave the issue of maize control to be fought out within Kenya.

Second, it was probably unwise to invite the Kenya Government to begin the adjustment process by liberalising imports in the presence of a large fiscal and balance-of-payments deficit, since to do so would have made those deficits worse; and once the liberalisation process began, it would have made economic sense to insist that vital capital goods and intermediates (which affect the entire cost structure, including that of exporters) be decontrolled first, rather than inviting the Government to liberalise in whatever order it chose, but as fast as possible, which was broadly the approach of the two SALs. Out of a large mass of research on the sequencing of policy reform (most of it unavailable to the designers of the Kenya SALs) the consensus has emerged that the following is at least one sensible approach to the order of liberalisation:[32]

1   Devalue the exchange rate to a competitive level.

2a Promote exports through *and*   2b Remove controls on level of
non-traditional export   internal interest rates so as to
subsidies, export pro-   achieve positive levels in real
cessing zones, export   terms.
insurance schemes and
government-sponsored
marketing.

3   Reduce public sector deficit to a level that eliminates reliance on foreign non-concessional sources of finance, but do *not* allow level of real development spending to fall.

4   Liberalise imports of essential capital and intermediate goods.

5a Liberalise other imports and *and* 5b Remove price controls.
rationalise tariff structure.

6   Remove controls on external capital account.

By contrast with this scheme, the sequence recommended by the Bank and Fund to the Kenya Government was (4 + 5a + 2a) → 1 → 2b → 3 → 5b, and the sequence actually adopted was 1 → 2b → 3 (without the proviso) → 5b, treating the liberalisation effort so far as negligible, which is a claim we shall argue in subsequent sections. As a consequence, the Kenya Government was faced with a request to undertake structural adjustment in the midst of stabilisation, which may be one reason why the structural adjustment programme made no more progress than it did.

It is at the level of political and administrative feasibility that the World Bank has most severely criticised its own efforts. The evaluation of SAL I insists that: 'the delays in implementation reflect overly optimistic timetables for the original action programme . . .'[33] and the evaluation of SAL II that: 'the structural adjustment programme was so wide-ranging that it was likely to be difficult for the country to implement unless it consisted almost entirely of policies already firmly rooted'.[34] However, it may not have been easy at the time to see that the policies were not 'firmly rooted'. SAL agreements are made between the World Bank and the Ministry of Finance, and the Ministry of Finance, in 1982, was firmly in the hands of Harris Mule, with backing from Ndegwa and Nyachae. It was not only the Bank's negotiators, but these technocrats within the Kenya Government, who saw in this period of economic crisis an opportune moment for pushing through a comprehensive reform package. The maize control condition, indeed, was inserted at Mule's suggestion, no doubt because such a reform might be easier to implement if the Bank could be cited as scapegoat than if it were presented as an independent initiative. The feasibility of the package, then, depended on a gamble by the three technocrats that they could both argue the reforms through and devise machinery for implementing them. They were to succeed much better, as we shall see, with the Fund's part of the package than with the Bank's.

16.3 THE SAL PHASE, 1980–4: IMPLEMENTATION

A summary of policy changes implemented by the Kenya Government in the areas requested by the Bank is set out in Table 16.4. Broadly, the picture is one of slippage in all areas.

On *trade liberalisation*, the detailed picture is as set out in Table 16.6. The conditionality of SAL I allowed the Kenya Government initially a free hand in the phasing of liberalisation, subject to the understanding that the complete programme, including tariff rationalisation, would be completed by December 1983. When it became apparent that nothing had been done in 1980 and 1981, apart from the removal of absolute prohibitions on import, the conditionality for SAL II was tightened to require 20 per cent of all items subject to quotas to be removed from quota status. This was done in June 1982, but when the balance of payments worsened in August the movement towards liberalisation was actually reversed, with all import permits being handed out on a basis of weekly foreign exchange allocations by the central bank. This system was relaxed the following year, but by 1986, as the Table shows, about half of all imports remained subject to some kind of restriction, by comparison with three-quarters when the SAL negotiations began. During the 1981–2 foreign exchange crisis there were increases in some tariffs, up to a maximum of 100 per cent, but there were also some cuts in the 1983 budget; overall, the level of effective protection provided by the tariff structure did not vary significantly during the SAL period, and it was estimated in 1986 at 90 per cent on average, with variations around this average ranging from minus 167 to plus 1019 per cent for individual industries.[35]

On export promotion, the letter of the conditions was fulfilled, but no more. An export compensation scheme had existed since the mid-1970s, and in the 1980 budget the available compensation was increased from 10 to 20 per cent of the value of exports (causing problems with the IMF, as we earlier saw); and a manufacturing-in-bond scheme was introduced in 1983. But in practice, payments under the export compensation scheme in 1985 represented less than 10 per cent of the value of eligible exports, and nearly half the actual payments were to two exporters – Kenya Canners and Bamburi Portland Cement. Likewise, many firms have applied to produce under the manufacturing-in-bond scheme but so far only ten have been granted permission. The proposed export insurance scheme which the

Table 16.6 Progress of import liberalisation, 1980–7

	Percentage of total imports in each import schedule:				Supportive/countervailing measures
	IA (quota free)	IB (licences issued item by item, but usually readily available)	IIA (bulk goods, permit requires ministerial approval)	IIB (imports competing with domestic industry, severely restricted)	
1980	24	19	43	14	
1981	23	20	46	11	
1982	25	19	46	10	During second half of year import permits allocated on basis of weekly foreign exchange allocations by central bank. All tariff increased 10%.
1983	36	21	32	11	
1984	30	17	45	6	Many tariffs lowered in June budget.
1985	48	13	38	5	Many tariffs lowered in June budget.
1986	48	10	35	7	
1987	51	11	31	7	

Source: Kenya, Ministry of Commerce and Industry.

Government 'expected to introduce' by September 1980,[36] was cancelled in 1982 ostensibly on doubts about whether the Government had the necessary administrative capacity to implement it.

On *agricultural marketing*, the Government was asked to ensure that policies would be set within the range of import and export parities, and that 'policies to encourage farmers to expand production' would be maintained. This was done, and a subsequent report was to confirm that 'all [Government] administered prices except beef are now [1986] approximately at world price levels';[37] however, as explained earlier, this had in any case been Kenya Government policy for many years, so the degree of coercion involved in complying with the condition cannot have been very large. It was otherwise with the maize marketing system. The report by the consultants Bookers, released in the summer of 1983, recommended that the National Cereals and Produce Board (NCPB) should retreat to the role of 'buyer and seller of last resort', releasing the bulk of the trade to private buyers. The Government announced in December 1983 that this recommendation was to be implemented but did not do so. In July 1984, however, it announced that a Kenya Grain Growers' Co-operative Union (KGGCU) was to be formed to market maize and wheat in competition with the NCPB, a course of action not considered in the consultants' report or in previous negotiations with the Bank.

The remaining conditions, on land tenure, energy, population, interest rates and external debt management, seem to have been treated internally within the Bank as of secondary importance, although this does not seem to have been made clear at the time to the Kenya Government. On interest rates and energy prices, the terms of the conditionality were met, in each case under simultaneous pressure from the IMF. On population, a National Population Council was set up, though no targets had been announced at the time the second tranche came up for release, but in a dramatic change from previous policy both the President and the Vice-president have taken every opportunity to emphasise their commitment to family planning. On land reform, nothing was done, and in spite of the importance attached to the issue by many commentators,[38] nobody seemed to care. Out of nine conditions, therefore, four had been fully implemented by 1984, two partially implemented and three not implemented. This is a slippage rate of 44 per cent, or exactly 50 per cent if the 'key' maize control and import liberalisation conditions are given double weight; in relation to the entire set of policy-based operations analysed in this chapter, the slippage rate rises to 62 per cent. This is a little but not horrendously in excess of the overall slippage rate of 40 per cent on all policy-based operations estimated by the World Bank in its recent report on adjustment lending,[39] but the mere fact that slippage was above average was worthy of note, because Kenya's bargaining power – in terms of the gravity of her economic position and her ability to secure alternative sources of finance – was a good deal worse than average, and in terms of a conventional bargaining model this should have made her unusually compliant with the Bank's conditionality. Kenya stands out as an example of a government which took a risky financial gamble and got away with it – case 3, *'slippage unpunished'* in the notation of Chapter 3.

Moderate as Kenya's slippage was in relative terms, the Bank's senior staff in Washington came to feel in 1983–4 that because there was no progress on maize decontrol, the 'key condition', a hard line must be taken. Release of the second tranche of SAL II was delayed by nine months from March till December 1983,[40] and finally authorised on Christmas Eve by an acting Senior Vice-president (Operations) on the strength of an undertaking by the Kenya Government that maize would shortly be decontrolled. However, the Bank was determined to send a firm signal, and in 1984 informed the Kenya Government that 'we do not see that sufficient progress has been made in implementing the structural adjustment programme to justify proceeding with a third SAL at the present time'. This was a severe, if temporary, blow since the Government's financial planning was based on the assumption that there would be at least three further Structural Adjustment Loans during the 1984–8 Plan period.[41]

In their evaluation of SAL II the Bank concluded in 1985 that 'the time allowed in the Letter of Development Policy may have made insufficient allowance for administrative constraints' and, as we have seen, that the conditions for SAL II were 'too wide ranging'.[42] More explicitly, the Project Completion Report SAL I draws attention to the fact that:

> the Kenya Government is better able to formulate development policies and take measures that do not require strong management, technical or organisational capacity. In policy discussions, high level Kenya Civil Servants generally demonstrate sophistication and technical competence. Below the top levels, however, these attributes are scarce. Moreover, jobs are narrowly defined and tasks which do not clearly fall within any particular office's terms of reference are not performed. Inter-unit communication and co-ordination are weak.[43]

This tells half the story. Sheer lack of sufficient trained manpower does explain slippage in external debt monitoring, the development of the forward budget and (possibly) export promotion, although the fact that the majority of exporters are of multinational or Kenyan-Asian, rather than Kenyan-African, origin clearly has not helped the export promotion effort. But in other areas the problem was not so much that the Government lacked the administrative capacity to implement the agreed reform programme, as that it lacked the political inclination to do so. This was clearly the case with land reform, which was scarcely in the interest of the large farmers who made up the bulk of the President's agricultural power base. More dramatically, it was also the case with maize decontrol. It is not clear what assurances the Ministry of Finance received from above concerning the feasibility of decontrol before they signed the SAL II agreement on the dotted line. What is certain is that during 1983 Simeon Nyachae, as permanent secretary in the President's office, was advised by the President that such a measure was not on and proceeded to block it, whilst at the same time doing everything possible to maintain a yielding and respectful posture towards the Bank. The 1984 drought, in which it was politically essential for the Government to be seen to be 'in charge' of the food situation and preventing 'profiteering' by private traders, put an end to any hopes of decontrol for the immediate future.

More puzzling in many ways is the slow progress on trade liberalisation, since the majority of established importers (who hold licences) are either Kenyan-Asian or representatives of multinationals, whereas the majority of would-be importers (who do not) are Kenyan-African entrepreneurs. There would thus appear to be a clear populist pressure for (and government interest in) the removal of controls along the lines recommended by the World Bank. It clearly did not help the cause of liberalisation, however, that the Bank was pushing for it in 1980 and 1981 when the balance-of-payments problem was still not under control, and any shift to the issuance of import licences 'on demand' appeared likely to aggravate the problem. Likewise, progress was delayed by the fact that the Ministry which was responsible for implementing the programme – Commerce and Industry, with a protectionist Kenya Association of Manufacturers breathing down its neck[44] – was not the Ministry which negotiated it. The issue of 'ownership' of structural adjustment programmes, as we shall see, is one which has preoccupied Bank staff enormously in recent years.

Two lessons come out of all this. The first is that timing is vital. The Bank was in complete agreement with the technocrats of the Kenya Government about what had to be done, but not about when it had to be done. The Bank, particularly in SAL II, wanted a time-bound schedule of reforms; the Kenya Government negotiators, aware of the opposition they were facing, wanted the freedom to move on each reform as and when they got the green light to tell them that such a measure was politically opportune. Thus the Fund's type of conditionality, in which the disbursement is linked to the achievement of *targets* (e.g. for money supply or government borrowing) suited the Government better than the Bank's, in which the disbursement is linked to the performance of specific *actions*. The former allows more room for manoeuvre.

This brings us to the second point. It has often been found by the Bank that price-related policy changes (sometimes referred to as 'push-button' changes) have proved easier to implement than institutional changes, which are administratively more complex.[45] Certainly this appears to be so in Kenya: the prices of crops, credit and foreign exchange are broadly 'right' in Kenya, as Table 16.5 bears witness; in the last two areas there has been major progress in the last ten years, and the Fund's relations with the Kenya Government have blossomed as a consequence. But these are variables which can be altered in an afternoon by one individual in the central bank or the Ministry of Agriculture, as the case may be:[46] which is not true of the decontrol of maize or the rationalisation of protection, which require the collaboration of thousands of people over a period of years. As a consequence, by a remarkable reversal, the Kenya Government's relations with the Bank sank during the early 1980s as its relations with the Fund improved. There is evidence that the deterioration took the Government by surprise: they knew that, in macroeconomic terms, they were running a tight ship, and they also knew that, if the World Bank was not able to lend effectively for development in Kenya, it was not clear where else in Africa it might do so. Whatever pique the Regional Vice-president for Africa might show, therefore, the strong cards remained in the Kenya Government's hand. By 1986, as we shall see, the Bank had acknowledged this.

291

16.4   THE SHIFT TO SECTORAL LENDING 1984–9

A phoney war between the Bank and the Kenya Government persisted through 1984 and much of 1985. Having administered a token slap on the wrist by terminating the SAL process, the Bank was however anxious to send out signals that would enable it to sustain a policy dialogue of some kind. Accordingly, it added US $20 million unilaterally to its current line of credit in favour of the Agricultural Finance Corporation,[47] sent out word that policy-based lending to Kenya would henceforth be given on a sectoral basis, and initiated negotiations on an agriculture-sector based operation in early 1985. As the Bank had a large portfolio of poorly-performing small-farmer projects,[48] most of them inherited from the era of poverty-based project lending, it made considerable sense to tackle these problems at the root by intervening in the policy-making process. Recognising from its experience during the SAL period the importance of involving the prospective implementing ministry, it invited the permanent secretary for agriculture to chair a set of inter-ministerial working parties relating to each piece of suggested policy reform. For its part, the Kenya Government was at last emerging from its long stabilisation episode and therefore in a position to think long-term, which it did through the Sessional Paper no. 1 of 1986, *Economic Management for Renewed Growth* (Kenya Government, 1986). This document could, with one or two exceptions, have been written by the World Bank,[49] and indeed one of its new initiatives – the promotion of intermediate technology and of the informal or 'indigenous' sector – was to become a major theme of the Bank's new African report, *From Crisis to Sustainable Growth*.[50] In many ways, it served to pre-empt future Bank initiatives by defining the range of possible economic policy manoeuvres in advance. Within the agricultural sector it undertook to:

(a)   promote the *increased use of fertilisers*, which it was estimated were only used by 6 per cent of smallholders,[51] (para. 7.31);

(b)   tighten the financial performance of the *Agricultural Finance Corporation*, which had an estimated 50 per cent of non-performing assets[52] (para. 7.33);

(c)   instil greater financial and *operational responsibility in parastatals* (para. 2.35).

These undertakings were to become key elements of the conditionality attached to the Agricultural Sector Adjustment Credit of June 1986. The Sessional Paper pointedly avoided any mention of the Bank's *bête noire*, but even the National Cereals and Produce Board was becoming a serious embarrassment to the Government on account of its growing trading losses, which by 1986 accounted for something like a quarter of the public sector financial deficit.[53] As a consequence the Minister of Finance announced, before negotiations with the Bank were concluded, that maize farmers were now to be allowed to sell direct to millers. In such an environment, negotiations proceeded smoothly. An Agricultural Sector Credit, for US $60 million (all of it tied to purchases of agricultural inputs such as fertiliser and pesticide)[54] was agreed in June 1986. The detailed conditionality is set out in Table 16.4; the reader will note that it makes imaginative use of ambiguity as an instrument for resolving potential conflict. In place of the hard edges of SAL II, the Government is now required to 'fully implement measures to improve fertiliser marketing', 'increase user charges for livestock services' and make 'satisfactory progress with the financial restructuring' of the National Irrigation Board, the South Nyanza Sugar Company and the National Cereals and Produce Board.[55]

For this reason, and also because less than three years have passed since the Credit was granted, it is difficult to provide an objective assessment of how well the conditions have been met. It is certainly true that fertiliser imports have risen – by 40 per cent in the first year after the agreement was signed – that the number of licensed fertiliser importers has risen (to around 300) and that fertiliser is now available in bags smaller than the previous 50 kg minimum.[56] However, maximum price announcements are still made too late to influence planting decisions and, in the Bank's view, do not make a sufficient allowance for import costs, although a perfectly respectable argument can be made for subsidising the purchase of fertiliser by small farmers on a temporary basis.[57] There remain problems on the demand side, in cases where farmers do not receive credit, or payment for their crop, on time.[58] But there is no doubt that the availability of fertiliser to small farmers has increased, in particular by comparison with the situation in the early 1980s when the application of conditionality by some donors was actually reducing it.[59]

Elsewhere there is little to report but muddle. The Agricultural Finance Corporation remains, as it was in colonial times, an instrument for redistributing income to large farmers, and its overdue rates have actually risen, to around 60 per cent, since the signature of the Credit; there is no indication of its having reoriented its operations in any way towards small farmers, but then the overt conditionality, by contrast with the gloss in the Bank's loan document, does not require it to do so.[60] But the AFC was always going to be a tough nut to crack, simply because the majority of its delinquent customers are those very large farmers who sustain the Government's power. The same forces which cause agricultural prices in Kenya, to the Bank's pleasure, to be at or above export parity levels[61] are those which cause the AFC, to its displeasure, to be incapable of reforming itself. The 'process of budget rationalisation' (i.e. the restraint of recurrent costs and the prioritisation of capital expenditures within the agricultural budget) has got nowhere, principally as the result of the dispersal of the Ministry of Agriculture's functions, following the March 1988 elections, between four separate ministries: Agriculture proper, Livestock, Supplies

293

and Marketing, and Science and Technology (which is now responsible for all research).[62] On parastatals, finally, the position is static, or rather cyclical. Each time a programme aid agreement is in the offing an announcement is made that one or more parastatals is to be privatised; once the money is in the bank, reasons are found to defer the decision. Thus it is stated in the Agricultural Sector Credit Loan agreement that 'Government has decided to divest the Cotton Lint and Seed Marketing Board' and that it will 'divest all of its cotton and ginning activities to the private and co-operative sectors'[63] by March 1987 as a condition of second tranche release, but, although the tranche has been released and the necessary enabling legislation has been passed, no assets have changed hands as of February 1990.[64] The loan agreement states that 'the Uplands Bacon Co. is now (June 1986) in the progress of divestiture' and 'procedures have been initiated to restore (it) to its former owners',[65] but after a period of closure it has restarted operations in the public sector, as (in the summer of 1989) has the Kenya Meat Commission. The NCPB, meanwhile, has now been three times in the present decade (and ten times in all)[66] around the same mulberry bush. Following the Minister of Finance's announcement in January 1986 that farmers were to be allowed to sell directly to farmers, the Minister for Agriculture, Mr Odongo Omamo, announced a year later that the Government had decided to restore the NCPB's monopoly, and that any farmers or millers found flouting the new directive would be prosecuted.[67] The reasons he gave were that the NCPB had unsold stocks and that if farmers no longer sold to the Board it was impossible to retrieve their outstanding AFC loan instalments from them. In June 1988, following the conclusion of a new agricultural sector package from the EEC, the Minister of Finance announced that with immediate effect small traders, co-operatives, and the KGGCU would be allowed to buy from farmers up to 20 per cent of the maize crop; but on 5 August the Minister for Supplies and Marketing, William ole Ntimama, ruled that only KGGCU and NCPB would be allowed to buy maize from farmers, and that commercial buyers would not be licensed to market maize for the time being. Formally, this was not a breach of the Bank's conditionality, which merely required 'progress with the restructuring' of the NCPB,[68] and restructuring there has certainly been, with three general managers in less than a year and widespread sackings amongst the middle management. But it is the case that, six years after the setting up of the Task Force on Divestiture, not only has none of the 147 existing parastatals been divested, but three new ones have been created.

What is clear is that the approach of the Bank (and some other external donors) to efficiency in parastatals is quite different from that of the Kenya Government. The Government approach, made explicit in the report of the Ndegwa Commission (Kenya Government, 1982) is to *increase* central control over parastatals, for example by integrating the pay and career structure in parastatals with those of the civil service,[69] including the forward and annual budgets of parastatals in the national budget and subjecting the development spending plans of parastatals to even closer central scrutiny; whereas the Bank approach is to *decrease* that control to the point where the Corporation is trading unburdened in the market.[70] The dispute risks distracting the attention of both parties from the main issue, which as a previous Bank publication has emphasised is 'not whether an enterprise is publicly or privately owned, but how it is managed'.[71] Whether, however, 'management' is something which can be directly influenced by conditional programme finance remains a contentious matter. In other countries covered by this study there seem to be clear cases where it has been (e.g. the Development Bank of the Philippines, see Chapter 12). But the Kenyan case seems to bear out the generalisation that institutional change is much harder to achieve by this means than 'getting prices right'. The Agricultural Sector Credit, which was even more 'institutional' than its SAL predecessors, certainly appears to have scored only one palpable hit (fertiliser policy) amidst four areas of conditionality, although assessment of the others is clouded by ambiguity in the original conditions. On the other hand, the Bank is clearly now willing to take a more long-term view of institutional change than it was at the end of SAL II, and is currently (late 1989) preparing a second agricultural sector operation.

In principle, the industrial sector ought to be more fertile soil for the Bank's policy advice than the agricultural; since whereas Kenya Africans stand to *lose* in the short term *vis-à-vis* other races by liberalisation in agriculture, they stand to *gain* by liberalisation of import controls. However, those who stand to gain – especially small-scale manufacturers – have weak voices by the side of the rent-holders who gain from the existing system – i.e. those who currently hold licences and those who receive kick-backs from issuing them.[72] In addition, the existing system itself has generated a large pipeline of pending licence applications – many of them from people who, in their anxiety to beat the system, have submitted applications three or four times over; hence the central bank has perfectly proper worries about the effect of any sudden liberalisation on foreign exchange reserves. As a result, the rate of decontrol during the 1980s was slow (see Table 16.6). Underneath the ice, however, the waters were moving: the Ministry of Finance was quite clearly aware of the empirical connection between protection and inefficiency,[73] and the 1986 Sessional Paper contained a commitment to: 'reorient trade policy so as to reduce the degree of protection afforded import-substituting activities and to increase the returns to non-traditional exports'.[74] Going beyond this, the Sessional Paper announced an intention to remove price controls on all goods except those for which the domestic market was monopolised, a step for which the Kenyan Association of Manufacturers had been pressing for some years.[75] Boosted by these signals of government – or at any rate Ministry of Finance – commitment, the World Bank initiated negotiations on an industrial sector package. To the two areas of reform already mentioned, the Bank added a worry from its own project portfolio – the performance of the two major development banks, the Industrial Development Bank (IDB) and Kenya Industrial Estates (KIE), whose inefficiencies had already been exposed by the Kenya Government's Task Force on Divestiture. Between them they had received six World Bank lines of credit to the value of US $81 million, but as a result of letting their lending be influenced by what the Bank called 'extraneous considerations'[76] their average rate of return had fallen below 2 per cent by 1987.[77] The Industrial Development Bank was in a particularly bad way, with 90 per cent of its loans in arrears in 1987;[78] because it was known to be in a bad way, it found itself unable to borrow on domestic markets, and was forced to borrow in appreciating overseas currencies, which its customers found even more difficult to repay, thus provoking a downward spiral in its financial position. The policy conditions prescribed for the Industrial Sector Credit, negotiated in the spring of 1988, (set out in Table 16.7) were thus a combination of rehabilitation of the Bank's own industrial portfolio, unfinished business from the SALs and Kenya Government initiative. In spite of the Bank's efforts since 1985 to take a softer negotiating position, the agreement was preceded by tough bargaining, particularly over the Bank's requirement of 'full liberalisation, except for a few items restricted for reasons of security and health, by June 1991'.[79] Once again the issue was not what should be done, but when, and in particular how much freedom of manoeuvre the Kenya Government should be allowed in trade policy. The first tranche of the Credit was released in June 1988 following the 'down payment' of a highly imaginative budget, aimed almost entirely at the industrial sector, which identified certain categories of manufacturing (woollen textiles, fruit juice, shoes) as potential 'export successes', raised protective duties on their output and reduced duty on their input. To the same end, tax exemptions for private capital investment expenditure were increased – to 100 per cent in the case of manufacture in bond – and a delicate bow was made to the informal sector via the announcement of a district development fund for artisans and the reduction of import duty on bicycles.[80] In addition, the price control provisions of the Credit have been met ahead of time.

What made an accommodation with the Bank at this time particularly urgent was that once again, as ten years previously, the Kenya Government was living with the consequences of a coffee boom which it intervened in too little and too late to sterilise.[81] The balance-of-payments deficit, by 1988, was once again running at around 8.5 per cent (see Table 16.3) and the speed of its deterioration had once again provoked recourse to an IMF Stand-by, which was negotiated in the normal amicable way but at the

Table 16.7 Conditionality attached to Bank/Fund programme finance currently in force, February 1989

Agreement	Conditionality	Observations
First Industrial Sector Adjustment Credit, US $110 m. May 1988	Implement unrestricted licensing for all items in current Schedules IB and IIA (see Table 16.6).	Number of rates reduced to 17 in 1988 Budget.
	Reduce number of tariff rates from 25 to 12.	Complete tax exemption for MIB operations provided in 1988 budget. Implemented, October 1988.
	Devise a simple import duty compensation scheme with wider coverage and greater level of reimbursement to exporters than existing one; improve incentives for manufacturing in bond (MIB); implement export processing zone.	Implemented, June 1989.
	Remove price controls on 10 products and gradually decontrol prices of all remaining items not falling under new monopolies bill.	Still under discussion, December 1990.
	Restructure development finance institutions: Industrial Development Bank and Kenya Industrial Estates.	Confirmation of measure already in force.
Enhanced Structural Adjustment Facility, February 1989	Review and adjust exchange rate to expand and diversify export base.	
	Restrict public sector deficit, in particular by increasing/introducing user charges in education and elsewhere in public sector.	
	Import liberalisation: licences for imports in Schedules I, II (formerly IIA) and IIIA (formerly IB) to be issued without restrictions.	Already part of ISAC conditionality.
	Export incentives, as per World Bank ISAC.	Already part of ISAC conditionality.

normal cost. By May 1989 this expensive loan had been replaced with a low-interest Extended Structural Adjustment Facility; the draft conditions attached to this Facility are reproduced in Table 16.7. This conditionality is, of course, jointly negotiated between Fund, Bank and recipient government but the Fund, building on its good relations with the Government, has taken a firm lead in selecting policy conditions from the Bank's existing 'portfolio' – including import liberalisation and restructuring of development finance institutions – in order to give them additional leverage. Additionally, a US $170 million Financial Sector Adjustment Credit, with conditions relating to capital market regulation and development, real interest rates and the public sector deficit was negotiated with the Bank in July 1989. Meanwhile, the Kenya Government felt sufficiently confident of its bargaining position in December 1989 that the late Foreign Minister, Robert Ouko, urged donors in general not to attach policy conditions to their aid, noting that 'not all of their conditions are feasible' and that Kenya had national policies which need not be similar to those of the donor agencies.[82] Such boldness was not contemplated even five years previously.

16.5 EFFECTIVENESS: INITIAL ASSESSMENT

Table 16.8 suggests that during the early adjustment period to 1986 (roughly corresponding to the period of the SALs in Kenya) growth of GDP and of agriculture was substantially less than what had been achieved in the previous period and what the World Bank had hoped for – even *without* structural adjustment. None the less, it was a great deal better than what was achieved elsewhere in sub-Saharan Africa, in low-income countries as a whole, or in neighbouring Tanzania, which ostentatiously did not 'adjust' until 1986 and in consequence received no programme finance from the Bank at this time. The latter is perhaps a more valid standard of comparison, since 'before and after' comparisons do not compare like with like and the World Bank's expectations are based on an arbitrary projection rather than any scientific measure of what could be expected.[83] The investment ratio deteriorated, because the burden of the Government's fiscal adjustment effort fell on the development budget and the private sector did not 'take up the slack'; the rate of export growth and balance of payments both improved from the previous period, world recession notwithstanding, and – it scarcely needs to be added – performed better than in all the various 'control groups'. During the 'recovery' period 1986–8 – from the Bank's point of view, the period of the Agriculture Sector Credit – the economy as a whole revived, as did the overall investment rate, but the agricultural sector, for what this is worth, performed less well than the projections of the Bank's appraisal document. However, this was a period during which growth of both GDP and agriculture in sub-Saharan Africa as a whole were *negative*, and by that

Table 16.8 Kenya: comparisons of economic performance during SAL/SECAL period with previous performance, plan projections and 'control groups'

	1976–80 actual	1981–6 planned with structural adjustment	1981–6 planned without structural adjustment	1981–6 actual	1986–90 planned with structural adjustment	1986–90 planned without structural adjustment	1986–88 actual	Tanzania	All sub-Saharan Africa	All low-income
Annual GDP growth:										
whole economy	5.5	4.3	3.8	3.2	—	—	5.0	0.9	1.8	2.3
agriculture	2.9	3.9	2.7	2.2	4.5	3.2	2.7	0.8[a]	1.2[a]	2.0[a]
Annual export growth:										
whole economy	2.4	4.7	4.0	2.5	—	—	4.1	−9.8[a]	−2.1[a]	0.6[a]
Current account/GDP	−7.4	—	—	−3.8	—	—	−6.2	—	−6.5	−7.0
Investment/GDP	26.0	—	—	20.6	—	—	24.5	17.6	17.1	18.1

Sources: All Kenyan actual figures from Kenya, *Economic Surveys*, various; 1981–6 planned figures from World Bank (1982); 1986–90 planned figures from World Bank (1988b); international comparisons from World Bank (1988b) Table 2.6: 45 and World Bank (1989b) Table 1.1: 4.

Notes: a = 1980–6.

standard performance must again be described as satisfactory.

If the Kenyan economy did better than other African or low-income countries, then, the next question is what part of this difference was due to World Bank *money*; what part to World Bank *conditions*; what part to *spontaneous policy change*; and what part to other factors such as price trends, weather, and the role of other extraneous agencies such as the IMF or private investors. With the data we have, rigorous inference is impossible. But two things seem fairly clear: the World Bank's money made a difference, and its conditionality did not. The Bank's programme finance came to assume a strategic role in the early 1980s because during the recession the Government ceased to be able to afford to borrow overseas on commercial terms, and concessional inflows from overseas came to support almost the entire development budget; and of these inflows, Bank SALs had a larger share than contributions from any other donor.[84] But of all the policy conditions attached to its money, listed in Table 16.4, it is difficult to name a single one *during the SAL period* which was implemented because of its pressure. Most of the successful pressure during this period – in particular on exchange rates and interest rates – came from the Fund, although on the latter issue there was, and still is, cross-conditionality with the Bank. During the later period (1986–8) the picture became a great deal more complex: the Bank's conditionality came to gain more leverage, certainly on fertiliser imports and possibly on the reform of development finance institutions; the Kenya Government brought in some initiatives of its own, for example the dismantling of price controls; on the other hand, the world price trend for Kenya in this period, by contrast with the previous period, became favourable as the result of the coffee boom, so a part of Kenya's relatively quick recovery may be externally, rather than internally, generated. If one accepts that within Africa 'the countries which have enjoyed high growth rates are those that have avoided major price distortions'[85] Kenya's relative freedom from such distortion, during the period under examination, owed much more to indigenous technocrats and to the political strength of the large farm lobby than to the influence of the Bank. At the institutional level – in particular in the computerisation of the national budget – the Bank certainly made a contribution, but institutional development is an objective which sits uncomfortably with quick-disbursing finance.

16.6 CONCLUSIONS

Kenya is a country in which growth, certainly by African standards, has been fast but structural change has been slow. The central features of the country's political economy before the Second World War – the domination of the economy and policy- making by large agrarian interests, the patchy and politically weak industrial sector, the dominance of racial issues in economic policy-making – persist today. The first of these factors explains why so much was expected of Kenya when it embarked on its adjustment phase at the beginning of the 1980s, the last two why it delivered – from the World Bank's point of view – so little.

The central fact of that adjustment experience was that the central bank and Ministry of Finance came to be dominated by a group of able technocrats who, however, were able to exercise little lasting control over instruments for which they were not directly responsible. It is common, of course, for the political bargaining power of the financial authorities to increase during periods of economic crisis; but what was achieved in Kenya in the early 1980s, namely the depoliticisation of the exchange rate and of the central bank interest rate, contrary to the experience of many other countries, was achieved both peacefully and durably. However, when these same authorities proceeded to put forward a blue-print for liberalising the entire economy, they underestimated both the duration of the economic slump and their own ability to push their plan through the rest of the political system. And the World Bank, so far from tempering their enthusiasm with realism, took advantage of its very strong bargaining position in 1982 to try and speed them up.

That they got nowhere, then, is not the fault of any one authority; and the Bank has learnt from its experience, both by simplifying the scope of its operations and by investing more effort in the building of interdepartmental consensus around specific policy measures. But the central problem remains: first, to sustain that interdepartmental consensus after disbursement when the benefit of the loan is felt to belong to the Ministry of Finance,[86] and second, if that is achieved, to overcome the opposition of the losers in the country at large, which will be particularly powerful if they are African and the potential gainers are Asian. Four examples of Bank-sponsored policy proposals which have so far not been implemented are illustrated in Table 16.9, and in each case we suggest that what has to be done to facilitate implementation is explicitly to compensate the losers, either through selective public expenditure or selective tax exemption.[87] It is, of course, important that such compensation appear to come from internal sources and not be represented as a 'World Bank bribe'. The alternative of simply waiting until the vested interests which are currently blocking reform lose their leverage may – in the absence of a radical change of government[88] – take a very long time.

Opinion is divided on how far the restrictive practices described in this chapter, and not overcome in the 1980s, represent a speck of dust which makes no difference to the performance of the machine, or the crucial obstruction which stands between Kenya and progress towards NIC status. Having espoused the latter view with great firmness in the early part of the 1980s, the World Bank now seems to be opting for a more pragmatic

Table 16.9 Losers from economic reform, and possible compensation measures

Policy change	Initial disbursement to	Implementing ministry	'Rents' lost by	Possible compensation through
Decontrol of maize		Supplies and Marketing	Large farmers with licences.	Selective rural investment (e.g. water supplies).
Elimination of import licensing	Ministry of Finance	Commerce	Importers with licences; civil servants who 'sell' licences.	Increase in civil service salaries?
Collection of bad loans to: Industrial Development Bank		Commerce	Industrialists with bad loans.	Increase in duty exemptions for exporters.
Agricultural Finance Corporation		Agriculture	Large farmers with bad loans.	Selective rural investment (e.g. roads, water supplies).

approach which acknowledges the minor importance of privatisation and import liberalisation in the revitalisation of low-income economies, and acknowledges the very real political and economic achievement of a relatively resource-poor country.

Acknowledgements

The author acknowledges with warmest thanks the help of the following people: in Washington, Pamela Cox, David Hatendi; in Nairobi, James Otieno, Michael Mills, Richard Anson, Harris Mule, and above all Bo Karlstrom, Michael Westlake, Terry Ryan.

GLOSSARY

AFC   Agricultural Finance Corporation
ASAC   Agricultural Sector Adjustment Credit

CLSMB	Cotton Lint and Seed Marketing Board
IDB	Industrial Development Bank
ISAC	Industrial Sector Adjustment Credit
KGGCU	Kenya Grain Growers' Co-operative Union
KIE	Kenya Industrial Estates
NCPB	National Cereals and Produce Board
NIB	National Irrigation Board
QR	Quantitative restriction
SAL	Structural Adjustment Loan
SONY	South Nyanza Sugar Company

NOTES

1 For this early period of industrialisation, see Swainson (1976a) or Mosley (1983, chapter 6).
2 See for example Swainson (1976b).
3 For the contrary view see Leys (1975). The quotation is from J. M. Kariuki, Assistant Minister for Education from 1971 to 1975 and a staunch populist critic of the Kenyatta family (the 'ten millionaires' referred to above). He was murdered in 1975.
4 See Mosley (1983, Table 3.6).
5 See Lipton (1977) and for a specifically African application of the argument, Bates (1981).
6 For the detail of this episode, see Killick (1984: 182–9).
7 This is criticised by Killick (1984) and defended by Collier et al. (1989) on the grounds that the rural smallholders who were the main beneficiaries of the boom had such a high propensity to save as to stabilise the boom automatically.
8 Typical ventures of this type, all financed by IBRD, were the new Nairobi airport, the new Nairobi-Nakuru highway and the Kiambere hydro-electric project on the Tana River.
9 In June 1979 the Kenyan Government took out a US $ 200 million Eurodollar loan, repayable over seven years at 1.5 per cent above the LIBOR rate. This was not an untypical deal (Killick, 1984: 202).
10 World Bank (1988a: 2).
11 *Source*: World Bank, *Annual Reviews of Project Performance Audit Results*, various from 1976 to 1984; raw data are reproduced in Duncan and Mosley (1984: Table 1). Note that these data refer to projects *evaluated* during the periods stated, and therefore implemented several years beforehand.
12 Duncan and Mosley (1984: 111), drawing on internal Bank portfolio reviews.
13 Symptomatically, disbursement of aid by the World Bank and other donors began to lag a long way behind commitments in the late 1970s and early 1980s (Duncan and Mosley, 1984: 31–3).
14 Non-traditional exports (mainly processed agricultural products and a variety of manufactures) declined from 61 per cent of total exports in 1975 to 45 per cent in 1980.
15 Kenya Government (1982: 7).
16 Ibid., p. 42.
17 Ibid., pp. 15–16.
18 By 1980, net imports of fuels were absorbing 20 per cent of the country's net export earnings by comparison with less than 1 per cent in 1973.
19 According to the Fund's lawyers, this subsidy constituted a 'multiple currency arrangement' and constituted a breach of the Fund's understanding with Fund staff, although it was subsequently to be acclaimed by the Bank's evaluators (World Bank, 1984: 87).

20 For some Kenyan examples of this, see page 292.
21 A major informational problem in 1979 was that the Kenya Ministry of Finance did
    not have full knowledge of what loan and grant arrangements the spending ministries
    had made with external donors or of what they had spent the previous year. This
    situation has now been remedied, which may be counted as one of the major
    administrative advances in the Kenya Government in the 1980s (see p. 300).
22 The forecasts and out-turns were these:

		1980	1981	1982
exports (US $ m)	appraisal estimate	1248	1379	1532
	actual	1261	1072	951
Debt service ratio (%)	appraisal estimate	15	16	16
	actual	11	19	23

23 World Bank (1984) *Project Completion Report*, paragraph 8, p. 50.
24 The release of the second tranche of SAL I was delayed from April to September of
    1980 until machinery for the monitoring of external debt was set up. The
    memorandum informing the Executive Directors that the second tranche had been
    released claimed that 'the vast majority of import prohibitions . . . have been
    eliminated and replaced by tariffs', which was simply wrong (see Table 16.6).
25 Land issues will be given special attention in preparation of the next development plan.
    Task forces will be established with terms of reference to review key land issues and
    will be given appropriate technical assistance. Analysis and recommendations will be
    reviewed by Government.
26 Private traders have always been allowed, since the beginning of controls in 1940, to
    move up to two bags of maize (400 lb) out of the district of origin without a permit
    from the district commissioner. In September 1983 the ceiling was lifted to ten bags
    (2,000 lb, or just under a ton); but it was lowered again to two bags in 1984 during
    the severe drought of that year.
27 C. J. Wilson, *Kenya Legislative Council Debates*, 15 April 1942, col. 18.
28 For the detail of these see Mosley (1986a: 110).
29 See Mosley and Toye (1988). The approach adopted here has been contested, on the
    ground that to reject a liberalising measure as 'politically infeasible' is to give the game
    away to existing vested interests, rather than confront them as economic efficiency
    requires.
30 As Bates has argued, the Kenya National Farmers' Union

    has helped to create a framework of public policies that provides an economic
    environment highly favourable to all farmers, whether small or large . . .
    planters, large farmers and agribusiness (here and in the Ivory Coast) have
    secured public policies that are highly favourable by comparison with those in
    other nations.

                                                                   (Bates, 1981: 94–5).

31 Kenya Government (1983) *Grain Marketing Study: Final Report*, 4 vols, prepared for
    the Ministry of Finance by Booker Agriculture International in association with
    Githongo and Associates, Annexe 5: 48. For development of this argument, for other
    crops in addition to maize, see Jabara (1985), Mosley (1986b) and World Bank (1986).
    Implementation of the concept of 'world prices' has been bedevilled in Kenya by

muddle within the World Bank as to how world prices should be translated into domestic equivalents. The Bank's most usual practice was to recommend that prices paid to grain farmers should be set at *import* parity levels; which makes sense for wheat, but not for maize, since in surplus years (e.g. 1985 to the present), Kenya does not import maize. On the basis of this belief the Bank initially leant on the Kenya Ministry of Agriculture to revise its pricing formulae for grain, but eventually became persuaded that Kenyan farmers were indeed being paid 'incentive prices'. My interpretation of agricultural marketing policy in Kenya owes a good deal to discussions with Mike Westlake; for his own interpretation of the concept of agricultural 'price distortion' with reference to Kenya see Westlake (1988).

32 For discussion of the order of liberalisation see Edwards (1984) and Williamson (1987).
33 World Bank (1984: 10).
34 World Bank (1985: 10).
35 World Bank (1988a: 14).
36 World Bank (1984: Annexe 1: 7): Letter of Development Policy from Minister of Finance to President of World Bank.
37 World Bank (1986: 21).
38 See Hunt (1984) and Godfrey (1987: 617–8).
39 World Bank (1986) p. 90, Table 4.3.
40 The aid administrations of the US and UK reinforced the Bank's posture by delaying disbursement of their own programme loans to Kenya during such time as the second tranche of SAL II was held up.
41 Kenya Government (1984: 109).
42 World Bank (1985: 17, 18).
43 World Bank (1984: 57). Recall the very similar point made by John Toye in relation to the Ghanaian civil service: Chapter 14: 187.
44 In 1985 Commerce and Industry were divided into separate Ministries, with import licensing the responsibility of the Ministry of Commerce. For more on the role of the KAM in relation to liberalisation see below.
45 See for example Nicholas (1988); for a contrary example, see our case study of the Philippines (Chapter 12).
46 However, Bo Karlstrom has emphasised (in relation to the exchange rate) that the distinction between 'push-button' and institutional reform is not necessarily clear and sharp.

> [The principle of a market-determined exchange rate] has been a gradual educational process, starting with the successive governors of the central bank and Ministers of Finance. Beyond that, the President and a number of key politicians had to be convinced. It took three years before the rate began to move down at a pace sufficient to pull down the weighted real rate. And there are recurrent and sometimes strong objections to the policy, particularly from politically well-connected importers. The educational process therefore has to continue in order to slowly build an export lobby. I would call this institutional building, although not involving a physical institution.
>
> (Personal communication)

47 World Bank (1986: 9).
48 Recall (p. 273) above, passage keyed by notes 10 and 11.
49 Consider the following statement of goals:

> It will be imperative that:
> – economic growth becomes the primary concern of economic policy;
> – agriculture remains the leading sector in stimulating economic growth and job creation;

- the great majority of new jobs be created, not in the cities or in large industry, but on farms and in small-scale industries and services, both rural and urban;
- most investment be directed to create a prosperous agriculture, to build rural market centres and towns, and otherwise to support informal sector growth;
- what investment does occur in modern industry must be highly productive, capable of employing workers at low cost and capable of competing in world markets with modest protection or subsidy; and
- Government policies and budget allocations be moved decisively, and soon, in these directions.

(Kenya Government, 1986: 2)

However, one important exception relates to the Kenya Government's stated determination in the Sessional Paper to promote plantings of tea and of high-quality ('Ruiru 11') coffee, which the Bank tried unsuccessfully to discourage. The discouragement was partly based on price forecasts for tea and coffee which in 1988/9 were proving as over-pessimistic as its forecasts for cocoa were over-optimistic. For general comment on Bank in-house commodity forecasts see John Toye's essay on Ghana (Chapter 14: 164, 196–7).

50 See World Bank (1989b).
51 World Bank (1986: Annexe IV: 60).
52 World Bank (1986: 13).
53 The before-tax losses of the NCPB, and before 1981 of the Maize and Produce Board, have been as follows (in K £'000).

	Maize Board/NCPB	*All 16 agricultural parastatals combined*
1978	3300	1600
1979	8700	14500
1980	13500	16300
1981	15200	27300
1982	16600	37200
1983	24200	37500
1984	12750	9500
1985	45000	52000
1986	54000	62000
1987	32000	48000

Sources: Grosh (1986: Table 5); NCPB annual reports.

54 Although such inputs are fungible, this represents, together with the prior consultation process, a genuine attempt to give the Ministry of Agriculture 'ownership' of its own sectoral programme. For a description of what can happen when the operating ministry is not thus involved, see the Ecuador case study (Chapter 19).
55 World Bank (1986: Annexe III).

56 Imports of fertilisers were as follows (in K£ million):

1983	1984	1985	1986	1987	1988
25.09	13.89	52.03	50.01	38.96	55.15

Source: *Economic Survey 1988*: 79.

The *Survey* comments, 'the fall in imports of fertilisers (in 1987) was due to the existence of carry-over stocks in 1987'.

57 The price announcement for the 1988 short rains crop was made in September (it should have been July) and the price was adjusted upwards by 20 per cent. According to the World Bank, this should have been 28 per cent, but there is a case for subsidising fertiliser consumption based on the proposition that small farmers use a sub-optimal quantity of fertiliser (as we saw, only 6 per cent used it in the mid-1980s) on account of (a) imperfect information about likely yield increases from its use; (b) imperfections in the capital market; (c) indivisibilities (e.g. the minimum size of bag, as mentioned in the text). By subsidising the fertiliser consumption of small farmers the Government can bring its usage nearer to the optimal level (and in principle finance this subsidy by taxing incremental crop output). For another case in which the pricing of fertiliser became a bone of contention between Bank and recipient government, see the Malawi case study (Chapter 15).

58 For discussion of these problems, see World Bank (1986): Annexe IV: Table 2.4).

59 Because the donor (USAID) would not allow the fertiliser to be used until agreement was reached on the price at which it was to be sold to farmers. For detail of this episode see Mosley (1986a).

60 In the loan document it is stated that 'AFC will set ceilings on the amount to be lent to individuals in the light of Government's objective of increasing credit availability for smaller farmers' (World Bank, 1986: 26) but in the formal conditionality agreement this becomes 'The Government will define AFC's budget population and loan ceilings' (*ibid.*: Annexe III: 48).

61 See passage keyed by note 27.

62 Water Development and Co-operatives had split off from their parent ministry in the 1970s. It has been alleged that the reason for the creation of the additional ministries was that the President needed the additional ministers (four per ministry) to guarantee a majority in Parliament.

63 World Bank (1986: Annexe V: Table 2.2).

64 As with the decontrol of maize trading, the political problem means that the most likely buyers of the cotton ginning equipment would be Asians.

65 World Bank (1986: Annexe V: Table 4.1, and Annexe IV: 67).

66 For the previous attempts see p. 284, and Mosley (1986a).

67 See for example 'No Move on Maize', *Weekly Review* (Nairobi), 12 August 1988.

68 See p. 281.

69 This in practice means a drop in the salaries of senior parastatal officers, which is already causing an exodus from the parastatal sector.

70 For an excellent discussion of this problem see Grosh (1986: 51–8).

71 World Bank (1983: Chapter 4). It has to be borne in mind that the objectives of 'management' will often be more diverse in a parastatal than in a commercial company; for example, the Kenya Meat Commission is a technically bankrupt parastatal, often proposed for privatisation, but if during the 1984 drought it had not fulfilled its obligation of buying every animal offered to it (at a subsidised price), many pastoralists might have starved, and environmental deterioration within the rangeland areas might have been even greater.

72 Potentially, such influence may be exerted at three separate points within the system: the Ministry of Commerce, which issues the licences; the inter-ministerial Import Committee, which gives instructions to issue licences; and the central bank, which issues foreign exchange.

73 In 1986, a sample survey conducted by the World Bank found that the efficient industries – food manufacturing, beverages, leather and wood products – had an average effective protection rate of 43 per cent whereas the average effective protection rate on the inefficient industries – textiles, steel and automobile assembly, which had negative value added in 1988 – was 255 per cent. The boundary between 'efficient' and 'inefficient' industries was a domestic resource cost co-efficient of one, which implies that domestic manufacture is as efficient as importing (World Bank, 1988a: 9).

74 Kenya Government (1986: 17).

75 In a report issued in September 1988 the Kenyan Association of Manufacturers claimed that price controls had 'created monopolies, caused disruption in production, decreased Kenya's export competitiveness, encouraged hoarding, served as a wage suppressant, discouraged or delayed investment in new and expanding business, and created an unnecessary, costly and unresponsive bureaucracy'. It also pointed out that inflation during the ten years prior to the expansion of price control in 1972 (at 2.3 per cent) had been well below its level during the fifteen years since (at 12.3 per cent). But it opposed the logical complementary suggestion that import controls should be lifted at the same time as price controls to ease the immediate effects of price decontrol (see Economist Intelligence Unit, Kenya, *Country Report no. 1 for 1989*: 9). As in the Philippines (see Chapter 12) the manufacturing lobby consistently refused to be impressed by the arguments for liberalisation which Bank representatives put before it.

76 World Bank (1988a: 7).

77 World Bank (1987: 23).

78 Ibid.

79 World Bank (1988a: 13).

80 For full details of the 1988 budget see Economist Intelligence Unit, Kenya, *Country Report no. 3, 1988*: 6–8.

81 More precisely, the fiscal adjustment was too little and too late (the 1987 and 1988 budgets were broadly neutral in macro terms); but the monetary adjustment, when it came, was severe, with a fall in the rate of monetary growth from 30 per cent in 1986 to 6 per cent in 1988 and the issue of a range of treasury bonds of varying maturities by the central bank. The latter is also evidence of a spontaneous effort towards financial deepening by the central bank, although there is as yet no free market in government debt.

82 Economist Intelligence Unit, Kenya, *Country Report no. 1, 1989*: 20.

83 See Volume 1, Chapter 6 and also Mosley (1987: Table 4 and pp. 6–8).

84 The share of external grants and loans in total government development expenditure rose from 39.9 to 84.8 per cent between 1979–80 and 1982–3; of this flow of external finance, World Bank policy-based lending comprised about a quarter.

85 World Bank (1989a: 27 and Tables 17 and 18).

86 This applies even after the switch from structural to sector adjustment lending, because sector loans do not bring about an increase in the budget of sectoral ministries (interviews, Ministries of Agriculture, Energy and Industry, 6–7 February 1989).

87 If one takes a pessimistic view, there is of course the risk that such compensation would increase the income of those already seeking rents and (given the correlation between wealth and political power) strengthen their ability to acquire rents, rather than increase their incentive to increase their income through the market.

88 For example of a reform process being expedited by a change of government – and by the disappearance of its rent-seeking 'cronies' from positions of influence – see the essays on Turkey and the Philippines in this volume.

BIBLIOGRAPHY

Bates, R. H. (1981) *Markets and States in Tropical Africa: The Political Basis of Agricultural Policies*, Berkeley, University of California Press.

Collier, P. *et al.* (1989) *Trade Shocks in Africa: A Study of the New Macro-economics of External Shocks*, unpublished paper, Oxford, Institute of Economics and Statistics.

Duncan, A. and Mosley, P. (1984) *Aid Effectiveness: Kenya Case Study*, unpublished report commissioned by Task Force on Concessional Flows of the World Bank/IMF Development Committee.

Edwards, S. (1984) *The Order of Liberalisation of the External Sector in Developing Countries*, Princeton, NJ, Princeton Papers in International Finance, no. 156.

Fei, J. and Ranis, G. (1988) *The Political Economy of Development Policy Change: A Comparative Study of Thailand and the Philippines*, unpublished paper, Economic Growth Center, Yale University.

Godfrey, M. (1987) 'Stabilisation and structural adjustment of the Kenyan economy, 1975–85: an assessment of performance', *Development and Change*, 18, 595–624.

Grosh, B. (1986) *Agricultural Parastatals since Independence: How Have They Performed?* University of Nairobi, Institute for Development Studies Working Paper 435.

Gsaenger, H. G. and Schmidt, G. (1877) *Decontrolling the Maize Marketing System in Kenya*, University of Nairobi, Institute for Development Studies Discussion Paper 254.

Hunt, D. (1984) *The Impending Crisis in Kenya: The Case for Land Reform.* Aldershot, Gower.

Jabara, C. L. (1985) 'Agricultural pricing policy in Kenya', *World Development*, 13, 601–26.

Kenya Government (1982) *Report and Recommendations of the Working Party on Government Expenditures* ('Ndegwa Report'), Nairobi, Government Printer.

Kenya Government (1984) *Development Plan 1984–8*, Nairobi, Government Printer.

Kenya Government (1986) *Economic Management for Renewed Growth*, Sessional Paper no. 1 of 1986, Nairobi, Government Printer.

Killick, T. (1984) 'Kenya, 1975–81', in T. Killick, *The IMF and Stabilisation: Developing Country Experiences*, London, Heinemann Educational Books, 164–216.

Leys, C. (1975) *Under-development in Kenya.* London, Heinemann Educational Books.

Lipton, M. (1977) *Why Poor People Stay Poor*, London, Maurice Temple Smith.

Mosley, P. (1983) *The Settler Economies: Studies in the Economic History of Kenya and Southern Rhodesia 1900–1960*, Cambridge, Cambridge University Press.

Mosley, P. (1986a) 'The politics of economic liberalisation: USAID and the World Bank in Kenya 1980–4', *African Affairs* 85, 107–19.

Mosley, P. (1986b) 'Agricultural performance in Kenya since 1970: has the World Bank got it right?' *Development and Change* 17, 513–30.

Mosley, P. (1987) *Conditionality as Bargaining Process: Structural Adjustment Lending, 1980–86*, Princeton, NJ, Princeton Essays in International Finance, 168.

Mosley, P. and Toye, J. (1988) 'The design of structural adjustment programmes', *Development Policy Review* (December).

Nicholas, P. (1988) *Report on Adjustment Lending*, Washington DC, World Bank.

Swainson, N. (1976a) *Company Formation in Kenya before 1945, with Particular Reference to the Role of Foreign Capital*, University of Nairobi, Institute for Development Studies, Working Paper 267.

Swainson, N. (1976b) *The Role of the State in Kenya's Post-war Industrialisation*, University of Nairobi, Institute for Development Studies, Working Paper 275.

Westlake, M. (1987) 'The measurement of agricultural price distortion in developing countries', *Journal of Development Studies*, vol. 23, no. 3, April.

Williamson, J. (1987) in V. Corbo, M. Goldstein and M. Khan (eds) *Growth-oriented Adjustment Programmes*, Washington DC, World Bank and IMF.

World Bank (1982) *Report of the President to the Executive Directors on a Proposed Second*

Structural Adjustment Operation (Report no. P–3322–KE), Washington DC, World Bank.

World Bank (1983) *World Development Report 1983*, Washington DC, World Bank.

World Bank (1984) *Program Performance Audit Report: Kenya First Structural Adjustment Credit* (Report no. 4934), Washington DC, World Bank, Operations Evaluation Department.

World Bank (1985) *Program Performance Audit Report: Kenya Second Structural Adjustment Loan and Credit* (Report no. 5682), Washington DC, World Bank, Operations Evaluation Department.

World Bank (1986) *Report of the President to the Executive Directors . . . on a Proposed Agricultural Sector Adjustment Credit* (Report no. P–4278–KE), Washington DC, World Bank.

World Bank (1987) *Kenya: Industrial Sector Policies for Investment and Export Growth* (Report no. 6711–KE) Washington DC, World Bank.

World Bank (1988a) *Report of the President to the Executive Directors . . . on a Proposed Industrial Sector Adjustment Credit*, Washington DC, World Bank.

World Bank (1988b) *Report on Adjustment Lending*, Country Economics Department (Report no. R88–199) Washington DC, World Bank.

World Bank (1989a) *Africa's Adjustment and Growth in the 1980s*, Washington DC and New York, World Bank and UNDP.

World Bank (1989b) *Sub-Saharan Africa: From Crisis to Sustainable Growth*, Washington DC, World Bank.

17

JAMAICA

Jane Harrigan

17.1 INTRODUCTION

Having received more IMF stabilisation packages since 1977 than any other country, three World Bank Structural Adjustment Loans and three Sectoral Adjustment Loans since 1982, and significant bilateral balance-of-payments support from USAID during the 1980s, the Jamaican economy provides the opportunity for an analysis of the interaction between different types of programme lending. This chapter focuses on various aspects of the relationship between Fund-based stabilisation programmes and Bank-guided adjustment programmes, and between multilateral and bilateral programme lending in the Jamaican economy during the 1980s. An attempt is made to use the Jamaican experience to draw general policy conclusions and recommendations regarding the future orientation and co-ordination of these various forms of programme lending activities.

The first two sections of the chapter present an overview of Jamaica's policy environment and economic performance in the 1960s and 1970s. The intention is to illustrate aspects of both domestic policy and the international economic environment which, by the late 1970s, gave rise to the need for an adjustment and stabilisation effort on the part of Jamaican policy-makers. In addition, the political economy context within which such efforts were to be implemented is outlined.

Sections four to six cover three discrete phases of the adjustment and stabilisation policies of the 1980s. The chronology chosen is not determined by the disbursement of various programme loans, but rather by changes which occurred in the relative bargaining power of the Jamaican Government and the lead donor agencies. Such changes were caused by the combined influence of both internal and external political and economic factors. These shifts in power had a critical impact on both the nature of the stabilisation and adjustment efforts undertaken, and on the relationships between the policy conditions attached to the various forms of multi- and bilateral programme lending. The concluding section summarises the salient lessons which emerge from the analysis of Jamaica's three phases of policy reform, with particular emphasis on issues relating to conflicting conditionalities and cross-conditionalities.

17.2   THE JAMAICAN ECONOMY, 1962–77: POLITICAL ECONOMY, POLICIES AND PERFORMANCE

In order to understand the structural adjustment process which occurred in Jamaica under the 1980–8 Jamaica Labour Party (JLP) Government, led by Edward Seaga, the process must be placed in a historical context going back to the early 1960s.

It is tempting to blame the economic crisis of the late 1970s largely on the expansionist fiscal policies of Michael Manley's 1972–80 People's National Party (PNP) Government (as has been done, for example, by Sharpley, 1984). However, the seeds of crisis had been sown much earlier in the form of the development strategies adopted during the 1960s. A series of exogenous shocks in the 1970s – the oil price crisis, a collapse in export prices, recession in OECD countries, and disequilibrium in international financial markets – exposed the fragility of the earlier successes of the post-independence strategy. This is not to deny that the crisis was greatly exacerbated by the lack of fiscal and monetary discipline displayed by the Manley Government. However, the adjustment required during the 1980s encompassed much more than reinculcating sound fiscal management.

At the time of independence in 1962, the Jamaican economy was relatively well endowed with agricultural resources, a good civil service, effective health and education systems, sound infrastructure and a nascent manufacturing sector. However, the economy was extremely open, relying heavily on imported inputs and with foreign exchange earning potential largely confined to the agricultural sector, in particular, bananas and sugar. Hence, the economy was highly vulnerable to external shocks, so requiring rapid policy response to changes in the international economic environment.

Following the conventional wisdom of economic theory in the 1960s, Jamaica adopted an Import Substituting Industrialisation (ISI) strategy in the form of a highly protectionist trade regime, using tariffs, quantitative restrictions, and an overvalued exchange rate to protect an inefficient, capital-intensive and monopolistic domestic manufacturing sector. The Government provided impetus to the ISI strategy by enacting various forms of incentive legislation, which included the granting of tax-holdings, export draw-back schemes, and subsidised factors, as well as the provision of Government-guaranteed debt to a range of public-enterprise activities. Under such a policy environment, manufacturing flourished during the 1960s and early 1970s whilst agriculture, facing unfavourable domestic terms of trade, and competition from heavily subsidised imported food items, stagnated. Nevertheless, 1962–72 represented a boom period. The

312

terms of trade remained favourable, and the 1960s witnessed a massive inflow of foreign capital in the form of investment in two newly-developing sectors, namely, tourism and the bauxite/alumina industry.

The advent of Manley's People's National Party (PNP) Government in 1972 did not represent, as some believe, a fundamental radicalisation of Jamaica's political economy, but rather an intensification of past policies.[1] The ISI strategy continued to be led by an increasingly interventionist government, the main difference being the greater level of social consciousness displayed by the latter. This took the form of attempts to alleviate the growing unemployment problem, through measures such as a land reform programme and the creation of farmers' co-operatives aimed at stimulating agricultural production, along with increased public expenditure on social services.

The fact that some Washington observers have characterised 1972 as a watershed in Jamaican politics indicates a lack of awareness of certain similarities between Jamaica's two political parties – both are based on Trade Union movements, and both have advocated an interventionist, state-led, development strategy. Indeed, the main difference between the JLP Government of the late 1960s, with Seaga as Minister of Finance, and the JLP Government of the 1980s with Seaga as Prime Minister, was that government intervention in the latter period, under the auspices of the World Bank's structural adjustment programme, focused on an export-oriented, as opposed to an ISI strategy. However, Seaga's scepticism regarding the potential of an unfettered private sector to respond to liberalisation incentives, and fears regarding the political dangers of allowing a rapid erosion of real wage levels, continued to be evident during the 1980s, and presented a major constraint to Jamaica's stabilisation and adjustment efforts.

When Manley's PNP Government came to power in 1972, it inherited an economy already showing signs of 'Dutch Disease' – increasing reliance had been placed on the growing bauxite/alumina industry as a reliable earner of the foreign exchange needed to finance imported inputs required by the domestic manufacturing sector. As early as the 1972 election, a basic policy problem had found its way into the psyche of both political parties in the form of an inability to envisage potential decay in this key foreign exchange earning sector. Despite the declining fortunes of the bauxite/alumina industry during 1979–82, the same myopia was displayed in the early 1980s. Until the second collapse of bauxite prices in 1985, Seaga, assisted by the over-optimism of both the IMF and World Bank, maintained faith in the recovery of the bauxite/alumina industry, and this faith helps to explain the somewhat half-hearted nature of stabilisation and adjustment policies undertaken prior to 1986.

Structural weaknesses in the economy were first exposed by the oil price shock of the early 1970s. In 1970, almost 99 per cent of Jamaica's fuel

313

needs were met by imported oil such that the oil price shock had a major impact on the country's trade balance. This was compounded by a rapid increase in the price of imported foodstuffs at a time when domestic agriculture was stagnating due to the effects of the earlier policy regime. Until the latter part of the 1970s, buoyancy in world sugar and bauxite/alumina prices prevented a sharp deterioration in the terms of trade. However, the declining fortunes of the bauxite/alumina industry from 1978 onwards and the impact of OECD recession on tourism resulted in a dramatic deterioration in the terms of trade during the latter part of the 1970s.[2] In such a highly-trade-dependent economy, with an average ratio of trade to GNP of over 100 per cent throughout the 1970s,[3] the adverse impact of such exogenous shocks on the balance of payments cannot be overstressed.

The Government's response to the first oil price shock was an attempt to form an International Bauxite Association (IBA) following the concept of the OPEC cartel, combined with the introduction of a 7–9 per cent variable production levy on the bauxite industry. To quote a key moderate member of Manley's Government at that time: 'OPEC had created a new international legitimacy for the concept of capturing rents for the South from the mineral sector', (personal interview, Washington DC, December 1988). Initially, the policy met with success. Revenue from a previously undertaxed sector of the economy increased fourfold, and in 1974 generated 20 per cent of Central Government revenue – an amount just sufficient to cover the increase in the oil import bill. However, Jamaica had overestimated the strength of the IBA. Other members did not follow suit with a similar levy, and with production costs in Jamaica increased by over 17 per cent as a result of the levy, multinational producers began to shift resources and production elsewhere. Consequently, both production and exports from the bauxite industry declined consistently from the 1974 peak and revenue from the levy declined in the immediate years after its imposition.

Rents extracted from the bauxite industry were predominantly used to finance government consumption rather than, as originally intended, to finance the capital accumulation needed to underpin the economy's productive sectors. Under such circumstances the Government budget increasingly became an expenditure rather than a financing budget. This expansionary fiscal policy, largely aimed at improving the country's social indicators, was conducted with little regard for either internal or external constraints. As a result, public finances deteriorated rapidly in the 1974 to 1976 period. The Government's current account moved from surplus, to a deficit equivalent to 6.4 per cent of GDP in 1976, whilst the overall deficit increased from 8.7 per cent of GDP to 19.5 per cent of GDP in the same period (Table 17.1).

The Government's financing gap was increasingly monetised by utilising

Table 17.1 Macroeconomic indicators, 1972–80

	1972	1973	1974	1975	1976	1977	1978	1979	1980
GDP growth rate (%)	2.3	1.2	−3.8	0.3	−6.5	−2.4	0.4	−1.7	−5.8
of which: Agriculture (%)	1.8	−8.5	4.9	1.7	0.7	2.9	9.7	−10.4	−4.3
Mining (%)	6.4	14.3	8.5	−20.2	−20.6	17.5	2.5	−1.6	9.9
Manufacturing (%)	11.7	0.7	−3.4	2.3	−4.4	−7.4	−4.7	−4.9	−11.6
Construction (%)	−2.9	−11.7	−5.4	−1.3	−20.0	−20.8	3.6	−0.6	28.3
Consumption as % of GDP	78.1	78.1	85.9	84.5	90.5	89.1	83.4	84.6	86.5
Investment as % of GDP	27.5	31.5	24.4	25.8	18.4	12.4	15.2	19.1	15.6
Unemployment (%)	23.6	21.4	21.8	19.9	20.5	24.6	23.0	24.4	27.9
Inflation: % rate of change of consumer price index (1975=100)	5.4	17.4	27.3	17.4	9.8	11.5	35.0	28.9	28.2
Imports (US $ million)	642.6	676.6	935.9	1123.5	912.8	746.8	864.7	1002.8	1172.6
Exports (US $ million)	391.3	390.2	706.2	851.6	632.5	733.6	738.1	814.7	952.2
Balance-of-payments on current account (US $ million)	N/A	−180.3	−78.5	−257.2	−308.8	−28.9	−86.8	−142.6	−166.9
Government current account deficit as % of GDP	N/A	−0.8	2.3	1.8	−6.4	−6.2	−2.8	−4.2	−7.7
Overall government deficit as % of GDP	−3.5	−5.6	−8.7	−9.8	−19.5	−17.4	−14.2	−12.5	−17.5
Bank of Jamaica net credit to Central Government	N/A	42.5	74.6	156.7	371.0	420.4	597.4	804.0	1369.9

Sources: World Bank (1984a, b) statistical appendices.
Note: Fiscal data is given for the fiscal year, hence 1972 covers 1 April 1972 to 31 March 1973, and so forth.

accommodations from the Central Bank of Jamaica, with net Bank credit to the Government increasing from J $74.6 million in 1974 to J $371 million in 1976 (Table 17.1). To facilitate this process, the Bank of Jamaica Law was amended such that the Bank was potentially obliged to fund one-third of the *total* government budget with no repayment periods specified. With government expenditure running at over 30 per cent of GDP, and one third of this fundable by high-powered Central Bank money, a recipe for double digit inflation was in place. By 1978, inflation was running at 35 per cent. The inflationary effects of the expansionary monetary policy were further fuelled by rapid increases in both import prices and nominal wages.

The effects of the government's loose monetary policy put considerable pressure on the balance of payments through the accommodation of increased import demand. In addition, the resulting inflationary spiral, combined with lack of exchange-rate adjustment, caused a decline in the international competitiveness of Jamaica's exports. This compounded the already severe effects of exogenous trade shocks, and as a result of the deteriorating balance of payments, the Bank of Jamaica's net international reserves fell from US $109.9 million in 1973 to minus US $556 million in 1980.

As foreign reserves became tighter, import licensing proliferated, such that by 1980 370 items were covered, compared to 60 in 1970. With both licence and foreign exchange allocation becoming more arbitrary, domestic production declined, giving rise to high levels of unemployment. In addition, evidence of economic mismanagement led to a flight of both human and investment capital, with foreign private capital flows deteriorating from US $91 million in 1973 to minus US $201 million in 1978. This rapid decline in investment led to a consistent fall in GDP, such that by 1980, real GDP stood 18 per cent below its 1973 peak (Table 17.1).

By 1976, it had already become obvious that economic problems had moved beyond the issues of management of monetary and fiscal parameters to issues relating to the deterioration of the economy's real resource base. Acknowledging this, Gladstone Bonnick, Deputy Governor of the Bank of Jamaica, attempted to persuade the Government to call an early election and devise a stabilisation package. Although the borrowing of petro-dollars from Trinidad and Tobago and Venezuela enabled the decision to be postponed, by the end of 1976 foreign exchange reserves were again depleted, to such an extent that an oil tanker was turned back from Kingston harbour. Within this context of crisis management, an election was called and exploratory negotiations were initiated with the IMF.

17.3   1977–80:   ECONOMIC CRISIS AND THE IMF

It is not possible to understand the Bank's structural adjustment programme of the 1980s without first analysing Jamaica's involvement with IMF stabilisation packages from 1977 onwards. Although it is true that no country (with the exception of the recent and much criticised case of Argentina) has received Bank programme aid without a Fund programme of some sort first being in place, the link between IMF and Bank activities has been particularly close in Jamaica. In particular, despite the large number of agreements between Jamaica and the Fund in the past fifteen years, relations between the Government and the Fund have often been exceedingly strained and this has had crucial implications for the programme lending activities of other donors, particularly the World Bank.

An analysis of the IMF involvement in the Jamaican economy during the last three years of the Manley regime, 1977–80, indicates two key political factors, one internal and one external, which impacted heavily upon the nature and success of the attempted stabilisation programmes. The internal factor took the form of the strength of the Trade Union Movement and the obstacle this posed both to the ability to effect a sustained real devaluation of the Jamaican dollar and to the ability to reduce real wage levels. The external factor took the form of political pressures on the US Carter Administration and the influence this had on the nature of the Washington multilaterals' and bilaterals' activities in Jamaica. Despite the fact that the bargaining strategies adopted by Seaga, in his dealings with both internal and external political forces, contrasted starkly with those of Manley, the same two factors continued to influence the stabilisation and adjustment policies of the 1980s.

When negotiations were initiated with the IMF in late 1976 Jamaica possessed a cadre of technicians and bureaucrats – Gladstone Bonnick at the Bank of Jamaica, E. Bell as the new Minister of Finance and R. Fletcher as Secretary to the Minister of Finance – who were both willing and able to devise a much needed stabilisation programme. This facilitated a highly internalised policy debate with the Fund. Following negotiations between the two parties, the Government adopted a comprehensive stabilisation programme which formed the basis of a one-year stand-by, the first tranche of US $22 million being drawn in July 1977.

As a prior condition of the agreement, a two-tier exchange rate was established in an attempt to legalise the parallel foreign exchange market. The result was a 37 per cent devaluation (Table 17.2), and was undoubtedly seen by the Fund as the first step towards a unified and devalued exchange rate. However, with the exception of exchange rate reform, there was little genuine attempt at stabilisation. This was largely due to internal political factors, with radical members of the PNP having

317

captured control of the party apparatus following the 1976 election. Consequently, public expenditure continued to increase, large public sector pay increases were awarded, and the Government continued drawing heavily on the Bank of Jamaica, the latter resulting in the resignation of one of the Government's lead negotiators, Gladstone Bonnick. By December 1977 it had become obvious that the restrictive stand-by targets for both the fiscal and external accounts would not be met. At this stage, the first evidence of an external political dimension to programme lending in Jamaica became apparent. Technocrats and politicians, both in Jamaica

Table 17.2 Jamaica dollar (J $) exchange rate (currency unit = US $)

Period	Rates	Comments
Up to April 1977	US $1.00 = J $0.909	
April 1977	Basic rate US $1.00 = J $0.909 Special rate US $1.00 = J $1.250	A dual exchange system introduced, resulting in the equivalent of a 37% devaluation. Essential imports and government and bauxite
May 1978	Basic rate US $1.00 = J $1.050 Special rate US $1.00 = J $1.350	sector imports remained on the former 'basic' rate, all other transactions were conducted at the 'special rate'. A crawling-peg also adopted in the form of small monthly devaluation to both rates, up until May 1978.
10 May 1978	US $1.00 = J $1.550	Exchange rate unified resulting in the equivalent of a 25% devaluation. Crawling-peg devaluations continued,
– May 1979	US $1.00 = J $1.781	totalling 15% by May 1979.
May 1979 – Jan. 1983	US $1.00 = J $1.781 Official rate US $1.00 = J $1.781	Fixed exchange rate in place May 1979 to Jan. 1983.
Jan. 1983 – Nov. 1983	Parallel rate US $1.00 = J $2.40–2.80	Introduction of a two-tier market, in the form of an official and a parallel rate, the latter to be determined by the commercial banks.
Nov. 1983	US $1.00 = J $3.15	Exchange rates unified determined by twice-weekly auctions.
Oct. 1985	US $1.00 = J $6.40	
Oct. 1985 – March 1988	US $1.00 = J $5.50	Exchange rate revalued via government intervention in the exchange auction, and maintained at its new level.

Source: Bank of Jamaica Statistical Digest, various issues.

318

and Washington, openly criticised the Fund for having coerced Jamaica into agreeing to harsh and unrealistic stabilisation targets. In particular, Andrew Young, a black congressman, and a key contact point between Jimmy Carter and black Americans, having recently returned from a Caribbean tour and speaking at the United Nations, vilified the IMF for pushing countries such as Jamaica into unnecessary austerity, and simultaneously criticised the US Government for providing inadequate supportive funding to the region.

Possibly due to the influence of the above types of criticism, the stand-by was abandoned and in its place a three-year Extended Fund Facility (EFF) was signed in May 1978 which provided a longer period for adjustment, and higher financing levels. However, despite the more flexible approach adopted by the Fund, and despite mounting criticism of US reluctance to provide aid to the Manley Government, the Carter Administration, ignoring requests from the Fund itself, refused to increase financial commitments to Jamaica. Although the stabilisation attempts of the late 1970s were to falter largely due to Manley's inability to control political radicals within the PNP, lack of supportive financing from bilaterals such as the USAID undoubtedly further reduced the chance of success.

Under the three year EFF, the short-lived two-tier foreign exchange system was replaced with a single rate, resulting in an immediate 15 per cent devaluation, which was to be followed by a crawling-peg of small monthly devaluations to total 15 per cent by May 1979 (Table 17.2). The Government's tight control of imports was allowed to continue, although many price controls on imported items were to be removed. In addition, a wages and incomes policy was agreed upon, limiting nominal wage increases to 15 per cent per annum. A sharp reduction in the Central Government deficit was targeted for fiscal year 1978/9, with government credit and foreign indebtedness ceilings also being imposed.

From the start, the political aspects of this second stabilisation programme were acknowledged by both the Fund and the Government. The Fund team encouraged a highly participatory style of negotiation, effectively insisting that the Government itself devise and define the stabilisation programme. In response, the Government attempted to develop a bipartisan approach by involving several key members of the JLP opposition. A close dialogue was also conducted between the Fund, the Government, and the Trade Union Movement, resulting in support from the latter for the wage and income policy. Manley himself personalised the stabilisation issues, publicly expressing his commitment at mass rallies with speeches explaining the need for price increases and wage restraint. The Government's letter of intent and the list of Fund conditions were published in the Jamaican press and circulated in political pamphlets. In return, Fund staff unprecedentedly presented part of Manley's political speech to the Fund's Board as a supporting document to illustrate the strength of government commitment to reform.

Within three months of the EFF agreement real wages in Jamaica had been cut by 30 per cent – a brutal adjustment by the standards of the 1970s.[4] However, by the second year of the EFF Manley, coming under growing pressure from radicals within the PNP and lacking a strong political coalition, was unable to sustain commitment to the stabilisation package. The party radicals both vilified and neutralised the more moderate government technocrats and bureaucrats,[5] despatched missions to the Eastern Bloc in search of finance, and began to put together their own alternative economic package.

The growing political and economic uncertainty, including knowledge of an impending election, exacerbated the haemorrhage of both human and investment capital. As economic activity stagnated, taxes failed to bring in the required revenue such that fiscal performance continued to deteriorate. Recession, capital flight, and high government deficits caused growing trade and current account deficits on the balance of payments (Table 17.1) and in December 1979 the Fund's net international reserves target was not met, resulting in the suspension of the Extended Fund Facility. Although attempts were made by Manley to sell a new Fund-based stabilisation package to moderates in the party, he was resoundingly defeated by the PNP Party Committee. Hence, the Government severed relations with the Fund and called a general election.

During a protracted and bloody election campaign, both moderates and radicals within the PNP criticised the Fund for lack of political impartiality, claiming that the severe austerity measures foisted on the PNP Government by the Fund had been intended to ensure the defeat of the former in the forthcoming election. They were supported in their claims by a lead negotiator from the Fund's team who circulated a memo to Fund staff expressing concern at impartiality and at US interference in Jamaican politics.

Following the lead of the radicals, Manley's election campaign was based upon a faith in a 'New International Economic Order', which dramatically changed the international parameters of what the Jamaican economy should be expected to adjust to. Hence, the election campaign encompassed wide ranging ideological issues regarding Jamaica's future economic and political path: 'The merits of the mixed versus the market economy;. . . an independent self-reliant approach versus an IMF-guided path; diversifying links to the socialist world versus entrenching ties with the West' (Edmondson, 1982: 589).

However, the political and economic events of the past years had not only severely polarised Jamaican society, they had also exerted considerable economic hardship on vast numbers of the population such that the election resulted in a landslide victory for Edward Seaga's JLP party.

Manley's defeat was a double-edged blow. Not only was he ousted from power by a trade union movement, whose support for stabilisation three years earlier he had apparently gained, large numbers of the poorer members of non-unionised Jamaican society, whose well-being had been the focus of his government's social programmes, contributed to his defeat. It is worth quoting at length a retrospective criticism of the policies of the late 1970s from one of the key moderates of the time, Gladstone Bonnick:

> An effective stabilisation package was postponed for too long, allowing a radicalisation by which the whole business of giving higher priority to politics than good economic administration became ingrained in the Executive. In addition, we failed to grasp soon enough the importance of a correct exchange rate policy, and eventually counselled approaches involving too much discretionary intervention and not enough automaticity in exchange rate adjustment. Finally, as a Trade Unionist Party, we were wedded to the idea that wages should always compensate for increases in the cost of living, without distinguishing between price increases caused by increased import costs and those due to domestic cost increases. In the former case, although profits and investment must be squeezed, we failed to appreciate that those who would bear the burden were not only high income rentiers, but, through falling employment, the unemployed, as well as those on fixed wages, and those in inefficiently unionised sectors – agriculture and public sector workers.
>   (Personal interview, Washington DC, December 1988)

It is remarkable, that less than one week after Seaga's resounding defeat in the February 1989 election, with a pattern of voting similar to that which ousted Manley in 1980, much the same set of retrospective criticisms are already being voiced against his stabilisation and adjustment policies. As will be seen, the issues of automatic exchange-rate adjustment, concern for real wages in unionised sectors, and the impact on the poor, continued to be the central political and economic constraints to a sustainable stabilisation and adjustment programme in Jamaica during the 1980s.

17.4 THE FIRST PHASE OF ADJUSTMENT, 1980–3: IMPORT-LED GROWTH

The newly-elected JLP Government immediately initiated fresh negotiations with the IMF, and by March 1981 a three-year Extended Fund Facility had been agreed upon. A marked feature of this new agreement was its relatively mild conditionality, including the lack of any conditions relating to devaluation, reductions in public sector employment or public sector expenditure reductions. However, ambitious targets were set for the reduction of the Government's budgetary deficit and improvements in the balance-of-payments performance. These targets were predominantly based upon optimistic projections regarding GDP growth rates, with output improvements forecast for most sectors of the economy. To facilitate higher growth rates a policy framework was devised aimed at reducing the Government's direct and regulatory involvement in the economy. This included the gradual removal of import restrictions, divestment or scaling-down of many state enterprises, and a general revision of the incentive structure in order to promote private sector export-led growth.

Jamaica's first Structural Adjustment Loan (SAL I) was agreed in 1982 and provided US $76.2 million in balance-of-payments support. This was followed in 1983 by SAL II, providing US $60.2 million. Preparatory work for the loans identified four areas of structural weakness in the economy: balance-of-payments difficulties caused by an overconcentrated export sector and the high import demands of protected domestic industry; serious fiscal imbalance; sluggish performance of both indus-trial and agricultural sectors; and an overregulated economy. To address these problems programmes were designed covering four areas of economic policy, namely, balance-of-payments management, savings and investment, industrial sector policies, and agricultural sector policies.

The focus of the adjustment programme is succinctly summarised in the Bank's own review of SALs I and II:

> Difficulties reflected the wide distortions of market forces within the economy, an excessive level of consumption, particularly by the public sector, low productivity, and an environment which had caused the flight of scarce capital and skilled manpower. The strategy was to stimulate economic growth through an expansion in exports, both through higher capacity utilization and by promoting new investments. The strategy also called for a gradual reduction in the role of the public sector, and for a parallel strengthening of the private sector.
>
> (World Bank, 1984b: 8)

SAL I, like the first Fund agreement under the new Seaga regime, was relatively mild in its conditionality. Many of the conditions related to the initiation of studies on key aspects of the economy, such as a competitiveness study, and an overview of state enterprises with detailed programmes to be devised once the results of the studies were available. This, in part, reflected the Bank's acknowledgement of the need for a 'learning period'. However, the need for such a strategy raises questions in terms of the realism of the Fund's expectation of a rapid supply response which formed the basis of the stabilisation targets.

Government compliance with SAL conditionality was high during SAL I and the first phase of SAL II, in the sense that:

322

On a strictly legal basis, Jamaica has complied with the conditions of both loans and . . . a broad range of policy measures have been instituted. Indeed, in several areas, progress has been more rapid than had originally been envisaged. For example, most import licensing has now been removed, some three years ahead of the original programme.

(World Bank, 1984b: 9)

However, the fact that the Bank itself qualifies compliance as being on a 'strictly legal basis', suggests that it was the 'letter', rather than the 'spirit', of the adjustment programme which was complied with. An analysis of policy implementation during the period indicates that failure 'in spirit' was largely the result of the government's unwillingness to implement an adequate stabilisation package in relation to both the balance of payments and fiscal management.

The balance-of-payments focus of SALs I and II consisted of an agreement to gradually relax the import licensing system, which was seen as a major impediment to export and productivity improvements. The initial move was made in early 1983, when the Government announced that exporters would be automatically issued with import licenses. This granting of licence priority to exporters coincided with a change in the exchange-rate system. The rapid deterioration in the balance of payments during 1982, combined with a growing black market in foreign currency, had forced the government and IMF to reach an agreement in terms of exchange rate reform. A two-tier exchange rate was again established, with a 'parallel' rate set by the commercial banks at the initial level of US $1.00 = J $2.70, and the former fixed rate maintained at US $1.00 = J $1.781 as the official rate to be used for a range of government, bauxite sector, and essential imports (Table 17.2).

Despite concessions made to the Fund in the form of the above exchange rate reform, the government held firm in its resistance to an upfront devaluation under a single fixed rate system. In addition, throughout 1983 the Government continued to intervene in the foreign exchange market in order to prevent a widening of the differential between the official and the parallel rates and refused to allow the scheduled transfer of a range of transactions from the official to the parallel rate.

The above resistance to comprehensive exchange rate reform partly undermined the effects of the import licensing reforms simultaneously implemented as a condition of the SAL programme. Worsening of the foreign exchange shortage during 1983 was counteracted by the imposition of greater control over the licensing system such that by the end of 1983, exporters were no longer being given priority treatment. In the Bank's own words: 'This programme was not a completely successful one, not least because of some of the difficulties with operating the parallel market exchange system' (World Bank, 1984b: 13).

SALs I and II also aimed at stimulating export-orientated industrial growth via the gradual removal of 364 quantitative import restrictions (QRs) which were to be replaced with a rationalised tariff system. Progress on this front was rapid, such that by January 1984, 186 of the 364 restrictions had been removed. The above moves towards a liberalised trade regime were accompanied by the establishment of an export incentives scheme. Exporters of non-traditional products to countries outside of the Caribbean Community (CARICOM) were permitted to retain 50 per cent of their hard-currency earnings. In addition, an Export Development Fund was to advance to exporters, in hard currency, 50 per cent of their potential export earnings. However, as with import licensing reforms, although the export-incentive reforms were carried-out according to 'the letter' of the SAL agreement, their effectiveness was partly neutralised by the Government's failure to abide by the general 'spirit' of the overall stabilisation and adjustment programme. Government intervention in the foreign exchange market during 1983 severely depleted the Bank of Jamaica's foreign reserves, such that the latter was unable to replenish the Export Development Fund, so rendering the latter inoperative.

The focus of agricultural sector policies under SALs I and II was similar to that for the industrial sector with the primary objective being the stimulation of export production, of both non-traditional crops and the traditional crops of bananas and sugar. The main weaknesses in the sector were identified as institutional, in the form of the External Marketing Organisations (EMOs). The Government complied well with SAL conditionality relating to the agricultural sector. An EMO reform programme was adopted, with progress made towards managerial reforms and the divestment of a range of non-marketing activities. In addition, an export parity-based formula was agreed upon for the six main export crops. A land reform programme was also launched under SAL I, with 8,940 acres of government-owned land sold or leased to private farmers in 1983.

Concern with savings and investment under the structural adjustment programme mainly concentrated on the issue of public sector savings by addressing the deficits of major public enterprises, with the question of Central Government expenditure and the overall public sector deficit being left to the IMF's stabilisation programme. Conditions under SAL I consisted of carrying out studies, whilst under SAL II a range of reforms were implemented to improve the performance of public enterprises involved in the public utilities and public transport system. These included large tariff increases, a drastic reduction in staffing levels, and privatisation of the Kingston Omnibus Company. Again, however, although the Government performed well in terms of implementing the reforms prescribed under the SAL loans, the objective of improving the overall position of public sector savings was not achieved due to the high slippage

Table 17.3 Macroeconomic indicators 1979–83

	1979	1980	1981	1982	1983
GDP growth rate (%)	−1.7	−5.8	2.5	1.2	2.5
of which: Agriculture (%)	−10.4	−4.3	2.3	−7.9	7.3
Mining (%)	−1.6	9.9	1.3	−29.0	0.6
Manufacture (%)	−4.9	−11.6	1.1	6.4	1.9
Construction (%)	−0.6	−28.3	0.4	15.9	6.7
Unemployment (%)	24.4	27.9	26.2	27.0	25.3
Inflation: % rate of change of consumer price index (1975 = 100)	28.9	28.2	11.9	6.5	16.7
Imports (US $ million)	1003	1173	1481	1376	1281
Exports (US $ million)	815	959	978	769	686
Balance-of-payments current account (US $ million)	−142.6	−166.9	−437.5	−460.6	−278.6
Government current account deficit as % of GDP	−4.2	−7.7	−3.4	−3.7	−10.0
Overall government deficit as % of GDP	−12.5	−17.5	−15.9	−14.1	−15.8

Note: For public sector financial data 1979 represents fiscal year 1 April 1979 to 31 March 1980, and so forth.
Sources: World Bank (1984a, b) Statistical Appendices; Davies (1986) Tables 4 and 9.

in terms of the Fund's fiscal stabilisation measures which resulted in a rapid deterioration in the finances of central government.

Despite the reforms carried out under SALs I and II and despite the improvement in GDP growth rates, economic performance between 1980 and the end of 1983 remained weak. This weakness was reflected in a continued deterioration of the trade balance and the government current account deficit, and failure to improve the overall government deficit as a percentage of GDP (Table 17.3).

The positive GDP growth rates of 1982 and 1983 resulted from increased availability of foreign exchange, and a return of investor confidence. However, as Table 17.3 indicates, growth within various sectors was erratic. The recovery was led by those sectors sensitive to exchange availability and confidence, namely construction, tourism and financial services. Although manufacturing output improved drastically in 1982, with a growth rate of 6.4 per cent in that year, its decline in the subsequent two years was equally dramatic, whilst performance of the agricultural and mining sectors was disappointing. The above trends in output suggest that the GDP recovery of the early 1980s represented a short-term boom, rather than a return to sustainable positive growth rates. Analysis of investment trends supports this view.

The negative trend in real investment expenditure of the late 1970s was reversed, such that 1980–3 saw an average increase of 11.7 per cent p.a. and an increasing share contributed by the private sector. Part of this represented restocking and replacement of capital equipment made possible by increased foreign exchange availability and the liberalisation of imports. Much, however, represented speculation in real estate during the construction boom of 1981 and 1982 and investments from US businesses trying to take advantage of CARICOM and the Kingston Free Trade Zone. Hence, despite increased investment levels, there was little in the way of genuine new productive private investment needed to diversify the export base and to relieve the chronic unemployment problem. Throughout the period, unemployment levels remained above the 25 per cent level (Table 17.3).

Trends in the balance of payments indicate that much of the growth of the 1980–3 period was essentially import-led. Following years of frustrated import demand the increased foreign exchange availability, including that provided by the Fund and Bank's balance-of-payments support, and the liberalisation of import licensing, led to a higher level of imports when compared with the import levels of the late 1970s (Table 17.3). Although part of the increase took the form of capital goods, the greatest increase was registered in food, consumer durables and transport equipment. At the same time, export performance was disappointing, with a sharp decline in bauxite/alumina exports in 1982 and 1983, and non-traditional exports failing to play the significant role in economic recovery which had been predicted by both the Bank and the Fund. The combined performance of imports and exports contributed to a sharp deterioration in the current account of the balance of payments in both 1981 and 1982.

The stabilisation programme also failed to bring about any significant improvement in the area of public finance. Between 1980 and 1983, the Central Government current deficit deteriorated from 7.7 per cent of GDP to 10.0 per cent of GDP, whilst the overall deficit as a percentage of GDP showed no improvement in 1983 when compared to 1981 and fell well short of the IMF targets for 1983. Poor performance was predominantly due to a dramatic fall in revenue from the bauxite levy and the inability to curb increases in current account expenditure, much of which related to higher interest payments on external debt and food subsidies, the latter being tolerated by both the Fund and the Bank as a facility necessary to soften the impact of devaluation on low income households.

In summary, the period 1980 to the end of 1983 was one of import-led growth. Although the Bank, in a retrospective analysis, suggests that this was to be expected:

This had been largely foreseen, since an explicit aim of the economic recovery programme had been to increase imports to stimulate economic activity, to be financed by a higher level of borrowing until the economy could be re-oriented towards growth.

(World Bank, 1984b: 6)

The form which imports took, namely, consumption and capital replacement goods, did little to reorientate the economy towards sustainable export-led growth.

In the Bank's own internal review of SALs I and II, the single most important reason for the disappointing economic performance was identified as the failure of the Fund's stabilisation programme:

> Overall, however, it is considered that the programme as designed was broadly appropriate and would have achieved most of its expected benefits if the stabilization program had been successful. . . Therefore, the largest risk of the proposed SAL III is the potential for the failure of the new stabilization program.
>
> (World Bank, 1984b: 11)

Such an assessment indicates an important weakness in terms of the co-ordination and sequencing of Bank and Fund operations in the Jamaican economy. The Bank-guided liberalisation of the trade regime, in the form of import licensing reform and the removal of quantitative restrictions, had occurred in advance of a significant devaluation and exchange rate reform under the Fund-guided stabilisation programme. As a result, much of the Bank's work, intended to provide export incentives and revive domestic agriculture, via reform of the trade and incentive regime, was neutralised. The upshot was import-led growth without a medium-term export supply response and lack of improvement in the balance of payments.

This begs an important question regarding the policy emphasis of the first two SALs, namely whether Bank staff were sufficiently active in terms of negotiations concerning exchange-rate policy. Although there was little in the way of disagreement between the Government and the Bank regarding the reforms to the trade regime covered by SAL conditionality, the corner-stone of successful reform constituted exchange-rate policy. Reluctance by the Government to implement such a reform was the most significant aspect of implicit disagreement regarding 'the spirit' of the adjustment programme. Resistance centred on the Government's concern at the manner in which devaluation, in such an open economy, rapidly translated into domestic price increases, implying a concomitant reduction in real wage levels, particularly for the poorer members of Jamaican society not protected by the institutional wage-bargaining of the strong Trade Union Movements. This predominantly political concern continued to prevail throughout the 1980s.

Despite the centrality of the exchange rate issue, the overriding impression, given by both Jamaican policy-makers and Bank staff, is that during the late 1970s and early 1980s, the Bank maintained a relatively low profile in such areas, allowing the lead to be taken by the Fund, to a greater extent than normally implied by the traditional Bank/Fund division of labour. Indeed, Jamaica's first two SALs were highly sectorally orientated, focusing on the manufacturing, agricultural and export sectors, and concentrating particularly on details of the trade regime, and as such, had more of the character of a series of simultaneous Sectoral Adjustment Loans (SECALs) than a full-blown structural adjustment programme. As a result, in the early 1980s the Bank tolerated a high level of slippage in terms of exchange rate and fiscal policy. It was not until 1986, when a tripartite Bank/Fund/USAID mission formulated a joint policy framework paper, that the Bank became significantly involved in stipulations regarding such macro-policy parameters.

The Bank's own assessment regarding the impact of unsuccessful stabilisation on the SAL objectives also raises a second important question regarding Bank/Fund interaction. Fund targets for the Government deficit, balance-of-payments performance, and foreign reserve accumulation, established under the Extended Fund Facility, involved dramatic improvements in these variables over a three-year period. Beliefs that such targets were attainable, in the absence of any conditions relating to devaluation, were partly based on optimistic expectations regarding GDP growth rates in all sectors of the economy. Hence, the IMF programme was unusual, not only in the mildness of its conditionality, but also in view of the fact that considerable emphasis was placed upon developments on the supply side of the economy in order to achieve Fund targets generally associated with short-term demand-side policies. Therefore, the traditional sequencing, whereby the success of short-term stabilisation is seen as a prerequisite for successful medium-term adjustment with growth, was reversed. Within this context, *rapid* success in the structural adjustment programme initiated by the World Bank in 1982 became crucial, not only to medium-term economic performance, but also to the short-term performance of the Jamaican economy in the form of attaining targets set by the stabilisation programme.

However, a degree of inconsistency emerges here. Bank staff clearly stated that in the early years of the adjustment programme 'a sharp deterioration in the current account of the balance of payments. . . was foreseen' since the programme was designed to 'increase imports to stimulate economic activity, to be financed by a higher level of borrowing until the economy could be reorientated towards exports'. Clearly, the implication of such a statement is that the success of supply-side reorientation would take *several* years to emerge.

Given the public criticism the Fund had encountered during the late 1970s for the harshness of targets set for the Jamaican economy, one has to ask why the above inconsistency between the Fund's 1981 EFF targets and the Bank's time horizon for the adjustment programme was apparently overlooked by both multilaterals. The question is particularly pertinent given the extent to which output growth rates fell short of Fund predictions, and the magnitude by which the EFF targets were missed, both of which are outlined in Table 17.4.

The answer to the above question is partly given by the excessive optimism of the Bank, Fund, and Government regarding expected growth rates in OECD countries, the expected levels of private capital inflows, and in particular the potential performance of the bauxite industry. Although bauxite earnings held up well in 1981, this was largely due to stockpiling on the part of the USA. However, 1982 and 1983 saw a 45 per cent drop in foreign currency earnings from the sector due to a sharp decline in both world demand and international prices. The effects were severe, not only in terms of the balance of payments, but also due to the impact on government revenues. In fiscal year 1980–1, levy revenues stood at 4.7 per cent of GDP and represented 20 per cent of total government revenue; by 1983–4 this had fallen to 2.5 per cent of GDP and 10 per cent of revenue. Questions must therefore be asked regarding the basis of the Bank and Fund predictions for this sector, since there were clear signs in 1981 of potential excess global capacity, which, combined with the effects of world depression, could be expected to have an adverse impact on the industry.

Had the Bank, Fund and Government paid greater heed to international forecasts emanating from the private sector of the bauxite/alumina industry, predictions for Jamaica's performance would undoubtedly have been far less optimistic. A similar tendency for Bank over-optimism regarding international commodity markets was identified in the Ghana case study, where a misplaced underlying assumption of the structural adjustment programme was the expectation of a strong performance in the cocoa sector. The question was raised in the Ghana context as to why, in the area of commodity price forecasting, the Bank fails to follow its own advice

Table 17.4 Actual and expected performance of the Jamaican economy, 1983–4

	Actual (1983–4)	IMF prediction/target (fiscal year 1983–4)
PRODUCTION		
Bauxite/alumina (million tonnes)	7.7	18
Sugar ('000 long tons)	193	330
Bananas ('000 long tons)	23	120
Non-traditional exports (US $ million)	153	220
FISCAL		
Total government expenditure as % of GDP	42.7	30
Government current account deficit as % of GDP	−10.0	1.0
Overall government deficit as % of GDP	−15.8	−10.0

Source: Davies (1986) Tables 6 and 7.
Note: Actual production data are given for the calendar year. The fiscal year runs from 1 April to 31 March.

regarding the efficiency gains of privatisation by refusing to rely on the expertise of private sector forecasting. The same question is equally applicable in Jamaica.

The issue of forecasting is not specific to Jamaica and Ghana, or to commodity prices. In the 1988 World Development Report, the Bank acknowledges that throughout the 1980s its own predictions regarding OECD growth rates produced forecasts in excess of twice the actual outturn. In view of this, the question arises as to what extent such over-optimism represents genuine forecasting errors as opposed to institutional-ised, self-serving optimism. The latter interpretation may be explained by internal pressures on the Bank relating to both the raising and the disbursement of funds. Lower OECD growth rate forecasts imply lower LDC growth rates so reducing the latter's capacity to service and capitalise debt obligations, including those due to the Bank. This in turn, has the potential to adversely affect the Bank's own credit ratings on the international bond market and hence its ability to raise finance. In terms of the disbursement of funds, low forecasts of OECD growth rates have two implications. First, they imply contractionary pressure on bilateral aid flows, so increasing the balance-of-payments support required from the Bank. Second, lower levels of bilateral aid imply a larger balance-of-payments gap, and hence a harsher LDC adjustment effort in order to make good such external imbalance, with this harshness being compounded by the prospect of lower export growth rates to OECD economies. The upshot of such a scenario is the need for larger Bank disbursements accompanied by more severe, and hence less feasible, policy reform conditions. Both factors reduce the chance of programme loans being approved by the Bank's Board of Directors.

The analysis of Jamaica's stabilisation and adjustment attempts in the early 1980s clearly indicates that the failure to achieve stabilisation impacted negatively on the objectives of the adjustment programme, which in turn, given the underlying assumptions of the Fund's stabilisation targets, intensified the failure of the latter. This, however, gives rise to a more fundamental question, namely why both institutions were willing to substantially increase their exposure in the Jamaican economy through stabilisation and adjustment programmes involving comparatively mild conditionality and high levels of policy reform slippage.

The mildness of conditions in the 1980–3 period arose from the combined effects of internal and external political factors. Seaga's landslide victory in the 1980 elections ostensibly represented an electoral endorse-ment for an IMF-guided stabilisation package. However, in reality, the victory was based upon a popular vote against the economic and political demise that had beset the latter years of the Manley regime, with the JLP exploiting this through the use of such election slogans as 'immediate deliverance from hardship and poverty'. In addition, Seaga's recent ousting of Shearer as leader of the JLP had left him with a weak internal power base. For both reasons, it would have been politically difficult for the newly-elected Government to immediately implement severe austerity measures particularly in the form of an immediate devaluation.

Hence, although agreement existed between the Government, Fund and Bank regarding the direction of reform i.e. a reorientation towards export-led growth, there was disagreement in terms of the desired pace of reform and the policy instruments to be used, particularly in terms of the use of exchange rate policies. That Seaga was able to gain concessions on the issue of devaluation, reflected in part Bank/Fund awareness of Jamaica's internal political situation. However, such concessions and the subsequent toleration of high levels of policy slippage also reflected the impact of external political factors which influenced the level of multi- and bilateral lending to Jamaica.

The JLP's election to power in 1980 coincided with the new Reagan Administration in the USA. Following the strongly anti-western stance of the latter years of the Manley regime, a new pro-Washington Seaga Government was warmly welcomed by the US Administration since it represented a major shift in the geopolitical alignment of forces in the Caribbean region. Seaga himself was well aware of such factors, and utilized them fully in forming Jamaica's new détente with Washington. Hence, in 1980 the USA was willing to respond to the earlier calls for increased funding levels to Jamaica, resulting in direct White House pressures on the multilaterals to disburse loans. In addition, the Director of the Bank's Latin American and Caribbean Department, who had resisted the calls for increased funding levels in the late 1970s, had been replaced, and within this highly political context a proposed Programme Loan to Jamaica was converted into the first Structural Adjustment Loan. Several Jamaican commentators have been highly critical of this political dimension to Jamaica's stabilisation and adjustment programmes:

> The Reagan Administration has been most supportive of the Seaga regime, both directly and indirectly. In terms of indirect support, it is widely known that on a number of occasions, the USA has intervened on Jamaica's behalf in the deliberations of multilateral organizations such as the IMF and the World Bank. As a result, such agencies have been most lenient in their provision of balance of payments and other financial support.
>
> (Davies, 1986: 89)

The early 1980s also witnessed a dramatic increase in US bilateral aid to Jamaica. Between 1980–1 and 1984–5 Jamaica received a total of US $678.5 million in concessionary support from the US, US $346.6 million of which was in the form of direct balance-of-payments support. At the same time, Canada, Japan and Italy also significantly increased their funding levels. Hence, not only was the Bank under considerable pressure from such Part 1 OECD countries on its Board to likewise increase financial support to Jamaica, but the existence of such high levels of bilateral finance made Bank and Fund loans relatively 'expensive' in terms of the degree of associated conditionality. This undoubtedly contributed to the Bank and Fund's reluctance to impose harsher conditionality on the Seaga regime, and to the tolerance of such slippage as the blatant government intervention in the foreign exchange market during 1983. In addition, the high levels of bilateral support reduced the pressure on Jamaica's balance of payments, which further undercut the force behind Bank and Fund conditionality and retarded the pace of policy reform. It is interesting to note, however, that neither the Bank nor the Fund placed any explicit pressure on USAID to reduce financing levels, despite the fact that several members of the US State Department were themselves expressing concern at the high levels of US financing being granted to the Seaga regime without eliciting any substantial macro-policy reform.

The above observations suggest that there is a need to review the interrelation between multi- and bilateral lending activities. The current tendency is to regard the Fund and the Bank as 'lenders of last resort', whose loans are designed to fill a recipient's residual financing gap *after* bilateral pledges have been estimated. However, this means that both the severity and leverage of multilateral conditionality is arbitrarily dependent on the levels of expected bilateral financing, since it is the latter which determines not only the magnitude of the financing gap to be bridged by the Bank and the Fund, but also the estimation of the extent of stabilisation and adjustment required in the recipient economy.

The interaction between financing levels and policy reform during the early 1980s in Jamaica highlights an inherent conflict contained within both multi- and bilateral programme lending. The granting of balance-of-payments support, by easing external constraints, reduces the immediate pressure to both stabilise and adjust the economy.[6] The dilemma becomes particularly acute, when, as in the Jamaican case, the balance-of-payments gap bridged by concessionary support is large and where disagreement exists between the donor and recipient regarding the pace of the reform programme. In recent years, the Bank itself has shown an increasing awareness of such dilemmas and its recent in-house review of structural adjustment lending (World Bank, 1988) sparked a major internal debate as to whether this type of Bank lending activity was increasingly becoming a soft form of balance-of-payments support which consequently undermined the force of adjustment and stabilisation pressures.

The above dilemma has crucial implications, not only regarding the incentives for immediate reform, but also for the subsequent *magnitude* of a delayed reform effort. In its bargaining with recipient governments, the Bank is quick to point out, when convincing a government to accept adjustment conditions, that a delayed adjustment effort is tantamount to harsher future adjustment requirements. However, the argument is double-edged in that the utilisation of Bank concessionary balance-of-payments support, *without* a concomitant genuine reform effort, *compounds* the magnitude of the future adjustment problem by adding to it the burden of higher debt servicing obligations. Bank, Fund, and USAID balance-of-payments support which was provided to Jamaica in the early 1980s provides a particularly stark example of this dilemma. By 1985, Jamaica's external debt stood at approximately US $3,300 million, which, using all established indicators, gives the country one of the highest per capita debt ratios in the world. Of this, nearly two-thirds was accounted for by central government, much of it being owed to multi- and bi-lateral agencies, including over 20 per cent due to the Fund. As a result, by 1984, debt servicing accounted for over 40 per cent of total government expenditures. Under such constraints, the policy options open to Jamaica in the subsequent phases of the delayed stabilisation and adjustment process were to be severely limited:

> Effectively, there is little room for economic initiatives on the part of the Government after debt-servicing requirements are met. Hence, the Government could be placed increasingly in a defensive position rather than that of an architect of economic policy.
>
> (Davies, 1986: 103)

As events from 1984 onwards were to illustrate, the high level of multi- and bilateral lending in the early 1980s and the associated weak conditionality brought about a situation involving an excessively harsh trade-off between various policy objectives. The use of devaluation as a stabilisation instrument aimed at improving the balance of payments increased fiscal pressures, since a growing amount of the government's domestic currency resources were consequently required to service debt,[7] so giving rise to a costly trade-off between the objectives of external and internal balance. In addition, the debt servicing burden meant that despite tax increases, growth in government expenditure in the post-1984 period did little to expand public sector capital investment in order to underpin the productive sectors of the economy[8] or to improve social services. Consequently, the achievement of stabilisation objectives had a high opportunity cost in terms of both the Bank's adjustment objective of medium-term growth and the government's objective of maintaining political stability.

The government's response to such harsh trade-offs and conflicts was a continued resistance to Fund pressure for a sustained devaluation. However, the alternative followed in the form of tight monetary policy and excessively high interest rates, not only failed to have the desired effect on the balance of payments, it also did much to undermine Bank attempts to foster higher private sector growth rates.

17.5 THE SECOND PHASE OF ADJUSTMENT, 1983–5: STABILISATION VERSUS ADJUSTMENT

The period from the end of 1983 through to the last quarter of 1985 was marked by a weakening in the bargaining position of the Jamaican government in its negotiations with both the Bank and the Fund. As a result, conditions associated with both the stabilisation and adjustment programmes were tightened and the level of compliance, particularly relating to Fund conditions, improved. However, the tight monetary policy used to effect the much delayed stabilisation programme came into direct conflict with the medium-term growth objectives of the Bank's adjustment programme. Consequently the only significant achievement was an improvement in the public sector deficit. The cost of this achievement was high in terms of growing internal political unrest and increased policy reform fatigue on the part of the Jamaican government both of which, by 1986, led to a major rift between the government and the multilaterals.

The disappointing outcome of the 1980–3 stabilisation and adjustment efforts was such that the Government failed to meet the IMF reserves targets in both March and September 1983. As a result, the Extended Fund Facility was abandoned in September, and a period of lengthy negotiations with the Fund commenced. As a precondition of a new Fund agreement the Government was required to unify the two-tier exchange rate in November 1983, with a single, flexible rate to be determined by twice-weekly auctions. These new arrangements resulted in an immediate devaluation, whilst subsequent auction demand and supply forces led to a continuous devaluation through to October 1985 (Table 17.2). Despite these reforms, the Fund was still unable to convince the Government to adopt a single, fixed rate, determined and supported by the Bank of Jamaica, with periodic 'upfront' devaluations in response to pre-established trigger mechanisms.

During the first half of 1984, whilst negotiations with the Fund continued, the Government's main concern continued to be the adverse impact of devaluation on domestic prices and real wage levels. In order to soften this negative social impact a range of measures were introduced which represented a reversal of earlier compliance with the conditions of SALs I and II. These included the reintroduction of a licensing regime which effectively amounted to quantitative controls on a wide range of non-fuel imports – a blatant violation of the spirit of the agreement to remove quantitative restrictions under SALs I and II – and the reintroduction of subsidies on a large number of basic imports, at an estimated budgetary cost of 1.3 per cent of GDP.

The high level of subsidies, combined with the absence of Fund financing, led to a rapid deterioration in fiscal performance in early 1984 with a growing budget deficit financed by increased government utilisation of domestic credit. The combined effects of monetary expansion and devaluation gave rise to an inflation rate of 31.2 per cent in 1984. By mid-1984, all key macroeconomic indicators had deteriorated resulting in a severe foreign exchange shortage and a growing level of arrears in public debt-servicing. Under such crisis conditions the Government's bargaining position was severely weakened, and in June 1984 a stand-by agreement was reached with the Fund involving much harsher conditions and targets than earlier agreements. Again, the level of bilateral financing was a crucial factor determining the relative bargaining strength of the Government and the multilaterals. Growing budgetary pressures in both the US and Canada suggested a sharp reduction in concessionary financing from both USAID and Canadian International Development Authority (CIDA) in the near future. This prospect, combined with mounting debt arrears, meant that the Government could no longer afford to be without Fund balance-of-payments support or to risk any delay in agreeing the Third Structural Adjustment Loan under negotiation with the Bank.

In addition to the continued, unimpeded, operation of the foreign exchange auction system, the new stand-by called for a sharp reduction in the budget deficit to 7.5 per cent of GDP in fiscal year 1984–5. This target was to be achieved by a 10–15 per cent reduction in Central Government employment, a sharp reduction in government capital expenditures, increased revenue inflows via tax increases and large price increases for public utilities, and a faster pace in divestment of state-owned enterprises. In addition, there was to be an immediate increase in the price of basic foods through elimination of the subsidies imposed earlier in the year, strict limits on credit expansion, wage increases were to be kept below the rate of inflation and the list of restricted imports was to be reduced.

This stand-by agreement contained several conditions generally associated with World Bank supply-side adjustment policies, most notably in the area of pricing policies and reforms to the trade regime. Indeed, the period from 1984 onwards was to see a concerted attempt, albeit unsuccessful, at greater co-ordination of the Jamaican activities of the Bank and the Fund. The SAL III agreement, for example, signed in November 1984, explicitly acknowledged the interrelation between the stabilisation and adjustment programmes and the adverse effects of previously unsuccessful stabilisation on the outcome of SALs I and II. Part of the President's report on the proposed SAL III was devoted to an analysis of 'The Proposed Third Structural Adjustment Loan and Relations with the IMF'. In this section, it was stated that: 'Because of the importance of the stabilisation programme, this has been taken into account explicitly in designing the next phase of the (SAL) programme, as well as the schedule for processing the proposed loan' (World Bank, 1984b: 19). In particular, the Bank believed that SAL III programmes designed to reduce government expenditure via the Public Sector Investment Programme, to conserve on energy imports, and to encourage the rapid expansion of both traditional and non-traditional exports, would enable stabilisation of both internal and external accounts whilst simultaneously permitting a raised level of economic production. As such, part of SAL III was explicitly designed to 'assist in the achievement of the goals of the stabilisation programme'.

SAL III provided US $55 million in balance of payments support. The main policy focus remained similar to that of SALs I and II, with the addition of reforms relating to energy sector policy. Appendix I outlines the range of reforms covered by the SAL III agreement. In terms of balance-of-payments management, the main condition related to the continuation in the scheduled removal of quantitative import restrictions. Policies regarding public sector savings and investment focused on previous targets set for the removal of operating deficits in five major public enterprises, along with the development of a three-year rolling Public Sector Investment Programme. In addition, major reforms to the tax system were to be implemented by 1985. Following the disappointing response of private sector investment and growth rates under the previous SALs, SAL III placed a greater emphasis on policies relating to private sector savings and investment. This took the form of an agreement to devise a programme of financial reform in the areas of the equity market, the interest rate structure and the housing finance system. Regarding the industrial sector, the main thrust of reform remained in the area of export incentives, with the launching of an export incentives study, the provision of technical assistance to exporters and an agreement to establish a tax drawback scheme for exporters. Action for the agricultural sector consisted of a continuation of reforms to the External Marketing Organisations, including divestment and deregulation, and progress in implementing an export-parity-based pricing formula for major crops. The new area of energy policy consisted of a stipulation that a study be conducted on future power generation policies with a subsequent energy action programme to be based upon the results of the study.

As under SALs I and II, the negotiations concerning SAL III conditionality were marked by a relative absence of disagreement between Bank staff and the government regarding the nature of the conditions. The one area where differences of opinion emerged under all three SALs related to the pace of privatisation, with the government resisting privatisation of certain public sector activities such as tourist establishments and sugar factories, arguing that in the current economic environment sales would take place at depressed prices. As a result, leasing and management agreements were reached with private entrepreneurs in place of privatisation in these sectors.

Despite the higher level of co-ordination between the Fund and the Bank in the drafting of their respective loans, and despite satisfactory compliance with SAL III conditionality, the policy instruments used by the government in its attempt to comply with the stabilisation targets largely

Table 17.5 Nominal interest rates, 1982–7

	1982–3	1983–4	1984–5	1985–6	1986–7	1987–8
Weighted average rate on commercial credits	15.8	16.6	18.8	25.4	25.6	21.3(est.)
Overall weighted average loan rate	16.5	17.2	19.3	26.0	26.9	25.4(est.)

Source: Bank of Jamaica Statistical Digest, September 1988

undermined the supply-orientated growth objectives of the Bank's programme. As in the early 1980s, the Government's predominant concern from 1984 onwards continued to be the adverse effects of devaluation in terms of the impact on real wages, and the impact on fiscal debt-servicing obligations. Hence, the policy mix chosen by the Government took the form of the implementation of extremely tight monetary policy. The rationale behind the policy was a belief in the 'monetary theory of the balance of payments', namely, that higher interest rates would both restrict domestic currency available for bidding at the foreign exchange auction, and attract higher levels of foreign private capital inflows, thereby reducing downward pressure on the exchange rate and easing the balance-of-payments growth constraint.

The monetary policy was carried out predominantly by a manipulation of interest rates through dramatic increases in both the statutory liquid asset ratio and the cash reserve ratio, which were raised to 48 per cent and 20 per cent respectively. In the context of Jamaica's narrow financial markets and with many commercial bank assets being held in the form of low-interest Treasury Bills which provided cheap finance to the public sector, the effect of the above policy was an increase in interest rates facing the private sector. By 1986, the weighted interest rate on commercial credits exceeded 25 per cent, whilst the overall weighted average loan rate stood at 26.9 per cent (Table 17.5).

In essence, the monetary policy followed in the 1984–6 period was intended to counteract demand pressures which the Government was unwilling to control through exchange rate flexibility, or through contractionary fiscal policy over and above that already required to meet the restrictive government deficit target of the stand-by agreement. The use of contractionary monetary policy therefore represented a decision to pass much of the burden of stabilisation on to the private sector. The Government itself openly acknowledged this trade-off during a one-day seminar in early 1985 in which Bank and Government officials met with representatives of the business community. Tight demand containment via high interest rates was explained as being a necessary short-term policy in order to reduce pressures on fiscal policy, particularly in view of the fact that a crisis point had been reached in the form of gross underfunding of government non-personnel expenditures. Such a policy statement clearly indicates that the decline in social welfare expenditures was a predominant Government concern.

Undoubtedly, this policy stance was influenced by the perceived political risks of carrying out a restrictive fiscal policy or a flexible exchange rate policy. A further factor, however, was Seaga's increasingly sceptical attitude towards the private sector in view of the latter's disappointing response to earlier incentive measures. To quote one Bank official: 'Seaga may have felt that the devaluation of 1984 offered the private sector enough incentive. He believed he had given them a chance and they had proved their inability to respond'. (Personal interview, Washington DC, December 1988). The extent of Seaga's scepticism and his intransigence on the issue of permitting a flexible exchange rate is highlighted by a rift which occurred between the Government and USAID in late 1985. The Head of the USAID Resident Mission had pressurised the business sector, in the form of the Private Sector of Jamaica Organization, to lobby the Government for a further devaluation. Seaga, angered by what he regarded as a confrontation stance on the part of USAID, responded by ordering the removal of the Mission Head from the country.

The response of the economy to the Government's monetary policy was profoundly disappointing, not least because it disproved the applicability of the monetary theory of the balance of payments to an LDC economy such as Jamaica's characterised by imperfect finance markets and high levels of uncertainty. Foreign investment failed to respond to high interest rates, and psychological factors continued to predominate in the foreign exchange auction with expectations of impending devaluation giving rise to sustained downward pressure on the exchange rate. By October 1985, the rate had fallen to an all time low of US $1.00=J $6.40.

In addition to failing to stabilise the exchange rate, the use of monetary policy instruments had a strong negative impact on the performance of the private sector. Despite the fact that rapid inflation gave rise to negative real interest rates through much of the period, the high nominal interest rates adversely affected investment levels. This occurred predominantly as a result of the effect of the high nominal rates on investors' expected internal rates of return. Consequently, the flow of new investment was curtailed, as illustrated by the fact that commercial bank credits increased by only J $500 million in 1985. In addition, a growing number of existing firms encountered liquidity and cash-flow problems, resulting in an increased bankruptcy rate, especially amongst smaller establishments. The adverse investment effects of the Government's monetary policy were reflected in the poor performance of GDP. The GDP growth rate fell to −0.9 per cent

Table 17.6   Macroeconomic indicators, 1983–5

	1983	1984	1985
GDP growth rate (%)	2.5	−0.9	−4.5
of which: Agriculture (%)	7.3	9.3	−3.4
Mining (%)	0.6	0.7	−19.5
Manufacturing (%)	1.9	−5.0	0.9
Construction (%)	6.7	−7.1	−14.3
Unemployment (%)	25.8	25.6	25.0
Inflation: % rate of change of consumer price index	16.7	31.2	23.1
Imports (US $ million)	1281	1183	1144
Exports (US $ million)	686	702	569
Balance-of-payments current account (US $ million)	−278.6	−246.7	−248.1
Overall government deficit as % of GDP	−15.8	−6.3	−5.3

Note: For public sector financial data 1983 represents fiscal year 1 April 1983 to 31 March 1984, and so forth.
Sources: Davies (1988) Table 8; World Bank (1984b) Statistical Appendices.

in 1984 and −4.5 per cent in 1985, with poor performance spread across all sectors of the economy (Table 17.6).

Despite downward pressure on the exchange rate, growing uncertainty regarding exchange rate management and restricted access to the exchange auction led many exporters to reorientate towards the domestic market. Traditional exports and tourism also fared badly, the latter due to increasing political unrest. In terms of traditional exports, the 1985 downturn in the bauxite industry, including the decision of ALCOA, a major multinational, to close down operations in Jamaica, had a profound impact on the balance of payments. With devaluation failing to have any impact on the inflow of imports, the balance of payments by the end of 1985 showed only a marginal improvement over 1983, with the current account deficit being almost twice as large as the IMF target (Table 17.6).

In response to the disappointing balance-of-payments performance, new import tariffs and stamp duties were placed on consumer, capital, and raw material goods as a way of controlling demand in lieu of quantitative restrictions. The effect of such measures, combined with the impact of devaluation and the sharp rise in public enterprise utility rates, was an escalation in the inflation rate, which doubled in 1984 compared to the previous year, reaching 31.2 per cent in 1984 and 23.1 per cent in 1985 (Table 17.6). In conjunction with the required restrictions on wage increases, this had a negative welfare effect on large numbers of the population with the lowest income groups no longer able to obtain basic necessities. The gravity of the welfare situation was acknowledged by the introduction of a Food Security Programme aimed at almost half of the country's population.

In September 1985, the Government again failed the IMF tests associated with the stand-by agreement and the latter was suspended. Both the Fund and Bank were forced to conclude that even though 1984–5 represented the best period to date in terms of government compliance with IMF orthodoxy regarding wages, prices, interest rates, public expenditure and the exchange rate (albeit that the latter was unintended compliance), the only notable achievement was an improvement in fiscal performance, with the Central Government overall deficit declining from 15.8 per cent of GDP in 1983–4 to 5.3 per cent in 1985–6.

The political costs of Government compliance and the poor economic outcome were high and this political dimension itself reinforced disappointing economic performance. The rapid removal in late 1984 of food subsidies introduced only a few months earlier, combined with escalating inflation, led to growing economic hardship and political unrest. The sharp increase in gasoline prices in early 1985, necessitated by the Government's agreement to pass price increases on to consumers, led to a day and a half of protests in which normal economic activity virtually ceased, requiring the intervention of the opposition PNP to restore normality. The imposition of stamp duties on imports, including basic foodstuffs, further heightened political tension and culminated in an unprecedented national strike in June 1985. The strike received support from virtually every trade union, including the powerful Bustamante Industrial Trade Union (BITU), upon which the Seaga JLP Government's power base depended. These indications of public unrest had a severe negative impact on both the tourist industry and the inflow of private investment.

The confrontational manner in which this unrest was manifested was partly due to the nature of Seaga's leadership style and partly due to the events surrounding the 1983 general election. Throughout both terms of office Seaga utilised a highly centralised, non-participatory, system of government in an attempt to subvert opposition to policy changes. This involved a lack of dialogue, not only with key interest groups such as the Trade Union Movement and the business community, but also with members of his own government, the latter being assisted by the fact that he himself had several Ministerial portfolios, including that of Minister of Finance.[9] The Trade Union Institute, which under Manley's PNP Administration had served as a forum for dialogue between the two opposing Labour Unions, effectively fell into disuse during the 1980s. All unions, including the BITU, were dealt with in a dismissive manner, as shown by the fact that it was not until April 1985 that the Government attempted any formal policy dialogue with the labour movement. Union opposition mounted, not only regarding the erosion of real wages, but also due to the perceived weakening of the unions' political power. In particular, the reductions in public sector employment and the privatisation of many Local Government activities under the IMF programme had diminished the power of the Jamaica Association of Local Government Officers Union (JALGO) which had previously constituted a key link between the Union Movement and the Government.

However, although the Union Movement actively participated in demonstrations against Government policy these were initiated and led by the opposition PNP, whose recourse to Parliamentary opposition had been reduced by the events of the 1983 general election. In the early part of 1983, opinion polls clearly indicated declining support for the JLP Government. However, the US invasion of Grenada, strongly backed by Jamaica, including provision of Jamaican troops, resulted in a surge of populist support for the Government not dissimilar to the post-Falkland revival of support for the Thatcher Government. Utilising this turn of events, Seaga hastily called a general election. However, the snap election announcement represented a violation of an earlier agreement between the Government and the Opposition, namely that the elections would not be held until the electoral register had been updated to include younger voters, most of whom were likely to be PNP supporters. Consequently, the PNP boycotted the election, and the new Parliament was a House without an opposition bench, all sixty seats being held by JLP members.

Rather than strengthening Seaga's political position the effect was to force the PNP to vocalise its disagreement with government policies in a non-institutional, and potentially more damaging, public way. The issue of devaluation, in particular, was aired and personalised by Manley and the PNP through the public media, with the price and wage effects of devaluation becoming an increasingly politicised issue. When the exchange rate hit its all time low in October 1985, this culminated in an all-night vigil and a march of thousands of people, led by Manley, on the Bank of Jamaica. Within a week the Government had implemented a revaluation, an unprecedented measure throughout the Fund's involvement in the Jamaican economy.

Disquiet emanated not only from the labour movement and the PNP, but also increasingly from the business community. Undoubtedly Seaga felt that there was little need to court the favours of this group, given that the events of the late 1970s had left the business sector profoundly disenchanted with Manley's PNP. Hence, as with other groups, there was little attempt to co-opt support for the policy reforms being implemented. However, the continuous juggling of the exchange rate regime led to growing demands for exchange rate stability from a business community finding itself operating in an environment of increased uncertainty. In addition, trade liberalisation measures carried out under the SAL programme had provoked a reaction from other CARICOM members, who, claiming that Jamaica's policies were undermining the 'favoured status' agreement of the CARICOM free market, imposed licences on a range of

Jamaica's imports. This action had a particularly adverse effect on Jamaica's non-traditional manufacturers.

The political and economic events of the two-year period to the end of 1985 clearly indicate that although successful stabilisation is a prerequisite for successful adjustment with growth, this cannot take the form of stabilisation at any cost. The *form* of stabilisation programme and the *type* of policy instruments used to effect it, are equally crucial to the success of adjustment efforts. In the joint Bank/Fund meeting at Seoul in October 1985, Bank staff openly acknowledged, during their appraisal of the effects of Jamaica's current economic policy on SAL goals, that the monetary policy had undermined the SAL programme in several ways. Private sector growth was deemed to be impossible with such high interest rates, particularly since the debt-equity structure of many Jamaican firms was heavily weighted towards debt reflecting, in many cases, incentive arrangements which had been implemented under the SAL programmes. Escalating inflation and exchange-rate uncertainty were also seen by the Bank as jeopardising the performance of private-sector manufacturing activities. In addition the introduction of the Food Security Programme, utilising imported food aid, partly neutralised Bank attempts to revive Jamaica's domestic agricultural sector. In short, there was an explicit acknowledgement of inconsistency between the Fund's stabilisation programme and the Bank's trade and liberalisation policies.

Bank awareness of the above inconsistencies is further illustrated by the form which Bank programme lending took in the post-1985 period. The completion of SAL III was followed by a series of Sectoral Adjustment Loans (SECALs), including a Trade and Finance Sectoral Loan. An explicit objective of the latter SECAL was to create a macro-policy environment, in terms of monetary and exchange rate policy, which was consistent with the on-going reform of the trade regime. This entailed an attempt to stabilise the exchange rate by an infusion of Bank of Jamaica foreign reserves into the auction system, and a reorientation of monetary policy towards open market operations. Measures such as a phasing-out of the non-cash portion of the liquid asset ratio were used both to achieve the reorientation and reduce interest rates in line with market forces.

In view of the events of Seoul and the Bank's explicit attempts to assist the stabilisation programme, one is forced to ask why an attempt was not made by the Fund to ensure the compatibility of the stabilisation and adjustment programmes. Although the monetary policy experiment was essentially initiated by the Government of Jamaica, the Fund acquiesced and tacitly approved, albeit with a warning that the policy was potentially recessionary. This indicates a general, and questionable, aspect of the Fund's policy stance, namely, a neutrality and indifference between the use of monetary and fiscal instruments, and to some extent the sharing of the burden between the private and public sectors, to achieve stabilisation.

Such a stance may be acceptable for Fund operations in a developed economy, where stabilisation can often be characterised, in the words of one Fund official, as a 'piggy-bank' exercise in that it is the monetary as opposed to the real parameters of the economy which are misaligned. However, the case of Jamaica clearly illustrates the dangers of such neutrality in the context of an LDC economy beset by a deterioration in the real resource base and requiring both stabilisation *and* adjustment.

The Jamaican experience also illustrates an important, although often overlooked, aspect of Bank and Fund bargaining positions in LDC economies. The overriding impression given by Jamaican policy-makers involved with both organisations is that throughout the course of the stabilisation and adjustment efforts, the Fund was both able and willing to pursue its interests more vigorously than the Bank. The explanation appears to be twofold. First, the need for stabilisation can be characterised as more of an immediate 'crisis management' situation than the need for structural adjustment, in that problems associated with the latter are more insidious and solutions more gradualist. Related to this is the fact that the bargaining position of the Fund is considerably strengthened in such a context by its ability to align with front-line Ministries, such as the Ministry of Finance, and with the Central or Reserve Bank, whose immediate concerns often relate to Fund-type parameters associated with such 'crisis management'. By contrast, the implementation, if not the construction, of the Bank's structural adjustment programmes generally falls to the 'downline' ministries such as the Ministry of Trade and Industry and the Ministry of Agriculture. Second, government policy-makers often find Fund-type arguments more easy to accept in that a technical theoretical apparatus exists to map causal links between policy instruments, such as devaluation, and policy outcomes, such as movements in foreign reserves. By contrast, the theoretical foundation of Bank-type reforms are more disputable, both theoretically and ideologically (Harrigan, 1988) partly due to their medium-term perspective, and partly due to the prevalence of market imperfections in LDC economies. Hence, the Bank is more frequently forced to take recourse to theoretical dogmatism which consequently undermines the leverage of its bargaining position. Both of these factors were reinforced in the Jamaican context by the fact that the Fund, unlike the Bank, maintains a Resident Mission in Kingston.

All of the above suggests a need for greater Bank/Fund co-operation in LDC economies. The emergence of tripartite Medium Term Policy Framework Papers, drafted jointly by the Fund, Bank and recipient government, and the Fund's recent introduction of a medium-term form of balance-of-payments support, namely, the Structural Adjustment Facility, are to be welcomed in this respect. However, the increased use of such an approach from the mid-1980s onwards gives rise to a new dilemma, in the form of the cross-conditionality issue. This issue became explosive in

Jamaica by the end of 1985, giving rise to important questions regarding crucial distinctions between different types of cross-conditionality.

17.6   THE THIRD PHASE OF ADJUSTMENT, 1986–8:   A FRESH LOOK AND SUCCESS AT LAST?

The period 1986–8, like the previous two periods, is defined by a realignment of bargaining forces which, in contrast to the 1983–5 period, strengthened the Government's position. Again, such a change was brought about by a combination of internal and external political and economic factors. The Government's new position gave rise to a public statement of disagreement with the Fund, Bank, and USAID regarding appropriate policies for the continued stabilisation and adjustment effort. It also caused a bitter dispute over the issue of cross-conditionality, and led to more than a year of government-implemented policies in direct defiance of the IMF.

Internal factors leading to the Government's new stance took the form of political unrest in response to the austerity measures of 1984 and 1985. In addition, the Government faced municipal elections in mid-1986, and the Opposition PNP had made it clear, given their boycott of the 1983 general elections, that the forthcoming local elections would be treated as a referendum on the macroeconomic policies of the Seaga Government. Hence, realising that by now the JLP was a minority party, Seaga was forced to re-evaluate relations with both the Bank and the Fund. The initial step came in October 1985 in the form of the Government's intervention in the exchange auction, following the Manley-led march on the Bank of Jamaica, resulting in a revaluation from US $1.00 = J $6.40 to US $1.00 = J $5.50 (Table 17.2), a policy move which was heavily exploited during the local election campaign as representing a policy reversal – a strong Government stance against the IMF.

Following the failure to meet the September 1985 stand-by targets, and the currency revaluation of October, Seaga launched a harsh attack on IMF policies during the joint Bank/Fund meetings in Seoul. His hand was strengthened by the Bank's own assessment, during the same meeting, of the impact of stabilisation policies on the objectives of the adjustment programme. Seaga's attack amounted to a call for an end to counter-productive and inflexible austerity measures, and their replacement with policies directly designed to stimulate economic growth. The new measures envisaged by the Government entailed leaving the revalued exchange rate unaltered, less tight monetary policy to stimulate investment, and a review of fiscal policy. High taxes were seen as a disincentive to investment whilst public expenditure was already severely squeezed. A significant feature of the government's new policy stance was the fact that it represented a fundamental U-turn in terms of the abandonment of the monetary policies initiated in 1984 and 1985 and an outright statement against further use of devaluation. In addition, it also indicated a growing consensus between the government and the Bank regarding the adverse impact of the earlier monetary-based stabilisation policies on economic growth. Indeed, the Bank openly expressed agreement with Seaga's views on monetary, fiscal, and investment policies.

The government's policy statement was backed by a request for a tripartite Fund/Bank/USAID Mission to reassess Jamaica's stabilisation and adjustment policies. The agreement by the three organisations to conduct a 'Fresh-Look Mission', as it subsequently became known, suggests an implicit acknowledgement that the policies of the past six years had failed to achieve their stated objectives. However, the Mission's recommendations indicated a belief that this was due to the Government's failure to abide by previous agreements as opposed to the inappropriateness of their design. This is shown by the fact that, with one exception, the Mission's recommendations were virtually identical to the conditions attached to the earlier stabilisation and adjustment packages. These included: the determination of the exchange rate by market forces; a reduction in the overall public sector deficit; and a restructuring of incentives to eliminate anti-agricultural and anti-export bias. The new area of focus related to the need to implement monetary policy aimed at reducing inflation and removing discriminatory interest rates to the private sector. In addition to its specific policy recommendations, the Mission report stated that the Government's desire to shift the economy immediately to a 5 per cent per annum growth path was not feasible, not least because the levels of aid required to bridge the balance-of-payments gap under such a growth scenario would not be forthcoming. To maintain external balance, the report advocated a continuation of restrictive demand management policies resulting in a projected near-term growth rate of under 2 per cent per annum.

Not surprisingly, the report was rejected by the Government. The events surrounding the rejection were particularly acrimonious. The Fund's response to the rejection was a call for an 'up-front' devaluation. Given the Mission's recommendation that the exchange rate be determined by market forces, and given the Fund's earlier acceptance of the October 1985 revaluation, the Government was understandably angered by what it regarded as an unnecessarily confrontational response. In addition, despite the apparent pre-Mission consensus of opinion between the Bank and the Government, Bank Mission staff failed to back the Government's case for the need to adopt an expansionary policy. The rift with the Bank was intensified by the Government's claim that its failure to meet the March 1986 IMF targets, and the consequent inability to draw on stand-by resources which was causing a build-up of arrears to the Fund, was a direct result of the Bank's withholding the disbursement of an agreed Sectoral

Adjustment Loan. The Government's claim represented a direct criticism of the use of cross-conditionality by the Fund, Bank and USAID. In the Government's own words:

> The build-up of arrears to the Fund is due largely to the delay in the disbursement of a World Bank loan of US$40 million, the first tranche of the Sector Adjustment Loan. If this had materialised, Jamaica would have met all the IMF performance criteria as at 31st March 1986. However, the World Bank tied the draw-down of these funds to our reaching agreement on the Tripartite Mission's Report, a condition which did not exist when our agreements with the Fund and the Bank were originally concluded.
>
> (Government of Jamaica, 1986: 19–20)

In response to the charge of cross-conditionality on the part of the Tripartite Mission, the Bank claimed that the Government's rejection of the Mission's report, and the failure to reach an agreement with the Fund, gave rise to a situation in which there was no medium-term macroeconomic policy framework within which to disburse the SECAL Loan.

The above instance was not the first case of cross-conditionality in Jamaica. In the early 1980s USAID had explicitly linked its disbursement of Programme aid in the form of Economic Support Funds (ESFs) to the conditions of the Bank's SALs, requiring either a recent Bank Board approval of a SAL loan, or a Bank letter certifying satisfactory progress of an on-going SAL programme. In 1982 such cross-conditionality had been effectively levered to speed up the pace of reform in terms of the implementation of a SAL I condition relating to export incentives. USAID refused to disburse a programme loan, at a time when such funds were essential to meeting the IMF reserves test, until the Government complied with the Bank's condition by granting preferential foreign exchange access to exporters. However the subsequent passing of the Kemp Amendment by the Reagan Administration prohibited USAID from further use of this explicit form of cross-conditionality. In terms of Bank/Fund interaction, the timing of Bank Board approval of all three SALs indicates cross-conditionality in the sense that on each occasion the Fund's Board, less than a month earlier, had approved either a stabilisation facility or an adjustment of the stand-by programme to bring Jamaica back into line with Fund requirements.

As the Jamaican government's statement makes clear, the objection was not to the use of cross-conditionality *per se*, but to a case of *retrospective* cross-conditionality ie. to 'a condition which did not exist' when the SECAL agreement was 'originally concluded'. Objections had not been raised to the earlier 'upfront' cross-conditionality between USAID and the Bank, nor to the cross-conditionality between Fund stand-bys and the three SALs. In the former case, USAID had made the use of such cross-conditionality clear at the outset. In the latter case, it is generally acknowledged that since Paris Club and commercial bank arrangements are explicitly contingent on a Fund agreement being in place, and since in the absence of such arrangements the Bank alone is usually unable to bridge the potential recipients' balance-of-payments financing gap, the recipient is consequently deemed uncreditworthy by the Bank.

The Jamaican dispute clearly indicates a need for the multilateral agencies to cease their prudishness regarding open acknowledgement of the use of cross-conditionality, and to devise and articulate clear policy statements on this issue. This is particularly necessary in view of the growing use of 'intermediate' and hybrid forms of programme lending, such as the Bank's SECALs and the Fund's medium-term Structural Adjustment Facility (SAF), where, as the Jamaica case illustrates, there is as yet no implicit understanding between donor and recipient regarding the interrelation of the attached conditionalities. A clear statement on this issue would avoid the situation whereby a recipient *unexpectedly* finds the disbursement of a programme loan withheld due to failure to fulfil conditions attached to another loan. Such retrospective cross-conditionality needs to be avoided, not only because of its ethical implications, but also due to the economic consequences. As the Bank and Fund themselves often point out, devising a stabilisation or adjustment programme is always difficult due to the need to forecast donor pledges and hence the magnitude of the future balance-of-payments gap which the programmes need to address. Retrospective cross-conditionality compounds this problem by introducing an extra, and unnecessary, element of uncertainty for LDC policy-makers attempting to make such forecasts and to devise appropriate programmes.

Following the rejection of the tripartite Mission's report, the Government drafted its own proposed stabilisation and adjustment programme (Government of Jamaica, 1986). In doing so, it bypassed the Fund's technical team, and presented the programme directly to the Fund's Board. This alternative programme indicated the essence of the disagreement between the Government and the Tripartite Mission to be the rejection of the Mission's recommendation that monetary policy be relaxed, compensated for by a demand-controlling flexible exchange rate. However, given that the earlier policy mix of using devaluation to contain demand whilst liberalising the trade regime to stimulate exports had been largely unsuccessful, resulting instead in import-led growth, the government was able to make a strong case against resumption of such a policy.

The government's case rested on the negative effects, in terms of uncertainty and speculation, which resulted from continued devaluation. In acknowledgement of growing criticism from the business community, the government argued that businesses were experiencing planning difficulties. Difficulties led to domestic price distortions, which, along with

347

devaluation-induced price increases, had suppressed demand to such an extent that capacity utilisation was at a level below that 'which could be considered normal and desirable for an economy in transition to export-led growth'. When combined with the institutional nature of wage bargaining, such factors gave rise to a severe cost-push inflationary spiral. Furthermore, expectations of devaluation discouraged producers from utilising export credit lines, which compounded downward speculative pressure on the exchange rate.

In addition, the government questioned the previous use of exchange rate policy in view of what it saw as structural barriers to exchange rate response, thereby challenging the assumption that the Marshall-Lerner price elasticity conditions applied to the Jamaican economy. In terms of the two major foreign exchange earners, the bauxite/alumina industry and tourism, the local cost component was relatively small, consisting mainly of labour costs with limited scope for further substitution towards local inputs. The position also stressed the essentially short-term nature of competitiveness gains since: 'Devaluation will trigger an almost simul-taneous movement in major factor costs because of the highly organised labour movement' (Government of Jamaica, 1986: Appendix 2: 3).

In the traditional agricultural export sector, it was pointed out that the overriding negative factor was local production bottle-necks as opposed to lack of international competitiveness. In terms of non-traditional exports, the government argued that Jamaica had already gained a competitive edge from past devaluations, although a 10 per cent tax rebate would be required to compensate for the October 1985 currency revaluation.

Whilst the policy dialogue regarding the exchange rate continued, the hiatus in an agreement with the Fund was marked by policy slippage in several key areas of direct relevance to the Bank's structural adjustment programme. The 1986–7 fiscal budget represented the first occasion under the Seaga regime in which a budget was prepared which did not require Fund approval. The budget called for a significant increase in public capital investment expenditures and reintroduced subsidies on a range of basic imports. The manner in which subsidies were introduced provides a good example of the Seaga government's frequently demonstrated ability to carry out the letter of its agreements with donors, whilst denying them in spirit. In accordance with the Bank's SAL and SECAL conditions, subsidies were not financed through central government finances. Instead, falling oil prices enabled the Government to place a cess on the Jamaica Public Service Company, the electricity parastatal. These funds were transferred directly to the Jamaica Commodity Trading Company (JCTC), a large importing and distribution parastatal, and were used by the latter to subsidise the price of basic food imports. The JCTC's own cess on car imports was likewise used to cross-subsidise food prices. In addition to slippage in the area of public finance, 1986 and 1987 saw a slowdown in the pace of the

Bank's tariff reform programme, with the government arguing that many of the proposed reforms would violate its agreements with other CARICOM nations.

Throughout 1986 the government's bargaining position was substantially strengthened by the benefits derived by the fall in oil prices. Not only did this ease the balance-of-payments position, it also improved government revenue by the equivalent of 2.1 per cent of GDP in 1986–7 due to the fact that the price reduction was not passed on to gasoline consumers. The use of interparastatal cross-subsidisation also eased domestic inflation. Hence:

> Mainly as a result of this simultaneous easing of pressure on the balance of payments and fiscal accounts, the Jamaica Government was able to bargain with the IMF without the need for an immediate agreement as had been the case on previous occasions.
>
> (Davies, 1988: 17)

Agreement with the Fund was eventually reached in March 1987. Although many of the Tripartite Mission's recommendations were embodied in the new agreement, including conditions relating to the Public Sector Investment Programme, tariff reform, public enterprise reform, and demand restraint, the government's views on exchange rate policy prevailed. However, provisions for devaluation were agreed to in the event of a decline in the real effective exchange rate caused by either increased inflation or wage increases in excess of 10 per cent, or in the event of violation of the quarterly international reserve targets.

The Fund's acceptance of a stand-by without the implementation of a devaluation was undoubtedly influenced by the lengthy and constructive dialogue which occurred between the Government and the multilaterals throughout 1986. However, one must also ask whether the Fund's decision, and the Bank's earlier provision of the SECAL loans, were influenced by factors relating to Jamaica's debt-servicing position. By early 1987 Jamaica's arrears to the Fund stood at US $90 million, whilst the proposed stand-by was scheduled to provide US $130 million. Indeed, the Jamaican government constantly stressed to the Fund the fact that a new agreement was needed in order to make the country current on Fund obligations:

> The non-receipt of projected Fund and Fund-related disbursements have resulted in severe cash-flow constraints and a consequential build-up in arrears to the Fund.

> The prospects of clearing off all arrears to the Fund are critically dependent on the draw-down of the World Bank loan of US$40 million.
>
> (Government of Jamaica, 1986: 20)

This aspect of the government's bargaining indicates a growing dilemma for multilateral lending activities in a highly indebted economy such as Jamaica. Continued provision of high levels of concessionary finance in the early 1980s, accompanied by insignificant policy reform, had given rise to a rapid expansion of Jamaica's debt obligations without stimulating the growth necessary to service such debt. This compounded the subsequent adjustment task in two ways. First, the fiscal implications of debt-servicing had reduced the flexibility of public-sector policy response. Second, the leverage of the donors' policy bargaining position was weakened by the growing pressure to disburse in order to avoid default on the part of the recipient. Jamaica's case indicates an exploitation on the part of recipients of this inter- and intra-donor disbursement dilemma.

The utilisation of such an approach in a recipient's bargaining lends support to a cynical interpretation of the Baker Plan as being a means of ensuring that the Bank and the bilaterals' programme aid finances repayments to the Fund. In this context, it is interesting to note that of Jamaica's three main lending agencies, the Fund, Bank, and USAID, the latter was by 1987 the only one in a position of providing a net positive resource flow. Hence, it is not surprising that in response to the 'disbursement dilemma', the American Executive Director presented the strongest opposition to the passing of the March 1987 stand-by by the Fund's Board.

Despite the fact that 1986 represented the year in which relations between the Seaga regime and the Washington institutions were at their most strained, the period following the March 1987 stand-by agreement was characterised by a speeding-up of the pace of policy reform, and the first signs of a positive economic response to stabilisation and adjustment policies. In addition, it was marked by a somewhat new approach to conditionality on the part of all three major donors.

Conditionality during this period was less confrontational, with all three agencies adopting what could be characterised as a 'soft-underbelly approach'. USAID, in particular, under a new Mission director, explicitly focused conditionality on areas which supported the Government's *own* economic reform programme, in contrast to its more activist approach on controversial issues such as exchange-rate policy in the pre-1986 period. The 1987 stand-by agreement was also based upon support for the Government's own stabilisation programme which had materialised from the long policy dialogues of 1986, and hence represented a much greater internalisation of policy conditions, particularly in regard to exchange-rate policies. The successful implementation of a wide range of policy reforms during this period would suggest that a 'second-best' donor policy which has the backing of government support can often achieve more than a 'perfect policy scenario' to which a government remains uncommitted. This is particularly so for the Bank's adjustment programmes where there is ample scope for a Government to undermine the spirit and thrust of reform policies without violating the letter of the conditionality agreement. Although an associated cost of such a 'second-best' strategy takes the form of funding fungible policy reforms, the alternative costs, as Jamaica's pre-1985 experience illustrates, may be higher in terms of the debt-servicing implications of donor balance-of-payments support without the anticipated implementation of reforms.

Since 1986, significant progress has occurred under the Bank's Trade and Financial Sector Loan in terms of rationalising monetary policy and ensuring a more appropriate mix in the government's use of monetary and fiscal instruments for demand control. Although Jamaica's traditional preference for using monetary policy to contain demand and maintain a stable exchange rate continues, there is now a much greater sharing of the stabilisation and adjustment burden between monetary and fiscal policy. This has enabled greater compatibility between stabilisation objectives relating to the balance of payments and the adjustment objectives of attaining medium-term growth.

Under the Bank's SECAL, monetary policy has shifted towards the use of open-market operations. As a result, nominal interest rates facing the private sector have been reduced (Table 17.5). In response, commercial bank credit to the private sector increased dramatically in 1987, and has continued to do so at a steady rate. In addition, initial moves have been made to disentangle fiscal and monetary policy, resulting in a reduction in the interest rate differential facing the private and public sector. This has therefore reduced the implicit private sector subsidisation of public expenditure and has created a better basis for financial resource competition between the two sectors. The use of monetary policy in the form of open-market operations between 1986–8 has also been successful both in stabilising the exchange rate, and in controlling inflation, the latter both directly via demand management, and indirectly via the domestic price effects of the stable exchange rate. From 1986 to mid-1988 inflation averaged 7.5 per cent compared to the double digit figures of earlier periods (Table 17.7). Not only has the dramatic decline in inflation enabled Jamaica to retain international competitiveness, the higher real interest rates resulting from reduced inflation have attracted an increased inflow of foreign capital. Increased domestic and foreign investment also reflects the positive psychological impact of both exchange rate stability and the improvement in public sector expenditure.

The effort to rationalise the monitoring of fiscal policy has brought about improved public sector savings, such that by 1987 the overall deficit of central government had been eliminated (Table 17.7). This achievement was assisted by accelerated reform under the Bank's Public Enterprise Sector loan, and by the divestment conditions associated with USAID programme loans, with divestment of cement, telecommunications and

Table 17.7   Macroeconomic indicators, 1986–8

	1986	1987	1988 (ests)
GDP growth rate (%)	1.9	5.2	3.3
of which: Agriculture (%)	−2.1	2.5	..
Mining (%)	6.6	4.9	..
Manufacturing (%)	3.7	5.2	..
Construction (%)	2.5	14.0	..
Unemployment (%)	25.5	..	..
Inflation: % rate of change of consumer price index	7.7	7.8	10.7
Imports (US $ million)	1030.4	1284.0	872.0
Exports (US $ million)	622.6	774.0	727.0
Balance-of-payments current account (US $ million)	−73.4	−133.0	−234.0
Current government deficit as % of GDP	−1.4	0.0	−5.8

Sources: Davies (1988)   Table 6; Bank of Jamaica, *Statistical Digest*, September 1988.
Note: For public sector financial data, 1986 represents fiscal year 1 April 1986 to 31 March 1987, and so forth.

hotel enterprises implemented via share offers to the general public.

The ongoing tariff reform programme has also proceeded rapidly under the auspices of the Bank's Trade and Financial sector Loan, with the introduction of a uniform, no-exemptions tariff structure, followed by a gradual reduction in tariff rates, such that by December 1988, the weighted average tariff level stood at 20 per cent. In recent years there has been evidence of a greater acceptance of such reforms by the business community. An important advantage of the shift from quantitative restrictions to tariffs is the fact that under the new system, rents, in the form of tariff revenues, accrue to the public sector as opposed to the private sector.

Partly as a result of the greater synchronisation between stabilisation and adjustment policies and the improved mix of fiscal and monetary policies, 1986–8 witnessed the first occurrence of positive GDP growth rates for longer than a twelve-month period since the mid-1970s, with positive performance spread across all sectors of the economy (Table 17.7). This provides the first evidence of a much-delayed private sector response to the Bank's structural adjustment programme. In particular, there has been a change of attitudes within the business community in the form of an acceptance of a new export-orientated trade regime, and a response to the new incentive structure in the form of increased exports to non-domestic, non-CARICOM markets. Between 1986 and October 1988, prior to hurricane Gilbert, the value of exports increased by 24 per cent (Table 17.7), whilst between 1985 and October 1988, the current account of the balance-of-payments deficit improved from US $248.1 million to US $103.1 million. In this respect, growth in the non-traditional export sector has been impressive, most notably in the textile industry. However, the basis of growth remains fragile, and it is too early, as yet, to say that Jamaica has reached a sustainable medium-term growth path.

Although there has been a positive private sector response, much of the recent improved economic performance has been due to exogenous factors. The fall in oil prices, buoyancy of the US tourist market, and a dramatic improvement in bauxite/alumina prices over the last year, have all contributed to improved GDP growth rates, whilst easing both the balance-of-payments and the fiscal deficit.

In addition, the impact of hurricane Gilbert in October 1988 and political pressures in the run up to the February 1989 general election, have both retarded the recent pace of reform. In particular, 1988 saw slippage in the area of fiscal reform, with the Government failing to carry out its agreement to introduce a general consumption tax, refusing to grant many price increases and increasing, yet again, the subsidisation of a wide range of basic food imports.

At least for the next few years success remains crucially dependent on a continuation of the favourable trends in Jamaica's external trade regime. This is particularly so in view of the fact that the export diversification process is still in its infancy with the impressive growth rate in non-traditional exports having occurred from a low base level. The external debt burden presents a major obstacle to future growth in view of the associated balance-of-payments and fiscal constraints, and represents a high cost of the early 1980s postponement of genuine stabilisation and adjustment efforts. Table 17.8 illustrates the magnitude of Jamaica's debt burden. In view of this constraint, the maintenance of positive growth rates over the next few years will require high levels of concessionary financing *combined* with a continuation of the adjustment programme.

A key issue facing the new PNP Government is how to balance the needs of exchange rate policy with the fiscal pressures of debt servicing and with the politically sensitive issue of real wage levels. There is growing

Table 17.8 Public debt indicators, 1985–7 (percentage ratios)

	1985	1986	1987
Actual debt service/GDP	20.6	25.4	30.5
Actual debt service/exports of goods & services	35.4	43.8	48.2
Debt service/total central government expenditures	43.6	43.6	41.3
Debt interest payments/central government recent expenditures	40.1	39.6	38.3
Debt amortization/central government capital expenditures	52.5	46.9	46.8

Source: Davies (1988) Tables 2 and 3.
Notes: The debt to fiscal expenditure ratios are for fiscal years, i.e. 1985 represents fiscal year 1 April 1985 to 31 March 1986 and so forth.

353

evidence that, despite the gains derived from the exchange rate stability of the past three years, greater flexibility is again needed in exchange rate management. In such a highly-open economy as Jamaica, virtually every form of economic activity requires access to foreign exchange. However, the Government continues to tightly manage and restrict access to the exchange auction and both domestic and foreign investment remain inhibited by such a system. Greater faith on the part of investors that assets could be readily converted into foreign currency would undoubtedly increase the pace of both investment and growth. However, a freeing-up of the exchange allocation system is constrained by the fact that, under present debt-servicing obligations, the Bank of Jamaica lacks the necessary reserves to cushion any initial speculative downward pressure on the exchange rate. The possibility of utilising concessionary donor funds to create an exchange support fund within the Bank of Jamaica is an issue which deserves close donor attention in future years.

Finally, exchange rate flexibility is necessary to ensure that Jamaica retains her international competitiveness. However, this raises the crucial question of real wage levels. Under both the Manley and Seaga regimes the policy area in which the Fund and Bank encountered greatest resistance related to the use of devaluation as a policy tool to increase competitiveness via real wage reduction. Real wages have fallen in recent years, and much of the growth in non-traditional exports has been facilitated by this factor. However, in view of growing competition from low wage economies such as Haiti, the Dominican Republic and China, the question arises as to whether Jamaica's recent strategy of using low real wages to attract foreign investment is a viable long-term strategy both in terms of the external economic, and domestic political environment. The landslide electoral victory of the PNP in early 1989 indicated the growing popular dissatisfaction with declining wages and living standards, and illustrates the difficulty of sustaining a low wage strategy in a competitive democracy.

The real wage issue in Jamaica is not new to the 1970s and 1980s. Since the work of Arthur Lewis in the late 1940s, (Lewis, 1949, 1950) the debate has raged regarding the viability of a low-wage industrial growth strategy for the Caribbean. However, the past fifteen years have added new dimensions to the disjunction between economic and political expediency. Virtually every Jamaican family now has at least one relative in the USA or UK earning comparatively high wages and salaries. This factor, combined with the influence of the foreign tourist industry, and the conspicuous consumption patterns of Jamaica's *nouveaux riches*, have given rise to strong demonstration effects. In addition, the growing political strength of the Trade Union Movement over the past two decades and the institutionalised nature of wage agreements act as a further barrier to real wage reduction. The political dilemma regarding viable adjustment strategies in Jamaica has been succinctly summarised by a member of the former PNP Administration:

354

Long-term followers of adjustment in the Caribbean don't have the political rhetoric of left-wing parties, who can point to international and domestic exploitation. Seaga's Government has had nothing as rhetoric, except the East Asian low wage example and the Thatcherite rhetoric of a public enterprise culture based on privatisation via public share subscriptions. In Jamaica – a highly unionised society, where few people are property owners – neither example makes much sense.

(Personal interview, Washington DC, December 1988)

Throughout the stabilisation and adjustment process in Jamaica, neither donors nor the government made adequate allowance for this political economy context within which programmes were to be implemented. As a result, opportunities for political coalition-building were overlooked.

The politically-powerful Trade Union movement represents, to a large extent, the elite of Jamaica's labour force. In addition, many of the implicit rents and subsidies which existed during the 1980s provided little benefit to the poorest sections of Jamaican society. This interest-group specific nature of government intervention, and the associated accrual of rents, contrasts to the situation in many sub-Saharan countries, where government interventions, such as food and input subsidies, have a long-established populist tradition of benefiting large numbers of the population, hence making it difficult to build coalitions to fight for policy change. In Jamaica, however, potential exists for a coalition in the form of the agricultural sector, exporters, the unemployed, and those in weakly-unionised sectors to fight for real wage reduction in *selected* sectors of the economy, and for the continued removal of the rents and subsidies which have given rise to a highly-skewed income distribution. That such potential was not harnessed owes partly to the highly-centralised, non-participatory style of government under the Seaga regime, by which interest groups, including those positively affected by policy reform, were essentially bypassed.

However, the feasibility of a labour-intensive, industrial, export-led growth path in the Caribbean also crucially depends on the ability to increase productivity, and thereby reduce the burden on real-wage reduction. The stabilisation and adjustment policies followed by Jamaica during the 1980s did little to bring about this much needed productivity increase. The adverse effect of the stabilisation policies of the mid-1980s on private sector investment, and lack of selectivity in reductions in government expenditure are partly to blame. In addition, the failure to follow 'adjustment with a human face' (Cornia, Jolly and Stewart, 1987), has further retarded this process. A marked feature of Jamaica's adjustment policies has been their negative impact on all main indicators of social well-being. Not only has this politically alienated large numbers of a potential pro-reform coalition, the falling standards of health, education, and other

355

welfare services have already begun to lower the productivity of 'human capital'.

The advent of the new PNP Government, under the campaign slogan of 'we put people first', the recent reappraisal of the Bank's adjustment policies in terms of welfare implications, and the initiation of a large Bank-sponsored social well-being programme in Jamaica, suggests that potential now exists to back the ongoing adjustment programme with a broad-based coalition of political support.

17.7 CONCLUSIONS

The high level of donor involvement in the Jamaican economy throughout the 1980s has enabled an analysis of the interactions and relationships between various forms of programme lending, such as stabilisation and adjustment programmes, and multilateral and bilateral programmes. The analysis has shown that adequate co-ordination and the appropriate sequencing of these multifarious forms of programme lending is essential if each is to achieve its objectives.

Critics of the Bank's structural adjustment programme in Jamaica point to the fact that, despite the range of reforms carried out since 1981, a substantial and positive private sector response to the new incentive structure did not emerge until the 1987–8 period. In this light, the appropriateness of the Bank's reform programme has been increasingly challenged. However, the long lag in supply-side responses arose not so much from the inappropriateness of SAL policies, as from the failure to implement a sustained and compatible stabilisation programme. In the early 1980s both domestic and foreign investment were held back by the failure to reduce the Government deficit and thereby release resources for the private sector. The manner in which this deficit was addressed under the auspices of a Fund stabilisation programme during the 1983–5 period, namely via the use of contractionary monetary policy characterised by excessively high interest rates, was equally inhibitive to private sector investment and growth. The lesson which emerges from this period is that Fund neutrality regarding the use of monetary, fiscal or exchange rate policies to attain stabilisation can be inimical to Bank-guided adjustment and growth efforts.

The increased level of co-ordination of Fund and Bank policies in the post-1985 period, in the form of a more appropriate mix of fiscal and monetary policy, indicates that Jamaica's private sector was both willing and able to respond to the new export-orientated incentive structure once it had reason to believe that prudence had been introduced to public sector expenditure policies. The post-1985 period therefore indicates that stabilisation and adjustment with growth are compatible providing the burden of contractionary demand policies falls upon consumption and on *selective* areas of public expenditure. The clear implication is that although liberalisation, incentive structures and international competitiveness, which receive the focus of the Bank's policy reform thrust, are necessary to the generation of export-led growth, they are not sufficient. Equally important are the areas of fiscal, monetary and exchange rate policies, generally characterised as the province of the Fund's short-term demand management programmes.

The Jamaican experience suggests that the traditional interpretation of the Bank/Fund division of labour regarding programme lending, whereby the Fund is seen as active in the area of short-term demand-side policies, and the Bank in medium-term supply-side policies, is not only misleading, but potentially damaging. The tendency to view the two policy areas as being of a separate genesis gives rise to the danger that they will be formulated in isolation. Although it is true that Fund policy *objectives* relate to the demand side of the economy, the fiscal, monetary and exchange rate *instruments* targeted at these objectives also impact on medium-term supply-side variables. Hence the danger of regarding 'demand-side' as being synonymous with 'short-term'. Both exchange-rate policy and monetary policy, for example, have important medium-term supply-side implications, the former impacting on exports via the determination of international competitiveness and access to foreign exchange, the latter by impacting on interest rates and hence on the flow of both domestic and foreign investment. Although such causal links may sound like truisms, their importance is often overlooked in the characterisation of Fund programmes as short-term demand management policies.

In light of the above, the general trend which has emerged in many of our country case studies, namely the convergence of Fund/Bank programme lending activities from the mid-1980s onwards, in the form of increased use of a tripartite Bank/Fund/Government medium-term policy framework approach, and the Fund's Structural Adjustment Facility (SAF) is to be welcomed. However, as the Jamaican case study has illustrated, this new approach has given rise to an intensification of the problems surrounding the issue of cross-conditionality. There is an urgent need for both multi- and bilateral agencies to come clean on this issue and devise a clear and explicit policy statement regarding the use of cross-conditionality. Without such a statement, the uncertainty surrounding the forecasting and planning tasks facing LDC policy-makers in their attempt to devise stabilisation and adjustment policies in response to projected financing gaps in the balance of payments, will be increasingly compounded by the occurrence of retrospective cross-conditionality.

Events in Jamaica in the early 1980s, in the form of a substantial increase in USAID finance, indicate that bilateral agencies remain susceptible to geopolitical factors in the determination of the direction and magnitude of aid flows. Although this is to be expected, it nevertheless has crucial implications for the activities of multilaterals. In particular, under such circumstances, multilateral financing becomes 'expensive' in terms of attached conditionalities and the leverage of associated policy reform is reduced. This problem is compounded by the fact that both donors and recipients tend to regard multilaterals, in the form of the Bank and the Fund, as 'lenders of last resort', whose role is to fill the estimated balance-of-payments financing gap after bilateral pledges have been forecast. This indicates a need for greater co-ordination between bilateral and multilateral programme lending activities. Recent moves in this direction are to be welcomed, but again with the proviso that this gives rise to the need for greater clarity on the issue of cross-conditionality.

Finally, the Jamaican experience suggests that the internalisation of policy reform is crucial to its success. A reform programme which does not have the genuine support of the recipient body politic often results in a lack of consistent and coherent policies. This is particularly so in the case of the Bank's structural adjustment programmes, which are characterised by a medium-term, gradualist, implementation so making slippage difficult to monitor. The Jamaican reform programme, prior to 1986, was marked by such a lack of consistency with frequent policy reversals in response to changes in the strength of the Government's bargaining position. The reversal of the policy of granting import licence priority to exporters which occurred in late 1983, the increased level of import restrictions during 1985, and the recourse to domestic price subsidies on imported foodstuffs in 1983 and 1985 provide examples of such policy reversal. In addition, as Table 17.2 indicates, exchange rate policy throughout this period was marked by lack of consistency. As the Seaga regime has demonstrated, it is relatively easy for a recipient to adhere to the letter of a SAL or SECAL agreement, whilst failing to abide by the spirit of the intended policy reform.

The cost of policy inconsistency is high in two respects. First, in addition to the direct negative causal links between the reversed policy instrument and its targeted policy objective, constant policy shifts give rise to an economic environment characterised by uncertainty. As a result, even during periods of low policy slippage, economic response, particularly from the private sector, may be slow due to pessimism regarding the consistency and sustainability of the policy reforms. The Seaga Government itself clearly acknowledged this neutralising effect of policy uncertainty in its arguments with the Tripartite Mission regarding exchange-rate stability. The positive private sector response to the more stable post-1985 economic environment, in which the multilaterals pursued a 'second-best' policy with government support, lends weight to this argument. Second, donor provision of balance-of-payments support which is not accompanied by genuine recipient commitment to policy reform compounds the magnitude of the future adjustment effort, not only in the sense of the Bank's dictum that 'delayed adjustment means harsher adjustment' but also in view of the debt-servicing burden created by such disbursements. In addition, such a practice has a tendency to create a vicious circle which gives rise to a 'disbursement dilemma'. As a country becomes more and more indebted to both multi- and bilateral agencies without generating the reform and growth necessary to service such debt, the pressure on the creditor agencies to disburse is intensified by the desire to keep the recipient current in its debt service obligations. As the events of 1986–7 in Jamaica indicated, this 'disbursement dilemma' can significantly strengthen the recipient's bargaining position, hence intensifying the potential for the vicious circle of disbursement without reform to continue. Under such circumstances, policy conditionality becomes little more than a vehicle used to carry disbursements through the Bank's Board of Directors, as opposed to the disbursement acting as the vehicle to carry the reforms through the recipient Government.

Although the past two years indicate that Jamaica has broken away from such a disbursement cycle, having instead implemented sustained and consistent adjustment and stabilisation policies which have enabled her to take the first steps on the medium-term growth path, the cost of the earlier cycle has been excessive. The future has been heavily mortgaged by debt obligations such that the range and flexibility of adjustment policy options facing the new PNP Government has been severely curtailed.

NOTES

1 See for example, Bonnick (1985) for an analysis showing the continuity, intensification and progression of Jamaica's economic policies from the mid-1960s through the first six years of the Manley Government. Also, Stone (1986) illustrates the broad consensus which existed between both political parties in the late 1960s and early 1970s in terms of the need to expand the state's resources and administrative capability in order to further social and economic objectives.

2 Balassa and McCarthy (1984) have calculated the adverse balance-of-payments effects of exogenous shocks in the form of declining terms of trade and increased interest rates, for thirty developing countries in the period 1979–82. Of these, Jamaica was found to be the second most severely affected.

3 The average ratio of trade to GNP is defined as the sum of import and export values divided by GNP.

4 The style of Manley's involvement with the IMF and Trade Union Movement, the initial support from the latter for a harsh wages and incomes policy, and Manley's subsequent electoral defeat, bear resemblance to the events in Britain during the 1976 'winter of discontent' when Denis Healey played a similar role to Manley in relation to the Trade Unions and IMF.

5 At this point it is important to note the hybrid nature of certain aspects of Jamaica's political system. Although the constitution follows the lines of the British system, a *de facto* American system has been increasingly adopted in the formation of the Executive, with many civil service and parastatal posts being essentially political appointments. Under both governments, this has enabled political policy formulators to influence

supposedly apolitical policy implementors.

6   Recall the finding of the regressions of Volume 1, Chapter 7, that programme finance money on its own tended to reduce growth rates, just as compliance with its *conditions* tended, with a lag, to increase them.

7   Davies, (1988: Table 5), provides data showing the impact of devaluation on Central Government external debt obligations. Between 1982 and 1985, external debt in US $ terms grew by 39 per cent whilst, when denominated in Jamaican dollars, the corresponding growth was 330 per cent, the difference being accounted for by the impact of devaluation. Hence, the rapid growth of debt servicing over this period was predominantly due to the effects of devaluation rather than to the growth in the stock of debt.

8   In a recent analysis of the effects of adjustment on six sub-Saharan economies, (Mosley and Smith, 1989), it was observed that the main burden of government expenditure reductions fell on the capital account as opposed to the recurrent accounts (see also Table 5.3, Volume 1). The main reason for this trend was identified as being the higher political risks associated with cutting recurrent expenditures, such as public sector wage and employment levels. The Jamaican case study has isolated another explanatory variable, namely, pressure on a government's recurrent expenditure in the form of debt servicing, resulting from the effects of high levels of balance-of-payments support, without a corresponding reform effort, combined with the use of devaluation to achieve stabilisation.

9   Stone (1986) provides a detailed account of the ways in which a democratic style of government was eroded during Seaga's tenure of office.

BIBLIOGRAPHY

Balassa, B. and McCarthy, F. (1984) *Adjustment Policies in Developing Countries, 1979–1983: An Update*, World Bank Staff Working Papers no. 675, Washington DC, World Bank.

Bonnick, G. (1985) Chapter in Harberger, (ed.) *World Economic Growth*.

Cornia, G.A., Jolly, R. and Stewart, F. (1987) *Adjustment with a Human Face*, UNICEF.

Davies, O. (1986) *An Analysis of the Management of the Jamaican Economy: 1972–1985*, Social and Economic Studies, 35(1), Institute of Social and Economic Research, University of the West Indies, Kingston, Jamaica.

Davies, O. (1988) *Adjustment and Stabilisation Policies in Jamaica: 1981–1987*, unpublished paper.

Edmondson, L. (1982) *Jamaica*, Latin American and Caribbean Contemporary Record, 1 (1981–2).

Government of Jamaica (1986) *Jamaica's Medium-Term Economic Performance: An Outline*, brief for the Executive Directors of the International Monetary Fund.

Harrigan, J. (1988) *Alternative Concepts of Conditionality*, Manchester Papers on Development, 4 (October 1988).

Lewis, A. (1949) *Industrial Development in the Caribbean*, official document for the Caribbean Commission.

Lewis, A. (1950) *The Industrialisation of the British West Indies*, Caribbean Economic Review, 2(1).

Mosley, P. and Smith, L. (1989) 'Structural Adjustment and Agricultural Performance in sub-Saharan Africa, 1981–87', *Journal of International Development* 1, July 1989: 311–55.

Sharpley, J. (1984) 'Jamaica: 1972–1980', in T. Killick (ed.) *The IMF and Stabilisation: Developing Country Experiences*, London, Heinemann.

BIBLIOGRAPHY

Stone, C. (1986) 'Democracy and the State', in Davies (ed.) *The State in Caribbean Society*, Department of Economics, University of the West Indies, monograph no. 2.

World Bank (1984a) *Jamaica: Recent Developments and Economic Prospects* (Report no. 4905–JM), Washington DC, World Bank.

World Bank (1984b) *Report and Recommendation of the President of the International Bank for Reconstruction and Development to the Executive Directors on a Proposed Loan to Jamaica for a Third Structural Adjustment Operation* (Report no. P–3889–J), Washington DC, World Bank.

World Bank (1988) *Report on Adjustment Lending*, Country Economics Department (Report no. R88–199), Washington DC, World Bank.

18

GUYANA

Jane Harrigan

18.1 INTRODUCTION

Guyana's first, and only, Structural Adjustment Loan, which became effective in March 1981, was one of the Bank's earliest structural adjustment operations. In terms of two key criteria, namely bringing about sustained economic reform and effecting improvements in macro-economic performance, the programme can only be judged to have been a failure. With the wisdom of hindsight, some degree of failure could be expected in what was, at the time, an early exercise in a radically new type of Bank lending activity. Indeed, the one clear achievement which emerges from Guyana's SAL is a considerable amount of 'learning by doing' on the part of Bank staff. The Bank's Program Performance Audit Report (World Bank, 1986a) is one of the most thoroughly self-critical appraisals of any SAL operation, containing important lessons which have been applied in many subsequent adjustment operations elsewhere.

The magnitude of the Guyanese SAL failure cannot, however, be attributed solely to the novelty of the exercise. SAL operations in Bolivia, Kenya, the Philippines, Senegal and Turkey preceded that in Guyana. Although the Bolivian and Senegalese programmes were discontinued, in Kenya, and particularly in the Philippines and Turkey, these early SALs formed the initial phase of successful medium-term adjustment operations.

The Structural Adjustment Loan to Guyana failed largely because it was an inappropriate policy reform vehicle for addressing the type of economic problems which confronted the country in the early 1980s. Guyana did not conform to the typical export-orientated third world economy for whom internal structural weaknesses were exposed and precipitated by the changing international economic environment of the late 1970s and early 1980s. Rather, the Guyanese economic crisis was essentially a *domestic production crisis* rooted in the internal political-economy environment of Guyana's experiment in co-operative socialism. This crisis took the form of massive mismanagement of the predominantly state-owned modes of production, resulting in rapid erosion of the country's infrastructure and a vicious cycle of declining capacity utilisation. Within this context the appropriateness of the Bank's adjustment programme – with its emphasis on a nascent private sector as the engine of export-orientated growth, with policies aimed at trade liberalisation which gave questionable foreign exchange priority to export activities, and with considerable faith placed in the ability of 'getting prices right' to stimulate the economy – was highly questionable. Although macroeconomic policy adjustments, especially in the area of public sector financial management, were urgently required in the early 1980s, equally essential was a considerable increase in traditional project finance combined with improvements in the implementation and management of projects in order to rehabilitate the country's infrastructure and public utility services and to revitalise the key sugar, rice and bauxite production sectors. Such needs suggest that a lead Bank role in generating increased investment via project loan commitments and active Bank involvement in sectoral rehabilitation through a series of Sectoral Adjustment Loans (SECALs) would have been more acceptable to the Guyanese authorities and more effective than an unfocused and over-ambitious SAL programme which was attempted in the context of a contractionist and unsustained IMF programme.

Analysis of Guyana's structural adjustment experience hence poses the question as to whether conventional Bank adjustment programmes, grounded in neo-classical theory which gives a central role to price and incentive variables, are appropriate for structurally adjusting an economy caught in a cycle of cumulative decline, as opposed to an economy which is growing, but growing inefficiently and erratically, or an economy which is static. For an economy faced with systemic decline, the quality, quantity and sectoral allocation of investment becomes the key immediate-term macroeconomic variable, suggesting the need for an alternative type of adjustment programme which draws upon Structuralist and Keynesian policies for structural transformation. Equally contentious in the Guyanese case is the conventional wisdom that an IMF stabilisation programme, focusing on the objectives of rapid attainment of internal and external balance, must always be a prerequisite for other forms of donor programme lending activities when the latter are aimed at achieving economic rehabilitation as opposed to radical changes in resource allocations.

18.2   THE EMERGENCE OF CO-OPERATIVE SOCIALISM, 1966–76

At independence in 1966 Guyana's economic activity was highly concentrated on the export of sugar, rice and bauxite. Most non-mining economic activity occurred along a narrow coastal strip where over 90 per cent of the population were located, whilst the vast interior remained undeveloped. Policy makers faced a difficult physical environment; a narrow resource base; a highly open economy with imports supplying almost all fuel needs, raw materials, consumer goods and capital goods – there being little in the way of interlinkages within the economy; and a populace which was racially polarised along political, economic and social lines.

The People's National Congress Party (PNC) independence Government, led by Forbes Burnham, and representing the minority Afro-Guyanese populace, lacked legitimacy, having been brought to power as a result of manoeuvres on the part of the British colonial authorities designed to ensure that the more radical Marxist Indo-Guyanese People's Progressive Party (PPP) would not come to power. From 1966 onwards the PNC has maintained its power through a combination of electoral fraud, brutal repression and political propaganda. As a result, post-independence economic policies have been determined largely by the political needs of a ruling party which lacks a legitimate power base rather than by the dictates of economic logic.

In 1970 Guyana declared itself a Co-operative Socialist Peoples' Republic. The move was largely a political propaganda attempt by the regime to counter the left-wing character of the political opposition and seek legitimacy by presenting itself as a radical, progressive, Third World socialist regime. The co-operative socialist development strategy embraced four principles: state control of the 'commanding heights of the economy', achieved through the nationalisation of both multinational and local assets; priority in production to satisfy the 'basic needs' (food, housing, health care and education) of the population; the formation of a trisectoral economy consisting of the public, private and co-operative sectors; and the declaration of the 'paramountcy of the ruling party', by which all organs of the state, including the Government, became agencies of the PNC party. Despite the avowed principles of Guyana's co-operative socialism, the proclamations amounted to little more than a thinly disguised endorsement of dictatorship. Instead of a tripartite structure, the 1970s witnessed the rise of a unisectoral economy, with economic and political power increasingly centralised in the PNC-dominated state, so creating an elitist form of 'state capitalism'. By 1976 the American/Canadian owned bauxite industry and the British-owned sugar industry had been nationalised and state enterprises dominated all areas of economic and financial activity, with the state accounting for 80 per cent of gross domestic capital formation. The small indigenous private sector remained limited to local trading, agricultural and small-scale manufacturing activities.

Throughout the 1970s the socialist model created growing management problems as the state sector became increasingly over-extended. Party personnel, with little commercial experience, managed the wide range of public sector enterprises, and exploited the considerable scope for nepotism and corruption. The resulting low value-added from this large state sector gave rise to widespread shortages of many basic commodities and the resulting high monopoly rents accruing to the political elite were rapidly converted into foreign assets as political uncertainty grew. Capital flight was accompanied by a flight of scarce human capital, with the 'brain drain' reaching crisis proportions by the mid-1970s. Inflows of private capital also dwindled, with private direct investment falling from US $9 million in 1970 to US $2.6 million in 1982.

The rapid expansion of state economic activity and the concomitant growth of the services sector enabled GDP growth rates to average 3.6 per cent per annum in the first half of the 1970s (Table 18.1). The 1974 sugar price boom and strengthening of the bauxite/alumina market temporarily over-compensated for the increase in oil and other import prices and the imposition of a sugar levy enabled windfall gains from the price boom to finance the rapid expansion of government economic activities and the associated high import bill, the latter more than doubling between 1972 and 1975. The accumulation of US $70 million in foreign exchange reserves enabled the Government to maintain high import levels and continue expanding the ambitious public investment programme initiated in 1975. However, with the balance of payments registering a record current account deficit of 27 per cent of GDP in 1976, this method of expenditure financing was unsustainable, and by the end of 1976 Guyana's gross foreign exchange reserves were almost completely depleted.

Table 18.1 Key macroeconomic indicators, 1971–6

	1971	1972	1973	1974	1975	1976
GDP growth (% p.a.)	3.5	−3.5	2.4	7.9	9.7	1.7
Sugar	14.1	−15.2	−9.0	23.4	−16.0	19.1
Rice	−15.2	−21.4	−18.2	30.8	8.8	−30.0
Bauxite/alumina	−3.1	−12.0	−2.4	9.2	−1.7	−12.5
Services	2.3	2.9	8.6	3.1	18.2	6.1
Exports (US $ millions)	N/A	165	158	293	378	294
Imports (US $ millions)	N/A	168	209	285	378	405
Balance-of-payments current acc. deficit (US $ millions)	N/A	15.3	66.1	17.5	18.0	140.9
Change in reserves (US $ million)	N/A	5.8	−25.0	29.3	42.8	−90.7
Central Government deficit as % GDP	N/A	N/A	N/A	N/A	10.9	35.0
Net domestic credit to public sector (G $ millions)	N/A	219	307	293	305	597

Source: World Bank (1984): Statistical Appendix.

365

Public sector finances also deteriorated rapidly. Public sector investment reached 40 per cent of GDP in 1976, whilst current expenditures on the social welfare programme, including heavy subsidisation of essential consumer goods and public services, also increased. The fall in sugar revenues, weak tax revenue performance and the growing operating losses of state enterprises were such that by 1976 gross public sector savings had fallen to 0.2 per cent of GDP and the Central Government deficit stood at 35 per cent of GDP (Table 18.1).

18.3 ECONOMIC CRISIS AND ATTEMPTED STABILISATION, 1977–80

The economic situation continued to deteriorate in 1977. Although the terms of trade remained unfavourable, the decline in export receipts, which fell by 5 per cent over the already low levels of 1976, was largely due to production problems rather than adverse price movements (Table 18.2). In particular, a four and a half month strike by sugar workers severely affected output in this key export sector. The necessary cut-back in import levels contributed to a real GDP decline of 3 per cent. Although public sector capital expenditures were cut by 40 per cent, public sector savings became negative in 1977 and the Government resorted entirely to external inflows, domestic borrowing and credit creation to finance public sector investment.

In the Bank's assessment, by early 1978 'the Government faced its worst economic crisis since independence'. Utilising unsustainable methods of financing public investment, facing a rapid build-up in foreign payments arrears, and experiencing mounting production problems due to the acute

Table 18.2 Key macroeconomic indicators, 1976–80

	1976	1977	1978	1979	1980
GDP growth (% p.a.)	1.7	−3.0	−2.9	−1.4	1.6
Sugar	19.1	−23.0	36.4	−8.6	−7.3
Rice	−30.0	88.5	−14.3	−21.4	18.2
Bauxite/alumina	−12.5	0.0	−13.0	−7.5	7.3
Exports (goods+NFS) (US $ millions)	294	279	314	311	409
Imports (goods+NFS) (US $ millions)	405	347	314	360	471
Balance-of-payments current acc. deficit as % GDP	27.0	19.5	6.4	17.0	17.9
Change in reserves (US $ million)	−90.7	−29.7	9.8	−48.6	−81.0
Central Government deficit as % GDP	35.0	15.6	12.9	19.8	30.4
Public sector deficit as % GDP	N/A	23.0	8.3	15.6	21.2
Public sector capital expenditure as % GDP	N/A	22.4	14.3	21.0	23.7

Source: World Bank (1984): Statistical Appendix.

scarcity of foreign exchange, the Government was forced to negotiate a one-year Stand-by arrangement with the IMF which became effective in August 1978. The Fund programme aimed at improving public sector finances via reductions in consumer subsidies including those on public enterprise goods and services, increased excise and import duties, and the introduction of public sector credit ceilings. In addition, interest rates were almost doubled in an attempt to stimulate private sector savings. These measures amounted to a massive economic deflation, with aggregate domestic demand reduced by over 20 per cent in real terms during 1978. The demand restraint and resource mobilisation resulted in improvements in both internal and external balance in line with the Fund programme targets. Public sector savings increased from -2 per cent of GDP in 1977 to 5 per cent in 1978 and the public sector deficit fell to 8.3 per cent of GDP, whilst the balance-of-payments current account deficit improved from 19.5 per cent of GDP to 6.4 per cent of GDP (Table 18.2).

In addition to the Stand-by, which provided SDR 15 million over a twelve month period, a Bank Programme Loan and Credit for US $10 million became effective at the end of 1978. As with most Bank Programme Loans in the 1970s the primary objective of the Guyanese Programme Loan was to provide financial and policy support for the Fund's short-term stabilisation programme. Consequently, the loan was weak on conditionality. Policy reform conditions focused on an export-orientated development strategy through improvements in the design and financing of the Public Sector Investment Programme.

Although the Government adhered to the 1978 Stand-by stabilisation measures, economic performance under the Programme Loan was extremely disappointing, such that, even at this early stage, doubts must be cast on the appropriateness of the Bank's programme lending activities in Guyana. The Bank had placed considerable faith in improvements in the Government's execution of the Public Sector Investment Programme, along with improvements in the terms of trade, as the main means by which growth would be resumed. Yet the extreme contractionary policies implemented under the Stand-by resulted in a severe cut-back in public sector fixed investment, with public sector capital expenditure falling to 14.3 per cent of GDP – the lowest level since independence. At the same time, with real demand reduced by over 20 per cent and with imports drastically curtailed, increased shortages of intermediate goods and spare parts led to a depletion of capital stock and a deterioration in the provision of infrastructure and utility services. As a result, real GDP fell by 2.9 per cent in 1978. Given the magnitude and manner of this domestic deflation and the resulting trends which occurred on the supply side of the economy, it is difficult to envisage how the conditions attached to the Bank's Programme Loan could have successfully promoted export-led growth.

As a result of the mounting production problems and increased losses facing public sector enterprises, public finances again deteriorated in 1979 (Table 18.2). Disappointing output trends combined with the impact of the second oil price shock also led to an increase in the current account deficit of the balance of payments which rose to 17 per cent of GDP in 1979. The short-lived improvements under the Stand-by led the Government to conclude a three-year Extended Fund Facility (EFF) with the IMF in June 1979 which, following the continued deterioration in public sector finances, was renegotiated in June 1980. Within this context the Bank decided to convert the proposed second Programme Loan into a more extensive and free-standing Structural Adjustment Loan and Credit and in so doing, acknowledged the 'Importance of reconciling the short-term exigencies of Guyana's adjustment process with the requirements for achieving consistent economic growth, and employment generation over the medium and longer term (World Bank, 1981: 3).

18.4   OBJECTIVES AND CONDITIONS OF THE SAL PROGRAMME

The Bank's decision to grant one of its earliest Structural Adjustment Loans to a country ideologically committed to co-operative socialism arose primarily from pressure to support the Fund's continued stabilisation effort in Guyana, the success of which was predicated on a rapid inflow of additional external resources. In comparison with the initial Programme Loan proposal, the SAL provided more extensive and tighter conditionality in order to address the structural constraints in the economy and an increased level of financing, with the loan amount raised from US $10 million to US $22 million.

The SAL was to support a Government programme which, in conjunction with the Fund's EFF, aimed at the dual objectives of restoring balance-of-payments stability and resuming economic growth and employment generation via the development of export activities. Structural constraints acting as impediments to the resumption of growth were identified by the Bank as being: insufficient attention to maintenance and rehabilitation of the country's physical infrastructure; poor implementation of the Public Sector Investment Programme; an over-rigid system of administered prices leading to inadequate incentives to producers and losses on the part of state enterprises; lack of encouragement for the private sector; inappropriate interest rate policies and weak domestic resource mobilisation; and scarcity of entrepreneurial talent, particularly in public sector enterprises, resulting from inadequate remuneration and high out-migration.

The SAL programme had a distinct short-run and long-run focus. The avowed short-term aim was essentially one of economic rehabilitation to be achieved by improved utilisation of existing productive capacity through the execution of a production-orientated Public Sector Investment Programme. The longer-term objective was to structurally transform the economy through: sustained growth in the agricultural and mining sectors; diversification of output towards non-traditional manufactures and increased processing of raw materials; restraint in the rate of growth of the Government sector; a reduction in fuel imports, primarily through the installation of a hydroelectric power plant; and an increase in the domestic value-added of the bauxite sector through the development of alumina smelting using hydroelectric power.

The outline of Guyana's SAL programme was unusual in comparison to most subsequent Bank SAL operations, not only in its clear division into the two distinct phases of rehabilitation and transformation, but also in that considerable emphasis was placed on the Public Sector Investment Programme (PSIP) in order to accomplish both phases of the adjustment programme. A massive inflow of donor finance was therefore crucial to the success of the SAL, with the Government expected to mobilise G $725 million, or 40 per cent of the finance required for the PSIP, from external sources. Equally essential was the ability of the Fund's EFF programme to mobilise domestic savings, especially in the public sector.

The atypical nature of the SAL's thrust was not reflected in the actual conditions attached to the loan. Rather, conditionality focused on the pricing policy of public sector enterprises and on institutional reforms designed to strengthen the private sector, with this sector, rather than the Public Sector Investment Programme, expected to provide an engine of export-led growth. A clear time frame to reflect the distinct short and long-term focus of the programme was also lacking. The Appendix provides a summary of SAL conditionality.

18.5 SAL PHASE ONE: IMPLEMENTATION AND PERFORMANCE

Government implementation of the SAL policy measures in the first year of the programme i.e. prior to the second tranche release in mid-1982, was characterised by a lack of urgency and commitment. In the energy sector, electricity tariffs were increased by 40 per cent in the first half of 1981 but during the latter part of the year neither the modest tariff increase scheduled under the SAL nor the sharp cost increases resulting from the mid-year devaluation of the Guyanese dollar were passed on to consumers. The required studies on the rationalisation of electricity and transport tariffs were slow to be initiated, with the Bank not having received terms of reference by early 1982. Experience in the rice sector was similar. Although the producer price of rice had been increased by 16 per cent prior to loan effectiveness, with a further 8 per cent increase in the first half of 1981, the increased profits accruing to the Rice Board as a result of the devaluation were not passed on to farmers, such that the producers' share of the export border parity price actually declined. Progress was also slow regarding the completion of a satisfactory study on future rice pricing strategies.

The major policy initiative designed to promote non-traditional exports and private sector industrial development, namely, the use of SAL finance to establish an Export Development Fund (EDF), was carried out in early 1982. However, the fact that the EDF became virtually the only source of foreign exchange available to private manufacturing enterprises, meant that it failed to finance incremental export activities as originally intended by the Bank. Although the Government initially adhered to the agreement to provide prompt issuing of import licences to EDF clients, no actions were taken towards the across-the-board simplification of import licensing procedures recommended by Bank staff. Since most imports required licences, the continued use of lengthy and discretionary licensing procedures in response to growing scarcity of foreign exchange exacerbated this shortage by retarding many production activities. Measures designed to promote exports were also implemented in the form of the establishment of an Export Unit in the Ministry of Trade but by mid-1982 little progress had been made in setting-up Industrial Promotion Councils to provide a forum for meetings between the private manufacturing sector and the Government or in the formulation of a long-term Export Action Programme. Similarly, the Government showed no urgency in complying with the condition of promulgating a revised Investment Code designed to strengthen and clarify the role of private sector investment.

Although the execution of the on-going Public Sector Investment Programme continued to be beset by financial, manpower and institutional problems during 1981 and 1982, Government compliance with conditions in this area was higher than in most. A satisfactory review of the 1981 PSIP was conducted with Bank staff and the programme was found acceptable in terms of its magnitude and sectoral composition. Improvements were also made in the quarterly monitoring of investment expenditures. Despite these achievements, public sector investment in 1981–2 stood at only US $278 million, compared to US $400 million envisaged under the SAL programme, with most of the shortfall occurring in early 1982. The inability to fully carry out the investment programme, which was a crucial component of the SAL development strategy, reflected an excessively optimistic projection of expected financial resources. The assumption that public sector savings would be able to provide 20 per cent of total financing requirements proved to be unfounded. The Government's poor compliance with SAL policy measures designed to strengthen the financial operations of the public enterprises including the reluctance to remove consumer subsidies, the weak production performance of the national sugar and bauxite companies, and the sharp increase in interest payments all contributed to a decline in public sector savings. Hence, despite large tax increases introduced under the Fund's EFF programme which resulted in a 23 per cent increase in government current revenues in 1981, the current account deficit continued to widen and the overall savings of the public sector, instead of reaching 8 per cent of GDP as assumed in the SAL projections, averaged −15 per cent of GDP. Financing problems also arose for the PSIP because the inflow of external resources was 30 per cent below expectation − caused by both the unavailability of domestic counterpart funds and the administrative and physical delays in project implementation.

Finally, although the Government complied with the sole SAL policy measure explicitly aimed at private sector resource mobilisation by increasing domestic interest rates by 1.5 per cent, high inflation meant that the real interest rate remained negative, such that the impact was minimal.

Overall, the government's level of compliance with SAL policy conditions was such that by December 1981, the scheduled date for the release of the second tranche, a Bank mission report on progress under the first phase of the loan was forced to conclude that:

> Difficult decisions are still to be made and the process of trans-formation and adjustment has barely started . . . The six major areas of concern in the SAL (electricity tariff, rice prices, investment code, import licensing, export promotion and public investment program) are the areas in which the Mission felt that the Government needed to take some action before the second tranche could be released.
>
> (Bank Office Memorandum, December 1981)

Weak implementation of SAL conditions, the failure to address the deep-rooted structural constraints in the Guyanese economy, and adverse movements in the terms of trade resulted in a continued deterioration in economic performance during 1981 and the first half of 1982 − as reflected by trends in all key macroeconomic indicators (Table 18.3). Following a short-lived output improvement in 1980 GDP again declined in 1981 whilst real per capita income fell by 6.5 per cent. Output in the key bauxite and rice sectors fell by 14.3 per cent and 2.6 per cent respectively and although sugar output increased by 11 per cent this was offset by a sharp fall in international sugar prices. Domestic demand, however, failed to adjust to the reduced levels of resource availability such that both the fiscal and balance-of-payments accounts continued to deteriorate (Table 18.3).

The overall deficit of the public sector reached 43 per cent of GDP in 1981, compared to 15.6 per cent in 1979. Over two-thirds of this deficit was financed by recourse to the domestic banking system with the rapid expansion of credit (30 per cent per annum in nominal terms between 1979–82) contributing to an inflation rate of 20 per cent in 1981. The

Table 18.3   Key macroeconomic indicators, 1980–5

	1980	1981	1982	1983	1984	1985
GDP growth (% p.a.)	1.6	−0.3	−10.4	−9.3	2.1	1.0
Sugar	−7.3	11.2	−4.0	−2.1	−4.3	0.0
Rice	18.2	−2.6	10.5	−11.9	24.3	−15.2
Bauxite/alumina	7.3	−14.3	−33.4	−42.1	11.4	18.4
Exports (US $ millions)	409	367	265	225	246	245
Imports (US $ millions)	471	491	338	316	285	322
Balance-of-payments current acc. deficit as % GDP	17.9	32.9	29.4	33.4	22.0	33.0
Debt:exports ratio	137	174	258	311	282	303
Central Government deficit as % GDP	30.4	36.6	69.4	47.4	68.9	60.3
Public sec. deficit as % GDP	21.2	43.2	43.5	56.1	50.0	61.1
Public sec. capital expenditure as % GDP	23.7	26.4	22.4	18.9	23.6	24.6

Source: World Bank (1986a):   Statistical Appendix.

balance-of-payments current account deficit also worsened in 1981 reaching 33 per cent of GDP, two-thirds of which was financed by net public capital inflows, such that by 1982 the debt:export ratio stood at 258 per cent. Despite a relatively favourable debt structure, with much of the new debt being of a non-commercial type, poor economic performance in the export sector gave rise to increasing debt servicing problems in the first half of 1982.

18.6   TECHNICAL DEFICIENCIES IN THE SAL LOAN

The failure of the first phase of the SAL programme to stem economic deterioration can partly be attributed to the Government's low compliance with the SAL conditions. This low compliance rate is explained by a variety of factors: lack of Government commitment and institutional capacity to implement the policy measures; the poorly devised nature of the programme, in particular, its unrealistic time frame and lack of specificity; and shortcomings in the Bank's administration and monitoring of the Loan.

During the preparatory stages of the Loan in 1980 there were already clear signs that the Government lacked the potential commitment to carry out many of the SAL policy reforms. Although the general objectives of the structural adjustment programme were set out in the Government's Letter on Development Policies (World Bank,   1986a: Annexe 1), this LDP was remarkably vague and failed to constitute an explicit Government statement on the programme's long-term objectives, specific short-term actions and quantifiable targets. Throughout the sixteen-page letter only one paragraph was devoted to the issue of expanding the role of the private sector and little mention was made of the need to reduce the scope and improve the efficiency of the large public sector. In addition, the Letter clearly stated the Government's intention to remove consumer subsidies only in those instances 'where income distributional considerations will permit.' The overall rhetorical tone of the LDP therefore reflected the Government's continued commitment 'to the establishment of co-operative socialism'. The only area in which the LDP reflected a strong concurrence with Bank views on development policies was in the considerable emphasis it placed on the ability of a range of individual projects within the Public Sector Investment Programme to bring about an improvement in output levels.

The unsatisfactory nature of the Government's Letter on Development Policies was the direct result of the hurried manner in which the SAL package was constructed. The Bank's decision to convert what was to be Guyana's Second Programme Loan into a more extensive Structural Adjustment Loan was taken in mid-August 1980, less than two months before the operation was scheduled to be presented to the Bank's Board. This Board deadline was maintained in order to synchronise the timing of the SAL as closely as possible with the Fund's EFF which had been approved in July 1980. Such a decision meant that the Bank failed to invest the time needed to establish Government consensus and commitment to what had become a wide-ranging reform programme. Such an investment was all the more crucial since the thrust of the SAL programme, which envisaged the private manufacturing sector as providing an engine of export-led growth, challenged many of the long-standing ideological precepts of the PNC regime. Yet many of the policy measures aimed at this sector, such as the drafting of a long-term Export Action Programme, were eleventh-hour additions to the revised programme and had not been adequately discussed with the Guyanese authorities.

Not only were SAL negotiations hurried, they were conducted with civil servants who lacked the necessary will and authority to make a clear commitment to the proposed policy changes. The lead negotiator, the Chairman of the State Planning Secretariat – the institution responsible for planning and implementing the SAL programme – held less than Cabinet rank and so lacked full *de jure* authority to pursue policy objectives which fell under the jurisdiction of other Ministries.

Despite the unsatisfactory nature of the LDP the Chairman made it clear that he would be unable to persuade high ranking Government officials to accept a revised LDP. Acknowledging the fact that 'The possibility of reaching full agreement with the Government might be jeopardised by pushing the GOG to make explicit policy changes which were deemed to be too politically sensitive to be spelled out in black and white' (World Bank, 1986a: 4). Bank staff nevertheless reached the 'Conclusion that a "privately understood" GOG policy agenda had been solidified and could be effectively pursued without the Borrower setting out an explicit publicly stated policy program' (World Bank, 1986a: 5).

The basis of this conclusion, however, is hard to identify since, in addition to the LDP, there were other clear signs of Government reservations over the design of the programme and in particular its focus on the private sector. For example, the Government successfully negotiated the reduction of the amount of SAL funds earmarked for the Export Development Fund from US $10 million to US $8 million, with the balance being switched to supporting the Government's budget. Furthermore, the Bank of Guyana refused to guarantee the foreign exchange integrity of the revolving EDF and opposed the proposal that a portion of EDF finance be reserved exclusively for the private sector. The government also insisted that the requirement to promptly issue import licences to EDF clients would only be carried out to the extent that 'it did not conflict with existing import regulations' and reservations were expressed regarding the appointment of an Industrial Adviser and the speed with which a revised Investment Code could be drafted.

In addition to the failure to obtain clear government approval of the SAL, there was little attempt to involve key interest groups in the process of formulating and supporting policy measures. No government consultations were held with private sector groups, such as the Guyana Manufacturers' Association, even though many important components of the programme were aimed at this sector. Similarly, the Guyana Electricity Corporation, a major beneficiary of the Loan, receiving 36 per cent of non-EDF allocations, was not consulted regarding the power sector components of the programme until July 1982 i.e. sixteen months after Loan effectiveness.

It is worth quoting at length the Bank's own retrospective assessment of the SAL preparations:

> The procedure used by the Bank was clearly defective. To invite one official to Washington to draft an LDP which, as in this case, includes actions and deadlines involving Ministry responsibilities beyond his knowledge and authority, is a prescription for failure. However, when Bank management found the draft letter to be excessively vague, the solution was to accept the draft and to provide a clearer, more comprehensive presentation in the President's Report. . . as if clarity of presentation to the Board were the major concern rather than establishing consensus within, and agreement with, the Government. This was tantamount to the Bank's accepting a program with minimal Borrower commitment and deciding to

forego an opportunity to build Government consensus and commitment to carrying out the program.

(World Bank, 1986a: 27)

The hurried manner in which the SAL programme was put together, the absence of a 'black and white' statement of government commitment and the reliance on a 'private understanding' with the authorities gave rise to a programme which lacked specificity in most of its conditions – 'Apart from the EDF, pricing, and certain ongoing programs such as energy conservation and expansion of the Export Promotion Unit, most proposed actions lacked detail so that it became unclear, and misunderstandings arose, as to what was required' (World Bank, 1986a: 9). In particular, conditions relating to the drafting of a long-term Export Action Programme, appointment of an Industrial Adviser, revision of the Guyana Investment Code, provision of credit to EDF exporters, simplification of import licensing arrangements, and monitoring of Public Sector Investment, were not spelt out in sufficient detail. Since most of these nebulous conditions related to actions in the private sector – the part of the programme to which the government was least committed – there was considerable scope for the Government to avoid full implementation of such conditions without actually violating the formal legal requirements of the Loan.

In addition to the vagueness of the conditions, the government's low level of compliance was facilitated by the unrealistic and confused time frame of the programme. In the Bank's own words:

The deadlines for launching specific actions were so unrealistic that half of the target dates agreed between GOG and the Bank and appended to the Letter on Development Policies had been passed before the Guyana SAL/C had become effective. As a result, much of the credibility that such target dates might have otherwise had was undermined from the very beginning and subsequent slippage became a normal course of events.

(World Bank, 1986a: 10)

Weaknesses in the programme's time-bound trigger targets and the monitoring of policy actions was compounded by the fact that the details of the tranching conditions often differed between various documents associated with the Loan. For example, Schedule 1 of the Loan Agreement contained a condition regarding 'interim adjustment of farmgate prices' which did not feature as a tranching condition in the President's Report, whilst the latter contained 'a study relating to the rationalisation of transport tariffs' and 'effective operation of the EDF' as tranching conditions which did not appear in the Loan Agreement. Similarly, several of the deadline dates for conditions, such as those relating to the drafting of

375

the Export Action Programme, differed between the LDP and the President's Report.

A further criticism which must be levied against the quality of the Bank's technical work in drafting and monitoring Guyana's SAL is the manner in which the SAL funds were disbursed. Despite the obvious problems with the government's level of commitment, the only up-front conditionality required prior to the release of the first tranche was an increase in the producer price of rice. In addition, US $8 million of the US $22 million loan and credit was allocated to the operation of the EDF with its release not being subject to any tranching conditions. The remaining US $14 million was to be released in two equal tranches. However, by the end of February 1982 the first tranche disbursement of US $7 million had been exceeded by US $1.2 million due to the 'mistaken assumption on the part of the Loan Department that the limit of US $7 million had been lifted' (World Bank, 1986a: 73). Although the Guyanese authorities were initially requested to refund the excess disbursement, the request was dropped by the Bank in view of Guyana's severe foreign exchange shortage. Such errors on the part of the Bank undoubtedly further undermined the effectiveness of tranching as a leverage mechanism in encouraging compliance with conditionality.

Finally, the SAL programme failed to adequately address the Government's lack of institutional capacity to implement the SAL reform measures. Although a Technical Assistance Loan accompanied the SAL, this loan failed to acknowledge the fact that improved public sector management was one of the country's highest priority needs in the early 1980s. Instead, it focused on the undertaking of studies, the provision of support for specific short-term tasks required to implement the conditions of the SAL and the belated addition of *ad hoc* management and training support for the bauxite sector. In addition, the SAL emphasis on the private sector gave rise to a tendency for Bank staff to view policy choices in terms of a vigorous private sector *or* public sector institutional development.

In fairness to the Bank, it must be pointed out that implementation problems under the first phase of the SAL were compounded by circumstances beyond the control of Bank staff. In particular, unexpected balance-of-payments support provided by Trinidad and Tobago, the preoccupation of top-ranking government officials with changes in the domestic political climate, and a deteriorating economic situation which gave rise to a crisis management mode of operation, all helped to reduce the Government's level of commitment to, and compliance with, the SAL programme.

Although Bank staff had rushed to complete the Guyana SAL in order to help bridge a balance-of-payments financing gap which existed under the Fund's EFF programme, the unexpected provision in early 1981 of a large

Oil Finance Facility from Trinidad and Tobago meant that Guyana did not need to draw on the SAL money until August 1981 – six months after the SAL Loan became effective – by which time only one and a half of the eight second tranche release conditions had been met. Not only did the Trinidad and Tobago finance temporarily reduce Guyana's urgent need for foreign exchange, the fact that there was no conditionality attached to the finance made the Bank's much smaller loan appear relatively 'expensive' in terms of the associated conditions.

Domestic political events also diverted government attention away from preparation and implementation of the SAL. The deteriorating economic conditions of the late 1970s had been capitalised upon by the PPP and other opposition groups. Growing unrest took the form of strikes and demonstrations amongst all ethnic groups, including Afro-Guyanese supporters of the Burnham regime and pro-PNP Trade Unions. The response to the failure of co-operative socialism to bolster the credibility of the Burnham regime was a decision to amend the constitution in October 1980 in a manner which entrenched Prime Minister Burnham's power by establishing him as the country's first Executive President. The subsequent elections of December 1980 were clouded by opposition allegations of massive fraud with the claims supported by a team of international observers. Within this context of growing political uncertainty the Guyanese Government placed low priority on the SAL negotiations. For example, the draft LDP was circulated to Cabinet Ministers during the run-up period to the elections and there was no Cabinet review of either the LDP or the draft Loan documents before their approval by the Bank's Board. Policy compliance was also retarded by the domestic political situation. Politicians were unwilling to exacerbate the growing food shortages and unemployment by implementing politically sensitive measures associated with the SAL and EFF such as the incomes policy, consumer subsidy removal and the passing-on of the costs of the mid-1981 devaluation to consumers. Removal of government regulatory controls, such as the issuing of import licences, although ostensibly opposed by the Government on the economic grounds of foreign exchange shortage, were undoubtedly also unacceptable since deregulation was tantamount to removing an important source of economic patronage which had been used to forge clientistic support for the PNP regime.

Alongside the political difficulties of 1980–1 the economic crisis continued to intensify. By mid-1981 exchange reserves were virtually zero causing an acute shortage of many imported goods. Such circumstances further reduced the priority attached to the implementation of the Bank and Fund programmes with the Government adopting instead a crisis management mode of operation which concentrated on tightening controls in order to eliminate the parallel market for imported commodities. In view of the severity of this economic crisis, the question arises as to why both the SAL and the EFF programmes, albeit that they were only implemented in a limited manner, failed to have *any* positive economic impact. This question regarding the appropriateness of the SAL policy prescriptions under the first phase of the programme was belatedly addressed by Bank staff in early 1982.

18.7 REAPPRAISAL OF SAL POLICIES: THE GOVERNMENT ACTION PROGRAMME

Inadequacies in the specification of SAL conditionality gave rise to considerable debate within the Bank in early 1982 regarding the extent to which compliance with conditions had been breached by Guyana and hence, whether or not the second tranche should be suspended. It is obvious however, from various Bank internal memoranda, that the debate concerned not only the technical level of compliance, but also the extent to which SAL policies had adequately addressed the structural problems facing the Guyanese economy.

Although a Bank mission of late 1981 recommended that the second tranche could be released providing some additional measures relating to the SAL agreement were carried out, this recommendation was resisted by the Director of the Latin and Caribbean Department 2. The reasons advanced for suspension of the second tranche make it clear that the Director's concern was not so much with the Government's level of compliance with the pre-existing agreement, but with the inadequacies of the policy reforms proposed by this agreement:

> It is obvious now that the policy actions envisaged in the SAL, while necessary, are not sufficient to make substantial progress towards economic viability. Much more is needed, particularly concerning the need to promote private investment and production and export growth. It is clear that the public sector is not likely to be able in the foreseeable future to manage efficiently all the public enterprises, the production of which is declining sharply. As things stand now . . . a deepening balance of payments crisis and public sector financial crisis, and the EFF arrangement hopelessly derailed . . . Guyana is entering a dangerous stage in which social and political disturbances should be expected. Until a basic understanding is reached with the Government on how to address this crisis, we should not agree to release the SAL second tranche. Since the Guyanese have not complied fully with all their SAL obligations, we have a legal right to do so.
>
> (Bank Office Memorandum, December 1981)

As a result of the above recommendation release of the second tranche was suspended in February 1982 and there followed a period in which a revised SAL programme was negotiated with the Guyanese authorities. The government was effectively asked to reach agreement on, and start implementing, new policy measures, which had not formed part of the original SAL agreement, in order to secure the release of the second tranche: 'The issue before the Bank is do we try to obtain more than is, strictly speaking, in the Loan Agreement or do we release the tranche on the grounds that the Government has complied with the measures agreed upon' (Bank Office Memorandum, December 1981). The need for such retrospective conditionality arose because the Bank itself, half way through the programme, and with well over half the funds already having been disbursed, had still not determined an appropriate adjustment package. In the words of the appraisal·mission:

> Our Structural Adjustment Loan, while it has accomplished a number of useful things, has only scratched the surface of the problem. There still remains the central problem: how to increase production upon which the finances of the public sector critically depend . . . This thus raised the fundamental issue of structural adjustment in Guyana.
> (Bank Office Memorandum, December 1981)

The Bank's reappraisal of SAL policies consisted of a belated acknowledgement that the first phase of the SAL had paid insufficient attention to a key production sector, namely bauxite/alumina, whose output, even at the depressed levels of 1982, still accounted for 42 per cent of total exports. It was realised that prospects for improving both government finances and the balance of payments were critically dependent on achieving recovery in bauxite output, which had declined almost continuously since the late 1970s. The rice sector was also seen as having its considerable potential neglected under the first phase of the SAL. In response to recent financing problems, the revised programme also placed less stress on the Public Sector Investment Programme as a means for achieving economic recovery. However, with the exception of the new sectoral emphasis and the down-grading of the PSIP, the Bank's revised policy proposals consisted of an intensification of, rather than a departure from, the earlier proposals, with even greater emphasis now being placed on a strengthening of the non-traditional private sector. An extensive reorganisation of the economy was therefore proposed under which the private sector, both domestic and foreign, would be allowed a significantly greater role, and the remaining public sector would be 'restructured' to ensure its efficient operation. Hence, as an additional condition for the release of the second tranche, the Bank insisted on a broad understanding on the roles of the public and private sectors in the Guyanese economy.

This understanding took the form of the publication in May 1982 of the Government Action Programme, which appropriately became known as the GAP. To achieve recovery in the bauxite sector the GAP announced that management operations would be transferred to a foreign firm in the form of a private partner with equity participation. In addition to this foreign financing to assist in rehabilitation of the sector's aged capital equipment, G $60 million of the government's 1982 investment programme was earmarked for investment in the bauxite sector. A series of reforms were also targeted on the rice sector. Wholesale reorganisation of the sector was proposed through the restructuring of the Guyana Rice Board (GRB) involving a reduction of its monopoly procurement and marketing powers. The GAP announced the Government's intention to: split the GRB into five Regional Boards; transfer the provision of inputs from the GRB to the private sector; sell the GRB's fleet of tractors and combines and smaller rice mills to private operators and co-operatives; review the GRB's external and domestic rice marketing and price arrangements; and transfer the Board's extension, research and credit provision functions to other government agencies.

The GAP also announced a range of policies aimed at strengthening the role of the private sector, particularly in export manufacturing activities. These included: a reiterated intention to provide the overdue revision of the Guyana Investment Code and appointment of an Industrial Adviser; provision of a regime of fiscal and other incentives, including waiving of consumption taxes on imported components and the introduction of a more general system of tax concessions; and priority allocation of both scarce electricity and foreign exchange supplies to the manufacturing sector. In order to help rehabilitate many potentially export-orientated public sector enterprises the GAP specified government plans to seek private equity participation in public enterprises involved in the fisheries, timber, glassworks, stockfeeds and pharmaceutical industries. In addition the Government was to refrain from starting new operations and would cease to carry the deficits of commercial-type public sector corporations.

In comparison with the earlier Letter on Development Policies, the GAP constituted a much firmer statement of the Government's specific policy intentions under the second phase of the SAL, with clear time deadlines appended to the various policy measures. Nevertheless, Bank staff expressed reservations regarding the Government's political ability and will to implement the revised second phase policies which amounted to an even greater challenge to the regime's enunciated ideology. As the SAL appraisal mission acknowledged:

> In approaching a program of effective structural adjustment we would essentially be telling the Guyanese that the nationalisation policies, rapid expansion of public sector activities and controls, and restriction of private sector activities have not worked. The general position outlined clearly challenges, however, the very foundations of independence and the country's current philosophy.
>
> (World Bank, 1986b)

It was also clear that the amount of finance available under the second tranche of the SAL, namely, US $5.8 million of the non-EDF component of the loan, was small both in relation to the financial needs of the country and in relation to the extensive policy changes the Government was expected to undertake in return for the finance: 'I also think that for convincing Mr. Burnham to agree with this course of action, the release of the SAL second tranche does not provide, in itself, enough leverage' (Bank Office Memorandum, December 1981).

The Bank's decision not to suspend the SAL operation, and to trust instead in government commitment to the GAP regardless of the poor implementation record under the first phase, was partly due to the complex relationship which had developed between the Bank's programme lending activities in Guyana and those of other agencies, and in particular, the IMF. The Bank appraisal mission had initially recommended that disbursal of the second tranche should only occur when the Fund's EFF had been 'put back on track'. However, the direction of this proposed cross-conditionality was effectively reversed by Fund staff, who insisted instead on the continuation of the structural adjustment programme as a precondition of a further stabilisation package:

> Following discussions with the IMF, it became clear to Bank staff that the Fund would be willing to proceed with negotiations on a new EFF only after they had assurances that the policy reforms proposed by the Bank would be adopted by the GOG. Hence, it was decided to release the second tranche upon receipt of the GAP and to insist upon the negotiation of a new EFF agreement as a precondition for the proposed future sector loans.
>
> (World Bank, 1986b: 13)

Hence, the unusual situation arose whereby a Bank structural adjustment operation was a prerequisite for negotiations between Guyana and the IMF.

In addition to this direct Fund pressure for the continuation of the SAL, there was considerable pressure created by Guyana's debt situation. The success of the stabilisation and adjustment operation was critically dependent on extensive aid flows from non-Bank sources. By early 1982 Guyana was already dangerously close to reaching an uncreditworthy status which threatened the flow of external finance. Hence, the disbursal of the SAL second tranche was urgently required in order to help prevent the deleterious effects of further default on debt payments.

With the cessation of both Fund support and the reduction in assistance from many bilateral donors, such debt-servicing pressures also help to explain the Government's agreement to prepare the GAP and to initiate a number of the GAP measures needed to facilitate the release of the second tranche. The latter was consequently released in June 1982 – the date on which the SAL was originally due to be closed – with the closing date being extended to June 1983. Following the disbursal, progress in formulating and carrying out the revised GAP programme stagnated:

> While the GAP document was detailed, target deadlines for the most part were not adhered to, and, to the extent steps were taken towards fulfilling actions under the GAP, follow-through was weak and few of the required actions were completed.
>
> (World Bank, 1986b: 13)

By late 1982 the GAP policy of securing managerial, technical, marketing and equity support for the bauxite sector had been initiated in the form of discussions with foreign companies. However, these companies were unwilling to become involved in the sector before undertaking diagnostic studies and were not prepared to consider equity participation in the short term. Although part of this reluctance was due to the depressed international market for bauxite products, there was a degree of mistrust regarding the Guyanese commitment to the project. The major multi-national, ALCAN, for example, pulled out of the discussions, and in the assessment of a Bank mission of September 1982, ALCAN's withdrawal was prompted by: 'The opposition of BIDCO's Chairman and a number of others within Government against a deal with ALCAN' (Bank Office Memorandum, September 1982). Nevertheless, by early 1983 the Government had concluded terms of reference with two US companies for the provision of technical assistance and marketing studies.

Progress was minimal under the second phase of the SAL in restructuring the rice sector and the eventual decentralisation of the Guyana Rice Board via the establishment of five Regional Boards did little to improve the efficiency of public sector management of the rice industry. The transfer of GRB's credit, research, and extension functions to other government agencies, namely GAIBANK and the Ministry of Agriculture also took place behind schedule and in an *ad hoc* manner. Little was achieved in terms of transferring many of GRB's responsibilities and assets to the private sector. GRB's mills, tractors and combines were not formally offered for sale to private operators, whilst its functions with regard to the importation and distribution of inputs, rather than being privatised, were handed over to two public companies – GNTC and Guyana Stores. Significant progress was initially made in reducing GRB's marketing monopoly with millers and farmers permitted to sell rice directly to domestic retailers and consumers in competition with GRB. However, following government complaints that such liberalisation had resulted in higher prices, lower quality and illegal exports, legislation regulating rice marketing and processing was enacted in 1984 such that rice could only be sold to millers licensed by the Government. Since the adoption of a permanent rice pricing strategy was closely linked to reform of the rice marketing arrangements, the Government's unwillingness to undertake sustained reforms in the latter area meant that price policy continued to take the form of *ad hoc* adjustments. Overall, the intended liberalisation of the rice sector failed to occur under the second phase of the SAL. The GRB, plagued by mismanagement, corruption and inefficiencies, continued to operate a major portion of the milling capacity, remained the sole exporter of rice and continued to be responsible for administering prices and licences issued by the Government such that the envisaged incentives to private millers and traders failed to materialise.

As in the bauxite and rice sectors, the Government's commitment to strengthening private sector participation in the manufacturing sector was equally weak and unsustained. A draft of the revised Investment Code was not completed until mid-1984, by which time government officials had made it clear to a Bank OED mission that they had no intention of finalising the Code and enacting it into law. Similarly, by the target date of September 1982 no progress had been made in devising a general tax incentive policy, in the introduction of a limited no-fund licensing scheme for imports to the manufacturing sector or the introduction of a foreign exchange retention scheme. The planned Representative Councils for Industry were not set up, the Government failed to appoint a high level Industrial Advisor and by 1984 regular government meetings with private sector representatives had been discontinued. Finally, although the Government hired a foreign consultant to advise on public enterprise operations, there was little achievement in terms of securing private management and equity participation in public enterprises outside of the bauxite sector.

Severe problems were also experienced in the operation of the Export Development Fund under the second phase of the SAL. At the end of September 1982, the Bank of Guyana, facing acute foreign exchange shortages, suspended foreign exchange disbursements to the EDF. This direct violation of the SAL Loan Agreement was taken unilaterally without consulting the EDF Board, private sector participants or Bank staff, with the latter only being informed ten days after the action had occurred. Bank acceptance of such a blatant violation of SAL conditionality was partly due to the realisation that the EDF had failed to operate efficiently due to 'deficient design' of the scheme. The failure to reinforce the EDF scheme with incentives to encourage wider participation by producers exporting to hard currency areas had resulted in excessive EDF demands on the limited exchange resources of the Bank of Guyana in order for the Fund to revolve. Following Bank pressure, the EDF resumed business in early 1983 on a quasi-revolving basis at one-tenth of its original size but with eligibility limited to hard currency exporters. Consequently, only five companies had access to EDF resources, two of these being public sector enterprises who received over 86 per cent of EDF disbursements during 1984. Hence, by the end of the SAL operation: 'The EDF, despite continuing but limited operations, was, for all intents and purposes, no longer functioning in support of private sector growth and expanded exports, as had been its original objective' (World Bank, 1986a: 16).

Implementation of the Public Sector Investment Programme faced the same problems under phase two of the SAL as under the first phase, namely, finance and manpower constraints. During 1982 the sharp deterioration in fiscal performance, lack of imported inputs and declining capital inflows, resulted in a reduction in public investment to G $351 million – a 33 per cent fall in real terms. Much of this reduction took the form of across-the-board reductions in the release of funds. These financial constraints were worsened by the Government's failure to use SAL counterpart funds to finance local currency costs of the PSIP. Furthermore, the poor success in improving project implementation and monitoring gave rise to slow physical project progress such that three major projects in irrigation and forestry, which accounted for a large share of PSIP expenditure, were significantly behind schedule and suffering large cost overruns. Revisions to the 1983 PSIP occurred through government identification of a 'core programme' of on-going major projects for which external financing would be available. In identifying this core emphasis was placed on projects in the agricultural, infrastructure and manufacturing export sectors which were compatible with the development thrust of the GAP. However, the core programme lacked any direct recognition of the crucial need for minimum rehabilitation investments in public sector enterprises, and allocations fell short of their minimum capital stock maintenance needs. As a result, the production and export performance of such enterprises, which still accounted for a large part of manufacturing activities, continued to deteriorate.

In summary, actions under phase two of the SAL aimed at stimulating private sector exports and adjusting the mix of private and public sector activity were inhibited by worsening foreign exchange shortages and by the Government's lack of commitment to measures designed to strengthen the private sector. The Bank's own retrospective analysis succinctly summarises the implementation performance in all areas of the second phase of the SAL programme:

> Despite the release of the second tranche, little progress was made during the second phase of the SAL/C. In particular, such progress as was achieved contributed little to the Action Programme goals of expanding private sector production and diverting resources to export.
>
> (World Bank, 1986a: vii)

As Bank staff had feared during the formulation of the GAP, sustained implementation of the revised SAL programme failed to materialise due to lack of financial leverage needed to persuade the Government to undertake a politically unpalatable reorientation of the economy. The political resistance to the proposed liberalisation and privatisation of the economy was expressed in statements from high ranking government officials in the period immediately following disbursal of the second tranche. An IMF mission of August 1982 presented the following observations in their back-to-office report:

> There has apparently emerged a serious rift in the ruling party on the issue of greater 'privatisation' of the economy and particularly on the question of the participation of foreign companies in the ownership and management of the bauxite sector. The Prime Minister, Mr. Ptolemy Reid, who is well respected in Party circles, has reportedly aligned himself with the group that opposes the 'recolonization' of the economy. Mr. Burnham, who in earlier discussions with the World Bank, had endorsed the idea of foreign participation, now seems somewhat ambiguous on the issue. In recent speeches he has repeated the theme that his Government will not 'surrender' the economy to multinationals and has even chided public officials for suggesting a return to the former dependence on the foreign multi-nationals.
>
> (IMF Office Memorandum, August 1982)

Such resistance was not only due to a bitter colonial experience, but also to the racial cleavages which pervaded the structure of Guyanese politics and economic activity. Whilst the PNP was essentially an Afro-Guyanese party, it was the Indo-Guyanese supporters of the opposition PPP who stood to gain most from freeing-up of the economy since most private small-scale rice farming, commercial and trading activities were conducted by the Asian community.

Given this level of political opposition to the central thrust of the SAL programme, a substantial inflow of foreign finance may have provided some leverage in persuading the Government to undertake a high political risk reform programme. Although the second tranche of the SAL amounted to only US $5.8 million, Bank staff, aware of the 'inadequate leverage' of the SAL alone, had anticipated the SAL forming part of a much larger multi-donor adjustment effort supported by the IMF, the Inter-American Development Bank, CIDA and further Bank power sector, agriculture sector and manufacturing sector loans, with the latter SECALs expected to amount to US $45 million in 1983–4.

The interaction of agencies involved in programme lending to Guyana illustrates the potential 'domino effect' that can arise from the implicit practice of cross-conditionality. Following the Fund mission's assessment of government commitment to the GAP, the EFF was formally suspended and no further Fund programme was put in place. The Fund was unwilling to commit itself to a new Guyanese programme until the amount of foreign assistance likely to be available held out hope for the success of a stabilisation package. However, this foreign assistance was itself implicitly contingent on a Fund programme being in place. Hence, the failure of the latter to materialise resulted in the suspension of Bank sector loan negotiations and the insertion of 'retrospective cross-conditionality' on the part of CIDA whereby the provision of a US $12 million credit, intended to support the SAL, was not disbursed due to the failure to establish a Fund programme.

Effectively, by mid-1982 a vicious circle had arisen whereby most donors were unwilling to commit further resources to Guyana until they had received clear signs that other donors were also willing to do so. Although the Fund abdicated its traditional lead role by insisting on the continuation of the SAL as a prerequisite for its own programme, hence forcing the Bank to take the lead by committing the second tranche of the SAL, other donors maintained their conventional view of the Fund as the 'green light' agency. Consequently, the Bank, having taken the risk of providing signals to the donor community, found these signals ignored due to the collapse of the Fund negotiations, so leaving the Bank in the position of having to continue a hopelessly under-funded adjustment programme.

The disappointing levels of foreign financial flows from mid-1982 onwards affected the Government's ability, as well as its will, to implement many of the SAL policy reforms. Donor funding for projects in the PSIP fell well short of Bank expectations and was a major contributor to the need to curtail public sector investment. Scarcity of foreign exchange also resulted in: the closure of the EDF; the inability to implement a foreign exchange retention scheme for private sector manufacturing exporters; and the Government's unwillingness to liberalise the import licensing scheme. Throughout the second phase of the SAL, government officials consistently pointed to the worsening foreign exchange situation as the reason for their failure to provide greater support to the private manufacturing sector.

18.8 OVERALL ASSESSMENT OF SAL IMPACT

In view of trends in all key macroeconomic indicators (Table 18.3) the Bank was forced to conclude that 'By nearly every economic indicator the SAL program as translated into economic performance, failed dismally' (World Bank, 1986a: 17). The magnitude of this failure is seen by the comparison in Table 18.4 between actual performance during the 1981–3 SAL period and the projected performance contained within the January 1981 President's Report (World Bank, 1981). Despite forecasts of real GDP growth of 3.5–6.0 per cent during 1981–3 GDP actually *declined* by an average of 6.8 per cent and by 1983 stood 18 per cent below the pre-

Table 18.4   SAL projections versus actual outcomes, 1981–3 (%)

	SAL projections		Actual
	High growth target 1981–3	Moderate growth target 1981–3	Average 1981–3
Growth rates (1977 prices)			
GDP (factor cost)	5.7	3.6	−6.8
Exports	10.8	8.7	−12.3
Imports	6.0	3.9	−14.1
Consumption per cap.	1.1	−0.1	−5.0
Change in terms of trade	3.1	3.1	−12.5
Ratio to GDP (current prices)			
Consumption	81.5	82.3	89.2
Investment	27.3	26.4	29.7
Gross dom. savings	18.5	17.7	10.7
Gross nat. savings	14.7	13.5	1.0
Exports	65.1	64.8	55.6
Imports	73.9	73.5	74.6
Resource gap	8.8	8.7	19.0
Current account deficit	12.6	12.9	31.9

Source: World Bank (1986a:)   Table 1.

SAL 1979 level. Furthermore, production fell in every sector which had received SAL financial allocations and the attention of SAL policy reform measures. The most dramatic decline occurred in the bauxite/alumina sector which had been the largest recipient of SAL allocations outside non-traditional manufactures. Between 1981 and 1983 output from this sector fell by 61.5 per cent and 1983 witnessed the complete closure of the alumina plant due to excessively high production costs and weak international demand for a Guyanese product of declining quality.

Regarding the central SAL objective of increasing both traditional exports and non-traditional manufactured exports, the impact was generally unfavourable, with total exports falling as a percentage of GDP and by 12.3 per cent in absolute terms compared to the SAL President's report's prediction of a 8.7–10.8 per cent growth. Exports from the traditional rice, sugar and bauxite sectors dropped significantly throughout the life of the SAL programme and fell considerably short of planned targets. Although manufactured exports improved during the first two years of the SAL, largely due to the operation of the EDF, much of this increase was accounted for by a single manufacturer producing stoves and refrigerators for the CARICOM market and utilising over 40 per cent of EDF disbursements during 1981–2. There was little, therefore, in the way of strengthening and diversifying private manufacturing export activities. Moreover, manufacturing exports fell by almost 50 per cent in 1983 following the Bank of Guyana's inability to maintain the foreign exchange integrity of the EDF.

Imports declined by an average of 14.1 per cent over the SAL period compared to Bank predictions of a 3.9–6.0 per cent growth rate. Despite this import cut-back the balance of payments failed to register any improvement with an average current account deficit of 31.9 per cent of GDP compared to the 12 per cent projected. As a result, there was no improvement in net reserves over the period and a rapid accumulation of debt servicing arrears, with the country defaulting on most of its bilateral medium- and long-term debts. This critical foreign exchange situation led to a shortage of imported goods. Within this context the failure to devalue the Guyanese dollar created an overvalued exchange rate and led to the rapid growth in an unofficial parallel foreign exchange market in which the price of foreign exchange was up to 150 per cent above the official rate. This parallel market was fuelled by illegal exports of gold, rice and manufactured goods and financed increasing amounts of consumer and producer imports as well as extensive capital flight.

Accounts of the public sector also failed to register any sustained improvement. Between 1981 and 1983 the public sector current account deficit increased from G $−288 million to G $−543 million – a total increase of 89 per cent – and the overall deficit had reached G $−816 million by 1983. Much of this deficit continued to be financed by recourse to the domestic banking system, with net domestic credit to the public sector increasing by 68 per cent between 1981–3. The structural adjustment programme also achieved little in the form of increasing the efficiency and size of the public sector investment programme. During 1981–3, public sector investment stood at only US $357 million compared to the US $628 million envisaged by the SAL. This decline reflected the failure of the SAL programme to stimulate increased flows of external assistance and its failure to produce any significant improvements in the preparation, co-ordination, implementation and monitoring of the PSIP.

Finally, the structural adjustment programme produced no positive social impact. Per capita real income fell by over 21 per cent during the life of the SAL and by 1983 was lower than it had been in 1970 and one-third below the level attained in 1975. Both employment and real wages also continued to decline.

In summary, the only positive impact of the Bank's programme took the form of a temporary increase in manufactured exports, but with this increase occurring from a low base and primarily due to the operations of a single enterprise. Hence, in the final analysis:

> The Guyana SAL failed to achieve its central objectives, namely, the resumption of economic growth and strengthening of the balance of payments by improving productive capacity, in particular exportable commodities and manufactured items produced by the private sector.
>
> (World Bank, 1986a: 20)

Following the closure of the SAL loan in 1984 there was, however, a temporary upturn in the economy, a part of which can be attributed to the lagged positive impact of a few SAL measures. In 1984 real GDP rose by 2.1 per cent. This was largely due to dramatic increases in the output of the bauxite and rice sectors which rose by 11.4 per cent and 24 per cent respectively. The 1984 increase in rice output was assisted by favourable weather conditions and by a 28 per cent increase in acreage planted, the latter being partly due to the substantial increases in rice producer prices implemented under the SAL programme. While external factors, in particular improved international demand for calcined bauxite, also predominated in the bauxite recovery, part can again be attributed to actions taken in the second phase of the SAL. Bank provision of technical, marketing and management assistance to the two public enterprises in the bauxite sector, BIDCO and GUYMINE, considerably strengthened their institutional capacity and efficiency. The process continued in March 1985 when BIDCO concluded a contract with an international company to provide both management and marketing services, but without equity participation. Although such measures in the bauxite sector had not formed part of the original SAL programme, the Bank considered that their results: 'may be the program's only unqualified success' (World Bank, 1986a: 19).

18.9 CRITIQUE OF BANK/FUND DIAGNOSIS AND PRESCRIPTIONS

In the foregoing analysis a variety of technical factors have been identified which help to explain the low level of government compliance with the SAL reform conditions and hence the disappointing impact of the programme. However, even had the Government complied fully with the SAL policy measures it is doubtful whether this would have resulted in a significant improvement in economic performance since the programme failed to fully address the primary need for physical rehabilitation of the country's capital and infrastructure.

The Bank's diagnostic work prior to the SAL indicated considerable concurrence with the view held by the Guyanese authorities, namely: 'When the "temporary balance of payments crisis" did not go away, the regime then acted as if this was in essence *the crisis* and proceeded to force a reduction in living standards in order to reduce demand' (Thomas, 1986: 74). Hence, for example, in the late 1970s the following assessment of structural problems is provided by the Bank: 'The Guyanese economy is in a position of severe structural disequilibrium brought about by fluctuating export and import prices and exacerbated by the economy's dependence on foreign trade and its small size' (World Bank, 1978: 14). Although Guyana's crisis was manifested in terms of balance-of-payments difficulties brought about by a decline in the export sector: 'Guyana did not conform to the typical export-orientated Third World model . . . economic crisis was not directly produced by shrinking export markets and falling prices and was not caused predominantly by the world economic crisis' (Thomas, 1988: 256).

In all three key export sectors, bauxite, rice and sugar, Guyana had access to preferential trade contracts and premium prices. Sugar was sold at a premium price under the EEC-ACP Protocol quota with similar arrangements for sales to the USA whilst contractual rice markets in the CARICOM region provided a premium price over two-thirds above the world level. In the case of bauxite, Guyana possessed a virtual monopoly in the world market of high grade calcined ore, serving over 90 per cent of the market in the early 1970s. However, by the late 1970s Guyana was unable to satisfy these markets and continued access to them was threatened by her inability to meet demand in terms of both quantity and quality. Production declines were such that by the early 1980s the preferential rice and sugar markets could not be serviced and the bauxite industry was supplying less than 50 per cent of world calcined demand, the market having been captured by lower-grade Chinese ore.

The Guyanese crisis, therefore, was essentially a *domestic production crisis* caused by economic mismanagement, failure to maintain capital equipment and infrastructure and the virtual collapse of all public utilities, giving rise to a vicious cycle of production decline. This domestic production crisis was characterised by gross underutilisation of capacity in all sectors of the economy, with industry using, on average, only 30–40 per cent of rated capacity in the late 1970s. The magnitude of this domestic production crisis is shown in Table 18.5, which compares peak output levels obtained in the 1970s with the output levels of the early 1980s.

Table 18.5 Major export sectors: physical output (thousands of tons)

	Peak Year	1979	1980	1981	1982	1983
Rice	212 (1977)	142	166	163	182	149
Sugar	369 (1971)	298	270	301	287	252
Dried bauxite	2290 (1970)	1059	1005	982	958	761
Calcined bauxite	778 (1975)	589	598	513	392	315
Alumina	312 (1970)	171	215	170	73	0

Source: Thomas (1988): Table 11.6.

Given the nature of Guyana's economic crisis, the immediate priority need in the early 1980s was to restore production levels in the traditional export sectors via a process of economic rehabilitation, including the rehabilitation of the supporting public utility services and infrastructure. Such needs did not call for a typical Bank adjustment package in which changes in price and institutional incentives are used to transform the structure and pattern of production. This conventional form of adjustment package is appropriate for countries facing sharp changes in their terms of trade and with a narrow and overexploited production base requiring diversification – as was the case in many sub-Saharan countries during the 1980s. With Guyana's traditional production base grossly underutilised due to a deterioration in the country's capital stock and with non-traditional sector activity accounting for only a small fraction of exports, the use of price and institutional incentives could do little to stimulate the supply side of the economy since the physical state of the supply side was in no condition to be able to respond to such stimuli. As Guyana's lead negotiator has appositely noted:

Conventional text-book economics is not written for economies in decline, but for static or growing economies. One can structurally adjust an economy which is growing but growing inefficiently, or an economy which is static. But an economy in cumulative decline forces one to confront a systemic problem. Such an economy requires transformation of a Keynesian type, in which the emphasis is on the quality and quantity of investment, particularly the stimulative role of public sector investment. The Bank's structural adjustment programmes however are rooted in the marginality theories of Neo-Classical text-book economics with their emphasis placed on price incentives, exchange rate adjustments and trade liberalisation.

(Personal interview, Washington DC, December 1988)

Although the SAL President's Report (World Bank, 1981) partially acknowledged the need for rehabilitation of the Guyanese economy, and, in view of the extent of government ownership of the means of production, stressed the Public Sector Investment Programme as a means for its achievement, this was not adequately reflected in the policy conditions attached to the Loan. Instead, the SAL conditions focused on price and institutional incentives directed at the non-traditional export sector in an attempt to alter the pattern of production. This sector also received the largest SAL lending allocation (36 per cent) of any individual sector. However, the Bank's belief that manufactured exports from the private sector could become 'the main engine of growth' is hard to reconcile with the sector's relative importance in the economy. In 1980, over 80 per cent of the economy was in the hands of the public sector and manufactured exports represented less than 5 per cent of total Guyanese exports. By contrast, 45 per cent of exports were accounted for by the publicly-owned bauxite industry. It was clearly not feasible to expect a sector which represented less than 5 per cent of exports to generate sufficient foreign exchange to sustain economic growth. The Bank itself, in a retrospective analysis of the SAL operation concluded likewise:

> Actions under a SAP need to be directed at a sufficiently large economic base to sustain a cross-sectoral adjustment process . . . With hindsight it is clear that without sustained bauxite production and exports it was improbable that sufficient foreign exchange could have been generated to enable the SAP, as it was designed, to succeed.
>
> (World Bank, 1986a: 22, 31)

Hence, non-traditional exports were unable to produce a sustained response since the continued decline of traditional exports gave rise to acute foreign exchange shortages resulting in the inability of manufacturers to obtain imported inputs, capital equipment and spare parts.

The priority need to rehabilitate traditional export activities and public utilities also casts doubt on Bank policy proposals which aimed at giving foreign exchange priority to the non-traditional private manufacturing sector. Within the context of a declining economy such as Guyana's, export liberalisation and the concomitant foreign exchange allocation priorities did not represent an efficient use of scarce foreign exchange resources. Rather, priority needs would have been better served by first ensuring that the Electricity Corporation and the bauxite, rice and sugar sectors had sufficient access to foreign exchange and by maintaining an import licensing system designed to avoid the importation of unnecessary luxury consumption goods. In accordance with the Theory of the Second Best, the Guyanese economy in the early 1980s illustrated the fact that in an imperfectly functioning economy, price and trade liberalisation *per se* does not necessarily create a more efficient pattern of resource allocation. The Guyanese authorities themselves recognised this fact and acted in accordance:

> The foreign exchange which was earned was being used for basic sustenance; beyond that the residual was channelled to the bauxite, sugar and rice sectors in an effort to boost earnings. In the light of the emerging foreign exchange crisis, certain liberalizing actions such as simplification of import licensing procedures, or actions for the non-traditional export sector such as the EDF credit scheme . . . lost their urgency or were seen by GOG as counter-productive.
>
> (World Bank, 1986a: 9)

Priorities were also overlooked by the Bank's excessive reliance on price changes to address the problems facing public sector enterprises. Although in some cases tariff increases temporarily increased the financial flow of

PSEs, the fundamental problem of dilapidated and outdated capital equipment remained and was exacerbated by the fact that PSE investments were particularly hard hit by the cut-backs in public sector investment. The only area in which price incentives were effective was in the rice sector where unremunerative producer prices had played an important part in the past production decline.

The above critique suggests that the correct sequence of policy reform involved addressing the production constraints in the traditional export sectors and revitalising public utilities and infrastructure *before* focusing on non-traditional sectors.

The rehabilitation of the traditional export sectors was essential, not only to the success of the structural adjustment programme, but also to the viability of a stabilisation programme aimed at improving public sector accounts and the balance of payments. The dilemma facing the Fund in its attempt to implement a stabilisation package was that, given the structure of the Guyanese economy, the scope for restoring equilibrium was extremely limited *until* such time as production levels were increased. Since the level of government revenues was already high – 32 per cent of GDP in 1982 – there was little room for increasing public revenues in order to improve the fiscal balance since the high tax burden and the depressed state of the economy meant that reliance on increased taxation threatened to have severe and counter-productive disincentive effects. The alternative option of cutting public expenditure also threatened to depress production in a manner adverse to fiscal balance since, under Guyana's socialist economic structure, most productive activities fell within the ambit of the public sector and required considerable increases in investment to restore their economic viability and to reduce their long-term drain on the Government budget. The limited options for achieving internal balance in a socialist economy caught in the process of cumulative production decline present any stabilisation attempt with a dilemma in the form of a vicious circle:

> Because sources of Government revenue dwindle when GDP falls, tax increases are imposed in an attempt to improve yields. This, however, further depresses economic activity and increases the tendency towards price inflation. The Government is then forced to reduce its outlays and this in turn negatively affects output and incomes.
>
> (Thomas, 1988: 264)

Faced with this dilemma, the main policy measure which the Government was forced to use in its unsuccessful attempts to improve public finances under the Fund's EFF programme was a 24 per cent reduction of employment throughout the public sector.

The Fund's acknowledgement that the scope for reducing Government capital expenditure was limited is reflected in the considerable emphasis that the EFF placed upon the Public Sector Investment programme:

393

The IMF's financial stabilisation program, which aimed at redressing the severe fiscal imbalance, depended on the structural adjustment program supported by the SAL/C in which an acceptable minimum level of public investment, consistent with the available finance and the needs of the private sector, was maintained.

(World Bank, 1986a: 83)

This emphasis on the need for public sector investment gave rise to an unusual division of labour in Bank and Fund monitoring of the Guyanese economy. It was anticipated that the Bank would be the lead financer in a massive medium-term investment programme, including projects to rehabilitate the economic infrastructure and to develop a large wood-pulp plant, a hydro-electric power station and an alumina smelter, with such investments during the 1980s expected to be roughly equivalent to Guyana's total GDP. Both the Bank and Fund realised that such an investment plan would give rise to a widening of the balance-of-payments current account deficit. Hence it was decided that the Fund would monitor fiscal and monetary variables whilst the widening current account deficit would be monitored entirely by the Bank on the basis of the quality of the investment programme.

The unconventional monitoring strategy devised by the Bank and Fund in 1980–2 was commendable since large-scale public sector investment was essential for restoring the productive viability of the economy. However, it raises serious questions as to whether a Fund stabilisation programme was feasible in the early 1980s, i.e. before the production response was forthcoming. Under these conditions, with the EFF having no conditions relating to the external balance, the Fund programme was forced to attempt a contraction of demand in only one sense – by bringing down government demand to reduce the fiscal gap. However, the ability to reduce government demand was limited and threatened the very success of the investment programme. As the events of 1978–9 had illustrated, the success of a Fund programme relying entirely on fiscal retrenchment was short-lived. Although under this earlier Stand-by, fiscal reform had initially resulted in a significant increase in tax revenue, the massive deflation of demand was such that in real terms revenues subsequently fell as a consequence of declining output levels.

The Fund's ability to contract the system was limited not only by the need for a massive public sector investment programme, but also because the efficacy of exchange rate adjustment as a stabilisation tool was questionable. Guyana was a small, open economy with little in the way of backward linkages. In the traditional sectors of the economy there was heavy reliance on imported inputs with domestic costs accounting for a small share of total costs. In addition, by 1982 most imports were being used for basic sustenance needs and to maintain output in the traditional sectors. Hence, the elasticity of import demand was low. Likewise, until industrial activities had been rehabilitated their potential to respond to price changes was limited such that export supply elasticities were also low. Hence, Guyana's elasticity parameters did not fulfil the Marshall-Lerner conditions for an effective devaluation. As the Bank noted:

> Given the depressed level of imports and the weight of bauxite and sugar in total exports, an across-the-board devaluation will probably have only a limited effect on the volume of exports, and, in the short-term, on the volume of imports. A supply response would only be forthcoming with regard to non-traditional exports (manufactures) and rice (if private exports are allowed).
>
> (World Bank, 1983: 41)

In summary, given the conditions in the Guyanese economy – the high government profile in production activities and the critical dependence of government revenues on production levels, the high tax burden, and the low trade elasticities – a conventional stabilisation programme consisting of fiscal retrenchment and exchange rate adjustment could do little to improve, on a permanent basis, the country's internal and external balance. Rather, any attempt to implement stabilisation policies prior to a production revival was bound to achieve only short-lived success and to intensify the political and economic aspects of the production crisis itself. The only way in which the fiscal balance and the balance of payments could be *permanently* improved was through the physical rehabilitation of the traditional export sectors upon which government and export revenues were critically dependent.

18.10 AN ALTERNATIVE ADJUSTMENT PROGRAMME

In view of the nature of Guyana's domestic production crisis a radical departure from convention was required in the formulation of an 'adjustment programme' in the broadest sense of the term. Such a departure involved reversing the normal sequencing of the various stages of such a programme and a postponement of stabilisation measures as follows:

STAGE 1:   Institution building and physical rehabilitation of the traditional sectors of the economy.

STAGE 2:   Stabilisation of internal and external accounts and liberalisation and diversification of the conventional SAL type.

The resources needed for stage 1 were considerable and a period of several years would be required before a positive production response could be expected. However, only *after* such a response had occurred did the stabilisation and liberalisation measures of stage 2 stand any chance of sustained success. In effect, therefore, under the first stage of this proposed programme, the donor community needed to accept, and provide financial support for, a *widening* of both the balance-of-payments current account deficit and the government deficit. Such a strategy is undoubtedly high risk in view of the disequilibrium implications of government failure to carry out the necessary institutional and rehabilitation reforms of stage 1. However, such a risk is not considerably greater than that associated with the SAL, which, with its faith in the private manufacturing sector as the engine of growth, represented, in the Bank's own words, a 'giant leap of faith' in terms of both economic and political feasibility.

It is questionable whether a Structural Adjustment Loan and an accompanying Technical Assistance Loan would provide the appropriate vehicle for addressing the first stage of the alternative programme. Some form of institutional strengthening was essential in order to overcome Guyana's severe institutional, administrative and managerial constraints which impeded the potential rehabilitation of the economy through the efficient implementation of a massive Public Sector Investment Programme. However, a Technical Assistance Loan, forming a component of a quick disbursing, crisis-orientated, SAL programme was not the appropriate vehicle for long-term institution building. Rather, a multisectoral institutional development loan was required and needed to be aimed at strengthening public sector management in the key bauxite, rice and sugar sectors and in national institutions involved in macroeconomic management – particularly the management of the Public Sector Investment Programme.

It is also doubtful whether a Structural Adjustment Loan would provide the most appropriate vehicle for the physical rehabilitation of the country's productive capital and infrastructure. A series of Sectoral Adjustment Loans (SECALs) combined with a large increase in project lending would be more effective since each of the major sectors of the Guyanese economy were very different in character and required specifically tailored rehabilitation projects. The bauxite sector was entirely controlled by a public corporation, BIDCO/GUYMINE. Agriculture, however, consisted of differing sub-sectors. The state enterprise GUYSUCO owned all sugar estates and produced the bulk of the cane crop and was responsible for all processing activities. Rice, other food crops and livestock on the other hand were produced by over 25,000 small private farms, yet most rice processing and marketing and all exports were in the hands of the Guyana Rice Board. The small manufacturing sector possessed a large number of small private producers who were tightly controlled by government regulations and dominated by several large private companies and a range of public trading corporations. Hence, as the Bank has subsequently noted:

> The discrete characters of the major sectors of the Guyanese economy
> with highly differentiated policy requirements suggests that a series

of policy-based sector loans might have been the preferred approach to a multi-sector SAP. There were few multi-sectoral policy initiatives . . . which could have been applied and made effective in improving economic performance across all major sectors. Each sector, with its private-public mix and unique history required differing policy and institutional reform approaches.

(World Bank, 1986a: 30)

The second phase of the SAL had a strong, discrete sectoral emphasis on bauxite and rice and the Bank's proposed lending programme for 1983–4 consisted of a series of sector loans to the agricultural, power, bauxite, and manufacturing sectors. However, although it was acknowledged that such SECALs would allow larger amounts of lending to be directed at particular problem areas, this new strategy was still a far cry from the alternative type of adjustment programme suggested above. The emphasis remained on sectoral policy reform in terms of price and incentive structures rather than on the prior need for rehabilitation and these proposed sectoral loans were explicitly made conditional on a new Fund stabilisation programme first being in place. By contrast, stage 1 of an alternative programme required a set of free-standing sectoral loans, dependent neither on a Fund programme nor upon each other, with emphasis on renewing and upgrading capital equipment, technological and marketing improvements and managerial reforms in order to realise the production potential in each sector of the economy. In addition, sectoral loans needed to be complemented by large increases in donor project finance to boost the Public Sector Investment Programme. Although under the SAL the Bank took an active role in mobilising resources through the Bank-sponsored Caribbean Group for Co-operation in Economic Development (CGCED) project loan disbursements during the life of the SAL declined and fell woefully short of even the minimum requirements for maintaining capital equipment and for completion of ongoing projects. The Government's reduced access to donor funds from mid-1982 onwards resulted in the abandonment of many high priority projects in the field of agriculture and energy, the most notable example being the termination due to lack of funding of the Upper Mazaruni hydro-power project which resulted in the abandonment and decay of millions of dollars' worth of equipment. The failure of the massive project lending to materialise in the manner envisaged by the Bank in 1980–1 meant that the balance-of-payments current account deficit continued to widen, but not, as expected, due to the effects of large investment inflows, but due to the continued and rapid decline of all key export sectors in the Guyanese economy. Yet the economy's capacity to respond to increased project finance was considerable. There was no shortage of viable projects with high internal rates of return – both new projects and rehabilitation-type projects. Hence, this form of lending activity under stage 1 of the proposed programme would have produced a much higher rate of return than was forthcoming from the actual SAL operation.

The sequencing of the alternative adjustment programme proposed above raises important issues regarding Bank/Fund interaction. It has been suggested by a former Bank staff member (Please, 1984: Chapter 7) that a clear decision should always be taken as to whether the Bank or the Fund will function as the lead agency in implementing a reform programme with the decision based on circumstances facing a recipient economy. Please's suggestion is that during times of 'crisis management' the Fund should take such a lead with emphasis being placed on economic stabilisation. Such a proposal, however, ignores the fact that it is in just such times of crisis management that the Bank is simultaneously called upon to provide assistance in the form of Structural Adjustment Loans. The Guyana case, however, suggests that there are clear circumstances when the Bank should function as the lead agency, namely, when a country faces a cumulative domestic production crisis such that physical rehabilitation is required prior to any successful stabilisation and liberalisation programmes. A lead Bank role in the rehabilitation process would need to take the form of Bank co-ordination of donor lending in the context of the priorities set by the Public Sector Investment Programme. In addition, the Bank would need to take an active part in encouraging donor flexibility regarding the use of committed funds and the provision of additional financial support to cover both foreign and local costs of the PSIP.

An alternative type of Guyanese adjustment programme along the lines suggested above promises to be not only economically viable, but also politically feasible. The institutional strengthening and physical rehabilitation of stage 1, in contrast to the Bank's SAL, present little in the way of a challenge to the ideology of Guyana's ruling regime. Indeed, the emphasis on rehabilitation through the medium of the Public Sector Investment Programme is closely akin to the Government's philosophy of National Economic Planning under which the Government assumes responsibility for growth by providing a 'big push' investment plan. An important condition, however, needed to avoid the disappointing outcome of the 1970s National Plans, is institutional strengthening combined with a high Bank profile in assisting with the co-ordination and monitoring of such a plan. Furthermore, increased levels of flexible project and programme aid finance could help public sector enterprises attain their productive potential without recourse to private foreign equity participation. Such equity schemes, as shown by the SAL, met with considerable political resistance and were economically unviable given the private sector's reluctance to become involved in enterprises in urgent need of substantial physical revamping.

The initial improvement in output which could be expected to be forthcoming from the rehabilitation stage of the programme would progressively generate additional resources for investment in order to make possible a permanent improvement in economic growth. At this stage of the transformation, in keeping with government ideology, consideration could be given to using the co-operative sector in order to promote the savings/investment process. It is remarkable, given its potential and its role in Guyana's economic ideology, that this third sector of the economy was entirely neglected by the Bank's SAL programme.

Finally, any attempt to implement a conventional stabilisation and liberalisation programme prior to an upturn in production was bound to meet with strong political resistance given the socio-political conditions in Guyana. The severe incomes, employment and pricing policies which were required to stabilise the economy in the face of continued production decline, threatened the greatest adverse impact on the black urban proletariat who constituted the major support group for the ruling PNP party. This problem was compounded by Guyana's socialist economic structure since resistance to the use of real wage and employment reduction to contract demand centred on the state which, following the post-independence nationalisation strategy, was the major employer of wage labour. As Guyana's lead negotiator has observed:

> When an economy is in decline, the role of prices tends to become over-extended. Under such circumstances, reliance on prices alone, including the price of labour, to stabilise the system requires massive price changes with major income distribution effects. Such effects were politically unacceptable to the Burnham regime.
> (Personal interview, Washington DC, December 1988)

By contrast, postponing the stabilisation attempt until output recovery is under way would lessen the need to rely entirely on politically unacceptable price, incomes and employment policies in order to achieve internal and external balance.

18.11 PROSPECTS FOR THE GUYANESE ECONOMY

Given a massive inflow of donor resources co-ordinated and monitored by the Bank, with donor acceptance of a temporary widening of the balance-of-payments current account deficit and support for the Government deficit, and with significant institutional strengthening, the process of rehabilitating the Guyanese economy would be relatively easy. The country possesses vast quantities of underexploited natural resources, has extensive excess capacity in all key export sectors which could, as in the 1970s, have preferential access to a wide range of international markets, and there is no shortage of viable projects with high potential rates of return. In addition, unlike many sub-Saharan countries, Guyana's main domestic food crops and main export crops are the same commodities – rice and sugar. Hence, the country does not face the need to structurally transform the pattern of agricultural production in order to generate foreign exchange. Neither does it face the potential dilemma of many sub-Saharan nations whereby a decline in commodity prices for the export crop creates a situation in which there is inadequate export revenue to finance the importation of net food requirements. It is perhaps for this reason that Guyana has survived for so long in the face of the chronic production crisis since in times of production decline the country has been able to retreat towards a closed economy model cutting back on agricultural exports in order to maintain domestic consumption levels.

Despite the fact that rehabilitation of the economy is both politically and economically viable, the prospects of it occurring seem as remote now as they did in 1982. The predominant view contained within the Bank's retrospective analysis of the SAL operation (World Bank, 1986a) is that it was the failure of IMF demand-side policies which nullified the envisaged supply-side impact of the SAL. Far from concluding that an alternatively sequenced adjustment programme, along the lines suggested above, is required, the Bank is now more strongly of the view that effective stabilisation is an essential prerequisite for further structural adjustment lending in Guyana: 'The experience of this SAL suggests that medium-term structural adjustment objectives may have to be set aside until a reasonable degree of economic stability has been achieved' (World Bank, 1986a: viii). Indeed, the consensus within the Bank now seems to be that by late 1981, following the collapse of the Fund's EFF, Guyana's structural adjustment operation should have been abandoned entirely rather than revised into an alternatively sequenced programme.

Although the above report acknowledges the crucial importance of sequencing in an overall adjustment process, the sequence suggested by the Bank is the *reverse* of that proposed above, with price-orientated stabilisation recommended in advance of rehabilitation:

> This report recommends that in any future dialogue with Guyana emphasis should be placed on the careful sequencing and phasing of the adjustment process which should essentially entail three phases: (a) stabilization phase; (b) rehabilitation phase; and (c) liberalization and growth phase. The first phase should result in the reduction of price distortions (including the exchange rate system); the second in improving capacity utilisation of the existing capital assets and the third in trade liberalization and reducing Government interventions in the economy.
>
> (World Bank, 1986a: 85)

Following this recommendation, Bank structural adjustment operations were abandoned entirely in 1984 due to the absence of a Fund programme and still have not resumed. Such operations, along with many other donor-lending activities, remain on ice until a Fund stabilisation programme is negotiated. Meanwhile, Guyana's domestic production crisis continues largely unabated. In the interim period, debt servicing arrears have mounted considerably. Although in the past year (1988–9) attempts have been made to mount a new Fund programme this has been made contingent on clearance of debt arrears. Given that Paris Club rescheduling is itself contingent on a Fund programme and given the acute scarcity of foreign exchange, Guyana's ability to clear arrears remains remote. Equally remote, given the magnitude of the necessary domestic demand deflation and the required levels of foreign financing, is the prospect of the negotiation of a viable Fund programme prior to any upturn in production levels. Hence, in the late 1980s, Guyana is faced, not only with the vicious circle of cumulative production decline, but also with the vicious and counter-productive cycle of donor cross-conditionality.

GLOSSARY

CARICOM	Caribbean Common Market
CIDA	Canadian International Development Authority
EDF	Export Development Fund
EFF	Extended Fund Facility
GAP	Government Action Programme
GIC	Guyana Investment Code
GOG	Government of Guyana
GRB	Guyana Rice Board
LDP	Letter of Development Policies
OED	Operations Evaluation Department (of World Bank)
PNC	Peoples' National Congress (Party)
PPP	Peoples' Progressive Party
PSE	Public Sector Enterprises
PSIP	Public Sector Investment Programme
SAL	Structural Adjustment Loan
SAP	Structural Adjustment Programme
SDR	Special Drawing Right (on IMF)
SECAL	Sectoral Adjustment Loan

BIBLIOGRAPHY

Hope, K. R. (1985) *Guyana: Politics and Development in an Emergent Socialist State*, Ontario, Canada, Mosaic Press.

Please, S. (1984) *The Hobbled Giant: Essays on the World Bank*, Boulder and London, Westview Press.

Thomas, C. (1986) 'The authoritarian state in Caribbean societies', in O. Davies (ed.) *The State in Caribbean Society*, Mona, Jamaica, Department of Economics, University of the West Indies.

Thomas, C. (1988) *The Poor and the Powerless: Economic Policy and Change in the Caribbean*, London, Latin America Bureau.

World Bank (1978) *President's Report on Proposed Program Loan and Credit to Guyana* (Report no. P–2378–GUA), Washington DC.

World Bank (1981) *President's Report on Proposed Structural Adjustment Loan and Credit to Guyana* (Report no. P–2935–GUA), Washington DC.

World Bank (1984) *Guyana: Recent Developments, Structural Adjustment and Prospects* (Report no. 4765–GUA), Washington DC.

World Bank (1986a) *Program Performance Audit Report Guyana – Structural Adjustment Loan and Credit* (Report no. SecM86–358), Washington DC.

World Bank (1986b) *Guyana: A Proposal for Economic Recovery* (Report no. 6501–GUA), Washington DC.

World Bank (1988) *Guyana: Policy Framework Paper* (Report no. SecM88–738), Washington DC.

APPENDIX

Table 18A.1 Guyana: the structural adjustment programme

Economic issues	Government response up to 1 January 1981	Proposed policy actions		Expected economic impact
		Measures	*IBRD monitoring*	
I				
Balance of payments				
A. Rising petroleum import bill which has contributed to declining terms of trade and erosion in real income levels, and exacerbated inflation.	Energy conservation measures and targets adopted by GUYMINE, GUYSUCO and other public corporations.	Continued execution of energy conservation programme by public corporations with periodic reports to Cabinet on progress. Adoption of a programme for the promotion of energy conservation measures by 1 July 1981.	Semi-annual progress reports beginning 1/81. Programme will be discussed with IBRD prior to adoption.	Limit growth of petroleum imports.
	Full transfer of fuel price increase to consumers. Closing of gasoline stations at weekends.	Continued full transfer of fuel price increases to consumers.	Progress review in April, 1981.	Encourage efficient use of scarce energy resources and limit growth of petroleum imports.
	Rehabilitation of steam boilers and improved maintenance of diesel generating sets of GEC is underway with technical assistance from the UK.	Completion of rehabilitation and improved maintenance by mid-1982.		Increased operating efficiency of GEC's plant which will reduce required fuel imports and improve financial position of company.
	Upgrading of GEC's management under way with technical assistance from the IBRD.	Continuation of programme through 1982.	Under continuous review through project supervision.	Increased operating efficiency of GEC's plant which will reduce required fuel imports and improve financial position of company.

Table 18A.1   Continued

Economic issues	Government response up to 1 January 1981	Proposed policy actions		Expected economic impact
		Measures	IBRD monitoring	
		Studies of opportunities for increased use of alternative energy sources.	Progress of studies to be assessed in April 1981.	Identification of potential substitutes for imported energy.
	Promotion of use of indigenous resources of energy under various investment projects.			
	Studies of electricity and transportation tariff structure under way.	Studies of electricity and transportation tariff structure completed and programme for execution agreed upon by 1 July 1981.	Progress of studies to be assessed in April 1981. Programme for execution of recommendations to be agreed upon in consultation with the Bank.	Establishment of tariff structures which will promote the most efficient use of energy resources.
B. Stagnant or declining export values.	Introduction of export action programme:	Expansion of export action programme:		
	1 *Sugar* – upgrading of equipment – introduction of disease-resistant cane varieties – wage incentive programme	1 *Sugar* – increased supplies of fertiliser and spare parts – expansion of wage incentive programme	Review in April 1981.	Increased production and export volume of sugar: increased savings of GUYSUCO.

		Review	Objective
2 *Rice* – new tractor fleet – increased support services	2 *Rice* – increased use of agricultural inputs	Review in April 1981.	Increased yields and consequent increase in production and export volume of rice.
– development of extension, storage and irrigation schemes	– continued progress in extension, storage and irrigation	Review through monitoring of investment programme.	Increased yields and consequent increase in production and export volume of rice. Increased acreage devoted to rice and consequent increase in production and export volume in spring crop.
– 19% increase in producer prices during preceding 12 months and 12–15% increase in producer prices for 1981 spring crop.	– continuation of USAID technical assistance programme	Review in April 1981.	Increased efficiency of marketing and development of sufficient export markets for expanded volume of rice production anticipated in mid-1980s.
3 *Bauxite/alumina* – earthmoving under way to enable continuous bauxite mining operations	3 *Bauxite/alumina* – earthmoving completed by mid-1982		Increase access to bauxite ore, thus increasing efficiency and level of bauxite production.
– contract with multinational to improve reliability of operations and to increase alumina production capacity signed in 1980.	– plant alumina capacity to be increased by 10% by 1983. – continuation of programme.		Expand alumina export volume. Improve efficiency of operations and increase export volume.

Table 18A.1 Continued

Economic issues	Government response up to 1 January 1981	Proposed policy actions		Expected economic impact
		Measures	IBRD monitoring	
	– introduction of programme to reduce down time of essential machinery and rehabilitation of processing plant.			
	4 Non-traditional manufactures – employment of consultant to prepare for establishment of Export Development Fund (EDF).	4 Non-traditional manufactures – Establishment of Export Development Fund (EDF) to provide foreign exchange and credit to manufacturing sector. The Fund would be operational by 28 February 1981.	Quarterly reports commencing April 1981 to fourth quarter of 1983.	Provision of foreign exchange to finance intermediate goods imports will facilitate expansion of manufactured exports.
		– Appointment of Industrial Development Adviser by July 1981.	Selection in consultation with the IBRD.	Adviser will recommend programme. Policies and institutional arrangements to strengthen industrial sector.
		– Increase professional staff of Export Promotion Unit to 4	Progress review in April 1981.	Development of export markets for non-traditional manufactures.

		persons by 31 March 1981. – Establishment of Export Promotion Council with representatives from public and private sectors.	Progress review in April 1981.	Development of export markets for non-traditional manufacturers.
	5 *Long-term export programme* – Decision to prepare an export long-term programme.	5 *Long-term export programme* – Completion of long-term export programme by 30 June 1981.	To be reviewed with Bank staff third quarter of 1981.	To promote continued export expansion over the longer term.
II *Investment* Delays, cost overruns and inefficiencies in public sector investment.	Establishment of system for monitoring investment expenditures through financial controls exercised by the State Planning Commission with quarterly reports to Project Monitoring Subcommittee of the Cabinet.	Continued close monitoring of progress of investment programme. Utilisation of external technical assistance to minimise potential bottlenecks to project execution.	Quarterly reports on progress of investment programme beginning January 1981. Detailed annual investment levels and financing plans to be agreed upon with IBRD. Substantive changes in composition to be reviewed with IBRD quarterly until December 1982.	Improved execution of investment programme and more rapid progress of major production projects.
	Formulation of Investment programme and financing plan in consultation with IBRD.	Expedition of decisions on contract awards by December 1981.	Progress review in April 1981.	Improved execution of investment programme and more rapid progress of major production projects.

Table 18A.1 Continued

Economic issues	Government response up to 1 January 1981	Proposed policy actions		Expected economic impact
		Measures	IBRD monitoring	
		Delegation of greater authority to project managers by December 1981.	Progress review in April 1981.	Improved execution of investment programme and more rapid progress of major production projects.
		Reorganisation of Ministry of Works to include specialised functions in engineering consultancy and additional construction capacity.	Progress review in April 1981.	Improved execution of investment programme and more rapid progress of major production projects.
Declining real levels of private investment.	Institution of private sector investment code.	Clarification and expansion of code by September 1981.	Progress review in April 1981.	Increase confidence of both indigenous and foreign private sector and promote expanded levels of private investment.
	Promotion of private foreign investment in oil, mineral and metal exploration and manufacturing operations.	Increase in credit resources available to private sector by December 1981.	Progress review in April 1981.	Increase financial resources available for private investment.
		Establishment of EDF. Industrial Adviser and Export Promotion Council.	Progress review in April 1981.	Increase output of exports, expansion of export markets and improved institution support for

	strengthening the industrial sector.

III *Downward trend in national savings*

A. Public sector savings.

Problem	Measures	Review	Objective
1 Persistent current budgetary deficit.	Tax measures in 1980 budget including broadening of consumption tax base, increase in tax rates and increases in excise taxes. Limitation of growth of current expenditures to 8% annual rate during 1976–80. Improvement in collection of income tax arrears during 1977–9. Continued improvements in tax collection and administration. Rigorous control of current expenditure levels through reduction of subsidies and limitations on increase in public employment.	Progress review in April 1981.	Gradual reduction in the flow of Central Government's current deficit from 9% in 1980 to 5% of GDP by 1985.
2 Low savings generated by public corporations.	Rationalisation of pricing policies for public corporations. Establishment of savings targets for all public corporations.	Progress review in April 1981.	Place corporations on economic basis. Increase public enterprise savings from 5% of GDP in 1980 to above 9% in 1983.
3 Declining real levels of private sector savings.	Increase in Bank deposit rates by 2 percentage points in 1980. Gradual movement toward positive real interest rates through annual upward adjustments of 1–2 percentage points.	Review in April 1981 of Government's proposed timing for interest rate adjustments.	Increased mobilisation of financial savings by banking system.

Table 18A.1 Continued

Economic issues	Government response up to 1 January 1981	Proposed policy actions		Expected economic impact
		Measures	IBRD monitoring	
IV Inappropriate pricing policies				
A. Low farmgate prices for rice resulting in a reduction in acreage devoted to the crop.	19% increases in producer prices for 1980 and further increase of 12–15% in rice prices for 1981 spring crop. Ongoing study on appropriate relation between farmgate prices, consumer prices and agricultural input subsidies.	Completion of study and adoption of system for periodic adjustment of input, farmgate and domestic consumer prices.	Recommendations of study to be reviewed by bank in third quarter of 1981.	Expanded export volume of rice.
	Increases in electricity and transportation tariffs of 65% and 30% respectively in 1980.	Further increases of electricity tariffs by 15% in February 1981. Additional measures as required to eliminate GEC's cash deficit by 1 July 1981. Continuous transfer of increase in fuel costs to consumers.	Semi-annual review of electricity and transport tariffs beginning 30 December 1980.	Encourage decreased use of scarce energy resources and improve financial position in public corporations.

V	*Institutional weaknesses*			
A.	External debt management.	Establishment in 1978 of Cabinet sub-committee to monitor external debt.	Continued monitoring and increased control over external borrowing of all public agencies.	Progress review in April 1981. Guyana already provides reports to External Debt Division of IBRD.	Better control and improved management of external debts.
B.	Public finance administration.	Procedure established for high level co-ordination between Ministry of Finance and State Planning Commission.	Strengthening of co-ordination at operational levels. Strengthening of accounting and auditing arrangements throughout public sector.	Progress review in April 1981.	Improve managerial efficiency and strengthen institutions.
C.	Import licensing system.	Simplification of import licensing procedures.	Completion of simplification of import licensing procedures in first quarter of 1981.	Review in April 1981.	Acceleration of import approval process.
VI	*Labour productivity*	Broadening of existing schemes for the provision of wage increases based on productivity.	Continued efforts to clarify and extend wage incentive scheme.	Progress review in April 1981.	Expansion in labour productivity. Increased worker satisfaction and reduction in number of work stoppages.
			Extension of on- and off-the-job training schemes	Progress review in April 1981.	Increases in labour productivity

Source: World Bank (1981.

19

ECUADOR

Paul Mosley

19.1 BACKGROUND

The main objective of this essay is to analyse the influence on policy and on the Ecuadorian economy of the phase of policy-based lending which began with the World Bank's Agricultural Sector Adjustment Loan of 1985. If either the political or the economic impact is to be understood, however, a little of the historical and political background must first be sketched in.

The early development of Ecuador, like that of many other former colonies of European settlement in Africa and Latin America,[1] was based on extensive grants of land by the colonial authority to individual settlers or to missions. In return for rights to land the grantee would take responsibility for development of the land's natural assets, for tax collection and local administration (Hurtado, 1981: 62–8). During the colonial period the development of the land's natural assets involved little beyond production for the local market, but after independence in 1830 the estates on the coast came to be developed increasingly for the production of export crops: first cocoa, then coffee, and finally, in the 1940s, bananas. The estates of the mountain areas (*Sierra*) remained tied to the production of wheat, wool and dairy products principally for the domestic market; but although in terms of economic importance they have always been subordinate to the coast, politically they have always been able to exercise a power of veto over any economic policy prejudicial to their interests. The judgement of a former President of Ecuador relating to the pre-1945 period:

> No Government, whatever its ideology, can exist without the support of the *latifundistas* in the Sierra or of the agro-exporting oligarchy which controls estate production and external trade.
>
> (Hurtado, 1981: 172)

retains a startling relevance to the determination of economic policy, and to the ability of external authorities to influence it, in the late 1980s.

The development both of estate agriculture and of other parts of the economy, contrary to the experience of other Latin American economies,

412

remained surprisingly free of foreign capital before the Second World War (Hurtado, 1981: 75). After 1945 overseas finance did arrive, in three waves: principally American investment in the banana and fishing industries at the coast; loans by development finance agencies such as the World Bank and IDB for the development of public utilities; and finally overseas direct investment in services and in the import substitution effort which finally got under way in the 1960s. Very little of the inward investment in the latter two categories was of American origin.[2] These investments had a profound influence on the structure of financial flows, but little on the structure of the economy: the import substitution effort was by Latin American standards both late and feeble, and as late as 1970 agriculture still accounted for over 80 per cent of exports. As Table 19.1 shows, Ecuador has always been, and remains in relation to other Latin American countries, heavily dependent on agriculture as a source of productive employment.

Table 19.1   Structure of production

| | Distribution of Gross Domestic Product and labour force (percentage shares) | | | | | |
| | Agriculture | | Industry | | Services etc. | |
	1965	1986	1965	1986	1965	1986
Ecuador: GDP	27	24	22	42	50	45
Labour force	55	39	19	20	26	42
Latin America: GDP	18	15	29	33	53	52
Labour force	48	33	21	25	31	42
Middle-income economies: GDP	22	15	33	36	45	48
Labour force	56	43	17	23	27	34

Source: World Bank, *World Development Report 1988*, Tables 3, 31.

In 1967 oil reserves were discovered, and in the early 1970s began to flow, in the eastern jungles of Ecuador. The discoveries came just in time to benefit from the oil price shocks of 1974 and 1979, and entirely transformed the structure of production, so that between the beginning of the 1970s and the middle 1980s petroleum exports had risen from a negligible proportion of GDP to over 70 per cent. As shown in Table 19.2, they are now falling back again.

Three aspects of the Government's response to the oil boom should be noted at this point. In the first place, legislation earmarked petroleum revenues for a wide variety of domestic expenditures which exceeded growth in petroleum revenues, whilst at the same time non-petroleum revenues declined,[3] leading to a series of large public sector deficits, most of them financed by the accumulation of external debt, as shown in Table

Table 19.2 Export composition (as percentage of total value)

	1970	Average 1978–80	Average 1983–5	1986
Petroleum (crude & products)	0.4	53.1	70.3	44.9
Bananas	35.5	8.9	6.1	12.0
Coffee (beans & products)	21.3	12.1	7.2	13.7
Cocoa (beans & products)	10.6	12.7	4.9	6.8
Prawns and fish (& products)	2.4	4.3	8.9	17.8
Other	29.8	8.9	2.6	4.8

Source: World Bank, *World Development Report 1987*,   Table 1.3, Banco Central del Ecuador.

19.3. Second, although these public sector deficits in due course fed through into the balance of payments, there was no attempt to adjust the exchange rate until the advent of the international debt crisis in 1982. Third, since oil was first discovered petrol has, as illustrated in Table 19.4, been sold to domestic consumers at a heavy subsidy, estimated to be at the level of 9 per cent of GDP in 1986, which is now built into the expectations of the electorate. Whereas other less developed countries experience food price riots, Ecuador has already experienced its first petrol price riot (in March 1986) and at the time of writing (September 1988) the Minister of Energy has just been unsuccessfully impeached[4] by the legislature for merely increasing the consumer price of petroleum in line with the rate of inflation.

It remains to introduce the two major actors in the drama. Ecuador has been a republic governed by an elective legislature since 1830, interrupted by four episodes of military government in 1925–31, 1937, 1963 and 1972–9. Political parties are a relatively new concept in Ecuador,[5] internal party discipline is relatively weak, and democratically elected presidents have always had to protect their power base by trying to assemble a package of policies which will have appeal outside their own party, and which in particular, as we saw, will command the support of both coast and *Sierra* interests. In relation to agriculture, which still supports 39 per cent of the electorate (Table 19.1) this implies a need to offer acceptable proposals to protect the incomes of mixed farmers in the *Sierra* (farming mostly wheat, cattle and sheep), export producers at the coast (farming cocoa, bananas, coffee and rice), and to make available agricultural inputs, in particular credit, at an acceptable cost.

The World Bank, as we earlier saw, lent to Ecuador in the 1960s and early 1970s principally for the development of the infrastructure,[6] but from that date onwards increasingly concentrated on investment in directly productive activities in agriculture and industry. By the early 1980s it had come to espouse the view that in Latin America as a whole the protection of

Table 19.3 Ecuador: main macroeconomic indicators, 1975–88

	1975–81	1982	1983	1984	1985	1986	1987	1988
Growth rate of real GDP (% per annum)	6.0	1.2	−2.8	4.0	4.5	2.9	−3.1	8.5
Growth rate of real agricultural exports (% per annum)	..	21.7	−16.7	13.1	20.9	15.6	18.3	13.5
Exports (% of GDP)	24.4	21.1	23.7	25.5	26.7	23.3	21.4	22.1
Imports (% of GDP)	26.6	23.3	19.7	21.8	21.1	17.4	21.8	22.4
Current account balance (% of GDP)	−5.6	−12.0	−3.1	−4.9	−1.1	−5.8	−13.3	−8.0
Public expenditure (% of GDP)	..	29.5	22.4	24.3	25.9	29.8	32.2	30.9
Public revenue (% of GDP)	..	22.9	22.4	23.7	27.8	24.7	21.7	29.6
Public sector deficit (−) or surplus (+) (% of GDP)	−3.8	−6.7	0.0	−0.6	1.9	−5.1	−10.5	−5.1
Inflation (%)	12.6	14.7	48.1	29.7	28.7	27.7	32.5	65.9
Debt (current $ billions)	..	6.2	6.9	7.2	7.8	8.6	9.6	11.0
Debt service ratio (% of GDP)	..	..	..	..	29.8	37.7	53.0	63.6

Table 19.4 Crude petroleum: export prices in relation to retail price of gasoline (US $ per barrel)

	FOB export price	Domestic price of gasoline
1980	35.2	6.0
1981	34.4	17.0
1982	32.5	16.4
1983	27.6	15.8
1984	27.4	15.3
1985	25.8	13.2
1986	12.8	12.6
1987	16.3	11.2
1988 (Jan.–Jun.)	13.6	10.4

Source: Banco Central del Ecuador.

import-substituting industrial sectors aimed at the home market had been pushed to excessive lengths, thereby causing damage not only to agriculture, via the cost of agricultural inputs, but also to industry itself by reducing its competitiveness in overseas markets (see for example *World Development Report 1983*, Chapter 4). This of course was a problem which affected the entire economy, and the instrument selected by the Bank to deal with it world-wide in the early 1980s was the Structural Adjustment Loan (see Volume 1, Chapter 2). But with two exceptions (Chile and Panama), Latin American Governments quickly showed reluctance to accept finance from the Bank in this form. Such acceptance would have involved a public commitment on the part of government to reduce its level of involvement in economic regulation and productive activity, normally coming on top of an already humiliating surrender to the IMF. As a consequence, it became quickly accepted within the Bank that the way to change economic policy in Latin America was by means of sector loans, which were politically less visible and could sometimes be negotiated at a level below the highest reaches of government. Often it was felt in addition that there existed distortions (such as the level of the internal oil price in Ecuador) so deep-seated as to be immovable by means of pressure from outside, which none the less precluded the offer of an orthodox Structural Adjustment Loan. The sector approach, then, quickly became the norm for the continent, and in agriculture six such operations have so far been authorised, to a total value of nearly $2 billion as illustrated in Table 19.5 below.

In Ecuador, which as an oil-producing economy was shielded from the initial effects of the world recession, the origin of the Bank's involvement in policy-based lending came with the oil price fall of 1982, which provoked a balance-of-payments deficit of the order of 12.9 per cent of gross national product (Table 19.3) and caused commercial banks to become reluctant to extend further credit to Ecuador. This left the Ecuadorian Government, which for several years had been budgeting and borrowing overseas on the presumption of a steady growth in oil revenues, dangerously exposed, and made clear the extent to which Ecuador's other sectors, in particular agriculture, had been ravaged by 'Dutch Disease'. In the next section we examine the way in which the Bank and the Government sought to negotiate a cure for this disease.

Table 19.5 World Bank agricultural sector operations in Latin America, 1985–9

| | Value of disbursements ($ million) | | | | | |
	1985	1986	1987	1988	1989	Total
Argentina	—	172	175	3	—	350
Brazil	—	—	450	40	10	500
Chile	—	150	100	—	—	250
Ecuador	—	50	50	—	—	100
Uruguay	30	30	—	—	—	60
Mexico	—	—	—	250	250	500
TOTAL	30	402	775	293	260	1760

Source: Bonilla (1988) 2.

416

19.2 THE NEGOTIATION PROCESS, 1983–5

The first proposals inside the Bank for an agriculture sector operation in Ecuador were made late in 1983, at a time when it was becoming clear that the country's balance-of-payments crisis was to be of lengthy duration and that it was becoming increasingly urgent to plan for the time when the oil ran out. A Bank report of that time noted that the country's agricultural land was under-utilised, with only 44 per cent of the available arable land and 62 per cent of potential pasture land being utilised (World Bank, 1984: 8); but if the past performance of the agricultural sector had been poor, this can be largely attributed to past governments' trade and pricing policies,[7] including high and highly variable tariff protection of industry, overvalued exchange rates, selective taxation of coffee, cocoa and banana exports and subsidisation of agricultural imports. It is clear that the Government of the time, a social-democratic coalition led by Osvaldo Hurtado, shared the diagnosis in considerable measure; between 1982 and mid-1984 the national currency, the sucre, was devalued by 65 per cent and import controls were removed on a number of items. Aware that it was swimming with the tide, the Bank drafted a modest set of reforms as conditionalities for an Agricultural Sector Loan in May 1984 (as set out in the left-hand part of Table 19.6) involving essentially the removal of taxation on the country's main agricultural exports, a restructuring of the public investment programme, a reform of the principal agricultural development bank (the Banco Nacional de Fomento), and finally certain limitations on the scope of official minimum producer prices. In the event, the Hurtado Government was replaced in the general election of August 1984 by a right-wing coalition under the presidency of Leon Febres Cordero, the president of the Chamber of Industries in the coastal state of Guayas. This coalition contained a number of bankers and exporters from the coast in ministerial positions, who included the Minister of Agriculture, Marcel Laniado, owner of the Banco del Pacifico, the second largest bank in Ecuador. Such a group might have been expected to perceive the advantages of a competitive exchange rate and trading policy, and indeed by the end of 1984 not only had the currency been further devalued in real terms and generous measures undertaken to attract foreign investment, but export taxes on the three major export crops – one of the major elements of the Bank's original draft proposal – had been removed. In spite of this, the response of the Bank's Latin America Department was to insist on a considerable toughening of the originally proposed reform programme. A mission was dispatched to Ecuador to negotiate such a programme between 22 April and 10 May 1985. The team consisted of two economists and a consultant on agricultural policy.

On the Ecuadorian side, most of the negotiation was done by Carlos Julio Emanuel (the Governor of the central bank), Francisco Swett (the

Table 19.6 Conditionality originally proposed and eventually agreed for Ecuador Agricultural Sector Adjustment Loan

(a) *Proposed, 1984*	(b) *Eventually approved, October 1985*
1 Formulation of an agricultural development policy statement.	1 Elimination of quotas and other quantitative restrictions on imports of agricultural products and inputs, and substitution by tariffs at levels to be agreed by the Bank and to be determined from the internal terms of trade study.
2 Preparation of an agricultural investment programme, with clearly defined priorities, including restructuring of existing investments.	2 Satisfactory 1986 public investment programme for agriculture.
3 Elimination of export taxes on cocoa, coffee and bananas* (and of import subsidies).	3 Satisfactory progress in improving policies affecting intersectoral terms of trade and export incentives.
4 Preparation of a long-term marketing programme.	4 Elimination of purchases of maize and rice by ENAC, or other public enterprises, to support minimum producer prices.
5 Formulation of a plan for restructuring extension services.	5 Elimination of maximum consumer price on wheat flour.
6 Adjustment of product pricing policy. Linking of official prices for export crops to border prices and retention of official minimum prices only for certain important products.	
7 Formulation of a programme for capitalising BNF and reorienting it towards increased medium and long-term lending.	6 Positive interest rates on lending including commissions, and other related changes for the agricultural and industrial sectors.

* Implemented later in 1984.

Minister of Finance) and Alberto Dahik (economic adviser to the President, subsequently to become Minister of Finance himself in 1986). All of these people were young technocrats with a broad commitment to liberalisation of the economy; and two of them, Swett and Dahik, had experience of working inside the IMF and the World Bank respectively. What is interesting is that the Minister of Agriculture, ostensibly the main beneficiary of the proposed package, spent less than an hour in the negotiations. But this reflects a key feature of the 'sectoral adjustment' form of finance, namely that the costs and benefits are unequally distributed. The benefits, in the form of money, come to the economy as a whole, and in particular to the central bank, since there is no restriction on the type of imports which a loan of this type can be used to finance;[8] the costs, in the form of political opposition, are borne by the Government agencies who are responsible for the implementation of particular elements of a conditionality package.

Over and above the policy changes sought in the Bank's original draft manifesto of 1984, the nettles which the negotiating team decided to grasp were in the area of agricultural interest rates and food-crop marketing. It wanted to replace the eighty-five different concessionary interest rates offered by the central bank to agriculture (Swett, 1989: 9) by one lending rate which would be positive in real terms; and it wanted to establish free trade in food crops. Formally, it asked for:

1 Elimination of quotas . . . on the imports of agricultural products, and substitution by tariffs;
2 elimination of the maximum consumer price on wheat flour;
3 elimination of purchases of maize and rice by ENAC, or other public enterprises to support minimum wholesale prices.

It backed up its recommendations by means of an econometric model which suggested that the proposed injection of finance on its own should raise agricultural production by 38 per cent in real terms within five years, rising to 71 per cent if prices were liberalised, and a uniform import tariff of 25 per cent substituted for the existing mixture of tariffs and qualitative restrictions.[9]

Taken together, these proposals amounted to an assault on the entire apparatus by which the Ecuador Government sought to win the support of certain sections of the rural population. In particular, they were guaranteed to antagonise all *Sierra* cereal farmers, and to make it difficult for the Government to retain any responsibility for food security. Whatever the extent of 'urban bias' may have been, it was an obvious political necessity, given the importance of the rural sector, for the Government to temper it by means of some highly visible actions in its favour, and as in other parts of the Third World (Bates, 1981) this was done by offering *selective* benefits to influential rural interests which might counterbalance the *general* deprivations imposed by unfavourable rural-urban terms of trade. Among the more important of these were the multiple selective interest rate concessions, various ostentatious rural investment projects and support prices on particular food crops backed by restrictions or prohibitions on imports (of which there were 600 in 1984 – Swett, 1989: 15). The scope of the interest rate concessions, which benefited large farmers in all areas, is set out in Table 19.7. The size of the price advantage granted to food-crop farmers by the combined operation of import restrictions and a national food storage and marketing association (ENAC) is set out in Table 19.8. In each case government action was conferring an economic benefit on specific groups of rural producers which could be categorised as a *rent*

(Krueger, 1974) in the sense of a return to resources which had been made artificially scarce by government action. In orthodox economic theory the removal of the Government control would increase national income, first by encouraging competition for the previously state-rationed resources (credit and the right to supply cereals, respectively) which would encourage those unsuccessful in the competition to switch to higher-yielding activities, and second by diverting the energies of agriculturalists from seeking rents (e.g. petitioning the central bank or the BNF for a loan at a privileged interest rate) to increasing their productivity. The assumptions of this theory only hold good, of course, if it is possible for the resources which currently earn rents to be switched into uses which yield higher incomes, and there is evidence that this may be difficult for wheat and maize farmers in the *Sierra*, who in effect have only two alternative uses for their land, namely potatoes plus whichever of the two crops they do not currently grow. Neither of these is likely to lead to a significant increase in yield. The likelihood is, therefore, that even if it had been possible to overcome the political obstacles to the dissolution of ENAC, of price regulation and of import controls, the consequent economic benefit would have been minor.

If the Bank's reform agenda now seems over-ambitious, it must be stressed that in making many of its requests for policy change, its negotiators were kicking at an open door. The Ecuadorian negotiating team wanted a floating exchange rate; they wanted to provide incentives to exporters; and they wanted a unified system of interest rates. The one thing which they did not want was the dissolution of ENAC, which they saw as a fundamental instrument for the attainment of food security. The Bank mission leader (an American) argued for the abandonment of support prices for cereals on the grounds that they were a drain on the domestic budget, and received the reply, 'so why then do you subsidise rice production in Louisiana?' But once the Ecuadorian Government negotiating team had made their position clear, they decided not to fight to the last. They made a token request for an increase in the amount of finance available,[10] explicitly suggesting that it might thereby be possible to buy more policy reform ('you cannot make a revolution with $100 million', was the phrase used); and when this was refused, gave in gracefully, and gladly accepted a bird in the hand. They needed the money urgently; they were agreed in spirit with a large part of the package; and they knew from their previous experience as Bank and Fund employees that if the conditions were drafted with sufficient care, there would be plenty of scope for a fudge when the time came to release the second tranche.[11]

At this point it becomes important to focus on the information available to the negotiating team. The Bank team appear to have been under the impression that: 'Purchases by ENAC and other public enterprises in order to support minimum prices of agricultural commodities were eliminated,

Table 19.7 Interest rates (end of period) (per cent)

	Dec. 1983	Dec. 1984	Dec. 1985	Dec. 1986	Dec. 1987	July 1988
Central Bank credit lines						
(a) Public sector** & FODERUMA*	9	11	11	11	11	11
(b) Preferential discounting operations and advances to BNF	12	13	13	13	18	18
(c) Ordinary discounting operations	16	18	18	21	21	21
(d) Advances on export	16	18	18	18	18	23
Private bank operations						
(a) Stabilisation credits	16	18	18	23	23	23
(b) Development bonds	16	18	18	18	23	23
(c) 90-day certificates of deposit	16–19		23–25$	23–29$	27–31$	38–39$
(d) Normal rate of advances	19	23	23	23	28	32
(e) Normal rate paid on savings deposits	16–19	20	20	20–24$	21–22$	21–22$
Annual inflation rate	48.1	29.7	28.7	27.7	32.5	(55.7)

Source: Banco Central del Ecuador, *Informacion Estadistica Mensual*, 15 August 1988 (except inflation rates, from Table 19.3).

Notes: *   Fund for Development in Marginal Rural Areas.
     **   Includes ENAC, ENPROVIT and BEV (see Glossary).
     $ Levels determined by market forces; figures shown illustrate range of fluctuation.

Table 19.8 Producer prices for main cereal crops, February 1987 (sucres per 100 lbs)

	Producer price	CIF import price	FOB export price
Wheat flour	283	179	—
Wheat grain	182	131	—
Maize	151	—	72
Rice (milled)	365	—	180

Source: Ecuador, Ministerio de Agricultura y Ganaderia.

except for two products, hard corn (maize) and rice', and that 'Agricultural lending rates were unified, except for differences justified by transaction costs, at 21 per cent for all agricultural loans with maturities of 90 days or more' (World Bank, 1985: 16). These beliefs were simply inaccurate. ENAC has at all times been involved in the purchase of not only maize and rice, but also soya beans, cotton and sugar. And interest rates, as demonstrated by Table 19.7, were in 1985 far from 'unified', with a rate of 11 per cent charged to ENAC and other public bodies, 13 per cent on central bank preferential discounting operations, 18 per cent on central bank export finance, and 23 per cent on ordinary agricultural loans by private banks. All of these were well below the year's inflation rate of 28.7 per cent, and hence negative in real terms. In addition there are discrepancies between the wording of the policy conditionality presented to the Executive Board (right-hand half of Table 19.6) and those agreed by the Ecuador Government in its Letter of Development Policy drafted on 13 September 1985 and appended to the loan document submitted to the Board. The formal conditionality of Table 19.6 asks for 'elimination of the maximum consumer price on wheat flour' whereas the Letter of Development Policy offers only to 'reduce the control of consumer prices'. The loan document's explicit request for 'positive interest rates on lending' becomes, in the Letter of Development Policy, an undertaking 'to improve resource allocation and mobilisation through interest rate policies'. But astonishingly, given the level of political resistance to any changes in the system of food marketing, there is no attempt by the Government to fudge on ENAC. The Letter of Development Policy contained an explicit undertaking to 'completely eliminate state intervention in the support of minimum prices for crops' (World Bank, 1985: Annexe V: 3).

Once the Letter of Development Policy (signed by the Minister of Agriculture and Minister of Finance) was received in Washington in late September, the loan was immediately approved by the Executive Board of the Bank, with considerable acclamation for what was obviously a radical programme. The first tranche of $50 million was disbursed in February 1986. The fact that Ecuador accepted so tight a set of conditions on the loan is consistent with the general proposition of this study that the nature of the conditionality package agreed between donor and recipient will tend to reflect the recipient's bargaining power (Mosley, 1987: Table 7: 21). As a small country, with a serious balance-of-payments crisis caused by the fall in the price of oil and a debt-service ratio already in excess of 30 per cent, Ecuador had minor bargaining power *vis-à-vis* the World Bank in relation to a Brazil, an Indonesia or even a Turkey. It retained, in spite of this, considerable room for manoeuvre, but as we shall see it chose to use this weapon not during the negotiation but during the implementation phase.

19.3 THE IMPLEMENTATION PROCESS, 1986–8

Within months of the signing of the Agricultural Sector Loan agreement, Ecuador was hit by a very sharp drop in the price of petroleum, which reduced the average FOB export price from $25.8 per barrel for calendar 1985 to $13.9 per barrel for calendar 1986.[12] Its immediate response was to seek an IMF Stand-by, and to raise taxes, in particular the level of domestic sales tax and the charges for electricity, water and telephone services, with the consequence that in 1986, taxes on goods and services were 38 per cent higher in real terms than in 1985 (World Bank, 1987a: 23). It also finally floated the exchange rate in August 1986, after four years of bringing the rate down in occasional steps, and freed interest rates on all transactions apart from central bank credit lines. To this extent the liberalisation promised by the incoming right-wing alliance of 1984 and devised by the technocrats who negotiated the Agricultural Sector Adjustment Loan was sustained.[13] However, a number of forces conspired to blunt the Government's appetite for any further radical changes in economic policy. The personal standing of President Febres Cordero, already weakened by an attempted coup and an unsuccessful attempt at constitutional change in mid-1986, was seriously damaged in August of that year when as the result of a mid-term election the legislative Congress came to be dominated by members of the opposition; the farcical events of February 1987, when the President was briefly kidnapped by guerrillas, did not help his endeavours to strengthen his personal image. The Finance Minister was impeached by Parliament in August 1986 for freeing, and thus raising, some interest rates. Most seriously, in March 1987, an earthquake ruptured the main oil-export pipeline, causing an interruption of exports for six months. As a consequence of these developments a weakened executive was confronted by a public sector deficit which, so far from responding to treatment, rose exponentially: by 1987 it was 12.5 per cent of GNP, and the IMF Stand-by had been suspended with only one tranche disbursed.[14]

These developments clearly weakened whatever resolve the Government initially had to implement the provisions of the World Bank's Agricultural Sector Loan. A summary of the picture on implementation as the World Bank saw it in the first half of 1987, is at Table 19.9; however, it needs to be read with care, since in the light of the Government's precarious financial position it was of the utmost importance for it to secure release of the second tranche of the Loan, normally scheduled to take place about a year after the initial disbursement. As a consequence, strategies of obfuscation and pleas of *force majeure* were used with considerable success to escape punishment for what, by the Bank's criteria, was not a good implementation performance.

Table 19.9 Ecuador: World Bank Agricultural Sector Loan: implementation of policy conditions, 1986–8

Original condition	Beneficiaries (+)/Losers (−) from application of condition	Level of implementation as assessed by World Bank	Comments	Developments since mid-1987
1 Elimination of quotas and other quantitative restrictions on the import of agricultural products and substitution by tariffs.	Cereal farmers (−) Urban consumers (+)	QRs have been eliminated on products comprising 46% of the value of controlled products in 1986 and replaced by tariffs. All remaining QRs except for that on wheat to be removed within 90 days.	No further QRs were removed during the 90-day period and some new ones (e.g. edible oil) were instituted.	Prohibitions or quotas now exist on 94 items covering 71.7% of total imports: but wheat import quota was removed in July 1988.
2 Satisfactory 1986 public investment programme for agriculture.	Santa Elena: coastal farmers (−)	Acceptable apart from the inclusion of one large, non-viable project (Santa Elena irrigation).	Santa Elena included in 1987 development budget, but not implemented due to lack of money.	Santa Elena now to be implemented with private Brazilian finance.
3 Satisfactory progress in improving policies affecting intersectoral terms of trade.	Market-oriented (mainly coastal) farmers (+)	Satisfactorily complied with by maintenance of a competitive exchange rate policy.	Agriculture/manufacturing terms of trade have declined from 103 (1983) to 82 (1986) (1975 = 100) (World Bank, 1988: 38).	Exchange rate regime transferred to 'crawling peg', with bi-weekly foreign exchange auctions, with effect from August 1988.
4 Satisfactory progress on studies affecting intersectoral terms of trade and export incentives.		Satisfactorily complied with by reduced discrimination in trade policy via reductions in QRs and tariffs.		See item 1 above.

5	Elimination of purchases of maize and rice by ENAC, or other public enterprises, to support minimum producer prices.	Cereal farmers (−)	Not implemented, but procurement prices for maize and rice held at 1985 level through 1986 and 1987.	(a) Holding the price was a blessing for ENAC, in view of large surplus crops (especially of rice) in 1986. (b) ENAC was also involved in substantial trade in sugar and soya during the years examined.	Large increases (c. 250%) in wholesale price of maize and rice in 1988.
6	Elimination of maximum consumer price on wheat flour.	Cereal farmers (−) Urban consumers (+)	Implemented, although a legal basis for price controls remains on the statute book.	The into-mill (ex-farm) price of wheat remains subject to control.	Maximum prices gazetted March 1988 for sugar, rice, milk and wheat grain, as well as wheat flour.
7	Positive interest rates on lending including commissions, and other related changes for the agricultural and industrial sectors.	Farmers receiving loans (−)	Parly complied with but non-Central Bank credit lines now carry market-determined interest rates.	All interest rates (except, briefly, 90-day certificates of deposit) remained negative in real terms.	Financial Sector Loan, signed December 1987, contains stiff convenant to maintain positive real interest rates; but as yet no progress.

Sources: Column 1 is transcribed from the right-hand half of Table 19.6; column 3 is from the World Bank document SecM 87–825, 'Release of the Second Tranche of the Agricultural Sector Loan to Ecuador', dated 10 July 1987.

Of the seven conditions to which the release of the second tranche was to be subjected, the Bank awarded the Ecuador Government a mark of Good on one condition (relating to inter-sectoral terms of trade), Satisfactory on two (the public investment programme and export incentives) and Unsatisfactory on four maximum prices (QR's on wheat, the phasing out of ENAC and positive interest rates). Using the score-sheet of Good = 2, Satisfactory = 1, Unsatisfactory = 0, this would give a score of 4/14, or 28 per cent implementation (72 per cent slippage). However, the Bank was able to find mitigating circumstances in all of the Unsatisfactory cases. We now consider each of the groups in sequence:

1 'Good implementation' (terms of trade condition): this was obtained partly by courtesy of the IMF, since as previously described the fall in the petroleum price in early 1986 forced the Government to call in the Fund, who in turn prescribed a floating exchange rate. The Ecuador Government had however been following a reasonably competitive exchange rate policy ever since 1984, with a real depreciation of 4 per cent in 1985 and 12 per cent in 1986. It is hard to ascribe this shift in policy, (which was modified in mid-1988 with the shift to a foreign exchange auction system) to World Bank pressure; rather it constituted a rational pursuit of self-interest for most members of the Febres Cordero Government which was dominated by coastal bankers and exporters, under the impetus of pressure from the Fund.

2 'Satisfactory implementation' (public investment programme): it has long been an important part of the Bank's role to increase efficiency at the microeconomic level by funding, and where necessary helping to design, projects; of late, this role has been expanded to embrace the entire investment portfolio of recipient governments. In recent years, one project in Ecuador has caused the Bank particular anxiety: this was a proposed $250 million irrigation project for the Santa Elena Pensinsula, at the western extremity of the country, which had become desiccated and sparsely populated. It was intended to construct a tunnel under the suburbs of the city of Guayaquil in order to bring water from the existing Daule-Peripa project (financed by IDB) to irrigate cotton, wheat and maize in the Santa Elena Peninsula. The Bank calculated in 1986 that the likely rate of return of the project was 0.6 per cent and the pay-back period 166 years (World Bank, 1987a: 52). However, the Minister for Agriculture, Marcel Laniado, a banker from the coast, retained a strong commitment to the project which his successors have inherited; as we have seen, Laniado was virtually excluded from the initial dialogue over conditionality in 1985. For the period in early 1987 during which the second tranche review was taking place it was possible for the Government, operating under severe financial constraint, to accurately claim that the project had been shelved.

However, in early 1988 it was announced that the project was to go ahead with joint finance from the IDB and a Brazilian private bank and construction by a Brazilian contractor. By picking up the tab for Santa Elena the IDB was, of course, financing a project with which the World Bank had explicitly asked the Ecuador Government not to go ahead.

3 *'Unsatisfactory implementation'* (all other conditions): here one approaches the heart of the matter since each of these instruments, considered as a barrier to efficiency by the World Bank, was at the same time a vital tool used by the Ecuadorian Government to purchase the loyalty of its rural clientele. The Ecuador Government's withdrawal of the *maximum consumer price of wheat flour*, as requested, was a piece of sleight-of-hand. For the key element of protection which cereal farmers wanted to retain was a *producer* price substantially above the level of import parity which, as Table 19.8 demonstrates, was made comfortably possible by the existence of an import quota and by the maintenance of support prices by ENAC. These support prices continued to protect the income of producers – including the President of the Republic who was a wheat farmer on a large scale – throughout the period of the Agricultural Sector Loan, so that when the consumer price ceiling was removed in early 1987 this had little impact on the apparatus of protection. It was a case of the letter of the condition being complied with, and not its spirit. Maximum consumer prices were in any case reimposed on wheat flour in early 1988, together with sugar, rice, millet and wheat grain.

The *import quota on wheat* was essentially a device to win the support of farmers in the *Sierra*; but the President himself, we have seen, was also a wheat farmer and miller, and is said to have described the Bank's request that the quota be removed as 'horse-shit'. Whatever the accuracy of this attribution, the quota remained in force throughout the lifetime of the Sector Adjustment Loan and the Febres Cordero Government. Ironically, it was repealed by the incoming Borja Government in July 1988, since by then the desire to reduce inflation – and to please urban consumers – had replaced the wishes of wheat farmers, whose loyalty the new President already had, as the major force acting on food import policy.

The privatisation of ENAC, as we have seen, was the one element in the Bank's conditionality which was genuinely thrust on to the Ecuador Government by the Bank negotiating team. ENAC is the parastatal which buys strategic stocks, and has a monopoly of the import and export, of rice, maize, sugar, soya and cotton; as we have seen, the Bank negotiating team were unaware of the factual extent of its scope even when the loan was being negotiated.[15] It accumulated losses over the years for the simple reason that the inflated support prices which it was obligated to pay to

427

Ecuadorian producers (see Table 19.8) were a long way above the prices at which it was able to export, so that any surplus crops (as with rice in 1986) were exported at a loss. By the end of 1985 ENAC had an outstanding debt to the Government of $35 million which was written off in December of that year through the issuance of a bond. But, as the main instrument by which the Ecuadorian Government could claim to be taking responsibility for food security in the country, ENAC was too powerful a card for the Government willingly to throw away. In the course of telling the World Bank supervisory team this, the Minister for Agriculture (by now Marcos Espinel) offered to hold procurement prices for maize and rice for 1987 at their 1986 level; but this, given the scale of the surplus realised on these crops in 1986, was less a concession to the World Bank than to financial rationality. In 1988 the Government announced increases in the wholesale price of maize and rice of the order of 250 per cent,[16] or about three times the rate of inflation since 1985. The Borja Government has since announced that it intends to strengthen ENAC, and is considering the possibility of trading in new products such as barley, wheat and seafoods (*El Comercio* (Quito) 29 September 1988).

The subsidised interest rates listed in Table 19.7 were another of the selective rural benefits most needed by the Government to counterbalance the 'urban bias' of its trade and public investment policies. The structure of rates is complex, with some of the central bank's subsidised lines of credit going to state agencies such as ENAC and ENPROVIT, some going to the Banco Nacional de Fomento (BNF) the main agricultural development bank, as concessionary rediscounts, and some going direct to the BNF's privileged clients. Many branches of the BNF have long been guilty of a rather relaxed attitude towards repayment – the BNF's arrears rate for 1987 was 21.9 per cent[17] – and the bank has needed periodic injections of government money, over and above the interest rate subsidy, to keep going.[18] There is no doubt that these difficulties arose from the practice of using subsidised credit in general, and the BNF in particular, as a means of buying political support as well as an instrument for economic development, and not only the World Bank, but the technocrats who negotiated the Sectoral Adjustment Loan, had a genuine desire to unify the structure of interest rates and free it from government controls. Both parties, however, seem to have quite genuinely underestimated the amount of work they had to do. The World Bank, as we saw, erroneously believed that even when the first tranche of the SECAL was released the structure of interest rates was 'unified except for differences justified by transaction costs'; and when the Minister of Finance, Alberto Dahik, went a small way towards meeting the Bank's requirements in August 1986 by freeing the rate of interest on savings deposits and loans of private banks (some 55 per cent of the total) he was immediately subjected to a vote of no confidence (*juicio politico*) by the opposition-dominated congress, which was successful by 39 votes to 22 and caused him to lose his job. The record of the impeachment process makes interesting reading for anybody who doubts the strength of populist feeling against a free market in credit in Ecuador. The Minister of Finance was accused of:

1 'Violating the constitution;
2 favouring the concentration of income and wealth within a small monopolistic group which controls exports in a manner prejudicial to small industry and the large majority of the Ecuadorian people, increasing the price of food and increasing unemployment';

and, of course:

3 'Surrendering to external interests'.[19]

Even after this ordeal had been undergone, it must be stressed, interest rates in real terms remained negative on all loans except 90-day certificates of deposit, and to that extent short of the Bank's requirements. But the experience appears to have cured the Cordero Government of any further desire to intervene in the process of financial reform. The unfinished business of the Agricultural Sector Loan was, however, picked up by a World Bank Financial Sector Loan, granted in December 1987 to the value of $100 million plus a further $50 million of linked finance from the Japanese Government. The negotiators of this loan lowered their sights on real interest rates, to the extent of simply requiring the level of interest rates on central bank preferential credit to be raised within 5 points of the market rate on 90-day certificates of deposit (World Bank, 1987b: 46), and then concentrated their attention on trying to restrict the volume of central bank-subsidised credit, insisting that no new lines of credit be opened by the central bank and that there be a decrease in central bank credits to the private sector of 35 per cent in real terms between December 1986 and December 1988. The actual fall was over 50 per cent (interview, World Bank, 9 November 1989). But the spread between concessional and free market rates remains well above that desired by the Bank[20] and the maintenance of concessional credit, in particular for small businesses and the opening up of new lands, remains an important plank in the policy of the Borja Government, and a number of concessional lines of credit remain open to large farm borrowers. As in the case of Santa Elena Irrigation, it is appropriate to mention that the World Bank's bargaining position in its attempt to extract policy change was weakened by the existence of another lender (again the Inter-American Development Bank) offering credits to the Banco Nacional de Fomento[21] without any insistence on changes in lending policy in return.

All in all, the World Bank team had a difficult job to do in persuading the authorities in Washington that the conditions for release of the second tranche had been fulfilled. It will however be remembered that decisions on the release of a second tranche, unlike decisions on the initial award of a loan, do not have to be referred to the full Executive Board, but need only be approved by the Senior Vice-president, Operations. In July 1987 when the decision to release the second tranche of the loan was taken, the World Bank was in the midst of internal reorganisation, and there was substantial sympathy for Ecuador on account of the earthquake suffered in March with consequent loss in oil production. Even so, the Ecuador Government must count itself lucky, given its widespread slippages on the agreed terms of the loan, to have secured its disbursement in full. One recalls, however, that in the period 1980–6 there was a delay in releasing the second tranche of 80 per cent of World Bank sectoral and structural adjustment loans, but that in 'almost all cases' [*sic*] the loans had been fully disbursed within a year of the due date for the release of the second tranche (Nicholas, 1988: iv). World Bank country desks are under strong pressure to spend, and thus earn a return on, the money that has been budgeted for their use (Volume 1, Chapters 3, 5), a fact that has not escaped the attention of those negotiating on behalf of recipient countries.

Before we pass to a discussion of the impact of the Agriculture Sector Loan, it will be useful to pull together the threads of our discussion of implementation, and to set it in continental perspective. The Director of the World Bank's Agricultural Department has recently lamented that in Latin America generally, agriculture sector reforms have been disappointing, in particular (i) because they have failed to recognise the extent to which vested interests were built up by the long-time use of import-substituting industrialisation policies and (ii) because they have not dealt with the adjustment problems associated with policy reform (Schuh, 1987: 1). More recently, in a review of the agriculture sector loans summarised in Table 19.5, Bonilla, an EDI consultant, has agreed that 'the process of preparing [agricultural sector adjustment programmes] seems to have been relatively circumscribed at the level of the institutions, functionaries and social groups involved. This has had repercussions at the implementation level'.[22]

The last two points can certainly be echoed in the context of Ecuador. A negotiation on an agricultural sector loan which virtually excludes the Minister for Agriculture can certainly be described as 'relatively circumscribed at the level of the institutions, functionaries and social groups involved', and there is strong informal evidence that Marcel Laniado, the Minister for Agriculture in 1985/6, neither approved of the Bank's conditionality on ENAC or interest rates nor did anything whatever to facilitate its implementation. Similarly, although a number of the *Sierra* farmers most vociferously opposed to the abolition of ENAC and import controls cannot be described as underprivileged, some of them can, and as earlier argued, in this particular reform it is not easy to find alternative productive activities to which they could 'adjust' if deprived of the opportunity to produce wheat or maize. In retrospect, it is quite astonishing that an agriculture sector programme which explicitly forecast a bigger gain for large farmers than for small farmers, and the possibility of a negative gain for the latter (see Table in note 9) should have avoided even drawing attention to the fact, let alone discussing the question of how the losers from the process of policy adjustment were to be compensated. In these respects, at least, the problems of the Ecuador SECAL were the problems of the Bank in Latin America writ large.

However, as we have seen, a number of the implementation difficulties which arose in Ecuador were specific to Ecuador. In particular, Ecuador is still – even after the oil boom – a relatively agrarian economy by Latin American standards, and although in Schuh's words 'vested interests have been built up by the long-time use of ISI policies' all over the continent, these vested interests are relatively weak in Ecuador, were not well represented in the Febres Cordero Government and – as witness the removal of export taxes and the floating of the exchange rate – were relatively quickly overcome. The vested interests which were threatened by the implementation of the Ecuador SECAL were created, not by policies of import-substituting industrialisation, but rather by attempts to protect privileged agrarian groups from its worse effects. Particularly prominent among these groups were cereal farmers in the *Sierra*, and the unfortunate thing about the Bank's attack on them is not that it was unsuccessful – which given the opposition of the President[23] and the Minister of Agriculture it was bound to be – but that it was marginal to the Bank's overriding objective of opening the economy and expanding export production. Given the Government's commitment to the food security objective, the limited involvement of cereal farmers in export production and the limited possibilities for converting them to such production, the Bank's concentration of its conditionality in the food-crop sector must be described as quixotic. Around the world, as will be apparent from other studies in this volume, the Bank put a quite disproportionate amount of human resources into tilting at this particular windmill when it might have been better advised, given the balance of economic benefits and political costs, to aim directly at the infrastructure and incentives for export production.[24]

In all of this it is all too easy to overemphasise the role of the World Bank as the agency which 'lays down the conditions'. What must be clearly spelled out is that there would have been no conditions to lay down if it had not been for the existence of a technocratic group within the Cordero Government willing to collaborate with the Bank in implementing liberal policies; and in many ways the relative failure of the Ecuador SECAL is not the Bank's failure, but the failure of this technocratic group to overcome resistance to their chosen policies within the Government and the country (Chapter 16 on Kenya makes an identical point). Here a further factor specific to Ecuador comes into play, namely the severe limits which its constitution places on the inroads which any such technocratic group can make without reference to legislation. In particular, it is perfectly possible (as in the United States) for the President to be confronted by a legislature dominated by the opposition party and able to block all his legislation, which was in fact the position of President Febres Cordero between August 1986 and August 1988. Still more important, all monetary policy is in Ecuador made not by the central bank but by a committee (the *Junta Monetaria*) consisting of a chairman nominated by the President, the Ministers of Industry, Commerce and Agriculture and representatives of the private banks, the Chamber of Commerce and the Chamber of Industries. The Governor of the central bank is not a member and has no vote: his role is executive and not policy-making. The opportunity which exists in other countries for the central bank to act in collusion with external finance agencies to liberalise monetary policies simply does not exist, therefore, in Ecuador. From the point of view of the present study this has particular relevance to possibilities for the achievement of positive real interest rates.

Finally, in the present context, the World Bank needs to be seen as but one of several agencies offering finance to Ecuador. Even in the present year (1989), with the Government in dispute with the IMF and the World Bank over the implementation of conditionality and in dispute with the IDB and private banks over debt repayment, the Ecuador Government has been able to secure credits from the Governments of Japan (general import support), South Korea (tractor imports), the United States (agricultural development), and private banks in Brazil and Argentina (Santa Elena irrigation and Quito abattoir respectively). And there is no doubt that the Ecuador economy is in a worse state, and therefore its government is in a weaker bargaining position, now than it was in 1985–7 when negotiations on the Agricultural Sector Loan were taking place. The ability of governments world-wide to switch to alternative sources of finance which demand less conditionality than the Bank or will finance projects which the Bank refuses to take on has constituted, particularly in the middle-income countries of Asia and Latin America, one of the major limitations on the Bank's bargaining power. The Bank has tried to obviate this limitation by pleas for co-ordination but with relatively little success; in this respect it has been undone by the very competitive forces which it strives so hard to unleash.

19.4 THE INFLUENCE OF ADJUSTMENT LENDING

This case study will not attempt any sophisticated assessment of the effects of World Bank programme lending: of the three methods available for assessment of impact, 'before and after', 'plan versus realisation', and 'with and without' (see Volume 1, Chapter 6), the last, and best, will be left on one side in this essay, for sheer lack of data. However, it will be instructive to examine what happened to the main indicators of economic performance in the period of the Agriculture Sector Loan, and to speculate on how far the conditions and the finance provided by the loan may have been responsible.

We begin with the 'before and after' method. Table 19.10 sets out details of growth rates, balance of payments and export performance during the period of the loan (1986–7) and during the previous three-year period (1983–5). We find that on three of these indicators (the growth rate of GDP, the balance of payments and the 'openness' of the economy, as measured by the exports-to-GDP ratio) the performance of the Ecuadorian economy was actually worse during the loan period than beforehand; however, a great deal of this deterioration in performance will have been due to two factors entirely extraneous to the agricultural sector, namely the collapse of the oil price in 1986 (see Table 19.4) and in 1987. Once we abstract from these disturbances the picture becomes much more encouraging: the growth rate of agricultural exports was nearly three times as great during the loan period as during the preceding three years.

Table 19.11 breaks down the growth of agricultural exports into its component parts.

It will be seen that nearly all of the growth during both periods is concentrated within two export products, bananas and prawns, with the latter suddenly jumping in 1987 to become Ecuador's main non-oil export. Tuna fish and 'others' (mainly rice) also registered impressive growth rates in the later part of the period but remained negligible in absolute terms. If one asks what was the contribution to this growth of the financial package provided by the World Bank, one recalls that that package contained two elements, the money and the policy conditions. Since most of the conditions, however, were not complied with (with one exception to be noted below) one is forced to the conclusion that it was the financial contribution of the SECAL which made the main contribution to Ecuadorian agricultural growth by releasing an import constraint. The

Table 19.10 Ecuador: economic performance, 1983–5 and 1986–7

| | (annual averages) | |
	1983–5	1986–7
Growth rate of GDP (%)	1.9	−0.1
Current balance-of-payments deficit (% of GNP)	3.0	9.5
Exports (as % of GNP)	25.3	22.3
Growth rate of real agricultural exports (%)	5.9	16.9

Source: Table 19.3.

Table 19.11 Ecuador: main agricultural exports, 1981–7 (values are in US $ millions
at 1981 prices: growth rates are in real terms)

		1982	1983	1984	1985	1986	1987
Bananas:	value	213	152	154	216	237	238
	growth rate	2.8	−28.7	1.3	40.2	9.7	0.1
Coffee:	value	140	142	134	148	194	184
	growth rate	33.3	1.4	−5.7	10.4	31.0	−5.2
Prawns:	value	113	148	146	137	213	329
	growth rate	46.1	30.9	−1.4	−6.2	55.4	54.4
Cocoa:	value	69	9	76	114	62	72
	growth rate	59.1	−655.0	666.0	50.0	−54.3	16.1
Tuna fish:	value	2	1	2	4	12	19
	growth rate	47.5	−27.1	55.8	93.9	287.8	58.3
Others:	value	8	4	6	7	8	17
	growth rate	−36.7	−45.0	32.2	18.0	3.2	23.5
All agricultural exports:							
	value	547	549	519	628	726	859
	growth rate	21.7	−16.2	13.1	20.9	15.6	18.3

SECAL provided almost 30 per cent of Ecuador's imported agricultural inputs over the years 1986–7 ($100 million out of an import bill of $315 million), hence it is tempting to say that some 5 per cent of the 16.9 per cent agricultural export growth achieved in 1986–7 may have been due to the World Bank loan, but this is to make heroic assumptions about substitution possibilities in agriculture. Even without spurious precision of this sort, however, it does seem possible to agree with Luzuriaga's judgement that 'The agricultural sector was the crucial factor in enabling the economy to confront and overcome the balance of payments crisis which began in the early months of 1987' (Luzuriaga, 1988: 3), and to ascribe a considerable part of this success to the Bank's finance. In addition, one policy change was crucial to the leap in exports during 1986–7, namely the maintenance of a competitive exchange rate policy, and ultimately the movement to a free exchange rate regime in August 1986.

This change, which, as we have seen, was much appreciated by the exporters themselves, was the one big policy success which the Bank team were able to report during the period of the Sector Adjustment Loan, although the credit for it must lie in large part with the International Monetary Fund, which provided an emergency Stand-by credit in July 1986 of which a floating exchange rate was a key condition. However, in conclusion we may note that the appraisal team's forecast, derived from a linear programming model, that programme finance would *add* 38 per cent to real agricultural production in the absence of policy change, is still some way short of accomplishment. The growth of total agricultural production has been lagging some way short of exports, and is estimated at 21 per cent over the three years 1986–8; if we repeat our previous arbitrary assumption and ascribe one-third of this to Bank finance, it follows that only 7 per cent of the planned 38 per cent growth has so far, at the end of 1988, been achieved. This is of course a rough short-term assessment of what was explicitly conceived as a medium-term adjustment measure.

19.5   CONCLUSIONS

It is easy to be wise after the event. The business of trying to change economic policy in sovereign countries is, as the World Bank has discovered over the last eight years, massively difficult, and it is extremely risky for anyone to pretend that he or she might have been able to do better in their place. On the other hand, it is incumbent on anyone who criticises an action, however sympathetically, to say what he would have done had he been the decision-maker. It is quite clear to the present author that when the terms of the conditionality agreement of the Ecuador SECAL were negotiated the World Bank should have (a) asked for more involvement from the Ministry of Agriculture in negotiating what was designated as an agriculture sector loan, (b) ignored the reform of the wheat industry, as involving a political cost quite out of proportion to any economic benefit, (c) concentrated more on the promotion of agricultural exports (bananas, coffee and especially seafood), (d) examined the distributional impact of its planned measures, (e) once the gains and losses were identified, devised measures to compensate the losers (e.g. selective rural investment to compensate rice producers hurt by the removal of an import quota), (f) on the specific matter of interest rates, asked for a gradual approach to positive real interest rates rather than asking for a jump from a real rate of −10 per cent to +2 per cent over one year. The final point raises a familiar theme of this book: World Bank policy-based lending seeks two objectives, quick disbursement and fulfilment of medium-term policy conditions, which may be quite incompatible. The intellectual case for a gradual approach to positive real interest rates is perfectly plausible, but was overridden in the case under discussion by the administrative convention that the second tranche of a sector loan should be disbursed within one year, and all the relevant conditions implemented before the second tranche is released. There would appear to be a strong case for medium-term disbursement of medium-term loans.

Within the Bank, as we have seen, there is a great deal of gloom about Latin American agriculture in general and about Ecuador in particular. This is unfortunate: the present loan provides a useful experimental case of a policy-based loan in which the *de facto* contribution was almost entirely confined to the financial element, but which appears, on the basis of a superficial analysis, to be considerable. There is no denying the importance of progress towards a better policy environment, if it can be identified and achieved. But policy-based lending is the art of the possible, and there is a great deal that can be done to strengthen the forces of production and commercialisation regardless of the policy environment. Implicitly, that appears to be recognised by other donors, and by commercial lenders, who are far more sparing in their requests for policy change. The World Bank Sector Adjustment Loan did a great deal to help the agricultural sector of Ecuador pull the economy out of a serious crisis caused by a collapse in export revenues. That is a proud claim, and one which could have been made consistently with the adoption of a much lower political profile.

Acknowledgements

The author acknowledges with warmest thanks the help of the following people: in Washington, Jose Enrique Fernandez, Katherine Sierra, Mateen Thobani; in Quito, Fausto Cascarte, Mario Crëspo, Alberto Dahik, Marlon Flores C., Francisco Hidalgo V., Carlos Luzuriaga, Gillian Marsh.

GLOSSARY

BEV	Banco Ecuatoriano de la Vivienda (National Housing Finance Corporation)
BNF	Banco Nacional de Fomento (literally, National Development Bank, but almost entirely concerned with agricultural loans)
EDI	Economic Development Institute (of the World Bank)
ENAC	Empresa Nacional de Almacenamiento y Comercializacion (National Enterprise for Storage and Marketing (of foodstuffs))
ENPROVIT	Empresa Nacional de Productos Vitales (National Enterprise for Essential Products)
FODERUMA	Fondo para el Desarollo de Regiones Rurales Marginales (Fund for Development in Marginal Rural Areas)
IDB	Inter-American Development Bank
Latifundistas	Large farmers
QR	Quantitative restriction
SECAL	Sectoral Adjustment Loan
Sierra	Andean (mountain) areas of Ecuador
USAID	United States Agency for International Development

NOTES

1 Including Kenya and Malawi, discussed in this volume of case studies.
2 During the 1970s, this percentage was estimated at 10 per cent (Hurtado, 1981: 319); the remainder was from Europe, Japan and, increasingly in the 1980s, other Latin American countries.
3 Between 1973 and 1981 revenues from taxes on petroleum increased from 3.9 to 8 per cent of GDP; over the same period government current expenditures (including debt service) increased from 16.1 to 21.4 per cent of GDP, while capital expenditures increased from 7.3 to 10.3 per cent of GDP. During the same period, non-petroleum revenues declined from 11.4 per cent of non-petroleum GDP in 1973 to 8.1 per cent in 1981.

4   *Juicio politico*: essentially a motion of no confidence in a Minister proposing a particular policy action, which requests the legislature to rescind that policy action and dismiss the Minister responsible. For detail of a *juicio politico* relating to the implementation of a World Bank-recommended policy condition on interest rates, see pages 428–9.

5   In particular, Jose Maria Velasco Ibarra, five times elected President of Ecuador between 1934 and 1972, openly despised the concept of political party, and assembled an *ad hoc* party machine purely to secure re-election each time that it was needed.

6   Seven of the nine loans and credits extended for transport were to improve the country's load network and two were to help finance expansion of the port of Guayaquil. Three power operations aimed at improving generation and distribution facilities in Quito. But since 1967, when the first livestock development loan was approved, the Bank group has made nine other loans and credit for agriculture and fisheries, seven loans to support industrial development, and two for pre-investment studies. These productive sector loans contributed, to the end of 1985, 52 per cent of total Bank lending to Ecuador.

7   World Bank (1984: 9). In 1983, rates of effective protection were worked out at 61 per cent for industry and 4 per cent for agriculture.

8   Payments by the Bank are made in reimbursement of import invoices certified by the central bank as having been paid. There is a restricted list which forbids Bank programme loan money being used directly for imports of, for example, firearms and explosives; but indirectly, all programme loans are fungible.

9   World Bank (1985: 21). The full set of predictions 'for a medium-term period, that is, within five years' was as follows:

Policy outcomes (percentage change from 1984 base levels)

Policy reforms	Farm incomes			Agricultural employment	Gross value of production
	small	medium	large		
Removal of fertiliser import constraint (proxy for removal of all agricultural input constraints made possible by loan)	−4	7	45	31	38
Plus liberalisation of prices	26	26	58	28	48
Plus cut in all import tariffs of					
10%	48	43	70	27	59
25%	74	75	91	15	71

10 This was $100 million, which was approximately equivalent to the size of the country's balance-of-payments deficit at the time, or a quarter of its annual bill for agricultural inputs.

11 Particularly important precedents were the electricity sector loan granted to Brazil in 1983, and the import development loan granted to Mexico in 1985, in both of which cases the Ecuador negotiating team believed that the conditionality had effectively been dodged.

12 Banco Central del Ecuador (1988) *Informacion Estadistica Mensual*, Table on page 41; see also Table 19.4 above.

13 The freeing of the exchange rate was acclaimed as 'a courageous act' in an open letter in *El Universo* for 1 September 1986, signed by Presidents of the Ecuadorian Exporters'

Federation and the individual exporters' associations for coffee, cocoa and prawns.

14 A contributory cause of the problem, apart from the collapse in oil revenues, was the fact that although the Government raised taxes in 1986 it abandoned very few of the expenditures which it had planned in 1984 on the basis of an oil price of US $26 per barrel. As a consequence, government expenditure as a proportion of GNP continued to rise; see Table 19.3.

15 See page 420. ENAC is physically located within the Ministry of Agriculture and the Ministry's Deputy Secretary (in English terms) for Agricultural Marketing is the Chairman of ENAC's Board of Directors.

16 On 12 September 1988 the price of rice (per 100 lbs) was revised from 1400 sucres (at which level it had been since November 1984) to 4400 sucres, and the price of maize from 1000 sucres (at which level it had been since April 1985) to 2500 sucres.

17 Banco Nacional de Fomento, *Informe de Labores 1987*, p. 30.

18 Announcing a government grant of US $3 million to rehabilitate the BNF, its director spoke of his intention to 'raise the bank from the dead' (*El Comercio* (Quito) 23 September 1988).

19 Transcript of parliamentary questions submitted to the Minister of Finance by Deputies Rene Mosquera, Enrique Ayala and Trajano Andrade, August 1986. From the record of the Ecuador National Congress.

20 In September 1988 the free market rate on 90-day certificates of deposit varied between 38 and 39 per cent, whereas the standard public-sector lending rate to farmers was 32 per cent (interview, Central Bank of Ecuador, 21 September 1988).

21 These totalled 7,142 million sucres in 1987, against central bank credits of 14,275 million sucres, of which only a part would be accounted for by World Bank lending.

22 Bonilla (1988: 6). One problem which further constrained the dialogue between the World Bank and the Ecuadorian Government was the absence of any World Bank country office in Quito, with the consequence that all information relating to the economy and to compliance with conditions had to be hurriedly gathered by visiting missions from Washington.

23 With hindsight the nickname given to the President, *Febres Cordero, el cordero del Banco Mundial* (*Cordero* is Spanish for sheep) seems particularly unkind, as in so many areas, especially those involved with cereal marketing, Cordero fought hard to restrict the Bank's pressure.

24 Compare for example the parallel case of the Kenyan Second Structural Adjustment Loan (Chapter 16) which involved an attempt, so far unsuccessful, to reform and ultimately privatise the National Cereals and Produce Marketing Board, an institution comparable to ENAC in functions and in the financial burden it imposed on government. The Malawi case (Chapter 15) also featured an underestimation by the Bank team of the importance of the food security objective to the government and an over-estimation of the response of agricultural production to liberalisation.

BIBLIOGRAPHY

Banco Central del Ecuador (1988) *Informacion Estadistica Mensual*, August issue.

Bates, R. (1981) *Markets and States in Tropical Africa: The Political Basis of Agricultural Policies*, Berkeley, University of California Press.

Bonilla, E. D. (1988) *Los Programas de Ajuste Sectorial Agropecuario: Reflexiones Sobre Algunas Experiencias en America del Sur* (Agricultural Sector Adjustment Programmes: reflections on some South American experiences), unpublished paper presented to review of World Bank Agricultural Sector operations in Latin America, San José, Costa Rica.

Hurtado, O. (1981) *El Poder Politico en el Ecuador*, Barcelona, Editorial Arial.

Instituto Interamericano de Co-operacion para la Agricultura (IICA) (1987) *Los Programas de Ajuste Estructural y Sectoral: Alcances para la Reactivacion y Desarollo de la Agricultura* (Programmes of Structural and Sectoral Adjustment: achievements in the rehabilitation and development of agriculture), San José, Costa Rica: IICA.

Krueger, A. (1974) 'The political economy of the rent-seeking society', *American Economic Review* 64 (June), 291–301.

Luzuriaga, C, (1988) *El Comportamiento del Sector Agropecuario 1984–88* (The Behaviour of the Agricultural Sector 1984–8), unpublished paper submitted to review of World Bank agricultural sector operations in Latin America, San José, Costa Rica.

Mosley, P. (1987) *Conditionality as Bargaining Process: Structural Adjustment Lending, 1980–86*, Princeton, NJ, Princeton Essays in International Finance, 168.

Nicholas, P. (1988) *Interim Report on Adjustment Lending*, Washington DC, World Bank Occasional Paper.

Schuh, G. E. (1987) *Agricultural Policy Reform in Latin America*, unpublished paper presented at Latin America meeting of International Agricultural Economics Association, Mexico City, 14–15 July.

Stern, E. (1983) 'World Bank financing of structural adjustment', in J. Williamson (ed.) *IMF Conditionality*, Washington DC, Institute for International Economics.

Swett, F. X. (1989) *Turnaround: the Political Economy of Development and Liberalisation in Ecuador 1984–88*, paper presented to Conference on the Political Economy of Liberalisation, Bogota, July.

World Bank (1984) *Ecuador: an Agenda for Recovery and Sustained Growth* (Report no. 5094–EC), Washington DC.

World Bank (1985) *Report of the President to the Executive Directors on a Proposed Loan of $100 million for an Agriculture Sector Program to the Republic of Ecuador* (Report no. P–4126–EC).

World Bank (1987a) *Ecuador: Country Economic Memorandum* (Report no. 6592–EC), Washington DC.

World Bank (1987b) *Financial Sector Adjustment Loan: President's Report*, Washington DC, December.

World Bank (1988) *Ecuador: Country Economic Memorandum*, Washington DC, August.

INDEX

References to material in the end-notes at the end of each chapter are indicated by the suffix n, thus: 438n